D1622772

# COMMON and SCIENTIFIC NAMES of FISHES

## from the UNITED STATES, CANADA, and MEXICO

### Sixth Edition

QL 627
.C66
2004

OCLC
2-17-06
#56325804

# COMMON and SCIENTIFIC NAMES of FISHES

## from the UNITED STATES, CANADA, and MEXICO

### Sixth Edition

Joseph S. Nelson, *Chair*
Edwin J. Crossman, Héctor Espinosa-Pérez,
Lloyd T. Findley, Carter R. Gilbert, Robert N. Lea,
and James D. Williams

*Committee on Names of Fishes*
A joint committee of the American Fisheries Society and
the American Society of Ichthyologists and Herpetologists

American Fisheries Society
Special Publication 29

Bethesda, Maryland
2004

The American Fisheries Society Special Publication series is a registered serial. A suggested citation format follows.

Nelson, J. S., E. J. Crossman, H. Espinosa-Pérez, L. T. Findley, C. R. Gilbert, R. N. Lea, and J. D. Williams. 2004. Common and scientific names of fishes from the United States, Canada, and Mexico. American Fisheries Society, Special Publication 29, Bethesda, Maryland.

Fish drawings on cover are from *Fishes of the World*, 3rd edition by Joseph S. Nelson, © 1994. This material is used by permission of John Wiley & Sons, Inc. Cover map by Amy J. Benson.

© 2004 by the American Fisheries Society

All rights reserved. Photocopying for internal or personal use, or for the internal or personal use of specific clients, is permitted by AFS provided that the appropriate fee is paid directly to Copyright Clearance Center (CCC), 222 Rosewood Drive, Danvers, Massachusetts 01923, USA; phone 978-750-8400. Request authorization to make multiple copies for classroom use from CCC. These permissions do not extend to electronic distribution or long-term storage of articles or to copying for resale, promotion, advertising, general distribution, or creation of new collective works. For such uses, permission or license must be obtained from AFS.

· Printed in the United States of America on acid-free paper.

Library of Congress Control Number 2004108335
ISBN 1-888569-61-1
ISSN 0097-0638

American Fisheries Society website address: www.fisheries.org

American Fisheries Society
5410 Grosvenor Lane, Suite 110
Bethesda, Maryland 20814-2199
USA

This book is dedicated to Edwin (Ed) J. Crossman (1929–2003).

In memory of our colleague Ed, for his friendship and moderating influence throughout our writing of this publication.

# CONTENTS

# CONTRIBUTORS

Joseph S. Nelson, Department of Biological Sciences, University of Alberta, Edmonton, Alberta, T6G 2E9, Canada; E-mail: joe.nelson@ualberta.ca or jsne@shaw.ca

Edwin J. Crossman (the late), formerly Curator Emeritus of the Centre for Biodiversity & Conservation Biology, Royal Ontario Museum, 100 Queen's Park, Toronto, Ontario, Canada.

Héctor Espinosa-Pérez, Colección Ictiológica, Departamento de Zoología, Instituto de Biología, Universidad Nacional Autónoma de México, A.P. 70-153, México, D.F., 04510 México; E-mail: hector@servidor.unam.mx

Lloyd T. Findley, Centro de Investigación en Alimentación y Desarrollo, A.C.-Unidad Guaymas, Carretera al Varadero Nacional km. 6.6, "Las Playitas", A.P. 284, Guaymas, Sonora, 85480 México; E-mail: lfindley@gys.megared.net.mx

Carter R. Gilbert, Florida Museum of Natural History, University of Florida, Gainesville, Florida 32611, USA; E-mail: carter@flmnh.ufl.edu

Robert N. Lea, California Department of Fish and Game, 20 Lower Ragsdale Drive, Monterey, California 93940-5738, USA; E-mail: rnlea2@aol.com

James D. Williams, U.S. Geological Survey, 7920 N.W. 71st Street, Gainesville, Florida 32653, USA; E-mail: jim_williams@usgs.gov

Committee on Names of Fishes
A joint committee of the American Fisheries Society and the American Society of Ichthyologists and Herpetologists

# LIST OF FAMILIES

Common names of families given in parentheses in English, Spanish, and French.

# INTRODUCTION

A major change in this sixth edition is the inclusion of species found in Mexico. The list now covers the fishes of Canada, the continental United States, and Mexico and represents the first modern document listing in one place of the entire ichthyofauna of North America. In addition, the English and Spanish common name is given for each freshwater and marine species found in Mexico, and the English and French common name for freshwater and marine species found in Quebec. Also, for freshwater species, the country of occurrence is given. Earlier lists were published in 1948, 1960, 1970, 1980, and 1991 (as American Fisheries Society Special Publications 1, 2, 6, 12, and 20, respectively). These lists have been widely used and have contributed substantially to the goal of achieving uniform use of common names and avoiding confusion in scientific names. This list recommends the scientific names to use and attempts to reflect as best possible in our judgment the current views of specialists on the various taxa. From 570 entries in the abbreviated 1948 list (comprising primarily the better known sport, commercial, and forage fishes), coverage increased to 1,892 species in 1960, 2,131 in 1970, 2,268 in 1980, and 2,428 species in 1991. The present edition includes 3,700 species, 3,694 fishes and six cephalochordates (or, to give a figure comparable to the 1991 list, 2,635 species in Canada and the continental United States, not including species of the newly added family of cephalochordates, the Branchiostomatidae). In this list, as in that of 1991, the joint American Fisheries Society/American Society of Ichthyologists and Herpetologists (AFS/ASIH) Committee on Names of Fishes has endeavored to include common names for all native (indigenous) and established introduced species in the region of coverage, even when the introduced species occur in very limited areas. The number of introduced species found in North American waters, both through intentional and accidental releases, continues to rise. For many introductions, although one or more specimens may have been collected, there is no evidence that the species has become established (e.g., that breeding populations exist), and these species are not listed (Fuller et al. 1999, listed and discussed these for the United States). In addition, some introduced species previously reported in North America are no longer present. Common names for those few hybrid fishes that are important in fishery management or in sport or commercial fisheries are given in Appendix 2.

Many of the additions to this sixth edition, other than those noted for Mexico, have resulted from the description of new species and range extensions discovered in surveys of our marine and fresh waters (including those to the western United States associated with the 1997–1998 El Niño oceanographic event and noted by R. N. Lea and R. H. Rosenblatt, 2000, CalCOFI Rep. 41:117–129). Recent systematic studies have led to the recognition of species previously thought to be junior synonyms and, conversely, have demonstrated that some species on previous lists are junior synonyms and are thus to be removed from the list. There are still many cases where there is uncertainty about whether a given taxon should be treated at the species level or lower (e.g., the subspecies level), particularly in the Cyprinidae, Catostomidae, Salmonidae, Percidae, Dactyloscopidae, and Labrisomidae (in some of these families, we expect there will be more nominal species recognized as valid than placed in synonymy). Differences of opinion may result among users employing different species concepts (e.g., see R. L. Mayden, 1999, J. Nematol. 31(2):95–116, and J. S. Nelson, 1999, Rev. Fish Biol. Fish. 9:277–280) and different lines of evidence (e.g., morphological versus molecular data). In accepting names of species as valid from various works such as faunal, taxonomic, and systematic studies, regardless of approach, we make little or no judgment on differing species concepts, stated or not, of the various authors. Species of uncertain status are dealt with on a case-by-case basis. However, in general, when dealing with conflicting conclusions in current literature, we feel that if a good probability exists of a species being valid that is currently recognized, it is better to err on the side of continuing to recognize it than not. Otherwise, we have been more conservative than some might prefer in considering many changes. In general, where there is ongoing research on the question known to us, we prefer to wait until the evidence is published before making a change. Further discussion on how we have proceeded is discussed below under various headings.

Comprehensive listing of all species in the area of coverage, North America, is attempted with the following exceptions. Many species that occur beyond our bathymetric (200-m bottom depth) and geographical limits have early life history stages that have been recorded from our continental shelf waters. These species are excluded from this list, as are many mesopelagic species that may occur over the outer shelf where deep waters occur very close to shore. For example, Scott and Scott (1988) described species where individuals (including eggs or larvae) occasionally come within our area, but they are omitted from the list. Other than further qualifications given in the next section, we have not limited the list. All species, ranging from small, secretive or rare fishes, to large, recreational/sport and commercial fishes, are of importance in documenting and understanding our biodiversity. Many of the species are used as laboratory experimental animals, are displayed or maintained in public or private aquaria, are used as bait, or are treated as objects of natural history inquiry or aesthetic appeal. Some species once disdained as "trash fish" are commercially harvested and highly valued today. Considerable attention is being focused on using the bycatch of fisheries, and as a result, species formerly discarded are now entering the market place. An increased environmental consciousness has focused attention on native fishes as indicators of the condition of freshwater and marine ecosystems. Endangered species are discussed in newspapers and popular magazines. Thus, this comprehensive listing will be of use to many interests. The book's organization and indexing are such that its comprehensiveness should still make it easy to use by those with special interests.

## Area of Coverage

The present list purports to include all species of fishes known with reproducing or self-sustaining populations from the fresh waters of continental Canada, the United States, and Mexico, and those marine species inhabiting contiguous shore waters on or above the continental shelf, to a bottom depth of 200 m (656 feet). We exclude species known only where the bottom depth exceeds 200 m, even if the fish is found shallower than 200 m. There are many species known in waters south of Mexico that will undoubtedly be recorded from

there in the future. This is especially true on the Atlantic side, where there are about 66 marine species known from Belize that have yet to be recorded from Mexico. Most of these will likely be added to the list at some time in the future as they can be expected to occur northward along the eastern side of the Yucatan Peninsula. In addition, six species are known from freshwater from Belize but not recorded from Mexico. In the Atlantic Ocean, as conventionally defined, the shore fishes from Greenland, eastern Canada and the United States, and the Mexican waters of the Gulf of Mexico and the Caribbean Sea adjacent to the Yucatan Peninsula southward to the Mexico-Belize border (as far as we were able to determine their faunas) are included. Species from Iceland, Bermuda, the Bahamas, Cuba, and the other West Indian islands are excluded unless they occur also in the region covered. In the Pacific, as conventionally defined, the area includes that part of the continental shelf from Bering Strait to the Mexico–Guatemala border, including the oceanic Revillagigedo Archipelago and Guadalupe Island, to 200 m depth in contiguous shore waters. It is especially difficult to know which species to include for oceanic islands lacking a continental shelf, where oceanic species may be found close to shore along with neritic species, and we have attempted in such cases to include only species normally associated with continental shelves. The Arctic shore waters of Alaska and Canada are included. Hawaii and Clipperton Island (atoll), with their large and strikingly different Indo-Pacific and endemic faunas, are not. Deep-sea fishes, whether benthic or mesopelagic, including vertically migrating species that temporarily enter the epipelagic zone, and strictly oceanic fishes are excluded unless they appear other than as presumed strays in our shelf waters. In practice, this line of distinction often is difficult to apply and becomes rather arbitrary, especially if egg and larval stages are considered. Pelagic fishes that enter waters over the continental shelf are included. We exclude species that are known in North America only from deeper than 200 m, even though they have been captured in extralimital areas where the bottom depth is shallower than 200 m. Users should thus exercise caution when inferring depth ranges of species (e.g., *Enchelycore anatina* (Lowe, 1838), commonly found in the eastern Atlantic well above 200 m, has been recorded in western Atlantic only at depths in excess of 200 m, and *Ophichthus menezesi* McCosker & Böhlke,

1984, to 169–209 m off Brazil, was found in the Gulf of Mexico off Florida only from 1,200 to 1,400 m).

Key abbreviations in the list provide a general guide to occurrence. An "**A**" denotes Atlantic Ocean and includes the Arctic Ocean east of the Boothia Peninsula (i.e., 95°W longitude), whereas "**AM**" denotes occurrence in Atlantic Ocean in Mexico but not recorded in Canada or the United States. A "**P**" refers to the Pacific Ocean and includes the western Arctic Ocean (Chukchi Sea and Beaufort Sea to west of the Boothia Peninsula), whereas "**PM**" denotes occurrence in Pacific Ocean in Mexico but not recorded in Canada or the United States. The list does not separately indicate species occurring in the Arctic Ocean (an "A" or a "P" may also, or solely, indicate an Arctic occurrence, such as *Triglops nybelini*, designated as "A-P" but known only from the Beaufort Sea in the Arctic [here considered "P"] eastward into the Atlantic Ocean ["A"] and absent from the Pacific Ocean). An "**F:**" indicates occurrence in freshwaters or other inland waters that are saline (e.g., Salton Sea, California). Some species so designated may refer to historical records, such as *Elops affinis* in the lower Colorado River and the Salton Sea. An "F:" designation followed by a "**C**" denotes freshwater Canada, whereas "**M**" denotes freshwater Mexico, and "**U**" denotes freshwater United States (contiguous states and/or Alaska). It should be noted that (i) marine species known off one coast shallower than 201 m but off the other coast deeper than 200 m are only indicated as occurring off the shallower coast (e.g., *Notacanthus chemnitzii* is listed as "A" only but is known off California from depths over 200 m); (ii) although two species may be noted as occurring in both marine and fresh waters, one may be primarily marine and the other primarily fresh water; and (iii) many species not otherwise noted in the list as "F" have been collected on occasion in estuarine water or in freshwater (e.g., W. F. Loftus, 2000, Fla. Sci. 63(1):27–47; F. J. Schwartz, 1992, *in* C. Cole and K. Turner, editors, Barrier island ecology of the mid-Atlantic Coast: a symposium, Technical Report, NPS/SERCAHA/NRTR-93/04:94–118; F. J. Schwartz, 2000, J. Elisha Mitchell Sci. Soc. 116(3):206–224). A bracketed "**[I]**" follows the letter indication of occurrence for any introduced (nonindigenous or exotic) species established within our area of coverage and may be used separately or collectively for the "A," "P," "F," "C," "U," and "M" designa-

tions (these are species introduced into the designated area through human activity, documented or inferred, directly or indirectly). This symbol is not used for introductions of a native species within each of the above designated areas (e.g., the introduction of *Salvelinus fontinalis* from eastern to western Canada), but continues to be employed for a species subsequently dispersing into a country from another into which it had been introduced (e.g., *Scardinius erythrophthalmus* is still considered as an introduction in both countries where it presently occurs). Unlike the 1991 edition, we indicate the successful introduction of species from one ocean to another (e.g., *Alosa sapidissima* and *Morone saxatilis* were successfully introduced into Pacific waters from the Atlantic, and their occurrence is thus indicated as "A-F:CU-P[I]" [such changes are not noted in Appendix 1]). A bracketed "**[X]**" indicates that the species is considered extinct. Species given in the 1991 edition that are still extant but known only from historical records and probably now extirpated in either Canada or the United States are still listed (e.g., *Erimystax x-punctatus* no longer exists in Canada but does occur in the United States and is listed as "F:CU"; *Catostomus bernardini* no longer exists in the United States but does occur in Mexico and is listed as "F:UM"). All Mexican species noted as "AM," "PM," or "F:M" are new to the list and, with few exceptions, are not otherwise annotated in Appendix 1. Species with the notation "A" or "P" and with a **name in Spanish and/or French** occur in Mexican and/or Quebec waters and elsewhere in the area of coverage, and they appeared in the 1991 list unless otherwise indicated as being new records (mainly California) by an accompanying asterisk (*).

## Family Names

Family names are important in identification and information retrieval. They are widely used in fishery literature, popular books on fishes, and dictionaries and encyclopedias. However, in some groups, ichthyologists vary widely in their interpretation of family limits. While we agree that changes in family names are to be avoided wherever possible, we also feel that the list should reflect, in our best judgment, the actual practices of current systematists. This has resulted in a considerable increase in the number of families recognized. Apart from this, we prefer to accept families added since the 1991 edition when the reasons are based on phylogenetic grounds or where the former family name suggests unlikely relationships. Appendix notes are generally provided where we have not made changes that some may think would be justified. We prefer not to make subjective or arbitrary changes such as splitting up a family known to be monophyletic. Thus, for example, we recognize the whitefishes, the grayling, and the trouts, salmons, and chars in one monophyletic family rather than in three separate families as preferred by some authors. In this example, splitting would create a loss of phylogenetic information that could be overcome by recognizing superfamilies or suborders. With lumping, as we do in this case, the loss in phylogenetic information can be corrected where deemed desirable by recognizing subfamilies. In general, with such difference, we opt for the older and conservative arrangement. New families added to the list are annotated in Appendix 1; however, families added because all species for our new area of coverage are in Mexico only are not otherwise annotated as being new. We recognize orders and some higher levels of classification but stress that this list is not intended to necessarily reflect what we consider to be the accepted views of relationships at the ordinal level. Not all changes at the ordinal level from the previous edition are annotated in Appendix 1.

## Common Names

Common names of species have had a long history, far exceeding that of scientific names, and as long as the public and biologists use them, we feel it behooves us to have a standardized and effective system for them. The Committee therefore aims to develop a body of common names—a single common name for each species—that reflects broad current usage; to create a richer, more meaningful, and colorful vernacular nomenclature; and to promote mechanisms that will add to the stability and universality of names applied to North American fishes. Common names of fishes, as used in this list, are applied to individual species. These names sometimes are employed as market names as well as for other purposes. However, some market names often apply to several species or differ for various reasons from the names adopted in this list, and they are not incorporated into this work. In the interests of an informed public, we strongly encourage the adoption of the common names presented herein whether by authors, merchants, or others, even if a name is thought to have little appeal (e.g., we discourage

the use of the regional market name "mullet," instead of sucker, when applied to members of the family Catostomidae). A summary of market names in English, as they apply to fishes (and invertebrates) marketed in the United States, is available in "The Seafood List, FDA's Guide to Acceptable Market Names for Seafood Sold in Interstate Commerce 1993, U.S. Food and Drug Administration," U.S. Government Printing Office (see also http://vm.cfsan.fda.gov/~frf/rfe0.html). In the present list, many names differ from those used in publications of the Food and Agriculture Organization of the United Nations (FAO). We hope that in the future there may be greater agreement.

The common name, as here employed, is viewed as a formal appellation to be used in lieu of the Latinized scientific name of a species. We stress that common names are not intended to duplicate the power of scientific names in reflecting phylogenetic relationships (see Principle 8 below). History confirms that common names are often more stable than scientific names (this is not widely appreciated). The following species had changes in only the scientific name between the 1980 and 1991 editions: rosyface chub — *Hybopsis rubrifrons* to *Notropis rubescens* and now (2004) back to *H. rubrifrons*; rainbow trout — *Salmo gairdneri* to *Oncorhynchus mykiss*; English sole — *Parophrys vetulus* to *Pleuronectes vetulus* and now back to *Parophrys vetulus*. Generic names in particular are subject to interpretation and vacillation and will remain necessarily so. Common names are usually more readily adaptable to lay uses than scientific names. There is clear need for standardization and uniformity in vernacular names not only for sport and commercial fishes, but as trade (market) names, for aquarium fishes, in legal terminology, and as substitutes for scientific names in popular or scientific writing. The Committee believes it desirable to establish a common name for each species of fishes occurring naturally or through introduction in the waters of Canada, the United States, and Mexico. The newly added common names in Spanish, as determined by committee members Espinosa-Pérez and Findley, are based on field experience, consultation with colleagues, and review of many sources in the literature. Principal sources consulted for the latter are marked with an asterisk (*) in the References section. Many of those also were consulted for possible adoption of names in English for Mexican species newly entering the list. For the common names in French for species of freshwater fishes in Quebec, we have relied primarily on J. F. Bergeron and J. Dubé, 2000, Liste historique des poissons d'eau douce du Québec, Gouvernement du Québec, Mars 2000. Names of marine species in Quebec are from Desrosiers et al. 1995, which is also useful for freshwater fishes. For catostomids of the genus *Moxostoma*, we follow J. F. Bergeron and J. Dubé, 2000 and A. Branchaud and R. E. Jenkins, 1999, Can. Field-Nat. 113(2):345–358, where *suceur* of previous lists was replaced by *chevalier*. Family names in French have been selected mainly by J. F. Bergeron (personal communication, May 2001–August 2003), from a variety of North American and European sources, including D. E. McAllister, 1990, A list of the fishes of Canada/Liste des poissons du Canada, Syllogeus 64, National Museum of Natural Sciences, Ottawa, and B. W. Coad, 1995, Encyclopedia of Canadian fishes, Canadian Museum of Nature and Canadian Sportfishing Productions, Inc., Ottawa.

Agreement on many names may be reached quickly, but others are attended by complications and marked disagreement may develop. This disagreement is especially true of fishes known by market (trade) names that differ from those more familiar to anglers, biologists, and others (e.g., what is known as "red snapper" on much of the West Coast may be a species of *Sebastes* and not the snapper *Lutjanus campechanus*). The use of different names in various parts of the geographic range of a species creates difficulties that seem solvable only through arbitration. Conversely, a given name may be employed in several places for diverse species. Although Committee action on such situations may not be expected to change local use quickly, it seems plainly improper to sanction use of one name for two or more different species. We stress that all users of fish common names are ill served, indeed perhaps misled, if names are used in an inconsistent manner.

After struggling with common names for many years, an earlier Committee on Names of Fishes realized the importance of establishing a set of guiding principles to be employed in the selection of English names. Such a code permits a more objective appraisal of the relative merits among several names than if selection were based primarily on personal experience and preference. Consideration of many vernacular names of fishes makes it apparent that few principles can be established for which there will be no exceptions. Many exceptions exist because at the time the Committee began to function, a majority of the larger and more abundant, hence "important," species in the United States and Canada had such firmly established common names that it would have been unrealistic to reject them just to conform to a newly established set of principles. The name for a species may often be decided by weighing the "pros" and "cons" among possible choices and selecting the one that best fits the aggregate of guiding criteria. The criteria that the Committee regards as appropriate to the selection of common names of fishes are repeated below from previous lists, with some modification.

## Principles Governing Selection of Common Names

1. *A single vernacular name in each appropriate language shall be accepted for each species.* In the 1991 edition, only one fish, *Coregonus artedi*, had two accepted common names; now there are no exceptions.

2. *No two species in the list shall have the same common name.* Commonly used names of extralimital species should be avoided for species in our area wherever possible.

3. *The expression "common" or its Spanish or French equivalent as part of a fish's name shall be avoided wherever possible.*

4. *Simplicity in names is favored.* In English and Spanish fish names, hyphens, suffixes, and apostrophes shall be omitted (e.g., smallmouth bass) except when they are orthographically essential (e.g., three-eye flounder), have a special meaning (e.g., C-O sole), are necessary to avoid possible misunderstanding (e.g., cusk-eel), or join two fish names, neither of which represents the fish in question, into a single name (e.g., the trout-perch, which is neither a trout nor a perch). Compounded modifying words, especially appropriate to English, including paired structures, should usually be treated as singular nouns in apposition with a group name (e.g., spottail shiner), but a plural modifier should usually be placed in adjectival form (e.g., spotted hake, blackbanded sunfish) unless its plural nature is obvious (e.g., fourspot flounder). Preference shall be given to names that are short and euphonious.

The compounding of brief, familiar words into a single name, written without a hyphen, may in some cases promote clarity and simplicity, especially in English (e.g., tomcod, goldfish, mudminnow), but the habitual practice of combining words, especially those that are lengthy, awkward, or unfamilar, shall be avoided.

5. *Common names shall not be capitalized in text use except for those elements that are proper names (nouns)* (e.g., rainbow trout, but Sacramento perch; carpita fantasma, but guayacón de Palenque; grand corégone, but anguille d'Amérique).

6. *Names intended to honor persons* (e.g., Allison's tuna, Julia's darter, Meek's halfbeak, blanquillo de Hubbs) *are discouraged in that they are without descriptive value.* In some groups, identical specific patronyms in the scientific names (sometimes honoring different persons sharing a surname) exist in related genera, and use of a patronym in the common name may be confusing. In a few instances, patronyms have become so incorporated into the vernacular that they are not treated or recognized as such. These names are accepted and not capitalized (e.g., guppy, lane snapper). This principle does not necessarily apply to the common names in French (e.g., the common name for *Liparis coheni* is limace de Cohen). However, in cases where a patronymic common name did not have an established "priority," an alternate nonpatronymic common name usually was chosen.

7. *Only clearly defined and well-marked taxonomic entities* (usually species) *shall be assigned common names.* While subspecies are not always suitable subjects for common names, some valid subspecies are so different in appearance (not just in geographic distribution) that they are distinguished readily by anglers, commercial fishermen, or laypersons, and for these, a common name constitutes an important aid in communication. However, and contrary to the 1991 edition where we recognized two subspecies of *Esox americanus*, for the sake of consistency, we have not provided scientific or common names for subspecies in this edition. Nevertheless, we recognize that subspecies, with their own evolutionary history in allopatry, have importance in evolutionary inquiry and may be given special protective status and be recognized in studies of biodiversity. When subspecies names are used, the common name for the species should apply to all subspecies of the taxon.

Hybrids are usually not given common names, but those important in fish management and which have established common names are treated in Appendix 2. Cultured varieties, phases, and morphological variants are not named even though they may be important in commercial trade and culture of aquarium fishes (e.g., the many varieties of goldfish and common carp; the spotted versus the golden color phases of the leopard grouper and the guineafowl puffer).

8. *The common name shall not be intimately tied to the scientific name.* The necessary vagaries of scientific nomenclature do not entail constant changing of common names. The unfortunate practice of applying a common name to each genus, a modifying name for each species, and still another modifier for each subspecies, while appealing in its simplicity, has the defect of inflexibility, and risks nonrecognition of a fish by discarding what may be a perfectly acceptable traditionally used name. We see that practice as simply an attempt to recreate in the vernacular name the scientific nomenclature. If a species is transferred from one genus to another, or shifted from species to subspecies status or vice versa, the common name ideally should remain unaffected. It is not a primary function of common names to indicate relationship. This principle continues to be misunderstood or rejected by those who advocate that common names of all members of a genus should incorporate the same "root" word(s) (e.g., that all *Oncorhynchus* be termed salmon, such as "rainbow salmon" and "steelhead salmon," and those of *Salvelinus* be termed char(r)s, such as "brook char"). We stress our belief that the stability of common names far outweighs any disadvantage in this regard. When two or more taxonomic groups (e.g., nominal species) are found to be identical (synonymous), one name shall be adopted for the combined group. See also Principle 13.

9. *Names shall not violate the tenets of good taste* (e.g., *names shall not contain offensive words*). Our changes of the names squawfish to pikeminnow for species of *Ptychocheilus*, and jewfish to goliath grouper, were made

with this principle in mind. These changes were made after receiving opinions from a number of individuals and receiving considerable support from others.

---

The preceding principles are largely in the nature of procedural dicta. Those below are criteria regarded as aids in the selection of suitable names.

10. *Colorful, romantic, fanciful, metaphorical, and otherwise distinctive and original names are especially appropriate.* Such terminology adds to the richness and breadth of the nomenclature and yields a harvest of satisfaction to the user. Examples of such names in English include madtom, Dolly Varden, midshipman, chilipepper, garibaldi, pumpkinseed, flier, angelfish, Moorish idol, and hogchoker; and in Spanish include bruja, guitarra, chucho, and lacha; and in French include tête-de-boule, crayon d'argent, and truite fardée.

11. *North American native names or their modifications are welcome for adoption as common names.* Those in current use include menhaden, eulachon, cisco, Chinook, mummichog, tautog, puyeki, and totoaba.

12. *Regardless of origin, truly vernacular names that are widespread and in common use by the public are to be retained wherever possible.* In addition to aboriginal names, many now well-known fish names utilized north of Mexico originated with nonEnglish-speaking fishermen: barracuda, cero, mojarra, pompano, sierra (all Spanish or modified from it); capelin (French); bocaccio (Italian); mako (Maori). Many excellent names have been developed by North American immigrants. Most of these conform to Principles 14 and 15 below. Care should be taken to avoid words that mean the same thing in related languages but differ slightly in spelling (e.g., sierra in Spanish and serra in Portuguese).

13. *Commonly employed names adopted from traditional English usage* (e.g., chub, minnow, trout, bass, perch, sole, flounder), *from Spanish* (e.g., cazón, sardina, carpa, mojarra, perca, lenguado) *and similarly from French* (e.g., méné and perche) *are given considerable latitude in taxonomic placement.* Adherence to customary practice is to be preferred if this does not conflict with the broad general us-

age of another name. Many names, however, have been applied to similarly appearing but often distantly related fishes in North America. For example, we find "bass" and "lenguado" in use for representatives of several families of spiny-rayed fishes, and "perch" and "perca" for even more. "Chub" appears in such unrelated groups as the Cyprinidae and Kyphosidae, and "mojarra" in the Cichlidae, Gerreidae and other families. The ocean whitefish or pierna, *Caulolatilus princeps*, sometimes referred to as "salmón" in northwestern Mexico, is not a salmonid, and the Pacific pompano (pámpano in Spanish), *Peprilus simillimus*, is not a carangid, yet each is best known to fishermen throughout its range by the name indicated. For widely known species, the Committee believes it preferable to recognize general use than to adopt bookish or pedantic substitutes. Thus, established practice with original usage should outweigh attempts at consistency. This is not well understood by some ichthyologists who feel that "perch" should not be used for an embiotocid, "trout" for a *Salvelinus*, "sardinita" for a characid, and "cazón" for a carcharhinid. Some problems have been avoided or minimized by joining English names to create new words (e.g., seatrout for sea trout, mudsucker for mud sucker, surfperch for surf perch); such combinations have gained wide acceptance since they were adopted by the Committee in its earlier lists.

14. *Structural attributes, color, and color pattern are desirable sources of names and are commonly so used.* Sailfin, flathead, slippery, giant, mottled, copper, tripletail for English, chato, jorobado, bocón, gigante, jabonero, pinto, cobrizo for Spanish, and citron, cuivré, fardé, and fossettes in French, and a multitude of other descriptors decorate fish names. Efforts should be made to select terms that are descriptively accurate, and to hold repetition of those most frequently employed (e.g., white [blanco, blanc], black [negro, noir], spotted [manchado, tacheté], banded [de cintas, barré]) to a minimum.

Following tradition for English names in North American ichthyology and herpetology, we have attempted to restrict use of "line" or "stripe" to mean longitudinal marks that parallel the body axis and "bar" or "band" to mean vertical or transverse marks.

15. *Ecological characteristics are useful in making good names.* Such terms should be properly descriptive. English (Spanish, French) modifiers such as reef (de arrecife, récif), coral (coralino, corail), sand (arenero, sable), rock (piedrero, roche), lake (de lago, lac), freshwater (dulciacuícola, dulcicole), and mountain (de la sierra, montagne) are well known in fish names.

16. *Geographic distribution provides suitable adjectival modifiers.* Poorly descriptive or misleading geographic characterizations (e.g., "Kentucky bass" for a wide-ranging species) should be corrected unless they are too entrenched in current usage (in the interests of stability, we have retained such names as Alaska blackfish even though this species is known to also occur in Russia, and "guatopote de Sonora" even though this livebearer commonly occurs beyond the limits of that state). In the interest of brevity, it is usually possible to delete words such as lake (lago, lac), river (río, fleuve), gulf (golfo, golfe), or sea (mar, mer), in the names of species (e.g., Colorado pikeminnow, not "Colorado River pikeminnow"; topote del Balsas, not "topote del Río Balsas").

17. *Generic names may be employed as common names outright* (e.g., gambusia, remora, tilapia, mola, torpedo, anchoa, brótula, guavina) *or in modified form* (e.g., molly, from *Mollienesia*). Once adopted, such names should be maintained even if the generic or higher level name is subsequently changed. These vernaculars should be written in Roman orthography (i.e., not in italics). Brevity and euphony are of special importance for names of this type, which probably will be adopted most often for aquarium fishes or other small and/or little-known fishes that do not already have a well-established vernacular nomenclature.

18. *The duplication of common names for fishes and other organisms should be avoided if possible, but names in wide general use need not be rejected on this basis alone.* For example, "buffalo" is employed for various artiodactyl mammals and for catostomid suckers of the genus *Ictiobus,* "zorro" (literally meaning fox) is used for alopiid sharks, and "mariposa" (literally meaning butterfly) is employed for chaetodontid butterflyfishes

and gymnurid butterfly rays. On the basis of prevailing use, such names are admissible as fish names without modification. However, we now have changed the name "dolphin," appropriately applied to several species of toothed cetaceans but also formerly employed for species of *Coryphaena*, to dolphinfish in order to avoid confusion.

## Relationship of Common and Scientific Names of Species

The primary purpose of this list is to recommend a common name in the appropriate language and to provide the generally accepted scientific name for all species of fishes in North America within the geographical limitations applied. Common names, we believe, can be stabilized by general agreement. Scientific names, on the other hand, will inevitably shift with advancing knowledge and in accordance with the views of taxonomists. With regard to usage, the nomenclature reflects the opinion of the Committee, which realizes that many users of this list are incompletely aware of the literature or are not interested in systematics or the rules of nomenclature, but simply seek a guide to technical names, common and/or scientific. The scientific nomenclature employed has been reviewed carefully with regard to spelling, authorities, and dates of original descriptions.

We stress that there are many groups in which there is disagreement on their classification or where the classification is poorly known. Also, there are often subjective differences of opinion between workers in designating rank of taxa. In addition, workers using a synthetic (i.e., nonphylogenetic) methodology may prefer to classify species with marked trophic, behavioral, or morphological specializations in monotypic genera (monotypic genera and families may also be recognized for taxa whose relationships are too poorly known to better classify, a philosophy to which we adhere). We prefer to accept phylogenetic conclusions when the work is firmly founded (see also discussion above under "Family Names" and "Common Names," particularly Principle 8).

## Plan of the List

The list is presented in a phylogenetic sequence of families of fishes as far as we know it from available research. Arrangement of the orders and families generally follows Nelson (1994), but there are some changes that reflect recent systematic studies. The classes and orders of recent fishes are indicated. In most cases, we give a single common name for each family in English, Spanish, and French. Exceptions include the family Salmonidae, the trouts and salmons family, which includes trouts, salmons, chars, whitefishes, and graylings.

Within families, genera and species are listed alphabetically; the occasional disadvantage of separating closely related forms within a family is regarded as more than offset by the greater ease of use. We adopt landscape format in this edition, versus portrait as in the previous editions, in order to present the common names of species in English, Spanish, and French on the same line. Each page of Part I consists of five columns, the first with the scientific name, the second the area of occurrence, the third the common name in English (regardless of area of occurrence), the fourth the common name in Spanish for those species in Mexico, and the fifth the common name in French for those species in Quebec.

We attempt to follow the new code of the International Commission of Zoological Nomenclature (ICZN) and, as such, employ original orthographies of species names (thus, the endings of some personal [patronymic] names will be -i or -ii as appropriate). The present code, as embodied in the fourth edition of the "International Code of Zoological Nomenclature" (hereafter referred to as the Code) was published in 1999 and took effect 1 January 2000. C. J. Ferraris and W. N. Eschmeyer, 2000, Copeia 2000(3):907–908, reviewed the new Code with reference to its effect on fish names.

In this edition, we continue to add, after the scientific name, the authority and the date of the original published description of the species. Authorities and dates are commonly needed by persons who may not have ready access to the original literature. Determination of the correct authority and the year of publication can often be complicated, especially for names proposed before 1900. Eschmeyer (1998), Gilbert (1998), and others have corrected many dates of description that appeared in the 1991 edition, and we have incorporated these corrections in the present list and noted them in Appendix 1. Our justifications for the spellings of Delaroche, Forsskål, Lacepède, and Lesueur were explained in the third (page 5) and fourth (page 8) editions. The attribution of names proposed in the M. E. Blochii Systema Ichthyologicae, 1801, by J. G. Schneider was explained in the fourth edition (page 8).

Use of the authority's name(s) reflects current interpretation of the new Code. In line with those rules, the author's name(s) directly follow(s) the specific name (written in italics). If the species, when originally described, was assigned to the same genus to which it is assigned herein, the author's name(s) is (are) not enclosed in parentheses; if the species was described in another genus, the author's name(s) appear(s) in parentheses. The date (as year) of publication is separated from the authority by a comma and is included within the parentheses where these are appropriate. For example, Mitchill originally named the brook trout, *Salmo fontinalis*, in a work published in 1814; it appears here as *Salvelinus fontinalis* (Mitchill, 1814). In the 1991 edition, parentheses were also placed around an author's name in cases where the species-group name was originally combined with an incorrect spelling or an unjustified emendation of the generic name. This is no longer appropriate, even though an unjustified emendation is an available name with its own authorship and date (Article 51.3.1 of the Code). Hence, parentheses are now removed for species described in such genera as *Rhinobatus* (now *Rhinobatos*), *Raia* (now *Raja*), *Lepidosteus* (now *Lepisosteus*), *Ophichthys* (now *Ophichthus*), *Nototropis* (now *Notropis*), *Amiurus* (now *Ameiurus*), *Hemirhamphus* (now *Hemiramphus*), *Opisthognathus* (now *Opistognathus*), and *Pomadasis* (now *Pomadasys*). Care in orthography must be taken because the same spelling may be used for an unjustified emendation and for an independent valid spelling; for example, *Ophichthys* is used both as an unjustified emendation of *Ophichthus* Ahl, 1789, a genus of ophichthid eels, and as *Ophichthys* Swainson, 1839, for a synbranchid eel (Eschmeyer 1998:2045).

Previous editions of the list have received widespread use and endorsement. Since the fifth edition was published in 1991, many users have communicated their suggested changes to the Committee, and each received consideration as we prepared the present edition. Stability in common names was given highest priority, and changes have been made only for substantial reasons. Scientific knowledge of fishes advanced rapidly during the 1990s. Many new species were described, many additional species were recorded within our boundaries, and numerous taxonomic/systematic revisions were completed. Addition of species has forced modifications or changes in some common names, and revisions often resulted in changes in scientific nomenclature. In some families (e.g., Cyprinidae), the changes are ongoing, incomplete, or in some cases conflicting. The Committee has chosen to be conservative in adopting such changes in the hope that reversals or vacillation will be avoided or minimized in future editions of the list.

Except for the many additions of species from Mexico, all new entries and all entries that depart in any way (scientific name, author(s), date of description, occurrence, and common name in English) from the 1991 edition are preceded by an asterisk (*). Information describing and explaining the change is given for each such entry in Appendix 1, identified by the page number on which the name appears in the list. Information formerly given in Appendix 1 of the 1970, 1980, and 1991 lists (pages 65–87, 68–92, and 71–96, respectively), documenting the changes between editions 2 and 3, between 3 and 4, and between 4 and 5, is not repeated in this edition.

A plus sign (+) before an entry indicates that, although the entry is unchanged, a comment will be found in Appendix 1 under that name. This includes taxa above the species level (e.g., family and order) where the name is unchanged but the composition of the taxon differs from that in the 1991 edition (e.g., by removal of taxa or transfers from other higher taxa).

Although most decisions of the Committee have been unanimous, many were made by majority opinion. Thus, no committee member necessarily subscribes to all decisions reached, but we respect that no one person has all the right answers. We realize that not all decisions will be "popular," but we hope that all users will appreciate our efforts. In many cases, information available to the Committee exceeded that found in the current literature. The Committee often struggled to reach justifiable decisions regarding inclusion of such information and has been cautious about adopting changes.

The alphabetical list of families on pages 1–6 serves also as a Table of Contents. The list, Part I, appears on pages 47–186, and the appendices follow in Part II, pages 187–256. Part III, References, Editions of the Names List, and Edition of the World List begins on page 257, Personal Communications begins on page 261, followed by the Index, beginning on page 265. Appendix 2 of the 1991 edition (Exotic Fishes) has not been included because of the availability of this information elsewhere (e.g., for the United States, http://nas.er.usgs.gov/fishes, and Fuller et al. 1999; and for North America, R. Claudi and J. Leach, editors, 1999, Nonindigenous freshwater organisms, vectors, biology and impacts, Lewis Publishers, Boca Raton, Florida).

## Index

The Index incorporates both scientific and common names in all three languages. Page references are given for common names herein adopted for classes, orders, families, and species. A single entry is included for each species; for example, brook trout is entered only under "trout, brook," but "trucha de arroyo" appears as such. There are a great many vernacular names of North American fishes, and extensive research would be necessary to assemble even a large fraction of them, some of which have not been used for many decades and are of historical interest only. In general, the Committee has not attempted to perform such an extensive search (although one member [LTF] has compiled a list of common names in Spanish and English currently containing more than 16,000 entries), but many of the more widely used names are included herein.

Page references are given for the scientific names here entered for classes, orders, families, genera, and species. Each species is entered only under its specific (trivial) name. For example, *Sciaenops ocellatus* may be located only under "*ocellatus, Sciaenops*," although an entry for "*Sciaenops*" directs the reader to the page on which entries in that genus begin. Scientific names of species that are not accepted for this list are excluded, except for those that appeared in the 1991 (fifth) edition and have since been placed in synonymy, as explained for such cases in Appendix 1.

## Acknowledgments

This list is the result of contributions made over nearly 60 years by the many past and present members of the Committee on Names of Fishes. To all of the former members, we are greatly indebted. Some have continued to contribute to the Committee's endeavors, and in this regard, we especially thank Reeve M. Bailey and C. Richard Robins. They have maintained a strong and helpful interest. Lasting contributions were made also by many specialists leading up to the second, third, fourth, and fifth editions, wherein their help was acknowledged. In preparing materials for this edition, we have received assistance, large and small, from many individuals. We have enjoyed the help of an astute advisory subcommittee, most of whose members met with us during various annual meetings of the American Society of Ichthyologists and Herpetologists where we also appreciated the help of local conference chairpersons for arranging meeting space. We owe a special debt of gratitude to the core members of the advisory group: William D. Anderson, Jr., Jacques F. Bergeron, George H. Burgess, Brooks M. Burr, Bruce B. Collette, Salvador Contreras-Balderas, William N. Eschmeyer, Robert E. Jenkins, Richard L. Mayden, John F. Morrissey, Lawrence M. Page, Richard H. Rosenblatt, Ramón Ruiz-Carus, William F. Smith-Vaniz, and Wayne C. Starnes.

The monumental three-volume "Catalog of Fishes" by W. N. Eschmeyer (editor) (Eschmeyer, 1998) brought to light many important nomenclatural changes and problems, and we have exchanged data continually with Bill. We especially appreciate his efforts on our behalf and that of the users of the List.

In addition to that advisory group, so many individuals assisted our task that it is impractical to list them all. Some, however, have been so continuously interested and constructively helpful in our task or had other major input as to merit special mention: Larry G. Allen, M. James Allen, James W. Atz, David Aurioles-Gamboa, Henry L. Bart, Robert J. Behnke, Louis Bernatchez, Ernesto Bolado, Herbert T. Boschung, Brian W. Bowen, John Clay Bruner, Warren E. Burgess, Morgan Busby, William A. Bussing, Donald G. Buth, Kent E. Carpenter, Robert C. Cashner, José Luis Castro-Aguirre, David Catania, Ted M. Cavender, Francois Chapleau, Brian W. Coad, Miles M. Coburn, Walter R. Courtenay, Jr., Angelica Daza-Zepeda, Jean Dubé, William N. Eschmeyer, David A. Etnier, Richard F. Feeney, Patricia Fuentes-Mata, Juan Pablo Gallo-Reynoso, Juan Manuel García-Caudillo, R. Grant Gilmore, Roberto González-Morales, David W. Greenfield, Thomas A. Greiner, Gary D. Grossman, Rocio Güereca, Phillip M. Harris, Ian J. Harrison, Karsten E. Hartel, Antony S. Harold, Philip A. Hastings, Phillip C. Heemstra, Dean A. Hendrickson, Michael H. Horn, C. Leticia Huidobro, Paul Humann, Tomio Iwamoto, Witold L. Klawe, Cynthia (Cindy) Klepadlo, Sven O. Kullander, Louise Lapierre, Robert J. Lavenberg, Kenneth J. Lazara, Michel Letendre, Ken Lindeman, Myrna I. López, Milton Love, Gérard Massé, Ann C. Matarese, Richard E. Matheson, Jr., John E. McCosker, Catherine (Kitty) W. Mecklenburg, Maurice (Scott) F. Mettee, the late Robert Rush Miller, the late W. L. Minckley, Jr., Randall D. Mooi, J. Manuel Nava-Romo, Leo G. Nico, Volker Niem, Steven M. Norris, Pere Oliver, James W. Orr, Alex E. Peden, Mauricia Pérez-Tello, Frank L. Pezold, Edward J. Pfeiler, Edwin P. Pister, Héctor G. Plascencia, Stuart G. Poss, Catherine Poussart, John E. Randall, Spring Randolph, James D. Reist, Claude Renaud, Robert H. Robins, Gorgonio Ruiz-Campos, Mark H. Sabaj, Juan Jacobo Schmitter-Soto, Jeffrey A. Seigel, Bernard Séret, David G. Smith, Gerald R. Smith, Victor G. Springer, Donald J. Stewart, Royal D. Suttkus, Christine Thacker, Bruce A. Thompson, Jorge Torre-Cosio, James C. Tyler, Albert M. van der Heiden, Carlos J. Villavicencio-Garayzar, H. J. Walker, Melvin L. Warren, Jr., Douglas C. Weaver, Edward O. Wiley, Jeffrey T. Williams, and Chris Wilson.

Travel funds for committee members to attend two marathon work sessions in Gainesville, Florida were provided by the American Fisheries Society. These meetings were held at the U.S. Geological Survey Lab, where the help of Sherry Bostick and other staff members was very much appreciated. We were also greatly assisted by local ichthyologists, most notably William F. Smith-Vaniz and George Burgess, and local hostess Nancy Gilbert. We also wish to thank our home institutions for subsidizing our efforts on this project, often including travel funds, secretarial help, duplicating facilities, and postal services; and for providing work space for Committee members. In this regard, LTF wishes to thank Inocencio Higuera and Alfonso Gardea of CIAD, and the continued support of Conservation International's "Bioregión Golfo de California" Program, especially María de los Ángeles Carvajal and Alejandro Robles. Special thanks are due to the Natural Sciences and Engineering Research Council of Canada for support by grant A5457 to JSN. Mark K. Nelson made the conversion from portrait format to landscape format in the draft. The staff, past and present, of the American Fisheries Society's International Headquarters has helped in many ways, particularly Betsy Fritz, Mary R. Frye, Janet Harry, Robert L. Kendall, Sally Kendall, Aaron Lerner, Beth D. McAleer, Robert Rand, Ghassan (Gus) Rassam, Catherine W. Richardson, and Beth Staehle; we are especially grateful for the dedicated and pleasant help of Deborah Lehman. The various presidents of the American Fisheries Society and of the American Society of Ichthyologists and Herpetologists have continuously offered encouragement to the Committee. We also wish to thank, on behalf of all past and present Committee members, the American Fisheries Society for their Distinguished Service Award at their 2000 annual meeting and for recognizing the importance of the Committee's work. Last, but far from least, we thank our families for their support.

We are grateful to many individuals who assisted with providing translations of the Introduction into Spanish and into French. The Introduction was translated into Spanish by Dr. Salvador Contreras-Balderas (Universidad Autónoma de Nuevo León, Monterrey, México) and Dr. Ramón Ruiz-Carus (Florida Fish and Wildlife Conservation Commission) and edited by HEP and LTF. The French translation was made by Denise Campillo and Jacqueline Lanteigne (Translation Bureau, Public Works and Government Services Canada), with the valuable help of Jacques F. Bergeron and Claude B. Renaud, the gracious contribution of the late Edwin J. Crossman and of Joseph S. Nelson, and funding from Fisheries and Oceans Canada.

# INTRODUCCIÓN

Esta sexta edición presenta un cambio importante, la inclusión de las especies distribuidas en México. Ahora la lista abarca los peces del Canadá, la zona continental de Estados Unidos, y México, siendo el primer documento que registra por completo en un solo lugar la ictiofauna de Norteamérica. Además se ofrece el nombre común en español e inglés de cada especie dulceacuícola y marina que se encuentra en México, y el nombre común en francés e inglés de cada especie dulceacuícola y marina que se halla en Quebec. Para las especies de agua dulce, se ofrece también el país donde se presentan. Las listas anteriores fueron publicadas en 1948, 1960, 1970, 1980, y 1991 (Publicaciones Especiales 1, 2, 6, 12, y 20, respectivamente, de la American Fisheries Society). Estas listas se han utilizado ampliamente y han contribuido sustancialmente a la meta de alcanzar el uso uniforme de nombres comunes y evitar la confusión en nombres científicos. La lista recomienda los nombres científicos a usar y procura reflejar de la mejor manera posible, a nuestro juicio, las opiniones recientes de los especialistas en diferentes taxa. Partiendo de los 570 registros en la lista abreviada de 1948 (que abarcó principalmente las especies deportivas, comerciales y forrajeras mejor conocidas), la cobertura aumentó a 1,892 especies en 1960, a 2,131 en 1970, a 2,268 en 1980 y hasta 2,428 especies en 1991. La presente edición incluye 3,700 especies, 3,694 peces y seis cefalocordados (o, dando un cálculo comparable a la lista de 1991, 2,635 especies en Canadá y la parte continental de Estados Unidos, no incluyendo especies de los cefalocordados de la familia Branchiostomatidae, nuevamente adicionada a la lista). En esta lista, como en la de 1991, el Comité (permanente) de los Nombres de Peces de la American Fisheries Society y la American Society of Ichthyologists and Herpetologists (AFS/ASIH) trabajó para incluir los nombres comunes de todas las especies nativas (autóctonas) y de las especies introducidas y establecidas en la región abarcada, incluso cuando las especies introducidas encontraron en áreas muy limitadas. El número de especies introducidas, por liberaciones intencionales y accidentales, en aguas norteamericanas continúa creciendo. En muchas introducciones, aunque uno o más especímenes

pudieron haber sido colectados, no existe evidencia que la especie se haya establecido (e.g., existencia de poblaciones reproductoras); dichas especies no se enlistan (Fuller et al. 1999, enlistan y discuten éstas para los Estados Unidos). Además, algunas de las especies introducidas mencionadas previamente en Norteamérica ya no están presentes. Los nombres comunes para los contados peces híbridos de importancia en manejo pesquero o pesca comercial o deportiva se presentan en el Apéndice 2.

Muchas de las adiciones a esta sexta edición, con excepción de aquellas anotadas para México, han resultado de la descripción de especies nuevas y extensiones de distribución descubiertas en muestreos de nuestras aguas marinas y dulceacuícolas (incluyendo aquellas en el occidente de los Estados Unidos asociadas con el evento de El Niño de 1997–1998 e indicadas por R. N. Lea y R. H. Rosenblatt, 2000, CalCOFI Rep. 41:117–129). Los estudios sistemáticos recientes han conducido al reconocimiento de especies que previamente fueron consideradas sinónimos menores, e inversamente, otros estudios han demostrado que ciertas especies en las listas anteriores si son sinónimos menores y por tanto fueron borradas de la presente lista. Aún hay muchos casos en donde existe incertidumbre acerca de si un taxon deber ser tratado al nivel de especie o por abajo (e.g., nivel de subespecie), particularmente en Cyprinidae, Catostomidae, Salmonidae, Percidae, Dactyloscopidae y Labrisomidae (en algunas de estas familias nosotros esperamos que más especies nominales sean reconocidas como válidas, que colocadas en sinonímia). Pueden existir diferencias de opinión por el empleo de los diferentes conceptos de especie al igual que por diferentes tipos de evidencia (e.g., morfológico *versus* datos moleculares; vea R. L. Mayden, 1999, J. Nematol. 31(2):95–116, y J. S. Nelson, 1999, Rev. Fish Biol. 9:277–280). Al aceptar como válidos los nombres de las especies de varios trabajos tales como estudios faunísticos, taxonómicos y sistemáticos, sin importar el enfoque, nosotros juzgamos poco o no juzgamos los diferentes conceptos de especie utilizados por los autores. Las especies de estatus incierto se tratan caso por caso. Sin embargo, en general, al ocuparnos de conclusiones que están en conflicto en la literatura actual, sentimos que si existe mayor probabilidad de que una especie siendo válida sea realmente reconocida, es mejor errar al reconocerla que errar por no hacerlo. De todas formas, hemos sido más conservadores de lo que algunos pudieran preferir al considerar muchos cambios. En general, cuando sabemos que hay una investigación en curso sobre un problema pertinente, nosotros preferimos esperar hasta que la evidencia se publique antes de realizar un cambio.

Se pretende mostrar un listado completo de todas las especies en el área de cobertura, Norteamérica, con las siguientes excepciones. Muchas especies que se encuentran más allá de nuestros límites batimétrico (200 m de profundidad al fondo) y geográfico tienen etapas tempranas de su ciclo de vida que han sido registradas en aguas de la plataforma continental. Estas especies se excluyen de la lista, al igual que muchas especies mesopelágicas que pueden encontrarse sobre la plataforma continental exterior, donde las aguas profundas están muy cerca de la costa. Por ejemplo, Scott y Scott (1988) describieron especies donde los individuos (incluyendo huevos o larvas) entran ocasionalmente a nuestra área; tales especies son omitidas de la presente lista. Con excepción de otras limitaciones indicadas en la siguiente sección, no se ha reducido la lista. Todas las especies, desde peces pequeños, crípticos o raros, hasta los grandes peces comerciales, recreativos y/o deportivos son de importancia para documentar y entender nuestra biodiversidad. Muchas de las especies se utilizan como animales experimentales de laboratorio, se exhiben o mantienen en acuarios públicos o privados, se utilizan como carnada, o son considerados como objetos de análisis de la historia natural o tienen un valor estético. Algunas especies que fueron despreciadas alguna vez como "peces basura", hoy se pescan comercialmente y son altamente valorados. Una atención especial se está prestando a usar la fauna acompañante de las pesquerías, y como resultado las especies antes desechadas ahora están entrando en el mercado. Una creciente concientización ambiental ha centrado su atención en los peces nativos como indicadores de la condición de ecosistemas dulceacuícolas y marinos. Las especies en peligro se discuten en periódicos y revistas populares. Así, este listado comprensivo será de utilidad a muchos interesados. La organización e índice del

libro son tales que a pesar de su complejidad, es fácil de usar por aquellos con objetivos particulares.

## Área de cobertura

La lista actual pretende incluir todas las especies de peces conocidos con poblaciones reproductivas o mantenidas por si mismas en las aguas continentales de Canadá, Estados Unidos, y México, así como aquellas especies marinas que habitan las aguas costeras sobre la plataforma continental, a una profundidad inferior a 200 m (656 pies). Excluimos a las especies conocidas solamente en donde la profundidad excede 200 m, incluso si el pez se encontró a menos de 200 m. Existen muchas especies registradas en aguas más al sur de México que sin duda serán capturadas en el futuro. Esto especialmente en el lado Atlántico, donde se conocen 66 especies marinas de Belice aun no registradas para México. Muchas de estas tendran que ser agregadas a la lista en un futuro, ya que se espera encontrarlas también al norte y al este de la península de Yucatán. También se conocen seis especies de agua dulce en Belice aun no registradas en México. En el Océano Atlántico, como se define convencionalmente, los peces de las costas de Groenlandia, este del Canadá y los Estados Unidos, y las aguas mexicanas del Golfo de México y del Mar Caribe adyacente a la península de Yucatán hasta la frontera México–Belice (hasta donde nosotros fuimos capaces de determinar sus faunas) fueron incluidas. Las especies de Islandia, Bermuda, las Bahamas, Cuba, y otras islas de las Antillas son excluidas a menos que se encuentren también en la región cubierta. En el Pacífico, como se define, el área comprende esa parte de la plataforma continental desde el estrecho de Bering hasta la frontera México–Guatemala, incluyendo el archipiélago oceánico de Revillagigedo y la Isla Guadalupe, hasta la profundidad de 200 m en aguas contiguas a la costa. Es especialmente difícil el decidir qué especies incluir de las islas oceánicas que carecen de plataforma continental en donde las especies oceánicas se pueden encontrar junto con las especies neríticas, en tales casos nosotros hemos procurado incluir solamente a las especies asociadas normalmente a la plataforma continental. Las aguas de las costas árticas de Alaska y Canadá son incluidas. Hawaii e Isla (atolón) Clipperton, con sus faunas sumamente diferentes del Indo-Pacífico y endémicas, no lo fueron. Los peces de mar profundo, sean bénticos o mesopelágicos, incluyendo especies que migran verticalmente y entran temporalmente la zona epipelágica, y los peces estrictamente oceánicos se excluyen, excepto cuando éstos aparecen no como apartados sobre la plataforma continental. En la práctica, esta línea de separación es difícil de aplicar y a menudo llega a ser algo arbitrario, especialmente si se consideran el huevo y las etapas larvarias. Los peces pelágicos que entran en las aguas sobre la plataforma continental fueron incluidos. Hemos excluido a las especies que solamente se conocen en Norteamérica de profundidades mayores a 200 m, aunque se conocen a las mismas en áreas extralimitales a nuestra cobertura en donde la profundidad de captura fue menor a 200 m. Los usuarios deben tener precaución cuando se tratan de inferir los intervalos de profundidad de las especies (e.g., *Enchelycore anatina* (Lowe, 1838), comúnmente encontrada en el Atlántico oriental a profundidades inferiores a 200 m, ha sido registrada en el Atlántico occidental sólamente en profundidades que exceden 200 m, y *Ophichthus menezesi* McCosker & Böhlke, 1984, descrita a profundidades de 169–209 m frente a Brasil, se ha encontrada frente a Florida en el Golfo de México pero sólo entre 1,200 y 1,400 m).

Las abreviaturas claves en la lista proporcionan una guía general de la presencia. Una "**A**" denota el Océano Atlántico e incluye el Océano Ártico al este de la península de Boothia (i.e., longitud 95°W), mientras que la "**AM**" denota presencia en el Océano Atlántico de México pero sin registro en Canadá o los Estados Unidos. Una "**P**" refiere al Océano Pacífico e incluye el Océano Ártico occidental (Mar de Chukchi y Mar de Beaufort al oeste de la península de Boothia), mientras que la "**PM**" denota presencia en el Océano Pacífico de México pero sin registro en Canadá o los Estados Unidos. La lista no indica por separado a las especies que se presentan en el Océano Ártico (una "A" o una "P" pueden indicar también o solamente indicar presencia ártica, tal como *Triglops nybelini*, designada como "A-P" pero conocida solamente del Mar de Beaufort en el Ártico [considerada aquí "P"] hacia el este en el Océano Atlántico ["A"] y ausente del Océano Pacífico). Una "**F:**" indica presencia en aguas dulces u otras aguas continentales salobres (e.g., Salton Sea [el Lago Salton], California). Algunas especies así señaladas pueden referirse a registros históricos, tales como *Elops affinis* en el bajo Río Colorado y en el Lago Salton. La designación

"F:" seguida por una "**C**" denota dulceacuícola de Canadá, mientras que "**M**" indica dulceacuícola de México, y "**U**" dulceacuícola de Estados Unidos (los estados contiguos y/o Alaska). Debe hacerse notar que (i) las especies marinas conocidas frente una costa a menos de 201 m pero de la otra costa a más de 200 m, se indican solamente como presentes frente la costa con el registro de profundidad menor (e.g., *Notacanthus chemnitzii* es designado solamente como "A" pero se sabe que se presenta en aguas de California a profundidades por debajo de 200 m; (ii) aunque dos especies puedan ser indicadas como presentes en aguas marinas y dulceacuícolas, una puede ser primariamente marina y la otra primariamente dulceacuícola; y (iii) muchas especies designadas en la lista como "F" han sido colectadas ocasionalmente en aguas estuarinas como en aguas dulce (e.g., W. F. Loftus, 2000, Fla. Sci. 63(1):27–47; F. J. Schwartz, 1992, *en* C. Cole y K. Turner (editores), Barrier island ecology of the mid-Atlantic Coast: a symposium, Technical Report, NPS/SERCAHA/NRTR-93/04:94–118; F. J. Schwartz, 2000, J. Elisha Mitchell Sci. Soc. 116(3):206–224). Una "**I**" entre corchetes, "**[I]**", indica la presencia de cualquier especie introducida (no autóctona o exótica) establecida dentro de nuestra área de cobertura y puede utilizarse por separado o colectivamente con "A", "P", "F", "C", "U", y "M" en las designaciones (éstas son especies introducidas en el área señalada debido a la actividad humana, documentada o deducida, directa o indirectamente). Este símbolo no se utiliza para las introducciones de una especie nativa dentro de cada una de las áreas designadas (e.g., la introducción de *Salvelinus fontinalis* del oriente al occidente de Canadá), pero se continúa usando para las especies que subsecuentemente se dispersaron de un país a otro (e.g., *Scardinius erythrophthalmus* se considera aun como una introducción en ambos países en donde actualmente se presenta). A diferencia de la edición de 1991, se indica la introducción exitosa de una especie de un océano a otro; e.g., *Alosa sapidissima* y *Morone saxatilis* fueron introducidas con éxito del Atlántico a las aguas del Pacífico y su presencia se indica como "A-F:CU-P[I]" (tales cambios no son indicados en el Apéndice 1). Una "**X**" entre corchetes, "**[X]**", indica que la especie es considerada extinta. Las especies indicadas en la edición de 1991 como existentes pero conocidas sólo de registros históricos y probablemente ahora extirpadas del Canadá o de los

Estados Unidos, son aun enlistadas (e.g., *Erimystax x-punctatus* que actualmente no se encuentra en Canadá pero todavía ocurre en Estados Unidos, se designa como "F:CU", y *Catostomus bernardini* que actualmente no se encuentra en Estados Unidos pero vive en México, se designa como "F:UM"). Todas las especies mexicanas designadas como la "AM", "PM", o "F:M" son nuevas en la lista y, con pocas excepciones, no se anotan de otra manera en el Apéndice 1. Las especies con la anotación "A" o "P" y con **un nombre en español y/o francés**, se presentan en aguas mexicanas y/o de Quebec y otras partes del área de cobertura y aparecieron en la lista de 1991, a menos que se indiquen como registros nuevos (principalmente de California) por un asterisco (*).

## Nombres de familias

Los nombres de las familias son importantes en la identificación y la recuperación de información. Se utilizan extensamente en literatura de la industria pesquera, libros populares sobre peces, diccionarios y enciclopedias. Sin embargo, en algunos grupos los ictiólogos varían extensamente en sus interpretaciones de cuales son los límites de una familia. Mientras que convenimos que los cambios en nombres de familia deben ser evitados cuando sea posible, nosotros también entendemos que la lista debe reflejar, a nuestro mejor juicio, la práctica actual de los ictiólogos sistemáticos. Esto ha dado lugar a un aumento considerable en el número de familias reconocidas. Aparte de esto, hemos preferido aceptar familias adicionales a las de la edición de 1991 cuando las razones están basadas en argumentos filogenéticos o donde el nombre utilizado anteriormente para la familia sugiere relaciones improbables (notas del apéndice generalmente son presentadas, dónde no hemos realizado cambios que algunos pueden pensar pudieran estar justificados). Preferimos no realizar cambios subjetivos o arbitrarios tales como la división de una familia conocida como monofilética. Así, por ejemplo, reconocemos los coregonos ("whitefishes"), el tímalo ("grayling"), las truchas, salmones, y salvelinos ("chars," incluyendo la trucha alpina) en una familia monofilética en lugar de tres familias separadas según lo prefieren algunos autores. En este ejemplo la separación crearía una pérdida de información filogenética que podría ser superada reconociendo superfamilias o subórdenes. Con el agrupamiento, como lo

hacemos en este caso, la pérdida en información filogenética puede ser corregida donde se juzga deseable reconociendo subfamilias. En general, con esta diferencia, optamos por el arreglo más antiguo y conservador. Las nuevas familias en la lista se indican en el Apéndice 1; sin embargo, cuando las familias que se agregaron por que todas las especies en nuestra nueva área de cobertura existen sólo en México, no se indican de otra manera como nuevas. Se reconocen órdenes y algunos niveles más altos de la clasificación, pero enfatizamos que esta lista no intenta reflejar necesariamente lo que consideramos son los puntos de vista aceptados a nivel de órden. No todos los cambios de la edición anterior a nivel órden se indican en el Apéndice 1.

## Nombres comunes

Los nombres comunes de las especies han tenido una historia larga, excediendo por mucho la de los nombres científicos, y mientras el público y los biólogos los utilizen, sentimos que nos corresponde el tener un sistema estandarizado y eficaz para ellos. El Comité por lo tanto se enfoca a desarrollar un cuerpo de nombres comunes—un nombre común único para cada especie—que refleje ampliamente su uso actual; crear una nomeclatura vernacular más rica, más significativa y colorida; y promover mecanismos que agregarán estabilidad y universalidad de los nombres aplicados a los peces norteamericanos. Los nombres comunes de los peces en esta lista se aplican a especies individuales. Estos nombres son empleados a veces como nombres de mercado así como para otros propósitos. Sin embargo, algunos nombres del mercado a menudo se aplican a especies diferentes o difieren por varias razones de los nombres adoptados en esta lista y no se han incorporado en este trabajo. En el interés de un público informado, nosotros recomendamos ampliamente la adopción de los nombres comunes presentados aquí, entre autores, comerciantes u otras personas, aun cuando se piensa que un nombre tiene poca aceptación (por ejemplo, no se recomienda el uso del nombre regional "lisa" en lugar de matalote, cuando se aplica a miembros de la familia Catostomidae). Un resumen de los nombres en inglés que se aplican a los peces (y a los invertebrados) en el mercado de los Estados Unidos, está disponible en "The Seafood List, FDA's Guide to Acceptable Market Names for Seafood Sold in Interstate Commerce 1993, U.S. Food and Drug Administration," U.S. Government Printing Office (véase también <http://vm.cfsan.fda.gov/~frf/rfe0.html>). En la presente lista, muchos nombres difieren de aquellos usados en las publicaciones de la Organización para la Alimentación y la Agricultura (FAO) de las Naciones Unidas. Esperamos que en el futuro pueda haber mayor acuerdo.

El nombre común, como se emplea aquí, se considera como una denominación formal que se utilizará en lugar del nombre científico en Latín (o latinizado) de una especie. Puntualizamos que los nombres comunes no intentan duplicar el poder de los nombres científicos para reflejar las relaciones filogenéticas (véase el Principio 8 mas adelante). La historia confirma que los nombres comunes son a menudo más estables que los nombres científicos (esto no es ampliamente considerado). Las siguientes especies sufrieron cambios solamente en el nombre científico entre las ediciones de 1980 y 1991: el ciprínido *Hybopsis rubrifrons* cambió a *Notropis rubescens* y ahora (2004) regresa a *H. rubrifrons*; la trucha arcoiris, *Salmo gairdneri*, cambió a *Oncorhynchus mykiss*; la platija limón, *Parophrys vetulus*, cambió a *Pleuronectes vetulus* y ahora regresa a *Parophrys vetulus*. Los nombres genéricos en particular están sujetos a la interpretación e incertidumbre y permanecerán necesariamente así. Los nombres comunes son más fáciles de adaptar al uso vernacular que los nombres científicos. Existe una clara necesidad de estandarizar y uniformizar los nombres vernáculos, no solamente para los peces deportivos y comerciales, sino los nombres de mercado (comerciales), los de los peces de ornato (de acuario), en la terminología legal, y como substitutos de nombres científicos en la literatura popular o científica. El Comité cree que es deseable establecer un nombre común único para cada especie de pez que se distribuye de forma natural o a través de la introducción en las aguas de Canadá, Estados Unidos, y México. Las nuevas adiciones de nombres comunes en español, según lo determinaron los miembros del Comité Espinosa-Pérez y Findley-Talbott, se basan en experiencia de campo, la consulta con colegas, y la revisión de muchas fuentes en la literatura. Las principales fuentes consultadas son indicadas con asterisco (*) en la sección de Referencias, y varias de ellas también fueron consultadas para nombres comunes potenciales para adoptar en inglés a las especies mexicanas que se enlistan por primera vez. Para los nombres comunes en francés de las especies de peces dulceacuícolas de Quebec,

hemos confiado principalmente en J. F. Bergeron y J. Dubé, 2000, Liste historique des poissons d'eau douce du Québec, Gouvernement du Québec, Mars 2000. Los nombres de las especies marinas en Quebec son de Desrosiers et al. 1995, que es también útil para peces dulceacuícolas. Para los catostómidos del género *Moxostoma* seguimos a J. F. Bergeron y J. Dubé, 2000, y A. Branchaud y R. E. Jenkins, 1999, Can. Field-Nat. 113(2):345–358, donde *suceur* de listas previas fue substituido por *chevalier*. Los nombres en francés de las familias han sido seleccionados principalmente por J. F. Bergeron (comunicaciones personales, mayo de 2001–agosto de 2003) de una variedad de fuentes norteamericanas y europeas, incluyendo D. E. McAllister, 1990, A list of fishes of Canada/Liste des poissons du Canadá, Syllogeus 64, y B. W. Coad, 1995, Encyclopedia of Canadian fishes, Canadian Museum of Nature and Canadian Sportfishing Productions, Inc., Ottawa.

El alcanzar un acuerdo para muchos nombres puede ser rápido, pero para otros puede haber complicaciones que pueden llegará discrepancias. Este discrepancia es especialmente palpable en peces conocidos por nombres de mercado (comerciales) que difieren de los nombres más familiares usados por pescadores deportivos, biólogos y otros (e.g., lo que se conoce como "red snapper" [huachinango rojo] en gran parte de la costa occidental de los Estados Unidos puede ser una especie de *Sebastes* y no el *Lutjanus campechanus*). El uso de nombres diferentes en varias partes del intervalo geográfico de una especie crea dificultades que parecen ser solucionables solo mediante arbitraje. Por el contrario, un nombre dado se puede emplear en varios lugares para referirse a diversas especies. Aunque la acción del Comité en tales situaciones no puede hacer que cambie el uso local rápidamente, parece claramente incorrecto sancionar el uso de un nombre para dos o más especies diferentes. Nosotros enfatizamos que todos los usuarios de nombres comunes son mal servidos, quizás engañados, si los nombres comunes se utilizan de forma inconsistente.

Después de trabajar con los nombres comunes por muchos años, uno de los anteriores Comités entendió la importancia de establecer un conjunto de principios que se emplearán para la selección de nombres (en aquel tiempo solo en inglés). Tal código permite una valoración más objetiva de los méritos relativos entre varios nombres que si la selección es basada principalmente en experiencias y preferencias personales. La gran cantidad de nombres vernáculos de peces hace evidente que pocos principios pueden ser establecidos para los cuales no habrá excepciones. Existen varias excepciones ya que cuando el Comité comenzó a funcionar, la mayoría de las especies grandes y abundantes, por lo tanto más "importantes", en los Estados Unidos y Canadá tenían nombres comunes firmemente establecidos, que habría sido ficticio rechazarlos solo de conformidad a unos principios recientemente establecidos. El nombre de una especie puede ser decidido a menudo pesando los "pros" y "contras" entre las opciones posibles, seleccionando el que se ajuste más a los criterios guía. Los criterios que el Comité considera apropiados para la selección de nombres comunes de peces se repiten de las listas previas con cierta modificación a continuación.

## Principios que rigen la selección de nombres comunes

1. *Un nombre vernáculo único en cada idioma apropiado será aceptado para cada especie.* En la edición de 1991, solo un pez, *Coregonus artedi*, tuvo dos nombres comunes aceptados; ahora no hay excepciones.

2. *Dos especies en la lista no tendrán el mismo nombre común.* Los nombres comunes usados para especies extralimitales deben evitarse en especies de nuestra área de cobertura cuando sea posible.

3. *La expresión "common" o su equivalente español (común) o francés debe evitarse como parte del nombre de un pez cuando sea posible.*

4. *Se favorecerá la simplicidad en los nombres.* En inglés y español los guiones, sufijos, y apóstrofos debieran ser omitidos (e.g., "smallmouth bass") excepto cuando éstos son esenciales ortográficamente (e.g., "three-eye flounder"), tienen un significado especial (e.g., "C-O sole"), son necesarios para evitar malentendidos (e.g., "cusk-eel"), o que unen dos nombres de peces, ninguno de los cuáles representa al pez aludido (e.g., "trout-perch", que no es ni trucha ni perca). Las palabras calificativas compuestas, apropiadas especialmente en inglés, incluyendo combinaciones, se deben usar generalmente como sustantivos singulares en aposición al nombre del grupo (e.g., "spottail shiner"), pero en el plural el modificante se debe poner generalmente en forma de adjetivo (e.g., "spotted hake", "blackbanded sunfish") a menos que su naturaleza plural sea obvia (e.g., "fourspot flounder"). Se dará preferencia a los nombres cortos y eufónicos.

Las combinaciones usando palabras cortas y familiares en un solo nombre, escrito sin guión, puede en algunos casos imprimir claridad y simplicidad, especialmente en inglés (e.g., "tomcod", "goldfish", "mudminnow"), pero la práctica habitual de combinar palabras, especialmente de nombres muy largos, desmañados, o no familiares, será evitada.

5. *Los nombres comunes no serán escritos con mayúscula en uso textual excepto en aquellos elementos que sean nombres propios (sustantivos)* (e.g., "rainbow trout" versus "Sacramento perch"; carpita fantasma versus guayacón de Palenque; "grand corégone" versus "anguille d'Amérique").

6. *Se recomienda no usar nombres que intentan honrar a personas* (e.g., "Allison's tuna", "Julia's darter", "Meek's halfbeak", blanquillo de Hubbs) *en tanto que no tienen valor descriptivo.* En algunos grupos existen nombres propios (patronímicos específicos) idénticos en los nombres científicos (a veces honrando a personas diferentes pero con el mismo apellido) de géneros relacionados, y el uso del mismo nombre (patronímico) en el nombre común puede causar confusión. En muy pocos casos el patronímico ha sido incorporado tanto al nombre vernacular, de forma tal que estos no son considerados o reconocidos como patronímicos. Estos nombres son aceptados pero no se escribirán con mayúscula (e.g., "guppy" [gupi], "lane snapper" [originalmente "Lane's snapper" o "pargo de Lane"]). Este principio no se aplica necesariamente a los nombres comunes en francés (e.g., el nombre común de *Liparis coheni* es "limace de Cohen"). Sin embargo, en casos donde el nombre común con patronímico no tuvo "prioridad" establecida, usualmente un nombre común alterno sin el patronímico fué seleccionado.

7. *Solamente a las entidades taxonómicas claramente definidas y demarcadas (generalmente especie) les serán asignadas nombres comunes.* Mientras que las subespecies no son siempre sujetos adecuados para recibir

nombres comunes, ciertas subespecies válidas son tan diferentes en aspecto (no solo en la distribución geográfica) que ellas son distinguidas fácilmente por pescadores deportivos y comerciales, o personas comunes y corrientes, y para éstas un nombre común constituye una ayuda importante en la comunicación. Sin embargo, y contrariamente a la edición de 1991 en donde se reconocieron dos subespecies de *Esox americanus*, actualmente (para ser consistentes) no hemos proporcionado los nombres científicos o comunes de las subespecies en esta edición. Sin embargo, reconocemos que las subespecies, con su propia historia evolutiva en alopatría, tienen importancia en investigaciones evolutivas, y puede asignárselas estatus de protección especial y reconocerse en estudios de biodiversidad. Cuando se utilicen los nombres de las subespecies, el nombre común para la especie debe aplicarse a todas las subespecies del taxón.

Generalmente los híbridos no reciben nombres comunes, pero aquellos de importancia en manejo pesquero y con nombres comunes establecidos son anotados en el Apéndice 2. Las variedades cultivadas, las variaciones morfológicas y fases no son incluidas aunque puedan ser importantes en el movimiento comercial y el cultivo de los peces de ornato o de acuario (e.g., las muchas variedades de carpa dorada y de carpa común; las fases moteadas y doradas de la cabrilla sardinera y del botete aletas punteadas).

8. *El nombre común no estará íntimamente ligado al nombre científico.* Los caprichos necesarios de la nomenclatura científica no implican cambiar los nombres comunes constantemente. La práctica desatinada de aplicar un nombre común a cada género, un nombre modificante para cada especie, y aun otro indicador para cada subespecie, aunque abroga por su simplicidad, tiene el defecto de la inflexibilidad, y arriesga el desconocimiento de un pez al desechar lo que puede ser un nombre usado tradicionalmente y perfectamente aceptable. Vemos esa práctica como simple intento de reconstruir con el nombre vernáculo la nomenclatura científica. Si una especie se transfiere de un género a otro, o es cambiada de especie a nivel de subespecie o viceversa, idealmente el nombre común debe permanecer sin cambio. No es

función primaria de los nombres comunes el indicar relaciones. Este principio continúa siendo malentendido o rechazado por los que abogan que los nombres comunes de todos los miembros de un género deben incorporar la misma "raiz" de palabra(s) (e.g., todos los *Oncorhynchus* seran llamados "salmon" tales como "rainbow salmon" y "steelhead salmon," y aquellos en *Salvelinus* se llamaran "chars" tal como "brook char"). Enfatizamos nuestra convicción que la estabilidad de los nombres comunes compensa por mucho cualquier desventaja al respecto. Cuando dos o más grupos taxonómicos (e.g., especies nominales) se encuentran como idénticos (sinónimos), un nombre será adoptado para el grupo combinado. Vea también el Principio 13.

9. *Los nombres no violarán las normas del buen gusto (e.g., los nombres no contendrán palabras ofensivas).* Nuestros cambios de los nombres "squawfish" a "pikeminnow" para las especies de *Ptychocheilus*, y de "jewfish" a "goliath grouper", fueron hechos con este principio en mente. Estos cambios fueron realizados después de recibir numerosas opiniones de individuos y de recibir el apoyo de otros.

---

Los principios precedentes son en gran parte como mandatos de procedimiento. Los criterios siguientes son considerados como de ayuda para la selección de nombres apropiados.

10. *Los nombres coloridos, románticos, imaginarios, metafóricos o de otra forma distintivos y originales son especialmente apropiados.* Tal terminología agrega riqueza y amplitud a la nomenclatura y da satisfacción al usuario. Ejemplos de tales nombres en inglés incluyen el madtom, Dolly Varden, midshipman, chilipepper, garibaldi, pumpkinseed, flier, angelfish, Moorish idol, y hogchoker; y en español, bruja, guitarra, chucho, y lacha; en francés tête-de-boule, crayon d'argent, and truite fardée.

11. *Los nombres nativos norteamericanos o sus modificaciones son bienvenidos como nombres comunes.* Algunos en uso incluyen menhaden, eulachon, cisco, Chinook, mummichog, tautog, puyeki, y totoaba.

12. *Sin importar el origen, los nombres verdaderamente vernáculos que son utilizados*

*ampliamente y en uso común por el público deben conservarse cuando sea posible.* Además de los nombres aborígenes, muchos nombres ahora bien conocidos al norte de la frontera México-EUA tienen su origen en los pescadores no angloparlantes: barracuda, cero, mojarra, pompano, sierra (todos del español o modificado de él); capelin (francés); bocaccio (italiano); mako (maorí). Muchos nombres excelentes han sido creados por inmigrantes norteamericanos. Muchos de éstos de conformidad con los Principios 14 y 15 abajo. Mucho cuidado debe tomarse para evitar palabras que significan la misma cosa en idiomas relacionados pero que difieren ligeramente en su ortografía (e.g., sierra en español y serra en portugués)

13. *Los nombres empleados comúnmente adoptados del uso tradicional en inglés* (e.g., chub, minnow, trout, bass, perch, sole, flounder), *en español* (e.g., cazón, sardina, carpa, mojarra, perca, lenguado) *y en francés* (e.g., méné y perche) *reciben considerable laxitud en su situación taxonómica.* La adherencia a la práctica acostumbrada debe ser preferida, si ésta no está en conflicto con el uso general de otro nombre. Muchos nombres, sin embargo, se han aplicado en Norteamérica a peces que son semejantes pero a menudo están lejanamente relacionados. Por ejemplo, encontramos "bass" y lenguado en el uso para los representantes de varias familias de peces, y "perch" y perca aun más. "Chub" aparece en grupos sin relación tales como Cyprinidae y Kyphosidae, y mojarra en Cichlidae, Gerreidae y otras familias. El "ocean whitefish" o pierna, *Caulolatilus princeps,* llamado a veces "salmón" en el noroeste de México, no es un salmónido, y el "Pacific pompano" (pámpano en español), *Peprilus simillimus,* no es un carángido, sin embargo cada uno es bien conocido por los pescadores con el nombre indicado en sus regiones. Para las especies ampliamente conocidas, el Comité cree preferible reconocer el uso general, que adoptar sustitutos pedantes. Así, la práctica establecida, de que el uso original debe prevalecer sobre los intentos de consistencia. Esto no es bien entendido por algunos ictiólogos que consideran que "perch" no debe ser utilizada para un embiotócido, "trout" para un *Salvelinus,* sardinita para un carácido, y cazón para un carcharhínido. Han

sido evitados o reducidos algunos problemas al unir nombres en inglés para crear nuevas palabras (e.g., seatrout por sea trout, mudsucker por mud sucker, surfperch por surf perch); tales combinaciones han ganado amplia aceptación desde que fueron adoptadas por el Comité en sus listas anteriores.

14. *Los atributos estructurales, el color, y el patrón del color son fuentes deseables de nombres y son usados comúnmente.* Sailfin, flathead, slippery, giant, mottled, copper, y tripletail en inglés; chato, jorobado, bocón, gigante, jabonero, pinto, y cobrizo en español; citron, cuivré, fardé, y fossettes en francés, y una multitud de otros adjetivos, adornan los nombres de los peces. Debe hacerse un esfuerzo para seleccionar términos descriptivos adecuados y cuando sea posible evitar la repetición de aquellos empleados con mayor frecuencia (e.g., blanco [blanc, white], negro [noir, black], manchado [tacheté, spotted], de bandas [barré, banded]).

Siguiendo la tradición para los nombres en inglés en la ictiología y herpetología norteamericana, hemos procurado restringir el uso de "line" o "stripe" para indicar marcas longitudinales que son paralelas al eje del cuerpo y "bar" o "band" para indicar marcas verticales o tranversales.

15. *Las características ecológicas son útiles para crear buenos nombres.* Tales términos deben ser apropiadamente descriptivos. Los adjetivos ingleses (españoles, o franceses) como reef (de arrecife, récif), coral (coralino, corail), sand (arenero, sable), rock (piedrero, roche), lake (de lago, lac), freshwater (dulceacuícola, dulcicole), y mountain (de la sierra, montagne) son bien conocidos en los nombres de los peces.

16. *La distribución geográfica proporciona adjetivos calificativos convinientes.* Las malas descripciones geográficas o las caracterizaciones engañosas (e.g., "Kentucky bass" para una especie de distribución amplia) se deben corregir a menos que estén demasiado arraigadas en el uso actual (en interés de la estabilidad se han conservado nombres tales como "Alaska blackfish" aunque esta especie, se sabe ahora, también se encuentra en Rusia, y guatopote de Sonora aunque esta poecílido se encuentra comúnmente fuera de los límites de ese estado). En bien de la brevedad, es

posible suprimir palabras tales como lago (lac, lake), río (fleuve, river), golfo (golfe, gulf), o mar (mer, sea) en los nombres de las especies (e.g., "Colorado pikeminnow", no "Colorado River pikeminnow"; topote del Balsas, no topote del Río Balsas).

17. *Los nombres genéricos se pueden emplear como nombres comunes* (e.g., gambusia, rémora, tilapia, mola, torpedo, anchoa, brótula, guavina) o en forma modificada (e.g., "molly", de *Mollienesia*). Una vez adoptados, tales nombres deben ser mantenidos, incluso si el nombre a nivel genérico o más rango es cambiado posteriormente. Estos nombres vernáculos se deben escribir en letra de molde (i.e., no en itálica o cursiva). La brevedad y eufonía son de importancia especial en los nombres de este tipo, que probablemente serán adoptados más a menudo para los peces de ornato o de acuario u otros peces pequeños y/o poco conocidos que no tienen establecida una nomenclatura vernácula.

18. *La duplicación de los nombres comunes de los peces y otros organismos debe ser evitada si es posible, pero los nombres en uso general amplio no necesitan ser rechazados sobre esta base solamente.* Por ejemplo, "buffalo" (búfalo) se emplea para varios mamíferos artiodáctilos y en inglés para los catostómidos ("suckers", matalotes) del género *Ictiobus*; zorro (que significa literalmente "fox") se utiliza para los tiburones alópiidos, y mariposa (que significa literalmente "butterfly") es empleada para los peces mariposa ("butterflyfishes") y rayas mariposa ("butterfly rays"). Con estas bases de uso preestablicido, tales nombres son admisibles como nombres de peces sin modificación. Sin embargo, hemos cambiado ahora el nombre "dolphin", apropiadamente aplicado a varias especies de cetáceos dentados, que también era empleado en las especies del género *Coryphaena*, a "dolphinfish" para evitar la confusión.

## Relación entre los nombres comunes y científicos de las especies

El propósito primario de esta lista es recomendar un nombre común en cada idioma apropiado, y proporcionar el nombre científico generalmente aceptado para todas las especies de peces en Norteamérica, dentro de los límites geográficos establecidos. Los nombres comunes, creemos, pueden ser estabilizados por acuerdo general. Los nombres científicos, por otra parte, cambiarán inevitablemente conforme avanza el conocimiento y de acuerdo con los puntos de vista de los taxónomos. Con respecto al uso, la nomenclatura refleja la opinión del Comité que está consciente de que muchos usuarios de esta lista no están enterados de la literatura o no están interesados en la sistemática o las reglas de la nomenclatura, pero buscan simplemente una guía de los nombres técnicos, comúnes y/o científicos. La nomenclatura científica empleada ha sido corregida cuidadosamente con respecto a la ortografía, autoridades y fechas de las descripciones originales.

Enfatizamos que hay muchos grupos en los cuales existe desacuerdo sobre su clasificación o donde la clasificación se conoce poco. También, hay a menudo diferencias subjetivas entre los investigadores al designar la jerarquía de los taxa. Además, los investigadores que utilizan una metodología sintética (i.e., no filogenética) pueden preferir clasificar a las especies de acuerdo a características tróficas, etológicas, o morfológicas en géneros monotípicos (géneros y familias monotípicas pueden reconocerse por ser taxa cuyas relaciones son poco conocidas para clasificarles mejor, una filosofía a la cual nos apegamos). Preferimos aceptar conclusiones filogenéticas cuando el trabajo está firmemente fundamentado (véase también la discusión anterior bajo "Nombres de Familia" y "Nombres Comunes", particularmente el Principio 8).

## Arreglo de la lista

La lista se presenta en una secuencia filogenética de las familias de peces como lo conocemos en base al conocimiento disponible. El arreglo de los órdenes y de las familias sigue generalmente a Nelson (1994), pero hay algunos cambios que reflejan los estudios sistemáticos recientes. Las clases y los órdenes de peces recientes son indicados. En la mayoría de los casos damos un solo nombre común para cada familia en inglés, español, y francés. Las excepciones incluyen la famila Salmonidae, la familia de las truchas y salmones, que incluye truchas, salmones, salvelinos ("chars"), coregonos ("whitefishes"), y tímalos ("graylings").

Dentro de las familias, los géneros y las especies se enlistan alfabéticamente; la desventaja de separar las formas relacionadas dentro de una familia se compensa por la mayor facilidad en el uso. En esta edición adoptamos el formato horizontal, en contraste con el vertical de las ediciones anteriores, para presentar los nombres comunes de las especies en inglés, español, y francés en el mismo renglón. Cada página de la Parte I consiste de cinco columnas, las primera con el nombre científico, la segunda el área de presencia, la tercera el nombre común en inglés (sin importar el área de presencia), la cuarta el nombre común en español para las especies en México, y la quinta el nombre común en francés para las especies en Quebec.

Hemos procurado seguir el nuevo código de la Comisión Internacional de la Nomenclatura Zoológica [International Commission of Zoological Nomenclatura, ICZN], y como tal emplear la ortografía original de los nombres de las especies (así las terminaciones de algunos nombres personales [patronímicos] serán -i o -ii como sea apropiado). El actual código, según lo incorporado a la cuarta edición del Código Internacional de la Nomenclatura Zoológica ["International Code of Zoological Nomeclature"] (de aquí en adelante referido como el Código) fue publicado en 1999 y entró en efecto el 1° de enero 2000. C. J. Ferraris y W. N. Eschmeyer, 2000, Copeia 2000(3):907–908, revisaron el nuevo Código en lo referente a su efecto sobre los nombres de los peces.

En esta edición continuamos agregando, después del nombre científico de la especie, la autoridad y la fecha de publicación de la descripción original. Las autoridades y las fechas son generalmente necesitadas por personas que no tienen acceso a la literatura original. Las determinaciones de la autoridad correcta y del año correcto de la publicación pueden a menudo ser complicadas, especialmente de los nombres propuestos antes de 1900. Eschmeyer (1998), Gilbert (1998), y otros han corregido muchas fechas de la descripción que aparecieron en la edición de 1991, y se han incorporado estas correcciones en la lista actual y anotándolas en el Apéndice 1. Nuestras justificaciones de la ortografía de los apellidos Delaroche, Forsskål, Lacepède y Lesueur fueron explicadas en la tercera (página 5) y cuarta (página 8) ediciones. La atribución de los nombres propuestos en el M. E. Blochii Systema Ichthyologicae, 1801, por J. G. Schneider fué explicada en la cuarta edición (página 8).

El uso del nombre(s) de la autoridad refleja la interpretación actualizada del nuevo Código. De acuerdo a esas reglas, después del nombre específico (escrito en itálica) sigue directamente el nombre del autor(es). Si la especie, cuando fue descrita originalmente, fue asignada al mismo género que se asigna aqui, el nombre(s) del autor(es) está(n) sin paréntesis; si la especie fue descrita en otro género, el nombre(s) del autor(es) aparece(n) en paréntesis. La fecha (año) de la publicación es separada de la autoridad por una coma y es incluida dentro del paréntesis donde ésto sea apropiado. Por ejemplo, Mitchill originalmente nombró la trucha de arroyo, *Salmo fontinalis*, en un trabajo publicado en 1814; aquí aparece como *Salvelinus fontinalis* (Mitchill, 1814). En la edición de 1991, los paréntesis también se pusieron alrededor del nombre del(os) autor(es) en los casos donde el nombre de grupo de la especie fue combinado originalmente con una ortografía incorrecta o una enmienda injustificada del nombre genérico. Esto no es apropiado ahora, aunque una enmienda injustificada resulta en un nombre disponible con su(s) propios autor(es) y fecha (Artículo 51.3.1 del Código). Por lo tanto, los paréntesis ahora se quitan de los nombres de los autores de las especies descritas en los géneros tales como *Rhinobatus* (ahora *Rhinobatos*), *Raia* (ahora *Raja*), *Lepidosteus* (ahora *Lepisosteus*), *Ophichthys* (ahora *Ophichthus*), *Nototropis* (ahora *Notropis*), *Amiurus* (ahora *Ameiurus*), *Hemirhamphus* (ahora *Hemiramphus*), *Opisthognathus* (ahora *Opistognathus*), y *Pomadasis* (ahora *Pomadasys*). Debe tenerse cuidado en la ortografía original porque la misma ortografía se puede utilizar para una enmienda injustificada y para una ortografía independientemente válida; por ejemplo, *Ophichthys* se utiliza como enmienda injustificada de *Ophichthus* Ahl, 1789, un género de las anguilas ofíctidos (tiesos), y como *Ophichthys* Swainson, 1839, para una anguila synbránchido (anguilas de lodo) (Eschmeyer 1998:2045).

Las ediciones anteriores de la lista han recibido amplia consulta y uso. Desde que la quinta edición fue publicada en 1991, muchos usuarios han comunicado al Comité sus sugerencias de cambios, y cada sugerencia fue considerada en la preparacion de la presente edición. La estabilidad en nombres comunes recibio la prioridad más alta y los cambios se han realizado solamente por razones sustanciales. El conocimiento científico de los peces avanzó rápidamente durante los años 90, en los que se describieron muchas especies nuevas, muchas especies adicionales se registraron dentro de nuestros límites geográficos, y se terminaron numerosas revisiones taxonómico-sistemáticas. La adición de especies ha obligado a modificar o cambiar algunos nombres comunes, y las revisiones produjeron a menudo cambios en la nomenclatura científica. En algunas familias (e.g., Cyprinidae) los cambios todavía se están llevando a cabo, están incompletos o, en algunos casos, están en conflicto. El Comité ha elegido ser conservador en adoptar tales cambios con la esperanza de que las revocaciones o dudas sean evitadas o reducidas al mínimo en las ediciones futuras de la lista.

A excepción de las muchas adiciones de especies de México, todas las nuevas entradas y todas las entradas que cambian en cualquier manera (nombre científico, autor(es), fecha de la descripción, presencia, y el nombre común en inglés) de la edición de 1991 son precedidas por un asterisco (*). La información que describe y que explica el cambio es dada para cada entrada en el Apéndice 1, identificándose por la página en la cual el nombre aparece en la lista. La información antiguamente presentada en el Apéndice 1 de las listas 1970, 1980, y 1991 (páginas 65–87, 68–92, y 71–96, respectivamente), documentando los cambios entre las ediciones 2 y 3, entre 3 y 4, y entre 4 y 5, no se repite en esta edición.

Un signo de más (+) antes de una entrada indica que, aunque la entrada permanece sin cambio, un comentario se encontrará en el Apéndice 1 bajo ese nombre. Esto incluye taxa por arriba del nivel de especie (e.g., familia y órden) donde el nombre está sin cambio pero la composición del taxon difiere de aquella en la edición de 1991 (e.g., por el retiro de taxa o de transferencias de otros taxa jerárquicamente más altos).

Aunque la mayoría de las decisiones del Comité han sido unánimes, muchas fueron hechas por opinión mayoritaria. Por lo que, ningún miembro del Comité se suscribe necesariamente a todas las decisiones alcanzadas, pero nosotros respetamos el que nadie tiene todas las respuestas correctas. Nosotros entendemos que no todas las decisiones serán apoyadas como "populares", pero esperamos que todos los usuarios aprecien nuestros esfuerzos. En muchos casos, la información disponible al Comité excedió a la existente en la literatura actual. El Comité a menudo luchó para alcanzar decisiones justificables con respecto a la inclusión de dicha información y ha sido cauteloso en adoptar cambios.

La lista alfabética de las familias en las páginas 1–6 sirve también como un índice de contenidos. La lista, Parte I, aparece en las páginas 47–186, y los apéndices siguen en la Parte II, páginas 187–256. La Parte III sobre las Referencias, las Ediciones de la Lista de los Nombres, y la Edición de la "Lista del Mundo" ["World List"] comienza en la pagina 257, y las Comunicaciones Personales comienzan en la página 261, seguida por el Índice, comenzando en la página 265. El Apéndice 2 de la edición de 1991 (Peces Exóticos) no se ha incluido debido a la disponibilidad de esta información en otros foros (e.g., para Estados Unidos, http://nas.er.usgs.gov/fishes, y Fuller et al. 1999; y para Norteamérica, R. Claudi and J. Leach (editores), 1999, "Nonindigenous freshwater organisms, vectors, biology and impacts," Lewis Publishers, Boca Raton, Florida).

## Índice

El Índice incorpora los nombres científicos y los nombres comunes en los tres idiomas. Se da referencias a las páginas para los nombres comunes adoptados para las clases, los órdenes, las familias, y las especies. Se incluye una sola entrada para cada especie; por ejemplo "brook trout" se inscribió solamente bajo "trout, brook", pero "trucha de arroyo" aparece como tal. Hay un gran número de nombres vernáculos de peces norteamericanos, y sería necesario realizar una investigación extensa incluso para incluir una fracción de ellos, algunos de esos nombres no se han utilizado en muchas décadas y solamente tienen interés histórico. En general, el Comité no ha intentado realizar una búsqueda tan extensa (aunque uno de los miembros [LTF] ha compilado una lista de nombres comunes en español e inglés que actualmente contiene más de 16,000 entradas), pero muchos de los nombres más ampliamente usados son incluidos en la presente lista.

Las páginas de referencia se dan para los nombres científicos aquí adoptados para clases, órdenes, familias, géneros, y especies. Cada especie aparece solamente bajo su nombre específico (trivial). Por ejemplo, *Sciaenops ocellatus* se puede localizar solamente bajo "*ocellatus, Sciaenops*", aunque una entrada para "*Sciaenops*" dirige al lector a la página en la que las entradas de ese género comienzan. Los nombres científicos de las especies que no son aceptados para esta lista se excluyen, excepto aquellos que aparecieron en 1991 (quinta edición) y han sido puestos en sinonimia desde entonces, según lo explicado para tales casos en el Apéndice 1.

## Reconocimientos

Esta lista es el resultado de contribuciones hechas por casi 60 años por los muchos miembros pasados y presentes del Comité de Nombres de Peces [Committee on Names of Fishes]. Estamos en deuda con todos los miembros anteriores. Algunos miembros han continuado contribuyendo en las tareas del Comité, y en este aspecto agradecemos especialmente a Reeve M. Bailey y C. Richard Robins. Ellos han mantenido un interés grande y provechoso. Contribuciones importantes fueron hechas también por muchos especialistas que condujeron a la segunda, tercera, cuarta, y quinta ediciones, en donde su ayuda fue reconocida. En la preparación de los materiales para esta edición hemos recibido ayuda grande y pequeña de muchos individuos. Hemos disfrutado del apoyo de un astuto subcomité consultivo, la mayoría de cuyos miembros se reunió con nosotros durante varias reuniones anuales de la American Society of Ichthyologists and Herpetologists, en donde también reconocemos la ayuda brindada por los presidentes locales de las conferencias por arreglar el local para nuestras reuniones. Debemos un reconocimiento especial a los miembros núcleos del subcomité consultivo: William D. Anderson, Jr., Jacques F. Bergeron, George H. Burgess, Brooks M. Burr, Bruce B. Collette, Salvador Contreras-Balderas, William N. Eschmeyer, Robert E. Jenkins, Richard L. Mayden, John F. Morrissey, Lawrence M. Page, Richard H. Rosenblatt, Ramón Ruiz-Carus, William F. Smith-Vaniz, and Wayne C. Starnes.

El monumental "Catalog of Fishes" en tres volúmenes por W. N. Eschmeyer (editor) (Eschmeyer 1998) aclaró muchos problemas y cambios importantes en la nomenclatura y nosotros hemos intercambiado datos continuamente con él. Apreciamos muy especialmente sus esfuerzos a nuestro favor y en el de los usuarios de la Lista.

Además del subcomité consultivo, tantos individuos nos asistieron en nuestra tarea que resulta impráctico enumerar a todos. Algunos, sin embargo, se interesaron continuamente y apoyaron en forma constructiva y provechosa nuestra tarea o colaboraron de manera importante y merecen mención especial: Larry G. Allen, M. James Allen, James W. Atz, David Aurioles-Gamboa, Henry L. Bart, Robert J. Behnke, Louis Bernatchez, Ernesto Bolado, Herbert T. Boschung, Brian W. Bowen, John Clay Bruner, Warren E. Burgess, Morgan Busby, William A. Bussing, Donald G. Buth, Kent E. Carpenter, Robert C. Cashner, José Luis Castro-Aguirre, David Catania, Ted M. Cavender, Francois Chapleau, Brian W. Coad, Miles M. Coburn, Walter R. Courtenay, Jr., Angelica Daza-Zepeda, Jean Dubé, William (Bill) N. Eschmeyer, David A. Etnier, Richard F. Feeney, Patricia Fuentes-Mata, Juan Pablo Gallo-Reynoso, Juan Manuel García-Caudillo, R. Grant Gilmore, Roberto González-Morales, David W. Greenfield, Thomas A. Greiner, Gary D. Grossman, Rocio Güereca, Ian J. Harrison, Karsten E. Hartel, Antony S. Harold, Philip A. Hastings, Phillip C. Heemstra, Dean A. Hendrickson, Michael H. Horn, C. Leticia Huidobro, Paul Humann, Tomio Iwamoto, Witold L. Klawe, Cynthia (Cindy) Klepadlo, Sven O. Kullander, Louise Lapierre, Robert J. Lavenberg, Kenneth J. Lazara, Michel Letendre, Ken Lindeman, Myrna I. López, Milton Love, Gérard Massé, Ann C. Matarese, Richard E. Matheson, Jr., John E. McCosker, Catherine (Kitty) W. Mecklenburg, Maurice (Scott) F. Mettee, el recién fallecido Robert Rush Miller, el recién fallecido W. L. Minckley, Jr., Randall D. Mooi, J. Manuel Nava-Romo, Leo G. Nico, Volker Niem, Steven M. Norris, Pere Oliver, James W. Orr, Alex E. Peden, Mauricia Pérez-Tello, Frank L. Pezold, Edward J. Pfeiler, Edwin P. Pister, Héctor G. Plascencia, Stuart G. Poss, Catherine Poussart, John E. Randall, Spring Randolph, James D. Reist, Claude Renaud, Robert H. Robins, Gorgonio Ruiz-Campos, Mark H. Sabaj, Juan Jacobo Schmitter-Soto, Jeffrey A. Seigel, Bernard Séret, David G. Smith, Gerald R. Smith, Victor G. Springer, Donald J. Stewart, Royal D. Suttkus, Christine Thacker, Bruce A. Thompson, Jorge Torre-Cosio, James C. Tyler, Albert M. van der Heiden, Carlos J. Villavicencio-Garayzar, H. J. Walker, Melvin L. Warren, Jr., Douglas C. Weaver, Edward O. Wiley, Jeffrey T. Williams, y Chris Wilson.

Los fondos para que los miembros del Comité viajaron para participar en dos sesiones maratónicas de trabajo en Gainesville, Florida, fueron proporcionados por la American Fisheries Society. Estas reuniones se realizaron en el U.S. Geological Survey Lab (Florida Caribbean Science Center), en donde reconocemos la ayuda de Sherry Bostick y otros miembros del personal. Asi también fuimos asistidos por ictiólogos locales, notablemente William F. Smith-Vaniz and George Burgess, y la anfitriona local Nancy Gilbert. También deseamos agradecer a nuestras propias instituciones por subvencionar nuestros esfuerzos en este proyecto, éstos a menudo incluyeron fondos para viajar, ayuda de secretaria, foto-copiado y servicios postales; y por proporcionar espacio de trabajo a los miembros del Comité. En este aspecto, LTF desea agradecer a Inocencio Higuera y Alfonso Gardea del CIAD, y el apoyo continuo del Programa "Bioregión Golfo de California" de Conservation Internacional, especialmente María de los Ángeles Carvajal y Alejandro Robles. Un agradecimiento especial se debe al Natural Sciences and Engineering Research Council of Canada por apoyar el grant A5457 a JSN. Mark K. Nelson hizo la conversión del manuscrito en formato vertical al horizontal. El personal, pasado y presente, de la American Fisheries Society's International Headquarters ha apoyado de muchas maneras, particularmente Betsy Fritz, Maria R. Frye, Janet Harry, Robert L. Kendall, Sally Kendall, Aaron Lerner, Beth D. McAleer, Robert Rand, Ghassan (Gus) Rassam, Catherine W. Richardson, Beth Staehle, y especialmente Deborah Lehman. Los varios presidentes de la American Fisheries Society y de la American Society of Ichthyologists and Herpetologists han ofrecido continuamente su estímulo al Comité. También deseamos agradecer, a nombre de todos los miembros de Comités del pasado y del presente, a la American Fisheries Society por concedernos el Premio por Servicio Distinguido en su reunión anual del 2000 y por reconocer la importancia del trabajo del Comité. Finalmente, pero no menos importante, agradecemos el apoyo de nuestras familias.

Queremos agradecer a muchas personas que ayudaron a traducir la Introducción al español y francés. La Introducción al español fue realizada por el Dr. Salvador Contreras-Balderas (Universidad Autónoma de Nuevo León, Monterrey, México) y el Dr. Ramón Ruiz-Carus (Comisión de Conservación de Florida Fish and Wildlife), corregida por HEP y LTF. La traducción al francés fue hecha por Denise Campillo y Jacqueline Lanteigne (Translation Bureau, Public Works and Government Services Canada), con la valiosa ayuda de Jacques F. Bergeron y Claude B. Renaud, la desinteresada contribución de nuestro amigo, recién fallecido Edwin J. Crossman, y de Joseph Nelson, y con el apoyo de Fisheries and Oceans Canada.

## En la siguiente Parte I, la lista principal, los siguientes signos y abreviaturas claves significan:

[1] **A** = Atlántico (ver Introducción para Océano Ártico aguas incluidas en A y P); **AM** = Atlántico en México pero no registrada en Estados Unidos o Canadá; **F:C** = Agua dulce Canadá; **F:M** = Agua dulce México; **F:U** = Agua dulce Estados Unidos (los estados continentales y/o Alaska); **P** = Pacífico (ver Introducción para Océano Ártico aguas incluidas en A y P); **PM** = Pacífico en México pero no registrada en Estados Unidos o Canadá; **[I]** = Introducida y establecida en nuestras aguas; **[X]** = Extinto.

[2] Muchos nuevos nombres en inglés fueron agregados para especies mexicanas que ingresan en la lista. Los nombres en español fueron agregados para las especies de agua dulce y marinas de México, y los nombres en francés fueron agregados para las especies de agua dulce y marinas en Quebec. "**En-**"; "**Sp-**"; y "**Fr-**" indican los nombres de las familias en inglés, español y francés, respectivamente.

* Cambio de la lista de 1991 (excepto las nuevas adiciones de especies de México); ver Apéndice 1 para explicación.

+ Comentario en Apéndice 1.

# INTRODUCTION

La grande nouveauté de cette sixième édition de la liste de poissons de l'American Fisheries Society est l'inclusion des espèces que l'on retrouve au Mexique. La liste comprend désormais les poissons du Canada, de la partie continentale des États-Unis et du Mexique, et représente le premier document moderne qui rassemble toute l'ichtyofaune de l'Amérique du Nord. Autre fait nouveau, nous donnons maintenant le nom vernaculaire anglais et espagnol pour chaque espèce dulcicole et marine retrouvée au Mexique, ainsi que le nom vernaculaire anglais et français pour les espèces dulcicoles et marines présentes au Québec. De plus, pour les espèces d'eau douce, nous signalons le pays où l'espèce existe. Des listes de poissons ont déjà été publiées en 1948, 1960, 1970, 1980 et 1991 (respectivement en tant que Publications spéciales 1, 2, 6, 12 et 20 de l'American Fisheries Society). Ces listes ont été largement utilisées, et elles ont nettement contribué à l'uniformisation de l'usage des noms vernaculaires tout en permettant d'éviter la confusion dans les noms scientifiques. La présente liste recommande les noms scientifiques à utiliser et tente de rendre compte autant que possible de ce qui nous semble être l'opinion actuelle des spécialistes des différents taxons. Des 570 entrées de la version abrégée de 1948 (qui comportait essentiellement les poissons les mieux connus de la pêche sportive et commerciale et les espèces-fourrages), la liste est passée à 1 892 espèces en 1960, 2 131 en 1970, 2 268 en 1980, puis 2 428 en 1991. La présente édition comprend 3 700 espèces, dont 3 694 poissons et six céphalocordés (soit, pour donner un chiffre comparable à celui de la liste de 1991, 2 635 espèces au Canada et dans la partie continentale des États-Unis, sans tenir compte de la famille de céphalocordés nouvellement ajoutée, les Branchiostomatidae). Pour cette liste, comme pour celle de 1991, le Comité conjoint American Fisheries Society/ American Society of Ichthyologists and Herpetologists (AFS/ASIH) sur les noms de poissons a tenté de trouver des noms vernaculaires pour toutes les espèces indigènes et pour les espèces introduites et établies dans la région couverte, même si ces dernières ne sont présentes que dans des zones très limitées. Le nombre d'espèces introduites que l'on trouve dans les eaux nord-américaines, par suite de lâchers intentionnels ou accidentels, est en hausse constante. Dans de nombreux cas, même si l'on a pu capturer un ou plusieurs spécimens, rien ne prouve que l'espèce se soit établie (p. ex. qu'il existe des populations reproductrices), aussi ces espèces n'apparaissent-elles pas dans la liste (Fuller et al. 1999, donnent une liste et une analyse de ces espèces introduites pour les États-Unis, et Contreras, 2000, l'a fait pour le Mexique). De plus, certaines espèces introduites déjà signalées en Amérique du Nord n'y sont plus présentes. Les noms vernaculaires des quelques poissons hybrides qui jouent un rôle important dans la gestion des pêches ou dans les pêches sportives ou commerciales apparaissent à l'annexe 2.

Bon nombre des ajouts de cette sixième édition, mis à part les espèces du Mexique, sont le résultat de la description de nouvelles espèces et de l'extension des aires de répartition découvertes au cours des relevés de nos eaux douces et marines (notamment les données signalées dans l'ouest des États-Unis en rapport avec l'événement océanographique El Niño de 1997 à 1998 et consignées par R. N. Lea et R. H. Rosenblatt, 2000, rapport CalCOFI 41:117–129). De récentes études systématiques ont mené à la reconnaissance comme espèces de taxons jusque-là considérés comme des synonymes plus récents et, inversement, ont démontré que certaines espèces nommées dans les listes antérieures sont en fait des synonymes plus récents et doivent donc être retirées de la liste. Il reste de nombreux cas d'incertitude quant au niveau auquel doit être assigné un taxon particulier (espèce ou niveau inférieur, p. ex. sous-espèce), particulièrement chez les Cyprinidae, Catostomidae, Salmonidae, Percidae, Dactyloscopidae et Labrisomidae (dans certaines de ces familles, nous pensons que les espèces nominales reconnues comme valides seront plus nombreuses que celles placées en synonymie). Des divergences d'opinion peuvent apparaître entre des utilisateurs faisant appel à différents concepts d'espèces (voir p. ex. R. L. Mayden, 1999, J. Nematol. 31(2):95–116, et J. S. Nelson, 1999, Rev. Fish Biol. Fish. 9:277–280) et à différents types de preuves (p. ex. données morphologiques vs données moléculaires). En acceptant comme valides les noms d'espèces tirés de divers travaux portant sur la faune, la taxinomie et la systématique, et quelle qu'en soit l'approche, nous ne portons pratiquement pas de jugement sur les différents concepts d'espèces, énoncés ou non, des divers auteurs. Les espèces dont la position taxinomique est incertaine sont traitées au cas par cas. Toutefois, quand nous examinons des conclusions contradictoires présentées dans des publications récentes, nous jugeons généralement que, si la probabilité est bonne qu'une espèce actuellement reconnue soit valide, il vaut mieux par prudence continuer à reconnaître cette espèce. Pour le reste, nous avons été dans de nombreux cas plus prudents que ne le souhaiteraient certains. De façon générale, si nous savons que des recherches sont en cours sur une question, nous préférons attendre que les preuves soient publiées avant d'apporter un changement. On trouvera ci-dessous, sous diverses rubriques, une analyse complémentaire de notre démarche.

Nous avons tenté d'établir une liste exhaustive de toutes les espèces de la zone couverte, l'Amérique du Nord, avec quelques exceptions. De nombreuses espèces présentes au-delà de nos limites bathymétriques (isobathe de 200 m) et géographiques manifestent à leurs premiers stades biologiques des formes qui ont été signalées dans les eaux de notre plateau continental. Ces espèces sont toutefois exclues de la liste, tout comme de nombreuses espèces mésopélagiques qui peuvent se retrouver à la bordure du plateau continental aux endroits où le talus est très proche du littoral. Par exemple, Scott et Scott (1988) décrivent certaines espèces dont des individus (y compris des œufs et des larves) entrent à l'occasion dans notre zone, mais ces espèces ne sont pas inscrites dans la liste. Mis à part d'autres restrictions précisées dans la section qui suit, nous n'avons pas limité la liste. Toutes les espèces, qu'il s'agisse de poissons de petite taille, discrets ou rares, ou de gros poissons bien connus des pêcheurs sportifs et commerciaux, ont leur importance pour la documentation et la connaissance de notre biodiversité. Bon nombre des espèces servent d'animaux de laboratoire, sont présentées ou gardées dans des aquariums publics ou privés, sont utilisées comme poissons-appâts, ou présentent une valeur esthétique ou un intérêt pour l'histoire naturelle. Certaines espèces autrefois jugées sans valeur et rejetées sont maintenant exploitées commercialement et considérées comme précieuses. On accorde une attention considérable à l'utilisation des prises accessoires des pêches, de sorte que certaines espèces jusque-là rejetées trouvent maintenant leur place sur le marché. Le développement de la conscience écologique a fait ressortir l'intérêt des poissons indigènes comme indicateurs de l'état des écosystèmes des eaux douces et marines. Les espèces en péril font l'objet d'articles dans les journaux et les magazines grand public. Notre liste exhaustive sera donc utile à de nombreux secteurs de la société. L'organisation et le mode d'indexation de l'ouvrage font que, malgré son exhaustivité, il restera facile à consulter pour les personnes ayant des intérêts particuliers.

## Zone couverte

La présente liste veut inclure toutes les espèces de poissons dont des populations reproductrices ou autonomes ont été signalées dans les eaux douces de la partie continentale du Canada, des États-Unis et du Mexique, ainsi que les espèces marines qui occupent les eaux littorales du plateau continental jusqu'à l'isobathe de 200 m (656 pi). Nous avons exclu les espèces qui vivent seulement aux endroits où la profondeur dépasse 200 m, même si on retrouve ces poissons à moins de 200 m de la surface. De nombreuses espèces connues dans les eaux situées au sud du Mexique vont certainement être signalées dans les eaux mexicaines dans l'avenir. C'est particulièrement le cas sur la façade atlantique, où environ 66 espèces marines des eaux du Belize n'ont pas encore été signalées dans les eaux mexicaines. La plupart de ces espèces vont vraisemblablement s'ajouter à la liste dans l'avenir étant donné qu'elles sont certainement présentes plus au nord, le long du littoral oriental de la péninsule du Yucatán. De plus, six espèces dulcicoles du Belize n'ont pas été signalées au Mexique. Dans l'Atlantique, selon sa définition conventionnelle, nous recensons les poissons côtiers du Groenland, de l'est du Canada et des États-Unis, et de la partie mexicaine des eaux du golfe du Mexique et de la mer des Antilles adjacentes à la péninsule du Yucatán, avec pour limite sud la frontière Mexique-Belize (pour autant que nous ayons pu en déterminer la faune). Les espèces des eaux de l'Islande, des Bermudes, des Bahamas, de Cuba et des autres îles des Antilles sont exclues, à moins qu'elles ne se retrouvent aussi dans la région couverte. Dans le Pacifique, selon sa définition conventionnelle, la zone couvre la partie du plateau continental allant du détroit de Béring à la frontière Mexique-Guatemala, y compris l'archipel océanique de Revillagigedo et l'île de Guadalupe, jusqu'à une profondeur de 200 m dans les eaux littorales contiguës. Il est particulièrement difficile de déterminer quelles sont les espèces à inclure pour les îles océaniques dépourvues de plateau continental, où on peut retrouver près de la côte des espèces océaniques en compagnie d'espèces néritiques, et nous avons tenté dans de tels cas de n'inclure que les espèces normalement associées aux plateaux continentaux. Les eaux du littoral arctique de l'Alaska et du Canada sont également englobées, alors que celles d'Hawaii et de l'atoll de Clipperton, qui possèdent des faunes riches et nettement différentes, à caractère indo-pacifique ou endémique, sont exclues. Les poissons des grands fonds, qu'ils soient benthiques ou mésopélagiques, y compris les espèces à migration verticale qui entrent temporairement dans la zone épipélagique, ainsi que les poissons strictement océaniques, sont exclus de la liste, sauf s'ils semblent être plus que des spécimens égarés dans les eaux de notre plateau continental. Dans la pratique, ce distinguo est souvent difficile à appliquer et devient plutôt arbitraire, surtout si l'on considère les stades des œufs et des larves. Nous incluons les poissons pélagiques qui entrent dans les eaux du plateau continental, mais nous excluons les espèces qui, dans les eaux de l'Amérique du Nord, sont connues pour vivre seulement à des profondeurs de plus de 200 m, même si elles ont été capturées ailleurs dans des zones où le fond se trouve à moins de 200 m de la surface. Les utilisateurs devront donc être prudents lorsqu'ils veulent établir la plage de profondeur occupée par une espèce: par exemple, *Enchelycore anatina* (Lowe, 1838), espèce communément observée dans l'est de l'Atlantique nettement au-dessus de 200 m, n'a été signalée dans l'ouest de l'Atlantique qu'à des profondeurs dépassant 200 m; *Ophichthus menezesi* McCosker et Böhlke, 1984, qui a été décrite comme présente à une profondeur de 169 à 209 m au large du Brésil, n'a été observée dans le golfe du Mexique, au large de la Floride, qu'à des profondeurs de 1 200 à 1 400 m.

Les abréviations employées dans la liste donnent une idée générale des eaux où se retrouve telle espèce. Un « **A** » signifie l'océan Atlantique, et inclut l'océan Arctique à l'est de la péninsule de Boothia (c.-à-d. 95° de longitude ouest), tandis que « **AM** » signale la présence dans l'Atlantique, dans les eaux du Mexique, mais pas dans celles du Canada ni des États-Unis. Le « **P** » désigne l'océan Pacifique et inclut l'ouest de l'océan Arctique (mer des Tchouktches et mer de Beaufort jusqu'à l'ouest de la péninsule de Boothia), tandis que « **PM** » signale la présence dans l'océan Pacifique, dans les eaux du Mexique mais pas dans celles du Canada ni des États-Unis. La liste ne désigne pas spécifiquement les espèces présentes dans l'océan Arctique (un « A » ou un « P » peut aussi, ou exclusivement, indiquer la présence d'une espèce dans l'Arctique, comme c'est le cas pour *Triglops nybelini*: désignée « AP », elle est connue seulement en mer de Beaufort dans l'Arctique [zone « P »] et vers l'est jusque dans l'océan Atlantique [« A »], mais elle est absente de l'océan Pacifique). Un « **F:** » indique la présence en eau douce ou dans d'autres eaux intérieures qui sont salées (p. ex. la mer Salton, en Californie). Certaines espèces sont parfois ainsi désignées à cause de mentions historiques, comme c'est le cas pour *Elops affinis* dans le cours inférieur du Colorado et la mer Salton. Une désignation « **F:** » suivie par un « **C** » dénote les eaux douces du Canada, tandis que « **M** » dénote les eaux douces du Mexique, et « **U** » les eaux douces des États-Unis (États contigus et/ou Alaska). Il faut noter que (i) une espèce marine connue sur une côte à une profondeur de moins de 201 m, mais sur l'autre côte à des profondeurs de plus de 200 m, est indiquée seulement comme présente sur la côte peu profonde (p. ex. *Notacanthus chemnitzii* est désignée comme « A » seulement, mais sa présence est connue au large de la Californie à des profondeurs de plus de 200 m); (ii) même si deux espèces peuvent être désignées comme présentes en eau de mer et en eau douce, l'une peut être principalement marine et l'autre principalement dulcicole; (iii) de nombreuses espèces non désignées par « F » ont été capturées à l'occasion en estuaire ou en eau douce (voir p. ex. W. F. Loftus, 2000, Fla. Sci. 63(1):27–47; F. J. Schwartz, 1992, *in* C. Cole et K. Turner (directeur de publication), Barrier island ecology of the mid-Atlantic Coast: a symposium. Rapport technique NPS/SERCAHA/NRTR-93/04: 94–118; F. J. Schwartz, 2000, J. Elisha Mitchell Sci. Soc. 116(3):206–224). L'abréviation « **[I]** » entre crochets suit la lettre indiquant les eaux où est présente une espèce introduite (exotique) établie dans la zone couverte par la liste, et peut être utilisée séparément ou conjointement aux abréviations « A », « P », « F », « C », « U » et « M » (il s'agit d'espèces introduites dans la zone désignée par suite de l'activité humaine, dont la présence est documentée ou supposée, et l'introduction directe ou indirecte). Ce symbole n'est pas utilisé pour les introductions d'une espèce qui est indigène dans une des zones désignées ci-dessus (p. ex. l'introduction de *Salvelinus fontinalis* de l'est à l'ouest du Canada), mais continue à être employé pour une espèce qui, introduite dans un pays, se disperse par la suite dans un autre pays (p. ex. *Scardinius erythrophthalmus* est encore considérée comme une espèce introduite dans les deux pays où elle est présente à l'heure actuelle). Contrairement à la démarche de l'édition de 1991, nous indiquons le succès de l'introduction d'une espèce d'un océan à l'autre; par exemple, *Alosa sapidissima* et *Morone saxatilis*, espèces de l'Atlantique, ont été introduites avec succès dans les eaux du Pacifique, et leur présence est donc indiquée par la désignation « AF:CUP[I] » (ces modifications ne sont pas notées à l'annexe 1). Le symbole « **[X]** » entre crochets indique que l'espèce est considérée comme disparue. Des espèces signalées dans l'édition de 1991 qui existent encore mais sont connues seulement par des mentions historiques, et ont probablement, à l'heure actuelle, disparu du Canada ou des États-Unis, sont encore inscrites dans la liste; par exemple, *Erimystax x-punctatus* n'existe plus au Canada, mais se retrouve aux États-Unis et est donc désignée comme « F:CU », tandis que *Catostomus bernardini* n'existe plus aux États-Unis mais se retrouve au Mexique et est donc désignée comme « F:UM ». Toutes les espèces mexicaines notées « AM », « PM » ou « F:M » sont nouvelles dans la liste, et, à quelques exceptions près, ne font pas l'objet d'une mention à l'annexe 1. Les espèces désignées « A » ou « P » et portant **un nom espagnol et/ou français** se retrouvent dans les eaux du Mexique et/ou du Québec, ainsi que dans le reste de la zone couverte, et elles étaient inscrites sur la liste de 1991, sauf indication contraire signalant par un astérisque (*) qu'il s'agit de nouvelles mentions (principalement en Californie).

## Noms de famille

Les noms de famille sont importants pour l'identification et la recherche d'information. Ils sont couramment employés en ichtyologie, dans les ouvrages de vulgarisation sur les poissons, dans les dictionnaires et les encyclopédies. Toutefois, pour certains groupes, les ichtyologistes interprètent de façon très variable les limites des familles. Si nous convenons qu'il faut éviter autant que possible le changement dans les noms de famille, nous pensons aussi que la liste doit refléter, au meilleur de notre jugement, les pratiques réelles de la systématique actuelle. C'est ainsi qu'on notera une augmentation considérable du nombre de familles reconnues. Par ailleurs, nous préférons accepter les familles ajoutées depuis l'édition de 1991 lorsque les raisons se fondent sur des arguments phylogénétiques, ou si le nom de famille antérieur suggère des relations improbables (des notes sont généralement fournies en annexe lorsque nous n'avons pas apporté des modifications qui auraient semblé justifiées à certains). Nous préférons ne pas apporter de changements subjectifs ou arbitraires, comme le fractionnement d'une famille dont on sait qu'elle est monophylétique. Ainsi, par exemple, nous plaçons les corégones et ciscos, les ombres, et les truites, saumons et ombles dans une seule famille monophylétique plutôt que dans trois familles séparées comme le font certains auteurs. Dans cet exemple, le fractionnement créerait une perte d'information phylogénétique, qui pourrait être compensée par la reconnaissance de superfamilles ou de sous-ordres. En rassemblant les taxons, comme nous le faisons dans ce cas, il est possible le cas échéant de corriger la perte d'informations phylogénétiques en reconnaissant l'existence de sous-familles. En général, l'approche que nous retenons correspond au mode de classification employé antérieurement. Les nouvelles familles ajoutées à la liste font l'objet de commentaires à l'annexe 1; toutefois, celles qui sont ajoutées du fait que toutes les espèces présentes dans la zone nouvellement couverte se trouvent au Mexique seulement ne sont pas signalées comme étant nouvelles. Nous reconnaissons les ordres et certains niveaux élevés de classification, mais soulignons que cette liste ne représente pas nécessairement ce que nous considérons comme l'opinion reçue sur les relations au niveau de l'ordre. Les modifications au niveau de l'ordre par rapport à l'édition précédente ne sont pas toutes commentées à l'annexe 1.

## Noms vernaculaires

Les noms vernaculaires des espèces existent depuis longtemps—beaucoup plus longtemps que les noms scientifiques—et, étant donné que le grand public et les biologistes les emploient, nous pensons qu'il nous incombe d'établir un système efficace et normalisé pour ces noms. Le Comité vise donc à élaborer un corpus de noms vernaculaires—un seul nom vernaculaire pour chaque espèce—qui correspond à l'usage le plus courant; à créer une nomenclature vernaculaire plus riche, plus signifiante et plus colorée; enfin, à promouvoir des mécanismes qui renforceront la stabilité et l'universalité des noms assignés aux poissons de l'Amérique du Nord. Les noms vernaculaires des poissons présentés dans cette liste s'appliquent à l'espèce. Ils sont parfois employés comme appellations commerciales, ainsi qu'à d'autres fins. Toutefois, certaines appellations commerciales visent souvent plusieurs espèces, ou diffèrent pour des raisons diverses des noms adoptés dans cette liste, et nous ne les avons donc pas retenues. Nous invitons fortement les auteurs, commerçants et autres intervenants, dans l'intérêt de l'information du public, à adopter les noms vernaculaires proposés ici, même si un nom semble présenter peu d'attrait commercial (par ex. nous désapprouvons l'emploi du nom anglais « mullet » pour les « suckers » ou meuniers, famille des Catostomidae). On trouvera un résumé des appellations commerciales appliquées en anglais aux poissons (et invertébrés) commercialisés aux États-Unis dans le document "The Seafood List, FDA's Guide to Acceptable Market Names for Seafood Sold in Interstate Commerce," 1993, U.S. Food and Drug Administration, U.S. Government Printing Office (voir aussi le site http://vm.cfsan.fda.gov/~frf/rfe0.html). Dans la présente liste, de nombreux noms différent de ceux qui apparaissent dans les publications de la FAO (Organisation des Nations Unies pour l'alimentation et l'agriculture). Nous espérons parvenir à davantage d'uniformité dans l'avenir.

Le nom vernaculaire, tel que nous l'entendons ici, est considéré comme une appellation officielle qui peut remplacer le nom scientifique latinisé d'une espèce. Nous soulignons que les noms vernaculaires ne visent pas à remplacer les noms scientifiques en signalant les relations phylogénétiques (voir le principe 8 ci-dessous). L'histoire confirme que les noms vernaculaires sont souvent plus stables que les noms scientifiques (fait qui n'est pas toujours reconnu). Voici quelques espèces dont seul le nom scientifique a changé entre les éditions de 1980 et de 1991 : le cyprinidé nommé en anglais rosyface chub — *Hybopsis rubrifrons* est devenu *Notropis rubescens* puis est redevenu (2004) *H. rubrifrons*; la truite arc-en-ciel (rainbow trout) est passée de *Salmo gairdneri* à *Oncorhynchus mykiss*; la sole anglaise (English sole) est passée de *Parophrys*

*vetulus* à *Pleuronectes vetulus*, pour revenir à *Parophrys vetulus*. Pour les noms de genre, en particulier, on note des flottements et des interprétations diverses, mais il doit en être ainsi. Les noms vernaculaires sont plus facilement adaptables aux usages courants que les noms scientifiques. Il est clairement nécessaire de normaliser et d'uniformiser les noms vernaculaires, pas seulement pour la pêche sportive et commerciale, mais pour la vente au consommateur, l'aquariophilie, la terminologie juridique, et pour remplacer les noms scientifiques dans les écrits populaires ou savants. Le Comité juge souhaitable d'établir un nom vernaculaire pour chaque espèce de poisson présente naturellement ou par suite d'une introduction dans les eaux du Canada, des États-Unis et du Mexique. Les noms vernaculaires espagnols nouvellement ajoutés ont été établis par deux membres du Comité, H. Espinosa-Pérez et L. T. Findley, à partir de leur expérience de travail de terrain, de la consultation de collègues et de l'examen de nombreuses sources publiées. Les sources principales consultées à cette fin sont signalées par un astérisque dans la section des Références; bon nombre de ces sources ont également été consultées en vue de l'adoption éventuelle de noms en anglais pour les espèces mexicaines nouvellement inscrites sur la liste. Pour les noms vernaculaires français des espèces d'eau douce du Québec, nous nous sommes appuyés principalement sur le document de J. F. Bergeron et J. Dubé, 2000, Liste historique des poissons d'eau douce du Québec, Gouvernement du Québec, mars 2000. Les noms des espèces marines du Québec sont tirés de Desrosiers et al. 1995, ouvrage également utile pour les poissons d'eau douce. Pour les catostomidés du genre *Moxostoma*, nous suivons J. F. Bergeron et J. Dubé, 2000, et A. Branchaud et R. E. Jenkins, 1999, Can. Field-Nat. 113(2):345–358, qui ont remplacé le *suceur* des listes antérieures par le *chevalier*. Les noms français des familles ont été choisis principalement par J. F. Bergeron (communication personnelle, mai 2001–août 2003), à partir de diverses sources nord-américaines et européennes, notamment D. E. McAllister, 1990, A list of the fishes of Canada/ Liste des poissons du Canada, Syllogeus 64, et B. W. Coad, 1995, Encyclopedia of Canadian fishes, Canadian Museum of Nature et Canadian Sport-fishing Productions, Inc., Ottawa.

Pour de nombreux noms, il est facile d'arriver à une entente, mais d'autres suscitent des difficultés, et parfois de nettes controverses. C'est particulièrement le cas des poissons dont les appellations commerciales diffèrent des noms couramment utilisés par les pêcheurs sportifs, les biologistes et d'autres personnes (p. ex. le poisson qu'on appelle « red snapper » sur la côte ouest est généralement une espèce de *Sebastes*, et non le vivaneau *Lutjanus campechanus*). L'emploi de noms différents dans diverses parties de l'aire géographique d'une espèce crée des difficultés qui ne semblent pouvoir se résoudre que par l'arbitrage. Par contre, un nom donné peut être employé à plusieurs endroits pour des espèces différentes. Si l'on ne peut s'attendre à ce que dans un tel cas l'intervention du Comité fasse changer rapidement l'usage local, il semble tout à fait incorrect de sanctionner l'usage d'un seul nom pour plusieurs espèces différentes. Nous soutenons que tous les utilisateurs des noms vernaculaires des poissons sont mal servis, et peut-être même induits en erreur, si ces noms sont employés de façon incohérente.

Après s'être acharné pendant de nombreuses années à établir des noms vernaculaires, un Comité antérieur sur les noms de poissons s'est rendu compte qu'il était important de formuler une série de principes directeurs pour choisir les noms. Une telle codification permet d'évaluer les mérites relatifs de plusieurs noms plus objectivement que si le choix était fondé avant tout sur l'expérience personnelle et sur les préférences. Lorsqu'on constate la multitude des noms vernaculaires de poissons, il apparaît qu'on ne peut guère établir de principes sans prévoir des exceptions. Il existe en fait de nombreuses exceptions, car au moment où le Comité a commencé à travailler, la majorité des espèces les plus grosses et les plus abondantes—donc les plus « importantes »—des États-Unis et du Canada possédaient des noms vernaculaires si fermement établis qu'il aurait été peu réaliste de les rejeter dans le seul but de respecter un principe nouvellement formulé. Pour s'entendre sur le nom d'une espèce, il faut souvent peser le pour et le contre de plusieurs choix possibles et retenir celui qui correspond le mieux à un ensemble de critères. Nous présentons ci-dessous les principes que le Comité juge appropriés pour le choix des noms vernaculaires des poissons; ils sont tirés des listes précédentes, avec quelques modifications.

## Principes régissant le choix des noms vernaculaires

1. *Un seul nom vernaculaire, dans chaque langue retenue, sera accepté pour une espèce.* Dans l'édition de 1991, un seul poisson, *Coregonus artedi*, avait deux noms vernaculaires acceptés; il n'y a maintenant plus d'exception.

2. *Le même nom vernaculaire ne peut être attribué à deux espèces de la liste.* Il faut autant que possible éviter de retenir pour des espèces de notre zone des noms couramment utilisés pour des espèces qui vivent en dehors de cette zone.

3. *Le qualificatif « commun » ou son équivalent anglais ou espagnol doit autant que possible être évité dans la composition du nom d'un poisson.*

4. *Il faut rechercher la simplicité.* En français, on accordera la préférence à des noms qui sont courts et euphoniques. Les noms composés de mots brefs et familiers vont dans le sens de la clarté et de la simplicité, et il vaut mieux éviter de combiner des mots longs, complexes ou peu familiers. En français, les noms composés peuvent comporter un trait d'union (p. ex. crapet-soleil, raseux-de-terre) ou des prépositions (dard de sable, achigan à petite bouche).

5. *On n'emploiera pas de majuscule dans les noms vernaculaires sauf pour les éléments qui sont des noms propres* (p. ex. grand corégone, mais anguille d'Amérique; rainbow trout, mais Sacramento perch; carpita fantasma, mais guayacón de Palenque).

6. *Les noms choisis pour honorer des personnes* (p. ex. Allison's tuna, Julia's darter, Meek's halfbeak, blanquillo de Hubbs) *sont à éviter car ils n'ont aucune valeur descriptive.* Pour certains groupes, on trouve dans les noms scientifiques des patronymes spécifiques identiques (parfois établis en l'honneur de différentes personnes qui ont le même nom de famille) désignant des poissons de genres apparentés, et l'emploi d'un patronyme dans le nom vernaculaire peut être une source de confusion. Dans quelques cas, les patronymes sont tellement intégrés aux noms vernaculaires anglais qu'ils ne sont plus traités ni reconnus comme tels. Ces noms sont acceptés et ne portent pas de majuscule (p. ex. guppy, lane snapper). Ce principe ne s'applique pas nécessairement aux noms vernaculaires français (p. ex. le nom vernaculaire de *Liparis*

*coheni* est limace de Cohen). Toutefois, lorsqu'un nom vernaculaire patronymique n'avait pas de « priorité » établie, on a généralement choisi un autre nom vernaculaire sans caractère patronymique.

7. *Seules les entités taxinomiques clairement définies et bien marquées* (généralement l'espèce) *se verront attribuer un nom vernaculaire.* Si les sous-espèces ne sont pas toujours susceptibles de porter un nom vernaculaire, certaines sous-espèces valides sont si différentes d'apparence (et pas seulement dans leur distribution géographique) qu'elles sont facilement reconnues par les pêcheurs sportifs ou commerciaux, ou même par des membres du grand public, et dans ce cas un nom vernaculaire représente une aide importante pour la communication. Toutefois, et contrairement à l'édition de 1991 où nous avions reconnu deux sous-espèces d'*Esox americanus*, nous n'avons pas, pour des raisons de cohérence, donné de nom scientifique ni de nom vernaculaire pour ces sous-espèces dans la présente édition. Nous reconnaissons toutefois que les sous-espèces, qui ont leur propre histoire évolutionnaire sur le plan de l'allopatrie, jouent un rôle important dans les recherches sur l'évolution, et peuvent donc recevoir un statut de protection particulière et être reconnues dans les études sur la biodiversité. Lorsqu'on a recours à des noms de sous-espèces, le nom vernaculaire de l'espèce doit s'appliquer à toutes les sous-espèces du taxon.

Les hybrides ne reçoivent généralement pas de nom vernaculaire, mais ceux qui sont importants dans la gestion des pêches et qui possèdent des noms vernaculaires bien établis sont traités à l'annexe 2. Les variétés d'élevage, les phases et les variantes morphologiques ne sont pas nommées même si elles peuvent être importantes pour le commerce et l'élevage des poissons d'aquarium (p. ex. les nombreuses variétés de carassin et de carpe; la phase ocellée et la phase dorée de *Mycteroperca rosacea* et d'*Arothron meleagris*).

8. *Le nom vernaculaire ne doit pas être étroitement lié au nom scientifique.* Les flottements nécessaires de la nomenclature scientifique ne nécessitent pas une adaptation constante des noms vernaculaires. La malheureuse pratique qui consiste à établir un nom vernaculaire pour chaque genre, puis un qualificatif pour chaque espèce, et un autre qualificatif pour chaque sous-espèce, bien que séduisante par sa simplicité, a le gros défaut d'être dénuée de souplesse, de sorte qu'un poisson risque de ne pas être reconnu parce qu'on a rejeté ce qui pouvait être un nom traditionnel parfaitement acceptable. Nous voyons dans cette pratique une simple tentative d'inscrire dans le nom vernaculaire la nomenclature scientifique. Si une espèce est transférée d'un genre à un autre, ou passe du statut d'espèce à celui de sous-espèce, ou vice-versa, le nom vernaculaire ne devrait en principe pas changer. Les noms vernaculaires n'ont pas comme fonction première d'indiquer la relation. Ce principe reste toutefois incompris ou rejeté par ceux qui soutiennent que les noms vernaculaires de tous les membres d'un genre devraient comprendre le même mot racine (p. ex. que tous les *Oncorhynchus* devraient s'appeler saumon, comme dans « saumon coho » et « saumon rose », et que tous les *Salvelinus* devraient s'appeler omble, comme dans « omble de fontaine », etc.). Nous insistons sur le fait que la stabilité des noms vernaculaires contrebalance nettement tous les inconvénients éventuels. Lorsque deux ou plusieurs groupes taxinomiques (p. ex. des espèces nominales) sont jugés identiques (synonymes), on adoptera un seul nom pour le groupe combiné. Voir aussi le principe 13.

9. *Les noms respecteront les règles du bon goût (p. ex. ils ne contiendront pas de termes jugés offensants).* C'est par exemple pour respecter ce principe que des noms anglais ont été changés (« squawfish » et « jewfish » ont été remplacés respectivement par « pikeminnow » et « goliath grouper »). Ces changements, apportés sur les conseils de diverses personnes, ont été accueillis très favorablement.

Les principes qui précèdent relèvent essentiellement des règles de procédure. Ceux qui suivent sont des critères qui pourront aider à choisir des noms appropriés.

10. *On recherchera de préférence des noms imagés, colorés, romantiques, fantaisistes, métaphoriques, ou intéressants par leur fraîcheur et leur originalité.* Une telle terminologie ajoute à la richesse et à l'en-

vergure de la nomenclature et procure une grande satisfaction à l'utilisateur. En voici quelques exemples: en français, tête-de-boule, crayon d'argent et truite fardée; en anglais, madtom, Dolly Varden, midshipman, chili-pepper, garibaldi, pumpkinseed, flier, angelfish, Moorish idol et hogchoker; en espagnol, bruja, guitarra, chucho et lacha.

11. *Les noms autochtones d'Amérique du Nord ou leurs modifications font d'excellents noms vernaculaires.* On utilise couramment en français des noms comme poulamon, achigan, ouitouche, maskinongé, ogac et touladi; en anglais, menhaden, eulachon, cisco, Chinook, mummichog, tautog; en espagnol, puyeki et totoaba.

12. *Quelle que soit leur origine, les noms réellement vernaculaires qui sont répandus et couramment utilisés dans le public doivent être retenus autant que possible.* Outre les noms autochtones, de nombreux noms bien connus employés au nord du Mexique ont une origine autre que le français ou l'anglais: barracuda, cero, mojarra, pompano, sierra (noms espagnols ou tirés de l'espagnol); bocaccio (italien); mako (maori). De très beaux noms ont été établis par des immigrants installés en Amérique du Nord. La plupart de ces noms se conforment aux principes 14 et 15 ci-dessous. Il faut cependant prendre garde d'éviter des mots qui signifient la même chose dans des langues proches mais diffèrent légèrement sur le plan de l'orthographe (p. ex. sierra en espagnol et serra en portugais).

13. *Des noms couramment employés dans l'usage traditionnel français* (p. ex. méné et perche), *anglais* (p. ex. chub, minnow, trout, bass, perch, sole, flounder), *espagnol* (p. ex. cazón, sardina, carpa, mojarra, perca, lenguado) *sont utilisés avec une latitude considérable en taxinomie.* Le respect des pratiques traditionnelles est préférable si cela n'entre pas en conflit avec l'usage généralisé d'un autre nom. Toutefois, bien des noms ont été appliqués en Amérique du Nord à des poissons d'apparence similaire mais souvent peu apparentés. Par exemple, les termes « bass » et « lenguado » sont utilisés pour des représentants de plusieurs familles de poissons à rayons épineux, et les noms « perch » et « perca » pour un nombre encore plus grand de familles. Le nom « chub » est employé dans des groupes aussi éloignés que les Cyprinidae et les Kyphosidae, tandis que « mojarra » se retrouve dans les familles Cichlidae, Gerreidae et autres. Le tile océanique (*Caulolatilus princeps*), parfois appelé « salmón » dans le nord-ouest du Mexique, n'est pas un salmonidé, et le pompano du Pacifique (« pámpano » en espagnol) (*Peprilus simillimus*) n'est pas un carangidé, et pourtant c'est sous ces noms que les pêcheurs connaissent ces poissons dans toute leur aire. Pour les espèces bien connues, le Comité juge préférable de reconnaître l'usage général plutôt que d'adopter des substituts savants ou pédants. Aussi l'utilisation bien établie d'un nom traditionnel doit-elle supplanter les efforts de cohérence. Ce principe n'est pas bien compris par certains ichtyologistes qui jugent que le nom de « perche » ne devrait pas être employé pour un embiotocidé, le nom de « truite » pour un *Salvelinus*, celui de « sardinita » pour un characidé, ni celui de « cazón » pour un carcharinidé. En anglais, on a pu éviter certains problèmes, ou les limiter, en créant des mots-valises (p. ex. seatrout pour sea trout, mudsucker pour mud sucker, surfperch pour surf perch). Ces combinaisons sont maintenant largement acceptées depuis qu'elles ont été adoptées par le Comité dans ses listes antérieures.

14. *Les attributs structuraux, la couleur et les motifs de la livrée sont de bonnes sources de noms, et sont souvent employés à cette fin.* Les noms de poissons s'agrémentent d'une multitude de descripteurs, par exemple citron, cuivré, caméléon et à fossettes en français; sailfin, flathead, slippery, giant, mottled, copper, tripletail en anglais; chato, jorobado, bocón, gigante, jabonero, pinto, cobrizo en espagnol. Il faut s'efforcer de choisir des termes qui sont exacts sur le plan descriptif, mais éviter la répétition de ceux qui sont le plus fréquemment employés (p. ex. blanc [white, blanco], noir [black, negro], tacheté [spotted, manchado], barré [banded, de cintas]).

Selon la tradition nord-américaine de création des noms vernaculaires en ichtyologie et en herpétologie, nous avons tenté de restreindre l'usage des termes « ligne » ou « rayure » aux marques longitudinales parallèles à l'axe du corps, et les termes « barre » ou « bande » aux marques verticales ou transversales.

15. *Les caractéristiques écologiques sont utiles pour créer de bons noms.* Ces termes doivent avoir un caractère descriptif précis. Certains déterminants sont utilisés couramment dans les noms de poissons, en français (en anglais, en espagnol), comme de récif (reef, de arrecife), de corail (coral, coralino), de sable (sand, arenoso), de roche (rock, piedrero), de lac (lake, de lago), dulcicole (freshwater, dulciacuícola), et de montagne (mountain, de la sierra).

16. *La répartition géographique peut donner de bons déterminants adjectivaux.* Les caractères géographiques peu descriptifs ou trompeurs (p. ex. « Kentucky bass » pour une espèce à très grande répartition) doivent être corrigés, sauf si l'usage est vraiment trop établi (à des fins de stabilité, nous avons gardé des noms comme « Alaska blackfish », bien que cet umbre soit aussi présent en Russie, et « guatopote de Sonora » même si cette poecilie se retrouve couramment hors des limites de l'État du même nom). Dans un souci de concision, il est généralement possible d'éliminer des mots comme lac (lake, lago), fleuve ou rivière (river, río), golfe (gulf, golfo) ou mer (sea, mar) dans le nom des espèces (p. ex. Colorado pikeminnow, au lieu de « Colorado River pikeminnow »; topote del Balsas, plutôt que « topote del Río Balsas »).

17. *Les noms génériques peuvent servir de noms vernaculaires directement* (p. ex. rémora, tilapia, mola, torpedo, anchoa, brótula, guavina) *ou sous une forme modifiée* (p. ex. alose à partir d'*Alosa*). Une fois adoptés, ces noms doivent être maintenus, même si le nom scientifique du genre ou du taxon supérieur est changé par la suite. Ces noms vernaculaires doivent être écrits en caractères romains (et non en italique). La concision et l'euphonie sont des caractères importants pour les noms de ce type, qui seront probablement le plus souvent appliqués à des poissons d'aquarium ou à d'autres espèces de petite taille ou peu connues pour lesquelles il n'existe pas encore de nomenclature vernaculaire bien établie.

18. *Le double emploi de noms vernaculaires pour des poissons et d'autres organismes doit être évité autant que possible, mais cet argument ne doit pas être invoqué seul pour rejeter certains noms couramment employés.* Par exemple, le mot « buffalo » est employé en anglais pour divers mammifères artiodactyles (le bison notamment) et pour les meuniers catostomidés (buffalos en français) du genre *Ictiobus*; « renard » ou, en espagnol, « zorro » désignent des requins de la famille Alopiidae, tandis que le nom « mariposa » (papillon en espagnol) sert aussi bien pour les poissons-papillons de la famille Chaetodontidae que pour les raies-papillons de la famille Gymnuridae. Étant donné que leur usage est bien établi, ces noms peuvent être retenus comme noms vernaculaires sans modification. Toutefois, nous avons modifié le nom anglais des espèces du genre *Coryphaena*, que nous appelons maintenant « dolphinfish » au lieu de « dolphin », nom qui désigne les dauphins (cétacés).

## Relation entre le nom vernaculaire et le nom scientifique d'une espèce

L'objectif premier de cette liste est de recommander un nom vernaculaire dans la langue pertinente et de fournir le nom scientifique généralement accepté pour toutes les espèces de poissons d'Amérique du Nord dans les limites géographiques fixées. Les noms vernaculaires peuvent, à notre avis, être établis par entente générale. Par contre, les noms scientifiques vont inévitablement évoluer avec le progrès des connaissances et selon l'opinion des taxinomistes. Pour ce qui concerne l'usage, la nomenclature reflète l'opinion du Comité, qui est conscient du fait que bon nombre des utilisateurs de cette liste ne sont pas très au courant de l'évolution des publications, ou ne sont pas intéressés par la systématique ou les règles de la nomenclature, mais cherchent simplement un guide des noms techniques, vernaculaires et/ou scientifiques. Nous avons soigneusement vérifié la nomenclature scientifique utilisée en ce qui concerne l'orthographe, les auteurs et la date de la description originale.

Nous devons souligner qu'il y a désaccord concernant la classification de nombreux groupes, ou encore que la classification présente des lacunes. On note aussi souvent entre les chercheurs des divergences d'opinion à caractère subjectif pour la désignation du rang des taxons. De plus, les chercheurs qui utilisent une méthodologie synthétique (c.-à-d. non phylogénétique) préféreront classer dans des genres monotypiques les espèces présentant des spécialisations marquées sur le plan trophique, comportemental ou morphologique (on peut aussi assigner à des genres et des familles monotypiques des taxons dont les relations sont trop mal connues pour permettre une meilleure classification, philosophie à laquelle nous adhérons). Nous préférons accepter des conclusions de nature phylogénétique quand les travaux sont solidement fondés (voir aussi l'analyse présentée dans les sections Noms de famille et Noms vernaculaires, particulièrement le principe 8).

## Plan de la liste

La liste se présente sous forme d'une série phylogénétique de familles de poissons établie au mieux des connaissances fournies par les recherches actuelles. L'organisation des ordres et des familles suit globalement Nelson (1994), à part certaines modifications correspondant à des études systématiques récentes. Les classes et les ordres des poissons récemment décrits sont indiqués. Dans la plupart des cas, nous donnons un seul nom vernaculaire pour chaque famille en anglais, en espagnol et en français; on notera certaines exceptions, notamment dans le cas de la famille Salmonidae, truites et saumons, qui englobe les truites, les saumons, les ombles, les corégones, les ciscos et les ombres.

Au sein des familles, les genres et les espèces sont présentés par ordre alphabétique; s'il peut être désavantageux à l'occasion de séparer des formes étroitement apparentées d'une même famille, cet inconvénient est largement compensé par une plus grande facilité de consultation. Nous avons adopté dans cette édition le mode de mise en page Paysage, plutôt que le mode Portrait des éditions précédentes, afin de pouvoir présenter sur la même ligne les noms vernaculaires des espèces en anglais, en espagnol et en français. Chaque page de la partie I comporte cinq colonnes, la première donnant le nom scientifique, la deuxième la zone de présence, la troisième le nom vernaculaire anglais (quelle que soit la zone de présence), la quatrième le nom vernaculaire espagnol pour les espèces du Mexique, et la cinquième le nom vernaculaire français pour les espèces du Québec.

Nous avons tenté de suivre le nouveau code de la Commission Internationale de Nomenclature Zoologique, et nous avons donc retenu les orthographes originales des noms d'espèces (de sorte que les suffixes de certains noms patronymiques seront le cas échéant -i ou -ii). Le nouveau code, qui est la quatrième édition du Code International de Nomenclature Zoologique (le « Code »), a été publié en 1999 et est entré en vigueur le 1er janvier 2000. On trouvera dans C. J. Ferraris et W. N. Eschmeyer, 2000, Copeia 2000(3):907–908, une analyse du Code en ce qui concerne son effet sur les noms des poissons.

Dans cette édition, nous continuons d'ajouter, après le nom scientifique, l'auteur et la date de publication de la description originale de l'espèce. L'auteur et la date sont des renseignements souvent nécessaires pour des personnes qui n'ont pas forcément accès aux publications originales. Il est parfois compliqué de déterminer qui est l'auteur exact et quelle est l'année de publication, particulièrement pour les noms proposés avant 1900. Eschmeyer (1998), Gilbert (1998) et d'autres ont corrigé de nombreuses dates de description qui apparaissaient dans l'édition de 1991, et nous avons intégré ces corrections à la présente liste, avec des notes à l'annexe 1. Nos justifications de la graphie des noms Delaroche, Forsskål, Lacepède et Lesueur ont été présentées dans la troisième édition (page 5) et la quatrième édition (page 8). L'attribution des noms proposés dans le M. E. Blochii Systema Ichthyologicae, 1801, par J. G. Schneider a été expliquée dans la quatrième édition (page 8).

L'utilisation du nom de l'auteur correspond à l'interprétation du Code actuel. Conformément à ces règles, le nom de l'auteur (ou des auteurs) suit directement le nom de l'espèce (écrit en italique). Si, dans sa description originale, l'espèce a été assignée au genre auquel elle est assignée ici, le nom de l'auteur est écrit sans parenthèses; si l'espèce a été décrite dans un autre genre, le nom de l'auteur apparaît entre parenthèses. La date (année) de publication est séparée du nom de l'auteur par une virgule et apparaît dans la parenthèse quand c'est nécessaire. Par exemple, Mitchill a au départ nommé l'omble de fontaine *Salmo fontinalis* dans un ouvrage publié en 1814; ce poisson apparaît ici sous le nom de *Salvelinus fontinalis* (Mitchill, 1814). Dans l'édition de 1991, les parenthèses étaient aussi placées autour du nom d'un auteur dans les cas où le nom du niveau espèce était au départ combiné à un nom de genre incorrectement orthographié ou faisant l'objet d'une émendation injustifiée. Cette pratique n'est plus acceptable, en dépit du fait qu'une émendation injustifiée est un nom disponible avec son propre auteur et sa propre date (article 51.3.1 du Code). C'est ainsi que nous avons maintenant enlevé les parenthèses pour des espèces décrites dans des genres comme *Rhinobatus* (maintenant *Rhinobatos*), *Raia* (maintenant *Raja*), *Lepidosteus* (maintenant *Lepisosteus*), *Ophichthys* (maintenant *Ophichthus*), *Nototropis* (maintenant *Notropis*), *Amiurus* (maintenant *Ameiurus*), *Hemirhamphus* (maintenant *Hemiramphus*), *Opisthognathus* (maintenant *Opistognathus*), et *Pomadasis* (maintenant *Pomadasys*). Il faut être très attentif à l'orthographe, car la même graphie peut servir pour une émendation injustifiée et pour une orthographe valide indépendante; par exemple, *Ophichthys* sert à la fois comme émendation injustifié d'*Ophichthus* Ahl, 1789, un genre appartenant à la famille des serpents de mer (ophichtidés), et pour *Ophichthys* Swainson, 1839, une anguille des mares de la famille des synbranchidés (Eschmeyer 1998:2045).

Les éditions antérieures de la liste ont été consultées et validées par un vaste lectorat. Depuis la publication de la cinquième édition, en 1991, de nombreux utilisateurs ont fait part au Comité de propositions de changement, dont chacune a été considérée lors de la préparation de la présente édition. La stabilité des noms vernaculaires a été jugée prioritaire, et les modifications n'ont été apportées qu'avec une solide justification. Les connaissances scientifiques sur les poissons ont fait de rapides progrès dans les années 1990. De nombreuses espèces nouvelles ont été décrites, de nombreuses autres espèces ont été signalées à l'intérieur de nos frontières, et une foule de révisions ont été apportées sur le plan de la taxinomie ou de la systématique. L'ajout d'espèces nous a obligés à modifier ou à remplacer certains noms vernaculaires, tandis que les révisions se sont souvent traduites par des changements dans la nomenclature scientifique. Dans certaines familles (p. ex. Cyprinidae), les modifications se poursuivent, sont incomplètes et dans certains cas contradictoires. Le Comité a adopté une ligne prudente dans l'adoption de ces changements, avec l'espoir que les retours en arrière ou les flottements seront évités ou limités dans les éditions futures de la liste.

À l'exception des nombreux ajouts d'espèces du Mexique, toutes les nouvelles entrées et toutes celles qui différent (nom scientifique, auteur[s], date de description, eaux où l'espèce est présente ou nom vernaculaire anglais) de l'édition de 1991 sont précédées d'un astérisque (*). Des renseignements décrivant et expliquant le changement sont fournis pour chacune de ces entrées à l'annexe 1, identifiés par le numéro de la page où apparaît le nom dans la liste. L'information donnée autrefois à l'annexe 1 dans les listes de 1970, 1980 et 1991 (pages 65–87, 68–92 et 71–96 respectivement), qui décrivait les changements apportés entre les éditions 2 et 3, 3 et 4, puis 4 et 5, n'a pas été reprise dans la présente édition.

Le signe plus (+) placé avant une entrée indique que, même si cette entrée n'a pas été modifiée, on trouvera à l'annexe 1 un commentaire à son sujet. Il peut s'agir notamment d'un taxon situé au-dessus du niveau de l'espèce (p. ex. famille et ordre) dont le nom n'est pas modifié mais dont la composition diffère par rapport à l'édition de 1991 (p. ex. suppression de taxons ou transfert d'autres taxons d'un niveau supérieur); on trouvera à cet effet un commentaire à l'annexe 1 en regard de ce nom.

Si la plupart des décisions du Comité ont été unanimes, un bon nombre d'entre elles ont fait l'objet d'une opinion majoritaire. Ainsi, aucun membre du Comité ne souscrit nécessairement à toutes les décisions prises, mais nous respectons le droit de chaque personne à ne pas détenir toutes les bonnes réponses. Nous comprenons que toutes les décisions ne seront pas accueillies favorablement, mais nous espérons que tous les utilisateurs apprécieront nos efforts. Dans de nombreux cas, l'information dont disposait le Comité dépassait celle que l'on trouve dans les travaux publiés. Le Comité a souvent dû débattre longuement pour arriver à une décision justifiable au sujet de l'inclusion de ce genre d'information, et c'est avec prudence qu'il a adopté des changements de cet ordre.

La liste alphabétique des familles qui apparaît aux pages 1 à 6 sert aussi de table des matières. La liste (partie I) apparaît aux pages 47–186, et les annexes suivent à la partie II, aux pages 187–256. La partie III commence à la page 257 avec les références, les éditions de la liste des noms de poissons, et l'édition de la liste des poissons du monde; puis vient la liste des communications personnelles à la page 261, suivie par l'index, qui commence à la page 265. L'annexe 2 de l'édition de 1991 (poissons exotiques) n'a pas été ajoutée, car cette information existe ailleurs (p. ex. pour les États-Unis, voir http://nas.er.usgs.gov/fishes et Fuller et al. 1999, et pour l'Amérique du Nord, voir R. Claudi et J. Leach [directeurs de publication], 1999, Nonindigenous freshwater organisms, vectors, biology and impacts, Lewis Publishers, Boca Raton, Florida).

## Index

L'index intègre les noms scientifiques et les noms vernaculaires dans les trois langues. Le renvoi aux pages est indiqué pour les noms vernaculaires adoptés ici pour les classes, les ordres, les familles et les espèces. L'index comporte une seule entrée pour chaque espèce; par exemple, le grand corégone est inscrit seulement sous l'entrée « corégone, grand ». Il existe pour les poissons d'Amérique du Nord un grand nombre de noms vernaculaires, et il aurait fallu une recherche très approfondie pour en réunir ne serait-ce qu'une bonne fraction; certains ne sont d'ailleurs plus usités depuis des décennies et présentent seulement un intérêt historique. En général, le Comité a renoncé à poursuivre une telle recherche (quoiqu'un membre [Lloyd T. Findley] ait établi une liste des noms vernaculaires espagnols et anglais qui contient présentement plus de 16 000 entrées), mais bon nombre des noms couramment employés se retrouvent dans la liste.

Pour les noms scientifiques, on trouvera un renvoi aux pages correspondant aux classes, aux ordres, aux familles, aux genres et aux espèces. Chaque espèce est inscrite seulement par son nom spécifique. Par exemple, on trouvera *Sciaenops ocellatus* seulement à l'entrée « *ocellatus, Sciaenops* », bien qu'une entrée à « *Sciaenops* » renvoie le lecteur à la page où commencent les entrées correspondant aux espèces de ce genre. Les noms scientifiques des espèces qui n'ont pas été retenus pour cette liste ne sont pas cités, sauf ceux qui apparaissaient dans la cinquième édition (1991), et qui ont donc été placés en synonymie; on trouvera une explication à ce sujet à l'annexe 1.

## Remerciements

La présente liste est le fruit des contributions apportées pendant près de 60 ans par les nombreux membres passés et présents du Comité sur les noms de poissons (Committee on Names of Fishes). Nous voulons exprimer notre gratitude à tous les anciens membres; certains d'entre eux ont continué à contribuer aux travaux du Comité, et à cet égard nous remercions spécialement Reeve M. Bailey et C. Richard Robins, qui manifestent toujours un intérêt constant et précieux. De nombreux spécialistes ont également apporté une contribution du-

rable à la publication des deuxième, troisième, quatrième et cinquième éditions, dans lesquelles leur aide est signalée. Pour la préparation de la présente édition, nous avons reçu une aide, grande ou petite, de nombreuses personnes. Nous avons eu la chance de pouvoir tirer parti de la perspicacité du sous-comité consultatif, dont la plupart des membres se sont joints à nous au cours de diverses réunions annuelles de l'American Society of Ichthyologists and Herpetologists, et nous voulons remercier les présidents de ces rencontres qui ont fourni des locaux pour nos réunions. Nous sommes particulièrement reconnaissants aux membres principaux du groupe consultatif: William D. Anderson, Jr., Jacques F. Bergeron, George H. Burgess, Brooks M. Burr, Bruce B. Collette, Salvador Contreras-Balderas, William N. Eschmeyer, Robert E. Jenkins, Richard L. Mayden, John F. Morrissey, Lawrence M. Page, Richard H. Rosenblatt, Ramón Ruiz-Carus, William F. Smith-Vaniz, and Wayne C. Starnes.

Le monumental ouvrage en trois volumes que constitue le "Catalog of Fishes" de W. N. Eschmeyer (directeur de publication) (Eschmeyer 1998) a fait ressortir de nombreux changements et des problèmes importants dans la nomenclature, et nous avons constamment échangé des données avec M. Eschmeyer. Nous voulons lui exprimer une gratitude toute spéciale en notre nom et au nom des utilisateurs de la liste.

Outre ce groupe consultatif, les personnes qui nous ont aidés sont si nombreuses que nous ne pouvons toutes les citer. Certaines, toutefois, ont été si constantes dans leur intérêt et leur aide constructive, ou ont apporté une contribution si grande qu'elles méritent une mention spéciale: Larry G. Allen, M. James Allen, James W. Atz, David Aurioles-Gamboa, Henry L. Bart, Robert J. Behnke, Louis Bernatchez, Ernesto Bolado, Herbert T. Boschung, Brian W. Bowen, John Clay Bruner, Warren E. Burgess, Morgan Busby, William A. Bussing, Donald G. Buth, Kent E. Carpenter, Robert C. Cashmer, José Luis Castro-Aguirre, David Catania, Ted M. Cavender, François Chapleau, Brian W. Coad, Miles M. Coburn, Walter R. Courtenay, Jr., Angelica Daza-Zepeda, Jean Dubé, William N. Eschmeyer, David A. Etnier, Richard F. Feeney, Patricia Fuentes-Mata, Juan Pablo Gallo-Reynoso, Juan Manuel García-Caudillo, R. Grant Gilmore, Roberto González-Morales, David W. Greenfield, Thomas A. Greiner, Gary D. Grossman, Rocio Güereca, Ian J. Harrison, Karsten E. Hartel, Antony S. Harold, Philip A.

Hastings, Phillip C. Heemstra, Dean A. Hendrickson, Michael H. Horn, C. Leticia Huidobro, Paul Humann, Tomio Iwamoto, Witold L. Klawe, Cynthia (Cindy) Klepadlo, Sven O. Kullander, Louise Lapierre, Robert J. Lavenberg, Kenneth J. Lazara, Michel Letendre, Ken Lindeman, Myrna I. López, Milton Love, Gérard Massé, Ann C. Matarese, Richard E. Matheson, Jr., John E. McCosker, Catherine (Kitty) W. Mecklenburg, Maurice (Scott) F. Mettee, feu Robert Rush Miller, feu W. L. Minckley, Jr., Randall D. Mooi, J. Manuel Nava-Romo, Leo G. Nico, Volker Niem, Steven M. Norris, Pere Oliver, James W. Orr, Alex E. Peden, Mauricia Pérez-Tello, Frank L. Pezold, Edward J. Pfeiler, Edwin P. Pister, Héctor G. Plascencia, Stuart G. Poss, Catherine Poussart, John E. Randall, Spring Randolph, James D. Reist, Claude B. Renaud, Robert H. Robins, Gorgonio Ruiz-Campos, Mark H. Sabaj, Juan Jacobo Schmitter-Soto, Jeffrey A. Seigel, Bernard Séret, David G. Smith, Gerald R. Smith, Victor G. Springer, Donald J. Stewart, Royal D. Suttkus, Christine Thacker, Bruce A. Thompson, Jorge Torre-Cosio, James C. Tyler, Albert M. van der Heiden, Carlos J. Villavicencio-Garayzar, H. J. Walker, Melvin L. Warren, Jr., Douglas C. Weaver, Edward O. Wiley, Jeffrey T. Williams, and Chris Wilson.

Les frais de voyage des membres du Comité qui ont participé aux deux séances-marathons de Gainesville (Floride) ont été couverts par l'American Fisheries Society. Ces réunions ont eu lieu au laboratoire du U.S. Geological Survey (Florida Caribbean Science Center), où l'aide de Sherry Bostick et d'autres membres du personnel a été précieuse. Nous avons également reçu une assistance importante de la part d'ichtyologistes de la région, notamment William F. Smith-Vaniz et George Burgess, ainsi que de notre hôtesse Nancy Gilbert. Nous voulons aussi remercier nos institutions d'attache qui ont subventionné nos travaux dans ce projet, et apporté leur aide sous la forme de frais de déplacement, d'aide administrative, de reprographie et de services postaux, ainsi que de locaux pour les membres du Comité. À cet égard, Lloyd T. Findley désire remercier Inocencio Higuera et Alfonso Gardea du CIAD, et souligner le soutien constant du programme « Bioregión Golfo de California » de Conservation International, et particulièrement de María de los Angeles Carvajal et Alejandro Robles. Un merci tout particulier va au Conseil de recherches en sciences naturelles et en génie du Canada pour l'aide fournie par le biais de la subvention A5457 à Joseph S. Nelson. Mark K. Nelson a converti le format de l'ébauche du mode Portrait au mode Paysage. Le personnel, ancien et présent, du bureau international de l'American Fisheries Society a apporté une aide très diverse, particulièrement Betsy Fritz, Mary R. Frye, Janet Harry, Robert L. Kendall, Sally Kendall, Aaron Lerner, Beth D. McAleer, Robert Rand, Ghassan (Gus) Rassam, Catherine W. Richardson et Beth Staehle; nous tenons à remercier tout spécialement Deborah Lehman de son aide précieuse et agréable. Les présidents de l'American Fisheries Society et de l'American Society of Ichthyologists and Herpetologists ont soutenu le comité de leurs encouragements constants. Nous désirons aussi remercier, au nom de tous les membres anciens et actuels du Comité, l'American Fisheries Society qui, en nous décernant lors de sa réunion annuelle de l'an 2000 la récompense du Distinguished Service Award, a reconnu publiquement l'importance du travail du Comité. Enfin, et d'une façon toute particulière, nous remercions nos familles de leur appui.

Nous sommes reconnaissants aux nombreuses personnes qui ont apporté leur aide pour la traduction de l'Introduction en espagnol et en français. Pour l'espagnol, la traduction a été faite par D$^r$ Salvador Contreras-Balderas (Universidad Autónoma de Nuevo León, Monterrey, México) et D$^r$ Ramón Ruiz-Carus (Florida Fish and Wildlife Conservation Commission), et revue par Héctor Espinosa-Pérez et Lloyd T. Findley. La traduction française a été faite par Denise Campillo et Jacqueline Lanteigne, Bureau de la traduction, Travaux publics et Services gouvernementaux Canada, avec l'aide précieuse de Jacques F. Bergeron et de Claude B. Renaud, l'aimable appui de feu Edwin J. Crossman et de Joseph S. Nelson, et le soutien financier de Pêches et Océans Canada.

## Note de la liste principale de la Partie I :

[1] **A** = Atlantique (voir dans l'Introduction comment les eaux de l'Arctique sont partagées entre A et P); **AM** = eaux mexicaines de l'Atlantique, espèce non signalée dans les eaux des États-Unis et du Canada; **F:C** = eaux douces du Canada; **F:M** = eaux douces du Mexique; **F:U** = eaux douces des États-Unis (États contigus et/ou Alaska); **P** = Pacifique (voir dans l'Introduction comment les eaux de l'Arctique sont partagées entre A et P); **PM** = eaux

mexicaines du Pacifique, espèce non signalée dans les eaux des États-Unis et du Canada; **[I]** = espèce introduite et établie dans nos eaux; **[X]** = espèce disparue.

[2] De nombreux noms anglais ont été ajoutés pour les espèces mexicaines nouvellement inscrites sur la liste. Des noms espagnols ont été ajoutés pour les espèces marines et dulcicoles du Mexique, et des noms français pour les espèces marines et dulcicoles du Québec. Les abréviations « **En-** », « **Sp-** » et « **Fr-** » indiquent respectivement les noms de famille en anglais, en espagnol et en français.

\* Changement apporté par rapport à la liste de 1991 (à l'exception des ajouts d'espèces du Mexique); voir explications à l'annexe 1 (en anglais).

+ Commentaire à l'annexe 1 (en anglais).

# Part I

## Scientific Name, Occurrence, and Accepted Common Name

| SCIENTIFIC NAME | OCCURRENCE[1] | COMMON NAME (ENGLISH, SPANISH, FRENCH)[2] |
|---|---|---|

*SUBPHYLUM CEPHALOCHORDATA
ORDER AMPHIOXIFORMES

*Branchiostomatidae—En-lancelets, Sp-anfioxos, Fr-lancelets

| | | |
|---|---|---|
| *Branchiostoma bennetti* Boschung & Gunter, 1966 | A | mud lancelet |
| *Branchiostoma californiense* Andrews, 1893 | P | California lancelet .............. anfioxo californiano |
| *Branchiostoma floridae* Hubbs, 1922 | A | Florida lancelet |
| *Branchiostoma longirostrum* Boschung, 1983 | A | shellhash lancelet .............. anfioxo conchalero |
| *Branchiostoma virginiae* Hubbs, 1922 | A | Virginia lancelet |
| *Epigonichthys lucayanus* (Andrews, 1893) | A | sharptail lancelet |

*SUBPHYLUM CRANIATA (VERTEBRATA)
CLASS MYXINI—HAGFISHES
ORDER MYXINIFORMES

Myxinidae—En-hagfishes, Sp-brujas, Fr-myxines

| | | |
|---|---|---|
| *Eptatretus deani* (Evermann & Goldsborough, 1907) | P | black hagfish .............. bruja pecosa |

[1] A = Atlantic (see Introduction for Arctic Ocean waters included in A and in P); **AM** = Atlantic Mexico but not recorded in United States or Canada; **F:C** = Freshwater Canada; **F:M** = Freshwater Mexico; **F:U** = Freshwater United States (contiguous states and/or Alaska); **P** = Pacific (see Introduction for Arctic Ocean waters included in A and in P); **PM** = Pacific Mexico but not recorded in United States or Canada; **[I]** = introduced and established in our waters; **[X]** = extinct.

[2] Many new English names added for Mexican species entering the list. Spanish names added for freshwater and marine species in Mexico, and French names added for freshwater and marine species in Quebec. "**En-**," "**Sp-**," and "**Fr-**" indicate family names in English, Spanish, and French, respectively.

\* Change from 1991 list (except for new additions of species from Mexico); see Appendix 1 for explanation.

⁺ Comment in Appendix 1.

| SCIENTIFIC NAME | OCCURRENCE[1] | COMMON NAME (ENGLISH, SPANISH, FRENCH)[2] |
|---|---|---|
| *Eptatretus fritzi* Wisner & McMillan, 1990 | PM | Guadalupe hagfish ... bruja de Guadalupe |
| *Eptatretus mcconnaugheyi* Wisner & McMillan, 1990 | P | shorthead hagfish ... bruja cabeza chica |
| *Eptatretus sinus* Wisner & McMillan, 1990 | PM | Cortez hagfish ... bruja de Cortés |
| *Eptatretus stoutii* (Lockington, 1878) | P | Pacific hagfish ... bruja pintada |
| +*Myxine glutinosa* Linnaeus, 1758 | A | Atlantic hagfish ... myxine du nord |

## CLASS CEPHALASPIDOMORPHI—LAMPREYS
## ORDER PETROMYZONTIFORMES

+Petromyzontidae—En-lampreys, Sp-lampreas, Fr-lamproies

| SCIENTIFIC NAME | OCCURRENCE[1] | COMMON NAME (ENGLISH, SPANISH, FRENCH)[2] |
|---|---|---|
| *Ichthyomyzon bdellium* (Jordan, 1885) | F:U | Ohio lamprey |
| *Ichthyomyzon castaneus* Girard, 1858 | F:CU | chestnut lamprey ... lamproie brune |
| *Ichthyomyzon fossor* Reighard & Cummins, 1916 | F:CU | northern brook lamprey ... lamproie du nord |
| *Ichthyomyzon gagei* Hubbs & Trautman, 1937 | F:U | southern brook lamprey |
| *Ichthyomyzon greeleyi* Hubbs & Trautman, 1937 | F:U | mountain brook lamprey |
| *Ichthyomyzon unicuspis* Hubbs & Trautman, 1937 | F:CU | silver lamprey ... lamproie argentée |
| *Lampetra aepyptera* (Abbott, 1860) | F:U | least brook lamprey |
| +*Lampetra appendix* (DeKay, 1842) | F:CU | American brook lamprey ... lamproie de l'est |
| *Lampetra ayresii* (Günther, 1870) | F:CU-P | river lamprey |
| *Lampetra camtschatica* (Tilesius, 1811) | F:CU-P | Arctic lamprey |
| *Lampetra geminis* (Alvarez, 1964) | F:M | Jacona lamprey ... lamprea de Jacona |
| *Lampetra hubbsi* (Vladykov & Kott, 1976) | F:U | Kern brook lamprey |
| *Lampetra lethophaga* Hubbs, 1971 | F:U | Pit-Klamath brook lamprey |
| +*Lampetra macrostoma* Beamish, 1982 | F:C | Vancouver lamprey |
| *Lampetra minima* Bond & Kan, 1973 | F:U | Miller Lake lamprey |
| *Lampetra richardsoni* Vladykov & Follett, 1965 | F:CU | western brook lamprey |
| *Lampetra similis* (Vladykov & Kott, 1979) | F:U | Klamath lamprey |
| *Lampetra spadicea* Bean, 1887 | F:M | Chapala lamprey ... lamprea de Chapala |
| +*Lampetra tridentata* (Gairdner, 1836) | F:CUM-P | Pacific lamprey ... lamprea del Pacífico |
| *Petromyzon marinus* Linnaeus, 1758 | A-F:CU | sea lamprey ... lamproie marine |

| SCIENTIFIC NAME | OCCURRENCE[1] | COMMON NAME (ENGLISH, SPANISH, FRENCH)[2] |
|---|---|---|

**+CLASS CHONDRICHTHYES**
(SUBCLASS HOLOCEPHALI + ELASMOBRANCHII)—CARTILAGINOUS FISHES

**ORDER CHIMAERIFORMES**

*Chimaeridae—En-shortnose chimaeras, Sp-quimeras, Fr-chimères

*Hydrolagus colliei* (Lay & Bennett, 1839) .............. P ............. spotted ratfish ...............quimera manchada

**ORDER HEXANCHIFORMES**

Chlamydoselachidae—En-frill sharks, Sp-tiburones anguila, Fr-requins-lézards

*Chlamydoselachus anguineus* Garman, 1884 .............. P ............. frill shark ...............tiburón anguila

Hexanchidae—En-cow sharks, Sp-tiburones cañabota, Fr-grisets

*Heptranchias perlo* (Bonnaterre, 1788) .............. A ............. sharpnose sevengill shark .......tiburón de siete branquias
*Hexanchus griseus* (Bonnaterre, 1788) .............. A-P ............. bluntnose sixgill shark .......tiburón de seis branquias
*Hexanchus nakamurai* Teng, 1962 .............. A ............. bigeye sixgill shark .............cazón de seis branquias
*Notorynchus cepedianus* (Péron, 1807) .............. P ............. broadnose sevengill shark.......tiburón pinto

**+ORDER SQUALIFORMES**

*Echinorhinidae—En-bramble sharks, Sp-tiburones espinosos, Fr-squales bouclés

+*Echinorhinus brucus* (Bonnaterre, 1788) .............. A ............. bramble shark
*Echinorhinus cookei* Pietschmann, 1928 .............. P ............. prickly shark ...............tiburón espinoso negro

+Squalidae—En-dogfish sharks, Sp-cazones aguijones, Fr-chiens de mer

*Cirrhigaleus asper* (Merrett, 1973) .............. A ............. roughskin dogfish
*Squalus acanthias* Linnaeus, 1758 .............. A-P ............. spiny dogfish ...............cazón espinoso común ... aiguillat commun
*Squalus cubensis* Howell Rivero, 1936 .............. A ............. Cuban dogfish ...............cazón aguijón cubano
*Squalus mitsukurii* Jordan & Snyder, 1903 .............. AM ............. shortspine dogfish ...............cazón aguijón galludo

| SCIENTIFIC NAME | OCCURRENCE[1] | COMMON NAME (ENGLISH, SPANISH, FRENCH)[2] |
|---|---|---|
| *Etmopteridae—En-lantern sharks, Sp-tiburones luceros, Fr-requins-lanternes | | |
| Centroscyllium fabricii (Reinhardt, 1825) | A | black dogfish .................. aiguillat noir |
| *Etmopterus bigelowi Shirai & Tachikawa, 1993 | A | blurred lantern shark |
| *Etmopterus gracilispinis Krefft, 1968 | A | broadband lantern shark |
| Euprotomicrus bispinatus (Quoy & Gaimard, 1824) | PM | pygmy shark ..................tiburón pigmeo |
| *Somniosidae—En-sleeper sharks, Sp-tiburones dormilones, Fr-somniosidés | | |
| *Centroscymnus coelolepis Barboza du Bocage & de Brito Capello, 1864 | A | Portuguese shark |
| Somniosus microcephalus (Bloch & Schneider, 1801) | A | Greenland shark ................laimargue |
| Somniosus pacificus Bigelow & Schroeder, 1944 | P | Pacific sleeper shark ...........tiburón dormilón del Pacifico |
| *Dalatiidae—En-kitefin sharks, Sp-tiburones carochos, Fr-laimargues | | |
| Dalatias licha (Bonnaterre, 1788) | A | kitefin shark |
| +Isistius brasiliensis (Quoy & Gaimard, 1824) | PM | cookiecutter shark ...............tiburón cigarro |

### *ORDER SQUATINIFORMES

| | | |
|---|---|---|
| Squatinidae—En-angel sharks, Sp-angelotes, Fr-anges de mer | | |
| *Squatina californica Ayres, 1859 | P | Pacific angel shark..............angelote del Pacífico |
| Squatina dumeril Lesueur, 1818 | A | Atlantic angel shark ............angelote del Atlántico |

### ORDER HETERODONTIFORMES

| | | |
|---|---|---|
| Heterodontidae—En-bullhead sharks, Sp-tiburones cornudos, Fr-requins cornus | | |
| *Heterodontus francisci (Girard, 1855) | P | horn shark ..................tiburón puerco |
| Heterodontus mexicanus Taylor & Castro-Aguirre, 1972 | PM | Mexican horn shark ...........tiburón perro |

| SCIENTIFIC NAME | OCCURRENCE[1] | COMMON NAME (ENGLISH, SPANISH, FRENCH)[2] |
|---|---|---|

**\*ORDER ORECTOLOBIFORMES**

\*Ginglymostomatidae—En-nurse sharks, Sp-gatas, Fr-requins-nourrices

| Ginglymostoma cirratum (Bonnaterre, 1788) | A-PM | nurse shark .......... tiburón gata |
|---|---|---|

\*Rhincodontidae—En-whale sharks, Sp-tiburones ballena, Fr-requins-baleines

| Rhincodon typus Smith, 1828 | A-P | whale shark .......... tiburón ballena |
|---|---|---|

**+ORDER LAMNIFORMES**

\*Mitsukurinidae—En-goblin sharks, Sp-tiburones duende, Fr-requins-lutins

| \*Mitsukurina owstoni Jordan, 1898 | P | goblin shark |
|---|---|---|

\*Pseudocarchariidae—En-crocodile sharks, Sp-tiburones cocodrilo, Fr-requins-crocodiles

| Pseudocarcharias kamoharai (Matsubara, 1936) | AM | crocodile shark .......... tiburón cocodrilo |
|---|---|---|

Odontaspididae—En-sand tigers, Sp-tiburones toro, Fr-requins-taureaux

| \*Carcharias taurus Rafinesque, 1810 | A-PM | sand tiger .......... tiburón arenero tigre |
|---|---|---|
| Odontaspis ferox (Risso, 1810) | AM-P | ragged-tooth shark .......... tiburón dientes de perro |
| +Odontaspis noronhai (Maul, 1955) | A | bigeye sand tiger |

\*Megachasmidae—En-megamouth sharks, Sp-tiburones bocones, Fr-requins à grande gueule

| Megachasma pelagios Taylor, Compagno & Struhsaker, 1983 | P | megamouth shark .......... tiburón bocón |
|---|---|---|

Alopiidae—En-thresher sharks, Sp-tiburones zorro, Fr-requins-renards

| Alopias pelagicus Nakamura, 1935 | PM | pelagic thresher .......... zorro pelágico |
|---|---|---|
| Alopias superciliosus (Lowe, 1841) | A-P | bigeye thresher .......... tiburón zorro ojón |
| Alopias vulpinus (Bonnaterre, 1788) | A-P | thresher shark .......... tiburón zorro común |

| SCIENTIFIC NAME | OCCURRENCE[1] | COMMON NAME (ENGLISH, SPANISH, FRENCH)[2] |
|---|---|---|
| +Cetorhinidae—En-basking sharks, Sp-tiburones peregrino, Fr-pèlerins | | |
| +Cetorhinus maximus (Gunnerus, 1765) | A-P | basking shark .... tiburón peregrino .... pèlerin |
| Lamnidae—En-mackerel sharks, Sp-jaquetones, Fr-requins-taupes | | |
| Carcharodon carcharias (Linnaeus, 1758) | A-P | white shark .... tiburón blanco |
| Isurus oxyrinchus Rafinesque, 1810 | A-P | shortfin mako .... mako |
| *Isurus paucus Guitart Manday, 1966 | A-P | longfin mako .... mako aletón |
| Lamna ditropis Hubbs & Follett, 1947 | P | salmon shark .... tiburón salmón |
| Lamna nasus (Bonnaterre, 1788) | A | porbeagle .... maraîche |
| *ORDER CARCHARHINIFORMES | | |
| +Scyliorhinidae—En-cat sharks, Sp-pejegatos, Fr-roussettes | | |
| Apristurus brunneus (Gilbert, 1892) | P | brown cat shark .... pejegato marrón |
| Cephaloscyllium ventriosum (Garman, 1880) | P | swell shark .... pejegato globo |
| Cephalurus cephalus (Gilbert, 1892) | PM | lollipop cat shark .... pejegato renacuajo |
| *Galeus arae (Nichols, 1927) | A | marbled cat shark |
| Parmaturus xaniurus (Gilbert, 1892) | P | filetail cat shark .... pejegato lima |
| Scyliorhinus retifer (Garman, 1881) | A | chain dogfish .... alitán mallero |
| *Pseudotriakidae—En-false cat sharks, Sp-musolones, Fr-requins à longue dorsale | | |
| *Pseudotriakis microdon de Brito Capello, 1868 | A | false cat shark |
| *Triakidae—En-hound sharks, Sp-cazones, Fr-émissoles | | |
| *Galeorhinus galeus (Linnaeus, 1758) | P | tope .... tiburón aceitoso |
| Mustelus californicus Gill, 1864 | P | gray smoothhound .... cazón mamón |
| Mustelus canis (Mitchill, 1815) | A | smooth dogfish .... cazón dientón |
| Mustelus dorsalis Gill, 1864 | PM | sharptooth smoothhound .... cazón tripa |

| SCIENTIFIC NAME | OCCURRENCE[1] | COMMON NAME (ENGLISH, SPANISH, FRENCH)[2] |
|---|---|---|
| *Mustelus henlei (Gill, 1863) | P | brown smoothhound............cazón hilacho |
| Mustelus lunulatus Jordan & Gilbert, 1882 | P | sicklefin smoothhound............cazón segador |
| *Mustelus norrisi Springer, 1939 | A | Florida smoothhound............cazón viuda |
| *Mustelus sinusmexicanus Heemstra, 1997 | A | Gulf smoothhound............cazón del Golfo |
| *Triakis semifasciata Girard, 1855 | P | leopard shark............tiburón leopardo |
| +Carcharhinidae—En-requiem sharks, Sp-tiburones gambuso, Fr-mangeurs d'hommes | | |
| Carcharhinus acronotus (Poey, 1860) | A | blacknose shark............tiburón cangüay |
| Carcharhinus albimarginatus (Rüppell, 1837) | PM | silvertip shark............tiburón puntas blancas |
| Carcharhinus altimus (Springer, 1950) | A-PM | bignose shark............tiburón narizón |
| Carcharhinus brachyurus (Günther, 1870) | P | narrowtooth shark............tiburón cobrizo |
| * Carcharhinus brevipinna (Müller & Henle, 1839) | A | spinner shark............tiburón curro |
| * Carcharhinus falciformis (Müller & Henle, 1839) | A-PM | silky shark............tiburón piloto |
| * Carcharhinus galapagensis (Snodgrass & Heller, 1905) | A-PM | Galapagos shark............tiburón de Galápagos |
| * Carcharhinus isodon (Müller & Henle, 1839) | A | finetooth shark............tiburón dentiliso |
| * Carcharhinus leucas (Müller & Henle, 1839) | A-F:UM-P | bull shark............tiburón toro |
| * Carcharhinus limbatus (Müller & Henle, 1839) | A-PM | blacktip shark............tiburón volador |
| * Carcharhinus longimanus (Poey, 1861) | A-P | oceanic whitetip shark............tiburón oceánico |
| * Carcharhinus obscurus (Lesueur, 1818) | A-P | dusky shark............tiburón gambuso |
| * Carcharhinus perezii (Poey, 1876) | A | reef shark............tiburón coralino |
| * Carcharhinus plumbeus (Nardo, 1827) | A-PM | sandbar shark............tiburón aleta de cartón |
| * Carcharhinus porosus (Ranzani, 1840) | A-PM | smalltail shark............tiburón poroso |
| * Carcharhinus signatus (Poey, 1868) | A | night shark............tiburón nocturno |
| * Galeocerdo cuvier (Péron & Lesueur, 1822) | A-P | tiger shark............tintorera |
| Nasolamia velox (Gilbert, 1898) | PM | whitenose shark............tiburón coyotito |
| Negaprion brevirostris (Poey, 1868) | A-PM | lemon shark............tiburón limón |
| Prionace glauca (Linnaeus, 1758) | A-P | blue shark............tiburón azul............requin bleu |
| Rhizoprionodon longurio (Jordan & Gilbert, 1882) | P | Pacific sharpnose shark............cazón bironche |
| Rhizoprionodon porosus (Poey, 1861) | AM | Caribbean sharpnose shark............cazón antillano |
| Rhizoprionodon terraenovae (Richardson, 1836) | A | Atlantic sharpnose shark............cazón de ley |
| Triaenodon obesus (Rüppell, 1837) | PM | whitetip reef shark............cazón coralero trompacorta |

| SCIENTIFIC NAME | OCCURRENCE[1] | COMMON NAME (ENGLISH, SPANISH, FRENCH)[2] |
|---|---|---|
| Sphyrnidae—En-hammerhead sharks, Sp-tiburones martillo, Fr-requins-marteaux | | |
| Sphyrna corona Springer, 1940 | PM | scalloped bonnethead ............cornuda coronada |
| Sphyrna lewini (Griffith & Smith, 1834) | A-P | scalloped hammerhead ............cornuda común |
| Sphyrna media Springer, 1940 | PM | scoophead ............cornuda cuchara |
| Sphyrna mokarran (Rüppell, 1837) | A-PM | great hammerhead ............cornuda gigante |
| +Sphyrna tiburo (Linnaeus, 1758) | A-P | bonnethead ............cornuda cabeza de pala |
| Sphyrna zygaena (Linnaeus, 1758) | A-P | smooth hammerhead ............cornuda prieta |

## *ORDER TORPEDINIFORMES

| SCIENTIFIC NAME | OCCURRENCE | COMMON NAME |
|---|---|---|
| *Narcinidae—En-electric rays, Sp-rayas eléctricas, Fr-narcinidés | | |
| Diplobatis ommata (Jordan & Gilbert, 1890) | PM | bullseye electric ray ............raya eléctrica diana |
| *Narcine bancroftii (Griffith & Smith 1834) | A | lesser electric ray ............raya eléctrica torpedo |
| Narcine entemedor Jordan & Starks, 1895 | PM | giant electric ray ............raya eléctrica gigante |
| Narcine vermiculatus Breder, 1928 | PM | vermiculate electric ray ............raya eléctrica rayada |
| *Torpedinidae—En-torpedo electric rays, Sp-torpedos, Fr-torpilles | | |
| Torpedo californica Ayres, 1855 | P | Pacific electric ray ............torpedo del Pacífico |
| Torpedo nobiliana Bonaparte, 1835 | A | Atlantic torpedo ............torpedo del Atlántico |

## *ORDER PRISTIFORMES

| SCIENTIFIC NAME | OCCURRENCE | COMMON NAME |
|---|---|---|
| Pristidae—En-sawfishes, Sp-peces sierra, Fr-poissons-scies | | |
| *Pristis pectinata Latham, 1794 | A-F:UM-PM | smalltooth sawfish ............pez sierra peine |
| *Pristis pristis (Linnaeus, 1758) | A-F:M-PM | largetooth sawfish ............pez sierra común |

## +ORDER RAJIFORMES

| SCIENTIFIC NAME | OCCURRENCE | COMMON NAME |
|---|---|---|
| +Rhinobatidae—En-guitarfishes, Sp-guitarras, Fr-guitares de mer | | |
| Rhinobatos glaucostigma Jordan & Gilbert, 1883 | PM | speckled guitarfish ............guitarra punteada |

| SCIENTIFIC NAME | OCCURRENCE[1] | COMMON NAME (ENGLISH, SPANISH, FRENCH)[2] |
|---|---|---|
| *Rhinobatos lentiginosus Garman, 1880 | A | Atlantic guitarfish......guitarra diablito |
| Rhinobatos leucorhynchus Günther, 1867 | PM | whitesnout guitarfish......guitarra trompa blanca |
| *Rhinobatos productus Ayres, 1854 | P | shove nose guitarfish......guitarra viola |
| Rhinobatos spinosus Günther, 1870 | PM | spiny guitarfish......guitarra espinosa |
| Zapteryx exasperata (Jordan & Gilbert, 1880) | P | banded guitarfish......guitarra rayada |

*Platyrhynidae—En-thornbacks, Sp-guitarras espinudas, Fr-guitares de mer épineuses

| | | |
|---|---|---|
| Platyrhinoidis triseriata (Jordan & Gilbert, 1880) | P | thornback......guitarra espinuda |

+Rajidae—En-skates, Sp-rayas, Fr-raies

| | | |
|---|---|---|
| *Amblyraja radiata (Donovan, 1808) | A | thorny skate......raie épineuse |
| Bathyraja aleutica (Gilbert, 1896) | P | Aleutian skate |
| Bathyraja interrupta (Gill & Townsend, 1897) | P | sandpaper skate |
| *Bathyraja lindbergi Ishiyama & Ishihara, 1977 | P | Commander skate |
| *Bathyraja maculata Ishiyama & Ishihara, 1977 | P | whiteblotched skate |
| +Bathyraja parmifera (Bean, 1881) | P | Alaska skate |
| *Bathyraja spinicauda (Jensen, 1914) | A | spinytail skate |
| *Bathyraja taranetzi (Dolganov, 1983) | P | mud skate |
| *Bathyraja violacea (Suvorov, 1935) | P | Okhotsk skate |
| *Dipturus bullisi (Bigelow & Schroeder, 1962) | A | lozenge skate......raya triangular |
| *Dipturus laevis (Mitchill, 1818) | A | barndoor skate......grande raie |
| *Dipturus olseni (Bigelow & Schroeder, 1951) | A | spreadfin skate......raya colona |
| Fenestraja sinusmexicanus (Bigelow & Schroeder, 1950) | AM | Gulf skate......raya pigmea |
| +Leucoraja caribbaea (McEachran, 1977) | AM | Maya skate......raya maya |
| *Leucoraja erinacea (Mitchill, 1825) | A | little skate......raie-hérisson |
| *Leucoraja garmani (Whitley, 1939) | A | rosette skate |
| *Leucoraja lentiginosa (Bigelow & Schroeder, 1951) | A | freckled skate......raya pecosa |
| *Leucoraja ocellata (Mitchill, 1815) | A | winter skate......raie tachetée |
| *Leucoraja virginica (McEachran, 1977) | A | Virginia skate |
| *Malacoraja senta (Garman, 1885) | A | smooth skate......raie à queue de velours |
| Raja ackleyi Garman, 1881 | A | ocellate skate......raya ocelada |

| SCIENTIFIC NAME | OCCURRENCE[1] | COMMON NAME (ENGLISH, SPANISH, FRENCH)[2] |
|---|---|---|
| *Raja binoculata Girard, 1855 | P | big skate .......................... raya bruja gigante |
| Raja cortezensis McEachran & Miyake, 1988 | PM | Cortez skate ........................ raya de Cortés |
| *Raja eglanteria Bosc, 1800 | A | clearnose skate .................. raya naricita |
| Raja equatorialis Jordan & Bollman, 1890 | PM | equatorial skate ................ raya ecuatorial |
| Raja inornata Jordan & Gilbert, 1881 | P | California skate ................. raya de California |
| *Raja rhina Jordan & Gilbert, 1880 | P | longnose skate ................. raya narigona |
| *Raja stellulata Jordan & Gilbert, 1880 | P | starry skate ...................... raya estrellada |
| Raja texana Chandler, 1921 | A | roundel skate .................... raya tigre |
| Raja velezi Chirichigno, 1973 | PM | rasptail skate .................... raya chillona |

*ORDER MYLIOBATIFORMES

*Dasyatidae—En-whiptail stingrays, Sp-rayas látigo, Fr-pastenagues

| | | |
|---|---|---|
| Dasyatis americana Hildebrand & Schroeder, 1928 | A | southern stingray ............ raya látigo blanca |
| Dasyatis centroura (Mitchill, 1815) | A | roughtail stingray |
| +Dasyatis dipterura (Jordan & Gilbert, 1880) | P | diamond stingray ............ raya látigo diamante |
| Dasyatis guttata (Bloch & Schneider, 1801) | AM | longnose stingray ............ raya látigo del Golfo |
| Dasyatis longa (Garman, 1880) | PM | longtail stingray .............. raya látigo largo |
| Dasyatis sabina (Lesueur, 1824) | A-F:UM | Atlantic stingray ............. raya látigo de espina |
| Dasyatis say (Lesueur, 1817) | A | bluntnose stingray .......... raya látigo chata |
| Himantura pacifica (Beebe & Tee-Van, 1941) | PM | Pacific whiptail stingray ...... raya coluda del Pacífico |
| Himantura schmardae (Werner, 1904) | AM | Caribbean whiptail stingray ...... raya coluda caribeña |
| *Pteroplatytrygon violacea (Bonaparte, 1832) | A-P | pelagic stingray .............. raya látigo obispo |

Urolophidae—En-round stingrays, Sp-rayas redondas, Fr-pastenagues à queue charnue

| | | |
|---|---|---|
| Urobatis concentricus Osburn & Nichols, 1916 | PM | reef stingray ................... raya redonda de arrecife |
| *Urobatis halleri (Cooper, 1863) | P | round stingray ................ raya redonda común |
| *Urobatis jamaicensis (Cuvier, 1816) | A | yellow stingray .............. raya redonda de estero |
| Urobatis maculatus Garman, 1913 | PM | Cortez stingray .............. raya redonda de Cortés |
| Urotrygon aspidura (Jordan & Gilbert, 1882) | PM | Panamic stingray ........... raya redonda panámica |

| SCIENTIFIC NAME | OCCURRENCE[1] | COMMON NAME (ENGLISH, SPANISH, FRENCH)[2] |
|---|---|---|
| *Urotrygon chilensis* (Günther, 1872) | PM | blotched stingray ..........raya redonda moteada |
| *Urotrygon munda* Gill, 1863 | PM | spiny stingray ..........raya redonda áspera |
| *Urotrygon nana* Miyake & McEachran, 1988 | PM | dwarf stingray ..........raya redonda enana |
| *Urotrygon rogersi* (Jordan & Starks, 1895) | PM | thorny stingray ..........raya redonda de púas |

*Gymnuridae—En-butterfly rays, Sp-rayas mariposa, Fr-raies-papillons

| SCIENTIFIC NAME | OCCURRENCE[1] | COMMON NAME (ENGLISH, SPANISH, FRENCH)[2] |
|---|---|---|
| *Gymnura altavela* (Linnaeus, 1758) | A | spiny butterfly ray ..........raya de papel |
| +*Gymnura crebripunctata* (Peters, 1869) | PM | longsnout butterfly ray ..........raya mariposa picuda |
| *Gymnura marmorata* (Cooper, 1864) | P | California butterfly ray ..........raya mariposa californiana |
| *Gymnura micrura* (Bloch & Schneider, 1801) | A | smooth butterfly ray ..........raya cola de rata |

+Myliobatidae—En-eagle rays, Sp-águilas marinas, Fr-aigles de mer

| SCIENTIFIC NAME | OCCURRENCE[1] | COMMON NAME (ENGLISH, SPANISH, FRENCH)[2] |
|---|---|---|
| *Aetobatus narinari* (Euphrasen, 1790) | A-PM | spotted eagle ray ..........chucho pintado |
| *Myliobatis californica* Gill, 1865 | P | bat ray ..........tecolote |
| +*Myliobatis freminvillei* Lesueur, 1824 | A | bullnose ray ..........águila nariz de vaca |
| *Myliobatis goodei* Garman, 1885 | A | southern eagle ray |
| *Myliobatis longirostris* Applegate & Fitch, 1964 | PM | longnose eagle ray ..........águila picuda |
| *Pteromylaeus asperrimus* (Gilbert, 1898) | PM | rough eagle ray ..........águila cueruda |

*Rhinopteridae—En-cownose rays, Sp-rayas gavilán, Fr-mourines

| SCIENTIFIC NAME | OCCURRENCE[1] | COMMON NAME (ENGLISH, SPANISH, FRENCH)[2] |
|---|---|---|
| *Rhinoptera bonasus* (Mitchill, 1815) | A | cownose ray ..........gavilán cubanito |
| *Rhinoptera steindachneri* Evermann & Jenkins, 1892 | PM | golden cownose ray ..........gavilán dorado |

Mobulidae—En-mantas, Sp-mantas, Fr-mantes

| SCIENTIFIC NAME | OCCURRENCE[1] | COMMON NAME (ENGLISH, SPANISH, FRENCH)[2] |
|---|---|---|
| *Manta birostris* (Walbaum, 1792) | A-P | giant manta ..........manta gigante |
| *Mobula hypostoma* (Bancroft, 1831) | A | devil ray ..........manta del Golfo |
| *Mobula japanica* (Müller & Henle, 1841) | P | spinetail mobula ..........manta arpón |
| *Mobula munkiana* Notarbartolo di Sciara, 1987 | PM | pygmy devil ray ..........manta chica |
| *Mobula tarapacana* (Philippi, 1893) | A-PM | sicklefin devil ray ..........manta cornuda |
| *Mobula thurstoni* (Lloyd, 1908) | PM | smoothtail mobula ..........manta doblada |

| SCIENTIFIC NAME | OCCURRENCE[1] | COMMON NAME (ENGLISH, SPANISH, FRENCH)[2] |
|---|---|---|

**CLASS ACTINOPTERYGII—THE RAY-FINNED FISHES**

**ORDER ACIPENSERIFORMES**

Acipenseridae—En-sturgeons, Sp-esturiones, Fr-esturgeons

| SCIENTIFIC NAME | OCCURRENCE[1] | COMMON NAME |
|---|---|---|
| Acipenser brevirostrum Lesueur, 1818 | A-F:CU | shortnose sturgeon |
| Acipenser fulvescens Rafinesque, 1817 | F:CU | lake sturgeon ........ esturgeon jaune |
| Acipenser medirostris Ayres, 1854 | F:CU-P | green sturgeon ........ esturión verde |
| *Acipenser oxyrinchus Mitchill, 1815 | A-F:CUM | Atlantic sturgeon ........ esturión del Atlántico ........ esturgeon noir |
| Acipenser transmontanus Richardson, 1836 | F:CU-P | white sturgeon ........ esturión blanco |
| Scaphirhynchus albus (Forbes & Richardson, 1905) | F:U | pallid sturgeon |
| +Scaphirhynchus platorynchus (Rafinesque, 1820) | F:U | shovelnose sturgeon |
| *Scaphirhynchus suttkusi Williams & Clemmer, 1991 | F:U | Alabama sturgeon |

Polyodontidae—En-paddlefishes, Sp-espátulas, Fr-spatules

| SCIENTIFIC NAME | OCCURRENCE[1] | COMMON NAME |
|---|---|---|
| +Polyodon spathula (Walbaum, 1792) | F:CU | paddlefish |

**+ORDER LEPISOSTEIFORMES**

Lepisosteidae—En-gars, Sp-pejelagartos, Fr-lépisostés

| SCIENTIFIC NAME | OCCURRENCE[1] | COMMON NAME |
|---|---|---|
| *Atractosteus spatula (Lacepède, 1803) | F:UM | alligator gar ........ catán |
| Atractosteus tropicus Gill, 1863 | F:M | tropical gar ........ pejelagarto |
| *Lepisosteus oculatus Winchell, 1864 | F:CUM | spotted gar ........ catán pinto ........ lépisosté tacheté |
| +Lepisosteus osseus (Linnaeus, 1758) | F:CUM | longnose gar ........ catán aguja ........ lépisosté osseux |
| Lepisosteus platostomus Rafinesque, 1820 | F:U | shortnose gar |
| Lepisosteus platyrhincus DeKay, 1842 | F:U | Florida gar |

**ORDER AMIIFORMES**

Amiidae—En-bowfins, Sp-amias, Fr-poissons-castors

| SCIENTIFIC NAME | OCCURRENCE[1] | COMMON NAME |
|---|---|---|
| Amia calva Linnaeus, 1766 | F:CU | bowfin ........ poisson-castor |

| SCIENTIFIC NAME | OCCURRENCE[1] | COMMON NAME (ENGLISH, SPANISH, FRENCH)[2] |
|---|---|---|
| | | *ORDER HIODONTIFORMES |
| | | Hiodontidae—En-mooneyes, Sp-ojos de luna, Fr-laquaiches |
| Hiodon alosoides (Rafinesque, 1819) | F:CU | goldeye ................laquaiche aux yeux d'or |
| Hiodon tergisus Lesueur, 1818 | F:CU | mooneye ................laquaiche argentée |
| | | +ORDER OSTEOGLOSSIFORMES |
| | | *Notopteridae—En-featherfin knifefishes, Sp-cuchillos de pluma, Fr-poissons-couteaux à nageoire plumeuse |
| *Chitala ornata (Gray, 1831) | F[I]:U | clown knifefish |
| | | ORDER ELOPIFORMES |
| | | +Elopidae—En-tenpounders, Sp-machetes, Fr-guinées |
| +Elops affinis Regan, 1909 | F:UM-P | machete ................machete del Pacífico |
| +Elops saurus Linnaeus, 1766 | A-F:UM | ladyfish ................machete del Atlántico |
| | | *Megalopidae—En-tarpons, Sp-sábalos, Fr-tarpons |
| Megalops atlanticus Valenciennes, 1847 | A-F:CUM | tarpon ................sábalo |
| | | ORDER ALBULIFORMES |
| | | Albulidae—En-bonefishes, Sp-macabíes, Fr-bananes de mer |
| +Albula nemoptera (Fowler, 1911) | PM | shafted bonefish ................macabí de hebra |
| *Albula species | P | Cortez bonefish ................macabí de Cortés |
| *Albula vulpes (Linnaeus, 1758) | A | bonefish ................macabí |
| | | Notacanthidae—En-spiny eels, Sp-anguilas espinosas, Fr-poissons-tapirs à épines |
| *Notacanthus chemnitzii Bloch, 1788 | A | snubnosed spiny eel |

| SCIENTIFIC NAME | OCCURRENCE[1] | COMMON NAME (ENGLISH, SPANISH, FRENCH)[2] |
|---|---|---|

## ORDER ANGUILLIFORMES

Anguillidae—En-freshwater eels, Sp-anguilas de río, Fr-anguilles d'eau douce

| | | |
|---|---|---|
| Anguilla rostrata (Lesueur, 1817) | A-F:CUM | American eel ....... anguila americana ..... anguille d'Amérique |

*Heterenchelyidae—En-mud eels, Sp-anguilas de fango, Fr-anguilles de vase

| | | |
|---|---|---|
| Pythonichthys asodes Rosenblatt & Rubinoff, 1972 | PM | Pacific mud eel ....... anguila de fango del Pacífico |

Moringuidae—En-spaghetti eels, Sp-anguilas fideo, Fr-anguilles-spaghettis

| | | |
|---|---|---|
| Moringua edwardsi (Jordan & Bollman, 1889) | A | spaghetti eel ....... morenita |
| Neoconger mucronatus Girard, 1858 | A | ridged eel ....... anguila fideo aquillada |

Chlopsidae—En-false morays, Sp-morenas falsas, Fr-fausses murènes

| | | |
|---|---|---|
| *Chilorhinus suensonii Lütken, 1852 | A | seagrass eel ....... morena falsa bembona |
| Chlopsis apterus (Beebe & Tee-Van, 1938) | PM | stripesnout false moray ....... morena falsa hocico rayado |
| Chlopsis bicolor Rafinesque, 1810 | A | bicolor eel ....... morena falsa dientona |
| Chlopsis dentatus (Seale, 1917) | AM | mottled false moray ....... morena falsa dientona |
| *Kaupichthys hyoproroides (Strömman, 1896) | A | false moray ....... morena falsa de arrecife |
| Kaupichthys nuchalis Böhlke, 1967 | A | collared eel ....... morena falsa de collar |

Muraenidae—En-morays, Sp-morenas, Fr-murènes

| | | |
|---|---|---|
| Anarchias galapagensis (Seale, 1940) | PM | hardtail moray ....... morena cola dura |
| Anarchias similis (Lea, 1913) | A | pygmy moray ....... morena enana |
| Channomuraena vittata (Richardson, 1845) | AM | broadbanded moray ....... morena cinturones |
| Echidna catenata (Bloch, 1795) | A | chain moray ....... morena cadena |
| Echidna nebulosa (Ahl, 1789) | PM | starry moray ....... morena estrellada |
| Echidna nocturna (Cope, 1872) | PM | palenose moray ....... morena pecosa |
| Enchelycore carychroa Böhlke & Böhlke, 1976 | A | chestnut moray ....... morena castaña |
| Enchelycore nigricans (Bonnaterre, 1788) | A | viper moray ....... morena víbora |
| Enchelycore octaviana (Myers & Wade, 1941) | PM | slenderjaw moray ....... morena octaviana |
| Gymnomuraena zebra (Shaw, 1797) | PM | zebra moray ....... morena cebra |
| Gymnothorax castaneus (Jordan & Gilbert, 1883) | PM | Panamic green moray ....... morena verde panámica |

| SCIENTIFIC NAME | OCCURRENCE[1] | COMMON NAME (ENGLISH, SPANISH, FRENCH)[2] | |
|---|---|---|---|
| Gymnothorax conspersus Poey, 1867 | A | saddled moray | morena pintita |
| Gymnothorax dovii (Günther, 1870) | PM | finespotted moray | morena pintita |
| Gymnothorax equatorialis (Hildebrand, 1946) | PM | spottail moray | morena cola pintada |
| Gymnothorax funebris Ranzani, 1839 | A | green moray | morena verde |
| Gymnothorax hubbsi Böhlke & Böhlke, 1977 | A | lichen moray | |
| Gymnothorax kolpos Böhlke & Böhlke, 1980 | A | blacktail moray | morena cola negra |
| *Gymnothorax maderensis (Johnson, 1862) | A | sharktooth moray | |
| Gymnothorax miliaris (Kaup, 1856) | A | goldentail moray | morena cola dorada |
| Gymnothorax mordax (Ayres, 1859) | P | California moray | morena de California |
| Gymnothorax moringa (Cuvier, 1829) | A | spotted moray | morena manchada |
| *Gymnothorax nigromarginatus (Girard, 1858) | A | blackedge moray | morena de margen negro |
| Gymnothorax ocellatus Agassiz, 1831 | AM | ocellated moray | morena ocelada |
| Gymnothorax panamensis (Steindachner, 1876) | PM | masked moray | morena mapache |
| Gymnothorax polygonius Poey, 1875 | A | polygon moray | morena poligona |
| Gymnothorax saxicola Jordan & Davis, 1891 | A | honeycomb moray | morena panal |
| Gymnothorax verrilli (Jordan & Gilbert, 1883) | PM | white-edged moray | morena de borde blanco |
| Gymnothorax vicinus (Castelnau, 1855) | A | purplemouth moray | morena amarilla |
| Monopenchelys acuta (Parr, 1930) | AM | redface moray | morena rubicunda |
| Muraena argus (Steindachner, 1870) | PM | Argus moray | morena Argos |
| Muraena clepsydra Gilbert, 1898 | PM | hourglass moray | morena clepsidra |
| Muraena lentiginosa Jenyns, 1842 | PM | jewel moray | morena pinta |
| Muraena retifera Goode & Bean, 1882 | A | reticulate moray | morena reticulada |
| *Muraena robusta Osório, 1911 | A | stout moray | |
| Scuticaria tigrina (Lesson, 1828) | PM | tiger reef eel | morena atigrada |
| Uropterygius macrocephalus (Bleeker, 1865) | PM | largehead moray | morena cabezona |
| Uropterygius macularius (Lesueur, 1825) | A | marbled moray | morena jaspeada |
| Uropterygius polystictus Myers & Wade, 1941 | PM | peppered moray | morena pintada |
| Uropterygius versutus Bussing, 1991 | PM | crafty moray | morena lista |

Synaphobranchidae—En-cutthroat eels, Sp-anguilas branquias bajas, Fr-anguilles égorgées

| | | | |
|---|---|---|---|
| Dysomma anguillare Barnard, 1923 | A | shortbelly eel | anguila panzacorta |
| *Synaphobranchus kaupii Johnson, 1862 | A | northern cutthroat eel | |

| SCIENTIFIC NAME | OCCURRENCE[1] | COMMON NAME (ENGLISH, SPANISH, FRENCH)[2] | |
|---|---|---|---|

+Ophichthidae—En-snake eels, Sp-tiesos, Fr-serpents de mer

| SCIENTIFIC NAME | OCCURRENCE[1] | English | Spanish |
|---|---|---|---|
| *Ahlia egmontis* (Jordan, 1884) | A | key worm eel | tieso de cayo |
| +*Aplatophis chauliodus* Böhlke, 1956 | A | tusky eel | |
| *Aprognathodon platyventris* Böhlke, 1967 | A | stripe eel | |
| *Apterichtus ansp* (Böhlke, 1968) | A | academy eel | |
| *Apterichtus equatorialis* (Myers & Wade, 1941) | PM | equatorial eel | tieso ecuatorial |
| *Apterichtus kendalli* (Gilbert, 1891) | A | finless eel | |
| *Bascanichthys bascanium* (Jordan, 1884) | A | sooty eel | tieso tiznado |
| *Bascanichthys bascanoides* Osburn & Nichols, 1916 | PM | sooty sand eel | tieso manchitas |
| *Bascanichthys panamensis* Meek & Hildebrand, 1923 | PM | Panamic sand eel | tieso panámico |
| *Bascanichthys scuticaris* (Goode & Bean, 1880) | A | whip eel | |
| *Callechelys bilinearis* Kanazawa, 1952 | AM | twostripe snake eel | tieso dos rayas |
| *Callechelys cliffi* Böhlke & Briggs, 1954 | PM | sandy ridgefin eel | tieso aquillado arenero |
| *Callechelys eristigma* McCosker & Rosenblatt, 1972 | PM | spotted ridgefin eel | tieso aquillado manchado |
| * *Callechelys guineensis* (Osório, 1893) | A | shorttail snake eel | tieso colicorta |
| * *Callechelys muraena* Jordan & Evermann, 1887 | A | blotched snake eel | tieso moteado |
| *Callechelys springeri* (Ginsburg, 1951) | A | ridgefin eel | |
| *Caralophia loxochila* Böhlke, 1955 | A | slantlip eel | |
| *Echiophis brunneus* | | | |
| (Castro-Aguirre & Suárez de los Cobos, 1983) | PM | fangjaw eel | tieso colmillón |
| *Echiophis intertinctus* (Richardson, 1848) | A | spotted spoon-nose eel | tieso cucharón manchado |
| *Echiophis punctifer* (Kaup, 1860) | A | snapper eel | tieso pecoso |
| *Ethadophis akkistikos* McCosker & Böhlke, 1984 | A | indifferent eel | |
| *Ethadophis byrnei* Rosenblatt & McCosker, 1970 | PM | ordinary eel | tieso de Cortés |
| *Ethadophis merenda* Rosenblatt & McCosker, 1970 | PM | snack eel | tieso merienda |
| * *Gordiichthys ergodes* McCosker, Böhlke & Böhlke, 1989 | A | irksome eel | tieso fastidioso |
| *Gordiichthys irretitus* Jordan & Davis, 1891 | A | horsehair eel | tieso pelo de burro |
| *Gordiichthys leibyi* McCosker & Böhlke, 1984 | A | string eel | tieso bobo |
| *Herpetoichthys fossatus* (Myers & Wade, 1941) | PM | mustachioed snake eel | tieso bigotón |
| *Ichthyapus ophioneus* (Evermann & Marsh, 1900) | A | surf eel | tieso alacrán |
| *Ichthyapus selachops* (Jordan & Gilbert, 1882) | PM | smiling sand eel | tieso sonriente |

| SCIENTIFIC NAME | OCCURRENCE[1] | COMMON NAME (ENGLISH, SPANISH, FRENCH)[2] | |
|---|---|---|---|
| *Letharchus rosenblatti* McCosker, 1974 | PM | black sailfin eel | tieso vela negro |
| *Letharchus velifer* Goode & Bean, 1882 | A | sailfin eel | |
| *Lethogoleos andersoni* McCosker & Böhlke, 1982 | A | forgetful snake eel | |
| *Leuropharus lasiops* Rosenblatt & McCosker, 1970 | PM | acned snake eel | tieso pustuloso |
| *Myrichthys aspetocheiros* McCosker & Rosenblatt, 1993 | PM | longfin spotted snake eel | tieso aletón |
| *Myrichthys breviceps* (Richardson, 1848) | A | sharptail eel | tieso afilado |
| *Myrichthys ocellatus* (Lesueur, 1825) | A | goldspotted eel | tieso manchas doradas |
| *Myrichthys pantostigmius* Jordan & McGregor, 1898 | PM | Clarion snake eel | tieso manchado de Clarión |
| *Myrichthys tigrinus* Girard, 1859 | P | tiger snake eel | tieso tigre |
| *Myrophis platyrhynchus* Breder, 1927 | AM | broadnose worm eel | tieso chato |
| *Myrophis punctatus* Lütken, 1852 | A | speckled worm eel | tieso gusano |
| *Myrophis vafer* Jordan & Gilbert, 1883 | P | Pacific worm eel | tieso lombriz |
| *Ophichthus apachus* McCosker & Rosenblatt, 1998 | PM | thin snake eel | tieso delgado |
| *Ophichthus cruentifer* (Goode & Bean, 1896) | A | margined snake eel | |
| *Ophichthus frontalis* (Garman, 1899) | PM | deathbanded snake eel | tieso funebre |
| *Ophichthus gomesii* (Castelnau, 1855) | A | shrimp eel | tieso camaronero |
| *Ophichthus hyposagmatus* McCosker & Böhlke, 1984 | A | faintsaddled snake eel | |
| *Ophichthus longipenis* McCosker & Rosenblatt, 1998 | PM | slender snake eel | tieso fino |
| *Ophichthus mecopterus* McCosker & Rosenblatt, 1998 | PM | longarmed snake eel | tieso brazo largo |
| *Ophichthus melanoporus* Kanazawa, 1963 | A | blackpored eel | |
| *Ophichthus omorgmus* McCosker & Böhlke, 1984 | A | dottedline snake eel | |
| *Ophichthus ophis* (Linnaeus, 1758) | A | spotted snake eel | |
| *Ophichthus puncticeps* (Kaup, 1860) | A | palespotted eel | |
| *Ophichthus rex* Böhlke & Caruso, 1980 | A | king snake eel | lairón |
| *Ophichthus triserialis* (Kaup, 1856) | P | Pacific snake eel | tieso del Pacífico |
| *Ophichthus zophochir* Jordan & Gilbert, 1882 | P | yellow snake eel | tieso amarillo |
| *Paraletharchus opercularis* (Myers & Wade, 1941) | PM | pouch snake eel | tieso bolsa |
| *Paraletharchus pacificus* (Osburn & Nichols, 1916) | PM | Pacific sailfin eel | tieso vela del Pacífico |
| *Phaenomonas pinnata* Myers & Wade, 1941 | PM | elastic eel | tieso elástico |
| *Pisodonophis daspilotus* Gilbert, 1898 | PM | blunt-toothed snake eel | tieso dientes romos |
| *Pseudomyrophis fugesae* McCosker, Böhlke & Böhlke, 1989 | A | diminutive worm eel | |

| SCIENTIFIC NAME | OCCURRENCE[1] | COMMON NAME (ENGLISH, SPANISH, FRENCH)[2] |
|---|---|---|
| *Pseudomyrophis micropinna* Wade, 1946 | PM | plain worm eel ... tieso enano |
| *Quassiremus nothochir* (Gilbert, 1890) | PM | redsaddled snake eel ... tieso bisagra |
| *Scytalichthys miurus* (Jordan & Gilbert, 1882) | PM | shorttail viper eel ... tieso víbora |
| *Muraenesocidae—En-pike congers, Sp-congrios picudos, Fr-congres-brochets | | |
| *Cynoponticus coniceps* (Jordan & Gilbert, 1882) | PM | conehead eel ... congrio espantoso |
| Nemichthyidae—En-snipe eels, Sp-anguilas tijera, Fr-poissons-avocettes | | |
| *Nemichthys scolopaceus* Richardson, 1848 | A-P | slender snipe eel ... tijera esbelta |
| Congridae—En-conger eels, Sp-congrios, Fr-congres | | |
| *Ariosoma anale* (Poey, 1860) | A | longtrunk conger |
| *Ariosoma balearicum* (Delaroche, 1809) | A | bandtooth conger ... congrio balear |
| *Ariosoma gilberti* (Ogilby, 1898) | PM | sharpnose conger ... congrio narigón |
| +*Bathycongrus bullisi* (Smith & Kanazawa, 1977) | AM | bullish conger ... congrio disparatado |
| *Bathycongrus dubius* (Breder, 1927) | A | dubious conger |
| *Bathycongrus macrurus* (Gilbert, 1891) | PM | shorthead conger ... congrio cabeza corta |
| *Bathycongrus varidens* (Garman, 1899) | PM | largehead conger ... congrio cabezón |
| +*Bathycongrus vicinalis* (Garman, 1899) | AM | neighbor conger ... congrio vecino |
| *Chiloconger dentatus* (Garman, 1899) | PM | thicklip conger ... congrio labioso |
| *Conger oceanicus* (Mitchill, 1818) | A | conger eel |
| *Conger triporiceps* Kanazawa, 1958 | A | manytooth conger ... congrio dentudo |
| *Gnathophis bathytopos* Smith & Kanazawa, 1977 | A | blackgut conger |
| *Gnathophis bracheatopos* Smith & Kanazawa, 1977 | A | longeye conger |
| *Gnathophis cinctus* (Garman, 1899) | P | hardtail conger ... congrio cola tiesa |
| *Gorgasia punctata* Meek & Hildebrand, 1923 | PM | peppered garden eel ... congrio punteado |
| *Heteroconger canabus* (Cowan & Rosenblatt, 1974) | PM | Cape garden eel ... congrio del Cabo |
| *Heteroconger digueti* (Pellegrin, 1923) | PM | Cortez garden eel ... congrio de Cortés |
| *Heteroconger longissimus* Günther, 1870 | A | brown garden eel |
| *Heteroconger luteolus* Smith, 1989 | A | yellow garden eel |
| *Heteroconger pellegrini* Castle, 1999 | PM | speckled garden eel ... congrio pecoso |

| SCIENTIFIC NAME | OCCURRENCE[1] | COMMON NAME (ENGLISH, SPANISH, FRENCH)[2] |
|---|---|---|
| *Parabathymyrus oregoni* Smith & Kanazawa, 1977 | AM | flapnose conger ... congrio nariz colgada |
| *Paraconger californiensis* Kanazawa, 1961 | PM | ringeye conger ... congrio anteojos |
| *Paraconger caudilimbatus* (Poey, 1867) | A | margintail conger ... congrio cola de bordes |
| +*Paraconger similis* (Wade, 1946) | PM | shorttail conger ... congrio colicorta |
| *Rhynchoconger flavus* (Goode & Bean, 1896) | A | yellow conger ... congrio amarillo |
| *Rhynchoconger gracilior* (Ginsburg, 1951) | A | whiptail conger ... congrio grácil |
| *Rhynchoconger nitens* (Jordan & Bollman, 1890) | PM | needletail conger ... congrio estilete |
| *Uroconger syringinus* Ginsburg, 1954 | A | threadtail conger ... congrio plumilla |
| *Xenomystax congroides* Smith & Kanazawa, 1989 | A | bristletooth conger |

Nettastomatidae—En-duckbill eels, Sp-serpentinas, Fr-anguilles à bec de canard

| SCIENTIFIC NAME | OCCURRENCE | COMMON NAME |
|---|---|---|
| *Facciolella equatorialis* (Gilbert, 1891) | P | dogface witch eel ... serpentina bruja |
| *Hoplunnis diomediana* Goode & Bean, 1896 | A | blacktail pikeconger ... serpentina albatros |
| *Hoplunnis macrura* Ginsburg, 1951 | A | freckled pikeconger ... serpentina cola grande |
| *Hoplunnis pacifica* Lane & Stewart, 1968 | PM | silver pikeconger ... serpentina plateada |
| *Hoplunnis tenuis* Ginsburg, 1951 | A | spotted pikeconger ... serpentina dientona |
| *Nettenchelys pygmaea* Smith & Böhlke, 1981 | A | pygmy pikeconger ... serpentina enana |
| *Saurenchelys cognita* Smith, 1989 | A | longface eel ... serpentina noble |

## ORDER CLUPEIFORMES

+Engraulidae—En-anchovies, Sp-anchoas, Fr-anchois

| SCIENTIFIC NAME | OCCURRENCE | COMMON NAME |
|---|---|---|
| *Anchoa analis* (Miller, 1945) | F:M-PM | longfin Pacific anchovy ... anchoa aletona del Pacífico |
| *Anchoa argentivittata* (Regan, 1904) | PM | silverstripe anchovy ... anchoa plateada |
| *Anchoa belizensis* (Thomerson & Greenfield, 1975) | F:M | Belize anchovy ... anchoa beliceña |
| *Anchoa cayorum* (Fowler, 1906) | A | key anchovy ... anchoa de cayo |
| *Anchoa colonensis* Hildebrand, 1943 | AM | narrowstriped anchovy ... anchoa rayita |
| *Anchoa compressa* (Girard, 1858) | P | deepbody anchovy ... anchoa alta |
| *Anchoa cubana* (Poey, 1868) | A | Cuban anchovy ... anchoa cubana |
| *Anchoa curta* (Jordan & Gilbert, 1882) | PM | short anchovy ... anchoa chaparra |
| *Anchoa delicatissima* (Girard, 1854) | P | slough anchovy ... anchoa delicada |

| SCIENTIFIC NAME | OCCURRENCE[1] | COMMON NAME (ENGLISH, SPANISH, FRENCH)[2] |
|---|---|---|
| Anchoa exigua Jordan & Gilbert, 1882 | PM | slender anchovy ... anchoa fina |
| Anchoa helleri (Hubbs, 1921) | PM | Gulf anchovy ... anchoa del Golfo |
| Anchoa hepsetus (Linnaeus, 1758) | A-F:M | striped anchovy ... anchoa legítima |
| Anchoa ischana (Jordan & Gilbert, 1882) | PM | sharpnose anchovy ... anchoa chicotera |
| Anchoa lamprotaenia Hildebrand, 1943 | A | bigeye anchovy ... anchoa ojuda |
| Anchoa lucida (Jordan & Gilbert, 1882) | PM | bright anchovy ... anchoa ojitos |
| *Anchoa lyolepis (Evermann & Marsh, 1900) | A | dusky anchovy ... anchoa mulata |
| Anchoa mitchilli (Valenciennes, 1848) | A-F:UM | bay anchovy ... anchoa de caleta |
| Anchoa mundeola (Gilbert & Pierson, 1898) | PM | false Panama anchovy ... anchoa panameña falsa |
| Anchoa mundeoloides (Breder, 1928) | PM | northern Gulf anchovy ... anchoa golfina |
| Anchoa nasus (Kner & Steindachner, 1867) | PM | bignose anchovy ... anchoa trompuda |
| Anchoa parva (Meek & Hildebrand, 1923) | AM-F:M | little anchovy ... anchoa parva |
| Anchoa scofieldi (Jordan & Culver, 1895) | PM | yellow anchovy ... anchoa amarilla |
| Anchoa walkeri Baldwin & Chang, 1970 | PM | persistent anchovy ... anchoa persistente |
| Anchovia clupeoides (Swainson, 1839) | AM | zabaleta anchovy ... anchoveta sardina |
| Anchovia macrolepidota (Kner, 1863) | PM | bigscale anchovy ... anchoveta escamuda |
| Anchoviella perfasciata (Poey, 1860) | A | flat anchovy ... anchoa chata |
| Cetengraulis edentulus (Cuvier, 1829) | AM | Atlantic anchoveta ... anchoveta rabo amarillo |
| Cetengraulis mysticetus (Günther, 1867) | P | anchoveta ... anchoveta bocona |
| Engraulis eurystole (Swain & Meek, 1885) | A | silver anchovy |
| Engraulis mordax Girard, 1854 | P | northern anchovy ... anchoveta norteña |

*Pristigasteridae—En-longfin herrings, Sp-sardinas machete, Fr-pristigastéridés

| | | |
|---|---|---|
| Ilisha fuerthii (Steindachner, 1875) | PM | hatchet herring ... sardina hacha |
| Neoopisthopterus tropicus (Hildebrand, 1946) | PM | tropical longfin herring ... sardinela pelada |
| Odontognathus panamensis (Steindachner, 1876) | PM | Panama longfin herring ... sardina machete panameña |
| Opisthopterus dovii (Günther, 1868) | PM | Pacific longfin herring ... sardina machete chata |
| Pliosteostoma lutipinnis (Jordan & Gilbert, 1882) | PM | yellowfin herring ... arenquilla aleta amarilla |

Clupeidae—En-herrings, Sp-sardinas, Fr-harengs

| | | |
|---|---|---|
| Alosa aestivalis (Mitchill, 1814) | A-F:CU | blueback herring |
| Alosa alabamae Jordan & Evermann, 1896 | A-F:U | Alabama shad |

| SCIENTIFIC NAME | OCCURRENCE[1] | COMMON NAME (ENGLISH, SPANISH, FRENCH)[2] | | |
|---|---|---|---|---|
| *Alosa chrysochloris* (Rafinesque, 1820) | A-F:U | skipjack herring | | |
| *Alosa mediocris* (Mitchill, 1814) | A-F:U | hickory shad | | |
| *Alosa pseudoharengus* (Wilson, 1811) | A-F:CU | alewife | | gaspareau |
| *Alosa sapidissima* (Wilson, 1811) | A-F:CU-P[I] | American shad | sábalo americano | alose savoureuse |
| *Brevoortia gunteri* Hildebrand, 1948 | A | finescale menhaden | sardina escamitas | |
| *\*Brevoortia patronus* Goode, 1878 | A | Gulf menhaden | sardina lacha | |
| *Brevoortia smithi* Hildebrand, 1941 | A | yellowfin menhaden | | |
| *Brevoortia tyrannus* (Latrobe, 1802) | A | Atlantic menhaden | | |
| *Clupea harengus* Linnaeus, 1758 | A | Atlantic herring | | hareng atlantique |
| *\*Clupea pallasii* Valenciennes, 1847 | P | Pacific herring | arenque del Pacífico | |
| *Dorosoma anale* Meek, 1904 | F:M | longfin gizzard shad | sardina del Papaloapan | |
| *Dorosoma cepedianum* (Lesueur, 1818) | A-F:CUM | gizzard shad | sardina molleja | alose à gésier |
| *Dorosoma petenense* (Günther, 1867) | A-F:UM-P[I] | threadfin shad | sardina maya | |
| *Dorosoma smithi* Hubbs & Miller, 1941 | F:M | Pacific gizzard shad | sardina norteña | |
| *Etrumeus teres* (DeKay, 1842) | A-P | round herring | sardina japonesa | |
| *Harengula clupeola* (Cuvier, 1829) | A | false pilchard | sardinita carapachona | |
| *Harengula humeralis* (Cuvier, 1829) | A | redear sardine | sardinita de ley | |
| *Harengula jaguana* Poey, 1865 | A-F:UM | scaled sardine | sardinita vivita escamuda | |
| *Harengula thrissina* (Jordan & Gilbert, 1882) | P | flatiron herring | sardinita plumilla | |
| *Jenkinsia lamprotaenia* (Gosse, 1851) | A | dwarf herring | sardinita flaca | |
| *Jenkinsia majua* Whitehead, 1963 | A | little-eye herring | sardinita ojito | |
| *Jenkinsia stolifera* (Jordan & Gilbert, 1884) | A | shortband herring | sardinita de cayo | |
| *Lile gracilis* Castro-Aguirre & Vivero, 1990 | F:M-PM | graceful herring | sardinita agua dulce | |
| *Lile nigrofasciata* Castro-Aguirre, Ruiz-Campos & Balart, 2002 | PM | blackstripe herring | sardinita raya negra | |
| *Lile stolifera* (Jordan & Gilbert, 1882) | PM | striped herring | sardinita rayada | |
| *Opisthonema bulleri* (Regan, 1904) | PM | slender thread herring | sardina crinuda azul | |
| *Opisthonema libertate* (Günther, 1867) | P | deepbody thread herring | sardina crinuda | |
| *Opisthonema medirastre* Berry & Barrett, 1963 | P | middling thread herring | sardina crinuda machete | |
| *\*Opisthonema oglinum* (Lesueur, 1818) | A-F:U | Atlantic thread herring | sardina vivita de hebra | |
| *+Sardinella aurita* Valenciennes, 1847 | A | Spanish sardine | sardina española | |
| *+Sardinops sagax* (Jenyns, 1842) | P | Pacific sardine | sardina monterrey | |

| SCIENTIFIC NAME | OCCURRENCE[1] | COMMON NAME (ENGLISH, SPANISH, FRENCH)[2] |
|---|---|---|

## ORDER GONORYNCHIFORMES

Chanidae—En-milkfishes, Sp-sabalotes, Fr-chanos

| | | |
|---|---|---|
| *Chanos chanos* (Forsskål, 1775) | P | milkfish ............ sabalote |

## ORDER CYPRINIFORMES

Cyprinidae—En-carps and minnows, Sp-carpas y carpitas, Fr-carpes et ménés

| | | |
|---|---|---|
| *Acrocheilus alutaceus* Agassiz & Pickering, 1855 | F:CU | chiselmouth |
| +*Agosia chrysogaster* Girard, 1856 | F:UM | longfin dace ............ pupo panzaverde |
| *Algansea aphanea* Barbour & Miller, 1978 | F:M | riffle chub ............ pupo del Ayutla |
| *Algansea avia* Barbour & Miller, 1978 | F:M | remote chub ............ pupo de Tepic |
| *Algansea barbata* Alvarez & Cortés, 1964 | F:M | Lerma chub ............ pupo del Lerma |
| *Algansea lacustris* Steindachner, 1895 | F:M | Pátzcuaro chub ............ acúmara |
| *Algansea monticola* Barbour & Contreras-Balderas, 1968 | F:M | mountain chub ............ pupo del Juchipila |
| *Algansea popoche* (Jordan & Snyder, 1899) | F:M | popoche chub ............ popocha |
| +*Algansea tincella* (Valenciennes, 1844) | F:M | spottail chub ............ pupo del Valle |
| +*Aztecula sallaei* (Günther, 1868) | F:M | Aztec chub ............ carpita azteca |
| +*Campostoma anomalum* (Rafinesque, 1820) | F:CUM | central stoneroller ............ rodapiedras del centro |
| *Campostoma oligolepis* Hubbs & Greene, 1935 | F:U | largescale stoneroller |
| *Campostoma ornatum* Girard, 1856 | F:UM | Mexican stoneroller ............ rodapiedras mexicano |
| *Campostoma pauciradii* Burr & Cashner, 1983 | F:U | bluefin stoneroller |
| *Carassius auratus* (Linnaeus, 1758) | F[I]:CUM | goldfish ............ carpa dorada ............ carassin |
| *Clinostomus elongatus* (Kirtland, 1841) | F:CU | redside dace |
| *Clinostomus funduloides* Girard, 1856 | F:U | rosyside dace |
| *Couesius plumbeus* (Agassiz, 1850) | F:CU | lake chub ............ méné de lac |
| *Ctenopharyngodon idella* (Valenciennes, 1844) | F[I]:UM | grass carp ............ carpa herbívora |
| *Cyprinella alvarezdelvillari* Contreras-Balderas & Lozano-Vilano, 1994 | F:M | Tepehuan shiner ............ carpita tepehuana |

| SCIENTIFIC NAME | OCCURRENCE[1] | COMMON NAME (ENGLISH, SPANISH, FRENCH)[2] |
|---|---|---|
| Cyprinella analostana Girard, 1859 | F:U | satinfin shiner |
| Cyprinella bocagrande (Chernoff & Miller, 1982) | F:M | largemouth shiner ... carpita bocagrande |
| Cyprinella caerulea (Jordan, 1877) | F:U | blue shiner |
| Cyprinella callisema (Jordan, 1877) | F:U | Ocmulgee shiner |
| Cyprinella callistia (Jordan, 1877) | F:U | Alabama shiner |
| Cyprinella callitaenia (Bailey & Gibbs, 1956) | F:U | bluestripe shiner |
| Cyprinella camura (Jordan & Meek, 1884) | F:U | bluntface shiner |
| Cyprinella chloristia (Jordan & Brayton, 1878) | F:U | greenfin shiner |
| Cyprinella formosa (Girard, 1856) | F:UM | beautiful shiner ... carpita yaqui |
| Cyprinella galactura (Cope, 1868) | F:U | whitetail shiner |
| Cyprinella garmani (Jordan, 1885) | F:M | gibbous shiner ... carpita jorobada |
| Cyprinella gibbsi (Howell & Williams, 1971) | F:U | Tallapoosa shiner |
| +Cyprinella labrosa (Cope, 1870) | F:U | thicklip chub |
| Cyprinella leedsi (Fowler, 1942) | F:U | bannerfin shiner |
| Cyprinella lepida Girard, 1856 | F:U | plateau shiner |
| Cyprinella lutrensis (Baird & Girard, 1853) | F:UM | red shiner ... carpita roja |
| Cyprinella nivea (Cope, 1870) | F:U | whitefin shiner |
| +Cyprinella ornata (Girard, 1856) | F:M | ornate shiner ... carpita adornada |
| Cyprinella panarcys (Hubbs & Miller, 1978) | F:M | Conchos shiner ... carpita del Conchos |
| Cyprinella proserpina (Girard, 1856) | F:UM | proserpine shiner ... carpita río del norte |
| Cyprinella pyrrhomelas (Cope, 1870) | F:U | fieryblack shiner |
| Cyprinella rutila (Girard, 1856) | F:M | Mexican red shiner ... carpita regiomontana |
| *Cyprinella spiloptera (Cope, 1867) | F:CU | spotfin shiner ... méné bleu |
| Cyprinella trichroistia (Jordan & Gilbert, 1878) | F:U | tricolor shiner |
| +Cyprinella venusta Girard, 1856 | F:UM | blacktail shiner ... carpita colinegra |
| +Cyprinella whipplei Girard, 1856 | F:U | steelcolor shiner |
| Cyprinella xaenura (Jordan, 1877) | F:U | Altamaha shiner |
| Cyprinella xanthicara (Minckley & Lytle, 1969) | F:M | Cuatro Cienegas shiner ... carpita de Cuatro Ciénegas |
| +Cyprinella zanema (Jordan & Brayton, 1878) | F:U | Santee chub |
| Cyprinus carpio Linnaeus, 1758 | F[I]:CUM | common carp ... carpa común ... carpe |
| *Dionda argentosa Girard, 1856 | F:UM | Manantial roundnose minnow .. carpa de manantial |

| SCIENTIFIC NAME | OCCURRENCE[1] | COMMON NAME (ENGLISH, SPANISH, FRENCH)[2] |
|---|---|---|
| *Dionda catostomops* Hubbs & Miller, 1977 | F:M | Pánuco minnow ... carpa de Tamasopo |
| *Dionda diaboli* Hubbs & Brown, 1957 | F:UM | Devils River minnow ... carpa diabla |
| *Dionda dichroma* Hubbs & Miller, 1977 | F:M | bicolor minnow ... carpa bicolor |
| *Dionda episcopa* Girard, 1856 | F:UM | roundnose minnow ... carpa obispa |
| *Dionda erimyzonops* Hubbs & Miller, 1974 | F:M | chubsucker minnow ... carpa del Mante |
| *Dionda ipni* (Alvarez & Navarro, 1953) | F:M | lantern minnow ... carpa veracruzana |
| *Dionda mandibularis* Contreras-Balderas & Verduzco-Martínez, 1977 | F:M | flatjaw minnow ... carpa quijarona |
| *Dionda melanops* Girard, 1856 | F:M | spotted minnow ... carpa manchada |
| \* *Dionda nigrotaeniata* (Cope, 1880) | F:U | Guadalupe roundnose minnow |
| *Dionda rasconis* (Jordan & Snyder, 1899) | F:M | blackstripe minnow ... carpa potosina |
| \* *Dionda serena* Girard, 1856 | F:U | Nueces roundnose minnow |
| *Eremichthys acros* Hubbs & Miller, 1948 | F:U | desert dace |
| + *Erimonax monachus* (Cope, 1868) | F:U | spotfin chub |
| *Erimystax cahni* (Hubbs & Crowe, 1956) | F:U | slender chub |
| \* *Erimystax dissimilis* (Kirtland, 1841) | F:U | streamline chub |
| *Erimystax harryi* (Hubbs & Crowe, 1956) | F:U | Ozark chub |
| *Erimystax insignis* (Hubbs & Crowe, 1956) | F:U | blotched chub |
| + *Erimystax x-punctatus* (Hubbs & Crowe, 1956) | F:CU | gravel chub |
| *Evarra bustamantei* Navarro, 1955 | F[X]:M | Mexican chub ... carpa xochimilca |
| *Evarra eigenmanni* Woolman, 1894 | F[X]:M | plateau chub ... carpa verde |
| *Evarra tlahuacensis* Meek, 1902 | F[X]:M | endorheic chub ... carpa de Tláhuac |
| *Exoglossum laurae* (Hubbs, 1931) | F:U | tonguetied minnow |
| \* *Exoglossum maxillingua* (Lesueur, 1817) | F:CU | cutlip minnow ... bec-de-lièvre |
| *Gila alvordensis* Hubbs & Miller, 1972 | F:U | Alvord chub |
| *Gila atraria* (Girard, 1856) | F:U | Utah chub |
| + *Gila bicolor* (Girard, 1856) | F:U | tui chub |
| *Gila boraxobius* Williams & Bond, 1980 | F:U | Borax Lake chub |
| *Gila brevicauda* Norris, Fischer & Minckley, 2003 | F:M | shorttail chub ... carpa colicorta |
| + *Gila coerulea* (Girard, 1856) | F:U | blue chub |
| *Gila conspersa* Garman, 1881 | F:M | Nazas chub ... carpa Mayrán |

| SCIENTIFIC NAME | OCCURRENCE[1] | COMMON NAME (ENGLISH, SPANISH, FRENCH)[2] |
|---|---|---|
| *Gila crassicauda* (Baird & Girard, 1854) | F[X]:U | thicktail chub |
| \* *Gila cypha* Miller, 1946 | F:U | humpback chub |
| *Gila ditaenia* Miller, 1945 | F:UM | Sonora chub ... carpa sonorense |
| + *Gila elegans* Baird & Girard, 1853 | F:UM | bonytail ... carpa elegante |
| *Gila eremica* DeMarais, 1991 | F:M | desert chub ... carpa del desierto |
| + *Gila intermedia* (Girard, 1856) | F:UM | Gila chub ... carpa del Gila |
| + *Gila minacae* Meek, 1902 | F:M | Mexican roundtail chub ... carpa cola redonda mexicana |
| *Gila modesta* (Garman, 1881) | F:M | Saltillo chub ... carpa de Saltillo |
| \* *Gila nigra* Cope, 1875 | F:U | headwater chub |
| *Gila nigrescens* (Girard, 1856) | F:UM | Chihuahua chub ... carpa de Chihuahua |
| \* *Gila orcuttii* (Eigenmann & Eigenmann, 1890) | F:U | arroyo chub |
| *Gila pandora* (Cope, 1872) | F:U | Rio Grande chub |
| *Gila pulchra* (Girard, 1856) | F:M | Conchos chub ... carpa del Conchos |
| *Gila purpurea* (Girard, 1856) | F:UM | Yaqui chub ... carpa púrpura |
| + *Gila robusta* Baird & Girard, 1853 | F:U | roundtail chub |
| \* *Gila seminuda* Cope & Yarrow, 1875 | F:U | Virgin chub |
| *Hemitremia flammea* (Jordan & Gilbert, 1878) | F:U | flame chub |
| + *Hesperoleucus symmetricus* (Baird & Girard, 1854) | F:U | California roach |
| + *Hybognathus amarus* (Girard, 1856) | F:UM | Rio Grande silvery minnow ... carpa Chamizal |
| *Hybognathus argyritis* Girard, 1856 | F:CU | western silvery minnow |
| *Hybognathus hankinsoni* Hubbs, 1929 | F:CU | brassy minnow ... méné laiton |
| *Hybognathus hayi* Jordan, 1885 | F:U | cypress minnow |
| *Hybognathus nuchalis* Agassiz, 1855 | F:U | Mississippi silvery minnow |
| *Hybognathus placitus* Girard, 1856 | F:U | plains minnow |
| *Hybognathus regius* Girard, 1856 | F:CU | eastern silvery minnow ... méné d'argent |
| \* *Hybopsis amblops* (Rafinesque, 1820) | F:U | bigeye chub |
| \* *Hybopsis amnis* (Hubbs & Greene, 1951) | F:U | pallid shiner |
| \* *Hybopsis hypsinotus* (Cope, 1870) | F:U | highback chub |
| \* *Hybopsis lineapunctata* Clemmer & Suttkus, 1971 | F:U | lined chub |
| \* *Hybopsis rubrifrons* (Jordan, 1877) | F:U | rosyface chub |
| \* *Hybopsis winchelli* Girard, 1856 | F:U | clear chub |

| SCIENTIFIC NAME | OCCURRENCE[1] | COMMON NAME (ENGLISH, SPANISH, FRENCH)[2] |
|---|---|---|
| *Hypophthalmichthys molitrix* (Valenciennes, 1844) | F[I]:UM | silver carp ............ carpa plateada |
| *Hypophthalmichthys nobilis* (Richardson, 1845) | F[I]:UM | bighead carp ............ carpa cabezona |
| *Iotichthys phlegethontis* (Cope, 1874) | F:U | least chub |
| +*Lavinia exilicauda* Baird & Girard, 1854 | F:U | hitch |
| *Lepidomeda albivallis* Miller & Hubbs, 1960 | F:U | White River spinedace |
| *Lepidomeda altivelis* Miller & Hubbs, 1960 | F[X]:U | Pahranagat spinedace |
| *Lepidomeda mollispinis* Miller & Hubbs, 1960 | F:U | Virgin spinedace |
| *Lepidomeda vittata* Cope, 1874 | F:U | Little Colorado spinedace |
| *Leuciscus idus* (Linnaeus, 1758) | F[I]:U | ide |
| *Luxilus albeolus* (Jordan, 1889) | F:U | white shiner |
| *Luxilus cardinalis* (Mayden, 1988) | F:U | cardinal shiner |
| *Luxilus cerasinus* (Cope, 1868) | F:U | crescent shiner |
| *Luxilus chrysocephalus* Rafinesque, 1820 | F:CU | striped shiner |
| *Luxilus coccogenis* (Cope, 1868) | F:U | warpaint shiner |
| *Luxilus cornutus* (Mitchill, 1817) | F:CU | common shiner ............ méné à nageoires rouges |
| *Luxilus pilsbryi* (Fowler, 1904) | F:U | duskystripe shiner |
| *Luxilus zonatus* (Agassiz, 1863) | F:U | bleeding shiner |
| *Luxilus zonistius* Jordan, 1880 | F:U | bandfin shiner |
| *Lythrurus alegnotus* (Snelson, 1972) | F:U | Warrior shiner |
| +*Lythrurus ardens* (Cope, 1868) | F:U | rosefin shiner |
| *Lythrurus atrapiculus* (Snelson, 1972) | F:U | blacktip shiner |
| *Lythrurus bellus* (Hay, 1881) | F:U | pretty shiner |
| *Lythrurus fasciolaris* (Gilbert, 1891) | F:U | scarlet shiner |
| *Lythrurus fumeus* (Evermann, 1892) | F:U | ribbon shiner |
| *Lythrurus lirus* Jordan, 1877) | F:U | mountain shiner |
| *Lythrurus matutinus* (Cope, 1870) | F:U | pinewoods shiner |
| *Lythrurus roseipinnis* (Hay, 1885) | F:U | cherryfin shiner |
| *Lythrurus snelsoni* (Robison, 1985) | F:U | Ouachita shiner |
| *Lythrurus umbratilis* (Girard, 1856) | F:CU | redfin shiner |
| +*Macrhybopsis aestivalis* (Girard, 1856) | F:UM | speckled chub ............ carpa pecosa |
| *Macrhybopsis australis* (Hubbs & Ortenburger, 1929) | F:U | prairie chub |

| SCIENTIFIC NAME | OCCURRENCE[1] | COMMON NAME (ENGLISH, SPANISH, FRENCH)[2] |
|---|---|---|
| *Macrhybopsis gelida* (Girard, 1856) | F:U | sturgeon chub |
| *Macrhybopsis hyostoma* (Gilbert, 1884) | F:U | shoal chub |
| *Macrhybopsis marconis* (Jordan & Gilbert, 1886) | F:U | burrhead chub |
| *Macrhybopsis meeki* (Jordan & Evermann, 1896) | F:U | sicklefin chub |
| *Macrhybopsis storeriana* (Kirtland, 1845) | F:CU | silver chub |
| *Macrhybopsis tetranema* (Gilbert, 1886) | F:U | peppered chub |
| *Margariscus margarita* (Cope, 1867) | F:CU | pearl dace ...... mulet perlé |
| +*Meda fulgida* Girard, 1856 | F:U | spikedace |
| *Moapa coriacea* Hubbs & Miller, 1948 | F:U | Moapa dace |
| *Mylocheilus caurinus* (Richardson, 1836) | F:CU | peamouth |
| *Mylopharodon conocephalus* (Baird & Girard, 1854) | F:U | hardhead |
| *Nocomis asper* Lachner & Jenkins, 1971 | F:U | redspot chub |
| *Nocomis biguttatus* (Kirtland, 1841) | F:CU | hornyhead chub |
| *Nocomis effusus* Lachner & Jenkins, 1967 | F:U | redtail chub |
| *Nocomis leptocephalus* (Girard, 1856) | F:U | bluehead chub |
| +*Nocomis micropogon* (Cope, 1865) | F:CU | river chub |
| *Nocomis platyrhynchus* Lachner & Jenkins, 1971 | F:U | bigmouth chub |
| *Nocomis raneyi* Lachner & Jenkins, 1971 | F:U | bull chub |
| *Notemigonus crysoleucas* (Mitchill, 1814) | F:CU | golden shiner ...... méné jaune |
| *Notropis aguirrepequenoi* Contreras-Balderas & Rivera-Teillery 1973 | F:M | Soto la Marina shiner ...... carpita del Pilón |
| *Notropis albizonatus* Warren & Burr 1994 | F:U | palezone shiner |
| *Notropis alborus* Hubbs & Raney, 1947 | F:U | whitemouth shiner |
| *Notropis altipinnis* (Cope, 1870) | F:U | highfin shiner |
| *Notropis amabilis* (Girard, 1856) | F:UM | Texas shiner ...... carpita texana |
| *Notropis amecae* Chernoff & Miller, 1986 | F[X]:M | Ameca shiner ...... carpita del Ameca |
| *Notropis ammophilus* Suttkus & Boschung, 1990 | F:U | orangefin shiner |
| *Notropis amoenus* (Abbott, 1874) | F:U | comely shiner |
| *Notropis anogenus* Forbes, 1885 | F:CU | pugnose shiner |
| *Notropis ariommus* (Cope, 1867) | F:U | popeye shiner |
| *Notropis asperifrons* Suttkus & Raney, 1955 | F:U | burrhead shiner |

| SCIENTIFIC NAME | OCCURRENCE[1] | COMMON NAME (ENGLISH, SPANISH, FRENCH)[2] |
|---|---|---|
| *Notropis atherinoides* Rafinesque, 1818 | F:CU | emerald shiner ... méné émeraude |
| *Notropis atrocaudalis* Evermann, 1892 | F:U | blackspot shiner |
| *Notropis aulidion* Chernoff & Miller, 1986 | F[X]:M | Durango shiner ... carpita de Durango |
| *Notropis baileyi* Suttkus & Raney, 1955 | F:U | rough shiner |
| *Notropis bairdi* Hubbs & Ortenburger, 1929 | F:U | Red River shiner |
| *Notropis bifrenatus* (Cope, 1867) | F:CU | bridle shiner ... méné d'herbe |
| *Notropis blennius* (Girard, 1856) | F:CU | river shiner |
| *Notropis boops* Gilbert, 1884 | F:U | bigeye shiner |
| *Notropis boucardi* (Günther, 1868) | F:M | Balsas shiner ... carpita del Balsas |
| *Notropis braytoni* Jordan & Evermann, 1896 | F:UM | Tamaulipas shiner ... carpita tamaulipeca |
| +*Notropis buccatus* (Cope, 1865) | F:U | silverjaw minnow |
| *Notropis buccula* Cross, 1953 | F:U | smalleye shiner |
| +*Notropis buchanani* Meek, 1896 | F:CUM | ghost shiner ... carpita fantasma |
| *Notropis cahabae* Mayden & Kuhajda, 1989 | F:U | Cahaba shiner |
| *Notropis calientis* Jordan & Snyder, 1899 | F:M | yellow shiner ... carpita amarilla |
| *Notropis candidus* Suttkus, 1980 | F:U | silverside shiner |
| *Notropis chalybaeus* (Cope, 1867) | F:U | ironcolor shiner |
| *Notropis chihuahua* Woolman, 1892 | F:UM | Chihuahua shiner ... carpita chihuahuense |
| *Notropis chiliticus* (Cope, 1870) | F:U | redlip shiner |
| +*Notropis chlorocephalus* (Cope, 1870) | F:U | greenhead shiner |
| *Notropis chrosomus* (Jordan, 1877) | F:U | rainbow shiner |
| +*Notropis cumingii* (Günther, 1868) | F:M | Atoyac chub ... carpita del Atoyac |
| *Notropis cummingsae* Myers, 1925 | F:U | dusky shiner |
| *Notropis dorsalis* (Agassiz, 1854) | F:CU | bigmouth shiner |
| *Notropis edwardraneyi* Suttkus & Clemmer, 1968 | F:U | fluvial shiner |
| *Notropis girardi* Hubbs & Ortenburger, 1929 | F:U | Arkansas River shiner |
| *Notropis greenei* Hubbs & Ortenburger, 1929 | F:U | wedgespot shiner |
| *Notropis harperi* Fowler, 1941 | F:U | redeye chub |
| *Notropis heterodon* (Cope, 1865) | F:CU | blackchin shiner ... menton noir |
| *Notropis heterolepis* Eigenmann & Eigenmann, 1893 | F:CU | blacknose shiner ... museau noir |
| *Notropis hudsonius* (Clinton, 1824) | F:CU | spottail shiner ... queue à tache noire |

| SCIENTIFIC NAME | OCCURRENCE[1] | COMMON NAME (ENGLISH, SPANISH, FRENCH)[2] |
|---|---|---|
| Notropis hypsilepis Suttkus & Raney, 1955 | F:U | highscale shiner |
| +Notropis jemezanus (Cope, 1875) | F:UM | Rio Grande shiner ... carpita del Bravo |
| Notropis leuciodus (Cope, 1868) | F:U | Tennessee shiner |
| Notropis longirostris (Hay, 1881) | F:U | longnose shiner |
| +Notropis lutipinnis (Jordan & Brayton, 1878) | F:U | yellowfin shiner |
| Notropis maculatus (Hay, 1881) | F:U | taillight shiner |
| Notropis mekistocholas Snelson, 1971 | F:U | Cape Fear shiner |
| Notropis melanostomus Bortone, 1989 | F:U | blackmouth shiner |
| *Notropis micropteryx (Cope, 1868) | F:U | highland shiner |
| Notropis moralesi de Buen, 1955 | F:M | Papaloapan chub ... carpita Tepelneme |
| Notropis nazas Meek, 1904 | F:M | Nazas shiner ... carpita del Nazas |
| Notropis nubilus (Forbes, 1878) | F:U | Ozark minnow |
| Notropis orca Woolman, 1894 | F[X]:UM | phantom shiner ... carpita de El Paso |
| Notropis ortenburgeri Hubbs, 1927 | F:U | Kiamichi shiner |
| Notropis oxyrhynchus Hubbs & Bonham, 1951 | F:U | sharpnose shiner |
| Notropis ozarcanus Meek, 1891 | F:U | Ozark shiner |
| *Notropis percobromus (Cope, 1871) | F:CU | carmine shiner |
| Notropis perpallidus Hubbs & Black, 1940 | F:U | peppered shiner |
| Notropis petersoni Fowler, 1942 | F:U | coastal shiner |
| Notropis photogenis (Cope, 1865) | F:CU | silver shiner |
| Notropis potteri Hubbs & Bonham, 1951 | F:U | chub shiner |
| Notropis procne (Cope, 1865) | F:U | swallowtail shiner |
| *Notropis rafinesquei Suttkus, 1991 | F:U | Yazoo shiner |
| +Notropis rubellus (Agassiz, 1850) | F:CU | rosyface shiner ... tête rose |
| Notropis rubricroceus (Cope, 1868) | F:U | saffron shiner |
| Notropis rupestris Page, 1987 | F:U | bedrock shiner |
| Notropis sabinae Jordan & Gilbert, 1886 | F:U | Sabine shiner |
| +Notropis saladonis Hubbs & Hubbs, 1958 | F[X]:M | Salado shiner ... carpita del Salado |
| Notropis scabriceps (Cope, 1868) | F:U | New River shiner |
| Notropis scepticus (Jordan & Gilbert, 1883) | F:U | sandbar shiner |
| Notropis semperasper Gilbert, 1961 | F:U | roughhead shiner |
| Notropis shumardi (Girard, 1856) | F:U | silverband shiner |

| SCIENTIFIC NAME | OCCURRENCE[1] | COMMON NAME (ENGLISH, SPANISH, FRENCH)[2] | | |
|---|---|---|---|---|
| +Notropis simus (Cope, 1875) | F:UM | bluntnose shiner | carpita chata | |
| Notropis spectrunculus (Cope, 1868) | F:U | mirror shiner | | |
| *Notropis stilbius Jordan, 1877 | F:U | silverstripe shiner | | |
| +Notropis stramineus (Cope, 1865) | F:CUM | sand shiner | carpita arenera | méné paille |
| *Notropis suttkusi Humphries & Cashner, 1994 | F:U | rocky shiner | | |
| Notropis telescopus (Cope, 1868) | F:U | telescope shiner | | |
| Notropis texanus (Girard, 1856) | F:CU | weed shiner | | |
| +Notropis topeka (Gilbert, 1884) | F:U | Topeka shiner | | |
| Notropis tropicus Hubbs & Miller, 1975 | F:M | pygmy shiner | carpita tropical | |
| Notropis uranoscopus Suttkus, 1959 | F:U | skygazer shiner | | |
| Notropis volucellus (Cope, 1865) | F:CU | mimic shiner | | méné pâle |
| Notropis wickliffi Trautman, 1931 | F:U | channel shiner | | |
| Notropis xaenocephalus (Jordan, 1877) | F:U | Coosa shiner | | |
| Opsopoeodus emiliae Hay, 1881 | F:CU | pugnose minnow | | |
| Oregonichthys crameri (Snyder, 1908) | F:U | Oregon chub | | |
| *Oregonichthys kalawatseti Markle, Pearsons & Bills, 1991 | F:U | Umpqua chub | | |
| Orthodon microlepidotus (Ayres, 1854) | F:U | Sacramento blackfish | | |
| Phenacobius catostomus Jordan, 1877 | F:U | riffle minnow | | |
| Phenacobius crassilabrum Minckley & Craddock, 1962 | F:U | fatlips minnow | | |
| Phenacobius mirabilis (Girard, 1856) | F:U | suckermouth minnow | | |
| Phenacobius teretulus Cope, 1867 | F:U | Kanawha minnow | | |
| Phenacobius uranops Cope, 1867 | F:U | stargazing minnow | | |
| Phoxinus cumberlandensis Starnes & Starnes, 1978 | F:U | blackside dace | | |
| +Phoxinus eos (Cope, 1862) | F:CU | northern redbelly dace | | ventre rouge du nord |
| Phoxinus erythrogaster (Rafinesque, 1820) | F:U | southern redbelly dace | | |
| *Phoxinus neogaeus Cope, 1867 | F:CU | finescale dace | | ventre citron |
| Phoxinus oreas (Cope, 1868) | F:U | mountain redbelly dace | | |
| *Phoxinus saylori Skelton, 2001 | F:U | laurel dace | | |
| Phoxinus tennesseensis Starnes & Jenkins, 1988 | F:U | Tennessee dace | | |
| Pimephales notatus (Rafinesque, 1820) | F:CU | bluntnose minnow | | ventre-pourri |
| Pimephales promelas Rafinesque, 1820 | F:CUM | fathead minnow | carpita cabezona | tête-de-boule |
| Pimephales tenellus (Girard, 1856) | F:U | slim minnow | | |

| SCIENTIFIC NAME | OCCURRENCE[1] | COMMON NAME (ENGLISH, SPANISH, FRENCH)[2] |
|---|---|---|
| *Pimephales vigilax* (Baird & Girard, 1853) | F:UM | bullhead minnow ... carpita cabeza de toro |
| +*Plagopterus argentissimus* Cope, 1874 | F:U | woundfin |
| *Platygobio gracilis* (Richardson, 1836) | F:CU | flathead chub |
| *Pogonichthys ciscoides* Hopkirk, 1974 | F[X]:U | Clear Lake splittail |
| *Pogonichthys macrolepidotus* (Ayres, 1854) | F:U | splittail |
| *\*Pteronotropis euryzonus* (Suttkus, 1955) | F:U | broadstripe shiner |
| *\*Pteronotropis grandipinnis* (Jordan, 1877) | F:U | Apalachee shiner |
| *\*Pteronotropis hubbsi* (Bailey & Robison, 1978) | F:U | bluehead shiner |
| *\*Pteronotropis hypselopterus* (Günther, 1868) | F:U | sailfin shiner |
| *\*Pteronotropis merlini* (Suttkus & Mettee, 2001) | F:U | orangetail shiner |
| *\*Pteronotropis signipinnis* (Bailey & Suttkus, 1952) | F:U | flagfin shiner |
| *\*Pteronotropis welaka* (Evermann & Kendall, 1898) | F:U | bluenose shiner |
| *\*Ptychocheilus grandis* (Ayres, 1854) | F:U | Sacramento pikeminnow |
| *\*Ptychocheilus lucius* Girard, 1856 | F:UM | Colorado pikeminnow ... carpa gigante del Colorado |
| *\*Ptychocheilus oregonensis* (Richardson, 1836) | F:CU | northern pikeminnow |
| *\*Ptychocheilus umpquae* Snyder, 1908 | F:U | Umpqua pikeminnow |
| *Relictus solitarius* Hubbs & Miller, 1972 | F:U | relict dace |
| *\*Rhinichthys atratulus* (Hermann, 1804) | F:CU | eastern blacknose dace ... naseux noir de l'est |
| +*Rhinichthys cataractae* (Valenciennes, 1842) | F:CUM | longnose dace ... carpita rinconera ... naseux des rapides |
| *\*Rhinichthys cobitis* (Girard, 1856) | F:UM | loach minnow ... carpita locha |
| *Rhinichthys deaconi* Miller, 1984 | F[X]:U | Las Vegas dace |
| *Rhinichthys evermanni* Snyder, 1908 | F:U | Umpqua dace |
| *\*Rhinichthys falcatus* (Eigenmann & Eigenmann, 1893) | F:CU | leopard dace |
| *\*Rhinichthys obtusus* Agassiz, 1854 | F:CU | western blacknose dace |
| *\*Rhinichthys osculus* (Girard, 1856) | F:CUM | speckled dace ... carpita pinta |
| *\*Rhinichthys umatilla* (Gilbert & Evermann, 1894) | F:CU | Umatilla dace |
| *Rhodeus sericeus* (Pallas, 1776) | F[I]:U | bitterling |
| *Richardsonius balteatus* (Richardson, 1836) | F:CU | redside shiner |
| *Richardsonius egregius* (Girard, 1858) | F:U | Lahontan redside |
| +*Scardinius erythrophthalmus* (Linnaeus, 1758) | F[I]:CU | rudd |
| *Semotilus atromaculatus* (Mitchill, 1818) | F:CU | creek chub ... mulet à cornes |
| *Semotilus corporalis* (Mitchill, 1817) | F:CU | fallfish ... ouitouche |

| SCIENTIFIC NAME | OCCURRENCE[1] | COMMON NAME (ENGLISH, SPANISH, FRENCH)[2] |
|---|---|---|
| Semotilus lumbee Snelson & Suttkus, 1978 | F:U | sandhills chub |
| Semotilus thoreauianus Jordan, 1877 | F:U | Dixie chub |
| *Snyderichthys copei (Jordan & Gilbert, 1881) | F:U | leatherside chub |
| Stypodon signifer Garman, 1881 | F[X]:M | stumptooth minnow ............ carpa de Parras |
| Tinca tinca (Linnaeus, 1758) | F[I]:CU | tench ............................................ tanche |
| +Yuriria alta (Jordan, 1880) | F:M | Jalisco chub ........................ carpa blanca |
| +Yuriria chapalae (Jordan & Snyder, 1899) | F:M | Chapala chub .................. carpa de Chapala |
| Catostomidae—En-suckers, Sp-matalotes, Fr-catostomes | | |
| Carpiodes carpio (Rafinesque, 1820) | F:UM | river carpsucker .................. matalote chato |
| Carpiodes cyprinus (Lesueur, 1817) | F:CU | quillback ................................ couette |
| Carpiodes velifer (Rafinesque, 1820) | F:U | highfin carpsucker |
| Catostomus ardens Jordan & Gilbert, 1881 | F:U | Utah sucker |
| +Catostomus bernardini Girard, 1856 | F:UM | Yaqui sucker .................. matalote yaqui |
| Catostomus cahita Siebert & Minckley, 1986 | F:M | Cahita sucker .................. matalote cahita |
| +Catostomus catostomus (Forster, 1773) | F:CU | longnose sucker .................... meunier rouge |
| *Catostomus clarkii Baird & Girard, 1854 | F:UM | desert sucker ................ matalote del desierto |
| Catostomus columbianus (Eigenmann & Eigenmann, 1893) | F:CU | bridgelip sucker |
| *Catostomus commersonii (Lacepède, 1803) | F:CU | white sucker .......................... meunier noir |
| *Catostomus discobolus Cope, 1871 | F:U | bluehead sucker |
| Catostomus fumeiventris Miller, 1973 | F:U | Owens sucker |
| Catostomus insignis Baird & Girard, 1854 | F:UM | Sonora sucker ................ matalote de Sonora |
| Catostomus latipinnis Baird & Girard, 1853 | F:U | flannelmouth sucker |
| Catostomus leopoldi Siebert & Minckley, 1986 | F:M | fleshylip sucker ............ matalote del Bavispe |
| Catostomus macrocheilus Girard, 1856 | F:CU | largescale sucker |
| Catostomus microps Rutter, 1908 | F:U | Modoc sucker |
| Catostomus nebuliferus Garman, 1881 | F:M | Nazas sucker ................ matalote del Nazas |
| Catostomus occidentalis Ayres, 1854 | F:U | Sacramento sucker |
| +Catostomus platyrhynchus (Cope, 1874) | F:CU | mountain sucker |
| +Catostomus plebeius Baird & Girard, 1854 | F:UM | Rio Grande sucker ............ matalote del Bravo |
| +Catostomus rimiculus Gilbert & Snyder, 1898 | F:U | Klamath smallscale sucker |
| +Catostomus santaanae (Snyder, 1908) | F:U | Santa Ana sucker |

| SCIENTIFIC NAME | OCCURRENCE[1] | COMMON NAME (ENGLISH, SPANISH, FRENCH)[2] |
|---|---|---|
| *Catostomus snyderi* Gilbert, 1898 | F:U | Klamath largescale sucker |
| *Catostomus tahoensis* Gill & Jordan, 1878 | F:U | Tahoe sucker |
| *Catostomus warnerensis* Snyder, 1908 | F:U | Warner sucker |
| *Catostomus wigginsi* Herre & Brock, 1936 | F:M | Opata sucker .......... matalote opata |
| *Chasmistes brevirostris* Cope, 1879 | F:U | shortnose sucker |
| +*Chasmistes cujus* Cope, 1883 | F:U | cui-ui |
| *Chasmistes liorus* Jordan, 1878 | F:U | June sucker |
| *Chasmistes muriei* Miller & Smith, 1981 | F[X]:U | Snake River sucker |
| +*Cycleptus elongatus* (Lesueur, 1817) | F:UM | blue sucker .......... matalote azul |
| *Cycleptus meridionalis* Burr & Mayden, 1999 | F:U | southeastern blue sucker |
| *Deltistes luxatus* (Cope, 1879) | F:U | Lost River sucker |
| +*Erimyzon oblongus* (Mitchill, 1814) | F:U | creek chubsucker |
| *Erimyzon sucetta* (Lacepède, 1803) | F:CU | lake chubsucker |
| *Erimyzon tenuis* (Agassiz, 1855) | F:U | sharpfin chubsucker |
| *Hypentelium etowanum* (Jordan, 1877) | F:U | Alabama hog sucker |
| *Hypentelium nigricans* (Lesueur, 1817) | F:CU | northern hog sucker |
| *Hypentelium roanokense* Raney & Lachner, 1947 | F:U | Roanoke hog sucker |
| *Ictiobus bubalus* (Rafinesque, 1818) | F:UM | smallmouth buffalo .......... matalote boquín |
| *Ictiobus cyprinellus* (Valenciennes, 1844) | F:CU | bigmouth buffalo |
| *Ictiobus labiosus* (Meek, 1904) | F:M | fleshylip buffalo .......... matalote bocón |
| *Ictiobus meridionalis* (Günther, 1868) | F:M | southern buffalo .......... matalote meridional |
| +*Ictiobus niger* (Rafinesque, 1819) | F:CUM | black buffalo .......... matalote negro |
| +*Minytrema melanops* (Rafinesque, 1820) | F:CU | spotted sucker |
| +*Moxostoma albidum* (Girard, 1856) | F:M | longlip jumprock |
| +*Moxostoma anisurum* (Rafinesque, 1820) | F:CU | silver redhorse .......... matalote blanco |
| +*Moxostoma ariommum* Robins & Raney, 1956 | F:U | bigeye jumprock |
| *Moxostoma austrinum* Bean, 1880 | F:UM | Mexican redhorse .......... matalote chuime ............ chevalier blanc |
| *Moxostoma breviceps* (Cope, 1870) | F:U | smallmouth redhorse |
| *Moxostoma carinatum* (Cope, 1870) | F:CU | river redhorse .......... chevalier de rivière |
| *Moxostoma cervinum* (Cope, 1868) | F:U | blacktip jumprock |
| *Moxostoma collapsum* (Cope, 1870) | F:U | notchlip redhorse |
| +*Moxostoma congestum* (Baird & Girard, 1854) | F:U | gray redhorse |

| SCIENTIFIC NAME | OCCURRENCE[1] | COMMON NAME (ENGLISH, SPANISH, FRENCH)[2] |
|---|---|---|
| +Moxostoma duquesnei (Lesueur, 1817) | F:CU | black redhorse |
| Moxostoma erythrurum (Rafinesque, 1818) | F:CU | golden redhorse |
| Moxostoma hubbsi Legendre, 1952 | F:C | copper redhorse ... chevalier cuivré |
| *Moxostoma lacerum (Jordan & Brayton, 1877) | F[X]:U | harelip sucker |
| +Moxostoma lachneri Robins & Raney, 1956 | F:U | greater jumprock |
| +Moxostoma macrolepidotum (Lesueur, 1817) | F:CU | shorthead redhorse ... chevalier rouge |
| Moxostoma mascotae Regan, 1907 | F:M | Mascota jumprock ... matalote de Mascota |
| Moxostoma pappillosum (Cope, 1870) | F:U | V-lip redhorse |
| *Moxostoma pisolabrum Trautman & Martin, 1951 | F:U | pealip redhorse |
| *Moxostoma poecilurum Jordan, 1877 | F:U | blacktail redhorse |
| *Moxostoma robustum (Cope, 1870) | F:U | robust redhorse |
| +Moxostoma rupiscartes Jordan & Jenkins, 1889 | F:U | striped jumprock |
| Moxostoma valenciennesi Jordan, 1885 | F:CU | greater redhorse ... chevalier jaune |
| *Thoburnia atripinnis (Bailey, 1959) | F:U | blackfin sucker |
| *Thoburnia hamiltoni Raney & Lachner, 1946 | F:U | rustyside sucker |
| *Thoburnia rhothoeca (Thoburn, 1896) | F:U | torrent sucker |
| *Xyrauchen texanus (Abbott, 1860) | F:UM | razorback sucker ... matalote jorobado |

Cobitidae—En-loaches, Sp-lochas, Fr-loches

| | | |
|---|---|---|
| Misgurnus anguillicaudatus (Cantor, 1842) | F[I]:U | oriental weatherfish |

## ORDER CHARACIFORMES

Characidae—En-characins, Sp-carácidos, Fr-characins

| | | |
|---|---|---|
| Astyanax aeneus (Günther, 1860) | F:M | banded tetra ... pepesca |
| Astyanax altior Hubbs 1936 | F:M | Yucatan tetra ... sardinita yucateca |
| Astyanax armandoi Lozano-Vilano & Contreras-Balderas, 1990 | F:M | Penjamo tetra ... sardinita de Pénjamo |
| *Astyanax mexicanus (De Filippi, 1853) | F:UM | Mexican tetra ... sardinita mexicana |
| Bramocharax caballeroi Contreras-Balderas & Rivera-Teillery, 1985 | F:M | Catemaco characin ... pepesca de Catemaco |

| SCIENTIFIC NAME | OCCURRENCE[1] | COMMON NAME (ENGLISH, SPANISH, FRENCH)[2] |
|---|---|---|
| *Brycon guatemalensis* Regan 1908 | F:M | macabi tetra ... sardinita macabí |
| *Hyphessobrycon compressus* (Meek, 1904) | F:M | Maya tetra ... sardinita plateada |
| +*Roeboides bouchellei* Fowler 1923 | F:M | crystal tetra ... sardinita cristal |

## ORDER SILURIFORMES

*Ictaluridae—En-North American catfishes, Sp-bagres de agua dulce, Fr-barbottes et barbues

| SCIENTIFIC NAME | OCCURRENCE[1] | COMMON NAME (ENGLISH, SPANISH, FRENCH)[2] |
|---|---|---|
| *Ameiurus brunneus* Jordan, 1877 | F:U | snail bullhead |
| *Ameiurus catus* (Linnaeus, 1758) | F:U | white catfish |
| *Ameiurus melas* (Rafinesque, 1820) | F:CUM[I] | black bullhead ... bagre torito negro |
| *Ameiurus natalis* (Lesueur, 1819) | F:CUM[I] | yellow bullhead ... bagre torito amarillo ... barbotte jaune |
| *Ameiurus nebulosus* (Lesueur, 1819) | F:CU | brown bullhead ... barbotte brune |
| *Ameiurus platycephalus* (Girard, 1859) | F:U | flat bullhead |
| *Ameiurus serracanthus* (Yerger & Relyea, 1968) | F:U | spotted bullhead |
| +*Ictalurus australis* (Meek, 1904) | F:M | Panuco catfish ... bagre del Pánuco |
| *Ictalurus balsanus* (Jordan & Snyder, 1899) | F:M | Balsas catfish ... bagre del Balsas |
| *Ictalurus dugesii* (Bean, 1880) | F:M | Lerma catfish ... bagre del Lerma |
| +*Ictalurus furcatus* (Lesueur, 1840) | F:UM | blue catfish ... bagre azul |
| *Ictalurus lupus* (Girard, 1858) | F:UM | headwater catfish ... bagre lobo |
| *Ictalurus mexicanus* (Meek, 1904) | F:M | Rio Verde catfish ... bagre del Verde |
| +*Ictalurus ochoterenai* (de Buen, 1946) | F:M | Chapala catfish ... bagre de Chapala |
| +*Ictalurus pricei* (Rutter, 1896) | F:UM | Yaqui catfish ... bagre yaqui |
| *Ictalurus punctatus* (Rafinesque, 1818) | F:CUM | channel catfish ... bagre de canal ... barbue de rivière |
| *Noturus albater* Taylor, 1969 | F:U | Ozark madtom |
| *Noturus baileyi* Taylor, 1969 | F:U | smoky madtom |
| *Noturus elegans* Taylor, 1969 | F:U | elegant madtom |
| *Noturus eleutherus* Jordan, 1877 | F:U | mountain madtom |
| *Noturus exilis* Nelson, 1876 | F:U | slender madtom |
| *Noturus flavater* Taylor, 1969 | F:U | checkered madtom |
| *Noturus flavipinnis* Taylor, 1969 | F:U | yellowfin madtom |
| *Noturus flavus* Rafinesque, 1818 | F:CU | stonecat ... barbotte des rapides |

| SCIENTIFIC NAME | OCCURRENCE[1] | COMMON NAME (ENGLISH, SPANISH, FRENCH)[2] |
|---|---|---|
| *Noturus funebris* Gilbert & Swain, 1891 | F:U | black madtom |
| *Noturus furiosus* Jordan & Meek, 1889 | F:U | Carolina madtom |
| *Noturus gilberti* Jordan & Evermann, 1889 | F:U | orangefin madtom |
| *Noturus gyrinus* (Mitchill, 1817) | F:CU | tadpole madtom ... chat-fou brun |
| *Noturus hildebrandi* (Bailey & Taylor, 1950) | F:U | least madtom |
| +*Noturus insignis* (Richardson, 1836) | F:C[I]U | margined madtom ... chat-fou liséré |
| *Noturus lachneri* Taylor, 1969 | F:U | Ouachita madtom |
| *Noturus leptacanthus* Jordan, 1877 | F:U | speckled madtom |
| *Noturus miurus* Jordan, 1877 | F:CU | brindled madtom |
| *Noturus munitus* Suttkus & Taylor, 1965 | F:U | frecklebelly madtom |
| *Noturus nocturnus* Jordan & Gilbert, 1886 | F:U | freckled madtom |
| *Noturus phaeus* Taylor, 1969 | F:U | brown madtom |
| *Noturus placidus* Taylor, 1969 | F:U | Neosho madtom |
| *Noturus stanauli* Etnier & Jenkins, 1980 | F:U | pygmy madtom |
| *Noturus stigmosus* Taylor, 1969 | F:CU | northern madtom |
| *Noturus taylori* Douglas, 1972 | F:U | Caddo madtom |
| *Noturus trautmani* Taylor, 1969 | F[X]:U | Scioto madtom |
| *Prietella lundbergi* Walsh & Gilbert, 1995 | F:M | phantom blindcat ... bagre ciego duende |
| *Prietella phreatophila* Carranza, 1954 | F:M | Mexican blindcat ... bagre ciego de Múzquiz |
| +*Pylodictis olivaris* (Rafinesque, 1818) | F:UM | flathead catfish ... bagre piltonte |
| *Satan eurystomus* Hubbs & Bailey, 1947 | F:U | widemouth blindcat |
| *Trogloglanis pattersoni* Eigenmann, 1919 | F:U | toothless blindcat |
| Clariidae—En-labyrinth catfishes, Sp-bagres laberintos, Fr-poissons-chats à labyrinths | | |
| *Clarias batrachus* (Linnaeus, 1758) | F[I]:U | walking catfish |
| Ariidae—En-sea catfishes, Sp-bagres marinos, Fr-poissons-chats marins | | |
| *Ariopsis assimilis* (Günther, 1864) | AM | Maya sea catfish ... bagre maya |
| *Ariopsis dasycephalus* (Günther, 1864) | PM | bigbelly sea catfish ... bagre barrigón |
| *Ariopsis felis* (Linnaeus, 1766) | A-F:UM | hardhead catfish ... bagre boca chica |
| *Ariopsis guatemalensis* (Günther, 1864) | PM | widehead sea catfish ... bagre cuatete |
| *Ariopsis kessleri* (Steindachner, 1877) | PM | sculptured sea catfish ... bagre esculpido |

| SCIENTIFIC NAME | OCCURRENCE[1] | COMMON NAME (ENGLISH, SPANISH, FRENCH)[2] |
|---|---|---|
| Ariopsis planiceps (Steindachner, 1877) | PM | flathead sea catfish ........ bagre cabeza chata |
| Ariopsis platypogon (Günther, 1864) | PM | cominate sea catfish ........ bagre cominate |
| Ariopsis seemanni (Günther, 1864) | PM | tete sea catfish ........ bagre tete |
| Bagre marinus (Mitchill, 1815) | A | gafftopsail catfish ........ bagre bandera |
| Bagre panamensis (Gill, 1863) | P | chihuil ........ bagre chihuil |
| Bagre pinnimaculatus (Steindachner, 1877) | PM | long-barbeled sea catfish ........ bagre barbón |
| +Cathorops aguadulce (Meek, 1904) | AM-F:M | estuarine sea catfish ........ bagre aguadulce |
| +Cathorops fuerthii (Steindachner, 1877) | PM | congo sea catfish ........ bagre congo |
| +Cathorops melanopus (Günther, 1864) | AM | dark sea catfish ........ bagre prieto |
| +Cathorops spixii (Agassiz, 1829) | AM | raspfin sea catfish ........ bagre cuinchi |
| Galeichthys peruvianus Lütken, 1874 | PM | Peruvian sea catfish ........ bagre de faja |
| Potamarius nelsoni (Evermann & Goldsborough, 1902) | AM-F:M | Lacandon sea catfish ........ bagre lacandón |
| Sciadeops troschelii (Gill, 1863) | PM | chili sea catfish ........ bagre chili |
| Sciades hymenorrhinus (Bleeker, 1862) | PM | flapnose sea catfish ........ bagre moreno |

*Doradidae—En-thorny catfishes, Sp-bagres sierra, Fr-poissons-chats épineux

| | | |
|---|---|---|
| *Platydoras armatulus (Valenciennes, 1840) | F[I]:U | southern striped Raphael |

*Pimelodidae—Er-longwhiskered catfishes, Sp-juiles, Fr-poissons-chats à longues moustaches

| | | |
|---|---|---|
| +Rhamdia guatemalensis (Günther, 1864) | F:M | pale catfish ........ juil descolorido |
| +Rhamdia laticauda (Kner, 1858) | F:M | rock catfish ........ juil de Jamapa |
| +Rhamdia macuspanensis Weber & Wilkens, 1998 | F:M | Olmec blind catfish ........ juil ciego olmeca |
| +Rhamdia parryi Eigenmann & Eigenmann, 1888 | F:M | Tonala catfish ........ juil de Tonalá |
| +Rhamdia reddelli Miller, 1984 | F:M | blindwhiskered catfish ........ juil ciego |
| +Rhamdia zongolicensis Wilkens, 1993 | F:M | Oaxaca catfish ........ juil oaxaqueño |

*Callichthyidae—En-callichthyid armored catfishes, Sp-coridoras, Fr-poissons-chats cuirassés

| | | |
|---|---|---|
| *Hoplosternum littorale (Hancock, 1828) | F[I]:U | brown hoplo |

*Loricariidae—En-suckermouth armored catfishes, Sp-plecóstomas, Fr-loricariidés

| | | |
|---|---|---|
| *Hypostomus plecostomus (Linnaeus, 1758) | F[I]:U | suckermouth catfish |
| *Pterygoplichthys anisitsi Eigenmann & Kennedy, 1903 | F[I]:U | southern sailfin catfish |

| SCIENTIFIC NAME | OCCURRENCE[1] | COMMON NAME (ENGLISH, SPANISH, FRENCH)[2] |
|---|---|---|
| *Pterygoplichthys disjunctivus* (Weber, 1991) | F[I]:U | vermiculated sailfin catfish |
| *Pterygoplichthys multiradiatus* (Hancock, 1828) | F[I]:UM | Orinoco sailfin catfish ............ plecóstoma del Orinoco |
| *Pterygoplichthys pardalis* (Castelnau, 1855) | F[I]:U | Amazon sailfin catfish |

**ORDER GYMNOTIFORMES**

*Gymnotidae—En-nakedback knifefishes, Sp-cuchillos, Fr-poissons-couteaux

| | | |
|---|---|---|
| *Gymnotus maculosus* Albert & Miller, 1995 | F:M | spotted knifefish ............ cuchillo |

**\*ORDER ESOCIFORMES**

+Esocidae—En-pikes, Sp-lucios, Fr-brochets

| | | |
|---|---|---|
| *Esox americanus* Gmelin, 1789 | F:CU | redfin pickerel ............ brochet d'Amérique |
| *Esox lucius* Linnaeus, 1758 | F:CU | northern pike ............ grand brochet |
| *Esox masquinongy* Mitchill, 1824 | F:CU | muskellunge ............ maskinongé |
| *Esox niger* Lesueur, 1818 | F:CU | chain pickerel ............ brochet maillé |

+Umbridae—En-mudminnows, Sp-peces del fango, Fr-umbres

| | | |
|---|---|---|
| *Dallia pectoralis* Bean, 1880 | F:U | Alaska blackfish |
| *Novumbra hubbsi* Schultz, 1929 | F:U | Olympic mudminnow |
| +*Umbra limi* (Kirtland, 1840) | F:CU | central mudminnow |
| *Umbra pygmaea* (DeKay, 1842) | F:U | eastern mudminnow |

**\*ORDER ARGENTINIFORMES**

Argentinidae—En-argentines, Sp-argentinas, Fr-argentines

| | | |
|---|---|---|
| *Argentina sialis* Gilbert, 1890 | P | Pacific argentine ............ argentina del Pacífico |
| *Argentina silus* (Ascanius, 1775) | A | Atlantic argentine |
| *Argentina striata* Goode & Bean, 1896 | A | striated argentine ............ argentina estriada |
| *Glossanodon pygmaeus* Cohen, 1958 | A | pygmy argentine |

| SCIENTIFIC NAME | OCCURRENCE[1] | COMMON NAME (ENGLISH, SPANISH, FRENCH)[2] |
|---|---|---|

+Bathylagidae—En-deepsea smelts, Sp-capellanes mesopelágicos, Fr-garcettes

| | | |
|---|---|---|
| +Leuroglossus schmidti Rass, 1955 | P | northern smoothtongue |
| +Leuroglossus stilbius Gilbert, 1890 | P | California smoothtongue .......lengualisa californiana |

Opisthoproctidae—En-spookfishes, Sp-peces duende, Fr-revenants

| | | |
|---|---|---|
| Macropinna microstoma Chapman, 1939 | P | barreleye |

+ORDER SALMONIFORMES

+Osmeridae—En-smelts, Sp-capellanes, Fr-éperlans

| | | |
|---|---|---|
| Allosmerus elongatus (Ayres, 1854) | P | whitebait smelt |
| Hypomesus nipponensis McAllister, 1963 | F[I]:U | wakasagi |
| +Hypomesus olidus (Pallas, 1814) | F:CU | pond smelt |
| *Hypomesus pretiosus (Girard, 1854) | F:CU-P | surf smelt |
| Hypomesus transpacificus McAllister, 1963 | F:U-P | delta smelt |
| Mallotus villosus (Müller, 1776) | A-F:C-P | capelin ........................capelan |
| +Osmerus mordax (Mitchill, 1814) | A-F:CU-P | rainbow smelt ..................éperlan arc-en-ciel |
| Spirinchus starksi (Fisk, 1913) | P | night smelt |
| Spirinchus thaleichthys (Ayres, 1860) | F:CU-P | longfin smelt |
| Thaleichthys pacificus (Richardson, 1836) | F:CU-P | eulachon |

+Salmonidae—En-trouts and salmons, Sp-truchas y salmones, Fr-truites et saumons

| | | |
|---|---|---|
| *Coregonus artedi Lesueur, 1818 | F:CU | cisco .......................................cisco de lac |
| Coregonus autumnalis (Pallas, 1776) | F:CU | Arctic cisco |
| +Coregonus clupeaformis (Mitchill, 1818) | A-F:CU | lake whitefish ............................grand corégone |
| *Coregonus hoyi (Milner, 1874) | F:CU | bloater |
| *Coregonus huntsmani Scott, 1987 | A-F:C | Atlantic whitefish |
| Coregonus johannae (Wagner, 1910) | F[X]:CU | deepwater cisco |
| Coregonus kiyi (Koelz, 1921) | F:CU | kiyi |
| Coregonus laurettae Bean, 1881 | F:CU | Bering cisco |

| SCIENTIFIC NAME | OCCURRENCE[1] | COMMON NAME (ENGLISH, SPANISH, FRENCH)[2] |
|---|---|---|
| Coregonus nasus (Pallas, 1776) | F:CU | broad whitefish |
| *Coregonus nigripinnis (Milner, 1874) | F:CU | blackfin cisco |
| *Coregonus pidschian (Gmelin, 1789) | F:U | humpback whitefish |
| *Coregonus reighardi (Koelz, 1924) | F[X]:CU | shortnose cisco |
| Coregonus sardinella Valenciennes, 1848 | F:CU | least cisco |
| +Coregonus zenithicus (Jordan & Evermann, 1909) | F:CU | shortjaw cisco |
| +Oncorhynchus chrysogaster (Needham & Gard, 1964) | F:M | Mexican golden trout .......... trucha dorada mexicana |
| *Oncorhynchus clarkii (Richardson, 1836) | F:CUM-P | cutthroat trout .......... trucha degollada .......... truite fardée |
| +Oncorhynchus gilae (Miller, 1950) | F:U | Gila trout |
| *Oncorhynchus gorbuscha (Walbaum, 1792) | F:CU-P | pink salmon |
| *Oncorhynchus keta (Walbaum, 1792) | F:CU-P | chum salmon |
| *Oncorhynchus kisutch (Walbaum, 1792) | F:CU-P | coho salmon .......... salmón plateado .......... saumon coho |
| +Oncorhynchus mykiss (Walbaum, 1792) | A[I]-F:CUM-P | rainbow trout .......... trucha arcoiris .......... truite arc-en-ciel |
| +Oncorhynchus nerka (Walbaum, 1792) | F:CU-P | sockeye salmon .......... saumon rouge |
| *Oncorhynchus tshawytscha (Walbaum, 1792) | F:CU-P | Chinook salmon .......... salmón boquinegra .......... saumon chinook |
| Prosopium abyssicola (Snyder, 1919) | F:U | Bear Lake whitefish |
| *Prosopium coulterii (Eigenmann & Eigenmann, 1892) | F:CU | pygmy whitefish |
| *Prosopium cylindraceum (Pennant, 1784) | F:CU | round whitefish .......... ménomini rond |
| Prosopium gemmifer (Snyder, 1919) | F:U | Bonneville cisco |
| Prosopium spilonotus (Snyder, 1919) | F:U | Bonneville whitefish |
| Prosopium williamsoni (Girard, 1856) | F:CU | mountain whitefish |
| +Salmo salar Linnaeus, 1758 | A-F:CU-P[I] | Atlantic salmon .......... saumon atlantique |
| Salmo trutta Linnaeus, 1758 | A[I]-F[I]:CU | brown trout .......... truite brune |
| +Salvelinus alpinus (Linnaeus, 1758) | A-F:CU-P | Arctic char .......... omble chevalier |
| *Salvelinus confluentus (Suckley, 1859) | F:CU-P | bull trout |
| +Salvelinus fontinalis (Mitchill, 1814) | A-F:CUM[I] | brook trout .......... trucha de arroyo .......... omble de fontaine |
| Salvelinus malma (Walbaum, 1792) | F:CU-P | Dolly Varden |
| Salvelinus namaycush (Walbaum, 1792) | F:CU | lake trout .......... touladi |
| *Stenodus leucichthys (Güldenstädt, 1772) | F:CU | inconnu |
| Thymallus arcticus (Pallas, 1776) | F:CU | Arctic grayling |

| SCIENTIFIC NAME | OCCURRENCE[1] | COMMON NAME (ENGLISH, SPANISH, FRENCH)[2] |
|---|---|---|

**ORDER STOMIIFORMES**

*Sternoptychidae—En-marine hatchetfishes, Sp-peces hacha, Fr-haches d'argent

| | | |
|---|---|---|
| *Maurolicus weitzmani* Parin & Kobyliansky, 1993 | A | Atlantic pearlside |
| *Polyipnus clarus* Harold, 1994 | A | slope hatchetfish |

*Phosichthyidae—En-lightfishes, Sp-peces luminosos, Fr-poissons étoilés

| | | |
|---|---|---|
| *Pollichthys mauli* (Poll, 1953) | A | stareye lightfish |

+Stomiidae—En-dragonfishes, Sp-peces demonios, Fr-dragons à écailles

| | | |
|---|---|---|
| *Chauliodus macouni* Bean, 1890 | P | Pacific viperfish ... víbora del Pacífico |
| *Stomias boa* (Risso, 1810) | A | boa dragonfish |
| *Tactostoma macropus* Bolin, 1939 | P | longfin dragonfish |

**ORDER AULOPIFORMES**

Aulopidae—En-flagfins, Sp-aulópidos, Fr-limberts

| | | |
|---|---|---|
| *Aulopus bajacali* Parin & Kotlyar, 1984 | PM | eastern Pacific flagfin ... lagarto del Pacífico oriental |
| *Aulopus filamentosus* (Bloch, 1792) | A | yellowfin aulopus |

Chlorophthalmidae—En-greeneyes, Sp-ojiverdes, Fr-yeux-verts

| | | |
|---|---|---|
| *Chlorophthalmus agassizi* Bonaparte, 1840 | A | shortnose greeneye ... ojiverde chato |
| *Parasudis truculenta* (Goode & Bean, 1896) | A | longnose greeneye ... ojiverde truculento |

Scopelarchidae—En-pearleyes, Sp-ojos de perla, Fr-yeux-perlés

| | | |
|---|---|---|
| *Benthalbella dentata* (Chapman, 1939) | P | northern pearleye ... perlado norteño |

Synodontidae—En-lizardfishes, Sp-chiles, Fr-poissons-lézards

| | | |
|---|---|---|
| *Saurida brasiliensis* Norman, 1935 | A | largescale lizardfish ... chile brasileño |
| *Saurida caribbaea* Breder, 1927 | A | smallscale lizardfish ... chile caribeño |
| *Saurida normani* Longley, 1935 | A | shortjaw lizardfish ... chile espinoso |

| SCIENTIFIC NAME | OCCURRENCE[1] | COMMON NAME (ENGLISH, SPANISH, FRENCH)[2] |
|---|---|---|
| Synodus evermanni Jordan & Bollman, 1890 | PM | spotted lizardfish ... chile cadena |
| Synodus foetens (Linnaeus, 1766) | A | inshore lizardfish ... chile apestoso |
| *Synodus intermedius (Spix & Agassiz, 1829) | A | sand diver ... chile manchado |
| Synodus lacertinus Gilbert, 1890 | PM | calico lizardfish ... chile lagarto |
| Synodus lucioceps (Ayres, 1855) | P | California lizardfish ... chile lucio |
| Synodus poeyi Jordan, 1887 | A | offshore lizardfish ... chile barbado |
| *Synodus saurus (Linnaeus, 1758) | A | bluestripe lizardfish |
| Synodus scituliceps Jordan & Gilbert, 1882 | PM | lance lizardfish ... chile arpón |
| Synodus sechurae Hildebrand, 1946 | PM | iguana lizardfish ... chile iguana |
| Synodus synodus (Linnaeus, 1758) | A | red lizardfish ... chile rojo |
| Trachinocephalus myops (Forster, 1801) | A | snakefish ... chile chato |

*Paralepididae—En-barracudinas, Sp-barracudinas, Fr-lussions

| | | |
|---|---|---|
| *Arctozenus risso (Bonaparte, 1840) | A | white barracudina ... lussion blanc |
| *Magnisudis atlantica (Krøyer 1868) | A-P | duckbill barracudina ... barracudina pico de pato |

Anotopteridae—En-daggertooths, Sp-dagas, Fr-pharaons

| | | |
|---|---|---|
| *Anotopterus nikparini Kukuev, 1998 | P | North Pacific daggertooth ... daga |
| Anotopterus pharao Zugmayer, 1911 | A | daggertooth |

Alepisauridae—En-lancetfishes, Sp-lanzones, Fr-cavalos

| | | |
|---|---|---|
| Alepisaurus brevirostris Gibbs, 1960 | A | shortnose lancetfish |
| Alepisaurus ferox Lowe, 1833 | A-P | longnose lancetfish ... lanzón picudo |

ORDER MYCTOPHIFORMES

+Myctophidae—En-lanternfishes, Sp-linternillas, Fr-poissons-lanternes

| | | |
|---|---|---|
| +Benthosema glaciale (Reinhardt, 1837) | A | glacier lanternfish |
| Ceratoscopelus townsendi (Eigenmann & Eigenmann, 1889) | P | dogtooth lampfish ... diente de perro |
| Diaphus theta Eigenmann & Eigenmann, 1890 | P | California headlightfish ... linternilla californiana |
| *Diogenichthys laternatus (Garman, 1899) | P | Diogenes lanternfish ... linternilla de Diogenes |

| SCIENTIFIC NAME | OCCURRENCE[1] | COMMON NAME (ENGLISH, SPANISH, FRENCH)[2] |
|---|---|---|
| Lampadena speculigera Goode & Bean, 1896 | A | mirror lanternfish |
| Lampanyctus crocodilus (Risso, 1810) | A | jewel lanternfish |
| Myctophum affine (Lütken, 1892) | A | metallic lanternfish |
| Myctophum punctatum Rafinesque, 1810 | A | spotted lanternfish |
| *Nannobrachium regale (Gilbert, 1892) | P | pinpoint lampfish ... linternilla puntita |
| *Notoscopelus resplendens (Richardson, 1845) | A-P | patchwork lampfish ... linternilla brillante |
| Protomyctophum crockeri (Bolin, 1939) | P | California flashlightfish ... linternilla luciérnaga |
| Stenobrachius leucopsarus (Eigenmann & Eigenmann, 1890) | P | northern lampfish ... linternilla norteña |
| Tarletonbeania crenularis (Jordan & Gilbert, 1880) | P | blue lanternfish ... linternilla azul |
| Triphoturus mexicanus (Gilbert, 1890) | P | Mexican lampfish ... linternilla mexicana |

## *ORDER LAMPRIDIFORMES

*Lamprididae—En-opahs, Sp-opahs, Fr-opahs

| | | |
|---|---|---|
| Lampris guttatus (Brünnich, 1788) | A-P | opah ... opah |

Stylephoridae—En-tube-eyes, Sp-ojilargos, Fr-stylephoridés

| | | |
|---|---|---|
| Stylephorus chordatus Shaw, 1791 | A | tube-eye |

Lophotidae—En-crestfishes, Sp-peces flecos, Fr-poissons crêtés

| | | |
|---|---|---|
| Eumecichthys fiski (Günther, 1890) | A | unicornfish |
| *Lophotus capellei Temminck & Schlegel, 1845 | P | North Pacific crestfish |
| *Lophotus lacepede Giorna, 1809 | A | crestfish ... fleco de gallo |

Trachipteridae—En-ribbonfishes, Sp-listoncillos, Fr-trachiptères

| | | |
|---|---|---|
| Desmodema lorum Rosenblatt & Butler, 1977 | P | whiptail ribbonfish ... listoncillo látigo |
| *Desmodema polystictum (Ogilby, 1898) | A | polka-dot ribbonfish |
| Trachipterus altivelis Kner, 1859 | P | king-of-the-salmon ... rey de los salmones |
| Trachipterus arcticus (Brünnich, 1788) | A | dealfish |
| Trachipterus fukuzakii Fitch, 1964 | P | tapertail ribbonfish ... listoncillo pabilo |
| *Zu cristatus (Bonelli, 1819) | A-P | scalloped ribbonfish ... listoncillo festón |

| SCIENTIFIC NAME | OCCURRENCE[1] | COMMON NAME (ENGLISH, SPANISH, FRENCH)[2] |
|---|---|---|
| | | Regalecidae—En-oarfishes, Sp-peces remo, Fr-régalées |
| *Regalecus glesne Ascanius, 1772 | A-P | oarfish..............rey de los arenques |
| **ORDER POLYMIXIIFORMES** | | |
| | | Polymixiidae—En-beardfishes, Sp-colas de maguey, Fr-poissons à barbe |
| Polymixia lowei Günther, 1859 | A | beardfish................cola de maguey |
| **+ORDER PERCOPSIFORMES** | | |
| | | Percopsidae—En-trout-perches, Sp-percas falsas, Fr-omiscos |
| Percopsis omiscomaycus (Walbaum, 1792) | F:CU | trout-perch..............omisco |
| Percopsis transmontana (Eigenmann & Eigenmann, 1892) | F:U | sand roller |
| | | Aphredoderidae—En-pirate perches, Sp-percas pirata, Fr-perches-pirates |
| Aphredoderus sayanus (Gilliams, 1824) | F:U | pirate perch |
| | | Amblyopsidae—En-cavefishes, Sp-peces cavernícolas, Fr-amblyopes |
| *Amblyopsis rosae (Eigenmann, 1898) | F:U | Ozark cavefish |
| Amblyopsis spelaea DeKay, 1842 | F:U | northern cavefish |
| Chologaster cornuta Agassiz, 1853 | F:U | swampfish |
| *Forbesichthys agassizii (Putnam, 1872) | F:U | spring cavefish |
| Speoplatyrhinus poulsoni Cooper & Kuehne, 1974 | F:U | Alabama cavefish |
| Typhlichthys subterraneus Girard, 1859 | F:U | southern cavefish |
| **ORDER OPHIDIIFORMES** | | |
| | | Carapidae—En-pearlfishes, Sp-perleros, Fr-aurins |
| Carapus bermudensis (Jones, 1874) | A | pearlfish..............perlero del Atlántico |
| Echiodon dawsoni Williams & Shipp, 1982 | A | chain pearlfish |

| SCIENTIFIC NAME | OCCURRENCE[1] | COMMON NAME (ENGLISH, SPANISH, FRENCH)[2] |
|---|---|---|
| Echiodon exsilium Rosenblatt, 1961 | PM | nocturnal pearlfish ............ perlero nocturno |
| Encheliophis dubius (Putnam, 1874) | PM | Pacific pearlfish ............ perlero del Pacífico |
| Encheliophis vermicularis Müller, 1842 | PM | finless pearlfish ............ perlero mocho |

Ophidiidae—En-cusk-eels, Sp-brótulas y congriperlas, Fr-donzelles

| SCIENTIFIC NAME | OCCURRENCE[1] | COMMON NAME (ENGLISH, SPANISH, FRENCH)[2] |
|---|---|---|
| *Brotula barbata (Bloch & Schneider, 1801) | A | Atlantic bearded brotula ......... brótula barbona |
| Brotula clarkae Hubbs, 1944 | PM | Pacific bearded brotula ...... lengua rosada |
| Brotula ordwayi Hildebrand & Barton, 1949 | PM | fore-spotted brotula ...... lengua pintada |
| Chilara taylori (Girard, 1858) | P | spotted cusk-eel...... congriperla moteada |
| Lepophidium brevibarbe (Cuvier, 1829) | A | blackedge cusk-eel ...... congriperla clarín |
| Lepophidium jeannae Fowler, 1941 | A | mottled cusk-eel ...... congriperla jaspeada |
| Lepophidium microlepis (Gilbert, 1890) | PM | finescale cusk-eel ...... congriperla plateada |
| Lepophidium negropinna Hildebrand & Barton, 1949 | PM | specklefin cusk-eel ...... congriperla pinta |
| Lepophidium pardale (Gilbert, 1890) | PM | leopard cusk-eel ...... congriperla leopardo |
| Lepophidium pheromystax Robins, 1960 | AM | upsilon cusk-eel ...... congriperla bigotona |
| Lepophidium profundorum (Gill, 1863) | A | fawn cusk-eel ...... congriperla amarilla |
| Lepophidium prorates (Jordan & Bollman, 1890) | PM | prowspine cusk-eel ...... congriperla cornuda |
| Lepophidium staurophor Robins, 1959 | AM | barred cusk-eel ...... congriperla rayada |
| Lepophidium stigmatistium (Gilbert, 1890) | PM | Mexican cusk-eel ...... congriperla mexicana |
| *Neobythites gilli Goode & Bean, 1885 | A | twospot brotula ...... brótula amarillenta |
| *Neobythites marginatus Goode & Bean, 1886 | A | stripefin brotula |
| Neobythites stelliferoides Gilbert, 1890 | PM | thread brotula ...... brótula de hebra |
| *Ophidion antipholus Lea & Robins, 2003 | A | longnose cusk-eel...... congriperla narizón |
| *Ophidion dromio Lea & Robins, 2003 | A | shorthead cusk-eel |
| Ophidion galeoides (Gilbert, 1890) | PM | spotfin cusk-eel ...... congriperla adornada |
| +Ophidion grayi (Fowler, 1948) | A | blotched cusk-eel |
| *Ophidion holbrookii Putnam, 1874 | A | bank cusk-eel...... congriperla de bajos |
| Ophidion imitator Lea, 1997 | PM | mimic cusk-eel ...... congriperla mimética |
| Ophidion iris Breder, 1936 | PM | brighteye cusk-eel ...... congriperla arcoiris |
| *Ophidion josephi Girard, 1858 | A | crested cusk-eel ...... congriperla crestada |
| Ophidion marginatum (DeKay, 1842) | A | striped cusk-eel |
| Ophidion nocomis Robins & Böhlke, 1959 | AM | letter opener...... congriperla nacarada |

| SCIENTIFIC NAME | OCCURRENCE[1] | COMMON NAME (ENGLISH, SPANISH, FRENCH)[2] |
|---|---|---|
| *Ophidion robinsi Fahay, 1992 | A | colonial cusk-eel |
| Ophidion scrippsae (Hubbs, 1916) | P | basketweave cusk-eel........congriperla canastera |
| Ophidion selenops Robins & Böhlke, 1959 | A | mooneye cusk-eel |
| Otophidium chickcharney Böhlke & Robins, 1959 | AM | ghost cusk-eel........congriperla fantasma |
| Otophidium dormitator Böhlke & Robins, 1959 | A | sleeper cusk-eel |
| Otophidium indefatigabile Jordan & Bollman, 1890 | PM | Panamic cusk-eel........congriperla cabezona |
| *Otophidium omostigma (Jordan & Gilbert, 1882) | A | polka-dot cusk-eel........congriperla lunareja |
| Parophidion lagochila Böhlke & Robins, 1959 | AM | harelip cusk-eel........congriperla labio leporino |
| Parophidion schmidti (Woods & Kanazawa, 1951) | A | dusky cusk-eel........congriperla parda |
| Petrotyx hopkinsi Heller & Snodgrass, 1903 | PM | velvetnose brotula........brótula hocico terciopelado |
| Petrotyx sanguineus (Meek & Hildebrand, 1928) | A | redfin brotula........brótula aletiroja |

Bythitidae—En-viviparous brotulas, Sp-bróltulas vivíparas, Fr-donzelles vivipares

| | | |
|---|---|---|
| Brosmophycis marginata (Ayres, 1854) | P | red brotula........brótula roja |
| Calamopteryx goslinei Böhlke & Cohen, 1966 | AM | longarm brotula........brótula aletona |
| +Calamopteryx robinsorum Cohen, 1973 | AM | teacher brotula........brótula del profesor |
| *Grammonus claudei (de la Torre y Huerta, 1930) | A | reef-cave brotula |
| *Grammonus diagrammus (Heller & Snodgrass, 1903) | P | purple brotula........brótula púrpura |
| Gunterichthys longipenis Dawson, 1966 | A | gold brotula |
| *Ogilbia cayorum Evermann & Kendall, 1898 | A | key brotula........brótula rojiza |
| +Ogilbia pearsei (Hubbs, 1938) | F:M | Mexican blind brotula........dama blanca ciega |
| Ogilbia ventralis Gill, 1863 | PM | Gulf brotula........brótula del Golfo |
| Stygnobrotula latebricola Böhlke, 1957 | A | black brotula |

+ORDER GADIFORMES

Macrouridae—En-grenadiers, Sp-granaderos, Fr-grenadiers

| | | |
|---|---|---|
| Albatrossia pectoralis (Gilbert, 1892) | P | giant grenadier |
| Caelorinchus caelorhincus (Risso, 1810) | A | saddled grenadier........granadero tristón |
| Caelorinchus caribbaeus (Goode & Bean, 1885) | A | blackfin grenadier........granadero caribeño |
| *Caelorinchus scaphopsis (Gilbert, 1890) | P | shoulderspot grenadier........granadero carepala |
| *Macrourus berglax Lacepède, 1801 | A | roughhead grenadier |

| SCIENTIFIC NAME | OCCURRENCE[1] | COMMON NAME (ENGLISH, SPANISH, FRENCH)[2] |
|---|---|---|
| *Malacocephalus occidentalis Goode & Bean, 1385 | A | western softhead grenadier ..... granadero carapacho |
| *Nezumia bairdii (Goode & Bean, 1877) | A | marlin-spike ..... grenadier du Grand Banc |
| Nezumia sclerorhynchus (Valenciennes, 1838) | A | bluntsnout grenadier |
| Nezumia stelgidolepis (Gilbert, 1890) | P | California grenadier |
| *Steindachneriidae—En-luminous hakes, Sp-molleras, Fr-steindachnériidés | | |
| Steindachneria argentea Goode & Bean, 1896 | A | luminous hake ..... mollera luminosa |
| +Moridae—En-codlings, Sp-moras y carboneros, Fr-moros | | |
| Antimora microlepis Bean, 1890 | P | Pacific flatnose ..... mora viola |
| *Laemonema barbatulum Goode & Bean, 1883 | A | shortbeard codling |
| Physiculus fulvus Bean, 1884 | A | metallic codling ..... carbonero metálico |
| Physiculus nematopus Gilbert, 1890 | PM | charcoal codling ..... carbonero de fango |
| Physiculus rastrelliger Gilbert, 1890 | P | hundred-fathom codling ..... carbonero negro |
| Physiculus talarae Hildebrand & Barton, 1949 | PM | Peruvian codling ..... carbonero peruano |
| +Bregmacerotidae—En-codlets, Sp-bacaletes, Fr-varlets | | |
| Bregmaceros atlanticus Goode & Bean, 1886 | A | antenna codlet ..... bacalete antena |
| Bregmaceros bathymaster Jordan & Bollman, 1890 | PM | East Pacific codlet ..... bacalete del Pacífico oriental |
| *Bregmaceros cantori Milliken & Houde, 1984 | A | striped codlet ..... bacalete rayado |
| Bregmaceros houdei Saksena & Richards, 1986 | A | stellate codlet |
| *Phycidae—En-phycid hakes, Sp-merluzas barbonas, Fr-phycidés | | |
| +Ciliata septentrionalis (Collett, 1875) | A | northern rockling |
| +Enchelyopus cimbrius (Linnaeus, 1766) | A | fourbeard rockling ..... motelle à quatre barbillons |
| +Urophycis chesteri (Goode & Bean, 1878) | A | longfin hake |
| Urophycis chuss (Walbaum, 1792) | A | red hake ..... merluche-écureuil |
| *Urophycis cirrata (Goode & Bean, 1896) | A | Gulf hake ..... merluza barbona del Golfo |
| *Urophycis earllii (Bean, 1880) | A | Carolina hake |
| Urophycis floridana (Bean & Dresel, 1884) | A | southern hake ..... merluza barbona floridana |
| Urophycis regia (Walbaum, 1792) | A | spotted hake ..... merluza barbona reina |
| Urophycis tenuis (Mitchill, 1814) | A | white hake ..... merluche blanche |

| SCIENTIFIC NAME | OCCURRENCE[1] | COMMON NAME (ENGLISH, SPANISH, FRENCH)[2] |
|---|---|---|
| \*Merlucciidae—En-merlucciid hakes, Sp-merluzas, Fr-merlus | | |
| Merluccius albidus (Mitchill, 1818) | A | offshore hake |
| Merluccius angustimanus Garman, 1899 | PM | Panama hake ... merluza panameña |
| Merluccius bilinearis (Mitchill, 1814) | A | silver hake ... merlu argenté |
| +Merluccius hernandezi Mathews, 1985 | PM | Cortez hake ... merluza de Cortés |
| Merluccius productus (Ayres, 1855) | P | Pacific hake ... merluza norteña |
| +Gadidae—En-cods, Sp-bacalaos, Fr-morues | | |
| \*Arctogadus borisovi Dryagin, 1932 | A-P | toothed cod |
| \*Arctogadus glacialis (Peters, 1872) | A-P | polar cod |
| Boreogadus saida (Lepechin, 1774) | A-P | Arctic cod ... saïda franc |
| +Brosme brosme (Ascanius, 1772) | A | cusk ... brosme |
| Eleginus gracilis (Tilesius, 1810) | P | saffron cod |
| Gadus macrocephalus Tilesius, 1810 | P | Pacific cod |
| Gadus morhua Linnaeus, 1758 | A | Atlantic cod ... morue franche |
| +Gadus ogac Richardson, 1836 | A-P | Greenland cod ... ogac |
| +Lota lota (Linnaeus, 1758) | F:CU | burbot ... lotte |
| Melanogrammus aeglefinus (Linnaeus, 1758) | A | haddock ... aiglefin |
| Microgadus proximus (Girard, 1854) | P | Pacific tomcod |
| Microgadus tomcod (Walbaum, 1792) | A-F:CU | Atlantic tomcod ... poulamon atlantique |
| \*Micromesistius poutassou (Risso, 1827) | A | blue whiting |
| +Molva molva (Linnaeus, 1758) | A | European ling |
| Pollachius virens (Linnaeus, 1758) | A | pollock ... goberge |
| Theragra chalcogramma (Pallas, 1814) | P | walleye pollock |

## ORDER BATRACHOIDIFORMES

| | | |
|---|---|---|
| Batrachoididae—En-toadfishes, Sp-peces sapo, Fr-poissons-crapauds | | |
| Batrachoides gilberti Meek & Hildebrand, 1928 | AM | large-eye toadfish ... sapo ojón |
| Batrachoides goldmani Evermann & Goldsborough, 1902 | F:M | Mexican freshwater toadfish ... sapo mexicano |
| Batrachoides waltersi Collette & Russo, 1981 | PM | multipored toadfish ... sapo peludo |

| SCIENTIFIC NAME | OCCURRENCE[1] | COMMON NAME (ENGLISH, SPANISH, FRENCH)[2] |
|---|---|---|
| *Opsanus beta (Goode & Bean, 1880) | A | Gulf toadfish ......... sapo boquiblanca |
| Opsanus dichrostomus Collette, 2001 | AM | bicolor toadfish ......... sapo bicolor |
| *Opsanus pardus (Goode & Bean, 1880) | A | leopard toadfish ......... sapo leopardo |
| Opsanus tau (Linnaeus, 1766) | A | oyster toadfish |
| Porichthys analis Hubbs & Schultz, 1939 | PM | darkedge midshipman ......... sapo de luto |
| Porichthys ephippiatus Walker & Rosenblatt, 1988 | PM | saddle midshipman ......... sapo ensillado |
| Porichthys greenei Gilbert & Starks, 1904 | PM | shorthead midshipman ......... sapo cabeza corta |
| Porichthys margaritatus (Richardson, 1844) | PM | pearlspot midshipman ......... sapo luminoso |
| Porichthys mimeticus Walker & Rosenblatt, 1988 | PM | mimetic midshipman ......... sapo mimético |
| Porichthys myriaster Hubbs & Schultz, 1939 | P | specklefin midshipman ......... sapo aleta pintada |
| Porichthys notatus Girard, 1854 | P | plainfin midshipman ......... sapo aleta lucia |
| Porichthys plectrodon Jordan & Gilbert, 1882 | A | Atlantic midshipman ......... doradilla |
| Sanopus johnsoni Collette & Starck, 1974 | AM | Cozumel toadfish ......... sapo de Cozumel |
| Sanopus reticulatus Collette, 1983 | AM | reticulate toadfish ......... sapo reticulado |
| Sanopus splendidus Collette, Starck & Phillips, 1974 | AM | splendid toadfish ......... sapo magnífico |

## ORDER LOPHIIFORMES

Lophiidae—En-goosefishes, Sp-rapes pescadores, Fr-baudroies

| | | |
|---|---|---|
| Lophiodes caulinaris (Garman, 1899) | P | spottedtail goosefish ......... rape rabo manchado |
| Lophiodes reticulatus Caruso & Suttkus, 1979 | A | reticulate goosefish ......... rape hocicón |
| *Lophiodes spilurus (Garman, 1899) | P | threadfin goosefish ......... rape de hebra |
| +Lophius americanus Valenciennes, 1837 | A | goosefish ......... baudroie d'Amérique |
| *Lophius gastrophysus Miranda-Ribeiro, 1915 | A | blackfin goosefish ......... rape pescador |

Artennariidae—En-frogfishes, Sp-ranisapos, Fr-antennaires

| | | |
|---|---|---|
| Antennarius avalonis Jordan & Starks, 1907 | P | roughjaw frogfish ......... ranisapo antenado |
| Antennarius multiocellatus (Valenciennes, 1837) | A | longlure frogfish ......... ranisapo ceboso |
| Antennarius ocellatus (Bloch & Schneider, 1801) | A | ocellated frogfish ......... ranisapo pescador |
| Antennarius pauciradiatus Schultz, 1957 | A | dwarf frogfish ......... ranisapo enano |
| Antennarius radiosus Garman, 1896 | A | singlespot frogfish ......... ranisapo uniocelado |

| SCIENTIFIC NAME | OCCURRENCE[1] | COMMON NAME (ENGLISH, SPANISH, FRENCH)[2] |
|---|---|---|
| *Antennarius sanguineus* Gill, 1863 | PM | sanguine frogfish ............... ranisapo sangrón |
| *Antennarius striatus* (Shaw, 1794) | A | striated frogfish ............... ranisapo estriado |
| *Antennatus strigatus* (Gill, 1863) | PM | bandtail frogfish ............... ranisapo rabo listado |
| *Histrio histrio* (Linnaeus, 1758) | A | sargassumfish ............... pez sargazo |
| Chaunacidae—En-gapers, Sp-gómitas Fr-crapauds de mer | | |
| *Chaunax stigmaeus* Fowler, 1946 | A | redeye gaper |
| Ogcocephalidae—En-batfishes, Sp-murciélagos, Fr-chauves-souris de mer | | |
| *Dibranchus atlanticus* Peters, 1876 | A | Atlantic batfish |
| *Halieutichthys aculeatus* (Mitchill, 1818) | A | pancake batfish ............... murciélago picudo |
| *Ogcocephalus corniger* Bradbury, 1980 | A | longnose batfish |
| *Ogcocephalus cubifrons* (Richardson, 1836) | A | polka-dot batfish ............... murciélago diablo |
| *Ogcocephalus declivirostris* Bradbury, 1980 | A | slantbrow batfish ............... murciélago inclinado |
| *Ogcocephalus nasutus* (Cuvier, 1829) | A | shortnose batfish ............... murciélago tapacaminos |
| *Ogcocephalus pantostictus* Bradbury, 1980 | A | spotted batfish ............... murciélago manchado |
| *Ogcocephalus parvus* Longley & Hildebrand, 1940 | A | roughback batfish ............... murciélago lomo áspero |
| *Ogcocephalus rostellum* Bradbury, 1980 | A | palefin batfish |
| *Zalieutes elater* (Jordan & Gilbert, 1882) | P | roundel batfish ............... murciélago biocelado |
| *Zalieutes mcgintyi* (Fowler, 1952) | A | tricorn batfish ............... murciélago tres cuernos |
| Himantolophidae—En-footballfishes, Sp-peces balón, Fr-poissons-football | | |
| *Himantolophus groenlandicus* Reinhardt, 1837 | A | Atlantic footballfish |
| *Himantolophus sagamius* (Tanaka, 1918) | P | Pacific footballfish |
| Ceratiidae—En-seadevils, Sp-peces anzuelo, Fr-poissons-pêcheurs | | |
| *Cryptopsaras couesii* Gill, 1883 | A-P | triplewart seadevil ............... anzuelo diablo |

*ORDER MUGILIFORMES

| | | |
|---|---|---|
| Mugilidae—En-mullets, Sp-lisas, Fr-muges | | |
| *Agonostomus monticola* (Bancroft, 1834) | A-F:UM-PM | mountain mullet ............... trucha de tierra caliente |

| SCIENTIFIC NAME | OCCURRENCE[1] | COMMON NAME (ENGLISH, SPANISH, FRENCH)[2] |
|---|---|---|
| *Chaenomugil proboscideus* (Günther, 1861) | PM | snouted mullet ... lisa hocicona |
| *Joturus pichardi* Poey, 1860 | AM | bobo mullet ... bobo |
| *Mugil cephalus* Linnaeus, 1758 | A-F:UM-P | striped mullet ... lisa rayada |
| *Mugil curema* Valenciennes, 1836 | A-F:UM-P | white mullet ... lisa blanca |
| \**Mugil gyrans* (Jordan & Gilbert, 1884) | A | whirligig mullet ... lisa carrusel |
| *Mugil hospes* Jordan & Culver, 1895 | PM | hospe mullet ... lisa hospe |
| *Mugil liza* Valenciennes, 1836 | A | liza |
| *Mugil setosus* Gilbert, 1892 | PM | liseta mullet ... lisa liseta |
| \**Mugil species* | A | redeye mullet |
| \**Mugil trichodon* Poey, 1875 | A | fantail mullet ... lisa amarilla |
| *Xenomugil thoburni* (Jordan & Starks, 1896) | PM | orange-eye mullet ... lisa agugú |

+ORDER ATHERINIFORMES

\*Atherinopsidae—En-New World silversides, Sp-charales y pejerreyes, Fr-poissons d'argent

| | | |
|---|---|---|
| *Atherinella alvarezi* (Díaz-Pardo, 1972) | F:M | Gulf silverside ... plateadito de Tacotalpa |
| *Atherinella ammophila* Chernoff & Miller, 1984 | F:M | La Palma silverside ... plateadito de La Palma |
| *Atherinella balsana* (Meek, 1902) | F:M | Balsas silverside ... plateadito del Balsas |
| *Atherinella callida* Chernoff, 1986 | F:M | cunning silverside ... plateadito del Refugio |
| *Atherinella crystallina* (Jordan & Culver, 1895) | F:M | blackfin silverside ... plateadito del Presidio |
| *Atherinella elegans* Chernoff, 1986 | F:M | Fuerte silverside ... plateadito del Fuerte |
| *Atherinella eriarcha* Jordan & Gilbert, 1882 | PM | longfin silverside ... plateadito plateado |
| *Atherinella guatemalensis* (Günther, 1864) | F:M | peppered silverside ... plateadito de Huamuchal |
| *Atherinella lisa* (Meek, 1904) | F:M | naked silverside ... plateadito del Hule |
| *Atherinella marvelae* (Chernoff & Miller, 1982) | F:M | Eyipantla silverside ... plateadito de Eyipantla |
| *Atherinella nepenthe* (Myers & Wade, 1942) | PM | pitcher silverside ... plateadito marino |
| *Atherinella pellosemion* Chernoff, 1986 | F:M | Mancuernas silverside ... plateadito del Mancuernas |
| *Atherinella sallei* (Regan, 1903) | F:M | large-eye silverside ... plateadito del Papaloapan |
| *Atherinella schultzi* (Alvarez & Carranza, 1952) | F:M | Chimalapa silverside ... plateadito de Chimalapa |
| *Atherinops affinis* (Ayres, 1860) | P | topsmelt ... pejerrey pescadillo |
| *Atherinopsis californiensis* Girard, 1854 | P | jacksmelt ... pejerrey mocho |

| SCIENTIFIC NAME | OCCURRENCE[1] | COMMON NAME (ENGLISH, SPANISH, FRENCH)[2] |
|---|---|---|
| *Chirostoma aculeatum* Barbour, 1973 | F:M | scowling silverside ........ charal cuchillo |
| *Chirostoma arge* (Jordan & Snyder, 1899) | F:M | largetooth silverside ........ charal del Verde |
| *Chirostoma attenuatum* Meek, 1902 | F:M | slender silverside ........ charal prieto |
| *Chirostoma bartoni* Jordan & Evermann, 1896 | F:M | Alberca silverside ........ charal de la Caldera |
| *Chirostoma chapalae* Jordan & Snyder, 1899 | F:M | smallmouth silverside ........ charal de Chapala |
| *Chirostoma charari* (de Buen, 1945) | F:M | least silverside ........ charal tarasco |
| *Chirostoma consocium* Jordan & Hubbs, 1919 | F:M | ranch silverside ........ charal de rancho |
| *Chirostoma contrerasi* Barbour, 2002 | F:M | Ajijic silverside ........ charal de Ajijic |
| *Chirostoma estor* Jordan, 1880 | F:M | pike silverside ........ pescado blanco |
| *Chirostoma grandocule* (Steindachner, 1894) | F:M | bigeye silverside ........ charal de lago |
| *Chirostoma humboldtianum* (Valenciennes, 1835) | F:M | shortfin silverside ........ charal de Xochimilco |
| *Chirostoma jordani* Woolman, 1894 | F:M | mesa silverside ........ charal |
| *Chirostoma labarcae* Meek, 1902 | F:M | sharpnose silverside ........ charal de La Barca |
| *Chirostoma lucius* Boulenger, 1900 | F:M | longjaw silverside ........ charal de la Laguna |
| *Chirostoma melanoccus* Alvarez, 1963 | F:M | blunthead silverside ........ charal de San Juanico |
| *Chirostoma mezquital* Meek, 1904 | F:M | Mezquital silverside ........ charal del Mezquital |
| *Chirostoma patzcuaro* Meek, 1902 | F:M | Patzcuaro silverside ........ charal pinto |
| *Chirostoma promelas* Jordan & Snyder, 1899 | F:M | blacknose silverside ........ charal boca negra |
| *Chirostoma riojai* Solórzano & López, 1966 | F:M | Toluca silverside ........ charal de Santiago |
| *Chirostoma sphyraena* Boulenger, 1900 | F:M | bigmouth silverside ........ charal barracuda |
| *Colpichthys hubbsi* Crabtree, 1989 | PM | delta silverside ........ pejerrey delta |
| *Colpichthys regis* (Jenkins & Evermann, 1889) | PM | false grunion ........ pejerrey charal |
| *Labidesthes sicculus* (Cope, 1865) | F:CU | brook silverside ........ crayon d'argent |
| *Leuresthes sardina* (Jenkins & Evermann, 1889) | PM | Gulf grunion ........ pejerrey sardina |
| *Leuresthes tenuis* (Ayres, 1860) | P | California grunion ........ pejerrey californiano |
| *Melanorhinus cyanellus* (Meek & Hildebrand, 1923) | PM | blackback silverside ........ pejerrey azulado |
| +*Membras gilberti* (Jordan & Bollman, 1890) | PM | landia silverside ........ pejerrey landia |
| *\*Membras martinica* (Valenciennes, 1835) | A-F:UM | rough silverside ........ pejerrey rasposo |
| *\*Menidia audens* Hay, 1882 | F:U | Mississippi silverside |
| *\*Menidia beryllina* (Cope, 1867) | A-F:UM | inland silverside ........ plateadito salado |
| *Menidia clarkhubbsi* Echelle & Mosier, 1982 | A | Texas silverside |

| SCIENTIFIC NAME | OCCURRENCE[1] | COMMON NAME (ENGLISH, SPANISH, FRENCH)[2] |
|---|---|---|
| *Menidia colei* Hubbs, 1936 | F:M | golden silverside ........ plateadito de Progreso |
| +*Menidia conchorum* Hildebrand & Ginsburg, 1927 | A | key silverside |
| *Menidia extensa* Hubbs & Raney, 1946 | F:U | Waccamaw silverside |
| *Menidia menidia* (Linnaeus, 1766) | A | Atlantic silverside ........................ capucette |
| *Menidia peninsulae* (Goode & Bean, 1879) | A | tidewater silverside ........ plateadito playero |
| *Poblana alchichica* de Buen, 1945 | F:M | Alchichica silverside ........ charal de Alchichica |
| *Poblana ferdebueni* Solórzano & López, 1965 | F:M | Chignahuapan silverside ........ charal de Almoloya |
| *Poblana letholepis* Alvarez, 1950 | F:M | La Preciosa silverside ........ charal de La Preciosa |
| *Poblana squamata* Alvarez, 1950 | F:M | Quechulac silverside ........ charal de Quechulac |

*Atherinidae—En-Old World silversides, Sp-tinícalos Fr-athérines

| | | |
|---|---|---|
| *Atherinomorus stipes* (Müller & Troschel, 1848) | A | hardhead silverside ........ tinícalo cabezón |
| *Hypoatherina harringtonensis* (Goode, 1877) | A | reef silverside ........ tinícalo de arrecife |

## *ORDER BELONIFORMES

Belonidae—En-needlefishes, Sp-agujones, Fr-aiguillettes

| | | |
|---|---|---|
| *Ablennes hians* (Valenciennes, 1846) | A-PM | flat needlefish ........ agujón sable |
| *Platybelone argalus* (Lesueur, 1821) | A-PM | keeltail needlefish ........ agujón de quilla |
| *Strongylura exilis* (Girard, 1854) | P | California needlefish ........ agujón californiano |
| *Strongylura hubbsi* Collette, 1974 | F:M | Maya needlefish ........ agujón maya |
| *Strongylura marina* (Walbaum, 1792) | A-F:UM | Atlantic needlefish ........ agujón verde |
| *Strongylura notata* (Poey, 1860) | A | redfin needlefish ........ agujón negro |
| *Strongylura timucu* (Walbaum, 1792) | A | timucu ........ agujón timucú |
| *Tylosurus acus* (Lacepède, 1803) | A | Atlantic agujon ........ agujón del Atlántico |
| *Tylosurus crocodilus* (Péron & Lesueur, 1821) | A-PM | houndfish ........ agujón lisero |
| +*Tylosurus pacificus* (Steindachner, 1876) | PM | Pacific agujon ........ agujón del Pacífico |

Scomberesocidae—En-sauries, Sp-papardas, Fr-balaous

| | | |
|---|---|---|
| *Cololabis saira* (Brevoort, 1856) | P | Pacific saury ........ paparda del Pacífico |
| *Scomberesox saurus* (Walbaum, 1792) | A | Atlantic saury |

| SCIENTIFIC NAME | OCCURRENCE[1] | COMMON NAME (ENGLISH, SPANISH, FRENCH)[2] | |
|---|---|---|---|
| **+Exocoetidae— En-flyingfishes, Sp-voladores, Fr-exocets** | | | |
| *Cheilopogon atrisignis (Jenkins, 1903) | PM | glider flyingfish | volador planeador |
| *Cheilopogon cyanopterus (Valenciennes, 1847) | A | margined flyingfish | volador azul |
| Cheilopogon dorsomacula (Fowler, 1944) | PM | blackspot flyingfish | volador lomo manchado |
| *Cheilopogon exsiliens (Linnaeus, 1771) | A | bandwing flyingfish | volador campechano |
| *Cheilopogon furcatus (Mitchill, 1815) | A-PM | spotfin flyingfish | volador ala manchada |
| *Cheilopogon heterurus (Rafinesque, 1810) | P | blotchwing flyingfish | volador ala lunada |
| *Cheilopogon melanurus (Valenciennes, 1847) | A | Atlantic flyingfish | volador blanquito |
| Cheilopogon papilio (Clark, 1936) | PM | butterfly flyingfish | volador mariposa |
| *Cheilopogon pinnatibarbatus (Bennett, 1831) | P | smallhead flyingfish | volador cabecita |
| Cheilopogon spilonotopterus (Bleeker, 1866) | PM | stained flyingfish | volador jaspeado |
| Cheilopogon xenopterus (Gilbert, 1890) | PM | whitetip flyingfish | volador puntas blancas |
| Cypselurus angusticeps Nichols & Breder, 1935 | PM | narrowhead flyingfish | volador isleño |
| Cypselurus callopterus (Günther, 1866) | PM | beautyfin flyingfish | volador bonito |
| Cypselurus comatus (Mitchill, 1815) | A | clearwing flyingfish | |
| Exocoetus monocirrhus Richardson, 1846 | PM | barbel flyingfish | volador barbudo |
| Exocoetus obtusirostris Günther, 1866 | A | oceanic two-wing flyingfish | volador flecha |
| Exocoetus volitans Linnaeus, 1758 | A-PM | tropical two-wing flyingfish | volador tropical |
| *Fodiator acutus (Valenciennes, 1847) | P | sharpchin flyingfish | volador picudo |
| Hirundichthys affinis (Günther, 1866) | A | fourwing flyingfish | volador golondrina |
| Hirundichthys marginatus (Nichols & Breder, 1928) | PM | bladewing flyingfish | volador ala navaja |
| *Hirundichthys rondeletii (Valenciennes, 1847) | A-P | blackwing flyingfish | volador ala negra |
| Hirundichthys speculiger (Valenciennes, 1847) | PM | mirrorwing flyingfish | volador espejo |
| +Oxyporhamphus micropterus (Valenciennes, 1847) | A-PM | smallwing flyingfish | volador alita |
| +Parexocoetus brachypterus (Richardson, 1846) | A | sailfin flyingfish | volador aletón |
| *Prognichthys occidentalis Parin, 1999 | A | bluntnose flyingfish | volador chato |
| Prognichthys sealei Abe, 1955 | PM | sailor flyingfish | volador marinero |
| Prognichthys tringa Breder, 1928 | PM | Panamic flyingfish | volador panámico |
| **\*Hemiramphidae—En-halfbeaks, Sp-pajaritos, Fr-demi-becs** | | | |
| Chriodorus atherinoides Goode & Bean, 1882 | A | hardhead halfbeak | pajarito cabezidura |

| SCIENTIFIC NAME | OCCURRENCE[1] | COMMON NAME (ENGLISH, SPANISH, FRENCH)[2] |
|---|---|---|
| *Euleptorhamphus velox* Poey, 1868 | A | flying halfbeak ........ agujeta voladora |
| *Euleptorhamphus viridis* (van Hasselt, 1823) | P | ribbon halfbeak ........ agujeta alargada |
| *Hemiramphus balao* Lesueur, 1821 | A | balao ........ agujeta balao |
| *Hemiramphus brasiliensis* (Linnaeus, 1758) | A | ballyhoo ........ agujeta brasileña |
| *Hemiramphus saltator* Gilbert & Starks, 1904 | P | longfin halfbeak ........ pajarito saltador |
| *Hyporhamphus gilli* Meek & Hildebrand, 1923 | PM | choelo halfbeak ........ pajarito cholo |
| *Hyporhamphus meeki* Banford & Collette, 1993 | A | false silverstripe halfbeak ........ agujeta flaca |
| *Hyporhamphus mexicanus* Alvarez, 1959 | F:M | Mexican halfbeak ........ pajarito mexicano |
| *Hyporhamphus naos* Banford & Collette, 2001 | P | Pacific silverstripe halfbeak ........ pajarito blanco del Pacífico |
| *Hyporhamphus rosae* (Jordan & Gilbert, 1880) | P | California halfbeak ........ pajarito californiano |
| *Hyporhamphus snyderi* Meek & Hildebrand, 1923 | PM | skipper halfbeak ........ pajarito choca |
| *Hyporhamphus unifasciatus* (Ranzani, 1842) | A | Atlantic silverstripe halfbeak ........ pajarito blanco del Atlántico |

## *ORDER CYPRINODONTIFORMES

### *Aplocheilidae—En-rivulines, Sp-almirantes, Fr-aplochéilidés

| | | |
|---|---|---|
| *Millerichthys robustus* (Miller & Hubbs, 1974) | F:M | Mexican rivulus ........ almirante mexicano |
| *Rivulus hartii* (Boulenger, 1890) | F[I]:U | giant rivulus |
| *Rivulus marmoratus* Poey, 1880 | A-F:UM | mangrove rivulus ........ almirante de manglar |
| *Rivulus tenuis* (Meek, 1904) | F:M | Maya rivulus ........ almirante del Hule |

### *Profundulidae—En-Middle American killifishes, Sp-escamudos, Fr-profundulidés

| | | |
|---|---|---|
| *Profundulus candalarius* Hubbs, 1924 | F:M | headwater killifish ........ escamudo de Comitán |
| *Profundulus hildebrandi* Miller, 1950 | F:M | Chiapas killifish ........ escamudo de San Cristóbal |
| *Profundulus labialis* (Günther, 1866) | F:M | largelip killifish ........ escamudo bocón |
| *Profundulus oaxacae* (Meek, 1902) | F:M | Oaxaca killifish ........ escamudo oaxaqueño |
| *Profundulus punctatus* (Günther, 1866) | F:M | brownspotted killifish ........ escamudo pinto |

### *Fundulidae—En-topminnows, Sp-sardinillas, Fr-fondules

| | | |
|---|---|---|
| *Adinia xenica* (Jordan & Gilbert, 1882) | A | diamond killifish |

| SCIENTIFIC NAME[1] | OCCURRENCE[1] | COMMON NAME (ENGLISH, SPANISH, FRENCH)[2] |
|---|---|---|
| Fundulus albolineatus Gilbert, 1891 | F[X]:U | whiteline topminnow |
| Fundulus bifax Cashner & Rogers, 1988 | F:U | stippled studfish |
| *Fundulus blairae Wiley & Hall, 1975 | F:U | western starhead topminnow |
| Fundulus catenatus (Storer, 1846) | F:U | northern studfish |
| Fundulus chrysotus (Günther, 1866) | F:U | golden topminnow |
| +Fundulus cingulatus Valenciennes, 1846 | F:U | banded topminnow |
| Fundulus confluentus Goode & Bean, 1879 | A-F:U | marsh killifish |
| Fundulus diaphanus (Lesueur, 1817) | F:CU | banded killifish ... fondule barré |
| +Fundulus dispar (Agassiz, 1854) | F:U | starhead topminnow |
| *Fundulus escambiae (Bollman, 1887) | F:U | russetfin topminnow |
| Fundulus euryzonus Suttkus & Cashner, 1981 | F:U | broadstripe topminnow |
| *Fundulus grandis Baird & Girard, 1853 | A-F:UM | Gulf killifish ... sardinilla del Pánuco |
| Fundulus grandissimus Hubbs, 1936 | AM-F:M | giant killifish ... sardinilla gigante |
| Fundulus heteroclitus (Linnaeus, 1766) | A-F:CU | mummichog ... choquemort |
| Fundulus jenkinsi (Evermann, 1892) | A-F:UM | saltmarsh topminnow ... sardinilla del Bravo |
| Fundulus julisia Williams & Etnier, 1982 | F:U | Barrens topminnow |
| *Fundulus kansae Garman, 1895 | F:U | northern plains killifish |
| Fundulus lima Vaillant, 1894 | F:M | Baja California killifish ... sardinilla peninsular |
| Fundulus lineolatus (Agassiz, 1854) | F:U | lined topminnow |
| Fundulus luciae (Baird, 1855) | A-F:U | spotfin killifish |
| +Fundulus majalis (Walbaum, 1792) | A | striped killifish |
| Fundulus notatus (Rafinesque, 1820) | F:CU | blackstripe topminnow |
| *Fundulus nottii (Agassiz, 1854) | F:U | bayou topminnow |
| Fundulus olivaceus (Storer, 1845) | F:U | blackspotted topminnow |
| Fundulus parvipinnis Girard, 1854 | F:UM-P | California killifish ... sardinilla chococo |
| Fundulus persimilis Miller, 1955 | AM-F:M | Yucatan killifish ... sardinilla yucateca |
| Fundulus pulvereus (Evermann, 1892) | A-F:UM | bayou killifish ... sardinilla mulata |
| Fundulus rathbuni Jordan & Meek, 1889 | F:U | speckled killifish |
| *Fundulus rubrifrons (Jordan, 1880) | F:U | redface topminnow |
| Fundulus sciadicus Cope, 1865 | F:U | plains topminnow |
| Fundulus seminolis Girard, 1859 | F:U | Seminole killifish |

| SCIENTIFIC NAME | OCCURRENCE[1] | COMMON NAME (ENGLISH, SPANISH, FRENCH)[2] |
|---|---|---|
| +*Fundulus similis* (Baird & Girard, 1853) | A-F:M | longnose killifish .................. sardinilla narigona |
| *Fundulus stellifer* (Jordan, 1877) | F:U | southern studfish |
| *Fundulus waccamensis* Hubbs & Raney, 1946 | F:U | Waccamaw killifish |
| +*Fundulus zebrinus* Jordan & Gilbert, 1883 | F:U | plains killifish |
| *Leptolucania ommata* (Jordan, 1884) | F:U | pygmy killifish |
| *Lucania goodei* Jordan, 1880 | F:U | bluefin killifish |
| *Lucania interioris* Hubbs & Miller, 1965 | F:M | Cuatro Ciénegas killifish ........ sardinilla de Cuatro Ciénegas |
| *Lucania parva* (Baird & Girard, 1855) | A-F:UM-P[I] | rainwater killifish ................. sardinilla de lluvia |

*Anablepidae—En-four-eyed fishes, Sp-cuatrojos, Fr-poissons à quatre yeux

| | | |
|---|---|---|
| +*Anableps dowi* Gill, 1861 | F:M | northern four-eye .................. cuatrojos |

Poeciliidae—En-livebearers, Sp-topotes y espadas, Fr-poecilies

| | | |
|---|---|---|
| *Belonesox belizanus* Kner, 1860 | A-F:U[I]M | pike killifish ....................... picudito |
| *Brachyrhaphis hartwegi* Rosen & Bailey, 1963 | F:M | Soconusco gambusia ............ guayacón de Soconusco |
| *Carlhubbsia kidderi* (Hubbs, 1936) | F:M | Champoton gambusia .......... guayacón de Champotón |
| *Gambusia affinis* (Baird & Girard, 1853) | A-F:C[I]UM | western mosquitofish .......... guayacón mosquito |
| *Gambusia alvarezi* Hubbs & Springer, 1957 | F:M | yellowfin gambusia ............. guayacón de San Gregorio |
| *Gambusia amistadensis* Peden, 1973 | F[X]:U | Amistad gambusia |
| *Gambusia atrora* Rosen & Bailey, 1963 | F:M | blackfin gambusia ............... guayacón de San Luis |
| *Gambusia aurata* Miller & Minckley, 1970 | F:M | golden gambusia .................. guayacón dorado |
| *Gambusia eurystoma* Miller, 1975 | F:M | widemouth gambusia ........... guayacón del Azufre |
| *Gambusia gaigei* Hubbs, 1929 | F:U | Big Bend gambusia |
| *Gambusia geiseri* Hubbs & Hubbs, 1957 | F:U | largespring gambusia |
| *Gambusia georgei* Hubbs & Peden, 1969 | F[X]:U | San Marcos gambusia |
| *Gambusia heterochir* Hubbs, 1957 | F[X]:U | Clear Creek gambusia |
| *Gambusia holbrooki* Girard, 1859 | A-F:U | eastern mosquitofish |
| *Gambusia hurtadoi* Hubbs & Springer, 1957 | F:M | crescent gambusia ............... guayacón de Hacienda de Dolores |
| *Gambusia krumholzi* Minckley, 1963 | F:M | spotfin gambusia ................. guayacón del Nava |
| *Gambusia longispinis* Minckley, 1962 | F:M | Cuatro Cienegas gambusia ...... guayacón de Cuatro Ciénegas |
| *Gambusia marshi* Minckley & Craddock, 1962 | F:M | robust gambusia .................. guayacón de Nadadores |
| *Gambusia nobilis* (Baird & Girard, 1853) | F:U | Pecos gambusia |

| SCIENTIFIC NAME | OCCURRENCE[1] | COMMON NAME (ENGLISH, SPANISH, FRENCH)[2] | |
|---|---|---|---|
| +*Gambusia panuco* Hubbs, 1926 | F:M | Panuco gambusia | guayacón del Pánuco |
| +*Gambusia regani* Hubbs, 1926 | F:M | Forlon gambusia | guayacón del Forlón |
| *Gambusia rhizophorae* Rivas, 1969 | A-F:U | mangrove gambusia | |
| *Gambusia senilis* Girard, 1859 | F:UM | blotched gambusia | guayacón del Bravo |
| *Gambusia sexradiata* Hubbs, 1936 | F:M | stippled gambusia | guayacón del sureste |
| *Gambusia speciosa* Girard, 1859 | F:UM | Tex-Mex gambusia | guayacón de Nuevo León |
| *Gambusia vittata* Hubbs, 1926 | F:M | Gulf gambusia | guayacón de Victoria |
| *Gambusia yucatana* Regan, 1914 | F:M | Yucatan gambusia | guayacón yucateco |
| *Heterandria bimaculata* (Heckel, 1848) | F:M | spottail killifish | guatopote manchado |
| +*Heterandria formosa* Agassiz, 1855 | F:U | least killifish | |
| *Heterandria jonesii* (Günther, 1874) | F:M | barred killifish | guatopote listado |
| *Heterophallus echeagarayi* (Alvarez, 1952) | F:M | Maya gambusia | guayacón maya |
| *Heterophallus milleri* Radda, 1987 | F:M | Grijalva gambusia | guayacón del Grijalva |
| *Heterophallus rachovii* Regan, 1914 | F:M | Coatzacoalcos gambusia | guayacón jarocho |
| *Phallichthys fairweatheri* Rosen & Bailey, 1959 | F:M | picotee livebearer | topo |
| *Poecilia butleri* Jordan, 1889 | F:M | Pacific molly | topote del Pacífico |
| *Poecilia catemaconis* Miller, 1975 | F:M | bicolor molly | topote de Catemaco |
| *Poecilia chica* Miller, 1975 | F:M | dwarf molly | topote del Purificación |
| *Poecilia formosa* (Girard, 1859) | F:UM | Amazon molly | topote amazona |
| +*Poecilia latipinna* (Lesueur, 1821) | A-F:C[I]UM | sailfin molly | topote velo negro |
| *Poecilia latipunctata* Meek, 1904 | F:M | Tamesi molly | topote del Tamesí |
| *Poecilia maylandi* Meyer, 1983 | F:M | Balsas molly | topote del Balsas |
| *Poecilia mexicana* Steindachner, 1863 | F:U[I]M | shortfin molly | topote del Atlántico |
| +*Poecilia orri* Fowler, 1943 | AM-F:M | mangrove molly | topote de manglar |
| *Poecilia petenensis* (Günther, 1866) | F:M | Peten molly | topote lacandón |
| *Poecilia reticulata* Peters, 1859 | F[I]:UM | guppy | gupi |
| *Poecilia sphenops* Valenciennes, 1846 | F:U[I]M | Mexican molly | topote mexicano |
| *Poecilia sulphuraria* (Alvarez, 1948) | F:M | sulphur molly | topote de Teapa |
| *Poecilia velifera* (Regan, 1914) | F:M | Yucatan molly | topote aleta grande |
| *Poeciliopsis baenschi* Meyer, Radda, Riehl & Feichtinger, 1986 | F:M | golden livebearer | guatopote dorado |
| *Poeciliopsis balsas* Hubbs, 1926 | F:M | Balsas livebearer | guatopote del Balsas |

| SCIENTIFIC NAME | OCCURRENCE[1] | COMMON NAME (ENGLISH, SPANISH, FRENCH)[2] |
|---|---|---|
| *Poeciliopsis catemaco* Miller, 1975 | F:M | Catemaco livebearer ................. guatopote blanco |
| *Poeciliopsis fasciata* (Meek, 1904) | F:M | San Jeronimo livebearer ......... guatopote de San Jerónimo |
| +*Poeciliopsis gracilis* (Heckel, 1848) | F:U[I]M | porthole livebearer ................. guatopote jarocho |
| *Poeciliopsis hnilickai* Meyer & Vogel, 1981 | F:M | upper Grijalva livebearer ......... guatopote de Ixtapa |
| *Poeciliopsis infans* (Woolman, 1894) | F:M | Lerma livebearer ................. guatopote del Lerma |
| *Poeciliopsis latidens* (Garman, 1895) | F:M | lowland livebearer ................. guatopote del Fuerte |
| *Poeciliopsis lucida* Miller, 1960 | F:M | clearfin livebearer ................. guatopote del Mocorito |
| +*Poeciliopsis lutzi* (Meek, 1902) | F:M | Oaxaca livebearer ................. guatopote oaxaqueño |
| *Poeciliopsis monacha* Miller, 1960 | F:M | headwater livebearer ......... guatopote del Mayo |
| +*Poeciliopsis occidentalis* (Baird & Girard, 1853) | F:UM | Gila topminnow ................. guatopote de Sonora |
| *Poeciliopsis pleurospilus* (Günther, 1866) | F:M | largespot livebearer ................. guatopote manchote |
| *Poeciliopsis presidionis* (Jordan & Culver, 1895) | F:M | Sinaloa livebearer ................. guatopote de Sinaloa |
| *Poeciliopsis prolifica* Miller, 1960 | F:M | blackstripe livebearer ......... guatopote culiche |
| +*Poeciliopsis scarlli* Meyer, Riehl, Dawes & Dibble, 1985 | F:M | Michoacan livebearer ......... guatopote michoacano |
| *Poeciliopsis turneri* Miller, 1975 | F:M | blackspotted livebearer ......... guatopote de La Huerta |
| +*Poeciliopsis turrubarensis* (Meek, 1912) | F:M | barred livebearer ................. guatopote del Pacífico |
| *Poeciliopsis viriosa* Miller, 1960 | F:M | chubby livebearer ................. guatopote gordito |
| *Priapella bonita* (Meek, 1904) | F:M | graceful priapella ................. guayacón bonito |
| *Priapella compressa* Alvarez, 1948 | F:M | Palenque priapella ................. guayacón de Palenque |
| *Priapella intermedia* Alvarez & Carranza, 1952 | F:M | isthmian priapella ................. guayacón de Chimalapa |
| *Priapella olmecae* Meyer & Espinosa-Pérez, 1990 | F:M | Olmec priapella ................. guayacón olmeca |
| *Xenodexia ctenolepis* Hubbs, 1950 | F:M | Grijalva studfish ................. topo del Grijalva |
| *Xiphophorus alvarezi* Rosen, 1960 | F:M | Chiapas swordtail ................. espada de Comitán |
| *Xiphophorus andersi* Meyer & Schartl, 1979 | F:M | spiketail platyfish ................. espada del Atoyac |
| *Xiphophorus birchmanni* Lechner & Radda, 1987 | F:M | sheepshead swordtail ......... espada del Tempoal |
| *Xiphophorus clemenciae* Alvarez, 1959 | F:M | Coatzacoalcos swordtail ......... espada de Clemencia |
| *Xiphophorus continens* Rauchenberger, Kallman & Morizot, 1990 | F:M | short-sword platyfish ......... espada de Quince |
| *Xiphophorus cortezi* Rosen, 1960 | F:M | delicate swordtail ................. espada fina |
| +*Xiphophorus couchianus* (Girard, 1859) | F:M | Monterrey platyfish ......... espada de Monterrey |
| *Xiphophorus evelynae* Rosen, 1960 | F:M | reticulate platyfish ......... espada del Necaxa |
| *Xiphophorus gordoni* Miller & Minckley, 1963 | F:M | Cuatro Cienegas platyfish ......... espada de Cuatro Ciénegas |

| SCIENTIFIC NAME | OCCURRENCE[1] | COMMON NAME (ENGLISH, SPANISH, FRENCH)[2] |
|---|---|---|
| *Xiphophorus hellerii Heckel, 1848 | F: U[I]M | green swordtail ... cola de espada |
| Xiphophorus maculatus (Günther, 1866) | F:U[I]M | southern platyfish ... espada sureña |
| Xiphophorus malinche | | |
| Rauchenberger, Kallman & Morizot, 1990 | F:M | highland swordtail ... espada de Malinche |
| +Xiphophorus meyeri Schartl & Schröder, 1988 | F:M | marbled swordtail ... espada de Múzquiz |
| Xiphophorus milleri Rosen, 1960 | F:M | Catemaco platyfish ... espada de Catemaco |
| Xiphophorus montezumae Jordan & Snyder, 1899 | F:M | Moctezuma swordtail ... espada de Moctezuma |
| Xiphophorus mutilineatus | | |
| Rauchenberger, Kallman & Morizot, 1990 | F:M | barred swordtail ... espada pigmea rayada |
| Xiphophorus nezahualcoyotl | | |
| Rauchenberger, Kallman & Morizot, 1990 | F:M | mountain swordtail ... espada montañes |
| Xiphophorus nigrensis Rosen, 1960 | F:M | Panuco swordtail ... espada pigmea El Abra |
| Xiphophorus pygmaeus Hubbs & Gordon, 1943 | F:M | pygmy swordtail ... espada pigmea delgada |
| Xiphophorus variatus (Meek, 1904) | F:U[I]M | variable platyfish ... espada de Valles |
| Xiphophorus xiphidium (Gordon, 1932) | F:M | swordtail platyfish ... espada del Soto La Marina |
| *Goodeidae—En-goodeids, Sp-mexcalpiques, Fr-goodéidés | | |
| Allodontichthys hubbsi Miller & Uyeno, 1980 | F:M | whitepatch splitfin ... mexcalpique de Tuxpan |
| Allodontichthys polylepis Rauchenberger, 1988 | F:M | finescale splitfin ... mexcalpique escamitas |
| Allodontichthys tamazulae Turner, 1946 | F:M | peppered splitfin ... mexcalpique de Tamazula |
| Allodontichthys zonistius (Hubbs, 1932) | F:M | bandfin splitfin ... mexcalpique de Colima |
| Alloophorus robustus (Bean, 1892) | F:M | bulldog goodeid ... chegua |
| Allotoca catarinae (de Buen, 1942) | F:M | Catarina allotoca ... tiro Catarina |
| Allotoca diazi (Meek, 1902) | F:M | Patzcuaro allotoca ... chorumo |
| Allotoca dugesii (Bean, 1887) | F:M | bumblebee allotoca ... tiro chato |
| Allotoca goslinei Smith & Miller, 1987 | F:M | banded allotoca ... tiro listado |
| Allotoca maculata Smith & Miller, 1980 | F:M | blackspot allotoca ... tiro manchado |
| Allotoca meeki (Alvarez, 1959) | F:M | Zirahuen allotoca ... tiro de Zirahuén |
| Allotoca regalis (Alvarez, 1959) | F:M | Balsas allotoca ... chorumo del Balsas |
| Allotoca zacapuensis Meyer, Rada & Domínguez, 2001 | F:M | Zacapu allotoca ... tiro de Zacapu |
| Ameca splendens Miller & Fitzsimons, 1971 | F:M | butterfly splitfin ... mexcalpique mariposa |
| Ataeniobius toweri (Meek, 1904) | F:M | bluetail splitfin ... mexcalpique cola azul |

| SCIENTIFIC NAME | OCCURRENCE[1] | COMMON NAME (ENGLISH, SPANISH, FRENCH)[2] |
|---|---|---|
| Chapalichthys encaustus (Jordan & Snyder, 1899) | F:M | barred splitfin ................... pintito de Ocotlán |
| +Chapalichthys pardalis Alvarez, 1963 | F:M | polka-dot splitfin ................ pintito de Tocumbo |
| +Chapalichthys peraticus Alvarez, 1963 | F[X]:M | alien splitfin ..................... pintito de San Juanico |
| Characodon audax Smith & Miller, 1986 | F:M | bold characodon ................. mexcalpique del Toboso |
| Characodon garmani Jordan & Evermann, 1898 | F[X]:M | Parras characodon ............... mexcalpique de Parras |
| Characodon lateralis Günther, 1866 | F:M | rainbow characodon ............ mexcalpique arcoíris |
| +Crenichthys baileyi (Gilbert, 1893) | F:U | White River springfish |
| +Crenichthys nevadae Hubbs, 1932 | F:U | Railroad Valley springfish |
| +Empetrichthys latos Miller, 1948 | F:U | Pahrump poolfish |
| +Empetrichthys merriami Gilbert, 1893 | F[X]:U | Ash Meadows poolfish |
| Girardinichthys multiradiatus (Meek, 1904) | F:M | darkedged splitfin ............... mexcalpique de Zempoala |
| Girardinichthys viviparus (Bustamante, 1837) | F:M | Chapultepec splitfin ............ mexcalpique |
| +Goodea atripinnis Jordan, 1880 | F:M | blackfin goodea ................. tiro |
| +Goodea gracilis Hubbs & Turner, 1939 | F:M | dusky goodea .................... tiro oscuro |
| +Goodea luitpoldii (Steindachner, 1894) | F:M | green goodea .................... tiro de Pátzcuaro |
| Hubbsina turneri de Buen, 1940 | F:M | highland splitfin ................. mexcalpique michoacano |
| Ilyodon cortesae (Paulo-Maya & Trujillo-Jiménez, 2000) | F:M | freckled splitfin ................. mexcalpique pecoso |
| +Ilyodon furcidens (Jordan & Gilbert, 1882) | F:M | goldbreast splitfin .............. mexcalpique de Armería |
| +Ilyodon lennoni Meyer & Förster, 1983 | F:M | Chacambero splitfin ............ mexcalpique de Chacambero |
| +Ilyodon whitei (Meek, 1904) | F:M | Balsas splitfin .................... mexcalpique cola partida |
| +Ilyodon xantusi (Hubbs & Turner, 1939) | F:M | Limones splitfin ................. mexcalpique de Los Limones |
| Skiffia bilineata (Bean, 1887) | F:M | twoline skiffia .................... tiro de dos rayas |
| +Skiffia francesae Kingston, 1978 | F:M | golden skiffia .................... tiro dorado |
| Skiffia lermae Meek, 1902 | F:M | olive skiffia ....................... tiro olivo |
| Skiffia multipunctata (Pellegrin, 1901) | F:M | splotched skiffia ................ tiro pintado |
| Xenoophorus captivus (Hubbs, 1924) | F:M | relict splitfin .................... mexcalpique viejo |
| Xenotaenia resolanae Turner, 1946 | F:M | leopard splitfin ................. mexcalpique leopardo |
| +Xenotoca eiseni (Rutter, 1896) | F:M | redtail splitfin .................. mexcalpique cola roja |
| +Xenotoca melanosoma Fitzsimons, 1972 | F:M | black splitfin .................... mexcalpique negro |
| Xenotoca variata (Bean, 1887) | F:M | jeweled splitfin ................. pintada |
| Zoogoneticus quitzeoensis (Bean, 1898) | F:M | picote splitfin .................... picote |
| Zoogoneticus tequila Webb & Miller, 1998 | F:M | Tequila splitfin ................. picote Tequila |

| SCIENTIFIC NAME | OCCURRENCE[1] | COMMON NAME (ENGLISH, SPANISH, FRENCH)[2] | |
|---|---|---|---|
| *Cyprinodontidae—En-pupfishes, Sp-cachorritos, Fr-cyprinodontes | | | |
| Cualac tessellatus Miller, 1956 | F:M | Media Luna pupfish | cachorrito de la Media Luna |
| Cyprinodon albivelis Minckley & Miller, 2002 | F:M | whitefin pupfish | cachorrito aletas blancas |
| +Cyprinodon alvarezi Miller, 1976 | F:M | Potosi pupfish | cachorrito de Potosí |
| *Cyprinodon arcuatus Minckley & Miller, 2002 | F[X]:U | Santa Cruz pupfish | |
| Cyprinodon artifrons Hubbs 1936 | AM-F:M | Yucatan pupfish | bolín petota |
| Cyprinodon atrorus Miller, 1968 | F:M | bolson pupfish | cachorrito del bolsón |
| Cyprinodon beltrani Alvarez, 1949 | F:M | blackfin pupfish | cachorrito lodero |
| Cyprinodon bifasciatus Miller, 1968 | F:M | Cuatro Cienega pupfish | cachorrito de Cuatro Ciénegas |
| Cyprinodon bobmilleri | | | |
| Lozano-Vilano & Contreras-Balderas, 1999 | F:M | San Ignacio pupfish | cachorrito de San Ignacio |
| Cyprinodon bovinus Baird & Girard, 1853 | F:U | Leon Springs pupfish | |
| Cyprinodon ceciliae | | | |
| Lozano-Vilano & Contreras-Balderas, 1993 | F[X]:M | Villa Lopez pupfish | cachorrito de Villa López |
| Cyprinodon diabolis Wales, 1930 | F:U | Devils Hole pupfish | |
| Cyprinodon elegans Baird & Girard, 1853 | F:U | Comanche Springs pupfish | |
| *Cyprinodon eremus Miller & Fuiman 1987 | F:UM | Sonoyta pupfish | cachorrito del Sonoyta |
| Cyprinodon escondius Strecker, 2002 | F:M | hidden pupfish | cachorrito escondido |
| Cyprinodon eximius Girard, 1859 | F:UM | Conchos pupfish | cachorrito del Conchos |
| Cyprinodon fontinalis Smith & Miller, 1980 | F:M | Carbonera pupfish | cachorrito de Carbonera |
| Cyprinodon inmemoriam | | | |
| Lozano-Vilano & Contreras-Balderas, 1993 | F[X]:M | Charco Azul pupfish | cachorrito de Charco Azul |
| Cyprinodon labiosus Humphries & Miller, 1981 | F:M | thicklip pupfish | cachorrito cangrejero |
| Cyprinodon latifasciatus Garman, 1881 | F[X]:M | Parras pupfish | cachorrito de Parras |
| +Cyprinodon longidorsalis | | | |
| Lozano-Vilano & Contreras-Balderas, 1993 | F:M | La Palma pupfish | cachorrito de La Palma |
| Cyprinodon macrolepis Miller, 1976 | F:M | bigscale pupfish | cachorrito escamudo |
| +Cyprinodon macularius Baird & Girard, 1853 | F:UM | desert pupfish | cachorrito del desierto |
| Cyprinodon maya Humphries & Miller, 1981 | F:M | Maya pupfish | cachorrito gigante |
| Cyprinodon meeki Miller, 1976 | F:M | Mezquital pupfish | cachorrito del Mezquital |
| Cyprinodon nazas Miller, 1976 | F:M | Nazas pupfish | cachorrito del Nazas |
| Cyprinodon nevadensis Eigenmann & Eigenmann, 1889 | F:U | Amargosa pupfish | |

| SCIENTIFIC NAME | OCCURRENCE[1] | COMMON NAME (ENGLISH, SPANISH, FRENCH)[2] |
|---|---|---|
| *Cyprinodon pachycephalus* Minckley & Minckley, 1986 | F:M | bighead pupfish.............. cachorrito cabezón |
| *Cyprinodon pecosensis* Echelle & Echelle, 1978 | F:U | Pecos pupfish |
| +*Cyprinodon pisteri* Miller & Minckley, 2002 | F:M | Palomas pupfish ........ cachorrito de Palomas |
| *Cyprinodon radiosus* Miller, 1948 | F:U | Owens pupfish |
| *Cyprinodon rubrofluviatilis* Fowler, 1916 | F:U | Red River pupfish |
| *Cyprinodon salinus* Miller, 1943 | F:U | Salt Creek pupfish |
| *Cyprinodon salvadori* Lozano-Vilano, 2002 | F:M | Bocochi pupfish ........ cachorrito de Bocochi |
| +*Cyprinodon simus* Humphries & Miller, 1981 | F:M | boxer pupfish .............. cachorrito boxeador |
| *Cyprinodon tularosa* Miller & Echelle, 1975 | F:U | White Sands pupfish |
| +*Cyprinodon variegatus* Lacepède, 1803 | A-F:UM | sheepshead minnow ............... bolín |
| *Cyprinodon verecundus* Humphries, 1984 | F:M | largefin pupfish ............. cachorrito aletón |
| +*Cyprinodon veronicae* Lozano-Vilano & Contreras-Balderas, 1993 | F:M | Charco Palma pupfish .......... cachorrito de Charco Palma |
| *Floridichthys carpio* (Günther, 1866) | A | goldspotted killifish |
| *Floridichthys polyommus* Hubbs, 1936 | AM | ocellated killifish ............. bolín yucateco |
| *Jordanella floridae* Goode & Bean, 1879 | F:U | flagfish |
| +*Jordanella pulchra* (Hubbs, 1936) | F:M | Progreso flagfish ........ cachorrito de Progreso |
| +*Megupsilon aporus* Miller & Walters, 1972 | F:M | Catarina pupfish ........ cachorrito enano de Potosí |

+ORDER BERYCIFORMES

*Anomalopidae—En-flashlightfishes, Sp-ojos de linterna, Fr-poissons-phares

| | | |
|---|---|---|
| *Phthanophaneron harveyi* (Rosenblatt & Montgomery, 1976)PM | | Panamic flashlightfish .......... ojo de linterna panámica |

Trachichthyidae—En-roughies, Sp-relojes, Fr-hoplites

| | | |
|---|---|---|
| *Gephyroberyx darwinii* (Johnson, 1866) | A | big roughy |

Berycidae—En-alfonsinos, Sp-alfonsinos, Fr-béryx

| | | |
|---|---|---|
| *Beryx decadactylus* Cuvier, 1829 | A | red bream |

Holocentridae—En-squirrelfishes, Sp-candiles, Fr-marignans

| | | |
|---|---|---|
| *Corniger spinosus* Agassiz, 1831 | A | spinycheek soldierfish |

| SCIENTIFIC NAME | OCCURRENCE[1] | COMMON NAME (ENGLISH, SPANISH, FRENCH)[2] |
|---|---|---|
| *Holocentrus adscensionis* (Osbeck, 1765) | A | squirrelfish...............candil de vidrio |
| *Holocentrus rufus* (Walbaum, 1792) | A | longspine squirrelfish..............candil rufo |
| +*Myripristis berndti* Jordan & Evermann, 1903 | PM | bigscale soldierfish...........soldado azotado |
| *Myripristis clarionensis* Gilbert, 1897 | PM | yellow soldierfish ...........soldado amarillo |
| *Myripristis jacobus* Cuvier, 1829 | A | blackbar soldierfish ...........soldado raya negra |
| *Myripristis leiognathus* Valenciennes, 1846 | PM | Panamic soldierfish ...........soldado panámico |
| *\*Neoniphon marianus* (Cuvier, 1829) | A | longjaw squirrelfish ...........carajuelo mariano |
| *Ostichthys trachypoma* (Günther, 1859) | A | bigeye soldierfish |
| *Plectrypops retrospinis* (Guichenot, 1853) | A | cardinal soldierfish...........candil cardenal |
| *\*Sargocentron bullisi* (Woods, 1955) | A | deepwater squirrelfish ...........carajuelo profundo |
| *\*Sargocentron coruscum* (Poey, 1860) | A | reef squirrelfish ...........carajuelo de arrecife |
| *\*Sargocentron poco* (Woods, 1965) | A | saddle squirrelfish |
| *\*Sargocentron suborbitalis* (Gill, 1863) | PM | tinsel squirrelfish ...........candil sol |
| *\*Sargocentron vexillarium* (Poey, 1860) | A | dusky squirrelfish ...........carajuelo oscuro |

## ORDER ZEIFORMES

Zeidae—En-dories, Sp-peces de San Pedro, Fr-Saint-Pierre

| | | |
|---|---|---|
| *\*Cyttopsis rosea* (Lowe, 1843) | A | red dory ...........San Pedro rojo |
| *Zenopsis conchifera* (Lowe, 1852) | A | buckler dory ...........San Pedro plateado |
| *Zenopsis nebulosa* (Temminck & Schlegel, 1845) | P | mirror dory |

Grammicolepidae—En-diamond dories, Sp-oropeles, Fr-poissons-palissades

| | | |
|---|---|---|
| *Grammicolepis brachiusculus* Poey, 1873 | A | thorny tinselfish |
| +*Xenolepidichthys dalgleishi* Gilchrist, 1922 | A | spotted tinselfish |

+Caproidae—En-boarfishes, Sp-verracos, Fr-sangliers

| | | |
|---|---|---|
| *Antigonia capros* Lowe, 1843 | A | deepbody boarfish ...........verraco alto |
| *Antigonia combatia* Berry & Rathjen, 1959 | A | shortspine boarfish |

| SCIENTIFIC NAME | OCCURRENCE[1] | COMMON NAME (ENGLISH, SPANISH, FRENCH)[2] |
|---|---|---|

## ORDER GASTEROSTEIFORMES

*Aulorhynchidae—En-tubesnouts, Sp-trompudos, Fr-trompes

| | | |
|---|---|---|
| *Aulorhynchus flavidus Gill, 1861 | P | tubesnout .......... trompudo sargacero |

+Gasterosteidae—En-sticklebacks, Sp-espinochos, Fr-épinoches

| | | |
|---|---|---|
| Apeltes quadracus (Mitchill, 1815) | A-F:CU | fourspine stickleback .......... épinoche à quatre épines |
| *Culaea inconstans (Kirtland, 1840) | F:CU | brook stickleback .......... épinoche à cinq épines |
| +Gasterosteus aculeatus Linnaeus, 1758 | A-F:CUM-P | threespine stickleback .......... espinocho .......... épinoche à trois épines |
| Gasterosteus wheatlandi Putnam, 1867 | A | blackspotted stickleback .......... épinoche tachetée |
| +Pungitius pungitius (Linnaeus, 1758) | A-F:CU-P | ninespine stickleback .......... épinoche à neuf épines |

Syngnathidae—En-pipefishes, Sp-peces pipa y caballitos de mar, Fr-hippocampes

| | | |
|---|---|---|
| Acentronura dendritica (Barbour, 1905) | A | pipehorse .......... caballito pipa |
| Anarchopterus criniger (Bean & Dresel, 1884) | A | fringed pipefish .......... pez pipa orlado |
| Anarchopterus tectus (Dawson, 1978) | A | insular pipefish .......... pez pipa isleño |
| Bryx dunckeri (Metzelaar, 1919) | A | pugnose pipefish .......... pez pipa ñato |
| Bryx veleronis Herald, 1940 | PM | offshore pipefish .......... pez pipa velero |
| Cosmocampus albirostris (Kaup, 1856) | A | whitenose pipefish .......... pez pipa hocico blanco |
| Cosmocampus arctus (Jenkins & Evermann, 1889) | P | snubnose pipefish .......... pez pipa chato |
| Cosmocampus brachycephalus (Poey, 1868) | A | crested pipefish .......... pez pipa crestado |
| Cosmocampus elucens (Poey, 1868) | A | shortfin pipefish .......... pez pipa aletilla |
| Cosmocampus hildebrandi (Herald, 1965) | A | dwarf pipefish |
| Cosmocampus profundus (Herald, 1965) | A | deepwater pipefish .......... pez pipa de lo alto |
| Doryrhamphus excisus Kaup, 1856 | PM | fantail pipefish .......... pez pipa chico |
| *Halicampus crinitus (Jenyns, 1842) | A | banded pipefish .......... pez pipa payaso |
| Hippocampus erectus Perry, 1810 | A | lined seahorse .......... caballito estriado |
| Hippocampus ingens Girard, 1858 | P | Pacific seahorse .......... caballito del Pacífico |
| +Hippocampus reidi Ginsburg, 1933 | A | longsnout seahorse .......... caballito hocico largo |
| Hippocampus zosterae Jordan & Gilbert, 1882 | A | dwarf seahorse .......... caballito enano |
| Microphis brachyurus (Bleeker, 1853) | A-F:UM | opossum pipefish .......... pez pipa culebra |

| SCIENTIFIC NAME | OCCURRENCE[1] | COMMON NAME (ENGLISH, SPANISH, FRENCH)[2] |
|---|---|---|
| Penetopteryx nanus (Rosén, 1911) | AM | worm pipefish ............ pez pipa gusano |
| Pseudophallus starksii (Jordan & Culver, 1895) | F:M-PM | yellowbelly pipefish ............ pez pipa de río |
| Syngnathus affinis Günther, 1870 | A | Texas pipefish ............ pez pipa texano |
| Syngnathus auliscus (Swain, 1882) | P | barred pipefish ............ pez pipa anillado |
| Syngnathus californiensis Storer, 1845 | P | kelp pipefish ............ pez pipa californiano |
| Syngnathus caribbaeus Dawson, 1979 | AM | Caribbean pipefish ............ pez pipa caribeño |
| Syngnathus carinatus (Gilbert, 1892) | PM | Cortez pipefish ............ pez pipa de Cortés |
| Syngnathus euchrous Fritzsche, 1980 | P | chocolate pipefish ............ pez pipa chocolate |
| Syngnathus exilis (Osburn & Nichols, 1916) | P | barcheek pipefish ............ pez pipa cachete rayado |
| Syngnathus floridae (Jordan & Gilbert, 1882) | A | dusky pipefish ............ pez pipa prieto |
| Syngnathus fuscus Storer, 1839 | A | northern pipefish ............ |
| Syngnathus insulae Fritzsche, 1980 | PM | Guadalupe pipefish ............ pez pipa de Guadalupe |
| Syngnathus leptorhynchus Girard, 1854 | P | bay pipefish ............ pez pipa de bahía |
| Syngnathus louisianae Günther, 1870 | A | chain pipefish ............ pez pipa cadena |
| Syngnathus makaxi Herald & Dawson, 1972 | AM | Yucatan pipefish ............ pez pipa yucateco |
| Syngnathus pelagicus Linnaeus, 1758 | A | sargassum pipefish ............ pez pipa oceánico |
| * Syngnathus scovelli (Evermann & Kendall, 1896) | A-F:U | Gulf pipefish ............ pez pipa del Golfo |
| Syngnathus springeri Herald, 1942 | A | bull pipefish ............ |

Aulostomidae—En-trumpetfishes, Sp-trompetas, Fr-trompettes

| | | |
|---|---|---|
| Aulostomus chinensis (Linnaeus, 1766) | PM | Chinese trumpetfish ............ trompeta china |
| * Aulostomus maculatus Valenciennes, 1837 | A | Atlantic trumpetfish ............ trompeta del Atlántico |

Fistulariidae—En-cornetfishes, Sp-cornetas, Fr-fistulaires

| | | |
|---|---|---|
| Fistularia commersonii Rüppell, 1838 | PM | reef cornetfish ............ corneta pintada |
| * Fistularia corneta Gilbert & Starks, 1904 | P | deepwater cornetfish ............ corneta flautera |
| Fistularia petimba Lacepède, 1803 | A | red cornetfish ............ corneta colorada |
| Fistularia tabacaria Linnaeus, 1758 | A | bluespotted cornetfish ............ corneta azul |

*Macroramphosidae— En-snipefishes, Sp-trompeteros, Fr-bécasses de mer

| | | |
|---|---|---|
| Macroramphosus gracilis (Lowe, 1839) | A-P | slender snipefish ............ trompetero flaco |
| Macroramphosus scolopax (Linnaeus, 1758) | A | longspine snipefish ............ trompetero copete |

| SCIENTIFIC NAME | OCCURRENCE[1] | COMMON NAME (ENGLISH, SPANISH, FRENCH)[2] |
|---|---|---|
| **ORDER SYNBRANCHIFORMES** | | |
| *Synbranchidae—En-swamp eels, Sp-anguillas de lodo, Fr-anguilles des mares | | |
| *Monopterus albus (Zuiew, 1793) | F[I]:U | Asian swamp eel |
| Ophisternon aenigmaticum Rosen & Greenwood, 1976 | F:M | obscure swamp eel...........anguila falsa |
| Ophisternon infernale (Hubbs, 1938) | F:M | blind swamp eel...........anguila ciega yucateca |
| Synbranchus marmoratus Bloch, 1795 | F:M | mottled swamp eel...........anguila de lodo |
| **ORDER SCORPAENIFORMES** | | |
| +Scorpaenidae—En-scorpionfishes, Sp-escorpiones y rocotes, Fr-scorpènes | | |
| Helicolenus dactylopterus (Delaroche, 1809) | A | blackbelly rosefish |
| Neomerinthe hemingwayi Fowler, 1935 | A | spinycheek scorpionfish...........rascacio mejilla espinosa |
| +Pontinus castor Poey, 1860 | A | longsnout scorpionfish |
| Pontinus furcirhinus Garman, 1899 | PM | red scorpionfish...........lapón rojo |
| Pontinus longispinis Goode & Bean, 1896 | A | longspine scorpionfish...........lapón mariposa |
| Pontinus nematophthalmus (Günther, 1860) | A | spinythroat scorpionfish...........lapón aleta baja |
| Pontinus rathbuni Goode & Bean, 1896 | A | highfin scorpionfish |
| Pontinus sierra (Gilbert, 1890) | PM | speckled scorpionfish...........lapón manchado |
| Pontinus vaughani Barnhart & Hubbs, 1946 | PM | spotback scorpionfish...........lapón lomo manchado |
| *Pterois volitans (Linnaeus, 1758) | A[I] | red lionfish |
| *Scorpaena agassizii Goode & Bean, 1896 | A | longfin scorpionfish...........escorpión aleta larga |
| Scorpaena albifimbria Evermann & Marsh, 1900 | A | coral scorpionfish...........escorpión coralino |
| *Scorpaena bergii Evermann & Marsh, 1900 | A | goosehead scorpionfish...........escorpión gansito |
| Scorpaena brachyptera Eschmeyer, 1965 | A | shortfin scorpionfish |
| Scorpaena brasiliensis Cuvier, 1829 | A | barbfish...........escorpión pardo |
| Scorpaena calcarata Goode & Bean, 1882 | A | smoothhead scorpionfish...........escorpión pelón |
| Scorpaena dispar Longley & Hildebrand, 1940 | A | hunchback scorpionfish...........escorpión jorobado |
| Scorpaena elachys Eschmeyer, 1965 | A | dwarf scorpionfish |
| Scorpaena grandicornis Cuvier, 1829 | A | plumed scorpionfish...........escorpión plumeado |
| Scorpaena guttata Girard, 1854 | P | California scorpionfish...........escorpión californiano |
| Scorpaena histrio Jenyns, 1840 | PM | player scorpionfish...........escorpión juguetón |

| SCIENTIFIC NAME | OCCURRENCE[1] | COMMON NAME (ENGLISH, SPANISH, FRENCH)[2] |
|---|---|---|
| *Scorpaena inermis* Cuvier, 1829 | A | mushroom scorpionfish ... escorpión hongo |
| *Scorpaena isthmensis* Meek & Hildebrand, 1928 | A | smoothcheek scorpionfish ... escorpión mejilla lisa |
| *Scorpaena mystes* Jordan & Starks, 1895 | P | stone scorpionfish ... escorpión roquero |
| *Scorpaena plumieri* Bloch, 1789 | A | spotted scorpionfish ... escorpión negro |
| *Scorpaena russula* Jordan & Bollman, 1890 | PM | reddish scorpionfish ... escorpión sapo |
| *Scorpaena sonorae* Jenkins & Evermann, 1889 | PM | Sonora scorpionfish ... escorpión de Sonora |
| *Scorpaenodes caribbaeus* Meek & Hildebrand, 1928 | A | reef scorpionfish ... escorpión de arrecife |
| *Scorpaenodes tredecimspinosus* (Metzelaar, 1919) | A | deepreef scorpionfish ... escorpión espinoso |
| *Scorpaenodes xyris* (Jordan & Gilbert, 1882) | P | rainbow scorpionfish ... escorpión arcoiris |
| *Sebastes aleutianus* (Jordan & Evermann, 1898) | P | rougheye rockfish |
| *Sebastes alutus* (Gilbert, 1890) | P | Pacific ocean perch |
| *Sebastes atrovirens* (Jordan & Gilbert, 1880) | P | kelp rockfish ... rocote sargacero |
| *Sebastes auriculatus* Girard, 1854 | P | brown rockfish ... rocote moreno |
| +*Sebastes aurora* (Gilbert, 1890) | P | aurora rockfish |
| *Sebastes babcocki* (Thompson, 1915) | P | redbanded rockfish |
| *Sebastes borealis* Barsukov, 1970 | P | shortraker rockfish |
| *Sebastes brevispinis* (Bean, 1884) | P | silvergray rockfish |
| *Sebastes carnatus* (Jordan & Gilbert, 1880) | P | gopher rockfish ... rocote amarillo |
| *Sebastes caurinus* Richardson, 1844 | P | copper rockfish ... rocote cobrizo |
| *Sebastes chlorostictus* (Jordan & Gilbert, 1880) | P | greenspotted rockfish ... rocote verde |
| *Sebastes chrysomelas* (Jordan & Gilbert, 1881) | P | black-and-yellow rockfish ... rocote mulato |
| *Sebastes ciliatus* (Tilesius, 1813) | P | dusky rockfish |
| *Sebastes constellatus* (Jordan & Gilbert, 1880) | P | starry rockfish ... rocote estrellado |
| *Sebastes cortezi* (Beebe & Tee-Van, 1938) | PM | Cortez rockfish ... rocote de Cortés |
| *Sebastes crameri* (Jordan, 1897) | P | darkblotched rockfish |
| *Sebastes dallii* (Eigenmann & Beeson, 1894) | P | calico rockfish ... rocote algodón |
| *Sebastes diploproa* (Gilbert, 1890) | P | splitnose rockfish ... rocote doble hocico |
| *Sebastes elongatus* Ayres, 1859 | P | greenstriped rockfish ... rocote reina |
| *Sebastes emphaeus* (Starks, 1911) | P | Puget Sound rockfish |
| *Sebastes ensifer* Chen, 1971 | P | swordspine rockfish ... rocote espada |
| *Sebastes entomelas* (Jordan & Gilbert, 1880) | P | widow rockfish ... rocote viuda |
| *Sebastes eos* (Eigenmann & Eigenmann, 1890) | P | pink rockfish ... rocote Santa María |

| SCIENTIFIC NAME | OCCURRENCE[1] | COMMON NAME (ENGLISH, SPANISH, FRENCH)[2] |
|---|---|---|
| Sebastes exsul Chen, 1971 | PM | buccaneer rockfish ........ rocote bucanero |
| +Sebastes fasciatus Storer, 1854 | A | Acadian redfish |
| *Sebastes flavidus (Ayres, 1862) | P | yellowtail rockfish |
| +Sebastes gilli (Eigenmann, 1891) | P | bronzespotted rockfish .......... rocote bronceado |
| *Sebastes glaucus Hilgendorf, 1880 | P | gray rockfish |
| Sebastes goodei (Eigenmann & Eigenmann, 1890) | P | chilipepper .......... rocote pimienta |
| Sebastes helvomaculatus Ayres, 1859 | P | rosethorn rockfish |
| Sebastes hopkinsi (Cramer, 1895) | P | squarespot rockfish .......... rocote a cuadros |
| Sebastes jordani (Gilbert, 1896) | P | shortbelly rockfish .......... rocote pancita |
| Sebastes lentiginosus Chen, 1971 | P | freckled rockfish .......... rocote pecoso |
| Sebastes levis (Eigenmann & Eigenmann, 1889) | P | cowcod .......... rocote vaquilla |
| Sebastes macdonaldi (Eigenmann & Beeson, 1893) | P | Mexican rockfish .......... rocote mexicano |
| Sebastes maliger (Jordan & Gilbert, 1880) | P | quillback rockfish |
| Sebastes melanops Girard, 1856 | P | black rockfish |
| Sebastes melanosema Lea & Fitch, 1979 | P | semaphore rockfish .......... rocote semáforo |
| Sebastes melanostomus (Eigenmann & Eigenmann, 1890) | P | blackgill rockfish .......... rocote agalla negra |
| *Sebastes mentella (Travin, 1951) | A | deepwater redfish .......... sébaste atlantique |
| Sebastes miniatus (Jordan & Gilbert, 1880) | P | vermilion rockfish .......... rocote bermejo |
| *Sebastes moseri Eitner, 1999 | P | whitespotted rockfish .......... rocote manchas blancas |
| Sebastes mystinus (Jordan & Gilbert, 1881) | P | blue rockfish .......... rocote azul |
| +Sebastes nebulosus Ayres, 1854 | P | China rockfish |
| Sebastes nigrocinctus Ayres, 1859 | P | tiger rockfish |
| Sebastes norvegicus (Ascanius, 1772) | A | golden redfish .......... sébaste orangé |
| Sebastes notius Chen, 1971 | PM | Guadalupe rockfish .......... rocote de Guadalupe |
| *Sebastes ovalis (Ayres, 1862) | P | speckled rockfish .......... rocote manchado |
| Sebastes paucispinis Ayres, 1854 | P | bocaccio .......... rocote bocaccio |
| Sebastes peduncularis Chen, 1975 | PM | Gulf rockfish .......... rocote del Golfo |
| Sebastes phillipsi (Fitch, 1964) | P | chameleon rockfish |
| Sebastes pinniger (Gill, 1864) | P | canary rockfish .......... rocote canario |
| Sebastes polyspinis (Taranetz & Moiseev, 1933) | P | northern rockfish |
| Sebastes proriger (Jordan & Gilbert, 1880) | P | redstripe rockfish |
| Sebastes rastrelliger (Jordan & Gilbert, 1880) | P | grass rockfish .......... rocote olivo |

| SCIENTIFIC NAME | OCCURRENCE[1] | COMMON NAME (ENGLISH, SPANISH, FRENCH)[2] |
|---|---|---|
| *Sebastes reedi* (Westrheim & Tsuyuki, 1967) | P | yellowmouth rockfish |
| *Sebastes rosaceus* Girard, 1854 | P | rosy rockfish ............... rocote rosado |
| *Sebastes rosenblatti* Chen, 1971 | P | greenblotched rockfish ....... rocote motas verdes |
| *Sebastes ruberrimus* (Cramer, 1895) | P | yelloweye rockfish ........... rocote ojo amarillo |
| *Sebastes rubrivinctus* (Jordan & Gilbert, 1880) | P | flag rockfish ............... rocote bandera |
| *Sebastes rufinanus* Lea & Fitch, 1972 | P | dwarf-red rockfish |
| *Sebastes rufus* (Eigenmann & Eigenmann, 1890) | P | bank rockfish ............... rocote rojo |
| *Sebastes saxicola* (Gilbert, 1890) | P | stripetail rockfish ......... rocote cola listada |
| *Sebastes semicinctus* (Gilbert, 1897) | P | halfbanded rockfish ......... rocote inspector |
| *Sebastes serranoides* (Eigenmann & Eigenmann, 1890) | P | olive rockfish ............... rocote falsa cabrilla |
| *Sebastes serriceps* (Jordan & Gilbert, 1880) | P | treefish .................... rocote presidiario |
| *Sebastes simulator* Chen, 1971 | P | pinkrose rockfish ........... rocote rosa |
| *Sebastes sinensis* (Gilbert, 1890) | PM | blackmouth rockfish ......... rocote boquinegra |
| *Sebastes spinorbis* Chen, 1975 | PM | spinyeye rockfish ........... rocote ojo espinoso |
| *Sebastes umbrosus* (Jordan & Gilbert, 1882) | P | honeycomb rockfish .......... rocote panal |
| *Sebastes variegatus* Quast, 1971 | P | harlequin rockfish |
| *Sebastes varispinis* Chen, 1975 | PM | hidden rockfish ............. rocote escondido |
| *Sebastes wilsoni* (Gilbert, 1915) | P | pygmy rockfish |
| *Sebastes zacentrus* (Gilbert, 1890) | P | sharpchin rockfish |
| *Sebastolobus alascanus* Bean, 1890 | P | shortspine thornyhead ....... chancharro alacrán |
| *Sebastolobus altivelis* Gilbert, 1896 | P | longspine thornyhead ........ chancharro espinoso |
| * *Sebastolobus macrochir* (Günther, 1877) | P | broadfin thornyhead |
| *Trachyscorpia cristulata* (Goode & Bean, 1896) | A | Atlantic thornyhead |

+Triglidae—En-searobins, Sp-vacas y rubios, Fr-grondins

| | | |
|---|---|---|
| *Bellator brachychir* (Regan, 1914) | A | shortfin searobin ........... rubio aleticorta |
| *Bellator egretta* (Goode & Bean, 1896) | A | streamer searobin ........... rubio gallardete |
| *Bellator gymnostethus* (Gilbert, 1892) | PM | nakedbelly searobin ......... vaca enana |
| *Bellator loxias* (Jordan, 1897) | PM | chevron searobin ............ vaca angelita |
| *Bellator militaris* (Goode & Bean, 1896) | A | horned searobin ............. rubio soldadito |
| *Bellator xenisma* (Jordan & Bollman, 1890) | P | splitnose searobin .......... vaca doble hocico |
| *Prionotus alatus* Goode & Bean, 1883 | A | spiny searobin ............... rubio espinoso |

| SCIENTIFIC NAME | OCCURRENCE[1] | COMMON NAME (ENGLISH, SPANISH, FRENCH)[2] |
|---|---|---|
| *Prionotus albirostris* Jordan & Bollman, 1890 | PM | whitesnout searobin ............ vaca cariblanca |
| *Prionotus birostratus* Richardson, 1844 | PM | twobeak searobin ............ vaca dospicos |
| *Prionotus carolinus* (Linnaeus, 1771) | A | northern searobin |
| *Prionotus evolans* (Linnaeus, 1766) | A | striped searobin |
| *Prionotus horrens* Richardson, 1844 | PM | bristly searobin ............ vaca polla |
| *Prionotus longispinosus* Teague, 1951 | A | bigeye searobin ............ rubio ojón |
| *Prionotus martis* Ginsburg, 1950 | A | barred searobin ............ rubio de barras |
| *Prionotus ophryas* Jordan & Swain, 1885 | A | bandtail searobin ............ rubio cola bandeada |
| *Prionotus paralatus* Ginsburg, 1950 | A | Mexican searobin ............ rubio mexicano |
| *Prionotus punctatus* (Bloch, 1793) | AM | bluewing searobin ............ rubio azul |
| *Prionotus roseus* Jordan & Evermann, 1887 | A | bluespotted searobin ............ rubio manchas azules |
| *Prionotus rubio* Jordan, 1886 | A | blackwing searobin ............ rubio aletinegra |
| *Prionotus ruscarius* Gilbert & Starks, 1904 | PM | rough searobin ............ vaca rasposa |
| *Prionotus scitulus* Jordan & Gilbert, 1882 | A | leopard searobin ............ rubio leopardo |
| *Prionotus stearnsi* Jordan & Swain, 1885 | A | shortwing searobin ............ rubio pequeño |
| *Prionotus stephanophrys* Lockington, 1881 | P | lumptail searobin ............ vaca voladora |
| *Prionotus tribulus* Cuvier, 1829 | A | bighead searobin ............ rubio cabezón |

*Peristediidae—En-armored searobins, Sp-vaquitas blindadas, Fr-malarmats

| | | |
|---|---|---|
| *Peristedion gracile* Goode & Bean, 1896 | A | slender searobin ............ vaquita blindada flaca |
| *Peristedion greyae* Miller 1967 | A | alligator searobin |
| *Peristedion miniatum* Goode, 1880 | A | armored searobin |
| *Peristedion paucibarbiger* Castro-Aguirre & García-Domínguez, 1984 | PM | Cortez searobin ............ vaquita blindada de Cortés |
| *Peristedion thompsoni* Fowler, 1952 | A | rimspine searobin |

Anoplopomatidae—En-sablefishes, Sp-bacalaos negros, Fr-morues noires

| | | |
|---|---|---|
| *Anoplopoma fimbria* (Pallas, 1814) | P | sablefish ............ bacalao negro |
| *Erilepis zonifer* (Lockington, 1880) | P | skilfish |

Hexagrammidae—En-greenlings, Sp-molvas, Fr-sourcils

| | | |
|---|---|---|
| *Hexagrammos decagrammus* (Pallas, 1810) | P | kelp greenling |

| SCIENTIFIC NAME | OCCURRENCE[1] | COMMON NAME (ENGLISH, SPANISH, FRENCH)[2] |
|---|---|---|
| Hexagrammos lagocephalus (Pallas, 1810) | P | rock greenling |
| Hexagrammos octogrammus (Pallas, 1814) | P | masked greenling |
| Hexagrammos stelleri Tilesius, 1810 | P | whitespotted greenling |
| Ophiodon elongatus Girard, 1854 | P | lingcod |
| +Oxylebius pictus Gill, 1862 | P | painted greenling |
| Pleurogrammus monopterygius (Pallas, 1810) | P | Atka mackerel |
| +Zaniolepis frenata Eigenmann & Eigenmann, 1889 | P | shortspine combfish ............ cepillo espina corta |
| *Zaniolepis latipinnis Girard, 1858 | P | longspine combfish ............ cepillo espina larga |

*Rhamphocottidae—En-grunt sculpins, Sp-charrascos gruñones, Fr-chabots grogneurs

| | | |
|---|---|---|
| *Rhamphocottus richardsonii Günther, 1874 | P | grunt sculpin |

+Cottidae—En-sculpins, Sp-charrascos espinosos, Fr-chabots

| | | |
|---|---|---|
| *Archistes biseriatus (Gilbert & Burke, 1912) | P | scaled sculpin |
| Artediellus atlanticus Jordan & Evermann, 1898 | A | Atlantic hookear sculpin ............hameçon atlantique |
| *Artediellus gomojunovi Taranetz, 1933 | P | spinyhook sculpin |
| *Artediellus ochotensis Gilbert & Burke, 1912 | P | Okhotsk hookear sculpin |
| *Artediellus pacificus Gilbert, 1896 | P | hookhorn sculpin |
| Artediellus scaber Knipowitsch, 1907 | P | hamecon |
| Artediellus uncinatus (Reinhardt, 1835) | A | Arctic hookear sculpin ............hameçon neigeux |
| Artedius corallinus (Hubbs, 1926) | P | coralline sculpin ............ charrasco coralino |
| Artedius fenestralis Jordan & Gilbert, 1883 | P | padded sculpin |
| Artedius harringtoni (Starks, 1896) | P | scalyhead sculpin |
| Artedius lateralis (Girard, 1854) | P | smoothhead sculpin ............ charrasco cabeza lisa |
| Artedius notospilotus Girard, 1856 | P | bonyhead sculpin ............ charrasco huesudo |
| Ascelichthys rhodorus Jordan & Gilbert, 1880 | P | rosylip sculpin |
| +Asemichthys taylori Gilbert, 1912 | P | spinynose sculpin |
| Chitonotus pugetensis (Steindachner, 1876) | P | roughback sculpin ............ charrasco espalda rugosa |
| Clinocottus acuticeps (Gilbert, 1896) | F:CU-P | sharpnose sculpin |
| *Clinocottus analis (Girard, 1858) | P | woolly sculpin ............ charrasco lanudo |
| Clinocottus embryum (Jordan & Starks, 1895) | P | calico sculpin ............ charrasco angaripola |
| *Clinocottus globiceps (Girard, 1858) | P | mosshead sculpin |

| SCIENTIFIC NAME | OCCURRENCE[1] | COMMON NAME (ENGLISH, SPANISH, FRENCH)[2] |
|---|---|---|
| *Clinocottus recalvus* (Greeley, 1899) | P | bald sculpin ..... charrasco pelón |
| +*Cottus aleuticus* Gilbert, 1896 | F:CU-P | coastrange sculpin |
| *Cottus asper* Richardson, 1836 | F:CU-P | prickly sculpin |
| *Cottus asperrimus* Rutter, 1908 | F:U | rough sculpin |
| *Cottus baileyi* Robins, 1961 | F:U | black sculpin |
| * *Cottus bairdii* Girard, 1850 | F:CU | mottled sculpin ..... chabot tacheté |
| * *Cottus beldingii* Eigenmann & Eigenmann, 1891 | F:U | Paiute sculpin |
| * *Cottus bendirei* (Bean 1881) | F:U | Malheur sculpin |
| * *Cottus caeruleomentum* Kinziger, Raesly & Neely, 2000 | F:U | Blue Ridge sculpin |
| *Cottus carolinae* (Gill, 1861) | F:U | banded sculpin |
| *Cottus cognatus* Richardson, 1836 | F:CU | slimy sculpin ..... chabot visqueux |
| *Cottus confusus* Bailey & Bond, 1963 | F:CU | shorthead sculpin |
| *Cottus echinatus* Bailey & Bond, 1963 | F[X]:U | Utah Lake sculpin |
| *Cottus extensus* Bailey & Bond, 1963 | F:U | Bear Lake sculpin |
| *Cottus girardi* Robins, 1961 | F:U | Potomac sculpin |
| *Cottus greenei* (Gilbert & Culver, 1898) | F:U | Shoshone sculpin |
| *Cottus gulosus* (Girard, 1854) | F:U | riffle sculpin |
| * *Cottus hubbsi* Bailey & Dimick 1949 | F:CU | Columbia sculpin |
| *Cottus hypselurus* Robins & Robison, 1985 | F:U | Ozark sculpin |
| *Cottus klamathensis* Gilbert, 1898 | F:U | marbled sculpin |
| *Cottus leiopomus* Gilbert & Evermann, 1894 | F:U | Wood River sculpin |
| *Cottus marginatus* (Bean, 1881) | F:U | margined sculpin |
| * *Cottus paulus* Williams, 2000 | F:U | pygmy sculpin |
| *Cottus perplexus* Gilbert & Evermann, 1894 | F:U | reticulate sculpin |
| *Cottus pitensis* Bailey & Bond, 1963 | F:U | Pit sculpin |
| *Cottus princeps* Gilbert, 1898 | F:U | Klamath Lake sculpin |
| *Cottus rhotheus* (Smith, 1882) | F:CU | torrent sculpin |
| *Cottus ricei* (Nelson, 1876) | F:CU | spoonhead sculpin ..... chabot à tête plate |
| *Cottus tenuis* (Evermann & Meek, 1898) | F:U | slender sculpin |
| *Enophrys bison* (Girard, 1854) | P | buffalo sculpin |
| * *Enophrys diceraus* (Pallas, 1788) | P | antlered sculpin |
| *Enophrys lucasi* (Jordan & Gilbert, 1898) | P | leister sculpin |

| SCIENTIFIC NAME | OCCURRENCE[1] | COMMON NAME (ENGLISH, SPANISH, FRENCH)[2] |
|---|---|---|
| Enophrys taurina Gilbert, 1914 | P | bull sculpin |
| *Gymnocanthus detrisus Gilbert & Burke, 1912 | P | purplegray sculpin |
| Gymnocanthus galeatus (Bean, 1881) | P | armorhead sculpin |
| Gymnocanthus pistilliger (Pallas, 1814) | P | threaded sculpin |
| *Gymnocanthus tricuspis (Reinhardt, 1830) | A-P | Arctic staghorn sculpin ............ tricorne arctique |
| Hemilepidotus hemilepidotus (Tilesius, 1811) | P | red Irish lord |
| Hemilepidotus jordani Bean, 1881 | P | yellow Irish lord |
| Hemilepidotus papilio (Bean, 1880) | P | butterfly sculpin |
| Hemilepidotus spinosus (Ayres, 1854) | P | brown Irish lord |
| Hemilepidotus zapus Gilbert & Burke, 1912 | P | longfin Irish lord |
| Icelinus borealis Gilbert, 1896 | P | northern sculpin |
| Icelinus burchami Evermann & Goldsborough, 1907 | P | dusky sculpin |
| Icelinus cavifrons Gilbert, 1890 | P | pit-head sculpin .......... charrasco cabeza bacha |
| Icelinus filamentosus Gilbert, 1890 | P | threadfin sculpin |
| Icelinus fimbriatus Gilbert, 1890 | P | fringed sculpin |
| Icelinus oculatus Gilbert, 1890 | P | frogmouth sculpin |
| Icelinus quadriseriatus (Lockington, 1880) | P | yellowchin sculpin ........ charrasco barbiamarilla |
| Icelinus tenuis Gilbert, 1890 | P | spotfin sculpin ......... charrasco aletimanchada |
| Icelus bicornis (Reinhardt, 1840) | A-P | twohorn sculpin |
| Icelus canaliculatus Gilbert, 1896 | P | blacknose sculpin |
| Icelus euryops Bean, 1890 | P | wide-eye sculpin |
| Icelus spatula Gilbert & Burke, 1912 | A-P | spatulate sculpin .............. icèle spatulée |
| Icelus spiniger Gilbert, 1896 | P | thorny sculpin |
| Icelus uncinalis Gilbert & Burke, 1912 | P | uncinate sculpin |
| Jordania zonope Starks, 1895 | P | longfin sculpin |
| Leiocottus hirundo Girard, 1856 | P | lavender sculpin ............ charrasco lavanda |
| Leptocottus armatus Girard, 1854 | F:CUM-P | Pacific staghorn sculpin ........ charrasco de astas |
| Megalocottus platycephalus (Pallas, 1814) | P | belligerent sculpin |
| *Microcottus sellaris (Gilbert, 1896) | P | brightbelly sculpin |
| Myoxocephalus aenaeus (Mitchill, 1814) | A | grubby ............ chaboisseau bronzé |
| Myoxocephalus jaok (Cuvier, 1829) | P | plain sculpin |
| +Myoxocephalus niger (Bean, 1881) | P | warthead sculpin |

| SCIENTIFIC NAME | OCCURRENCE[1] | COMMON NAME (ENGLISH, SPANISH, FRENCH)[2] |
|---|---|---|
| Myoxocephalus octodecemspinosus (Mitchill, 1814) | A | longhorn sculpin ...... chaboisseau à dix-huit épines |
| Myoxocephalus polyacanthocephalus (Pallas, 1814) | P | great sculpin |
| +Myoxocephalus quadricornis (Linnaeus, 1758) | A-F:CU-P | fourhorn sculpin ...... chaboisseau à quatre cornes |
| +Myoxocephalus scorpioides (Fabricius, 1780) | A-P | Arctic sculpin |
| Myoxocephalus scorpius (Linnaeus, 1758) | A-P | shorthorn sculpin ...... chaboisseau à épines courtes |
| *Myoxocephalus stelleri Tilesius, 1811 | P | frog sculpin |
| *Myoxocephalus thompsonii (Girard, 1851) | F:CU | deepwater sculpin ...... chabot de profondeur |
| +Myoxocephalus verrucosus (Bean, 1881) | P | warty sculpin |
| Oligocottus maculosus Girard, 1856 | P | tidepool sculpin |
| Oligocottus rimensis (Greeley, 1899) | P | saddleback sculpin ...... charrasco ensillado |
| Oligocottus rubellio (Greeley, 1899) | P | rosy sculpin ...... charrasco rosado |
| Oligocottus snyderi Greeley, 1898 | P | fluffy sculpin ...... charrasco peludo |
| Orthonopias triacis Starks & Mann, 1911 | P | snubnose sculpin ...... charrasco chato |
| Paricelinus hopliticus Eigenmann & Eigenmann, 1889 | P | thornback sculpin |
| Phallocottus obtusus Schultz, 1938 | P | spineless sculpin |
| *Porocottus mednius (Bean, 1898) | P | Aleutian fringed sculpin |
| Radulinus asprellus Gilbert, 1890 | P | slim sculpin ...... charrasco flaco |
| Radulinus boleoides Gilbert, 1898 | P | darter sculpin |
| Radulinus vinculus Bolin, 1950 | P | smoothgum sculpin |
| *Rastrinus scutiger (Bean, 1890) | P | roughskin sculpin |
| Ruscarius creaseri (Hubbs, 1926) | P | roughcheek sculpin ...... charrasco cachetirugoso |
| Ruscarius meanyi Jordan & Starks, 1895 | P | Puget Sound sculpin |
| Scorpaenichthys marmoratus (Ayres, 1854) | P | cabezon ...... cabezón |
| Sigmistes caulias Rutter, 1898 | P | kelp sculpin |
| Sigmistes smithi Schultz, 1938 | P | arched sculpin |
| *Stelgistrum beringianum Gilbert & Burke, 1912 | P | smallplate sculpin |
| *Stelgistrum concinnum Andriashev, 1935 | P | largeplate sculpin |
| Synchirus gilli Bean, 1890 | P | manacled sculpin |
| Thyriscus anoplus Gilbert & Burke, 1912 | P | sponge sculpin |
| *Trichocottus brashnikovi Soldatov & Pavlenko, 1915 | P | hairhead sculpin |
| Triglops forficatus (Gilbert, 1896) | P | scissortail sculpin |
| *Triglops macellus (Bean, 1884) | P | roughspine sculpin |

| SCIENTIFIC NAME | OCCURRENCE[1] | COMMON NAME (ENGLISH, SPANISH, FRENCH)[2] |
|---|---|---|
| *Triglops metopias Gilbert & Burke, 1912 | P | highbrow sculpin |
| Triglops murrayi Günther, 1888 | A | moustache sculpin ... faux-trigle armé |
| Triglops nybelini Jensen, 1944 | A-P | bigeye sculpin |
| *Triglops pingelii Reinhardt, 1837 | A-P | ribbed sculpin |
| Triglops scepticus Gilbert, 1896 | P | spectacled sculpin |
| *Triglops xenostethus Gilbert, 1896 | P | scalybreasted sculpin |
| *Hemitripteridae—En-searavens, Sp-charrascos cuervo, Fr-hémitriptères | | |
| Blepsias bilobus Cuvier, 1829 | P | crested sculpin |
| +Blepsias cirrhosus (Pallas, 1814) | P | silverspotted sculpin |
| Hemitripterus americanus (Gmelin, 1789) | A | sea raven ... hémitriptère atlantique |
| Hemitripterus bolini (Myers, 1934) | P | bigmouth sculpin |
| *Nautichthys oculofasciatus (Girard, 1858) | P | sailfin sculpin |
| Nautichthys pribilovius (Jordan & Gilbert, 1898) | P | eyeshade sculpin |
| Nautichthys robustus Peden, 1970 | P | shortmast sculpin |
| Agonidae—En-poachers, Sp-bandidos, Fr-poissons-alligators | | |
| Agonopsis sterletus (Gilbert, 1898) | P | southern spearnose poacher ... bandido narigón |
| Agonopsis vulsa (Jordan & Gilbert, 1880) | P | northern spearnose poacher |
| Anoplagonus inermis (Günther, 1860) | P | smooth alligatorfish |
| *Aspidophoroides monopterygius (Bloch, 1786) | A-P | alligatorfish ... poisson-alligator atlantique |
| Bathyagonus alascanus (Gilbert, 1896) | P | gray starsnout |
| Bathyagonus infraspinatus (Gilbert, 1904) | P | spinycheek starsnout |
| Bathyagonus nigripinnis Gilbert, 1890 | P | blackfin poacher |
| Bathyagonus pentacanthus (Gilbert, 1890) | P | bigeye poacher |
| *Bothragonus swanii (Steindachner, 1876) | P | rockhead |
| *Chesnonia verrucosa (Lockington, 1880) | P | warty poacher |
| *Hypsagonus mozinoi (Wilimovsky & Wilson, 1979) | P | kelp poacher |
| Hypsagonus quadricornis (Cuvier, 1829) | P | fourhorn poacher |
| *Leptagonus decagonus (Bloch & Schneider, 1801) | A-P | Atlantic poacher ... agone atlantique |
| *Leptagonus frenatus (Gilbert, 1896) | P | sawback poacher |
| *Leptagonus leptorhynchus (Gilbert, 1896) | P | longnose poacher |

| SCIENTIFIC NAME | OCCURRENCE[1] | COMMON NAME (ENGLISH, SPANISH, FRENCH)[2] |
|---|---|---|
| *Occella dodecaedron* (Tilesius, 1813) | P | Bering poacher |
| *Odontopyxis trispinosa* Lockington, 1880 | P | pygmy poacher.....bandido enano |
| *Pallasina barbata* (Steindachner, 1876) | P | tubenose poacher |
| *Percis japonica* (Pallas, 1769) | P | dragon poacher |
| *Podothecus accipenserinus* (Tilesius, 1813) | P | sturgeon poacher |
| *Podothecus veternus* Jordan & Starks, 1895 | P | veteran poacher |
| +*Stellerina xyosterna* (Jordan & Gilbert, 1880) | P | pricklebreast poacher.....bandido pechoespinoso |
| *Ulcina olrikii* (Lütken, 1876) | A-P | Arctic alligatorfish |
| *Xeneretmus latifrons* (Gilbert, 1890) | P | blacktip poacher.....bandido penacho |
| *Xeneretmus leiops* Gilbert, 1915 | P | smootheye poacher |
| *Xeneretmus ritteri* Gilbert, 1915 | P | stripefin poacher.....bandido bandera |
| *Xeneretmus triacanthus* (Gilbert, 1890) | P | bluespotted poacher.....bandido manchas azules |

*Psychrolutidae—En-fathead sculpins, Sp-cabezas gordas, Fr-chabots veloutés

| SCIENTIFIC NAME | OCCURRENCE[1] | COMMON NAME (ENGLISH, SPANISH, FRENCH)[2] |
|---|---|---|
| *Cottunculus microps* Collett, 1875 | A | polar sculpin.....cotte polaire |
| *Dasycottus setiger* Bean, 1890 | P | spinyhead sculpin |
| *Eurymen gyrinus* Gilbert & Burke, 1912 | P | smoothcheek sculpin |
| *Malacocottus kincaidi* Gilbert & Thompson, 1905 | P | blackfin sculpin |
| *Malacocottus zonurus* Bean, 1890 | P | darkfin sculpin |
| *Psychrolutes paradoxus* Günther, 1861 | P | tadpole sculpin |
| *Psychrolutes sigalutes* (Jordan & Starks, 1895) | P | soft sculpin |

+Cyclopteridae—En-lumpfishes, Sp-peces grumo, Fr-poules de mer

| SCIENTIFIC NAME | OCCURRENCE[1] | COMMON NAME (ENGLISH, SPANISH, FRENCH)[2] |
|---|---|---|
| *Aptocyclus ventricosus* (Pallas, 1769) | P | smooth lumpsucker |
| *Cyclopteropsis mcalpini* (Fowler, 1914) | A | Arctic lumpsucker |
| *Cyclopterus lumpus* Linnaeus, 1758 | A | lumpfish.....grosse poule de mer |
| *Eumicrotremus andriashevi* Perminov, 1936 | P | pimpled lumpsucker |
| *Eumicrotremus asperrimus* (Tanaka, 1912) | P | Siberian lumpsucker |
| *Eumicrotremus barbatus* (Lindberg & Legeza, 1955) | P | papillose lumpsucker |
| *Eumicrotremus derjugini* Popov, 1926 | A-P | leatherfin lumpsucker |
| *Eumicrotremus eggvinii* Koefoed, 1956 | A | Eggvin lumpsucker |
| *Eumicrotremus gyrinops* (Garman, 1892) | P | Alaskan lumpsucker |

| SCIENTIFIC NAME | OCCURRENCE[1] | COMMON NAME (ENGLISH, SPANISH, FRENCH)[2] |
|---|---|---|
| *Eumicrotremus orbis* (Günther, 1861) | P | Pacific spiny lumpsucker |
| *Eumicrotremus phrynoides* Gilbert & Burke, 1912 | P | toad lumpsucker |
| *Eumicrotremus spinosus* (Fabricius, 1776) | A-P | Atlantic spiny lumpsucker ......... petite poule de mer atlantique |
| *Eumicrotremus terraenovae* Myers & Böhlke, 1950 | A | Newfoundland spiny lumpsucker |
| *Lethotremus muticus* Gilbert, 1896 | P | docked snailfish |
| *Liparidae—En-snailfishes, Sp-peces babosos, Fr-limaces de mer | | |
| *Careproctus candidus* Gilbert & Burke, 1912 | P | bigeye snailfish |
| *Careproctus furcellus* Gilbert & Burke, 1912 | P | emarginate snailfish |
| *Careproctus gilberti* Burke, 1912 | P | smalldisk snailfish |
| *Careproctus longipinnis* Burke, 1912 | A | longfin snailfish ......... limace à longues nageoires |
| *Careproctus melanurus* Gilbert, 1892 | P | blacktail snailfish ......... baboso colinegra |
| *Careproctus ostentum* Gilbert, 1896 | P | microdisk snailfish |
| *Careproctus phasma* Gilbert, 1896 | P | spectral snailfish |
| *Careproctus rastrinus* Gilbert & Burke, 1912 | P | salmon snailfish |
| *Careproctus reinhardti* (Krøyer, 1862) | A | sea tadpole ......... petite limace de mer |
| *Careproctus scottae* Chapman & DeLacy, 1934 | P | peachskin snailfish |
| *Careproctus spectrum* Bean, 1890 | P | stippled snailfish |
| *Crystallichthys cyclospilus* Gilbert & Burke, 1912 | P | blotched snailfish |
| *Liparis atlanticus* (Jordan & Evermann, 1898) | A | Atlantic seasnail ......... limace atlantique |
| *Liparis beringianus* (Gilbert & Burke, 1912) | P | Bering snailfish |
| *Liparis bristolensis* (Burke, 1912) | P | Bristol snailfish |
| *Liparis callyodon* (Pallas, 1814) | P | spotted snailfish |
| *Liparis catharus* Vogt, 1973 | P | purity snailfish |
| *Liparis coheni* Able, 1976 | A | Gulf snailfish ......... limace de Cohen |
| *Liparis cyclopus* Günther, 1861 | A | ribbon snailfish |
| *Liparis dennyi* Jordan & Starks, 1895 | P | marbled snailfish |
| *Liparis fabricii* Krøyer, 1847 | A-P | gelatinous seasnail ......... limace gélatineuse |
| *Liparis florae* (Jordan & Starks, 1895) | P | tidepool snailfish |
| *Liparis fucensis* Gilbert, 1896 | P | slipskin snailfish |
| *Liparis gibbus* Bean, 1881 | A-P | variegated snailfish ......... limace marbrée |
| *Liparis greeni* (Jordan & Starks, 1895) | P | lobefin snailfish |

| SCIENTIFIC NAME | OCCURRENCE[1] | COMMON NAME (ENGLISH, SPANISH, FRENCH)[2] |
|---|---|---|
| *Liparis inquilinus* Able, 1973 | A | inquiline snailfish ......... limace des pétoncles |
| *Liparis marmoratus* Schmidt, 1950 | P | festive snailfish |
| *Liparis megacephalus* (Burke, 1912) | P | bighead snailfish |
| *Liparis micraspidophorus* (Burke, 1912) | P | thumbtack snailfish |
| *Liparis mucosus* Ayres, 1855 | P | slimy snailfish ......... baboso mucoso |
| *Liparis ochotensis* Schmidt, 1904 | P | Okhotsk snailfish |
| *Liparis pulchellus* Ayres, 1855 | P | showy snailfish |
| *Liparis rutteri* (Gilbert & Snyder, 1898) | P | ringtail snailfish |
| *Liparis tunicatus* Reinhardt, 1837 | A-P | kelp snailfish ......... limace des laminaires |
| *Lipariscus nanus* Gilbert, 1915 | P | pygmy snailfish |
| *Nectoliparis pelagicus* Gilbert & Burke 1912 | P | tadpole snailfish |
| *Paraliparis calidus* Cohen, 1968 | A | lowfin snailfish |
| *Paraliparis deani* Burke, 1912 | P | prickly snailfish |

### ORDER DACTYLOPTERIFORMES

+Dactylopteridae—En-flying gurnards, Sp-alones, Fr-grondins volants

| | | |
|---|---|---|
| *Dactylopterus volitans* (Linnaeus, 1758) | A | flying gurnard ......... alón volador |

### +ORDER PERCIFORMES

+Centropomidae—En-snooks, Sp-robalos, Fr-centropomes

| | | |
|---|---|---|
| *Centropomus armatus* Gill, 1863 | PM | longspine snook ......... robalo espina larga |
| *Centropomus ensiferus* Poey, 1860 | A-F:UM | swordspine snook ......... robalo de espolón |
| *Centropomus medius* Günther, 1864 | PM | blackfin snook ......... robalo aleta prieta |
| +*Centropomus mexicanus* Bocourt, 1868 | AM-F:M | largescale fat snook ......... robalo gordo |
| +*Centropomus nigrescens* Günther, 1864 | PM | black snook ......... robalo negro |
| *Centropomus parallelus* Poey, 1860 | A-F:UM | smallscale fat snook ......... chucumite |
| *Centropomus pectinatus* Poey, 1860 | A-F:UM | tarpon snook ......... constantino |
| *Centropomus poeyi* Chávez, 1961 | AM-F:M | Mexican snook ......... robalo prieto |
| *Centropomus robalito* Jordan & Gilbert, 1882 | PM | yellowfin snook ......... robalo aleta amarilla |

| SCIENTIFIC NAME | OCCURRENCE[1] | COMMON NAME (ENGLISH, SPANISH, FRENCH)[2] |
|---|---|---|
| *Centropomus undecimalis* (Bloch, 1792) | A-F:UM | common snook ............ robalo blanco |
| *Centropomus unionensis* Bocourt, 1868 | PM | humpback snook ............ robalo serrano |
| *Centropomus viridis* Lockington, 1877 | PM | white snook ............ robalo plateado |
| | | *Moronidae—En-temperate basses, Sp-lobinas norteñas, Fr-bars |
| *Morone americana* (Gmelin, 1789) | A-F:CU | white perch ............ baret |
| *Morone chrysops* (Rafinesque, 1820) | F:CU | white bass ............ bar blanc |
| *Morone mississippiensis* Jordan & Eigenmann, 1887 | F:U | yellow bass |
| *Morone saxatilis* (Walbaum, 1792) | A-F:CU-P[I] | striped bass ............ lobina estriada ............ bar rayé |
| | | *Acropomatidae—En-lanternbellies, Sp-farolitos, Fr-macondes |
| *Synagrops bellus* (Goode & Bean, 1896) | A | blackmouth bass |
| *Synagrops spinosus* Schultz, 1940 | A | keelcheek bass ............ farolito cachetiquillada |
| * *Synagrops trispinosus* Mochizuki & Sano, 1984 | A | threespine bass ............ farolito tres espinas |
| | | *Symphysanodontidae—En-slopefishes, Sp-pargos del talud, Fr-symphysanodontidés |
| *Symphysanodon berryi* Anderson, 1970 | A | slope bass |
| | | *Polyprionidae—En-wreckfishes, Sp-náufragos, Fr-polyprions |
| * *Polyprion americanus* (Bloch & Schneider, 1801) | A | wreckfish |
| *Stereolepis gigas* Ayres, 1859 | P | giant sea bass ............ pescara |
| | | Serranidae—En-sea basses and groupers, Sp-cabrillas y meros, Fr-serrans |
| * *Alphestes afer* (Bloch, 1793) | A | mutton hamlet |
| + *Alphestes immaculatus* Breder, 1936 | PM | Pacific mutton hamlet ............ guaseta del Pacífico |
| + *Alphestes multiguttatus* (Günther, 1867) | PM | rivulated mutton hamlet ............ guaseta rayada |
| *Anthias nicholsi* Firth, 1933 | A | yellowfin bass ............ mero aleta amarilla |
| *Anthias tenuis* Nichols, 1920 | A | threadnose bass ............ mero naricita |
| * *Anthias woodsi* Anderson & Heemstra, 1980 | A | swallowtail bass |
| *Bathyanthias mexicanus* (Schultz, 1958) | A | yellowtail bass ............ mero cola amarilla |
| * *Centropristis fuscula* Poey, 1861 | A | twospot sea bass |

| SCIENTIFIC NAME | OCCURRENCE[1] | COMMON NAME (ENGLISH, SPANISH, FRENCH)[2] |
|---|---|---|
| *Centropristis ocyurus* (Jordan & Evermann, 1887) | A | bank sea bass .......... cabrilla de banco |
| *Centropristis philadelphica* (Linnaeus, 1758) | A | rock sea bass .......... cabrilla serrana |
| *Centropristis striata* (Linnaeus, 1758) | A | black sea bass |
| *Cephalopholis cruentata* (Lacepède, 1802) | A | graysby .......... cherna enjambre |
| *Cephalopholis fulva* (Linnaeus, 1758) | A | coney .......... cabrilla roja |
| *Cephalopholis panamensis* (Steindachner, 1877) | PM | Panama graysby .......... cabrilla enjambre |
| *Dermatolepis dermatolepis* (Boulenger, 1895) | P | leather bass .......... mero cuero |
| *Dermatolepis inermis* (Valenciennes, 1833) | A | marbled grouper |
| *Diplectrum bivittatum* (Valenciennes, 1828) | A | dwarf sand perch .......... serrano guabino |
| *Diplectrum eumelum* Rosenblatt & Johnson, 1974 | PM | orange-spotted sand perch .......... serrano carabonita |
| *Diplectrum euryplectrum* Jordan & Bollman, 1890 | PM | bighead sand perch .......... serrano extranjero |
| *Diplectrum formosum* (Linnaeus, 1766) | A | sand perch .......... serrano arenero |
| *Diplectrum labarum* Rosenblatt & Johnson, 1974 | PM | highfin sand perch .......... serrano espinudo |
| *Diplectrum macropoma* (Günther, 1864) | PM | Mexican sand perch .......... serrano mexicano |
| *Diplectrum maximum* Hildebrand, 1946 | P | greater sand perch .......... serrano de altura |
| *Diplectrum pacificum* Meek & Hildebrand, 1925 | PM | Pacific sand perch .......... serrano cabaicucho |
| *Diplectrum rostrum* Bortone, 1974 | PM | bridled sand perch .......... serrano frenado |
| *Diplectrum sciurus* Gilbert, 1892 | PM | squirrel sand perch .......... serrano ardilla |
| *Epinephelus acanthistius* (Gilbert, 1892) | P | Gulf coney .......... baqueta |
| *Epinephelus adscensionis* (Osbeck, 1765) | A | rock hind .......... cabrilla payaso |
| *Epinephelus analogus* Gill, 1863 | P | spotted cabrilla .......... cabrilla pinta |
| *Epinephelus cifuentesi* Lavenberg & Grove, 1993 | PM | olive grouper .......... cabrilla gallina |
| *Epinephelus drummondhayi* Goode & Bean, 1878 | A | speckled hind .......... mero pintarroja |
| *Epinephelus exsul* (Fowler, 1944) | PM | tenspine grouper .......... cabrilla diez espinas |
| *Epinephelus flavolimbatus* Poey, 1865 | A | yellowedge grouper .......... mero extraviado |
| *Epinephelus guttatus* (Linnaeus, 1758) | A | red hind .......... cabrilla colorada |
| *Epinephelus itajara* (Lichtenstein, 1822) | A-PM | goliath grouper .......... mero guasa |
| *Epinephelus labriformis* (Jenyns, 1840) | PM | flag cabrilla .......... cabrilla piedrera |
| *Epinephelus morio* (Valenciennes, 1828) | A | red grouper .......... cherna americana |
| *Epinephelus mystacinus* (Poey, 1852) | A | misty grouper |
| *Epinephelus nigritus* (Holbrook, 1855) | A | warsaw grouper .......... mero negro |
| *Epinephelus niphobles* Gilbert & Starks, 1897 | P | star-studded grouper .......... baqueta ploma |

| SCIENTIFIC NAME | OCCURRENCE[1] | COMMON NAME (ENGLISH, SPANISH, FRENCH)[2] |
|---|---|---|
| Epinephelus niveatus (Valenciennes, 1828) | A | snowy grouper ......... cherna pintada |
| Epinephelus striatus (Bloch, 1792) | A | Nassau grouper ......... mero del Caribe |
| Gonioplectrus hispanus (Cuvier, 1828) | A | Spanish flag ......... cherna bandera |
| Hemanthias aureorubens (Longley, 1935) | A | streamer bass ......... cabrilla cinta |
| Hemanthias leptus (Ginsburg, 1952) | A | longtail bass ......... cabrilla robalo |
| +Hemanthias peruanus (Steindachner, 1875) | PM | splittail bass ......... cabrilla doblecola |
| *Hemanthias signifer (Garman, 1899) | P | hookthroat bass ......... cabrilla doncella |
| *Hemanthias vivanus (Jordan & Swain, 1885) | A | red barbier ......... barbero rojo |
| *Hypoplectrus aberrans Poey, 1868 | A | yellowbelly hamlet |
| *Hypoplectrus gemma Goode & Bean, 1882 | A | blue hamlet |
| *Hypoplectrus guttavarius (Poey, 1852) | A | shy hamlet |
| *Hypoplectrus indigo (Poey, 1851) | A | indigo hamlet |
| *Hypoplectrus nigricans (Poey, 1852) | A | black hamlet ......... mero carbonero |
| *Hypoplectrus puella (Cuvier, 1828) | A | barred hamlet ......... mero barril |
| +Hypoplectrus unicolor (Walbaum, 1792) | A | butter hamlet ......... mero mantequilla |
| Liopropoma carmabi (Randall, 1963) | A | candy basslet |
| *Liopropoma eukrines (Starck & Courtenay, 1962) | A | wrasse basslet |
| Liopropoma fasciatum Bussing, 1980 | PM | rainbow basslet ......... cabrilla arcoiris |
| Liopropoma longilepis Garman, 1899 | PM | scalyfin basslet ......... cabrilla aleta escamosa |
| *Liopropoma mowbrayi Woods & Kanazawa, 1951 | A | cave basslet ......... cabrilla de cueva |
| *Liopropoma rubre Poey, 1861 | A | peppermint basslet ......... cabrilla menta |
| *Mycteroperca acutirostris (Valenciennes, 1828) | A | western comb grouper ......... cherna peineta |
| *Mycteroperca bonaci (Poey, 1860) | A | black grouper ......... cherna negrillo |
| *Mycteroperca interstitialis (Poey, 1860) | A | yellowmouth grouper ......... cherna boca amarilla |
| *Mycteroperca jordani (Jenkins & Evermann, 1889) | P | Gulf grouper ......... baya |
| *Mycteroperca microlepis (Goode & Bean, 1879) | A | gag ......... abadejo |
| Mycteroperca phenax Jordan & Swain, 1884 | A | scamp ......... abadejo garropa |
| Mycteroperca prionura Rosenblatt & Zahuranec, 1967 | PM | sawtail grouper ......... cabrilla chiruda |
| *Mycteroperca rosacea (Streets, 1877) | PM | leopard grouper ......... cabrilla sardinera |
| *Mycteroperca tigris (Valenciennes, 1833) | A | tiger grouper ......... cabrilla gato |
| *Mycteroperca venenosa (Linnaeus, 1758) | A | yellowfin grouper ......... guacamayo |
| Mycteroperca xenarcha Jordan, 1888 | P | broomtail grouper ......... cabrilla plomuda |

| SCIENTIFIC NAME | OCCURRENCE[1] | COMMON NAME (ENGLISH, SPANISH, FRENCH)[2] |
|---|---|---|
| Paralabrax auroguttatus Walford, 1936 | PM | goldspotted sand bass .......... cabrilla extranjera |
| Paralabrax clathratus (Girard, 1854) | P | kelp bass ...... cabrilla sargacera |
| Paralabrax loro Walford, 1936 | PM | parrot sand bass ...... cabrilla cachete amarillo |
| Paralabrax maculatofasciatus (Steindachner, 1853) | P | spotted sand bass ...... cabrilla de roca |
| Paralabrax nebulifer (Girard, 1854) | P | barred sand bass ...... cabrilla verde de arena |
| *Paranthias colonus (Valenciennes, 1846) | P | Pacific creolefish ...... sandía |
| *Paranthias furcifer (Valenciennes, 1828) | A | Atlantic creolefish ...... rabirrubia del Golfo |
| Plectranthias garrupellus Robins & Starck, 1961 | A | apricot bass |
| Pronotogrammus eos Gilbert, 1890 | PM | bigeye bass ...... serrano ojón |
| *Pronotogrammus martinicensis (Guichenot, 1868) | A | roughtongue bass ...... serrano lengua rasposa |
| Pronotogrammus multifasciatus Gill, 1863 | P | threadfin bass ...... serrano baga |
| Pseudogramma gregoryi (Breder, 1927) | A | reef bass ...... jaboncillo arrecifal |
| Pseudogramma thaumasium (Gilbert, 1900) | PM | Pacific reef bass ...... jaboncillo ocelado |
| Rypticus bicolor Valenciennes, 1846 | PM | mottled soapfish ...... jabonero moteado |
| Rypticus bistrispinus (Mitchill, 1818) | A | freckled soapfish ...... jabonero pecoso |
| Rypticus courtenayi McCarthy, 1979 | PM | Socorro soapfish ...... jabonero de Socorro |
| Rypticus maculatus Holbrook, 1855 | A | whitespotted soapfish ...... jabonero albipunteado |
| Rypticus nigripinnis Gill, 1861 | PM | twice-spotted soapfish ...... jabonero doble punteado |
| *Rypticus saponaceus (Bloch & Schneider, 1801) | A | greater soapfish ...... jabonero grande |
| *Rypticus subbifrenatus Gill, 1861 | A | spotted soapfish ...... jabonero punteado |
| Schultzea beta (Hildebrand, 1940) | A | school bass ...... serrano escolar |
| Serraniculus pumilio Ginsburg, 1952 | A | pygmy sea bass ...... serrano pigmeo |
| *Serranus aequidens Gilbert, 1890 | P | deepwater serrano ...... serrano de agua profunda |
| Serranus annularis (Günther, 1880) | A | orangeback bass ...... serrano naranja |
| Serranus atrobranchus (Cuvier, 1829) | A | blackear bass ...... serrano oreja negra |
| *Serranus baldwini (Evermann & Marsh, 1899) | A | lantern bass ...... serrano linterna |
| Serranus chionaraia Robins & Starck, 1961 | A | snow bass |
| Serranus huascarii Steindachner, 1900 | PM | flag serrano ...... serrano bandera |
| Serranus notospilus Longley, 1935 | A | saddle bass ...... serrano ensillado |
| *Serranus phoebe Poey, 1851 | A | tattler ...... serrano diana |
| Serranus psittacinus Valenciennes, 1846 | PM | barred serrano ...... serrano guaseta |
| Serranus socorroensis Allen & Robertson, 1992 | PM | Socorro serrano ...... serrano de Socorro |

| SCIENTIFIC NAME | OCCURRENCE[1] | COMMON NAME (ENGLISH, SPANISH, FRENCH)[2] |
|---|---|---|
| *Serranus subligarius* (Cope, 1870) | A | belted sandfish ............ serrano aporreado |
| *Serranus tabacarius* (Cuvier, 1829) | A | tobaccofish ............ serrano jácome |
| *Serranus tigrinus* (Bloch, 1790) | A | harlequin bass ............ serrano arlequín |
| *Serranus tortugarum* Longley, 1935 | A | chalk bass ............ serrano pálido |
| Grammatidae—En-basslets, Sp-cabrilletas, Fr-grammatidés | | |
| *Gramma linki* Starck & Colin, 1978 | AM | yellowcheek basslet ............ cabrilleta mejilla amarilla |
| *\*Gramma loreto* Poey, 1868 | AM | fairy basslet ............ loreto |
| *Gramma melacara* Böhlke & Randall, 1963 | AM | blackcap basslet ............ cabrilleta violeta |
| *Lipogramma anabantoides* Böhlke, 1960 | A | dusky basslet |
| *+Lipogramma evides* Robins & Colin, 1979 | AM | banded basslet ............ cabrilleta cinteada |
| *Lipogramma trilineatum* Randall, 1963 | A | threeline basslet ............ cabrilleta tres rayas |
| +Opistognathidae—En-jawfishes, Sp-bocones, Fr-tout-en-gueule | | |
| *Lonchopisthus micrognathus* (Poey, 1860) | A | swordtail jawfish ............ bocón rayado |
| *Lonchopisthus sinuscalifornicus* Castro-Aguirre & Villavicencio-Garayzar, 1988 | PM | longtail jawfish ............ bocón cola larga |
| *Opistognathus aurifrons* (Jordan & Thompson, 1905) | A | yellowhead jawfish ............ bocón cabeza amarilla |
| *\*Opistognathus lonchurus* Jordan & Gilbert, 1882 | A | moustache jawfish ............ bocón bigote |
| *\*Opistognathus macrognathus* Poey, 1860 | A | banded jawfish |
| *\*Opistognathus maxillosus* Poey, 1860 | A | mottled jawfish ............ bocón moteado |
| *+Opistognathus megalepis* Smith-Vaniz, 1972 | AM | largescale jawfish ............ bocón escamón |
| *\*Opistognathus melachasme* Smith-Vaniz, 1972 | AM | megamouth jawfish ............ megabocón |
| *+Opistognathus mexicanus* Allen & Robertson, 1991 | PM | Mexican jawfish ............ bocón mexicano |
| *\*Opistognathus nothus* Smith-Vaniz, 1997 | A | yellowmouth jawfish |
| *+Opistognathus punctatus* Peters, 1869 | PM | finespotted jawfish ............ bocón punteado |
| *Opistognathus rhomaleus* Jordan & Gilbert, 1881 | PM | giant jawfish ............ bocón gigante |
| *\*Opistognathus robinsi* Smith-Vaniz, 1997 | A | spotfin jawfish |
| *Opistognathus rosenblatti* Allen & Robertson, 1991 | PM | bluespotted jawfish ............ bocón manchas azules |
| *Opistognathus scops* (Jenkins & Evermann, 1889) | PM | bullseye jawfish ............ bocón ocelado |
| *\*Opistognathus whitehursti* (Longley, 1927) | A | dusky jawfish ............ bocón prieto |

| SCIENTIFIC NAME | OCCURRENCE[1] | COMMON NAME (ENGLISH, SPANISH, FRENCH)[2] |
|---|---|---|
| +Centrarchidae—En-sunfishes, Sp-lobinas, Fr-achigans et crapets | | |
| Acantharchus pomotis (Baird, 1855) | F:U | mud sunfish |
| Ambloplites ariommus Viosca, 1936 | F:U | shadow bass |
| Ambloplites cavifrons Cope, 1868 | F:U | Roanoke bass |
| Ambloplites constellatus Cashner & Suttkus, 1977 | F:U | Ozark bass |
| Ambloplites rupestris (Rafinesque, 1817) | F:CU | rock bass ... crapet de roche |
| +Archoplites interruptus (Girard, 1854) | F:U | Sacramento perch |
| Centrarchus macropterus (Lacepède, 1801) | F:U | flier |
| Enneacanthus chaetodon (Baird, 1855) | F:U | blackbanded sunfish |
| Enneacanthus gloriosus (Holbrook, 1855) | F:U | bluespotted sunfish |
| Enneacanthus obesus (Girard, 1854) | F:U | banded sunfish |
| +Lepomis auritus (Linnaeus, 1758) | F:CU | redbreast sunfish |
| Lepomis cyanellus Rafinesque, 1819 | F:CUM[I] | green sunfish ... pez sol |
| Lepomis gibbosus (Linnaeus, 1758) | F:CU | pumpkinseed ... crapet-soleil |
| +Lepomis gulosus (Cuvier, 1829) | F:C[I]UM[I] | warmouth ... mojarra golosa |
| Lepomis humilis (Girard, 1858) | F:CU | orangespotted sunfish |
| Lepomis macrochirus Rafinesque, 1819 | F:CUM | bluegill ... mojarra oreja azul ... crapet arlequin |
| Lepomis marginatus (Holbrook, 1855) | F:U | dollar sunfish |
| +Lepomis megalotis (Rafinesque, 1820) | F:CUM | longear sunfish ... mojarra gigante ... crapet à longues oreilles |
| Lepomis microlophus (Günther, 1859) | F:UM | redear sunfish ... mojarra oreja roja |
| *Lepomis miniatus Jordan, 1877 | F:U | redspotted sunfish |
| +Lepomis punctatus (Valenciennes, 1831) | F:U | spotted sunfish |
| Lepomis symmetricus Forbes, 1883 | F:U | bantam sunfish |
| *Micropterus cataractae Williams & Burgess, 1999 | F:U | shoal bass |
| Micropterus coosae Hubbs & Bailey, 1940 | F:U | redeye bass |
| Micropterus dolomieu Lacepède, 1802 | F:CU | smallmouth bass ... achigan à petite bouche |
| Micropterus notius Bailey & Hubbs, 1949 | F:U | Suwannee bass |
| Micropterus punctulatus (Rafinesque, 1819) | F:U | spotted bass |
| +Micropterus salmoides (Lacepède, 1802) | F:CUM | largemouth bass ... lobina negra ... achigan à grande bouche |
| *Micropterus treculii (Vaillant & Bocourt, 1874) | F:U | Guadalupe bass |
| Pomoxis annularis Rafinesque, 1818 | F:CU | white crappie |
| Pomoxis nigromaculatus (Lesueur, 1829) | F:CUM | black crappie ... mojarra negra ... marigane noire |

| SCIENTIFIC NAME | OCCURRENCE[1] | COMMON NAME (ENGLISH, SPANISH, FRENCH)[2] |
|---|---|---|
| | | Percidae—En-perches, Sp-percas, Fr-perches et dards |
| *Ammocrypta beanii Jordan, 1877 | F:U | naked sand darter |
| +Ammocrypta bifascia Williams, 1975 | F:U | Florida sand darter |
| +Ammocrypta clara Jordan & Meek, 1885 | F:U | western sand darter |
| +Ammocrypta meridiana Williams, 1975 | F:U | southern sand darter |
| *Ammocrypta pellucida (Agassiz, 1863) | F:CU | eastern sand darter ............dard de sable |
| +Ammocrypta vivax Hay, 1882 | F:U | scaly sand darter |
| *Crystallaria asprella (Jordan, 1878) | F:U | crystal darter |
| Etheostoma acuticeps Bailey, 1959 | F:U | sharphead darter |
| Etheostoma aquali Williams & Etnier, 1978 | F:U | coppercheek darter |
| *Etheostoma artesiae (Hay, 1881) | F:U | redspot darter |
| Etheostoma asprigene (Forbes, 1878) | F:U | mud darter |
| Etheostoma australe Jordan, 1889 | F:M | Conchos darter ............perca del Conchos |
| Etheostoma baileyi Page & Burr, 1982 | F:U | emerald darter |
| Etheostoma barbouri Kuehne & Small, 1971 | F:U | teardrop darter |
| Etheostoma barrenense Burr & Page, 1982 | F:U | splendid darter |
| *Etheostoma basilare Page, Hardman & Near, 2003 | F:U | corrugated darter |
| *Etheostoma bellator Suttkus & Bailey, 1993 | F:U | Warrior darter |
| Etheostoma bellum Zorach, 1968 | F:U | orangefin darter |
| *Etheostoma bison Ceas & Page, 1997 | F:U | Buffalo darter |
| +Etheostoma blennioides Rafinesque, 1819 | F:CU | greenside darter |
| Etheostoma blennius Gilbert & Swain, 1887 | F:U | blenny darter |
| Etheostoma boschungi Wall & Williams, 1974 | F:U | slackwater darter |
| *Etheostoma brevirostrum Suttkus & Etnier, 1991 | F:U | holiday darter |
| *Etheostoma burri Ceas & Page, 1997 | F:U | brook darter |
| Etheostoma caeruleum Storer, 1845 | F:CU | rainbow darter ............dard arc-en-ciel |
| Etheostoma camurum (Cope, 1870) | F:U | bluebreast darter |
| *Etheostoma cervus Powers & Mayden, 2003 | F:U | Chickasaw darter |
| *Etheostoma chermocki Boschung, Mayden & Tomelleri, 1992 | F:U | vermilion darter |
| *Etheostoma chienense Page & Ceas, 1992 | F:U | relict darter |
| Etheostoma chlorobranchium Zorach, 1972 | F:U | greenfin darter |

| SCIENTIFIC NAME | OCCURRENCE[1] | COMMON NAME (ENGLISH, SPANISH, FRENCH)[2] |
|---|---|---|
| *Etheostoma chlorosoma (Hay, 1881) | F:U | bluntnose darter |
| *Etheostoma chuckwachatte Mayden & Wood, 1993 | F:U | lipstick darter |
| Etheostoma cinereum Storer, 1845 | F:U | ashy darter |
| Etheostoma collettei Birdsong & Knapp, 1969 | F:U | creole darter |
| +Etheostoma collis (Hubbs & Cannon, 1935) | F:U | Carolina darter |
| *Etheostoma colorosum Suttkus & Bailey, 1993 | F:U | coastal darter |
| Etheostoma coosae (Fowler, 1945) | F:U | Coosa darter |
| *Etheostoma corona Page & Ceas, 1992 | F:U | crown darter |
| Etheostoma cragini Gilbert, 1885 | F:U | Arkansas darter |
| Etheostoma crossopterum Braasch & Mayden, 1985 | F:U | fringed darter |
| Etheostoma davisoni Hay, 1885 | F:U | Choctawhatchee darter |
| *Etheostoma denoncourti Stauffer & van Snik, 1997 | F:U | golden darter |
| *Etheostoma derivativum Page, Hardman & Near, 2003 | F:U | stone darter |
| Etheostoma ditrema Ramsey & Suttkus, 1965 | F:U | coldwater darter |
| *Etheostoma douglasi Wood & Mayden, 1993 | F:U | Tuskaloosa darter |
| *Etheostoma duryi Henshall, 1889 | F:U | blackside snubnose darter |
| Etheostoma edwini (Hubbs & Cannon, 1935) | F:U | brown darter |
| Etheostoma etnieri Bouchard, 1977 | F:U | cherry darter |
| *Etheostoma etowahae Wood & Mayden, 1993 | F:U | Etowah darter |
| Etheostoma euzonum (Hubbs & Black, 1940) | F:U | Arkansas saddled darter |
| Etheostoma exile (Girard, 1859) | F:CU | Iowa darter .......... dard à ventre jaune |
| Etheostoma flabellare Rafinesque, 1819 | F:CU | fantail darter ....................... dard barré |
| Etheostoma flavum Etnier & Bailey, 1989 | F:U | saffron darter |
| Etheostoma fonticola (Jordan & Gilbert, 1886) | F:U | fountain darter |
| *Etheostoma forbesi Page & Ceas, 1992 | F:U | Barrens darter |
| Etheostoma fragi Distler 1968 | F:U | Strawberry darter |
| Etheostoma fricksium Hildebrand, 1923 | F:U | Savannah darter |
| Etheostoma fusiforme (Girard, 1854) | F:U | swamp darter |
| Etheostoma gracile (Girard, 1859) | F:U | slough darter |
| Etheostoma grahami (Girard, 1859) | F:UM | Rio Grande darter .......... perca del Bravo |
| *Etheostoma gutselli (Hildebrand, 1932) | F:U | Tuckasegee darter |
| Etheostoma histrio Jordan & Gilbert, 1887 | F:U | harlequin darter |

| SCIENTIFIC NAME | OCCURRENCE[1] | COMMON NAME (ENGLISH, SPANISH, FRENCH)[2] |
|---|---|---|
| *Etheostoma hopkinsi* (Fowler, 1945) | F:U | Christmas darter |
| *Etheostoma inscriptum* (Jordan & Brayton, 1878) | F:U | turquoise darter |
| *Etheostoma jessiae* (Jordan & Brayton, 1878) | F:U | blueside darter |
| +*Etheostoma jordani* Gilbert, 1891 | F:U | greenbreast darter |
| *Etheostoma juliae* Meek, 1891 | F:U | yoke darter |
| *Etheostoma kanawhae* (Raney, 1941) | F:U | Kanawha darter |
| *Etheostoma kantuckeense* Ceas & Page, 1997 | F:U | Highland Rim darter |
| *Etheostoma kennicotti* (Putnam, 1863) | F:U | stripetail darter |
| *Etheostoma lachneri* Suttkus & Bailey, 1994 | F:U | Tombigbee darter |
| *Etheostoma lawrencei* Ceas & Burr, 2002 | F:U | headwater darter |
| *Etheostoma lepidum* (Baird & Girard, 1853) | F:U | greenthroat darter |
| *Etheostoma longimanum* Jordan, 1888 | F:U | longfin darter |
| *Etheostoma lugoi* Norris & Minckley, 1997 | F:M | tufa darter .......... perca de toba |
| *Etheostoma luteovinctum* Gilbert & Swain, 1887 | F:U | redband darter |
| *Etheostoma lynceum* Hay, 1885 | F:U | brighteye darter |
| *Etheostoma maculatum* Kirtland, 1840 | F:U | spotted darter |
| *Etheostoma mariae* (Fowler, 1947) | F:U | pinewoods darter |
| *Etheostoma microlepidum* Raney & Zorach, 1967 | F:U | smallscale darter |
| *Etheostoma microperca* Jordan & Gilbert, 1888 | F:CU | least darter |
| *Etheostoma moorei* Raney & Suttkus, 1964 | F:U | yellowcheek darter |
| *Etheostoma neopterum* Howell & Dingerkus, 1978 | F:U | lollypop darter |
| *Etheostoma niangue* Gilbert & Meek, 1887 | F:U | Niangua darter |
| *Etheostoma nigripinne* Braasch & Mayden, 1985 | F:U | blackfin darter |
| +*Etheostoma nigrum* Rafinesque, 1820 | F:CU | johnny darter .......... raseux-de-terre noir |
| *Etheostoma nuchale* Howell & Caldwell, 1965 | F:U | watercress darter |
| *Etheostoma obeyense* Kirsch, 1892 | F:U | barcheek darter |
| *Etheostoma okaloosae* (Fowler, 1941) | F:U | Okaloosa darter |
| *Etheostoma olivaceum* Braasch & Page, 1979 | F:U | sooty darter |
| *Etheostoma olmstedi* Storer, 1842 | F:CU | tessellated darter .......... raseux-de-terre gris |
| *Etheostoma oophylax* Ceas & Page, 1992 | F:U | guardian darter |
| *Etheostoma osburni* (Hubbs & Trautman, 1932) | F:U | candy darter |
| *Etheostoma pallididorsum* Distler & Metcalf, 1962 | F:U | paleback darter |

| SCIENTIFIC NAME | OCCURRENCE[1] | COMMON NAME (ENGLISH, SPANISH, FRENCH)[2] |
|---|---|---|
| *Etheostoma parvipinne* Gilbert & Swain, 1887 | F:U | goldstripe darter |
| \**Etheostoma percnurum* Jenkins, 1994 | F:U | duskytail darter |
| *Etheostoma perlongum* (Hubbs & Raney, 1946) | F:U | Waccamaw darter |
| \**Etheostoma phytophilum* Bart & Taylor, 1999 | F:U | rush darter |
| *Etheostoma podostemone* Jordan & Jenkins, 1889 | F:U | riverweed darter |
| *Etheostoma pottsii* (Girard, 1859) | F:M | Mexican darter ..................... perca mexicana |
| *Etheostoma proeliare* (Hay, 1881) | F:U | cypress darter |
| \**Etheostoma pseudovulatum* Page & Ceas, 1992 | F:U | egg-mimic darter |
| *Etheostoma punctulatum* (Agassiz, 1854) | F:U | stippled darter |
| +*Etheostoma pyrrhogaster* Bailey & Etnier, 1988 | F:U | firebelly darter |
| *Etheostoma radiosum* (Hubbs & Black, 1941) | F:U | orangebelly darter |
| *Etheostoma rafinesquei* Burr & Page, 1982 | F:U | Kentucky darter |
| \**Etheostoma ramseyi* Suttkus & Bailey, 1994 | F:U | Alabama darter |
| \**Etheostoma raneyi* Suttkus & Bart, 1994 | F:U | Yazoo darter |
| *Etheostoma rubrum* Raney & Suttkus, 1966 | F:U | bayou darter |
| *Etheostoma rufilineatum* (Cope, 1870) | F:U | redline darter |
| *Etheostoma rupestre* Gilbert & Swain, 1887 | F:U | rock darter |
| *Etheostoma sagitta* (Jordan & Swain, 1883) | F:U | arrow darter |
| *Etheostoma sanguifluum* (Cope, 1870) | F:U | bloodfin darter |
| \**Etheostoma scotti* Bauer, Etnier & Burkhead, 1995 | F:U | Cherokee darter |
| *Etheostoma segrex* Norris & Minckley, 1997 | F:M | Salado darter ..................... perca del Salado |
| \**Etheostoma sellare* (Radcliffe & Welsh, 1913) | F[X]:U | Maryland darter |
| *Etheostoma serrifer* (Hubbs & Cannon, 1935) | F:U | sawcheek darter |
| *Etheostoma simoterum* (Cope, 1868) | F:U | snubnose darter |
| *Etheostoma smithi* Page & Braasch, 1976 | F:U | slabrock darter |
| +*Etheostoma spectabile* (Agassiz, 1854) | F:U | orangethroat darter |
| *Etheostoma squamiceps* Jordan, 1877 | F:U | spottail darter |
| *Etheostoma stigmaeum* (Jordan, 1877) | F:U | speckled darter |
| *Etheostoma striatulum* Page & Braasch, 1977 | F:U | striated darter |
| \**Etheostoma susanae* (Jordan & Swain, 1883) | F:U | Cumberland darter |
| \**Etheostoma swaini* (Jordan, 1884) | F:U | Gulf darter |
| *Etheostoma swannanoa* Jordan & Evermann, 1889 | F:U | Swannanoa darter |

| SCIENTIFIC NAME | OCCURRENCE[1] | COMMON NAME (ENGLISH, SPANISH, FRENCH)[2] |
|---|---|---|
| *Etheostoma tallapoosae* Suttkus & Etnier, 1991 | F:U | Tallapoosa darter |
| *Etheostoma tecumsehi* Ceas & Page, 1997 | F:U | Shawnee darter |
| +*Etheostoma tetrazonum* (Hubbs & Black, 1940) | F:U | Missouri saddled darter |
| *Etheostoma thalassinum* (Jordan & Brayton, 1878) | F:U | seagreen darter |
| +*Etheostoma tippecanoe* Jordan & Evermann, 1890 | F:U | Tippecanoe darter |
| *Etheostoma trisella* Bailey & Richards, 1963 | F:U | trispot darter |
| *Etheostoma tuscumbia* Gilbert & Swain, 1887 | F:U | Tuscumbia darter |
| *Etheostoma uniporum* Distler, 1968 | F:U | current darter |
| *Etheostoma variatum* Kirtland, 1840 | F:U | variegate darter |
| +*Etheostoma virgatum* (Jordan, 1880) | F:U | striped darter |
| *Etheostoma vitreum* (Cope, 1870) | F:U | glassy darter |
| *Etheostoma vulneratum* (Cope, 1870) | F:U | wounded darter |
| *Etheostoma wapiti* Etnier & Williams, 1989 | F:U | boulder darter |
| +*Etheostoma whipplei* (Girard, 1859) | F:U | redfin darter |
| *Etheostoma zonale* (Cope, 1868) | F:U | banded darter |
| *Etheostoma zonifer* (Hubbs & Cannon, 1935) | F:U | backwater darter |
| *Etheostoma zonistium* Bailey & Etnier, 1988 | F:U | bandfin darter |
| *Gymnocephalus cernuus* (Linnaeus, 1758) | F[I]:CU | ruffe |
| *Perca flavescens* (Mitchill, 1814) | F:CU | yellow perch .......... perchaude |
| *Percina antesella* Williams & Etnier, 1977 | F:U | amber darter |
| *Percina aurantiaca* (Cope, 1868) | F:U | tangerine darter |
| *Percina aurolineata* Suttkus & Ramsey, 1967 | F:U | goldline darter |
| *Percina aurora* Suttkus & Thompson, 1994 | F:U | pearl darter |
| *Percina austroperca* Thompson, 1995 | F:U | southern logperch |
| *Percina brevicauda* Suttkus & Bart, 1994 | F:U | coal darter |
| *Percina burtoni* Fowler, 1945 | F:U | blotchside logperch |
| +*Percina caprodes* (Rafinesque, 1818) | F:CU | logperch .......... fouille-roche zébré |
| +*Percina carbonaria* (Baird & Girard, 1853) | F:U | Texas logperch |
| +*Percina copelandi* (Jordan, 1877) | F:CU | channel darter .......... fouille-roche gris |
| *Percina crassa* (Jordan & Brayton, 1878) | F:U | Piedmont darter |
| +*Percina cymatotaenia* (Gilbert & Meek, 1887) | F:U | bluestripe darter |

| SCIENTIFIC NAME | OCCURRENCE[1] | COMMON NAME (ENGLISH, SPANISH, FRENCH)[2] |
|---|---|---|
| Percina evides (Jordan & Copeland, 1877) | F:U | gilt darter |
| *Percina fulvitaenia Morris & Page, 1981 | F:U | Ozark logperch |
| Percina gymnocephala Beckham, 1980 | F:U | Appalachia darter |
| *Percina jenkinsi Thompson, 1985 | F:U | Conasauga logperch |
| *Percina kathae Thompson, 1997 | F:U | Mobile logperch |
| *Percina lenticula Richards & Knapp, 1964 | F:U | freckled darter |
| *Percina macrocephala (Cope, 1867) | F:U | longhead darter |
| Percina macrolepida Stevenson, 1971 | F:UM | bigscale logperch ........ perca escamona |
| Percina maculata (Girard, 1859) | F:CU | blackside darter |
| Percina nasuta (Bailey, 1941) | F:U | longnose darter |
| *Percina nevisense (Cope, 1870) | F:U | chainback darter |
| Percina nigrofasciata (Agassiz, 1854) | F:U | blackbanded darter |
| Percina notogramma (Raney & Hubbs, 1948) | F:U | stripeback darter |
| Percina oxyrhynchus (Hubbs & Raney, 1939) | F:U | sharpnose darter |
| Percina palmaris (Bailey, 1940) | F:U | bronze darter |
| Percina pantherina (Moore & Reeves, 1955) | F:U | leopard darter |
| +Percina peltata (Stauffer, 1864) | F:U | shield darter |
| Percina phoxocephala (Nelson, 1876) | F:U | slenderhead darter |
| Percina rex (Jordan & Evermann, 1889) | F:U | Roanoke logperch |
| Percina roanoka (Jordan & Jenkins, 1889) | F:U | Roanoke darter |
| Percina sciera (Swain, 1883) | F:U | dusky darter |
| Percina shumardi (Girard, 1859) | F:CU | river darter |
| Percina squamata (Gilbert & Swain, 1887) | F:U | olive darter |
| *Percina stictogaster Burr & Page, 1993 | F:U | frecklebelly darter |
| *Percina suttkusi Thompson, 1997 | F:U | Gulf logperch |
| Percina tanasi Etnier, 1976 | F:U | snail darter |
| Percina uranidea (Jordan & Gilbert, 1887) | F:U | stargazing darter |
| +Percina vigil (Hay, 1882) | F:U | saddleback darter |
| *Sander canadensis (Griffith & Smith, 1834) | F:CU | sauger ......... doré noir |
| *Sander lucioperca (Linnaeus, 1758) | F[I]:U | zander |
| *Sander vitreus (Mitchill, 1818) | F:CU | walleye ......... doré jaune |

| SCIENTIFIC NAME | OCCURRENCE[1] | COMMON NAME (ENGLISH, SPANISH, FRENCH)[2] |
|---|---|---|
| Priacanthidae—En-bigeyes, Sp-catalufas, Fr-beauclaires | | |
| Cookeolus japonicus (Cuvier, 1829) | A | bulleye ................... catalufa aleta larga |
| *Heteropriacanthus cruentatus (Lacepède, 1801) | A-PM | glasseye snapper ........ catalufa roquera |
| Priacanthus alalaua Jordan & Evermann, 1903 | PM | Hawaiian bigeye ......... catalufa alalahua |
| Priacanthus arenatus Cuvier, 1829 | A | bigeye................... catalufa ojón |
| Pristigenys alta (Gill, 1862) | A | short bigeye ............ catalufa de lo alto |
| Pristigenys serrula (Gilbert, 1891) | P | popeye catalufa ......... catalufa semáforo |
| Apogonidae—En-cardinalfishes, Sp-cardenales, Fr-poissons-cardinaux | | |
| Apogon affinis (Poey, 1875) | A | bigtooth cardinalfish ... cardenal dientón |
| Apogon atricaudus Jordan & McGregor, 1898 | PM | plain cardinalfish ...... cardenal sencillo |
| Apogon aurolineatus (Mowbray, 1927) | A | bridle cardinalfish ..... cardenal frenado |
| Apogon binotatus (Poey, 1867) | A | barred cardinalfish ..... cardenal rayado |
| Apogon dovii Gunther, 1861 | PM | tailspot cardinalfish ... cardenal colimanchada |
| Apogon evermanni Jordan & Snyder, 1904 | AM | oddscale cardinalfish ... cardenal coralero |
| Apogon gouldi Smith-Vaniz, 1977 | AM | deepwater cardinalfish .. cardenal de lo alto |
| Apogon guadalupensis (Osburn & Nichols, 1916) | P | Guadalupe cardinalfish .. cardenal mexicano |
| Apogon lachneri Böhlke, 1959 | A | whitestar cardinalfish .. cardenal estrella blanca |
| Apogon leptocaulus Gilbert, 1972 | A | slendertail cardinalfish | 
| Apogon maculatus (Poey, 1860) | A | flamefish ............... cardenal manchado |
| *Apogon pacificus (Herre, 1935) | P | pink cardinalfish ....... cardenal morro listado |
| Apogon phenax Böhlke & Randall, 1968 | A | mimic cardinalfish ...... cardenal mimético |
| Apogon pillionatus Böhlke & Randall, 1968 | A | broadsaddle cardinalfish. cardenal colirrayada |
| Apogon planifrons Longley & Hildebrand, 1940 | A | pale cardinalfish ....... cardenal pálido |
| Apogon pseudomaculatus Longley, 1932 | A | twospot cardinalfish .... cardenal dos puntos |
| Apogon quadrisquamatus Longley, 1934 | A | sawcheek cardinalfish ... cardenal espinoso |
| Apogon retrosella (Gill, 1862) | PM | barspot cardinalfish .... cardenal de Cortés |
| Apogon townsendi (Breder, 1927) | A | belted cardinalfish ..... cardenal cincho |
| Astrapogon alutus (Jordan & Gilbert, 1882) | A | bronze cardinalfish ..... cardenal bronceado |
| *Astrapogon puncticulatus (Poey, 1867) | A | blackfin cardinalfish ... cardenal punteado |
| *Astrapogon stellatus (Cope, 1867) | A | conchfish ............... cardenal del cobo |
| *Phaeoptyx conklini (Silvester, 1915) | A | freckled cardinalfish ... cardenal pecoso |

| SCIENTIFIC NAME | OCCURRENCE[1] | COMMON NAME (ENGLISH, SPANISH, FRENCH)[2] |
|---|---|---|
| Phaeoptyx pigmentaria (Poey, 1860) | A | dusky cardinalfish .......... cardenal prieto |
| Phaeoptyx xenus (Böhlke & Randall, 1968) | A | sponge cardinalfish .......... cardenal esponjero |
| +Malacanthidae—En-tilefishes, Sp-blanquillos, Fr-tiles | | |
| *Caulolatilus affinis Gill, 1865 | P | Pacific golden-eyed tilefish ...... conejo |
| Caulolatilus chrysops (Valenciennes, 1833) | A | goldface tilefish .......... blanquillo ojo amarillo |
| Caulolatilus cyanops Poey, 1866 | A | blackline tilefish .......... domingo |
| +Caulolatilus hubbsi Dooley, 1978 | P | enigmatic tilefish .......... blanquillo enigmático |
| Caulolatilus intermedius Howell Rivero, 1936 | A | anchor tilefish .......... blanquillo payaso |
| Caulolatilus microps Goode & Bean, 1878 | A | blueline tilefish .......... blanquillo lucio |
| *Caulolatilus princeps (Jenyns, 1840) | P | ocean whitefish .......... pierna |
| Lopholatilus chamaeleonticeps Goode & Bean, 1879 | A | tilefish .......... conejo amarillo |
| *Malacanthus plumieri (Bloch, 1786) | A | sand tilefish .......... matajuelo blanco |
| Pomatomidae—En-bluefishes, Sp-anjovas, Fr-tassergals | | |
| Pomatomus saltatrix (Linnaeus, 1766) | A | bluefish .......... anjova |
| Nematistiidae—En-roosterfishes, Sp-papagallos, Fr-plumières | | |
| Nematistius pectoralis Gill, 1862 | P | roosterfish .......... papagallo |
| Echeneidae—En-remoras, Sp-rémoras, Fr-rémoras | | |
| Echeneis naucrates Linnaeus, 1758 | A-P | sharksucker .......... rémora rayada |
| *Echeneis neucratoides Zuiew, 1786 | A | whitefin sharksucker .......... rémora filoblanco |
| Phtheirichthys lineatus (Menzies, 1791) | A-P | slender suckerfish .......... rémora delgada |
| *Remora albescens (Temminck & Schlegel, 1850) | A-P | white suckerfish .......... rémora blanca |
| Remora australis (Bennett, 1840) | A-P | whalesucker .......... rémora ballenera |
| Remora brachyptera (Lowe, 1839) | A-P | spearfish remora .......... rémora robusta |
| Remora osteochir (Cuvier, 1829) | A-P | marlinsucker .......... rémora marlinera |
| Remora remora (Linnaeus, 1758) | A-P | remora .......... rémora tiburonera |
| Rachycentridae—En-cobias, Sp-cobias, Fr-cobilos | | |
| Rachycentron canadum (Linnaeus, 1766) | A | cobia .......... cobia |

| SCIENTIFIC NAME | OCCURRENCE[1] | COMMON NAME (ENGLISH, SPANISH, FRENCH)[2] | |
|---|---|---|---|
| *Coryphaenidae—En-dolphinfishes, Sp-dorados, Fr-coryphènes | | | |
| *Coryphaena equiselis Linnaeus, 1758 | A-PM | pompano dolphinfish | dorado enano |
| *Coryphaena hippurus Linnaeus, 1758 | A-P | dolphinfish | dorado |
| Carangidae—En-jacks, Sp-jureles y pámpanos, Fr-carangues | | | |
| Alectis ciliaris (Bloch, 1787) | A-PM | African pompano | pámpano de hebra |
| +Caranx bartholomaei Cuvier, 1833 | A | yellow jack | cojinuda amarilla |
| Caranx caballus Günther, 1868 | P | green jack | jurel bonito |
| *Caranx caninus Günther, 1867 | P | Pacific crevalle jack | jurel toro |
| +Caranx crysos (Mitchill, 1815) | A | blue runner | cojinuda negra |
| +Caranx dentex (Bloch & Schneider, 1801) | A | white trevally | |
| +Caranx hippos (Linnaeus, 1766) | A | crevalle jack | jurel común |
| Caranx latus Agassiz, 1831 | A | horse-eye jack | jurel blanco |
| Caranx lugubris Poey, 1860 | A-PM | black jack | jurel negro |
| Caranx melampygus Cuvier, 1833 | PM | bluefin trevally | jurel aleta azul |
| Caranx orthogrammus Jordan & Gilbert, 1882 | PM | island jack | jurel isleño |
| +Caranx otrynter Jordan & Gilbert, 1883 | PM | threadfin jack | jurel chicuaca |
| +Caranx ruber (Bloch, 1793) | A | bar jack | cojinuda carbonera |
| *Caranx sexfasciatus Quoy & Gaimard, 1825 | P | bigeye trevally | jurel voraz |
| *Caranx vinctus Jordan & Gilbert, 1882 | P | cocinero | cocinero |
| Chloroscombrus chrysurus (Linnaeus, 1766) | A | Atlantic bumper | horqueta del Atlántico |
| Chloroscombrus orqueta Jordan & Gilbert, 1883 | P | Pacific bumper | horqueta del Pacífico |
| Decapterus macarellus (Cuvier, 1833) | A-PM | mackerel scad | macarela caballa |
| Decapterus macrosoma Bleeker, 1851 | PM | shortfin scad | macarela alicorta |
| *Decapterus muroadsi (Temminck & Schlegel, 1844) | P | amberstripe scad | macarela plátano |
| Decapterus punctatus (Cuvier, 1829) | A | round scad | macarela chuparaco |
| Decapterus tabl Berry, 1968 | A | redtail scad | |
| *Elagatis bipinnulata (Quoy & Gaimard, 1825) | A-PM | rainbow runner | macarela salmón |
| Gnathanodon speciosus (Forsskål, 1775) | PM | golden trevally | jurel dorado |
| Hemicaranx amblyrhynchus (Cuvier, 1833) | A | bluntnose jack | jurelito chato |
| Hemicaranx leucurus (Günther, 1864) | PM | yellowfin jack | jurelito aletiamarilla |

| SCIENTIFIC NAME | OCCURRENCE[1] | COMMON NAME (ENGLISH, SPANISH, FRENCH)[2] |
|---|---|---|
| Hemicaranx zelotes Gilbert, 1898 | PM | blackfin jack ... jurelito chocho |
| Naucrates ductor (Linnaeus, 1758) | A-P | pilotfish ... pez piloto |
| Oligoplites altus (Günther, 1868) | PM | longjaw leatherjack ... piña bocona |
| Oligoplites refulgens Gilbert & Starks, 1904 | PM | shortjaw leatherjack ... piña flaca |
| *Oligoplites saurus (Bloch & Schneider, 1801) | A-PM | leatherjack ... piña sietecueros |
| Selar crumenophthalmus (Bloch, 1793) | A-PM | bigeye scad ... charrito ojón |
| *Selene brevoortii (Gill, 1863) | P | Mexican lookdown ... jorobado mexicano |
| +Selene brownii (Cuvier, 1816) | AM | Caribbean moonfish ... jorobado luna |
| +Selene orstedii Lütken, 1880 | PM | Mexican moonfish ... jorobado carite |
| *Selene peruviana (Guichenot, 1866) | P | Pacific moonfish ... jorobado papelillo |
| Selene setapinnis (Mitchill, 1815) | A | Atlantic moonfish ... jorobado caballa |
| Selene vomer (Linnaeus, 1758) | A | lookdown ... jorobado penacho |
| Seriola dumerili (Risso, 1810) | A | greater amberjack ... medregal coronado |
| *Seriola fasciata (Bloch, 1793) | A | lesser amberjack ... medregal listado |
| *Seriola lalandi Valenciennes, 1833 | P | yellowtail jack ... medregal rabo amarillo |
| Seriola peruana Steindachner, 1881 | PM | fortune jack ... medregal fortuno |
| Seriola rivoliana Valenciennes, 1833 | A-P | almaco jack ... medregal limón |
| Seriola zonata (Mitchill, 1815) | A | banded rudderfish ... medregal rayado |
| Trachinotus carolinus (Linnaeus, 1766) | A | Florida pompano ... pámpano amarillo |
| Trachinotus falcatus (Linnaeus, 1758) | A | permit ... pámpano palometa |
| Trachinotus goodei Jordan & Evermann, 1896 | A | palometa ... pámpano listado |
| Trachinotus kennedyi Steindachner, 1876 | PM | blackblotch pompano ... pámpano gitano |
| Trachinotus paitensis Cuvier, 1832 | P | paloma pompano ... pámpano paloma |
| *Trachinotus rhodopus Gill, 1863 | P | gafftopsail pompano ... pámpano fino |
| Trachinotus stilbe (Jordan & MacGregor, 1898) | PM | steel pompano ... pámpano acerado |
| Trachurus lathami Nichols, 1920 | A | rough scad ... charrito garretón |
| Trachurus symmetricus (Ayres, 1855) | P | jack mackerel ... charrito chícharo |
| *Uraspis helvola (Forster, 1801) | PM | whitemouth jack ... jurel lengua blanca |
| +Uraspis secunda (Poey, 1860) | A-P | cottonmouth jack ... jurel volantín |

Bramidae—En-pomfrets, Sp-tristones, Fr-castagnoles

| | | |
|---|---|---|
| *Brama brama (Bonnaterre, 1788) | A | Atlantic pomfret |

| SCIENTIFIC NAME | OCCURRENCE[1] | COMMON NAME (ENGLISH, SPANISH, FRENCH)[2] |
|---|---|---|
| *Brama caribbea* Mead, 1972 | A | Caribbean pomfret......tristón del Caribe |
| *Brama dussumieri* Cuvier, 1831 | A | lowfin pomfret |
| *Brama japonica* Hilgendorf, 1878 | P | Pacific pomfret......tristón del Pacífico |
| *Brama orcini* Cuvier, 1831 | P | bigtooth pomfret |
| *Pteraclis aesticola* (Jordan & Snyder, 1901) | P | Pacific fanfish......abanico del Pacífico |
| *Pterycombus brama* Fries, 1837 | A | Atlantic fanfish |
| *Taractes asper* Lowe, 1843 | P | rough pomfret |
| *Taractes rubescens* (Jordan & Evermann, 1887) | A | keeltail pomfret......tristón coliquillada |
| *Taractichthys longipinnis* (Lowe, 1843) | A | bigscale pomfret......tristón aletudo |
| *Taractichthys steindachneri* (Döderlein, 1884) | P | sickle pomfret......tristón segador |
| | | |
| Emmelichthyidae—En-rovers, Sp-andorreros, Fr-poissons-rubis | | |
| | | |
| *Emmelichthys ruber* (Trunov, 1976) | A | red rover |
| *Erythrocles monodi* Poll & Cadenat, 1954 | A | crimson rover |
| | | |
| +Lutjanidae—En-snappers, Sp-pargos y huachinangos, Fr-vivaneaux | | |
| | | |
| +*Apsilus dentatus* Guichenot, 1853 | A | black snapper......pargo lamparita |
| *Etelis oculatus* (Valenciennes, 1828) | A | queen snapper......pargo cachucho |
| *Hoplopagrus guentherii* Gill, 1862 | PM | barred pargo......pargo coconaco |
| *Lutjanus analis* (Cuvier, 1828) | A | mutton snapper......pargo criollo |
| *Lutjanus apodus* (Walbaum, 1792) | A | schoolmaster......pargo canchix |
| *Lutjanus aratus* (Günther, 1864) | PM | mullet snapper......pargo raicero |
| *Lutjanus argentiventris* (Peters, 1869) | P | amarillo snapper......pargo amarillo |
| *Lutjanus buccanella* (Cuvier, 1828) | A | blackfin snapper......pargo sesí |
| *Lutjanus campechanus* (Poey, 1860) | A | red snapper......huachinango del Golfo |
| *Lutjanus colorado* Jordan & Gilbert, 1882 | P | colorado snapper......pargo colorado |
| *Lutjanus cyanopterus* (Cuvier, 1828) | A | cubera snapper......pargo cubera |
| *Lutjanus griseus* (Linnaeus, 1758) | A-F:UM | gray snapper......pargo mulato |
| *Lutjanus guttatus* (Steindachner, 1869) | PM | spotted rose snapper......pargo lunarejo |
| *Lutjanus inermis* (Peters, 1869) | PM | golden snapper......pargo rabirrubia |
| *Lutjanus jocu* (Bloch & Schneider, 1801) | A | dog snapper......pargo caballera |
| *Lutjanus jordani* (Gilbert, 1898) | PM | whipper snapper......pargo colmillón |

| SCIENTIFIC NAME | OCCURRENCE[1] | COMMON NAME (ENGLISH, SPANISH, FRENCH)[2] |
|---|---|---|
| *Lutjanus mahogoni* (Cuvier, 1828) | A | mahogany snapper — pargo ojón |
| *Lutjanus novemfasciatus* Gill, 1862 | P | Pacific dog snapper — pargo prieto |
| *Lutjanus peru* (Nichols & Murphy, 1922) | P | Pacific red snapper — huachinango del Pacífico |
| *Lutjanus purpureus* (Poey, 1866) | A | Caribbean red snapper — pargo rojo |
| *Lutjanus synagris* (Linnaeus, 1758) | A | lane snapper — pargo biajaiba |
| *Lutjanus viridis* (Valenciennes, 1846) | PM | blue-and-gold snapper — pargo azul-dorado |
| *Lutjanus vivanus* (Cuvier, 1828) | A | silk snapper — huachinango ojo amarillo |
| +*Ocyurus chrysurus* (Bloch, 1791) | A | yellowtail snapper — rubia |
| *Pristipomoides aquilonaris* (Goode & Bean, 1896) | A | wenchman — huachinango navaja |
| *Pristipomoides freemani* Anderson, 1966 | A | slender wenchman |
| *Pristipomoides macrophthalmus* (Müller & Troschel, 1848) | AM | cardinal snapper — pargo panchito |
| *Rhomboplites aurorubens* (Cuvier, 1829) | A | vermilion snapper — besugo |

Lobotidae—En-tripletails, Sp-dormilonas, Fr-croupias

| | | |
|---|---|---|
| *Lobotes pacificus* Gilbert, 1898 | P | Pacific tripletail — dormilona del Pacífico |
| *Lobotes surinamensis* (Bloch, 1790) | A | Atlantic tripletail — dormilona del Atlántico |

Gerreidae—En-mojarras, Sp-mojarras, Fr-blanches

| | | |
|---|---|---|
| *Diapterus auratus* Ranzani, 1842 | A-F:UM | Irish pompano — mojarra guacha |
| *Diapterus aureolus* (Jordan & Gilbert, 1882) | PM | golden mojarra — mojarra palometa |
| *Diapterus peruvianus* (Cuvier, 1830) | F:M-PM | Peruvian mojarra — mojarra aletas amarillas |
| *Diapterus rhombeus* (Cuvier, 1829) | AM-F:M | rhombic mojarra — mojarra de estero |
| *Eucinostomus argenteus* Baird & Girard, 1855 | A-F:M | spotfin mojarra — mojarra plateada |
| *Eucinostomus currani* Zahuranec, 1980 | F:M-P | Pacific flagfin mojarra — mojarra tricolor |
| *Eucinostomus dowii* (Gill, 1863) | P | Pacific spotfin mojarra — mojarra manchita |
| +*Eucinostomus entomelas* Zahuranec, 1980 | PM | darkspot mojarra — mojarra mancha negra |
| *Eucinostomus gracilis* (Gill, 1862) | PM | graceful mojarra — mojarra charrita |
| *Eucinostomus gula* (Quoy & Gaimard, 1824) | A | silver jenny — mojarra española |
| *Eucinostomus harengulus* Goode & Bean, 1879 | A-F:UM | tidewater mojarra — mojarra costera |
| *Eucinostomus havana* (Nichols, 1912) | A | bigeye mojarra — mojarra cubana |
| *Eucinostomus jonesii* (Günther, 1879) | A | slender mojarra — mojarra flaca |

| SCIENTIFIC NAME | OCCURRENCE[1] | COMMON NAME (ENGLISH, SPANISH, FRENCH)[2] | |
|---|---|---|---|
| +Eucinostomus lefroyi (Goode, 1874) | A | mottled mojarra | mojarra pinta |
| +Eucinostomus melanopterus (Bleeker, 1863) | A-F:M | flagfin mojarra | mojarra de ley |
| Eugerres axillaris (Günther, 1864) | F:M-PM | black axillary mojarra | mojarra malacapa |
| Eugerres brasilianus (Cuvier, 1830) | AM | Brazilian mojarra | mojarra brasileña |
| Eugerres brevimanus (Günther, 1864) | PM | shortfin mojarra | mojarra aleta corta |
| Eugerres lineatus (Humboldt, 1821) | F:M-PM | streaked mojarra | mojarra china |
| Eugerres mexicanus (Steindachner, 1863) | F:M | Mexican mojarra | mojarra mexicana |
| *Eugerres plumieri (Cuvier, 1830) | A-F:UM | striped mojarra | mojarra rayada |
| +Gerres cinereus (Walbaum, 1792) | A-F:M-PM | yellowfin mojarra | mojarra trompetera |

Haemulidae—En-grunts, Sp-burros y roncos, Fr-grogneurs

| SCIENTIFIC NAME | OCCURRENCE[1] | COMMON NAME (ENGLISH, SPANISH, FRENCH)[2] | |
|---|---|---|---|
| Anisotremus caesius (Jordan & Gilbert, 1882) | PM | silvergray grunt | burro mojarro |
| *Anisotremus davidsonii (Steindachner, 1876) | P | sargo | sargo rayado |
| Anisotremus dovii (Günther, 1864) | PM | blackbarred grunt | burro rompepaila |
| Anisotremus interruptus (Gill, 1862) | PM | burrito grunt | burro bacoco |
| Anisotremus pacifici (Günther, 1864) | PM | carruco grunt | burro carruco |
| *Anisotremus surinamensis (Bloch, 1791) | A | black margate | burriquete |
| Anisotremus taeniatus Gill, 1861 | PM | Panamic porkfish | burro bandera |
| Anisotremus virginicus (Linnaeus, 1758) | A | porkfish | burro payaso |
| Conodon nobilis (Linnaeus, 1758) | A | barred grunt | ronco canario |
| * Conodon serrifer Jordan & Gilbert, 1882 | P | armed grunt | ronco ofensivo |
| Haemulon album Cuvier, 1830 | A | margate | ronco jallao |
| Haemulon aurolineatum Cuvier, 1830 | A | tomtate | ronco jeníguaro |
| Haemulon bonariense Cuvier, 1830 | AM | black grunt | ronco prieto |
| Haemulon carbonarium Poey, 1860 | A | caesar grunt | ronco carbonero |
| Haemulon chrysargyreum Günther, 1859 | A | smallmouth grunt | ronco boquichica |
| * Haemulon flaviguttatum Gill, 1862 | P | Cortez grunt | burro de Cortés |
| Haemulon flavolineatum (Desmarest, 1823) | A | French grunt | ronco condenado |
| Haemulon macrostomum Günther, 1859 | A | Spanish grunt | |
| Haemulon maculicauda (Gill, 1862) | PM | spottail grunt | burro rasposo |
| Haemulon melanurum (Linnaeus, 1758) | A | cottonwick | ronco lomo manchado |
| Haemulon parra (Desmarest, 1823) | A | sailors choice | boquilla |

| SCIENTIFIC NAME | OCCURRENCE[1] | COMMON NAME (ENGLISH, SPANISH, FRENCH)[2] |
|---|---|---|
| *Haemulon plumierii (Lacepède, 1801) | A | white grunt ........ chac-chí |
| Haemulon sciurus (Shaw, 1803) | A | bluestriped grunt ........ ronco carite |
| Haemulon scudderii Gill, 1862 | PM | mojarra grunt ........ burro pecoso |
| Haemulon sexfasciatum Gill, 1862 | PM | graybar grunt ........ burro almejero |
| Haemulon steindachneri (Jordan & Gilbert, 1882) | PM | Latin grunt ........ burro latino |
| Haemulon striatum (Linnaeus, 1758) | A | striped grunt ........ ronco pinto |
| +Haemulopsis axillaris (Steindachner, 1869) | PM | yellowstripe grunt ........ ronco callana |
| +Haemulopsis elongatus (Steindachner, 1879) | PM | elongate grunt ........ ronco alargado |
| +Haemulopsis leuciscus (Günther, 1864) | PM | raucous grunt ........ ronco ruco |
| +Haemulopsis nitidus (Steindachner, 1869) | PM | shining grunt ........ ronco brillante |
| Microlepidotus brevipinnis (Steindachner, 1869) | PM | brassy grunt ........ ronco bronceado |
| Microlepidotus inornatus Gill, 1862 | P | wavyline grunt ........ ronco rayadillo |
| +Orthopristis cantharinus (Jenyns, 1840) | PM | sheephead grunt ........ teniente |
| Orthopristis chalceus (Günther, 1864) | PM | humpback grunt ........ burrito corcovado |
| Orthopristis chrysoptera (Linnaeus, 1766) | A-F:UM | pigfish ........ corocoro armado |
| Orthopristis reddingi Jordan & Richardson, 1895 | PM | bronzestriped grunt ........ burrito rayado |
| Pomadasys bayanus Jordan & Evermann, 1898 | F:M-PM | purplemouth grunt ........ roncacho boquimorada |
| Pomadasys branickii (Steindachner, 1879) | PM | sand grunt ........ roncacho arenero |
| Pomadasys crocro (Cuvier, 1830) | A-F:M | burro grunt ........ corocoro crocro |
| Pomadasys macracanthus (Günther, 1864) | PM | longspine grunt ........ roncacho gordo |
| Pomadasys panamensis (Steindachner, 1876) | PM | Panamic grunt ........ roncacho mapache |
| Xenichthys xanti Gill, 1863 | PM | longfin salema ........ chula |
| *Xenistius californiensis (Steindachner, 1876) | P | salema ........ salema |

Inermiidae—En-bonnetmouths, Sp-bogas, Fr-inermiidés

| | | |
|---|---|---|
| Emmelichthyops atlanticus Schultz, 1945 | A | bonnetmouth |
| *Inermia vittata Poey, 1860 | A | boga |

Sparidae—En-porgies, Sp-plumas, Fr-dorades

| | | |
|---|---|---|
| Archosargus probatocephalus (Walbaum, 1792) | A-F:UM | sheephead ........ sargo chopa |
| Archosargus rhomboidalis (Linnaeus, 1758) | A | sea bream ........ sargo amarillo |
| Calamus arctifrons Goode & Bean, 1882 | A | grass porgy |

| SCIENTIFIC NAME | OCCURRENCE[1] | COMMON NAME (ENGLISH, SPANISH, FRENCH)[2] |
|---|---|---|
| *Calamus bajonado (Bloch & Schneider, 1801) | A | jolthead porgy — pluma |
| Calamus brachysomus (Lockington, 1880) | P | Pacific porgy — pluma marotilla |
| Calamus calamus (Valenciennes, 1830) | A | saucereye porgy |
| Calamus campechanus Randall & Caldwell, 1966 | AM | Campeche porgy — pluma campechana |
| Calamus leucosteus Jordan & Gilbert, 1885 | A | whitebone porgy — pluma golfina |
| Calamus nodosus Randall & Caldwell, 1966 | A | knobbed porgy — mojarrón pecoso |
| Calamus penna (Valenciennes, 1830) | A | sheepshead porgy — pluma manchada |
| Calamus pennatula Guichenot, 1868 | AM | pluma porgy — pluma del Caribe |
| Calamus proridens Jordan & Gilbert, 1884 | A | littlehead porgy — pluma jorobada |
| Diplodus argenteus (Valenciennes, 1830) | A | silver porgy |
| *Diplodus holbrookii (Bean, 1878) | A | spottail pinfish — sargo cotonero |
| Lagodon rhomboides (Linnaeus, 1766) | A-F:UM | pinfish — xlavitia |
| Pagrus pagrus (Linnaeus, 1758) | A | red porgy — sargo rojo |
| *Stenotomus caprinus Jordan & Gilbert, 1882 | A | longspine porgy — sargo espinudo |
| Stenotomus chrysops (Linnaeus, 1766) | A | scup |

Polynemidae—En-threadfins, Sp-barbudos, Fr-capitaines

| SCIENTIFIC NAME | OCCURRENCE[1] | COMMON NAME (ENGLISH, SPANISH, FRENCH)[2] |
|---|---|---|
| Polydactylus approximans (Lay & Bennett, 1839) | P | blue bobo — barbudo seis barbas |
| Polydactylus octonemus (Girard, 1858) | A | Atlantic threadfin — barbudo ocho barbas |
| Polydactylus oligodon (Günther, 1860) | A | littlescale threadfin — barbudo siete barbas |
| Polydactylus opercularis (Gill, 1863) | P | yellow bobo — barbudo nueve barbas |
| Polydactylus virginicus (Linnaeus, 1758) | A | barbu — barbudo barbú |

Sciaenidae—En-drums and croakers, Sp-corvinas y berrugatas, Fr-tambours

| SCIENTIFIC NAME | OCCURRENCE[1] | COMMON NAME (ENGLISH, SPANISH, FRENCH)[2] |
|---|---|---|
| Aplodinotus grunniens Rafinesque, 1819 | F:CUM | freshwater drum — roncador de agua dulce — malachigan |
| Atractoscion nobilis (Ayres, 1860) | P | white seabass — corvina cabaicucho |
| Bairdiella armata Gill, 1863 | PM | armed croaker — ronco armado |
| +Bairdiella batabana (Poey, 1860) | A | blue croaker — ronco azul |
| Bairdiella chrysoura (Lacepède, 1802) | AM-F:UM | silver perch — ronco amarillo |
| Bairdiella ensifera (Jordan & Gilbert, 1882) | PM | swordspine croaker — ronco barbirrubia |
| +Bairdiella icistia (Jordan & Gilbert, 1882) | F[I]:U-PM | bairdiella — ronco roncacho |
| Bairdiella ronchus (Cuvier, 1830) | AM | ground croaker — ronco rayado |

| SCIENTIFIC NAME | OCCURRENCE[1] | COMMON NAME (ENGLISH, SPANISH, FRENCH)[2] | |
|---|---|---|---|
| +Bairdiella sanctaeluciae (Jordan, 1890) | A | striped croaker | ronco caribeño |
| Cheilotrema saturnum (Girard, 1858) | P | black croaker | corvinata negra |
| Corvula macrops (Steindachner, 1876) | PM | vacuoqua croaker | corvineta vacuoqua |
| Cynoscion albus (Günther, 1864) | PM | queen corvina | corvina chiapaneca |
| *Cynoscion arenarius Ginsburg, 1930 | A | sand seatrout | corvina arenera |
| Cynoscion jamaicensis (Vaillant & Bocourt, 1883) | AM | Jamaica weakfish | corvina jamaica |
| Cynoscion nannus Castro-Aguirre & Arvizu-Martínez, 1976. | PM | dwarf corvina | corvina enana |
| *Cynoscion nebulosus (Cuvier, 1830) | A-F:U | spotted seatrout | corvina pinta |
| *Cynoscion nothus (Holbrook, 1848) | A | silver seatrout | corvina plateada |
| Cynoscion othonopterus Jordan & Gilbert, 1882 | PM | Gulf corvina | corvina golfina |
| *Cynoscion parvipinnis Ayres, 1861 | P | shortfin corvina | corvina aleta corta |
| Cynoscion phoxocephalus Jordan & Gilbert, 1882 | PM | sharpnose corvina | corvina picuda |
| Cynoscion regalis (Bloch & Schneider, 1801) | A | weakfish | |
| Cynoscion reticulatus (Günther, 1864) | PM | striped corvina | corvina rayada |
| Cynoscion squamipinnis (Günther, 1867) | PM | scalyfin corvina | corvina aguada |
| Cynoscion stolzmanni (Steindachner, 1879) | PM | yellowtail corvina | corvina coliamarilla |
| +Cynoscion xanthulus Jordan & Gilbert, 1882 | F[I]:U-PM | orangemouth corvina | corvina boquinaranja |
| Elattarchus archidium (Jordan & Gilbert, 1882) | PM | bluestreak drum | corvineta gallinita |
| Equetus lanceolatus (Linnaeus, 1758) | A | jackknife-fish | payasito obispo |
| *Equetus punctatus (Bloch & Schneider, 1801) | A | spotted drum | payasito punteado |
| Genyonemus lineatus (Ayres, 1855) | P | white croaker | corvineta blanca |
| +Isopisthus remifer Jordan & Gilbert, 1882 | PM | bigeye corvina | corvina ojona |
| Larimus acclivis Jordan & Bristol, 1898 | PM | steeplined drum | boquinete |
| Larimus argenteus (Gill, 1863) | PM | silver drum | boquinete chato |
| Larimus effulgens Gilbert, 1898 | PM | shining drum | boquinete boca de novia |
| Larimus fasciatus Holbrook, 1855 | A | banded drum | boquinete listado |
| Larimus pacificus Jordan & Bollman, 1890 | PM | Pacific drum | boquinete del Pacífico |
| Leiostomus xanthurus Lacepède, 1802 | A-F:UM | spot | croca |
| Menticirrhus americanus (Linnaeus, 1758) | A | southern kingfish | berrugato zorro |
| Menticirrhus elongatus (Günther, 1864) | PM | slender kingfish | berrugato fino |
| *Menticirrhus littoralis (Holbrook, 1847) | A | Gulf kingfish | berrugato del Golfo |
| Menticirrhus nasus (Günther, 1868) | PM | highfin kingfish | berrugato real |

| SCIENTIFIC NAME | OCCURRENCE[1] | COMMON NAME (ENGLISH, SPANISH, FRENCH)[2] |
|---|---|---|
| *Menticirrhus paitensis* Hildebrand, 1946 | PM | Paita kingfish ... berrugato chulo |
| *Menticirrhus panamensis* (Steindachner, 1875) | PM | Panama kingfish ... berrugato panameño |
| *Menticirrhus saxatilis* (Bloch & Schneider, 1801) | A | northern kingfish ... berrugato ratón |
| *Menticirrhus undulatus* (Girard, 1854) | P | California corbina ... berrugato californiano |
| *Micropogonias altipinnis* (Günther, 1864) | PM | golden croaker ... chano sureño |
| +*Micropogonias ectenes* (Jordan & Gilbert, 1882) | PM | slender croaker ... chano mexicano |
| *Micropogonias megalops* (Gilbert, 1890) | PM | Gulf croaker ... chano norteño |
| *Micropogonias undulatus* (Linnaeus, 1766) | A-F:UM | Atlantic croaker ... gurrubata |
| *Nebris occidentalis* Vaillant, 1897 | PM | Pacific smalleye croaker ... corvina guavina |
| *Odontoscion dentex* (Cuvier, 1830) | A | reef croaker |
| *Odontosion xanthops* Gilbert, 1898 | PM | yelloweye croaker ... corvineta ojiamarillo |
| *Ophioscion scierus* (Jordan & Gilbert, 1884) | PM | dusky croaker ... corvineta parda |
| *Ophioscion strabo* Gilbert, 1897 | PM | squint-eyed croaker ... corvineta bizca |
| *Ophioscion typicus* Gill, 1863 | PM | racer croaker ... corvineta corredora |
| *Ophioscion vermicularis* (Günther, 1867) | PM | wormlined croaker ... corvineta cococha |
| *Paralonchurus goodei* Gilbert, 1898 | PM | angel croaker ... corvineta ángel |
| * *Pareques acuminatus* (Bloch & Schneider, 1801) | A | high-hat ... payasito largo |
| *Pareques fuscovittatus* (Kendall & Radcliffe, 1912) | PM | festive drum ... payasito lindo |
| * *Pareques iwamotoi* Miller & Woods, 1988 | A | blackbar drum ... payasito rayado |
| * *Pareques umbrosus* (Jordan & Eigenmann, 1889) | A | cubbyu ... payasito prieto |
| +*Pareques viola* (Gilbert, 1898) | PM | rock croaker ... payasito gungo |
| *Pogonias cromis* (Linnaeus, 1766) | A | black drum ... tambor negro |
| * *Roncador stearnsii* (Steindachner, 1876) | P | spotfin croaker ... roncador aleta manchada |
| *Sciaenops ocellatus* (Linnaeus, 1766) | A-F:UM | red drum ... corvineta ocelada |
| *Seriphus politus* Ayres, 1860 | P | queenfish ... corvineta reina |
| *Stellifer chrysoleuca* (Günther, 1867) | PM | shortnose stardrum ... corvinilla chata |
| *Stellifer ericymba* (Jordan & Gilbert, 1882) | PM | hollow stardrum ... corvinilla hueca |
| *Stellifer illecebrosus* Gilbert, 1898 | PM | silver stardrum ... corvinilla plateada |
| *Stellifer lanceolatus* (Holbrook, 1855) | A | star drum ... corvinilla lanza |
| *Stellifer walkeri* Chao, 2001 | PM | professor stardrum ... corvinilla del profesor |
| *Stellifer wintersteenorum* Chao, 2001 | PM | amigo stardrum ... corvinilla amigable |
| *Totoaba macdonaldi* (Gilbert, 1890) | PM | totoaba ... totoaba |

| SCIENTIFIC NAME | OCCURRENCE[1] | COMMON NAME (ENGLISH, SPANISH, FRENCH)[2] |
|---|---|---|
| *Umbrina analis* Günther, 1868 | PM | longspine croaker ...... berrugata espinuda |
| *Umbrina bussingi* López, 1980 | PM | bigeye croaker ...... berrugata ojona |
| *Umbrina coroides* Cuvier, 1830 | A | sand drum ...... berrugata arenera |
| *Umbrina dorsalis* Gill, 1862 | PM | longfin croaker ...... berrugata aleta larga |
| *Umbrina roncador* Jordan & Gilbert, 1882 | P | yellowfin croaker ...... berrugata aleta amarilla |
| *Umbrina wintersteeni* Walker & Radford, 1992 | PM | Cortez croaker ...... berrugata de Cortés |
| *Umbrina xanti* Gill, 1862 | PM | surf croaker ...... berrugata roncadora |

Mullidae—En-goatfishes, Sp-chivos, Fr-surmulets

| SCIENTIFIC NAME | OCCURRENCE[1] | COMMON NAME (ENGLISH, SPANISH, FRENCH)[2] |
|---|---|---|
| *Mulloidichthys dentatus* (Gill, 1862) | PM | Mexican goatfish ...... chivo barbón |
| *Mulloidichthys martinicus* (Cuvier, 1829) | A | yellow goatfish ...... chivo amarillo |
| *Mullus auratus* Jordan & Gilbert, 1882 | A | red goatfish ...... chivo colorado |
| *Pseudupeneus grandisquamis* (Gill, 1863) | P | bigscale goatfish ...... chivo escamudo |
| *Pseudupeneus maculatus* (Bloch, 1793) | A | spotted goatfish ...... chivo manchado |
| *Upeneus parvus* Poey, 1852 | A | dwarf goatfish ...... chivo rayuelo |

Pempheridae—En-sweepers, Sp-barrenderos, Fr-poissons-balayeurs

| SCIENTIFIC NAME | OCCURRENCE[1] | COMMON NAME (ENGLISH, SPANISH, FRENCH)[2] |
|---|---|---|
| *Pempheris schomburgkii* Müller & Troschel, 1848 | A | glassy sweeper ...... barrendero transparente |

Chaetodontidae—En-butterflyfishes, Sp-peces mariposa, Fr-poissons-papillons

| SCIENTIFIC NAME | OCCURRENCE[1] | COMMON NAME (ENGLISH, SPANISH, FRENCH)[2] |
|---|---|---|
| *Chaetodon capistratus* Linnaeus, 1758 | A | foureye butterflyfish ...... mariposa ocelada |
| *Chaetodon humeralis* Günther, 1860 | P | threebanded butterflyfish ...... mariposa muñeca |
| *Chaetodon ocellatus* Bloch, 1787 | A | spotfin butterflyfish ...... mariposa perla amarilla |
| *Chaetodon sedentarius* Poey, 1860 | A | reef butterflyfish ...... mariposa parche |
| *Chaetodon striatus* Linnaeus, 1758 | A | banded butterflyfish ...... mariposa rayada |
| *Forcipiger flavissimus* Jordan & McGregor, 1898 | PM | forcepsfish ...... mariposa hocicona |
| *Johnrandallia nigrirostris* (Gill, 1862) | PM | barberfish ...... mariposa barbero |
| *Prognathodes aculeatus* (Poey, 1860) | A | longsnout butterflyfish ...... mariposa narigona |
| *Prognathodes aya* (Jordan, 1886) | A | bank butterflyfish ...... mariposa de banco |
| *Prognathodes falcifer* (Hubbs & Rechnitzer, 1958) | P | scythe butterflyfish ...... mariposa guadaña |
| *Prognathodes guyanensis* (Durand, 1960) | A | Guyana butterflyfish |

| SCIENTIFIC NAME | OCCURRENCE[1] | COMMON NAME (ENGLISH, SPANISH, FRENCH)[2] |
|---|---|---|
| **Pomacanthidae—En-angelfishes, Sp-ángeles, Fr-demoiselles** | | |
| *Centropyge argi* Woods & Kanazawa, 1951 | A | cherubfish ............ angelote pigmeo |
| +*Holacanthus bermudensis* Goode, 1876 | A | blue angelfish ............ chabelita azul |
| *Holacanthus ciliaris* (Linnaeus, 1758) | A | queen angelfish ............ ángel reina |
| *Holacanthus clarionensis* Gilbert, 1891 | PM | Clarion angelfish ............ ángel de Clarión |
| *Holacanthus passer* Valenciennes, 1846 | PM | king angelfish ............ ángel real |
| *Holacanthus tricolor* (Bloch, 1795) | A | rock beauty ............ chabelita tricolor |
| *Pomacanthus arcuatus* (Linnaeus, 1758) | A | gray angelfish ............ gallineta café |
| *Pomacanthus paru* (Bloch, 1787) | A | French angelfish ............ gallineta negra |
| *Pomacanthus zonipectus* (Gill, 1862) | P | Cortez angelfish ............ ángel de Cortés |
| **Pentacerotidae—En-armorheads, Sp-espartanos, Fr-têtes casquées** | | |
| *\*Pseudopentaceros wheeleri* Hardy, 1983 | P | North Pacific armorhead |
| **Kyphosidae—En-sea chubs, Sp-chopas, Fr-kyphoses** | | |
| *Girella nigricans* (Ayres, 1860) | P | opaleye ............ chopa verde |
| *Girella simplicidens* Osburn & Nichols, 1916 | PM | Gulf opaleye ............ chopa ojo azul |
| *\*Hermosilla azurea* Jenkins & Evermann, 1889 | P | zebraperch ............ chopa bonita |
| *Kyphosus analogus* (Gill, 1862) | P | blue-bronze chub ............ chopa rayada |
| *Kyphosus elegans* (Peters, 1869) | PM | Cortez sea chub ............ chopa de Cortés |
| *Kyphosus incisor* (Cuvier, 1831) | A | yellow chub ............ chopa amarilla |
| *Kyphosus lutescens* (Jordan & Gilbert, 1882) | PM | Revillagigedo sea chub ............ chopa de Revillagigedo |
| *Kyphosus sectatrix* (Linnaeus, 1758) | A | Bermuda chub ............ chopa blanca |
| *\*Medialuna californiensis* (Steindachner, 1876) | P | halfmoon ............ chopa medialuna |
| *Sector ocyurus* (Jordan & Gilbert, 1882) | P | bluestriped chub ............ chopa salema |
| **\*Kuhliidae—En-flagtails, Sp-daras, Fr-crocros** | | |
| *Kuhlia mugil* (Forster, 1801) | PM | barred flagtail ............ dara bandera |
| **Cirrhitidae—En-hawkfishes, Sp-halcones, Fr-poissons-éperviers** | | |
| *Amblycirrhitus pinos* (Mowbray, 1927) | A | redspotted hawkfish ............ halcón rayadito |

| SCIENTIFIC NAME | OCCURRENCE[1] | COMMON NAME (ENGLISH, SPANISH, FRENCH)[2] |
|---|---|---|
| *Cirrhitichthys oxycephalus* (Bleeker, 1855) | PM | coral hawkfish............halcón de coral |
| *Cirrhitus rivulatus* Valenciennes, 1846 | PM | giant hawkfish............chino mero |
| *Oxycirrhites typus* Bleeker, 1857 | PM | longnose hawkfish............halcón narigón |
| *Elassomatidae—En-pygmy sunfishes, Sp-solecitos, Fr-crapets-pygmées | | |
| *Elassoma alabamae* Mayden, 1993 | F:U | spring pygmy sunfish |
| *Elassoma boehlkei* Rohde & Arndt, 1987 | F:U | Carolina pygmy sunfish |
| *Elassoma evergladei* Jordan, 1884 | F:U | Everglades pygmy sunfish |
| *Elassoma okatie* Rohde & Arndt, 1987 | F:U | bluebarred pygmy sunfish |
| *Elassoma okefenokee* Böhlke, 1956 | F:U | Okefenokee pygmy sunfish |
| *Elassoma zonatum* Jordan, 1877 | F:U | banded pygmy sunfish |
| +Cichlidae—En-cichlids, Sp-tilapias y mojarras de agua dulce, Fr-cichlidés | | |
| *Astronotus ocellatus* (Agassiz, 1831) | F[I]:U | oscar |
| *Cichla ocellaris* Bloch & Schneider, 1801 | F[I]:U | butterfly peacock bass |
| *Cichlasoma affine* (Günther, 1862) | F:M | golden cichlid............mojarra dorada |
| *Cichlasoma argenteum* Allgayer, 1991 | F:M | white cichlid............mojarra pozolera |
| *Cichlasoma bartoni* (Bean, 1892) | F:M | Media Luna cichlid............mojarra caracolera |
| *Cichlasoma beani* (Jordan, 1889) | F:M | Sinaloa cichlid............mojarra de Sinaloa |
| *Cichlasoma bifasciatum* (Steindachner, 1864) | F:M | twoband cichlid............mojarra panza colorada |
| *Cichlasoma bimaculatum* (Linnaeus, 1758) | F[I]:U | black acara |
| *Cichlasoma breidohri* Werner & Stawikowski, 1987 | F:M | Angostura cichlid............mojarra de Angostura |
| *Cichlasoma bulleri* (Regan, 1905) | F:M | Sarabia cichlid............mojarra del Sarabia |
| *Cichlasoma callolepis* (Regan, 1904) | F:M | San Domingo cichlid............mojarra de San Domingo |
| *Cichlasoma carpintis* (Jordan & Snyder, 1899) | F:M | lowland cichlid............mojarra tampiqueña |
| *Cichlasoma citrinellum* (Günther, 1864) | F[I]:U | midas cichlid |
| *Cichlasoma cyanoguttatum* (Baird & Girard, 1854) | F:UM | Rio Grande cichlid............mojarra del norte |
| *Cichlasoma deppii* (Heckel, 1840 ) | F:M | Nautla cichlid............mojarra del sur |
| *Cichlasoma ellioti* (Meek, 1904) | F:M | spotcheek cichlid............chescla |
| *Cichlasoma fenestratum* (Günther, 1860) | F:M | blackstripe cichlid............mojarra del La Lana |
| *Cichlasoma friedrichsthalii* (Heckel, 1840) | F:M | yellowjacket............mojarra del San Juan |
| *Cichlasoma gibbiceps* (Steindachner, 1864) | F:M | Teapa cichlid............mojarra del Teapa |

| SCIENTIFIC NAME | OCCURRENCE[1] | COMMON NAME (ENGLISH, SPANISH, FRENCH)[2] | |
| --- | --- | --- | --- |
| Cichlasoma grammodes Taylor & Miller, 1980 | F:M | Chiapa de Corzo cichlid | mojarra del Chiapa de Corzo |
| Cichlasoma guttulatum (Günther, 1864) | F:M | Amatitlan cichlid | mojarra de Amatitlán |
| Cichlasoma hartwegi Taylor & Miller, 1980 | F:M | tailbar cichlid | mojarra del Río Grande de Chiapa |
| Cichlasoma helleri (Steindachner, 1864) | F:M | yellow cichlid | mojarra amarilla |
| Cichlasoma heterospilum Hubbs, 1936 | F:M | Montecristo cichlid | mojarra de Montecristo |
| Cichlasoma intermedium (Günther, 1862) | F:M | Peten cichlid | mojarra del Petén |
| Cichlasoma irregulare (Günther, 1862) | F:M | arroyo cichlid | canchay |
| Cichlasoma istlanum (Jordan & Snyder, 1899) | F:M | redside cichlid | mojarra del Balsas |
| Cichlasoma labridens (Pellegrin, 1903) | F:M | blackcheek cichlid | mojarra huasteca |
| Cichlasoma lentiginosum (Steindachner, 1864) | F:M | freckled cichlid | mojarra gachupina |
| Cichlasoma macracanthum (Günther, 1864) | F:M | blackthroat cichlid | mojarra de Guamuchal |
| +Cichlasoma managuense (Günther, 1867) | F[I]:UM | jaguar guapote | mojarra de Managua |
| Cichlasoma meeki (Brind, 1918) | F:U[I]M | firemouth cichlid | mojarra boca de fuego |
| Cichlasoma mincklevi Kornfield & Taylor, 1983 | F:M | Cuatro Ciénegas cichlid | mojarra de Cuatro Ciénegas |
| Cichlasoma motaguense (Günther, 1867) | F:M | Motagua cichlid | mojarra del Motagua |
| Cichlasoma nebuliferum (Günther, 1860) | F:M | Papaloapan cichlid | mojarra del Papaloapan |
| Cichlasoma nigrofasciatum (Günther, 1867) | F[I]:UM | convict cichlid | mojarra convicto |
| Cichlasoma nourissati (Allgayer, 1989) | F:M | bluemouth cichlid | mojarra labios gruesos |
| Cichlasoma octofasciatum (Regan, 1903) | F:U[I]M | Jack Dempsey | mojarra castarrica |
| Cichlasoma pantostictum Taylor & Miller, 1983 | F:M | Chairel cichlid | mojarra de Chairel |
| Cichlasoma pasionis Rivas, 1962 | F:M | blackgullet cichlid | mojarra de La Pasión |
| Cichlasoma pearsei (Hubbs, 1936) | F:M | pantano cichlid | mojarra zacatera |
| Cichlasoma regani Miller, 1974 | F:M | Almoloya cichlid | mojarra del Almoloya |
| Cichlasoma rheophilus (Seegers & Staeck, 1985) | F:M | Palenque cichlid | mojarra de Palenque |
| Cichlasoma robertsoni Regan, 1905 | F:M | Honduras cichlid | mojarra hondureña |
| *Cichlasoma salvini (Günther, 1862) | F:U[I]M | yellowbelly cichlid | guapote tricolor |
| Cichlasoma socolofi Miller & Taylor 1984 | F:M | Chiapas cichlid | mojarra del Misalá |
| Cichlasoma spilurum (Günther, 1862) | F:M | blue-eye cichlid | mojarra yucateca |
| Cichlasoma steindachneri Jordan & Snyder, 1899 | F:M | slender cichlid | mojarra del Ojo Frío |
| Cichlasoma synspilum Hubbs, 1935 | F:M | redhead cichlid | mojarra paleta |
| Cichlasoma tamasopoensis (Artigas Azas, 1993) | F:M | Tamasopo cichlid | mojarra del Tamasopo |
| Cichlasoma trimaculatum (Günther, 1867) | F:M | threespot cichlid | mojarra prieta |

| SCIENTIFIC NAME | OCCURRENCE[1] | COMMON NAME (ENGLISH, SPANISH, FRENCH)[2] |
|---|---|---|
| *Cichlasoma ufermanni* (Allgayer, 2002) | F:M | Usumacinta cichlid ............ mojarra del Usumacinta |
| *Cichlasoma urophthalmus* (Günther, 1862) | A-F:U[I]M | Mayan cichlid ............ mojarra del sureste |
| *Cichlasoma zonatum* Meek, 1905 | F:M | Oaxaca cichlid ............ mojarra oaxaqueña |
| *Geophagus surinamensis* (Bloch, 1791) | F[I]:U | redstriped eartheater |
| *Hemichromis guttatus* Günther, 1862 | F[I]:M | spotted jewelfish ............ pez joya manchado |
| *Hemichromis letourneuxi* Sauvage, 1880 | F[I]:CU | African jewelfish |
| *Heros severus* Heckel, 1840 | F[I]:U | banded cichlid |
| *Oreochromis aureus* (Steindachner, 1864) | F[I]:UM | blue tilapia ............ tilapia azul |
| *Oreochromis mossambicus* (Peters, 1852) | F[I]:UM-P[I] | Mozambique tilapia ............ tilapia mosambica |
| *Oreochromis niloticus* (Linnaeus, 1758) | F[I]:UM | Nile tilapia ............ tilapia del Nilo |
| *Oreochromis urolepis* (Norman, 1922) | F[I]:U | Wami tilapia |
| *Petenia splendida* Günther, 1862 | F:M | giant cichlid ............ tenguayaca |
| *Sarotherodon melanotheron* Rüppell, 1852 | F[I]:U | blackchin tilapia |
| *Tilapia mariae* Boulenger, 1899 | F[I]:U | spotted tilapia |
| *Tilapia zillii* (Gervais, 1848) | F[I]:U | redbelly tilapia |

Embiotocidae—En-surfperches, Sp- mojarras vivíparas, Fr-perches vivipares

| SCIENTIFIC NAME | OCCURRENCE[1] | COMMON NAME (ENGLISH, SPANISH, FRENCH)[2] |
|---|---|---|
| *Amphistichus argenteus* Agassiz, 1854 | P | barred surfperch ............ mojarra de bandas |
| *Amphistichus koelzi* (Hubbs, 1933) | P | calico surfperch ............ mojarra angaripola |
| *Amphistichus rhodoterus* (Agassiz, 1854) | P | redtail surfperch |
| *Brachyistius frenatus* Gill, 1862 | P | kelp perch ............ mojarra sargacera |
| *Cymatogaster aggregata* Gibbons, 1854 | F:CUM-P | shiner perch ............ mojarra brillosa |
| *Embiotoca jacksoni* Agassiz, 1853 | P | black perch ............ mojarra negra |
| *Embiotoca lateralis* Agassiz, 1854 | P | striped seaperch ............ mojarra azul |
| *Hyperprosopon anale* Agassiz, 1861 | P | spotfin surfperch ............ mojarra aletimanchada |
| *Hyperprosopon argenteum* Gibbons, 1854 | P | walleye surfperch ............ mojarra ojona |
| *Hyperprosopon ellipticum* (Gibbons, 1854) | P | silver surfperch ............ mojarra ovalada |
| *Hypsurus caryi* (Agassiz, 1853) | P | rainbow seaperch ............ mojarra arcoiris |
| *Hysterocarpus traskii* Gibbons, 1854 | F:U | tule perch |
| *Micrometrus aurora* (Jordan & Gilbert, 1880) | P | reef perch ............ mojarra de arrecife |
| *Micrometrus minimus* (Gibbons, 1854) | P | dwarf perch ............ mojarra enana |
| *Phanerodon atripes* (Jordan & Gilbert, 1880) | P | sharpnose seaperch ............ mojarra picuda |

| SCIENTIFIC NAME | OCCURRENCE[1] | COMMON NAME (ENGLISH, SPANISH, FRENCH)[2] |
|---|---|---|
| Phanerodon furcatus Girard, 1854 | P | white seaperch .......... mojarra lomo rayado |
| Rhacochilus toxotes Agassiz, 1854 | P | rubberlip seaperch .......... mojarra labios de hule |
| Rhacochilus vacca (Girard, 1855) | P | pile perch .......... mojarra muellera |
| Zalembius rosaceus (Jordan & Gilbert, 1880) | P | pink seaperch .......... mojarra rosada |

Pomacentridae—En-damselfishes, Sp-castañetas y jaquetas, Fr-sergents

| SCIENTIFIC NAME | OCCURRENCE[1] | COMMON NAME (ENGLISH, SPANISH, FRENCH)[2] |
|---|---|---|
| Abudefduf declivifrons (Gill, 1862) | PM | Mexican night sergeant .......... petaca mexicana |
| Abudefduf saxatilis (Linnaeus, 1758) | A | sergeant major .......... petaca rayada |
| Abudefduf taurus (Müller & Troschel, 1848) | A | night sergeant .......... petaca toro |
| *Abudefduf troschelii (Gill, 1862) | P | Panamic sergeant major .......... petaca banderita |
| *Azurina hirundo Jordan & McGregor, 1898 | P | swallow damselfish .......... castañuela golondrina |
| *Chromis alta Greenfield & Woods, 1980 | P | silverstripe chromis .......... castañeta alta |
| +Chromis atrilobata Gill, 1862 | PM | scissortail chromis .......... castañeta cola de tijera |
| Chromis cyanea (Poey, 1860) | A | blue chromis .......... castañeta azul |
| *Chromis enchrysura Jordan & Gilbert, 1882 | A | yellowtail reeffish .......... castañeta coliamarilla |
| Chromis insolata (Cuvier, 1830) | A | sunshinefish .......... castañeta sol |
| *Chromis limbaughi Greenfield & Woods, 1980 | PM | blue-and-yellow chromis .......... castañeta mexicana |
| Chromis multilineata (Guichenot, 1853) | A | brown chromis .......... castañeta parda |
| Chromis punctipinnis (Cooper, 1863) | P | blacksmith .......... castañeta herrera |
| Chromis scotti Emery, 1968 | A | purple reeffish .......... castañeta púrpura |
| Hypsypops rubicundus (Girard, 1854) | P | garibaldi .......... jaqueta garibaldi |
| Microspathodon bairdii (Gill, 1862) | PM | bumphead damselfish .......... jaqueta vistosa |
| Microspathodon chrysurus (Cuvier, 1830) | A | yellowtail damselfish .......... jaqueta coliamarilla |
| Microspathodon dorsalis (Gill, 1862) | PM | giant damselfish .......... jaqueta gigante |
| Stegastes acapulcoensis (Fowler, 1944) | PM | Acapulco damselfish .......... jaqueta acapulqueña |
| *Stegastes adustus (Troschel, 1865) | A | dusky damselfish .......... jaqueta prieta |
| *Stegastes diencaeus (Jordan & Rutter, 1897) | A | longfin damselfish .......... jaqueta miel |
| Stegastes flavilatus (Gill, 1862) | PM | beaubrummel .......... jaqueta de dos colores |
| Stegastes leucorus (Gilbert, 1892) | PM | whitetail damselfish .......... jaqueta rabo blanco |
| *Stegastes leucostictus (Müller & Troschel, 1848) | A | beaugregory .......... jaqueta bonita |
| *Stegastes partitus (Poey, 1868) | A | bicolor damselfish .......... jaqueta bicolor |
| *Stegastes planifrons (Cuvier, 1830) | A | threespot damselfish .......... jaqueta de tres puntos |

| SCIENTIFIC NAME | OCCURRENCE[1] | COMMON NAME (ENGLISH, SPANISH, FRENCH)[2] |
|---|---|---|
| *Stegastes rectifraenum* (Gill, 1862) | PM | Cortez damselfish ............ jaqueta de Cortés |
| *Stegastes redemptus* (Heller & Snodgrass, 1903) | PM | Clarion damselfish ............ jaqueta azafranada |
| \* *Stegastes variabilis* (Castelnau, 1855) | A | cocoa damselfish ............ jaqueta castaña |

Labridae—En-wrasses, Sp-doncellas y señoritas, Fr-labres

| SCIENTIFIC NAME | OCCURRENCE[1] | COMMON NAME (ENGLISH, SPANISH, FRENCH)[2] |
|---|---|---|
| *Bodianus diplotaenia* (Gill, 1862) | PM | Mexican hogfish ............ vieja mexicana |
| *Bodianus pulchellus* (Poey, 1860) | A | spotfin hogfish ............ vieja lomo negro |
| *Bodianus rufus* (Linnaeus, 1758) | A | Spanish hogfish ............ vieja española |
| *Clepticus parrae* (Bloch & Schneider, 1801) | A | creole wrasse ............ doncella mulata |
| \* *Decodon melasma* Gomon, 1974 | P | blackspot wrasse ............ viejita manchada |
| *Decodon puellaris* (Poey, 1860) | A | red hogfish ............ doncella de lo alto |
| *Doratonotus megalepis* Günther, 1862 | A | dwarf wrasse ............ doncella enana |
| *Halichoeres adustus* (Gilbert, 1890) | PM | black wrasse ............ señorita negra |
| *Halichoeres aestuaricola* Bussing, 1972 | PM | mangrove wrasse ............ señorita de manglar |
| *Halichoeres bathyphilus* (Beebe & Tee-Van, 1932) | A | greenband wrasse ............ doncella cintaverde |
| *Halichoeres bivittatus* (Bloch, 1791) | A | slippery dick ............ doncella rayada |
| *Halichoeres caudalis* (Poey, 1860) | A | painted wrasse ............ doncella pintada |
| *Halichoeres chierchiae* di Caporiacco, 1947 | PM | wounded wrasse ............ señorita herida |
| *Halichoeres cyanocephalus* (Bloch, 1791) | A | yellowcheek wrasse ............ |
| *Halichoeres dispilus* (Günther, 1864) | PM | chameleon wrasse ............ señorita camaleón |
| *Halichoeres garnoti* (Valenciennes, 1839) | A | yellowhead wrasse ............ doncella cabeciamarilla |
| *Halichoeres insularis* Allen & Robertson, 1992 | PM | Socorro wrasse ............ señorita de Socorro |
| *Halichoeres maculipinna* (Müller & Troschel, 1848) | A | clown wrasse ............ doncella payaso |
| *Halichoeres melanotis* (Gilbert, 1890) | PM | golden wrasse ............ señorita dorada |
| *Halichoeres nicholsi* (Jordan & Gilbert, 1882) | PM | spinster wrasse ............ señorita solterona |
| *Halichoeres notospilus* (Günther, 1864) | PM | banded wrasse ............ señorita listada |
| *Halichoeres pictus* (Poey, 1860) | A | rainbow wrasse ............ doncella arcoiris |
| *Halichoeres poeyi* (Steindachner, 1867) | A | blackear wrasse ............ doncella orejinegra |
| *Halichoeres radiatus* (Linnaeus, 1758) | A | puddingwife ............ doncella azulada |
| *Halichoeres semicinctus* (Ayres, 1859) | P | rock wrasse ............ señorita piedrera |
| *Iniistius pavo* (Valenciennes 1840) | PM | peacock razorfish ............ cuchillo pavo real |
| *Lachnolaimus maximus* (Walbaum, 1792) | A | hogfish ............ boquinete |

| SCIENTIFIC NAME | OCCURRENCE[1] | COMMON NAME (ENGLISH, SPANISH, FRENCH)[2] |
|---|---|---|
| *Novaculichthys taeniourus* (Lacepède, 1801) | PM | rockmover wrasse .......... cuchillo dragón |
| +*Oxyjulis californica* (Günther, 1861) | P | señorita .......... señorita californiana |
| *Polylepion cruentum* Gomon, 1977 | PM | bleeding wrasse .......... vieja sangradora |
| *Pseudojuloides inornatus* (Gilbert, 1890) | PM | Cape wrasse .......... señorita del Cabo |
| *Semicossyphus pulcher* (Ayres, 1854) | P | California sheephead .......... vieja californiana |
| *Tautoga onitis* (Linnaeus, 1758) | A | tautog |
| *Tautogolabrus adspersus* (Walbaum, 1792) | A | cunner .......... tanche-tautogue |
| *Thalassoma bifasciatum* (Bloch, 1791) | A | bluehead .......... cara de cotorra |
| *Thalassoma grammaticum* Gilbert, 1890 | PM | sunset wrasse .......... señorita crepúsculo |
| *Thalassoma lucasanum* (Gill, 1862) | PM | Cortez rainbow wrasse .......... arcoiris de Cortés |
| *Thalassoma virens* Gilbert, 1890 | PM | emerald wrasse .......... señorita esmeralda |
| *\*Xyrichtys martinicensis* Valenciennes, 1840 | A | rosy razorfish .......... cuchillo llorón |
| *Xyrichtys mundiceps* Gill, 1862 | PM | Cape razorfish .......... cuchillo desnudo |
| *\*Xyrichtys novacula* (Linnaeus, 1758) | A | pearly razorfish .......... cuchillo perlino |
| *\*Xyrichtys splendens* Castelnau, 1855 | A | green razorfish .......... cuchillo de lunar |

Scaridae—En-parrotfishes, Sp-loros, Fr-poissons-perroquets

| SCIENTIFIC NAME | OCCURRENCE[1] | COMMON NAME (ENGLISH, SPANISH, FRENCH)[2] |
|---|---|---|
| *Calotomus carolinus* (Valenciennes, 1840) | PM | stareye parrotfish .......... pococho perico |
| *Cryptotomus roseus* Cope, 1871 | A | bluelip parrotfish .......... loro chimuelo |
| *\*Nicholsina denticulata* (Evermann & Radcliffe, 1917) | P | loosetooth parrotfish .......... pococho beriquete |
| *\*Nicholsina usta* (Valenciennes, 1840) | A | emerald parrotfish .......... loro esmeralda |
| *\*Scarus coelestinus* Valenciennes, 1840 | A | midnight parrotfish .......... loro de medianoche |
| +*Scarus coeruleus* (Bloch, 1786) | A | blue parrotfish .......... loro azul |
| *Scarus compressus* (Osburn & Nichols, 1916) | PM | azure parrotfish .......... loro chato |
| *Scarus ghobban* Forsskål, 1775 | PM | bluechin parrotfish .......... loro barbazul |
| *Scarus guacamaia* Cuvier, 1829 | A | rainbow parrotfish .......... loro guacamayo |
| *\*Scarus iseri* (Bloch, 1789) | A | striped parrotfish .......... loro listado |
| *Scarus perrico* Jordan & Gilbert, 1882 | PM | bumphead parrotfish .......... loro jorobado |
| *Scarus rubroviolaceus* Bleeker, 1847 | PM | bicolor parrotfish .......... loro bicolor |
| *Scarus taeniopterus* Desmarest, 1831 | A | princess parrotfish |
| *\*Scarus vetula* Bloch & Schneider, 1801 | A | queen parrotfish .......... loro reina |
| *Sparisoma atomarium* (Poey, 1861) | A | greenblotch parrotfish .......... loro mancha verde |

| SCIENTIFIC NAME | OCCURRENCE[1] | COMMON NAME (ENGLISH, SPANISH, FRENCH)[2] |
|---|---|---|
| *Sparisoma aurofrenatum* (Valenciennes, 1840) | A | redband parrotfish ................ loro manchado |
| *Sparisoma chrysopterum* (Bloch & Schneider, 1801) | A | redtail parrotfish ............... loro verde |
| *Sparisoma radians* (Valenciennes, 1840) | A | bucktooth parrotfish ............ loro dientuso |
| *Sparisoma rubripinne* (Valenciennes, 1840) | A | yellowtail parrotfish ........... loro coliamarilla |
| *Sparisoma viride* (Bonnaterre, 1788) | A | stoplight parrotfish ............ loro brilloso |

Bathymasteridae—En-ronquils, Sp-roncos pelones, Fr-ronquilles

| | | |
|---|---|---|
| *Bathymaster caeruleofasciatus* Gilbert & Burke, 1912 | P | Alaskan ronquil |
| *Bathymaster leurolepis* McPhail, 1965 | P | smallmouth ronquil |
| *Bathymaster signatus* Cope, 1873 | P | searcher |
| *Rathbunella alleni* Gilbert, 1904 | P | stripefin ronquil ................ ronco pelón aletirrayada |
| *Rathbunella hypoplecta* (Gilbert, 1890) | P | bluebanded ronquil ............ ronco pelón rayado |
| *Ronquilus jordani* (Gilbert, 1889) | P | northern ronquil |

+Zoarcidae—En-eelpouts, Sp-viruelas, Fr-lycodes

| | | |
|---|---|---|
| *Bothrocara brunneum* (Bean, 1890) | P | twoline eelpout ................ viruela dos rayas |
| *Bothrocara pusillum* (Bean, 1890) | P | Alaska eelpout |
| *Eucryphycus californicus* (Starks & Mann, 1911) | P | persimmon eelpout |
| *Gymnelus hemifasciatus* Andriashev, 1937 | P | halfbarred pout |
| *Gymnelus popovi* (Taranetz & Andriashev, 1935) | P | Aleutian pout |
| *Gymnelus retrodorsalis* Le Danois, 1913 | A-P | aurora pout |
| *Gymnelus viridis* (Fabricius, 1780) | A-P | fish doctor ....................... unernak caméléon |
| *Lycenchelys paxillus* (Goode & Bean, 1879) | A | common wolf eel |
| *Lycenchelys verrillii* (Goode & Bean, 1877) | A | wolf eelpout |
| *Lycodapus fierasfer* Gilbert, 1890 | P | blackmouth eelpout |
| *Lycodapus mandibularis* Gilbert, 1915 | P | pallid eelpout |
| *Lycodapus parviceps* Gilbert, 1896 | P | smallhead eelpout |
| *Lycodapus psarostomatus* Peden & Anderson, 1981 | P | specklemouth eelpout |
| *Lycodes brevipes* Bean, 1890 | P | shortfin eelpout |
| *Lycodes concolor* Gill & Townsend, 1897 | P | ebony eelpout |
| *Lycodes cortezianus* (Gilbert, 1890) | P | bigfin eelpout |
| *Lycodes diapterus* Gilbert, 1892 | P | black eelpout |

| SCIENTIFIC NAME | OCCURRENCE[1] | COMMON NAME (ENGLISH, SPANISH, FRENCH)[2] |
|---|---|---|
| *Lycodes esmarkii Collett, 1875 | A | greater eelpout ..... lycode d'Esmark |
| *Lycodes fasciatus (Schmidt, 1904) | P | banded eelpout |
| Lycodes jugoricus Knipowitsch, 1906 | P | shulupaoluk |
| Lycodes lavalaei Vladykov & Tremblay, 1936 | A | Newfoundland eelpout ..... lycode du Labrador |
| Lycodes mucosus Richardson, 1855 | A-P | saddled eelpout |
| *Lycodes pacificus Collett, 1879 | P | blackbelly eelpout ..... viruela panza negra |
| Lycodes palearis Gilbert, 1896 | P | wattled eelpout |
| *Lycodes pallidus Collett, 1879 | A-P | pale eelpout ..... lycode pâle |
| Lycodes polaris (Sabine, 1824) | A-P | Canadian eelpout ..... lycode polaire |
| *Lycodes raridens Taranetz & Andriashev, 1937 | P | marbled eelpout |
| Lycodes reticulatus Reinhardt, 1835 | A-P | Arctic eelpout ..... lycode arctique |
| *Lycodes rossi Malmgren, 1865 | P | threespot eelpout |
| Lycodes turneri Bean, 1879 | A-P | polar eelpout |
| *Lycodes vahlii Reinhardt, 1831 | A | checker eelpout ..... lycode à carreaux |
| Lyconema barbatum Gilbert, 1896 | P | bearded eelpout ..... viruela barbona |
| Melanostigma atlanticum Koefoed, 1952 | A | Atlantic soft pout ..... mollasse atlantique |
| Melanostigma pammelas Gilbert, 1896 | PM | midwater eelpout ..... viruela carbonera |
| *Zoarces americanus (Bloch & Schneider, 1801) | A | ocean pout ..... loquette d'Amérique |

Stichaeidae—En-pricklebacks, Sp-peces abrojo, Fr-stichées

| SCIENTIFIC NAME | OCCURRENCE[1] | COMMON NAME (ENGLISH, SPANISH, FRENCH)[2] |
|---|---|---|
| *Acantholumpenus mackayi (Gilbert, 1896) | P | blackline prickleback |
| Alectrias alectrolophus (Pallas, 1814) | P | stone cockscomb |
| Alectridium aurantiacum Gilbert & Burke, 1912 | P | lesser prickleback |
| Allolumpenus hypochromus Hubbs & Schultz, 1932 | P | Y-prickleback |
| *Anisarchus medius (Reinhardt, 1837) | A-P | stout eelblenny |
| Anoplarchus insignis Gilbert & Burke, 1912 | P | slender cockscomb |
| Anoplarchus purpurescens Gill, 1861 | P | high cockscomb |
| Bryozoichthys lysimus (Jordan & Snyder, 1902) | P | nutcracker prickleback |
| Bryozoichthys marjorius McPhail, 1970 | P | pearly prickleback |
| Cebidichthys violaceus (Girard, 1854) | P | monkeyface prickleback ..... abrojo cara de mono |
| Chirolophis ascanii (Walbaum, 1792) | A | Atlantic warbonnet ..... toupet marbré |

| SCIENTIFIC NAME | OCCURRENCE[1] | COMMON NAME (ENGLISH, SPANISH, FRENCH)[2] |
|---|---|---|
| *Chirolophis decoratus* (Jordan & Snyder, 1902) | P | decorated warbonnet |
| *Chirolophis nugator* (Jordan & Williams, 1895) | P | mosshead warbonnet |
| *Chirolophis snyderi* (Taranetz, 1938) | P | bearded warbonnet |
| *Chirolophis tarsodes* (Jordan & Snyder, 1902) | P | matcheek warbonnet |
| *Ernogrammus walkeri* Follett & Powell, 1988 | P | masked prickleback |
| *Esselenichthys carli* (Follett & Anderson, 1990) | P | threeline prickleback | abrojo tres rayas |
| *Esselenichthys laurae* (Follett & Anderson, 1990) | P | twoline prickleback | abrojo dos rayas |
| *Eumesogrammus praecisus* (Krøyer, 1837) | A-P | fourline snakeblenny | quatre-lignes atlantique |
| *Gymnoclinus cristulatus* Gilbert & Burke, 1912 | P | trident prickleback |
| *Kasatkia seigeli* Posner & Lavenberg, 1999 | P | sixspot prickleback |
| *Leptoclinus maculatus* (Fries, 1837) | A-P | daubed shanny | lompénie tachetée |
| *Lumpenella longirostris* (Evermann & Goldsborough, 1907) | P | longsnout prickleback |
| *Lumpenus fabricii* Reinhardt, 1836 | A-P | slender eelblenny | lompénie élancée |
| *Lumpenus lampretaeformis* (Walbaum, 1792) | A | snakeblenny | lompénie-serpent |
| *Lumpenus sagitta* Wilimovsky, 1956 | P | snake prickleback |
| *Phytichthys chirus* (Jordan & Gilbert, 1880) | P | ribbon prickleback |
| *Plagiogrammus hopkinsii* Bean, 1894 | P | crisscross prickleback |
| *Plectobranchus evides* Gilbert, 1890 | P | bluebarred prickleback |
| *Poroclinus rothrocki* Bean, 1890 | P | whitebarred prickleback |
| *Stichaeus punctatus* (Fabricius, 1780) | A-P | Arctic shanny |
| *Ulvaria subbifurcata* (Storer, 1839) | A | radiated shanny | ulvaire deux-lignes |
| *Xiphister atropurpureus* (Kittlitz, 1858) | P | black prickleback | abrojo negro |
| *Xiphister mucosus* (Girard, 1858) | P | rock prickleback |
| Cryptacanthodidae—En-wrymouths, Sp-risueños, Fr-terrassiers | | |
| *Cryptacanthodes aleutensis* (Gilbert, 1896) | P | dwarf wrymouth |
| *Cryptacanthodes giganteus* (Kittlitz, 1858) | P | giant wrymouth |
| *Cryptacanthodes maculatus* Storer, 1839 | A | wrymouth | terrassier tacheté |
| Pholidae—En-gunnels, Sp-espinosos de marea, Fr-sigouines | | |
| *Apodichthys flavidus* Girard, 1854 | P | penpoint gunnel |
| *Apodichthys fucorum* Jordan & Gilbert, 1880 | P | rockweed gunnel | espinoso de marea zacatero |

| SCIENTIFIC NAME | OCCURRENCE[1] | COMMON NAME (ENGLISH, SPANISH, FRENCH)[2] |
|---|---|---|
| *Pholis clemensi* Rosenblatt, 1964 | P | longfin gunnel |
| +*Pholis fasciata* (Bloch & Schneider, 1801) | A-P | banded gunnel |
| *Pholis gunnellus* (Linnaeus, 1758) | A | rock gunnel ................ sigouine de roche |
| *Pholis laeta* (Cope, 1873) | P | crescent gunnel |
| *Pholis ornata* (Girard, 1854) | P | saddleback gunnel |
| *Pholis schultzi* Schultz, 1931 | P | red gunnel |
| *Rhodymenichthys dolichogaster* (Pallas, 1814) | P | stippled gunnel |
| *Ulvicola sanctaerosae* Gilbert & Starks, 1897 | P | kelp gunnel .......... espinoso de marea sargacero |
| Anarhichadidae—En-wolffishes, Sp-peces lobo, Fr-poissons-loups | | |
| *Anarhichas denticulatus* Krøyer, 1845 | A-P | northern wolffish |
| *Anarhichas lupus* Linnaeus, 1758 | A | Atlantic wolffish .................. loup atlantique |
| *Anarhichas minor* Olafsen, 1772 | A | spotted wolffish ................. loup tacheté |
| *Anarhichas orientalis* Pallas, 1814 | P | Bering wolffish |
| *Anarrhichthys ocellatus* Ayres, 1855 | P | wolf-eel |
| Ptilichthyidae—En-quillfishes, Sp-peces pua, Fr-fouette-queues | | |
| *Ptilichthys goodei* Bean, 1881 | P | quillfish |
| Zaproridae—En-prowfishes, Sp-peces proa, Fr-zaproridés | | |
| *Zaprora silenus* Jordan, 1896 | P | prowfish |
| Scytalinidae—En-graveldivers, Sp-peces topo, Fr-blennies fouisseuses | | |
| *Scytalina cerdale* Jordan & Gilbert, 1880 | P | graveldiver |
| Trichodontidae—En-sandfishes, Sp-areneros, Fr-trichodontes | | |
| *Arctoscopus japonicus* (Steindachner, 1881) | P | sailfin sandfish |
| *Trichodon trichodon* (Tilesius, 1813) | P | Pacific sandfish |
| Percophidae—En-flatheads, Sp-picos de pato, Fr-platêtes | | |
| *Bembrops anatirostris* Ginsburg, 1955 | A | duckbill flathead .............. pico de pato |
| *Bembrops gobioides* (Goode, 1880) | A | goby flathead .............. pico de pala |

| SCIENTIFIC NAME | OCCURRENCE[1] | COMMON NAME (ENGLISH, SPANISH, FRENCH)[2] |
|---|---|---|
| Ammodytidae—En-sand lances, Sp-peones, Fr-lançons | | |
| Ammodytes americanus DeKay, 1842 | A | American sand lance ..........lançon d'Amérique |
| +Ammodytes dubius Reinhardt, 1837 | A | northern sand lance |
| Ammodytes hexapterus Pallas, 1814 | P | Pacific sand lance |
| +Ammodytoides gilli (Bean, 1895) | PM | Panamic sand lance .............. peón panámico |
| Uranoscopidae—En-stargazers, Sp-miracielos, Fr-uranoscopes | | |
| *Astroscopus guttatus Abbott, 1860 | A | northern stargazer |
| Astroscopus y-graecum (Cuvier, 1829) | A | southern stargazer .............. miracielo del sureste |
| *Astroscopus zephyreus Gilbert & Starks, 1897 | P | Pacific stargazer .............. miracielo perro |
| Gnathagnus egregius (Jordan & Thompson, 1905) | A | freckled stargazer |
| Kathetostoma albigutta (Bean, 1892) | A | lancer stargazer .............. miracielo sargacero |
| Kathetostoma averruncus Jordan & Bollman, 1890 | P | smooth stargazer .............. miracielo buldog |
| Tripterygiidae—En-triplefins, Sp-tres aletas, Fr-triptérygiidés | | |
| Axoclinus carminalis (Jordan & Gilbert, 1882) | PM | carmine triplefin .............. tres aletas carmín |
| Axoclinus lucillae Fowler, 1944 | PM | Panamic triplefin .............. tres aletas bigote |
| Axoclinus multicinctus Allen & Robertson, 1992 | PM | multibarred triplefin .............. tres aletas listado |
| Axoclinus nigricaudus Allen & Robertson, 1991 | PM | Cortez triplefin .............. tres aletas colinegra |
| Crocodilichthys gracilis Allen & Robertson, 1991 | PM | lizard triplefin .............. lagartija tres aletas |
| Enneanectes altivelis Rosenblatt, 1960 | A | lofty triplefin .............. tres aletas de barras |
| Enneanectes atrorus Rosenblatt, 1960 | AM | blackedge triplefin .............. tres aletas orlado |
| Enneanectes boehlkei Rosenblatt, 1960 | A | roughhead triplefin .............. tres aletas rugoso |
| Enneanectes jordani (Evermann & Marsh, 1899) | AM | mimic triplefin .............. tres aletas escondido |
| Enneanectes pectoralis (Fowler, 1941) | A | redeye triplefin .............. tres aletas aletón |
| Enneanectes reticulatus Allen & Robertson, 1991 | PM | flag triplefin .............. tres aletas bandera |
| Enneanectes sexmaculatus (Fowler, 1944) | PM | delicate triplefin .............. tres aletas manchada |
| Dactyloscopidae—En-sand stargazers, Sp-miraestrellas, Fr-télescopes | | |
| Dactylagnus mundus Gill, 1863 | PM | giant stargazer .............. miraestrellas gigante |
| Dactylagnus parvus Dawson, 1976 | PM | Panamic stargazer .............. miraestrellas panámica |

| SCIENTIFIC NAME | OCCURRENCE[1] | COMMON NAME (ENGLISH, SPANISH, FRENCH)[2] |
|---|---|---|
| *Dactyloscopus amnis* Miller & Briggs, 1962 | PM | riverine stargazer ... miraestrellas ribereña |
| *Dactyloscopus byersi* Dawson, 1969 | PM | notchtail stargazer ... miraestrellas coliranurada |
| *Dactyloscopus crossotus* Starks, 1913 | A | bigeye stargazer |
| *Dactyloscopus fimbriatus* (Reid, 1935) | PM | fringed stargazer ... miraestrellas orlada |
| *Dactyloscopus foraminosus* Dawson, 1982 | A | reticulate stargazer |
| *Dactyloscopus lunaticus* Gilbert, 1890 | PM | moonstruck stargazer ... miraestrellas lunática |
| *Dactyloscopus metoecus* Dawson, 1975 | PM | Mexican stargazer ... miraestrellas mexicana |
| *Dactyloscopus minutus* Dawson, 1975 | PM | tiny stargazer ... miraestrellas chiquita |
| *Dactyloscopus moorei* (Fowler, 1906) | A | speckled stargazer |
| *Dacyloscopus pectoralis* Gill, 1861 | PM | whitesaddle stargazer ... miraestrellas fisgona |
| *Dactyloscopus tridigitatus* Gill, 1859 | A | sand stargazer ... miraestrellas ojilargo |
| *Gillellus arenicola* Gilbert, 1890 | PM | sandloving stargazer ... miraestrellas fina |
| *Gillellus greyae* Kanazawa, 1952 | A | arrow stargazer ... miraestrellas flecha |
| *Gillellus healae* Dawson, 1982 | A | masked stargazer |
| *Gillellus ornatus* Gilbert, 1892 | PM | ornate stargazer ... miraestrellas ornada |
| *Gillellus searcheri* Dawson, 1977 | PM | Searcher stargazer ... miraestrellas rayada |
| *Gillellus semicinctus* Gilbert, 1890 | PM | halfbanded stargazer ... miraestrellas mediafranjada |
| *Gillellus uranidea* Böhlke, 1968 | A | warteye stargazer ... miraestrellas ojiverrugado |
| *Heteristius cinctus* (Osburn & Nichols, 1916) | PM | banded stargazer ... miraestrellas vendada |
| *Myxodagnus macrognathus* Hildebrand, 1946 | PM | longjaw stargazer ... miraestrellas bocona |
| *Myxodagnus opercularis* Gill, 1861 | PM | dart stargazer ... miraestrellas virote |
| *Platygillellus rubrocinctus* (Longley, 1934) | A | saddle stargazer |

*Labrisomidae—En-labrisomid blennies, Sp-trambollos, Fr-labrisomidés

| SCIENTIFIC NAME | OCCURRENCE[1] | COMMON NAME (ENGLISH, SPANISH, FRENCH)[2] |
|---|---|---|
| *Alloclinus holderi* (Lauderbach, 1907) | P | island kelpfish ... trambollo isleño |
| *Cryptotrema corallinum* Gilbert, 1890 | P | deepwater blenny ... trambollo de profundidad |
| *Cryptotrema seftoni* Hubbs, 1954 | PM | hidden blenny ... trambollo escondido |
| *Dialommus macrocephalus* (Günther, 1861) | PM | foureye rockskipper ... trambollo listo |
| *Exerpes asper* (Jenkins & Evermann, 1889) | PM | sargassum blenny ... trambollo sargacero |
| +*Haptoclinus apectolophus* Böhlke & Robins, 1974 | AM | uncombed blenny ... trambollo despeinado |
| *Labrisomus bucciferus* Poey, 1868 | A | puffcheek blenny ... trambollo fumador |

| SCIENTIFIC NAME | OCCURRENCE[1] | COMMON NAME (ENGLISH, SPANISH, FRENCH)[2] |
|---|---|---|
| Labrisomus gobio (Valenciennes, 1836) | A | palehead blenny ....... trambollo caripálida |
| Labrisomus guppyi (Norman, 1922) | A | mimic blenny ....... trambollo mímico |
| Labrisomus haitiensis Beebe & Tee-Van, 1928 | A | longfin blenny ....... trambollo príncipe |
| Labrisomus kalisherae (Jordan, 1904) | A | downy blenny ....... trambollo velloso |
| Labrisomus multiporosus Hubbs, 1953 | PM | porehead blenny ....... trambollo cabeza porosa |
| Labrisomus nigricinctus Howell Rivero, 1936 | A | spotcheek blenny ....... trambollo lunado |
| Labrisomus nuchipinnis (Quoy & Gaimard, 1824) | A | hairy blenny ....... trambollo peludo |
| +Labrisomus socorroensis Hubbs, 1953 | PM | misspelled blenny ....... trambollo de Socorro |
| Labrisomus striatus Hubbs, 1953 | PM | green blenny ....... trambollo listado |
| Labrisomus wigginsi Hubbs 1953 | PM | Baja blenny ....... trambollo bajacaliforniano |
| Labrisomus xanti Gill, 1860 | PM | largemouth blenny ....... chalapo |
| Malacoctenus aurolineatus Smith, 1957 | A | goldline blenny ....... trambollo lineado |
| Malacoctenus boehlkei Springer, 1959 | AM | diamond blenny ....... trambollo diamantino |
| Malacoctenus ebisui Springer, 1959 | PM | fishgod blenny ....... trambollo dorado |
| Malacoctenus erdmani Smith, 1957 | AM | imitator blenny ....... trambollo imitador |
| Malacoctenus gigas Springer, 1959 | PM | Sonora blenny ....... trambollo de Sonora |
| Malacoctenus gilli (Steindachner, 1867) | AM | dusky blenny ....... trambollo pardo |
| Malacoctenus hubbsi Springer, 1959 | PM | redside blenny ....... trambollo rojo |
| Malacoctenus macropus (Poey, 1868) | A | rosy blenny ....... trambollo rosado |
| Malacoctenus margaritae (Fowler, 1944) | PM | margarita blenny ....... trambollo margarita |
| Malacoctenus tetranemus (Cope, 1877) | PM | throatspotted blenny ....... trambollo pintado |
| Malacoctenus triangulatus Springer, 1959 | A | saddled blenny ....... trambollo ensillado |
| Malacoctenus versicolor (Poey, 1876) | AM | barfin blenny ....... trambollo multicolor |
| Malacoctenus zacae Springer, 1959 | PM | Zaca blenny ....... trambollo aletiamarilla |
| Malacoctenus zonifer (Jordan & Gilbert, 1882) | PM | glossy blenny ....... trambollo brilloso |
| Nemaclinus atelestos Böhlke & Springer, 1975 | A | threadfin blenny |
| Paraclinus altivelis (Lockington, 1881) | PM | topgallant blenny ....... trambollito juanete |
| Paraclinus beebei Hubbs, 1952 | PM | pink blenny ....... trambollito clavel |
| Paraclinus cingulatus (Evermann & Marsh, 1899) | A | coral blenny ....... trambollito coralino |
| Paraclinus ditrichus Rosenblatt & Parr, 1969 | PM | leastfoot blenny ....... trambollito pocas patas |
| Paraclinus fasciatus (Steindachner, 1876) | A | banded blenny ....... trambollito ocelado |

| SCIENTIFIC NAME | OCCURRENCE[1] | COMMON NAME (ENGLISH, SPANISH, FRENCH)[2] |
|---|---|---|
| Paraclinus grandicornis (Rosén, 1911) | A | horned blenny ... trambollito pelón |
| Paraclinus infrons Böhlke, 1960 | A | bald blenny ... trambollito de arrecife |
| Paraclinus integripinnis (Smith, 1880) | P | reef finspot ... |
| Paraclinus magdalenae Rosenblatt & Parr, 1969 | PM | Magdalena blenny ... trambollito de Magdalena |
| Paraclinus marmoratus (Steindachner, 1876) | A | marbled blenny ... |
| Paraclinus mexicanus (Gilbert, 1904) | PM | Mexican blenny ... trambollito mexicano |
| Paraclinus naeorhegmis Böhlke, 1960 | AM | surf blenny ... trambollito de la resaca |
| Paraclinus nigripinnis (Steindachner, 1867) | A | blackfin blenny ... trambollito aletinegra |
| Paraclinus sini Hubbs, 1952 | PM | flapscale blenny ... trambollito frondoso |
| Paraclinus stephensi Rosenblatt & Parr, 1969 | PM | professor blenny ... trambollito del maestro |
| Paraclinus tanygnathus Rosenblatt & Parr, 1969 | PM | longjaw blenny ... trambollito adornado |
| Paraclinus walkeri Hubbs 1952 | PM | San Quintin blenny ... trambollito de San Quintín |
| Starksia atlantica Longley, 1934 | AM | smootheye blenny ... trambollito ojiliso |
| Starksia cremnobates (Gilbert, 1890) | PM | fugitive blenny ... trambollito fugaz |
| Starksia fasciata (Longley, 1934) | AM | blackbar blenny ... trambollito barra oscura |
| Starksia grammilaga Rosenblatt & Taylor, 1971 | PM | pinstriped blenny ... trambollito estilográfo |
| Starksia guadalupae Rosenblatt & Taylor, 1971 | PM | Guadalupe blenny ... trambollito de Guadalupe |
| Starksia hoesei Rosenblatt & Taylor, 1971 | PM | hose blenny ... trambollito manguera |
| Starksia lepicoelia Böhlke & Springer, 1961 | AM | blackcheek blenny ... trambollito carinegro |
| Starksia lepidogaster Rosenblatt & Taylor, 1971 | PM | scalybelly blenny ... trambollito panza escamosa |
| Starksia nanodes Böhlke & Springer, 1961 | AM | dwarf blenny ... trambollito enano |
| Starksia occidentalis Greenfield, 1979 | AM | occidental blenny ... trambollito occidental |
| Starksia ocellata (Steindachner, 1876) | A | checkered blenny ... |
| Starksia posthon Rosenblatt & Taylor, 1971 | PM | brownspotted blenny ... trambollito moteado |
| Starksia sluiteri (Metzelaar, 1919) | AM | spotted blenny ... trambollito manchado |
| Starksia spinipenis (Al-Uthman, 1960) | PM | phallic blenny ... trambollito macho |
| Starksia starcki Gilbert, 1971 | A | key blenny ... |
| Xenomedea rhodopyga Rosenblatt & Taylor, 1971 | PM | redrump blenny ... trambollito nalga roja |

*Clinidae—En-kelp blennies, Sp-sargaceros, Fr-clinies

| | | |
|---|---|---|
| +Gibbonsia elegans (Cooper, 1864) | P | spotted kelpfish ... sargacero manchado |
| Gibbonsia metzi Hubbs, 1927 | P | striped kelpfish ... sargacero rayado |

| SCIENTIFIC NAME | OCCURRENCE[1] | COMMON NAME (ENGLISH, SPANISH, FRENCH)[2] |
|---|---|---|
| Gibbonsia montereyensis Hubbs, 1927 | P | crevice kelpfish .......... sargacero de Monterey |
| Heterostichus rostratus Girard, 1854 | P | giant kelpfish .......... sargacero gigante |

*Chaenopsidae—En-tube blennies, Sp-trambollos tubícolas, Fr-chaenopsidés

| SCIENTIFIC NAME | OCCURRENCE[1] | COMMON NAME (ENGLISH, SPANISH, FRENCH)[2] |
|---|---|---|
| Acanthemblemaria aspera (Longley, 1927) | A | roughhead blenny |
| Acanthemblemaria balanorum Brock, 1940 | PM | clubhead barnacle blenny ....... tubícola espinudo |
| Acanthemblemaria chaplini Böhlke, 1957 | A | papillose blenny |
| Acanthemblemaria crockeri Beebe & Tee-Van, 1938 | PM | browncheek blenny .......... tubícola cachetón |
| Acanthemblemaria greenfieldi Smith-Vaniz & Palacio, 1974 | AM | stalk blenny .......... tubícola palito |
| Acanthemblemaria macrospilus Brock, 1940 | PM | Mexican barnacle blenny .......... tubícola mexicano |
| Acanthemblemaria mangognatha Hastings & Robertson, 1999 | PM | Revillagigedo barnacle blenny .......... tubícola mango |
| Acanthemblemaria spinosa Metzelaar, 1919 | AM | spinyhead blenny .......... tubícola cabeza espinosa |
| Chaenopsis alepidota (Gilbert, 1890) | P | orangethroat pikeblenny .......... tubícola lucio |
| Chaenopsis coheni Böhlke, 1957 | PM | Cortez pikeblenny .......... tubícola picudo |
| Chaenopsis limbaughi Robins & Randall, 1965 | A | yellowface pikeblenny |
| +Chaenopsis ocellata Poey, 1865 | A | bluethroat pikeblenny .......... tubícola afilado |
| *Chaenopsis roseola Hastings & Shipp, 1981 | A | freckled pikeblenny |
| Cirriemblemaria lucasana (Stephens, 1963) | PM | plume blenny .......... tubícola plumoso |
| Coralliozetus angelicus (Böhlke & Mead, 1957) | PM | angel blenny .......... tubícola ángel |
| Coralliozetus boehlkei Stephens, 1963 | PM | barcheek blenny .......... tubícola cachete rayado |
| Coralliozetus micropes (Beebe & Tee-Van, 1938) | PM | zebraface blenny .......... tubícola cara de cebra |
| Coralliozetus rosenblatti Stephens, 1963 | PM | spikefin blenny .......... tubícola espiga |
| Ekemblemaria myersi Stephens, 1963 | PM | reef-sand blenny .......... tubícola de cejas |
| Emblemaria atlantica Jordan & Evermann, 1898 | A | banner blenny |
| Emblemaria hypacanthus (Jenkins & Evermann, 1889) | PM | Gulf signal blenny .......... tubícola flamante |
| *Emblemaria pandionis Evermann & Marsh, 1900 | A | sailfin blenny .......... tubícola dragón |
| Emblemaria piratica Ginsburg, 1942 | PM | sailfin signal blenny .......... tubícola bandera |
| Emblemaria piratula Ginsburg & Reid, 1942 | A | pirate blenny |
| Emblemaria walkeri Stephens, 1963 | PM | elusive signal blenny .......... tubícola fugaz |
| *Emblemariopsis bahamensis Stephens, 1961 | A | blackhead blenny .......... tubícola cabezinegro |

| SCIENTIFIC NAME | OCCURRENCE[1] | COMMON NAME (ENGLISH, SPANISH, FRENCH)[2] |
|---|---|---|
| *Emblemariopsis diaphana Longley, 1927 | A | glass blenny |
| Emblemaricpsis occidentalis Stephens, 1970 | AM | redspine blenny — tubícola espina roja |
| Emblemariopsis pricei Greenfield, 1975 | AM | seafan blenny — tubícola gorgonio |
| Emblemariopsis signifera (Ginsburg, 1942) | AM | flagfin blenny — tubícola aletón |
| *Hemiemblemaria simula Longley & Hildebrand, 1940 | A | wrasse blenny |
| Neoclinus blanchardi Girard, 1858 | P | sarcastic fringehead — tubícola chusco |
| Neoclinus stephensae Hubbs, 1953 | P | yellowfin fringehead — tubícola aletiamarilla |
| Neoclinus uninotatus Hubbs, 1953 | P | onespot fringehead — tubícola mancha singular |
| Protemblemaria bicirris (Hildebrand, 1946) | PM | warthead blenny — tubícola tupido |
| Stathmonotus gymnodermis Springer, 1955 | AM | naked blenny — tubícola esperanza |
| Stathmonotus hemphilli Bean, 1885 | A | blackbelly blenny |
| Stathmonotus lugubris Böhlke, 1953 | PM | Mexican worm blenny — tubícola lombríz |
| Stathmonotus sinuscalifornici (Chabanaud, 1942) | PM | Gulf worm blenny — tubícola gusano |
| Stathmonotus stahli (Evermann & Marsh, 1899) | A | eelgrass blenny — tubícola anguila |

Blenniidae—En-combtooth blennies, Sp-borrachos, Fr-blennies à dents de peigne

| SCIENTIFIC NAME | OCCURRENCE[1] | COMMON NAME (ENGLISH, SPANISH, FRENCH)[2] |
|---|---|---|
| +Chasmodes bosquianus (Lacepède, 1800) | A | striped blenny |
| *Chasmodes longimaxilla Williams, 1983 | A | stretchjaw blenny — borracho bocón |
| Chasmodes saburrae Jordan & Gilbert, 1882 | A | Florida blenny |
| Entomacrodus chiostictus (Jordan & Gilbert, 1882) | PM | notchfin blenny — borracho aleta mocha |
| Entomacrodus nigricans Gill, 1859 | A | pearl blenny — borracho perlado |
| Hypleurochilus bermudensis Beebe & Tee-Van, 1933 | A | barred blenny — borracho de barras |
| *Hypleurochilus caudovittatus Bath, 1994 | A | zebratail blenny |
| +Hypleurochilus geminatus (Wood, 1825) | A | crested blenny |
| *Hypleurochilus multifilis (Girard, 1858) | A | featherduster blenny — borracho plumero |
| *Hypleurochilus pseudoaequipinnis Bath, 1994 | A | oyster blenny — borracho ostionero |
| Hypleurochilus springeri Randall, 1966 | A | orangespotted blenny |
| Hypsoblennius brevipinnis (Günther, 1861) | PM | barnaclebill blenny — borracho vacilón |
| Hypsoblennius gentilis (Girard, 1854) | P | bay blenny — borracho de bahía |
| Hypsoblennius gilberti (Jordan, 1882) | P | rockpool blenny — borracho de poza |
| Hypsoblennius hentz (Lesueur, 1825) | A | feather blenny |
| Hypsoblennius invemar Smith-Vaniz & Acero, 1980 | A | tessellated blenny |

| SCIENTIFIC NAME | OCCURRENCE[1] | COMMON NAME (ENGLISH, SPANISH, FRENCH)[2] |
|---|---|---|
| *Hypsoblennius ionthas* (Jordan & Gilbert, 1882) | A | freckled blenny |
| *Hypsoblennius jenkinsi* (Jordan & Evermann, 1896) | P | mussel blenny ........ borracho mejillonero |
| *Hypsoblennius proteus* (Krejsa, 1960) | PM | Socorro blenny ........ borracho de Socorro |
| *Lupinoblennius nicholsi* (Tavolga, 1954) | A | highfin blenny ........ borracho aletón |
| *\*Lupinoblennius vinctus* (Poey, 1867) | A | mangrove blenny |
| *\*Ophioblennius macclurei* (Silvester, 1915) | A | redlip blenny ........ borracho labio rojo |
| *Ophioblennius steindachneri* Jordan & Evermann, 1898 | PM | Panamic fanged blenny ........ borracho mono |
| *Parablennius marmoreus* (Poey, 1876) | A | seaweed blenny ........ borracho marmóreo |
| *\*Plagiotremus azaleus* (Jordan & Bollman, 1890) | P | sabertooth blenny ........ diente sable |
| *Scartella cristata* (Linnaeus, 1758) | A | molly miller ........ borracho peineta |

Icosteidae—En-ragfishes, Sp-peces harapo, Fr-icostéidés

| | | |
|---|---|---|
| *Icosteus aenigmaticus* Lockington, 1880 | P | ragfish |

+Gobiesocidae—En-clingfishes, Sp-chupapiedras, Fr-crampons

| | | |
|---|---|---|
| *Acyrtops amplicirrus* Briggs, 1955 | AM | flarenostril clingfish ........ chupapiedra nariz crestada |
| *\*Acyrtops beryllinus* (Hildebrand & Ginsburg, 1926) | A | emerald clingfish |
| +*Acyrtus artius* Briggs, 1955 | AM | papillate clingfish ........ chupapiedra papilosa |
| +*Acyrtus rubiginosus* (Poey, 1868) | AM | red clingfish ........ chupapiedra roja |
| *Arcos erythrops* (Jordan & Gilbert, 1882) | PM | rockwall clingfish ........ chupapiedra de cantil |
| *Arcos macrophthalmus* (Günther, 1861) | AM | padded clingfish ........ chupapiedra acojinada |
| *Derilissus kremnobates* Fraser, 1970 | AM | whiskereye clingfish ........ chupapiedra ojo estriado |
| *Gobiesox adustus* Jordan & Gilbert, 1882 | PM | Panamic clingfish ........ chupapiedra panámica |
| *Gobiesox aethus* (Briggs, 1951) | PM | Clarion clingfish ........ chupapiedra de Clarión |
| *Gobiesox barbatulus* Starks, 1913 | AM | lappetlip clingfish ........ chupapiedra aristada |
| *Gobiesox canidens* (Briggs, 1951) | PM | Socorro clingfish ........ chupapiedra de Socorro |
| *Gobiesox eugrammus* Briggs, 1955 | P | lined clingfish ........ chupapiedra estriada |
| *Gobiesox fluviatilis* Briggs & Miller, 1960 | F:M | mountain clingfish ........ cucharita de río |
| *Gobiesox juniperoserrai* Espinosa-Pérez & Castro-Aguirre, 1996 | F:M | peninsular clingfish ........ cucharita peninsular |
| *Gobiesox maeandricus* (Girard, 1858) | P | northern clingfish ........ chupapiedra norteña |
| *Gobiesox marijeanae* Briggs, 1960 | PM | lonely clingfish ........ chupapiedra solita |

| SCIENTIFIC NAME | OCCURRENCE[1] | COMMON NAME (ENGLISH, SPANISH, FRENCH)[2] | |
|---|---|---|---|
| Gobiesox mexicanus Briggs & Miller, 1960 | F:M | Mexican clingfish | cucharita mexicana |
| Gobiesox papillifer Gilbert, 1890 | P | bearded clingfish | chupapiedra barbona |
| Gobiesox pinniger Gilbert, 1890 | PM | tadpole clingfish | chupapiedra renacuajo |
| *Gobiesox punctulatus (Poey, 1876) | A | stippled clingfish | chupapiedra punteada |
| Gobiesox rhessodon Smith, 1881 | P | California clingfish | chupapiedra californiana |
| Gobiesox schultzi Briggs, 1951 | PM | smoothlip clingfish | chupapiedra labioliso |
| Gobiesox strumosus Cope, 1870 | A | skilletfish | cazoleta |
| Pherallodiscus funebris (Gilbert, 1890) | PM | northern fraildisc clingfish | chupapiedra discofrágil norteña |
| Pherallodiscus varius Briggs, 1955 | PM | southern fraildisc clingfish | chupapiedra discofrágil sureña |
| *Rimicola cabrilloi Briggs, 2002 | P | Channel Islands clingfish | |
| Rimicola dimorpha Briggs, 1955 | P | southern clingfish | chupapiedra chiquita |
| Rimicola eigenmanni (Gilbert, 1890) | P | slender clingfish | chupiedra flaca |
| Rimicola muscarum (Meek & Pierson, 1895) | P | kelp clingfish | chupapiedra sargacera |
| Rimicola sila Briggs, 1955 | PM | Guadalupe clingfish | chupapiedra de Guadalupe |
| Tomicodon absitus Briggs, 1955 | PM | distant clingfish | chupapiedra lejana |
| Tomicodon boehlkei Briggs, 1955 | PM | Cortez clingfish | chupapiedra de Cortés |
| Tomicodon eos (Jordan Gilbert, 1882) | PM | rosy clingfish | chupapiedra rosada |
| Tomicodon fasciatus (Peters, 1860) | AM | barred clingfish | chupapiedra de barras |
| Tomicodon humeralis (Gilbert, 1890) | PM | Sonora clingfish | chupapiedra de Sonora |
| Tomicodon myersi Briggs, 1955 | PM | blackstripe clingfish | chupapiedra raya negra |
| Tomicodon petersii (Garman, 1875) | PM | hourglass clingfish | chupapiedra clepsidra |
| Tomicodon zebra (Jordan & Gilbert, 1882) | PM | zebra clingfish | chupapiedra cebra |

Callionymidae—En-dragonets, Sp-dragoncillos, Fr-dragonnets

| | | | |
|---|---|---|---|
| Diplogrammus pauciradiatus (Gill, 1865) | A | spotted dragonet | |
| *Foetorepus agassizii (Goode & Bean, 1888) | A | spotfin dragonet | |
| *Foetorepus goodenbeani Nakabo & Hartel, 1999 | A | palefin dragonet | |
| *Paradiplogrammus bairdi (Jordan, 1888) | A | lancer dragonet | dragoncillo coralino |
| *Synchiropus atrilabiatus (Garman, 1899) | P | blacklip dragonet | dragoncillo de asta |

Eleotridae—En-sleepers, Sp-guavinas, Fr-dormeurs

| | | | |
|---|---|---|---|
| Dormitator latifrons (Richardson, 1844) | F:M-P | Pacific fat sleeper | puyeki |

| SCIENTIFIC NAME | OCCURRENCE[1] | COMMON NAME (ENGLISH, SPANISH, FRENCH)[2] |
|---|---|---|
| *Dormitator maculatus (Bloch, 1792) | A-F:UM | fat sleeper ... naca |
| *Eleotris amblyopsis (Cope, 1871) | A-F:UM | largescaled spinycheek sleeper ... |
| *Eleotris perniger (Cope, 1871) | A-F:UM | smallscaled spinycheek sleeper ... dormilón oscuro |
| *Eleotris picta Kner, 1863 | F:UM-PM | spotted sleeper ... guavina espinosa |
| Erotelis armiger (Jordan & Richardson, 1895) | F:M-PM | flathead sleeper ... guavina machada |
| Erotelis smaragdus (Valenciennes, 1837) | A-F:M | emerald sleeper ... guavina cabeza plana |
| Gobiomorus dormitor Lacepède, 1800 | A-F:UM | bigmouth sleeper ... guavina de concha |
| Gobiomorus maculatus (Günther, 1859) | F:M-PM | Pacific sleeper ... guavina bocón |
| Gobiomorus polylepis Ginsburg, 1953 | F:M-PM | finescale sleeper ... dormilón manchado |
| *Guavina guavina (Valenciennes, 1837) | AM-F:UM | guavina ... guavina cristalina |
| | | guavina |
| +Gobiidae—En-gobies, Sp-gobios, Fr-gobies | | |
| Aboma etheostoma Jordan & Starks, 1895 | PM | scaly goby ... gobio escamoso |
| Acanthogobius flavimanus (Temminck & Schlegel, 1845) | F[I]:UM-P[I] | yellowfin goby ... gobio extranjero |
| Aruma histrio (Jordan, 1884) | PM | slow goby ... gobio lento |
| *Awaous banana (Valenciennes, 1837) | F:UM | river goby ... gobio de río |
| Barbulifer antennatus Böhlke & Robins 1968 | AM | whiskered goby ... gobio antenado |
| Barbulifer ceuthoecus (Jordan & Gilbert, 1884) | A | bearded goby |
| Barbulifer mexicanus Hoese & Larsen, 1985 | PM | saddlebanded goby ... gobio alambrón |
| Barbulifer pantherinus (Pellegrin, 1901) | PM | panther goby ... gobio pantera |
| Bathygobius curacao (Metzelaar, 1919) | A | notchtongue goby ... gobio jaspeado |
| Bathygobius mystacium Ginsburg, 1947 | A | island frillfin ... gobio bandeado |
| Bathygobius ramosus Ginsburg, 1947 | PM | Panamic frillfin ... mapo panámico |
| Bathygobius soporator (Valenciennes, 1837) | A | frillfin goby ... mapo aguado |
| Bollmannia boqueronensis Evermann & Marsh, 1899 | A | white-eye goby |
| Bollmannia communis Ginsburg, 1942 | A | ragged goby ... gobio andrajoso |
| Bollmannia eigenmanni (Garman, 1896) | A | shelf goby |
| Bollmannia macropoma Gilbert, 1892 | PM | frailscale goby ... gobio pedernal |
| Bollmannia marginalis Ginsburg, 1939 | PM | apostrophe goby ... gobio sellado |

| SCIENTIFIC NAME | OCCURRENCE[1] | COMMON NAME (ENGLISH, SPANISH, FRENCH)[2] |
|---|---|---|
| *Bollmannia ocellata* Gilbert, 1892 | PM | pennant goby ............pennant goby ............gobio penacho |
| *Bollmannia stigmatura* Gilbert, 1892 | PM | tailspot goby ............gobio colimanchado |
| *Bollmannia umbrosa* Ginsburg, 1939 | PM | dusky goby ............gobio prieto |
| *Chriolepis benthonis* Ginsburg 1953 | AM | deepwater goby ............gobio de agua profunda |
| *Chriolepis cuneata* Bussing, 1990 | PM | rail goby ............gobio carril |
| *Chriolepis minutillus* Gilbert, 1892 | PM | rubble goby ............gobio conchalero |
| * *Chriolepis vespa* Hastings & Bortone, 1981 | A | wasp goby |
| *Chriolepis zebra* Ginsburg, 1938 | PM | gecko goby ............gobio salamanquesa |
| *Clevelandia ios* (Jordan & Gilbert, 1882) | F:U-P | arrow goby ............gobio flecha |
| *Coryphopterus alloides* Böhlke & Robins, 1960 | A | barfin goby |
| *Coryphopterus dicrus* Böhlke & Robins, 1960 | A | colon goby ............gobio dos puntos |
| *Coryphopterus eidolon* Böhlke & Robins, 1960 | A | pallid goby ............gobio pálido |
| *Coryphopterus glaucofraenum* Gill, 1863 | A | bridled goby ............gobio de riendas |
| *Coryphopterus hyalinus* Böhlke & Robins, 1962 | A | glass goby ............gobio cristal |
| *Coryphopterus lipernes* Böhlke & Robins, 1962 | A | peppermint goby |
| * *Coryphopterus personatus* (Jordan & Thompson, 1905) | A | masked goby ............gobio mapache |
| *Coryphopterus punctipectophorus* Springer, 1960 | A | spotted goby ............gobio punteado |
| *Coryphopterus thrix* Böhlke & Robins, 1960 | A | bartail goby ............gobio listado |
| + *Coryphopterus tortugae* (Jordan, 1904) | A | sand goby |
| *Coryphopterus urospilus* Ginsburg, 1938 | PM | redlight goby ............gobio semáforo |
| * *Ctenogobius boleosoma* (Jordan & Gilbert, 1882) | A-F:UM | darter goby ............madrejuile |
| * *Ctenogobius claytonii* (Meek, 1902) | A-F:UM | Mexican goby ............gobio mexicano |
| * *Ctenogobius fasciatus* Gill, 1858 | F:U | blotchcheek goby |
| *Ctenogobius manglicola* (Jordan & Starks, 1895) | PM | mangrove goby ............gobio de manglar |
| * *Ctenogobius pseudofasciatus* (Gilbert & Randall, 1971) | A-F:U | slashcheek goby |
| * *Ctenogobius saepepallens* (Gilbert & Randall, 1968) | A | dash goby |
| * *Ctenogobius sagittula* (Günther, 1861) | P | longtail goby ............gobio aguzado |
| * *Ctenogobius shufeldti* (Jordan & Eigenmann, 1887) | A-F:U | freshwater goby |
| * *Ctenogobius smaragdus* (Valenciennes, 1837) | A | emerald goby |
| * *Ctenogobius stigmaticus* (Poey, 1860) | A | marked goby |
| * *Ctenogobius stigmaturus* (Goode & Bean, 1882) | A | spottail goby |

| SCIENTIFIC NAME | OCCURRENCE[1] | COMMON NAME (ENGLISH, SPANISH, FRENCH)[2] |
|---|---|---|
| *Elacatinus digueti* (Pellegrin, 1901) | PM | banded cleaning goby ......... gobio barbero |
| *Elacatinus evelynae* (Böhlke & Robins, 1968) | AM | sharknose goby ............... gobio tiburoncito |
| *Elacatinus genie* (Böhlke & Robins, 1968) | AM | cleaning goby .................. gobio limpiador |
| *Elacatinus horsti* (Metzelaar, 1922) | A | yellowline goby |
| *Elacatinus illecebrosus* (Böhlke & Robins, 1968) | AM | barsnout goby ................. gobio seductor |
| *Elacatinus janssi* Bussing, 1981 | PM | spotback goby ............... gobio lomopintado |
| *Elacatinus limbaughi* Hoese & Reader, 2001 | PM | widebanded cleaning goby ...... gobio insólito |
| *Elacatinus louisae* (Böhlke & Robins, 1968) | AM | spotlight goby ................... gobio farol |
| *Elacatinus macrodon* (Beebe & Tee-Van, 1928) | A | tiger goby ...................... gobio tigre |
| *Elacatinus oceanops* Jordan, 1904 | A | neon goby |
| *Elacatinus prochilos* (Böhlke & Robins 1968) | AM | broadstripe goby .............. gobio bordeado |
| *Elacatinus puncticulatus* (Ginsburg, 1938) | PM | redhead goby ............. gobio cabeza roja |
| *Elacatinus xanthiprora* (Böhlke & Robins, 1968) | A | yellowprow goby |
| *Enypnias seminudus* (Günther, 1861) | PM | silt goby ..................... gobio cienoso |
| *Eucyclogobius newberryi* (Girard, 1856) | F:U-P | tidewater goby |
| *Evermannia longipinnis* (Steindachner, 1879) | PM | enigmatic goby ............. gobio enigmático |
| *Evermannia zosterura* (Jordan & Gilbert, 1882) | PM | bandedtail goby ............ gobio colirrayada |
| *Evermannichthys spongicola* (Radcliffe, 1917) | A | sponge goby ............... gobio esponjero |
| *Evorthodus lyricus* (Girard, 1858) | A-F:M | lyre goby ......................... tismiche |
| *Evorthodus minutus* Meek & Hildebrand, 1928 | PM | small goby .................... gobio pequeño |
| *Gillichthys mirabilis* Cooper, 1864 | F:UM-P | longjaw mudsucker ......... chupalodo grande |
| *Gillichthys seta* (Ginsburg, 1938) | PM | shortjaw mudsucker ......... chupalodo chico |
| *Ginsburgellus novemlineatus* (Fowler, 1950) | AM | ninelined goby ............. gobio nueve rayas |
| *Gnatholepis thompsoni* Jordan, 1904 | A | goldspot goby ............ gobio puntadorada |
| *Gobioides broussonetii* Lacepède, 1800 | A-F:UM | violet goby ................... gobio violeta |
| *Gobionellus microdon* (Gilbert, 1892) | PM-F:M | palmtail goby ............. gobio cola de palma |
| *Gobionellus oceanicus* (Pallas, 1770) | A | highfin goby ............... madrejuile flecha |
| *Gobiosoma bosc* (Lacepède, 1800) | A-F:UM | naked goby ................... gobio desnudo |
| *Gobiosoma chiquita* (Jenkins & Evermann, 1889) | PM | Sonora goby .................. gobio chiquito |
| *Gobiosoma ginsburgi* Hildebrand & Schroeder, 1928 | A | seaboard goby |
| *Gobiosoma grosvenori* (Robins, 1964) | A | rockcut goby |

| SCIENTIFIC NAME | OCCURRENCE[1] | COMMON NAME (ENGLISH, SPANISH, FRENCH)[2] |
|---|---|---|
| *Gobiosoma longipala* Ginsburg, 1933 | A | twoscale goby ... gobio blanco y negro |
| *Gobiosoma nudum* (Meek & Hildebrand, 1928) | PM | knobchin goby ... gobio bulto |
| *Gobiosoma paradoxum* (Günther, 1861) | PM | paradox goby ... gobio paradoja |
| *\*Gobiosoma robustum* Ginsburg, 1933 | A | code goby ... gobio clave |
| *Gobiosoma yucatanum* Dawson, 1971 | AM | Yucatan goby ... gobio yucateco |
| *Gobulus crescentalis* (Gilbert, 1892) | PM | crescent goby ... gobio creciente |
| *Gobulus hancocki* Ginsburg, 1938 | PM | sandtop goby ... gobio invertido |
| *Gobulus myersi* Ginsburg, 1939 | A | paleback goby ... gobio blanco y negro |
| *Gymneleotris seminudus* (Günther, 1864) | PM | splitbanded goby ... gobio mejilla manchada |
| *Ilypnus gilberti* (Eigenmann & Eigenmann, 1889) | P | cheekspot goby ... gobio brillante |
| *Ilypnus luculentus* Ginsburg, 1938 | PM | bright goby ... gobio frío |
| *Lepidogobius lepidus* (Girard, 1858) | P | bay goby ... gobio sargacero |
| *Lethops connectens* Hubbs, 1926 | P | halfblind goby ... gobio gallo |
| +*Lophogobius cyprinoides* (Pallas, 1770) | A-F:UM | crested goby ... gobio bonito |
| *Lythrypnus dalli* (Gilbert, 1890) | P | bluebanded goby ... gobio enano |
| *Lythrypnus elasson* Böhlke & Robins, 1960 | A | dwarf goby ... gobio isleño |
| *Lythrypnus insularis* Bussing, 1990 | PM | distant goby ... gobio insular |
| *Lythrypnus nesiotes* Böhlke & Robins, 1960 | A | island goby ... gobio reo |
| *Lythrypnus phorcellus* Böhlke & Robins, 1960 | A | convict goby ... gobio coquetón |
| *Lythrypnus pulchellus* Ginsburg, 1938 | PM | gorgeous goby ... gobio ligero |
| *Lythrypnus rhizophora* (Heller & Snodgrass, 1903) | PM | spottedcheek goby ... gobio marcado |
| *Lythrypnus spilus* Böhlke & Robins, 1960 | A | bluegold goby ... gobio cebra |
| *Lythrypnus zebra* (Gilbert, 1890) | P | zebra goby ... gobio de Balboa |
| *Microgobius brevispinis* Ginsburg, 1939 | PM | Balboa goby ... gobio escamas redondas |
| *Microgobius carri* Fowler, 1945 | A | Seminole goby ... gobio emblema |
| *Microgobius cyclolepis* Gilbert, 1890 | PM | roundscale goby ... gobio chato |
| *Microgobius emblematicus* (Jordan & Gilbert, 1882) | PM | emblem goby ... gobio payaso |
| *Microgobius erectus* Ginsburg, 1938 | PM | erect goby ... gobio de Miraflores |
| *Microgobius gulosus* (Girard, 1858) | A-F:U | clown goby |
| *Microgobius microlepis* Longley & Hildebrand, 1940 | A | banner goby |
| *Microgobius miraflorensis* Gilbert & Starks, 1904 | PM-F:M | Miraflores goby |

| SCIENTIFIC NAME | OCCURRENCE[1] | COMMON NAME (ENGLISH, SPANISH, FRENCH)[2] |
|---|---|---|
| *Microgobius tabogensis* Meek & Hildebrand, 1928 | PM | Taboga goby ................ gobio de Taboga |
| *Microgobius thalassinus* (Jordan & Gilbert, 1883) | A | green goby |
| *Neogobius melanostomus* (Pallas, 1814) | F[I]:CU | round goby .................. gobie à taches noires |
| *Nes longus* (Nichols, 1914) | A | orangespotted goby ......... gobio camaronícola |
| *Oxyurichthys stigmalophius* (Mead & Böhlke, 1958) | A | spotfin goby ............. gobio aleta manchada |
| *Palatogobius paradoxus* Gilbert, 1971 | A | mauve goby |
| *Parrella ginsburgi* Wade, 1946 | PM | darkblotch goby .............. gobio lunarejo |
| *Parrella lucretiae* (Eigenmann & Eigenmann, 1888) | PM | maculated goby ............ gobio maculado |
| *Parrella maxillaris* Ginsburg, 1938 | PM | doublestripe goby .......... gobio veteado |
| *Priolepis hipoliti* (Metzelaar, 1922) | A | rusty goby .................. gobio oxidado |
| *Proterorhinus marmoratus* (Pallas, 1814) | F[I]:CU | tubenose goby |
| *Psilotris alepis* Ginsburg, 1953 | AM | scaleless goby ........... gobio sin escamas |
| *Psilotris batrachodes* Böhlke, 1963 | AM | toadfish goby ............... gobio sapito |
| *Psilotris celsus* Böhlke, 1963 | A | highspine goby ........... gobio espina alta |
| *Pycnomma semisquamatum* Rutter, 1904 | PM | secret goby ................. gobio furtivo |
| *Quietula guaymasiae* Jenkins & Evermann, 1889 | PM | Guaymas goby ........... gobio guaymense |
| *Quietula y-cauda* (Jenkins & Evermann, 1889) | P | shadow goby ........... gobio sombreado |
| *Rhinogobiops nicholsii* (Bean, 1882) | P | blackeye goby ................ gobio triste |
| *Risor ruber* (Rosén, 1911) | A | tusked goby ................ gobio boquita |
| *Sicydium gymnogaster* Ogilvie-Grant, 1884 | F:M | smoothbelly goby ......... dormilón de Veracruz |
| *Sicydium multipunctatum* Regan, 1906 | F:M | multispotted goby ......... dormilón pecoso |
| *Tridentiger barbatus* (Günther, 1861) | F[I]:U-P[I] | Shokihaze goby |
| *Tridentiger bifasciatus* Steindachner, 1881 | F[I]:U | shimofuri goby |
| *Tridentiger trigonocephalus* (Gill, 1859) | P[I] | chameleon goby |
| *Typhlogobius californiensis* Steindachner, 1879 | P | blind goby .................. gobio ciego |
| *Varicus marilynae* Gilmore, 1979 | A | orangebelly goby |

Microdesmidae—En-wormfishes, Sp-peces lombriz, Fr-poissons-lombrics

| | | |
|---|---|---|
| *Cerdale floridana* Longley, 1934 | A | pugjaw wormfish |
| *Clarkichthys bilineatus* (Clark, 1936) | PM | flagtail wormfish ........... pez lombriz colibandera |
| *Microdesmus affinis* Meek & Hildebrand, 1928 | PM | olivaceous wormfish ......... pez lombriz oliváceo |

| SCIENTIFIC NAME | OCCURRENCE[1] | COMMON NAME (ENGLISH, SPANISH, FRENCH)[2] |
|---|---|---|
| *Microdesmus carri* Gilbert, 1966 | AM | stippled wormfish ............ pez lombriz punteado |
| *Microdesmus dipus* Günther, 1864 | PM | banded wormfish ............ pez lombriz rayado |
| *Microdesmus dorsipunctatus* Dawson, 1968 | PM | spotback wormfish ............ pez lombriz lomo punteado |
| *Microdesmus lanceolatus* Dawson, 1962 | A | lancetail wormfish |
| *Microdesmus longipinnis* (Weymouth, 1910) | A | pink wormfish |
| *Microdesmus retropinnis* Jordan & Gilbert, 1882 | PM | rearfin wormfish ............ pez lombriz aletatrasera |
| *Microdesmus suttkusi* Gilbert, 1966 | PM | spotside wormfish ............ pez lombriz manchado |

*Ptereleotridae—En-dartfishes, Sp-gobios dardos, Fr-ptéréléotridés

| | | |
|---|---|---|
| *Ptereleotris calliura* (Jordan & Gilbert, 1882) | A | blue dartfish ............ gobio dardo azul |
| *Ptereleotris carinata* Bussing, 2001 | PM | Panamic dartfish ............ gobio dardo panámico |
| *Ptereleotris helenae* (Randall, 1968) | A | hovering dartfish |

Ephippidae—En-spadefishes, Sp-peluqueros, Fr-chèvres de mer

| | | |
|---|---|---|
| *Chaetodipterus faber* (Broussonet, 1782) | A | Atlantic spadefish ............ chabela |
| *Chaetodipterus zonatus* (Girard, 1858) | P | Pacific spadefish ............ chambo |
| *Parapsettus panamensis* Steindachner, 1876 | PM | Panama spadefish ............ zapatero |

Luvaridae—En-louvars, Sp-emperadores, Fr-louvereaux

| | | |
|---|---|---|
| *Luvarus imperialis* Rafinesque, 1810 | A-P | louvar ............ emperador |

*Zanclidae—En-Moorish idols, Sp-ídolos moros, Fr-cochers

| | | |
|---|---|---|
| +*Zanclus cornutus* (Linnaeus, 1758) | PM | Moorish idol ............ ídolo moro |

Acanthuridae—En-surgeonfishes, Sp-cirujanos, Fr-poissons-chirurgiens

| | | |
|---|---|---|
| +*Acanthurus achilles* Shaw, 1803 | PM | Achilles tang ............ cirujano encendido |
| *Acanthurus bahianus* Castelnau, 1855 | A | ocean surgeon ............ cirujano pardo |
| *Acanthurus chirurgus* (Bloch, 1787) | A | doctorfish ............ cirujano rayado |
| *Acanthurus coeruleus* Bloch & Schneider, 1801 | A | blue tang ............ cirujano azul |
| *Acanthurus nigricans* (Linnaeus, 1758) | PM | goldrim surgeonfish ............ cirujano cariblanco |
| *Acanthurus triostegus* (Linnaeus, 1758) | PM | convict surgeonfish ............ cirujano reo |

| SCIENTIFIC NAME | OCCURRENCE[1] | COMMON NAME (ENGLISH, SPANISH, FRENCH)[2] |
|---|---|---|
| *Acanthurus xanthopterus* Valenciennes, 1835 | PM | yellowfin surgeonfish......cirujano aleta amarilla |
| *Prionurus laticlavius* (Valenciennes, 1846) | PM | razor surgeonfish......cochinito barbero |
| *Prionurus punctatus* Gill, 1862 | PM | yellowtail surgeonfish......cochinito punteado |
| Sphyraenidae—En-barracudas, Sp-barracudas, Fr-barracudas | | |
| *Sphyraena argentea* Girard, 1854 | P | Pacific barracuda......barracuda plateada |
| *\*Sphyraena barracuda* (Edwards, 1771) | A | great barracuda......barracuda |
| *Sphyraena borealis* DeKay, 1842 | A | northern sennet |
| *\*Sphyraena ensis* Jordan & Gilbert, 1882 | P | Mexican barracuda......barracuda mexicana |
| *Sphyraena guachancho* Cuvier, 1829 | A | guaguanche......tolete |
| *Sphyraena idiastes* Heller & Snodgrass, 1903 | PM | pelican barracuda......barracuda pelícano |
| *Sphyraena lucasana* Gill, 1863 | PM | Cortez barracuda......barracuda de Cortés |
| *+Sphyraena picudilla* Poey, 1860 | A | southern sennet......picudilla |
| *Gempylidae—En-snake mackerels, Sp-escolares, Fr-escolars | | |
| *\*Diplospinus multistriatus* Maul, 1948 | A | striped escolar......escolar rayado |
| *Epinnula magistralis* Poey, 1854 | AM | domine......dominó |
| *Gempylus serpens* Cuvier, 1829 | A-P | snake mackerel......escolar de canal |
| *Lepidocybium flavobrunneum* (Smith, 1843) | A-P | escolar......escolar negro |
| *Nealotus tripes* Johnson, 1865 | A-PM | black snake mackerel......escolar listado |
| *\*Neoepinnula americana* (Grey, 1953) | A | American sackfish......escolar americano |
| *Nesiarchus nasutus* Johnson, 1862 | A | black gemfish......escolar narigudo |
| *\*Ruvettus pretiosus* Cocco, 1833 | A-P | oilfish......escolar clavo |
| +Trichiuridae—En-cutlassfishes, Sp-sables, Fr-sabres de mer | | |
| *Assurger anzac* (Alexander, 1917) | P | razorback scabbardfish......sable aserrado |
| *\*Benthodesmus pacificus* Parin & Becker, 1970 | P | North Pacific frostfish......cintilla del Pacífico |
| *\*Benthodesmus simonyi* (Steindachner, 1891) | A | North Atlantic frostfish......cintilla del Atlántico |
| *\*Evoxymetopon taeniatus* Poey, 1863 | A | channel scabbardfish |
| *\*Lepidopus altifrons* Parin & Collette, 1993 | A | crested scabbardfish |
| *Lepidopus fitchi* Rosenblatt & Wilson, 1987 | P | Pacific scabbardfish......pez cinto |

| SCIENTIFIC NAME | OCCURRENCE[1] | COMMON NAME (ENGLISH, SPANISH, FRENCH)[2] |
|---|---|---|
| +*Trichiurus lepturus* Linnaeus, 1758 | A | Atlantic cutlassfish ........ sable del Atlántico |
| +*Trichiurus nitens* Garman, 1899 | P | Pacific cutlassfish ........ sable del Pacífico |

Scombridae—En-mackerels, Sp-macarelas, Fr-maquereaux

| SCIENTIFIC NAME | OCCURRENCE[1] | COMMON NAME (ENGLISH, SPANISH, FRENCH)[2] |
|---|---|---|
| *Acanthocybium solandri* (Cuvier, 1832) | A-PM | wahoo ........ peto |
| *Allothunnus fallai* Serventy, 1948 | P | slender tuna ........ atún lanzón |
| *Auxis rochei* (Risso, 1810) | A-P | bullet mackerel ........ melvera |
| *Auxis thazard* (Lacepède, 1800) | A-P | frigate mackerel ........ melva |
| *Euthynnus affinis* (Cantor, 1849) | P | kawakawa ........ bacoreta oriental |
| *Euthynnus alletteratus* (Rafinesque, 1810) | A | little tunny ........ bacoreta |
| *Euthynnus lineatus* Kishinouye, 1920 | P | black skipjack ........ barrilete negro |
| *Katsuwonus pelamis* (Linnaeus, 1758) | A-P | skipjack tuna ........ barrilete listado |
| *Sarda chiliensis* (Cuvier, 1832) | P | Pacific bonito ........ bonito del Pacífico oriental |
| *Sarda orientalis* (Temminck & Schlegel, 1844) | PM | striped bonito ........ bonito mono |
| *Sarda sarda* (Bloch, 1793) | A | Atlantic bonito ........ bonito del Atlántico |
| +*Scomber australasicus* Cuvier, 1832 | PM | spotted chub mackerel ........ macarela pintoja |
| *Scomber colias* Gmelin, 1789 | A | Atlantic chub mackerel ........ maquereau blanc |
| *Scomber japonicus* Houttuyn, 1782 | P | Pacific chub mackerel ........ macarela estornino |
| *Scomber scombrus* Linnaeus, 1758 | A | Atlantic mackerel ........ maquereau bleu |
| *Scomberomorus brasiliensis* Collette, Russo & Zavala-Camin, 1978 | AM | serra ........ serra |
| *Scomberomorus cavalla* (Cuvier, 1829) | A | king mackerel ........ carito |
| *Scomberomorus concolor* (Lockington, 1879) | P | Gulf sierra ........ sierra golfina |
| *Scomberomorus maculatus* (Mitchill, 1815) | A | Spanish mackerel ........ sierra común |
| *Scomberomorus regalis* (Bloch, 1793) | A | cero ........ sierra |
| *Scomberomorus sierra* Jordan & Starks, 1895 | P | Pacific sierra ........ sierra del Pacífico |
| *Thunnus alalunga* (Bonnaterre, 1788) | A-P | albacore ........ albacora |
| *Thunnus albacares* (Bonnaterre, 1788) | A-P | yellowfin tuna ........ atún aleta amarilla |
| *Thunnus atlanticus* (Lesson, 1831) | A | blackfin tuna ........ atún aleta negra |
| *Thunnus obesus* (Lowe, 1839) | A-P | bigeye tuna ........ patudo |
| *Thunnus orientalis* (Temminck & Schlegel, 1844) | P | Pacific bluefin tuna ........ atún cimarrón |
| *Thunnus thynnus* (Linnaeus, 1758) | A | bluefin tuna ........ atún aleta azul ........ thon rouge |

| SCIENTIFIC NAME | OCCURRENCE[1] | COMMON NAME (ENGLISH, SPANISH, FRENCH)[2] |
|---|---|---|
| **Xiphiidae—En-swordfishes, Sp-espadas, Fr-espadons** | | |
| Xiphias gladius Linnaeus, 1758 | A-P | swordfish...pez espada |
| **Istiophoridae—En-billfishes, Sp-picudos, Fr-voiliers** | | |
| *Istiophorus platypterus (Shaw, 1792) | A-P | sailfish...pez vela |
| Makaira indica (Cuvier, 1832) | P | black marlin...marlin negro |
| *Makaira mazara (Jordan & Snyder 1901) | P | Indo-Pacific blue marlin...marlin azul del Indo-Pacífico |
| *Makaira nigricans Lacepède, 1802 | A | blue marlin...marlin azul |
| Tetrapturus albidus Poey, 1860 | A | white marlin...marlin blanco |
| Tetrapturus angustirostris Tanaka, 1915 | P | shortbill spearfish...marlin trompa corta |
| Tetrapturus audax (Philippi, 1887) | P | striped marlin...marlin rayado |
| Tetrapturus pfluegeri Robins & de Sylva, 1963 | A | longbill spearfish...marlin trompa larga |
| ***Centrolophidae—En-medusafishes, Sp-cojinobas, Fr-pompiles** | | |
| *Centrolophus medusophagus (Cocco, 1829) | A | brown ruff |
| *Centrolophus niger (Gmelin, 1789) | A | black ruff |
| Hyperoglyphe bythites (Ginsburg, 1954) | A | black driftfish |
| Hyperoglyphe perciformis (Mitchill, 1818) | A | barrelfish |
| Icichthys lockingtoni Jordan & Gilbert, 1880 | P | medusafish...cojinoba medusa |
| ***Nomeidae—En-driftfishes, Sp-derivantes, Fr-physaliers** | | |
| *Cubiceps capensis (Smith, 1845) | A | Cape cigarfish |
| Cubiceps paradoxus Butler, 1979 | P | longfin cigarfish...derivante colón |
| Cubiceps pauciradiatus Günther, 1872 | A-PM | bigeye cigarfish...derivante ojón |
| *Nomeus gronovii (Gmelin, 1789) | A | man-of-war fish...derivante fragata portuguesa |
| Psenes cyanophrys Valenciennes, 1833 | A | freckled driftfish...derivante rayado |
| Psenes maculatus Lütken, 1880 | A | silver driftfish |
| Psenes pellucidus Lütken, 1880 | A-P | bluefin driftfish...derivante aleta azul |
| Psenes sio Haedrich 1970 | PM | twospine driftfish...derivante dos espinas |

| SCIENTIFIC NAME | OCCURRENCE[1] | COMMON NAME (ENGLISH, SPANISH, FRENCH)[2] |
|---|---|---|
| *Ariommatidae—En-ariommatids, Sp-pastorcillos, Fr-poissons pailletés | | |
| *Ariomma bondi* Fowler, 1930 | A | silver-rag .............. pastorcillo lucía |
| *Ariomma melanum* (Ginsburg, 1954) | A | brown driftfish .............. pastorcillo café |
| *Ariomma regulus* (Poey, 1868) | A | spotted driftfish .............. pastorcillo aquillado |
| *Tetragonuridae—En-squaretails, Sp-colicuadrados, Fr-tétragonures | | |
| *Tetragonurus atlanticus* Lowe, 1839 | A | bigeye squaretail |
| *Tetragonurus cuvieri* Risso, 1810 | P | smalleye squaretail .............. colicuadrado ojito |
| +Stromateidae—En-butterfishes, Sp-palometas, Fr-stromatées | | |
| *Peprilus burti* Fowler, 1944 | A | Gulf butterfish .............. palometa del Golfo |
| *Peprilus medius* (Peters, 1869) | PM | Pacific harvestfish .............. palometa |
| *Peprilus ovatus* Horn, 1970 | PM | Cortez butterfish .............. palometa de Cortés |
| *Peprilus paru* (Linnaeus, 1758) | A | harvestfish .............. palometa pámpano |
| *Peprilus simillimus* (Ayres, 1860) | P | Pacific pompano .............. palometa plateada |
| *Peprilus snyderi* Gilbert & Starks, 1904 | PM | salema butterfish .............. palometa salema |
| *Peprilus triacanthus* (Peck, 1804) | A | butterfish .............. stromatée à fossettes |
| *Belontiidae—En-gouramies, Sp-guramis, Fr-gouramies | | |
| *Trichopsis vittata* (Cuvier, 1831) | F[I];U | croaking gourami |
| *Channidae—En-snakeheads, Sp-cabezas de serpiente, Fr-têtes-de-serpent | | |
| *Channa marulius* (Hamilton, 1822) | F[I];U | bullseye snakehead |
| ORDER PLEURONECTIFORMES | | |
| +Bothidae—En-lefteye flounders, Sp-lenguados chuecos, Fr-turbots | | |
| *Bothus constellatus* (Jordan, 1889) | PM | Pacific eyed flounder .............. lenguado hoja |
| *Bothus leopardinus* (Günther, 1862) | PM | Pacific leopard flounder .............. lenguado leopardo del Pacífico |
| *Bothus lunatus* (Linnaeus, 1758) | A | peacock flounder .............. lenguado lunado |
| *Bothus mancus* (Broussonet, 1782) | PM | tropical flounder .............. lenguado tropical |

| SCIENTIFIC NAME | OCCURRENCE[1] | COMMON NAME (ENGLISH, SPANISH, FRENCH)[2] |
|---|---|---|
| *Bothus ocellatus* (Agassiz, 1831) | A | eyed flounder — chueco playón |
| *Bothus robinsi* Topp & Hoff, 1972 | A | twospot flounder — chueco dos manchas |
| *Engyophrys sanctilaurentii* Jordan & Bollman, 1890 | P | speckledtail flounder — lenguado colimanchada |
| *Engyophrys senta* Ginsburg, 1933 | A | spiny flounder — lenguado ojicornudo |
| *Monolene antillarum* Norman, 1933 | A | slim flounder |
| *Monolene asaedai* Clark, 1936 | PM | dark flounder — lenguado carbón |
| *Monolene dubiosa* Garman, 1899 | PM | Acapulco flounder — lenguado acapulqueño |
| *Monolene maculipinna* Norman, 1933 | PM | Pacific deepwater flounder — lenguado de profundidad |
| *Monolene sessilicauda* Goode, 1880 | A | deepwater flounder |
| *Perissias taeniopterus* (Gilbert, 1890) | PM | flag flounder — lenguado bandera |
| *Trichopsetta ventralis* (Goode & Bean, 1885) | A | sash flounder — lenguado de punto |

*Scophthalmidae—En-turbots, Sp-rodaballos, Fr-scophthalmidés

| | | |
|---|---|---|
| *Scophthalmus aquosus* (Mitchill, 1815) | A | windowpane — turbot de sable |

*Paralichthyidae—En-sand flounders, Sp-lenguados areneros, Fr-flétans de sable

| | | |
|---|---|---|
| *Ancylopsetta dendritica* Gilbert, 1890 | PM | threespot sand flounder — lenguado tresojos |
| *Ancylopsetta dilecta* (Goode & Bean, 1883) | A | three-eye flounder — lenguado tres manchas |
| *Ancylopsetta quadrocellata* Gill, 1864 | A | ocellated flounder — lenguado cuatro manchas |
| *Citharichthys abbotti* Dawson, 1969 | AM | Veracruz whiff — lenguado veracruzano |
| *Citharichthys arctifrons* Goode, 1880 | A | Gulf Stream flounder — lenguado golfino |
| *Citharichthys arenaceus* Evermann & Marsh, 1900 | A | sand whiff |
| *Citharichthys cornutus* (Günther, 1880) | A | horned whiff — lenguado cornudo |
| *Citharichthys dinoceros* Goode & Bean, 1886 | A | spined whiff — lenguado espinoso |
| *Citharichthys fragilis* Gilbert, 1890 | P | Gulf sanddab — lenguado flaco |
| *Citharichthys gilberti* Jenkins & Evermann, 1889 | PM | bigmouth sanddab — lenguado tapadera |
| *Citharichthys gordae* Beebe & Tee-Van, 1938 | PM | mimic sanddab — lenguado escondido |
| *Citharichthys gymnorhinus* Gutherz & Blackman, 1970 | A | anglefin whiff |
| *Citharichthys macrops* Dresel, 1885 | A | spotted whiff — lenguado manchado |
| *Citharichthys mariajorisae* van der Heiden & Mussot, 1995 | PM | five-rayed sanddab — lenguado cinco radios |
| *Citharichthys platophrys* Gilbert, 1891 | PM | small sanddab — lenguado frentón |
| *Citharichthys sordidus* (Girard, 1854) | P | Pacific sanddab — lenguado moteado |

| SCIENTIFIC NAME | OCCURRENCE[1] | COMMON NAME (ENGLISH, SPANISH, FRENCH)[2] | |
|---|---|---|---|
| *Citharichthys spilopterus* Günther, 1862 | A-F:U | bay whiff | lenguado pardo |
| *Citharichthys stigmaeus* Jordan & Gilbert, 1882 | P | speckled sanddab | lenguado pecoso |
| *Citharichthys uhleri* Jordan, 1889 | AM | voodoo whiff | lenguado albimoteado |
| *Citharichthys xanthostigma* Gilbert, 1890 | P | longfin sanddab | lenguado alón |
| *Cyclopsetta chittendeni* Bean, 1895 | A | Mexican flounder | lenguado mexicano |
| *Cyclopsetta fimbriata* (Goode & Bean, 1885) | A | spotfin flounder | lenguado aleta sucia |
| *Cyclopsetta panamensis* (Steindachner, 1876) | PM | Panamic flounder | lenguado panámico |
| *Cyclopsetta querna* Jordan & Bollman, 1890 | PM | toothed flounder | lenguado dientón |
| +*Etropus crossotus* Jordan & Gilbert, 1882 | A-PM | fringed flounder | lenguado ribete |
| *Etropus cyclosquamus* Leslie & Stewart, 1986 | A | shelf flounder | |
| *Etropus microstomus* (Gill, 1864) | A | smallmouth flounder | |
| *Etropus peruvianus* Hildebrand, 1946 | PM | Peruvian flounder | lenguado zapatilla |
| *Etropus rimosus* Goode & Bean, 1885 | A | gray flounder | lenguado sombreado |
| *Gastropsetta frontalis* Bean, 1895 | A | shrimp flounder | lenguado gambero |
| *Hippoglossina bollmani* Gilbert, 1890 | PM | spotted flounder | lenguado pintado |
| *Hippoglossina stomata* Eigenmann & Eigenmann, 1890 | P | bigmouth sole | lenguado bocón |
| *Hippoglossina tetrophthalma* (Gilbert, 1890) | PM | foureye flounder | lenguado cuatrojos |
| *Paralichthys aestuarius* Gilbert & Scofield, 1898 | PM | Cortez halibut | lenguado de Cortés |
| *Paralichthys albigutta* Jordan & Gilbert, 1882 | A | Gulf flounder | lenguado panzablanca |
| *Paralichthys californicus* (Ayres, 1859) | P | California halibut | lenguado californiano |
| *Paralichthys dentatus* (Linnaeus, 1766) | A | summer flounder | |
| *Paralichthys lethostigma* Jordan & Gilbert, 1884 | A-F:U | southern flounder | lenguado limpio |
| *Paralichthys oblongus* (Mitchill, 1815) | A | fourspot flounder | |
| *Paralichthys squamilentus* Jordan & Gilbert, 1882 | A | broad flounder | lenguado huarachón |
| *Paralichthys woolmani* Jordan & Williams, 1897 | PM | dappled flounder | lenguado huarache |
| *Syacium gunteri* Ginsburg, 1933 | A | shoal flounder | lenguado arenoso |
| *Syacium latifrons* (Jordan & Gilbert, 1882) | PM | beach flounder | lenguado playero |
| *Syacium longidorsale* Murakami & Amaoka, 1992 | PM | pompadour flounder | lenguado copetón |
| *Syacium micrurum* Ranzani, 1842 | A | channel flounder | lenguado anillado |
| *Syacium ovale* (Günther, 1864) | PM | oval flounder | lenguado ovalado |
| *Syacium papillosum* (Linnaeus, 1758) | A | dusky flounder | lenguado moreno |
| *Xystreurys liolepis* Jordan & Gilbert, 1880 | P | fantail sole | lenguado cola de abanico |

| SCIENTIFIC NAME | OCCURRENCE[1] | COMMON NAME (ENGLISH, SPANISH, FRENCH)[2] |
|---|---|---|
| | | Pleuronectidae—En-righteye flounders, Sp-platijas, Fr-plies |
| +*Atheresthes evermanni* Jordan & Starks, 1904 | P | Kamchatka flounder |
| +*Atheresthes stomias* (Jordan & Gilbert, 1880) | P | arrowtooth flounder |
| +*Embassichthys bathybius* (Gilbert, 1890) | P | deepsea sole ........ platija de profundidad |
| *Eopsetta jordani* (Lockington, 1879) | P | petrale sole ........ platija petrale |
| *Glyptocephalus cynoglossus* (Linnaeus, 1758) | A | witch flounder ........ plie grise |
| *Glyptocephalus zachirus* Lockington, 1879 | P | rex sole ........ platija rey |
| *Hippoglossoides elassodon* Jordan & Gilbert, 1880 | P | flathead sole |
| *Hippoglossoides platessoides* (Fabricius, 1780) | A | American plaice ........ plie canadienne |
| *Hippoglossoides robustus* Gill & Townsend, 1897 | P | Bering flounder |
| *Hippoglossus hippoglossus* (Linnaeus, 1758) | A | Atlantic halibut ........ flétan atlantique |
| *Hippoglossus stenolepis* Schmidt, 1904 | P | Pacific halibut ........ alabato del Pacífico |
| *Isopsetta isolepis* (Lockington, 1880) | P | butter sole |
| *Lepidopsetta bilineata* (Ayres, 1855) | P | rock sole |
| *Lepidopsetta polyxystra* Orr & Matarese, 2000 | P | northern rock sole |
| *Limanda aspera* (Pallas, 1814) | P | yellowfin sole |
| *Limanda ferruginea* (Storer, 1839) | A | yellowtail flounder ........ limande à queue jaune |
| *Limanda proboscidea* Gilbert, 1896 | P | longhead dab |
| *Limanda sakhalinensis* Hubbs, 1915 | P | Sakhalin sole |
| *Lyopsetta exilis* (Jordan & Gilbert, 1880) | P | slender sole ........ platija flaca |
| *Microstomus pacificus* (Lockington, 1879) | P | Dover sole ........ platija resbalosa |
| *Parophrys vetulus* (Girard, 1854) | P | English sole ........ platija limón |
| *Platichthys stellatus* (Pallas, 1788) | F:CU-P | starry flounder |
| *Pleuronectes glacialis* Pallas, 1776 | P | Arctic flounder |
| *Pleuronectes putnami* (Gill, 1864) | A | smooth flounder ........ plie lisse |
| *Pleuronectes quadrituberculatus* Pallas, 1814 | P | Alaska plaice |
| *Pleuronichthys coenosus* Girard, 1854 | P | C-O sole ........ platija de fango |
| *Pleuronichthys decurrens* Jordan & Gilbert, 1881 | P | curlfin sole ........ platija aleta de rizo |
| *Pleuronichthys guttulatus* Girard, 1856 | P | diamond turbot ........ platija diamante |
| *Pleuronichthys ocellatus* Starks & Thompson, 1910 | PM | ocellated turbot ........ platija ocelada |
| *Pleuronichthys ritteri* Starks & Morris, 1907 | P | spotted turbot ........ platija moteada |

| SCIENTIFIC NAME | OCCURRENCE[1] | COMMON NAME (ENGLISH, SPANISH, FRENCH)[2] |
|---|---|---|
| *Pleuronichthys verticalis* Jordan & Gilbert, 1880 | P | hornyhead turbot ... platija cornuda |
| *Psettichthys melanostictus* Girard, 1854 | P | sand sole |
| *Pseudopleuronectes americanus* (Walbaum, 1792) | A | winter flounder ... plie rouge |
| +*Reinhardtius hippoglossoides* (Walbaum, 1792) | A-P | Greenland halibut ... platija negra ... flétan du Groenland |
| \*Poecilopsettidae—En-bigeye flounders, Sp-lenguados ojones, Fr-plies à grands yeux | | |
| \*Poecilopsetta beanii* (Goode, 1881) | A | deepwater dab ... lenguado ojón |
| \*Achiridae—En-American soles, Sp-lenguados suelas, Fr-soles américaines | | |
| +*Achirus klunzingeri* (Steindachner, 1879) | PM | brown sole ... suela plomiza |
| *Achirus lineatus* (Linnaeus, 1758) | A | lined sole ... suela listada |
| *Achirus mazatlanus* (Steindachner, 1869) | PM | Pacific lined sole ... tepalcate |
| *Achirus scutum* (Günther, 1862) | PM | network sole ... comal |
| +*Achirus zebrinus* Clark, 1936 | PM | Tehuantepec sole ... suela cebra |
| \*Gymnachirus melas* Nichols, 1916 | A | naked sole ... suela desnuda |
| *Gymnachirus nudus* Kaup, 1858 | AM | flabby sole ... suela fofa |
| *Gymnachirus texae* (Gunter, 1936) | A | fringed sole ... suela texana |
| *Trinectes fimbriatus* (Günther, 1862) | PM | whitespotted sole ... suela pintada |
| *Trinectes fonsecensis* (Günther, 1862) | F:M-PM | spottedfin sole ... suela rayada |
| *Trinectes inscriptus* (Gosse, 1851) | A | scrawled sole |
| *Trinectes maculatus* (Bloch & Schneider, 1801) | A-F:U | hogchoker ... suela tortilla |
| *Trinectes paulistanus* Miranda-Ribeiro, 1915 | AM | southern hogchoker ... suela carioca |
| \*Soleidae—En-soles, Sp-suelas soles, Fr-soles | | |
| *Aseraggodes herrei* Seale, 1940 | PM | reticulated sole ... sol reticulado |
| \*Cynoglossidae—En-tonguefishes, Sp-lenguas, Fr-soles-langues | | |
| *Symphurus arawak* Robins & Randall, 1965 | A | Caribbean tonguefish ... lengua caribeña |
| *Symphurus atramentatus* Jordan & Bollman, 1890 | PM | halfspotted tonguefish ... lengua mediomanchada |
| *Symphurus atricaudus* (Jordan & Gilbert, 1880) | P | California tonguefish ... lengua californiana |
| \*Symphurus billykrietei* Munroe, 1998 | A | chocolatebanded tonguefish ... lengua boba |
| *Symphurus callopterus* Munroe & Mahadeva, 1989 | PM | chocolate tonguefish ... lengua chocolate |

| SCIENTIFIC NAME | OCCURRENCE[1] | COMMON NAME (ENGLISH, SPANISH, FRENCH)[2] |
|---|---|---|
| *Symphurus chabanaudi* Mahadeva & Munroe, 1990 | PM | darkcheek tonguefish......lengua cachete prieto |
| *Symphurus civitatium* Ginsburg, 1951 | A | offshore tonguefish......lengua gatita |
| *Symphurus diomedeanus* (Goode & Bean, 1885) | A | spottedfin tonguefish......lengua filonegro |
| *Symphurus elongatus* (Günther, 1868) | PM | elongate tonguefish......lengua esbelta |
| *Symphurus fasciolaris* Gilbert, 1892 | PM | banded tonguefish......lengua listada |
| *Symphurus gorgonae* Chabanaud, 1948 | PM | dwarf tonguefish......lengua enana |
| *Symphurus leei* Jordan & Bollman, 1890 | PM | blacktail tonguefish......lengua colinegra |
| *Symphurus marginatus* (Goode & Bean, 1886) | A | margined tonguefish |
| *Symphurus melanurus* Clark, 1936 | PM | drab tonguefish......lengua lucia |
| *Symphurus melasmatotheca* Munroe & Nizinski, 1990 | PM | darkbelly tonguefish......lengua tripa negra |
| *Symphurus minor* Ginsburg, 1951 | A | largescale tonguefish |
| *Symphurus oligomerus* Mahadeva & Munroe, 1990 | PM | whitetail tonguefish......lengua coliblanca |
| *Symphurus parvus* Ginsburg, 1951 | A | pygmy tonguefish......lengua pigmea |
| *Symphurus pelicanus* Ginsburg, 1951 | A | longtail tonguefish......lengua colilarga |
| *Symphurus piger* (Goode & Bean, 1886) | A | deepwater tonguefish......lengua perezosa |
| *Symphurus plagiusa* (Linnaeus, 1766) | A | blackcheek tonguefish......lengua gris |
| *Symphurus prolatinaris* Munroe, Nizinski & Mahadeva, 1991 | PM | halfstriped tonguefish......lengua narigona |
| *Symphurus pusillus* (Goode & Bean, 1885) | A | northern tonguefish |
| *Symphurus stigmosus* Munroe, 1998 | A | blotchfin tonguefish |
| *Symphurus undecimplerus* Munroe & Nizinski, 1990 | PM | imitator tonguefish......lengua imitador |
| *Symphurus urospilus* Ginsburg, 1951 | A | spottail tonguefish......lengua colipunteada |
| *Symphurus williamsi* Jordan & Culver, 1895 | PM | yellow tonguefish......lengua amarillenta |

ORDER TETRAODONTIFORMES

Triacanthodidae—En-spikefishes, Sp-cochis espinosos, Fr-triacanthodidés

| | | |
|---|---|---|
| *Hollardia meadi* Tyler, 1966 | A | spotted spikefish |
| *Parahollardia lineata* (Longley, 1935) | A | jambeau......cochi rombo |

+Balistidae—En-triggerfishes, Sp-cochitos, Fr-balistes

| | | |
|---|---|---|
| *Balistes capriscus* Gmelin, 1789 | A | gray triggerfish......pejepuerco blanco |

| SCIENTIFIC NAME | OCCURRENCE[1] | COMMON NAME (ENGLISH, SPANISH, FRENCH)[2] |
|---|---|---|
| *Balistes polylepis* Steindachner, 1876 | P | finescale triggerfish ............ cochi |
| *Balistes vetula* Linnaeus, 1758 | A | queen triggerfish ............ cochino |
| *Canthidermis maculata* (Bloch, 1786) | A-PM | rough triggerfish ............ cochito manchado |
| *Canthidermis sufflamen* (Mitchill, 1815) | A | ocean triggerfish ............ sobaco lija |
| *Melichthys niger* (Bloch, 1786) | A-P | black durgon ............ cochito negro |
| *Pseudobalistes naufragium* (Jordan & Starks, 1895) | PM | blunthead triggerfish ............ cochito bota |
| *Sufflamen verres* (Gilbert & Starks, 1904) | PM | orangeside triggerfish ............ cochito naranja |
| *Xanthichthys mento* (Jordan & Gilbert, 1882) | P | redtail triggerfish ............ cochito cuadriculado |
| *Xanthichthys ringens* (Linnaeus, 1758) | A | sargassum triggerfish ............ cocuyo |

*Monacanthidae—En-filefishes, Sp-lijas, Fr-poissons-bourses

| SCIENTIFIC NAME | OCCURRENCE[1] | COMMON NAME (ENGLISH, SPANISH, FRENCH)[2] |
|---|---|---|
| * *Aluterus heudelotii* Hollard, 1855 | A | dotterel filefish ............ lija jaspeada |
| *Aluterus monoceros* (Linnaeus, 1758) | A-PM | unicorn filefish ............ lija barbuda |
| * *Aluterus schoepfii* (Walbaum, 1792) | A | orange filefish ............ lija naranja |
| *Aluterus scriptus* (Osbeck, 1765) | A-PM | scrawled filefish ............ lija trompa |
| *Cantherhines dumerilii* (Hollard, 1854) | PM | barred filefish ............ lija vagabunda |
| * *Cantherhines macrocerus* (Hollard, 1853) | A | whitespotted filefish |
| *Cantherhines pullus* (Ranzani, 1842) | A | orangespotted filefish ............ lija colorada |
| *Monacanthus ciliatus* (Mitchill, 1818) | A | fringed filefish ............ lija de clavo |
| *Monacanthus tuckeri* Bean, 1906 | A | slender filefish ............ lija reticulada |
| * *Stephanolepis hispidus* (Linnaeus, 1766) | A | planehead filefish ............ lija áspera |
| * *Stephanolepis setifer* (Bennett, 1831) | A | pygmy filefish ............ lija de hebra |

Ostraciidae—En-boxfishes, Sp-peces cofre, Fr-coffres

| SCIENTIFIC NAME | OCCURRENCE[1] | COMMON NAME (ENGLISH, SPANISH, FRENCH)[2] |
|---|---|---|
| * *Acanthostracion polygonia* Poey, 1876 | A | honeycomb cowfish ............ torito hexagonal |
| * *Acanthostracion quadricornis* (Linnaeus, 1758) | A | scrawled cowfish ............ torito cornudo |
| *Lactophrys bicaudalis* (Linnaeus, 1758) | A | spotted trunkfish ............ chapín pintado |
| *Lactophrys trigonus* (Linnaeus, 1758) | A | trunkfish ............ chapín búfalo |
| *Lactophrys triqueter* (Linnaeus, 1758) | A | smooth trunkfish ............ chapín baqueta |
| * *Lactoria diaphana* (Bloch & Schneider, 1801) | P | spiny boxfish ............ cofre espinoso |
| *Ostracion meleagris* Shaw, 1796 | PM | spotted boxfish ............ cofre moteado |

| SCIENTIFIC NAME | OCCURRENCE[1] | COMMON NAME (ENGLISH, SPANISH, FRENCH)[2] |
|---|---|---|
| +Tetraodontidae—En-puffers, Sp-botetes, Fr-sphéroïdes | | |
| Arothron hispidus (Linnaeus, 1758) | PM | stripebelly puffer ........ botete panza rayada |
| Arothron meleagris (Lacèpede, 1798) | PM | guineafowl puffer ........ botete aletas punteadas |
| *Canthigaster jamestyleri Moura & Castro, 2002 | A | goldface toby |
| Canthigaster punctatissima (Günther, 1870) | PM | spotted sharpnose puffer ........ botete bonito |
| *Canthigaster rostrata (Bloch, 1786) | A | sharpnose puffer ........ tamborín narizón |
| +Lagocephalus laevigatus (Linnaeus, 1766) | A | smooth puffer ........ botete grande |
| Lagocephalus lagocephalus (Linnaeus, 1758) | A-P | oceanic puffer ........ botete oceánico |
| Sphoeroides annulatus (Jenyns, 1842) | P | bullseye puffer ........ botete diana |
| Sphoeroides dorsalis Longley, 1934 | A | marbled puffer ........ botete jaspeado |
| Sphoeroides lispus Walker, 1996 | PM | naked puffer ........ botete liso |
| Sphoeroides lobatus (Steindachner, 1870) | P | longnose puffer ........ botete verrugoso |
| Sphoeroides maculatus (Bloch & Schneider, 1801) | A | northern puffer |
| Sphoeroides nephelus (Goode & Bean, 1882) | A | southern puffer ........ botete fruta |
| Sphoeroides pachygaster (Müller & Troschel, 1848) | A | blunthead puffer ........ botete chato |
| Sphoeroides parvus Shipp & Yerger, 1969 | A | least puffer ........ botete xpú |
| Sphoeroides sechurae Hildebrand, 1946 | PM | Peruvian puffer ........ botete peruano |
| *Sphoeroides spengleri (Bloch, 1785) | A | bandtail puffer ........ botete collarete |
| Sphoeroides testudineus (Linnaeus, 1758) | A | checkered puffer ........ botete sapo |
| Sphoeroides trichocephalus (Cope, 1870) | PM | pygmy puffer ........ botete enano |
| *Diodontidae—En-porcupinefishes, Sp-peces erizo, Fr-poissons porcs-épics | | |
| *Chilomycterus antennatus (Cuvier, 1816) | A | bridled burrfish |
| +Chilomycterus antillarum Jordan & Rutter, 1897 | A | web burrfish ........ guanábana caribeña |
| *Chilomycterus atringa (Linnaeus, 1758) | A | spotted burrfish |
| *Chilomycterus reticulatus Linnaeus, 1758 | P | spotfin burrfish ........ pez erizo enano |
| *Chilomycterus schoepfii (Walbaum, 1792) | A | striped burrfish ........ guanábana rayada |
| Diodon eydouxii Brisout de Barneville, 1846 | PM | pelagic porcupinefish ........ pez erizo pelágico |
| Diodon holocanthus Linnaeus, 1758 | A-P | balloonfish ........ pez erizo mapache |
| Diodon hystrix Linnaeus, 1758 | A-P | porcupinefish ........ pez erizo pecoso |

| SCIENTIFIC NAME | OCCURRENCE[1] | COMMON NAME (ENGLISH, SPANISH, FRENCH)[2] |
|---|---|---|
| Molidae—En-molas, Sp-molas, Fr-poissons-lune | | |
| *Mola lanceolata (Liénard, 1840) | A-PM | sharptail mola ............ mola coliaguda |
| Mola mola (Linnaeus, 1758) | A-P | ocean sunfish ...... mola ............................ môle |
| Ranzania laevis (Pennant, 1776) | A-P | slender mola ...... mola flaca |

# PART II

## Appendix 1
## Changes from 1991 Edition and Comments

The comments and explanatory notes below are keyed to the appropriate scientific name as indicated by an asterisk (*) or plus sign (+) in the main list, Part I. Entries are in the same order as in the list and are grouped, for convenience, by page. Information provided in Pages 65–87 *in* the Appendix in the Third Edition, 1970, American Fisheries Society, Special Publication 6, Bethesda, Maryland, in Pages 68–92 *in* Appendix 1 in the Fourth Edition, 1980, American Fisheries Society, Special Publication 12, Bethesda, Maryland, and in Pages 71–96 *in* Appendix 1 in the Fifth Edition, 1991, American Fisheries Society, Special Publication 20, Bethesda, Maryland, is not repeated here. Literature citations occur in either standard form (e.g., author, year) with the cited work given in "References," or in text form. Abbreviations of journal names are those used in the 2002 edition of Biosis® Serial Sources, Volume 2002, Biosis, Philadelphia. In the following notes, the fourth edition of the International Code of Zoological Nomenclature is referred to as the "Code," whereas "ICZN" refers to the International Commission on Zoological Nomenclature, author of the Code. Changes from the 1991 edition or comments that relate to fishes from the United States or Canada are noted here along with a few notes for pertinent Mexico-only species, all of which are new to the list.

### Page 47

Cephalochordata. The lancelets have been included in this edition. The scientific names are based on S. G. Poss and H. T. Boschung, 1996, Lancelets (Cephalochordata: Branchiostomatidae): how many species are valid? Isr. J. Zool. 42(Supplement 1996):13–66, Jerusalem, Laser Pages Publishing Ltd., and the common names in English were provided by H. T. Boschung and S. G. Poss (personal communications, 1999, 2002).

Branchiostomatidae. See Cephalochordata.

Craniata (Vertebrata). All taxa conventionally termed fishes, together with the tetrapods, belong in this subphylum. The terms Craniata and Vertebrata are regarded as synonyms by some workers, while others use them for different levels of classification (e.g., Vertebrata is used for all craniates except the hagfishes, a descriptively appealing use of the term since hagfishes lack any trace of vertebrae).

### Page 48

*Eptatretus mcconnaugheyi*. This new species was described from California and Mexico by R. L. Wisner and C. B. McMillan, 1990, Fish. Bull. 88(4):790. They also noted the occurrence of two other new species of Pacific hagfishes, *E. fritzi* from Guadalupe Island, Mexico (p. 791), and *E. sinus* from the Gulf of California (p. 792), which appear to occur just within our depth of coverage, 200 m.

*Eptatretus stoutii*. Original spelling ends with -*ii*.

*Myxine glutinosa*. This species, as previously recognized, is assumed to occur across the North Atlantic Ocean, but R. L. Wisner and C. B. McMillan, 1995, Fish. Bull. 93:530–550, provided diagnostic characters to distinguish a western Atlantic species, *Myxine limosa* Girard, 1859, and an eastern Atlantic species. However, the results of F. H. Martini, M. P. Lesser, and J. B. Heiser, 1998, Fish. Bull. 96:516–524, did not support a clean division between North Atlantic populations of *M. glutinosa*, and they recommended "that until and unless molecular data indicate otherwise, the species name *M. glutinosa* be retained as encompassing both eastern and western North Atlantic populations."

Petromyzontidae. The nominal species *Lampetra meridionale*, *L. folletti*, and *L. alaskensis* were not recognized in the 1980 (Appendix 1:68) or 1991 edition. We follow the advice of C. B. Renaud (personal communication, 1999) in continuing not to recognize their validity until proposed studies suggest otherwise. Alaska populations of *L. appendix* are recognized as *L. alaskensis*, the Alaskan brook lamprey, in Mecklenburg et al. (2002) (the spelling *alaskensis* versus *alaskense* is followed, based on the advice of R. M. Bailey, personal communication, January 2003). Some species of *Lampetra* are recognized in the nominal genera *Entosphenus*, *Lethenteron*, and

*Tetrapleurodon* in some works (these are here considered as subgenera, as in Nelson 1994). We retain these in *Lampetra* pending publication of a follow-up paper, based on total evidence with taxonomic recommendations, to the cladistic study based on morphological evidence by H. S. Gill, C. B. Renaud, F. Chapleau, R. L. Mayden, and I. C. Potter, 2003, Copeia 2003(3):687–703.

*Lampetra appendix*. See Petromyzontidae.

*Lampetra ayresii*. Original spelling ends with -*ii*.

*Lampetra camtschatica*. M. Kottelat, 1997, European freshwater fishes, Biologia (Bratislava) 52(Supplement 5):1–271, showed that the previously recognized *L. japonica* (Martens, 1868) is a junior synonym of this species. While the ICZN could have been petitioned to conserve *japonica*, we feel that now with the Kottelat publication and use of *camtschatica* (usually as *Lethenteron japonicum*, as employed by Kottelat) in other publications, it is too late to act. We know of no attempt to apply to the ICZN to suppress the older name.

*Lampetra macrostoma*. Page and Burr (1991) and Mayden et al. (1992) gave the common name as lake lamprey, and R. J. Beamish, 2001, Can. Field-Nat. 115(1):127–130, gave it as Vancouver Island lake lamprey (the species appears to be limited to two lakes on Vancouver Island).

*Lampetra minima*. This species, formerly thought to be extinct, was reported from at least two subdrainages of the upper Klamath basin, Oregon, by C. M. Lorion, D. F. Markle, S. B. Reid, and M. F. Docker, 2000, Copeia 2000(4):1019–1028.

*Lampetra tridentata*. Although Richardson provided the main description (W. N. Eschmeyer, personal communication, August 2000) and is given as the author in Eschmeyer (1998), we prefer to continue to recognize Gairdner as the author because he was responsible for the name and the description of life color and also because in the original description, Richardson listed this species as "*Petromyzon tridentatus* Gairdner." It is often difficult to be certain who was responsible for some early descriptions, and we believe we should normally follow authorship as given in the original descriptions.

### Page 49

Chondrichthyes. For the subclass Elasmobranchii, the recognition of seven orders and 23 families of sharks (Chlamydoselachidae through Sphyrnidae) follows Compagno's (1999) classification (which is basically phenetic), whereas recognition of four orders and 12 families of rays (Narcinidae through Mobulidae) follows McEachran and Fechhelm (1998) (with addition of the North Pacific family Platyrhinidae). In following a more split classification in this edition, three more orders of sharks and three more orders of rays are now recognized from our area than in the 1991 edition. The order Squatiniformes was formerly included in the Squaliformes; Orectolobiformes and Carcharhiniformes in the Lamniformes; and Torpediniformes, Pristiformes, and Myliobatiformes in the Rajiformes. The term "ray" is used as a collective term for members of the families Narcinidae to Mobulidae (in four orders). Thus, skates are members of one particular family of rays, the Rajidae, although Compagno (1999) included skates in their own order (with three families). Compagno placed the species of *Bathyraja* from our area in the Arhynchobatidae, which was considered a subfamily of Rajidae by J. D. McEachran and K. A. Dunn, 1998, Copeia 1998(2):271–290. Although the ordinal and family classification of the chondrichthyans is subject to change, we adopt the arrangement indicated as a better reflection of relatively stable usage and probable relationships than the scheme previously followed. L. J. V. Compagno, 2001, Sharks of the world, FAO species catalogue for fishery purposes, No. 1, Volume 2, FAO, Rome, presented a tentative cladistic classification of the orders in an annotated catalog of bullhead, mackerel, and carpet sharks, which presents a still different phylogenetic sequence for some orders and families. This is not followed here because the published series on sharks is not yet complete. Changes in the classification proposed by J. D. McEachran, K. A. Dunn, and T. Miyake, 1996, Interrelationships of the batoid fishes (Chondrichthyes: Batoidea), Pages 63–84 *in* M. L. J. Stiassny, L. R. Parenti, and G. D. Johnson, editors, Interrelationships of fishes, Academic Press, San Diego, California, are not made here because of the provisional nature of the suggestions and the likelihood that further changes will soon be made.

Chimaeridae. The common name of this family is modified because there are two other families of chimaeras.

*Heptranchias perlo*. Added to the list on basis of occurrence from off North Carolina to northern Gulf of Mexico and occurrence in relatively shallow depths noted in L. J. V. Compagno, 1984, FAO species catalogue, Sharks of the world, FAO Fish. Synop. 125(4)(1):17–18.

*Hexanchus griseus*. Additional qualifier given to common name following Compagno (1999).

*Hexanchus nakamurai*. This species, less common than *H. griseus*, has been reported off Florida in depths shallower than 200 m. Recognition under the name as given follows T. Taniuchi and H. Tachikawa, 1991, Jpn. J. Ichthyol. 38(1):57–60, and Compagno (1999). The species in our area was recognized by some workers (e.g., L. J. V. Compagno, 1984, FAO species catalogue, Sharks of the world, FAO Fish. Synop. 125(4)(1):20–21) under the name *H. vitulus* Springer & Waller, 1969, even after it was regarded as conspecific with Teng's 1962 taxon, because of doubts about whether Teng's description was formally published.

*Notorynchus cepedianus*. Correction of spelling of author. Additional qualifier given to common name following Compagno (1999).

Squaliformes. See Chondrichthyes above.

Echinorhinidae. See Squalidae below.

*Echinorhinus brucus*. Presence of this benthic shark in our area shallower than 200 m requires confirmation because the record for inclusion in the 1960 and subsequent editions is based on a dead specimen found washed ashore at Provincetown, Massachusetts, around the turn of the 1900s; it is known from deeper waters off our area (G. H. Burgess, personal communication, June 2001) and from shallower than 200 m in other areas.

Squalidae. Some species in this family in the 1991 edition are now placed in Echinorhinidae, Etmopteridae, Somniosidae, and Dalatiidae, following the classification of Compagno (1999) and practice of many authors. The family common names in English occur in such publications as Compagno (1999).

*Cirrhigaleus asper*. Formerly recognized in *Squalus*. Generic change based on S. Shirai, 1992, Squalean phylogeny, a new framework of squaloid sharks and related taxa, Hokkaido University Press, Sapporo, Japan. Records exist from Mexican waters in the Gulf of Mexico from 196 to 224 m (UF 28535).

Page 50

Etmopteridae. See Squalidae above.

*Etmopterus bigelowi*. Added to the list based on S. Shirai and H. Tachikawa, 1993, Copeia 1993(2):483–495, who gave the common name as blurred smooth-dogfish. The common name is based on that given by L. J. V. Compagno, 2003 (dated 2002), Sharks, Pages 357–505 *in* K. E. Carpenter, editor, The living marine resources of the western central Atlantic, FAO species identification guide for fishery purposes, Volume 1, FAO, Rome. Known previously from western Atlantic as *E. pusillus* (Lowe, 1839), which is not known from our area (G. H. Burgess, personal communication, July 2002).

*Etmopterus gracilispinis*. Common name changed from the poorly known name broadband dogfish to that used by Compagno (1999).

Somniosidae. See Squalidae above.

*Centroscymnus coelolepis*. Parentheses are removed from the authors' names and change of spelling of authors' names.

Dalatiidae. See Squalidae above.

*Isistius brasiliensis*. Occurrence of this normally deepwater, oceanic shark in the Pacific off Guadalupe Island is based on finding its distinctive wounds on two species of pinnipeds that do not dive past 200-m depth there (J. P. Gallo, personal communication, May 2001). A specimen was also found dead off Miami, Florida (UF 232954); this species, which is known to extend into epipelagic waters, is known in the Atlantic off our area but only at more than 200-m depth (G. H. Burgess, personal communication, June 2001).

Squatiniformes. See Chondrichthyes above.

*Squatina californica*. Geographic modifier inadvertently omitted in 1991 edition.

*Heterodontus francisci*. Date of publication correction.

Page 51

Orectolobiformes. See Chondrichthyes above.

Ginglymostomatidae. See Rhincodontidae below.

Rhincodontidae. Nurse sharks are recognized in their own family, Ginglymostomatidae, separate from the now monotypic Rhincodontidae, with appropriate changes in family common names. The family common name previously used was carpet sharks.

Lamniformes. See Chondrichthyes above.

Mitsukurinidae. Added to the list for the species noted.

*Mitsukurina owstoni.* J. K. Ugoretz and J. A. Seigel, 1999, Calif. Fish Game 85(3):118–120, reported on a goblin shark taken by drift gillnet from near surface waters off San Clemente Island, California. We have no records of this species above 200-m depth from Mexico.

Pseudocarchariidae. Added to the list for the species noted.

*Carcharias taurus.* For a discussion of the recognition of *Carcharias* rather than *Odontaspis* for *C. taurus* (also recognized by some as *Eugomphodus taurus*), see Nelson (1994:51). Although some recent authors recognize *Odontaspis*, the senior synonym, and *Carcharias* as congeneric, we follow Compagno (1999) in considering *Carcharias* to be a valid genus.

*Odontaspis noronhai.* Has been recorded from the Gulf of Mexico off Texas very close to the Mexican boundary, but as yet there are no verified records from Mexico.

Megachasmidae. See Cetorhinidae below.

## Page 52

Cetorhinidae. Megamouth sharks are recognized in their own family, Megachasmidae, separate from the now monotypic Cetorhinidae.

*Cetorhinus maximus.* Author's name sometimes spelled Gunner; we retain the Latinized Gunnerus, as used in the original description and in the 1991 edition. Northern Gulf of California population apparently is extirpated.

*Isurus paucus.* Although previously known from Mexican Pacific waters, two specimens of longfin mako were captured off the northern Channel Islands, California (D. A. Ebert, 2001, Calif. Fish Game 87(3):117–121).

Carcharhiniformes. See Chondrichthyes above.

Scyliorhinidae. False cat sharks are recognized in their own family, Pseudotriakidae, separate from the Scyliorhinidae.

*Galeus arae.* Added on the basis of voucher material from our area from 100-m depth (Florida Museum of Natural History).

Pseudotriakidae. See Scyliorhinidae above.

*Pseudotriakis microdon.* Correction of author.

Triakidae. See Carcharhinidae below.

*Galeorhinus galeus.* L. J. V. Compagno, 1988, Sharks of the order Carcharhiniformes, Princeton University Press, Princeton, New Jersey, provided data for his proposal in 1984 to synonymize *G. zyopterus* Jordan & Gilbert, 1883, soupfin shark, with *G. galeus.* This was accepted in L. J. V. Compagno, F. Krupp, and W. Schneider *in* Fischer et al. (1995, Volume II:734) and Compagno (1999), and we follow this synonymy here. We accept the term tope as the common name because of its long and consistent application to *G. galeus,* rather than "tope shark," as used in Compagno's publications, or "soupfin shark," although the latter is the English name used historically and exclusively for this species on the Pacific Coast.

## Page 53

*Mustelus henlei.* Date of publication correction.

*Mustelus norrisi.* Date of publication correction.

*Mustelus sinusmexicanus.* This new species was described from the Gulf of Mexico by P. C. Heemstra, 1997, Bull. Mar. Sci. 60(3):918.

*Triakis semifasciata.* Date of publication correction.

Carcharhinidae. Hound sharks are recognized in their own family, Triakidae, separate from the Carcharhinidae.

*Carcharhinus brevipinna.* Date of publication correction.

*Carcharhinus falciformis.* Correction of author and date of publication.

*Carcharhinus galapagensis.* Added on the basis of unpublished documented records off the east coast of Florida (G. H. Burgess, personal communication, January 2001). It was previously known from Mexican waters.

*Carcharhinus isodon.* Correction of author.

*Carcharhinus leucas.* Correction of author and date of publication.

*Carcharhinus limbatus.* Correction of author and date of publication.

*Carcharhinus obscurus.* Date of publication correction.

*Carcharhinus perezii.* Original spelling ends with -*ii*.

*Galeocerdo cuvier.* Correction of spelling of author.

## Page 54

*Sphyrna tiburo.* C. F. Jensen and F. J. Schwartz, 1994, Journal of the Elisha Mitchell Scientific Society 110(1):46–48, and W. F. Loftus, 2000, Fla. Sci. 63(1):27–47, noted occurrence in freshwater and estuarine habitats.

Torpediniformes. See Chondrichthyes above.

Narcinidae. See Torpedinidae below.

*Narcine bancroftii*. M. R. de Carvalho, 1999, A systematic revision of the electric ray genus *Narcine* Henle, 1834 (Chondrichthyes: Torpediniformes: Narcinidae), and the higher-level relationships of the orders of elasmobranch fishes (Chondrichthyes), Ph.D. thesis, The City University of New York, New York, has shown that the species in our area is not *N. brasiliensis* (Olfers, 1831), described from off southern Brazil, but *N. bancroftii*, previously considered a synonym of *N. brasiliensis* (M. R. de Carvalho, personal communication, February 2002). This was recognized by J. D. McEachran and M. R. de Carvalho, 2003 (dated 2002), Narcinidae, Pages 518–523 *in* K. E. Carpenter, editor, The living marine resources of the western central Atlantic, FAO species identification guide for fishery purposes, Volume 1, FAO, Rome. We retain the common name previously used in our area. Authorship and the *-ii* ending of specific name are as advised by W. N. Eschmeyer (personal communication, February 2002), based on checking the original publication.

Torpedinidae. Some electric rays are recognized in their own family, Narcinidae, separate from the Torpedinidae. The family common names electric rays (referred to as numbfishes in Compagno 1999) and torpedo electric rays have been adopted with the recognition of *Narcine* and *Torpedo* in separate families. The family common name previously used for Torpedinidae was electric rays.

Pristiformes. See Chondrichthyes above.

*Pristis pectinata*. Change in distribution; this species has been captured in the lower Mississippi River and the St. Johns River of Florida (McEachran and Fechhelm 1998).

*Pristis pristis*. Parentheses are added to the author's name since Linnaeus described this species in *Squalus*. This species has been recognized in our area under the names *P. microdon* Latham, 1794, and *P. perotteti* Müller & Henle, 1841; pending a revision of largetooth sawfishes worldwide, we accept the advice of G. H. Burgess (personal communication, January 2001) and treat all as conspecific under the earliest name, as done in the 1991 edition.

Rajiformes. See Chondrichthyes above.

Rhinobatidae. Formerly recognized as also containing *Platyrhinoidis triseriata*, now placed in Platyrhynidae.

### Page 55

*Rhinobatos lentiginosus*. Parentheses are removed from the author's name.

*Rhinobatos productus*. Parentheses are removed from the author's name.

Platyrhynidae. See Rhinobatidae and Chondrichthyes above.

Rajidae. See Chondrichthyes above. Further changes in generic placement are expected based on the research by J. D. McEachran and K. A. Dunn, 1998, Copeia 1998(2):271–290. The Pacific species *Bathyraja trachura* (Gilbert, 1892), roughtail skate, has been removed from the list as we find no records from above 200-m depth.

*Amblyraja radiata*. Date of publication correction. J. D. McEachran and K. A. Dunn, 1998, Copeia 1998(2):271–290, elevated *Amblyraja* and several other subgenera of *Raja* to genus-group names.

*Bathyraja lindbergi*. Added because of occurrence within our area in eastern Bering Sea and off Aleutian Islands (Mecklenburg et al. 2002).

*Bathyraja maculata*. Added because of occurrence within our area in eastern Bering Sea and off Aleutian Islands (Mecklenburg et al. 2002).

*Bathyraja parmifera*. *Bathyraja rosispinis* (Gill & Townsend, 1897), the flathead skate, recognized in the 1991 edition, was considered a junior synonym of *B. parmifera* by M. Stehmann, 1986, *in* T. Uyeno, R. Arai, T. Taniuchi, and K. Matsuura, editors, Indo-Pacific fish biology, Ichthyological Society of Japan, Tokyo. This synonymy is also recommended by J. D. McEachran (personal communication, 1998).

*Bathyraja spinicauda*. Change in generic placement follows J. D. McEachran and K. A. Dunn, 1998, Copeia 1998(2):271–290.

*Bathyraja taranetzi*. Added because of occurrence within our area along eastern Bering Sea outer shelf and upper slope and off Aleutian Islands. Species included as junior synonyms are the previously listed *B. hubbsi* Ishihara & Ishiyama, 1985, mud skate, based on work of H. Ishihara, and the nominal species *Rhinoraja longi* Raschi & McEachran, 1991, Aleutian dotted skate (J. D. McEachran, personal communication, September 2000; Mecklenburg et al. 2002). Date of publication accepted as 1983, rather than the usually cited 1985, because of a description (in the genus *Rhinoraja*) in Dolganov's widely cited 1983 guide, Manual for identification of cartilaginous fishes of far-eastern seas of USSR and adjacent waters, TINRO, Vladivostok, Russia (In Russian) (C. W. Mecklenburg, personal communication, August 2000).

*Bathyraja violacea*. Added because of occurrence within our area in eastern Bering Sea (Mecklenburg et al. 2002).

*Dipturus bullisi*. Added on the basis of a voucher specimen from our area from 125-m depth (Florida Museum of Natural History) and recorded from Mexico by J. L. Castro-Aguirre and H. Espinosa Pérez, 1996, VII, Listados faunísticos de México, Universidad Nacional Autónoma de México, México, D.F.

*Dipturus laevis*. See *Amblyraja radiata*. Date of publication correction.

*Dipturus olseni*. See *Amblyraja radiata*.

*Leucoraja caribbaea*. Included in the Mexican fauna on basis of corrected depth information for the holotype (UF 231707) (G. H. Burgess, personal communication, January 2001). See *L. garmani*.

*Leucoraja erinacea*. See *Amblyraja radiata*.

*Leucoraja garmani*. See *Amblyraja radiata*. This species was recognized with four subspecies by J. D. McEachran, 1977, Bull. Mar. Sci. 27(3):423–439, which were treated as distinct species by McEachran and Fechhelm (1998:162). All four, *L. caribbaea*, *L. garmani*, *L. lentiginosa*, and *L. virginica*, occur in our area (G. H. Burgess, personal communication, January 2001).

*Leucoraja lentiginosa*. See *L. garmani*.

*Leucoraja ocellata*. See *Amblyraja radiata*. Date of publication correction.

*Leucoraja virginica*. See *L. garmani*.

*Malacoraja senta*. See *Amblyraja radiata*.

Page 56

*Raja binoculata*. Date of publication correction.

*Raja eglanteria*. Date of publication correction.

*Raja rhina*. Parentheses are removed from the authors' names.

*Raja stellulata*. Parentheses are removed from the authors' names.

Myliobatiformes. See Chondrichthyes above.

Dasyatidae. Butterfly rays are recognized in their own family, Gymnuridae, separate from the Dasyatidae. The family common names in English follow Compagno (1999) and Smith-Vaniz et al. (1999).

*Dasyatis dipterura*. Eschmeyer (1998:483) noted that treatment of this species by K. Nishida and K. Nakaya in 1990 as a junior synonym of *D. brevis* (Garman, 1880) is incorrect (*D. dipterura* has date priority).

*Pteroplatytrygon violacea*. Formerly placed in *Dasyatis*, we follow McEachran and Fechhelm (1998) in this change of genus.

*Urobatis halleri*. Formerly placed in *Urolophus*, we follow J. D. McEachran *in* Fischer et al. (1995, Volume II:789) and Compagno (1999) in this change of genus.

*Urobatis jamaicensis*. Formerly placed in *Urolophus*, we follow McEachran and Fechhelm (1998) and Compagno (1999) in this change of genus.

Page 57

Gymnuridae. See Dasyatidae above.

*Gymnura crebripunctata*. W. D. Smith, J. L. Bizzarro, J. F. Márquez-Farias, J. Nielsen, and M. Shivji, 2003, Abstract, Page 15 *in* Resumenes: Foro de intercambio científico sobre tiburones y rayas, Instituto Nacional de la Pesca, 29–30 Mayo 2003, Guaymas, Sonora, México, presented morphometric and genetic evidence that this species is a junior synonym of *G. marmorata* and are preparing a manuscript for publication (W. D. Smith, personal communication, October 2003). We recognize *G. crebripunctata* pending publication of this work.

*Gymnura micrura*. Correction of author.

Myliobatidae. Formerly considered to include the genus *Rhinoptera*. The families Myliobatidae, Rhinopteridae, and Mobulidae were treated as a subfamily of Dasyatidae by J. D. McEachran, K. A. Dunn, and T. Miyake, 1996, Interrelationships of the batoid fishes (Chondrichthyes: Batoidea), Pages 63–84 *in* M. L. J. Stiassny, L. R. Parenti, and G. D. Johnson, editors, Interrelationships of fishes, Academic Press, San Diego, California. The present recognition of families follows McEachran and Fechhelm (1998) and Compagno (1999).

*Aetobatus narinari*. Generic name spelling correction.

*Myliobatis freminvillei*. Although the original spelling of the specific name ends in *–ii,* we retain the spelling –*ei*, which is in prevailing usage and required by the Code, whether deemed to be a justified emendation (Article 33.2.3.1) or a correct original spelling (Article 33.3.1).

Rhinopteridae. See Myliobatidae above.

*Manta birostris*. Adjective added to common name to distinguish it from other mantas.

*Mobula tarapacana*. McEachran and Fechhelm (1998:196) noted the occurrence of this worldwide species in the Flower Gardens Banks (= Flower Garden Reefs) off Texas.

*Mobula thurstoni*. Based on a revisionary study of the genus *Mobula* by G. Notarbartolo-di-Sciara, 1987, Zool. J. Linn. Soc. 91:1–91 (p. 46), *M. thurstoni*, included in previous editions (since 1960) as occurring off California (as "P"), was found to be based on a misidentification of *M. japanica*. We note that prior listings are incorrect. However, *M. thurstoni* does occur in the Gulf of California and off mainland Mexico and accordingly is listed as "PM."

### Page 58

*Acipenser oxyrinchus*. This spelling of the specific name (versus *oxyrhynchus*) is the one used in the original species description by Mitchill (1815) and thus, by the rule of original orthography, the correct one. Also date of publication correction. Occurrence in Mexico based on a 1991 sight record, thought to be of this species, from the eastern Big Bend area of the Rio Grande/Río Bravo, Texas/Coahuila (S. P. Platania, personal communication, January 2003, and a 1991 manuscript report by S. P. Platania, D. A. Young, and B. M. Burr), as also noted in Miller et al. (in press). This record likely is based on a stray from the Gulf of Mexico; the possibility that the individual was introduced is highly unlikely. E. Artyukhin and P. Vecsei, 1999, J. Appl. Ichthyol. (Special Issue) 15(4–5):35–37, concluded that this species is best considered conspecific with *A. sturio*, but we await further study of this question before making change.

*Scaphirhynchus platorynchus*. There is a confirmed record from the Rio Grande, dating from 1874, from Albuquerque, New Mexico (E. D. Cope and H. C. Yarrow, 1875, U.S. Geological and Geographical Explorations and Survey West of 100th Meridian 5(6)), with two voucher specimens (USNM 15994). There is also a specimen in the BMNH from the Rio Grande, but with imprecise locality data. We believe it highly likely that this species, known in Mexico as the esturión, was once native to the entire Río Bravo/Rio Grande basin in Mexico, but do not include it as part of the Mexican fauna because of the absence of confirmed records.

*Scaphirhynchus suttkusi*. This new and rare species was described from the Mobile basin of Alabama and Mississippi by J. D. Williams and G. H. Clemmer, 1991, Bulletin of the Alabama Museum of Natural History 10:19. It was redescribed by R. L. Mayden and B. R. Kuhajda, 1996, Copeia 1996(2):241–273.

*Polyodon spathula*. Extirpated in Canada (Ontario); last reported in 1917.

Lepisosteiformes. Extant gar and the fossil Semionotidae are often recognized in the same order, either under the ordinal name Lepisosteiformes or Semionotiformes. Pending ongoing studies by L. Grande on the interrelationships of this group, we follow L. Grande and W. E. Bemis, 1998, Society of Vertebrate Paleontology Memoir 4 (Supplement to J. Vertebr. Paleontol. 18(1)), p. 634, who separated the two groups into different orders, Lepisosteiformes and Semionotiformes.

*Atractosteus spatula*. Generic name change. E. O. Wiley, 1976, Univ. Kans. Mus. Nat. Hist. Misc. Publ. 64, gave generic rank to the two phyletic lineages of gars. We now adopt this proposal. Occasionally occurs along coast of Gulf of Mexico.

*Lepisosteus oculatus*. Parentheses are removed from the author's name.

*Lepisosteus osseus*. Occasionally occurs along Atlantic and Gulf of Mexico coasts.

### Page 59

Hiodontiformes. Recognition of this order rather than Osteoglossiformes, as formerly done for Hiodontidae, follows L. Guo-Qing and M. V. H. Wilson, 1996, Phylogeny of Osteoglossomorpha, Pages 163–174 *in* M. L. Stiassny, L. R. Parenti and G. D. Johnson, editors, Interrelationships of fishes, Academic Press, San Diego, California.

Osteoglossiformes. Change in composition from Hiodontidae (see Hiodontiformes above) to Notopteridae.

Notopteridae. Added to the list for the species noted.

*Chitala ornata*. First reported in 1994 by an angler and subsequently collected in 1996 from Lake Osborne, Palm Beach County, Florida, by the Florida Fish and Wildlife Conservation Commission (FWC) personnel. FWC monitoring confirms that clown knifefish persist in low numbers, with fewer than 100 individuals documented between 1994 and 2003 (P. Shafland, personal communication, June 2003). We consider it probably established. Voucher specimens collected from Lake Osborne are deposited in the Florida Museum of Natural History, UF 120072.

Elopidae. Recognition of Megalopidae as a separate family follows J. S. Nelson, 1984:97, Fishes of the world, 2nd edition, John Wiley & Sons, New York (and Nelson 1994).

*Elops affinis*. Common in Mexican marine and fluvial waters; occurrence in freshwater in the United States based on historical records from the lower Colorado River area, including the Salton Sea. The river now only rarely flows into the Gulf of California. There are recent marine records from southern California.

*Elops saurus*. There possibly is an undescribed species of *Elops,* with fewer myomeres in the larval stage than *E. saurus,* in the Gulf of Mexico and along the Atlantic Coast (D. G. Smith, 1989, Fishes of the western North Atlantic, Memoir, Sears Foundation for Marine Research, Part 9(2):961–972). Whether adults also occur in U.S. waters is unkown.

Megalopidae. See Elopidae above.

*Albula nemoptera*. The type locality is in the Caribbean Sea, and this species may occur in Mexican waters of the Gulf of Mexico and/or Caribbean Sea, but voucher material is apparently lacking (see Castro-Aguirre et al. 1999).

*Albula* species. See *A. vulpes.*

*Albula vulpes*. In the 1991 edition, only this species was recognized, with occurrence on both coasts. We now know it to occur only in the Atlantic, with other species in the eastern Pacific (E. Pfeiler, 1996, Copeia 1996(1):181–183; J. Colborn, R. E. Crabtree, J. B. Shaklee, E. Pfeiler, and B. W. Bowen, 2001, Evolution 55(4):807–820). Molecular studies suggest that there are also at least two other species in our area: one (the lesser bonefish = "*Albula* sp. B" in the above-mentioned Colborn et

al., 2001, reference), in the Florida Keys, has been characterized morphologically (R. E. Crabtree and B. W. Bowen, 1997, Page 106 *in* Abstracts, 77th Annual Meeting of the American Society of Ichthyologists and Herpetologists, June 26–July 2, 1997, University of Washington, Seattle), and one (in the list as *Albula* species; = "*Albula* sp. A" in the above-mentioned Colborn et al., 2001, reference) occurs throughout the Gulf of California and occasionally off California (E. C. Starks, 1918, Calif. Fish Game 4(2):58–65; J. E. Fitch, 1950, Calif. Fish Game 36(1):3–6; R. N. Lea and R. H. Rosenblatt, 2000, CalCOFI Rep. 41:117–129; E. Pfeiler, D. Padrón, and R. E. Crabtree, 2000, J. Fish Biol. 56:448–453). There is also a southern form of eastern Pacific *Albula* in the Gulf of Panama (Colborn et al., 2001, cited above). The nomenclature of these forms has yet to be resolved, but a name is available, *A. esuncula* (Garman, 1899; see P. J. P. Whitehead, 1986, Cybium 10:211–230), for one of the eastern Pacific species. Allen and Robertson (1994) and Castro-Aguirre et al. (1999) mistakenly applied the name *A. neoguinaica* Valenciennes, 1847 (a junior synonym of *A. forsteri* Valenciennes, 1847, as given in J. E. Randall and M.-L. Bauchot, 1999, Cybium 23(1):79–83) to one or both form(s) in the eastern Pacific, but those names apply to an Indo-West Pacific species (Colborn et al., 2001, cited above).

*Notacanthus chemnitzii*. Date of publication correction, original spelling ends with *–ii,* and common name changed to distinguish it from other spiny eels.

### Page 60

Heterenchelyidae. Added to the list for the species noted, *Pythonichthys asodes* [CIAD 90-22, CIAD 90-24 (CIAD 90-24 now SIO 95-28, SIO 97-3)] (A. M. van der Heiden and H. Plascencia and R. H. Rosenblatt, personal communications, November 2001).

*Chilorhinus suensonii*. Original spelling ends with *-ii.*

*Kaupichthys hyoproroides*. Correction of spelling of author's name.

### Page 61

*Gymnothorax maderensis*. Correction of spelling of specific name.

*Gymnothorax nigromarginatus*. Date of publication correction.

*Muraena robusta*. Correction of spelling of author's name and of date of publication.

*Synaphobranchus kaupii*. Original spelling ends with *-ii*.

### Page 62

Ophichthidae. This list is probably incomplete for species in Atlantic Mexico; many species are known from above 200-m depth from leptocephalous larvae only and, as noted by D. G. Smith (personal communication, February 2002), "Leptocephali are usually a good indicator of the presence of eel species that are cryptic or difficult to collect as adults." The following species, which are not included in our list, have been recorded from within our area of coverage only as leptocephali (M. M. Leiby, 1989, Fishes of the western North Atlantic, Memoir, Sears Foundation for Marine Research, Part 9(2):764–897): *Asarcenchelys longimanus, Gordiichthys randalli, Letharchus aliculatus, Mixomyrophis pusillipinna, Ophichthus menezesi* (one adult has been obtained off Florida deeper than 200 m), *O. spinicauda, Phaenomonas longissima, Pseudomyrophis frio, Quassiremus ascensionis,* and *Stictorhinus potamius*. The following species are included in our list as occurring only in United States waters, but leptocephali have been recorded from Mexico: *Aprognathodon platyventris, Apterichtus kendalli, Bascanichthys scuticaris, Caralophia loxochila,* and *Pseudomyrophis fugesae*. The following species are indicated on our list to occur only in Mexican waters, but leptocephali have been recorded from United States waters: *Callechelys bilinearis* and *Myrophis platyrhynchus*. Absence of verified adults from the areas indicated is most likely a collecting artifact, and adults may be expected to occur in areas from which they so far have not been recorded.

*Aplatophis chauliodus*. Has been recorded from the Gulf of Mexico off Texas (ANSP 116366), very close to the Mexican boundary, but as yet there are no verified records from Mexico.

*Callechelys guineensis*. Specific name spelling correction and date of publication correction (however, the year may be 1894, according to Eschmeyer 1998:690).

*Callechelys muraena*. Date of publication correction.

*Gordiichthys ergodes*. Correction of author.

### Page 63

*Lethogoleos andersoni*. Generic name spelling correction.

*Myrichthys breviceps*. Date of publication correction.

*Myrichthys tigrinus*. *Myrichthys tigrinus* was resurrected to species status by J. E. McCosker and R. H. Rosenblatt, 1993, Proc. Calif. Acad. Sci. 48(8):153–169, from the *M. maculosus* complex, which is now represented by four species. *Myrichthys maculosus* (Cuvier, 1816) is Indo-West Pacific in distribution and does not occur in our area. The common name tiger snake eel, although seemingly inappropriate in English for this blotched snake eel, was originally applied to the eastern Pacific *M. tigrinus* and is retained for that taxon. *Myrichthys maculosus* as listed in the previous edition was composed of four populations or subspecies.

*Myrophis punctatus*. Date of publication correction.

*Ophichthus gomesii*. Original spelling ends with *-ii*.

*Ophichthus zophochir*. Parentheses are removed from the authors' names.

*Pseudomyrophis fugesae*. Date of publication correction.

### Page 64

Muraenesocidae. Added to the list for the species noted.

*Bathycongrus bullisi*. Known depth of occurrence above 200-m depth is not definite.

*Bathycongrus dubius*. Added to list on basis of records from less than 200-m depth (D. G. Smith, 1989, Fishes of the western North Atlantic, Memoir, Sears Foundation for Marine Research, Part 9(1):460–567, as *Rhechias dubia*, and D. G. Smith, personal communication, May 2001).

*Bathycongrus vicinalis*. Known depth of occurrence above 200-m depth is not definite.

*Conger oceanicus*. Date of publication correction.

*Gnathophis cinctus*. *Gnathophis catalinensis* (Wade, 1946), Catalina conger, was indicated by S. R. Charter, 1966, Page 101 *in* The early stages of fishes in the California current region, CalCOFI Atlas No. 33, to be a junior synonym of *G. cinctus*. The common name in English is from D. G. Smith *in* Fischer et al. (1995, Volume II:1034).

*Heteroconger longissimus*. The previously recognized *H. halis* (Böhlke, 1957), brown garden eel, is probably conspecific with this species, previously regarded as occurring only in the eastern Atlantic (J. C. Tyler and B. E. Luckhurst, 1994, Northeast Gulf Sci. 13(2):89–99; G. González-Lorenzo, A. Brito, J. M. Falcón, and P. Pascual-Alayón, 1995, Bull. Mar. Sci. 57(2):550–555).

### Page 65

*Paraconger similis*. Formerly placed in *Chiloconger*, D. G. Smith and E. S. Karmovskaya, 2003, Zootaxa 348:1–19, placed this species in *Paraconger*.

*Rhynchoconger flavus*. We follow D. G. Smith, 1989, Fishes of the western North Atlantic, Memoir, Sears Foundation for Marine Research, Part 9(1):525–526, in regarding *Hildebrandia* as a junior synonym of *Rhynchoconger*. Specific name ending changed accordingly.

*Rhynchoconger gracilior*. See *R. flavus*.

*Facciolella equatorialis*. The formerly recognized *F. gilbertii* (Garman, 1899) [as *F. gilberti*] was treated as a synonym of this species in J. S. Grove and R. J. Lavenberg, 1997, The fishes of the Galápagos Islands, Stanford University Press, Stanford, California, an action endorsed by D. G. Smith (personal communication, January 2001). The same common name is retained except that the hyphen is removed.

*Hoplunnis diomediana*. The generic name is feminine (D. G. Smith, personal communication, November 2002), and the specific name ending is changed accordingly. Hyphen removed from common name.

*Hoplunnis macrura*. See *H. diomediana* for change in common name.

*Hoplunnis tenuis*. See *H. diomediana* for change in common name.

*Nettenchelys pygmaea*. Described from the Gulf of Mexico in D. G. Smith, J. E. Böhlke, and P. H. J. Castle, 1981, Proc. Biol. Soc. Wash. 94(2):533–560, but inadvertently omitted from the 1991 edition.

Engraulidae. Two additional species may belong on the list. *Anchoa parri* (Hildebrand, 1943), mystery anchovy or anchoa misteriosa, was described from the northern Gulf of California, but it has not been seen since its original collection; generic placement as shown or in *Anchoviella* is uncertain. *Engraulis japo-nicus* Temminck & Schlegel, 1846, Japanese anchovy, may occur in our area off the western Aleutian Islands based on Mecklenburg et al. (2002).

### Page 66

*Anchoa lyolepis*. *Anchoa nasuta* Hildebrand & Carvalho, 1948, longnose anchovy, recognized in the 1991 list, was placed in synonymy with *A. lyolepis* by P. J. P. Whitehead, G. J. Nelson, and T. Wongratana, 1988, FAO species catalogue, Clupeoid fishes of the world (suborder Clupeoidei), Part 2, FAO Fish. Synop. 125(7)(2):305–579.

Pristigasteridae. Added to the list for the species noted.

### Page 67

*Brevoortia patronus*. The term "Gulf" in the common name is treated as a proper noun, and we infer that the name was originally proposed for the species' occurrence in the Gulf of Mexico.

*Clupea pallasii*. Original spelling ends with *-ii*.

*Opisthonema oglinum*. Date of publication correction.

*Sardinella aurita*. *Sardinella brasiliensis* (Steindachner, 1879), the orangespot sardine, included in previous lists, is removed based on studies by R. R Wilson, Jr. and P. D. Alberdi, Jr., 1991, Can. J. Fish. Aquat. Sci., 48:792–798, and M. D. Tringali and R. R. Wilson, Jr., 1993, Fish. Bull. 91:362–370 (summarized by McEachran and Fechhelm 1998: 346), who found no consistent genetic differences among populations of *Sardinella* within our area of coverage and determined that all are *S. aurita*. They also found that populations of *Sardinella* from the southwestern Atlantic differ genetically from those elsewhere in the western Atlantic. Since the type locality of *S. brasiliensis* (together with its replacement name *S. janeiro* (Eigenmann, 1894), as *brasiliensis* is preoccupied by *Clupea brasiliensis* Bloch & Schneider, 1801) is Rio de Janeiro, Brazil, it is likely that the name *janeiro* is the name properly applied to the south Atlantic populations.

*Sardinops sagax*. Some workers recognize populations off the west coast of North America as a sister species, *S. caeruleus* (Girard, 1854) (e.g., P. J. P. Whitehead and R. Rodríguez-Sánchez *in* Fischer et al. 1995, Volume II:1023); we follow R. H. Parrish, R. Serra, and W. S. Grant, 1989, Can. J. Fish. Aquat. Sci. 46(11):2019–2036, who considered these populations to be conspecific.

### Page 68

*Agosia chrysogaster*. Placed in the genus *Rhinichthys* by D. A. Woodman, 1992, Systematic relationships within the cyprinid genus *Rhinichthys*, Pages 374–391 *in* R. L. Mayden, editor, Systematics, historical ecology, and North American freshwater fishes, Stanford University Press, Stanford, California. However, A. M. Simons and R. L. Mayden, 1999, Copeia 1999(1):13–21, recommended continued placement in the monotypic genus *Agosia*, as done in the 1991 edition of this list, until relationships are further clarified.

*Algansea tincella*. The nominal species *Notropis josealvarezi* Cortés, 1986, listed in Espinosa-Pérez et al. 1993, is thought to be a junior synonym of this species (R. R. Miller, personal communication *in* Gilbert 1998:98).

*Aztecula sallaei*. This species, placed in *Aztecula* by R. L. Mayden, 1989, Univ. Kans. Mus. Nat. Hist. Misc. Publ. 80, and Mayden et al. (1992), is often recognized in *Notropis* (e.g., Espinosa-Pérez et al. 1993).

*Campostoma anomalum*. W. L. Pflieger, 1997, Fishes of Missouri, Missouri Department of Conservation, Jefferson City, recognized *C. pullum* (Agassiz, 1854), currently regarded as a subspecies of *C. anomalum*, as a valid species. We defer recognition of *C. pullum* pending publication of a taxonomic study by, for example, D. A. Etnier and H. T. Boschung (in preparation and outlined in an addendum to the 2001 second printing of D. A. Etnier and W. C. Starnes, 1994 [dated 1993], The fishes of Tennessee, The University of Tennessee Press, Knoxville). Etnier and Boschung's study show that *C. pullum* has the widest distribution of the stonerollers, extending from Canada in the Great Lakes drainage to Mexico, with *C. anomalum* confined to the United States east of the Mississippi River. Additional changes in stoneroller taxonomy may be forthcoming in studies by D. A. Etnier and W. C. Starnes (W. C. Starnes, personal communication, June 2002). Pflieger (1997, see above) employed the descriptively appropriate name "central stoneroller" for *C. pullum*, the name used in the 1980 and 1991 lists for *C. anomalum*. If formal recog-

nition were given to *C. pullum*, "central stoneroller" might be the preferred name with a substitute name being needed for *C. anomalum*.

*Clinostomus elongatus*. Date of publication correction following Gilbert (1998:75).

### Page 69

*Cyprinella labrosa*. See *Hybopsis* below.

*Cyprinella ornata*. Recognized by Mayden et al. (1992) and Gilbert (1998:25, 127) in the genus *Codoma*, in which it was originally described. We retain it in *Cyprinella* until evidence is published for the change.

*Cyprinella spiloptera*. Date of publication correction.

*Cyprinella venusta*. A. Y. Kristmundsdóttir and J. R. Gold, 1996, Copeia 1996:773–783, suggested that further taxonomic study of this species may be warranted and noted that the clades represented by the nominal species *C. eurystoma* (Jordan, 1877) and *C. stigmatura* (Jordan, 1877) (recognized as valid species in Gilbert 1998:78, 151) may be found with further study to merit species recognition.

*Cyprinella whipplei*. Although the original spelling ends with *–ii*, we retain the spelling *–ei*, which is in prevailing usage and deemed to be a justified emendation following Article 33.2.3.1 of the Code (also see Eschmeyer 1998: Online version, February 2002).

*Cyprinella zanema*. See *Hybopsis* below.

*Dionda argentosa*. Recognized as a valid species in R. L. Mayden, R. H. Matson, and D. M. Hillis, 1992, Speciation in the North American genus *Dionda* (Teleostei: Cypriniformes), Pages 710–746 *in* R. L. Mayden, editor, Systematics, historical ecology, and North American freshwater fishes, Stanford University Press, Stanford, California, and in Gilbert (1998:43).

### Page 70

*Dionda nigrotaeniata*. Recognized as a valid but unnamed species in R. L. Mayden, R. H. Matson, and D. M. Hillis, 1992, Speciation in the North American genus *Dionda* (Teleostei: Cypriniformes), Pages 710–746 *in* R. L. Mayden, editor, Systematics, historical ecology, and North American freshwater fishes, Stanford University Press, Stanford, California; Gilbert (1998:120) determined that the name *nigrotaeniata* is available for this population.

*Dionda serena*. Recognized as a valid species in R. L. Mayden, R. H. Matson, and D. M. Hillis, 1992, Speciation in the North American genus *Dionda* (Teleostei: Cypriniformes), Pages 710–746 *in* R. L. Mayden, editor, Systematics, historical ecology, and North American freshwater fishes, Stanford University Press, Stanford, California, and in Gilbert (1998:147).

*Erimonax monachus*. Placed in the monotypic genus *Erimonax* (Jordan, 1924) by Mayden et al. (1992) because of its uncertain relationships. The analysis of R. E. Broughton and J. R. Gold, 2000, Copeia 2000(1):1–10, suggests it does not belong in *Cyprinella*, but placement is uncertain because of the limited sample of outgroup taxa. Recognized in the 1991 edition as *C. monacha,* and variously by other authors in the genera *Hybopsis* and *Erimystax*.

*Erimystax dissimilis*. Date of publication correction following Gilbert (1998:72).

*Erimystax x-punctatus*. Extirpated from Canada (Ontario); last reported there in 1958.

*Exoglossum maxillingua*. We recommend the common name be changed from cutlips minnow to cutlip minnow.

*Gila bicolor*. P. M. Harris and D. F. Markle (personal communication, August 2001) have unpublished evidence placing *G. bicolor*, along with two other species, *G. alvordensis and G. boraxobius*, in the genus *Siphateles*; they also have evidence that *G. bicolor* consists of several allopatric species. *Siphateles* was considered a subgenus of *Gila* in the 1970 and subsequent lists; it was first re-elevated as a genus, for *G. bicolor*, by A. M. Simons and R. L. Mayden, 1998, Mol. Phylogenet. Evol. 9:308–329. The above three species are recognized in *Siphateles* by G. R. Smith, T. E. Dowling, K. W. Gobalet, T. Lugaski, D. K. Shiozawa, and R. P. Evans, 2002, Great basin aquatic systems history, Pages 175–234 *in* R. Hershler, D. B. Madsen, and D. R. Currey, editors, Smithsonian Contributions to Earth Sciences 33. In addition, these authors recognize *G. coerulea* in the genus *Klamathella* and make changes to other taxa not noted here.

*Gila coerulea*. See *G. bicolor.*

Page 71

*Gila cypha*. Date of publication correction.

*Gila elegans*. Extirpated from Mexico (lower Colorado River).

*Gila intermedia*. See *G. nigra.*

*Gila minacae*. See *G. robusta.*

*Gila nigra*. Recognized by W. L. Minckley and B. D. DeMarais, 2000, Copeia 2000(1):251–256, as a species of hybrid origin, found in the Gila River basin of Arizona and New Mexico; it was formerly regarded as a subspecies of either *G. intermedia* or *G. robusta*.

*Gila orcuttii*. Original spelling ends with *-ii.*

*Gila robusta*. See *G. nigra*. This is a highly variable species, and several nominal species may be elevated from synonymy in the future. Indeed, *G. minacae*, of northern Mexico and perhaps formerly occurring in Arizona, is recognized as a valid species in Miller et al. (in press) and is recognized here as well. Although *G. robusta*, in the strict taxonomic sense (carpa cola redonda in Miller et al., in press), probably occurred in Mexico in the lower Colorado River and in the headwaters of the Río San Pedro, Sonora, in the past, there are apparently no verified records of present occurrence (S. M. Norris, personal communication, April 2003; Miller et al., in press).

*Gila seminuda*. Previously regarded as a subspecies of *G. robusta*, *G. seminuda* was considered a valid species of hybrid origin by B. D. DeMarias, T. E. Dowling, M. E. Douglas, W. L. Minckley, and P. C. Marsh, 1992, Proc. Nat. Acad. Sci. 89(7):2747–2751 (also see Gilbert 1998:146).

*Hesperoleucus symmetricus*. As noted in the 1991 edition (p. 75), there are reasons to consider this species congeneric with *Lavinia exilicauda*. Evidence exists from several workers strengthening this view (D. G. Buth, T. E. Dowling, and W. J. Jones, personal communication, May 2001), but we defer making the change until the information is published.

*Hybognathus amarus*. Believed to be extirpated from Mexico where it once occurred in the Río Bravo (= Rio Grande; S. Contreras-Balderas and S. M. Norris, personal communications, May 2003).

*Hybopsis amblops*. Many additional species recognized here in the genera *Cyprinella* (namely *C. labrosa* and *C. zanema*) and *Notropis*, as in the 1991 edition, are placed in *Hybopsis* in R. L. Mayden, 1989, Univ. Kans. Mus. Nat. Hist. Misc. Publ. 80, Mayden (1991), Mayden et al. (1992), and E. O. Wiley and T. A. Titus, 1992, Occas. Pap. Mus. Nat. Hist. Univ. Kans. 152. However, M. M. Coburn and T. M. Cavender, 1992, Interrelationships of North American cyprinid fishes, Pages 328–373 *in* R. L. Mayden, editor, Systematics, historical ecology, and North American freshwater fishes, Stanford University Press, Stanford, California, in their study of interrelationships of North American cyprinid fishes, recommended submerging species of *Hybopsis* into *Notropis* until the interrelationships are better known. In the study of R. E. Broughton and J. R. Gold, 2000, Copeia 2000(1):1–10, *C. labrosa* and *C. zanema* fall within the *Cyprinella* clade. We recognize only six species in *Hybopsis* in the strict sense (see also Jenkins and Burkhead, 1994:345), a monophyletic group termed the *H. amblops* species group in M. J. Grose and E. O Wiley, 2002, Copeia 2002(4):1092–1097, but we acknowledge that this arrangement is subject to change.

*Hybopsis amnis.* See *H. amblops.*

*Hybopsis hypsinotus.* See *H. amblops.*

*Hybopsis lineapunctata.* See *H. amblops.*

*Hybopsis rubrifrons.* When the genera *Hybopsis* and *Notropis* were synonymized under the latter name in the 1991 edition (p. 77), *N. rubrifrons* (Jordan, 1877) became a junior homonym of *N. rubrifrons* (Cope, 1865), and a replacement name, *N. rubescens* Bailey, 1991, was erected. With the generic recognition of *Hybopsis*, Jordan's species name again became available and Bailey's name became a junior synonym. See *H. amblops.*

*Hybopsis winchelli.* See *H. amblops.* M. J. Grose and E. O. Wiley, 2002, Copeia 2002(4):1092–1097, noted the existence of an undescribed sister species to *H. winchelli* in western Florida and southeastern Alabama.

## Page 72

*Lavinia exilicauda.* See *Hesperoleucus symmetricus.*

*Luxilus zonatus.* Correction of author.

*Lythrurus alegnotus.* Formerly considered a subspecies of *L. bellus.* Recognized as a valid species for reasons summarized in Gilbert (1998:37).

*Lythrurus ardens.* See *L. fasciolaris* and *L. matutinus.*

*Lythrurus fasciolaris.* Formerly synonymized under the name *L. ardens.* Recognized as a valid species based on genetic studies by W. W. Dimmick, K. L. Fiorino, and B. M. Burr, 1996, Copeia 1996(4):818 and summarized in Gilbert (1998:42, 79). We adopt the common name scarlet shiner on the advice of H. T. Boschung (personal communication, 1999), not scarletfin shiner as in Mayden et al. (1992) or rosefin shiner (already used for *L. ardens*) as in Dimmick, Fiorino, and Burr, 1996:818 (the latter authors used blueside shiner for *L. ardens*).

*Lythrurus matutinus.* Formerly synonymized under the name *L. ardens.* Recognized as a valid species based on genetic studies by W. W. Dimmick, K. L. Fiorino, and B. M. Burr, 1996, Copeia 1996(4):818 and summarized in Gilbert (1998:42, 110).

*Macrhybopsis aestivalis.* See *M. australis, M. hyostoma, M. marconis,* and *M. tetranema.*

*Macrhybopsis australis.* Formerly synonymized under the name *M. aestivalis.* Recognized as a valid species for reasons summarized in Gilbert (1998:46–47) and D. J. Eisenhour, 1999, Copeia 1999(4):969–980. Common name suggested by D. J. Eisenhour, 1997, Systematics, variation, and speciation of the *Macrhybopsis aestivalis* complex (Cypriniformes:Cyprinidae) west of the Mississippi River, Ph.D. dissertation, Southern Illinois University, Carbondale.

## Page 73

*Macrhybopsis hyostoma.* Formerly synonymized under the name *M. aestivalis.* Recognized as a valid species for reasons summarized in Gilbert (1998:93–94). Also recognized as a valid species by D. J. Eisenhour, 1999, Copeia 1999(4):969–980, and G. R. Luttrell, A. A. Echelle, W. L. Fisher, and D. J. Eisenhour, 1999, Copeia 1999(4):981–989. The generic name is feminine (Eschmeyer and Bailey 1990), requiring a change to the feminine ending from that in the literature. Common name suggested by D. J. Eisenhour (personal communication, April 2002; see *M. australis*).

*Macrhybopsis marconis.* Formerly synonymized under the name *M. aestivalis.* Recognized as a valid species for reasons summarized in Gilbert (1998:110) and D. J. Eisenhour, 1999, Copeia 1999(4):969–980. Common name suggested by D. J. Eisenhour in his Ph.D. dissertation (see *M. australis*).

*Macrhybopsis storeriana.* Date of publication correction following Gilbert (1998:152).

*Macrhybopsis tetranema.* Formerly synonymized under the name *M. aestivalis.* Recognized as a valid species for reasons summarized in Gilbert (1998:155) and given in D. J. Eisenhour, 1999, Copeia 1999(4):969–980, and G. R. Luttrell, A. A. Echelle, W. L. Fisher, and D. J. Eisenhour, 1999, Copeia 1999(4):981–989. The generic name is feminine (Eschmeyer and Bailey 1990), requiring a change to the feminine ending from that in the literature. Common name suggested by D. J. Eisenhour in his Ph.D. dissertation (see *M. australis*).

*Margariscus margarita.* Parentheses are added to the author's name; also date of publication correction. The subspecies *M. margarita nachtriebi* (Cox, 1896), northern pearl dace, is recognized as a valid species in R. M. Bailey, W. C. Latta, and G. R. Smith, in press, An atlas of Michigan fishes with keys and illustrations for their identification, Univ. Mich. Mus. Zool. Spec. Publ. 2. We feel that independent confirmation is required before accepting this proposal.

*Meda fulgida.* Almost certainly once occurred in the upper Río San Pedro (Gila River drainage) in Mexico, and the type locality is very near the international boundary (S. M. Norris, personal communication, April 2003), but confirmed records are lacking.

*Nocomis biguttatus.* Date of publication correction following Gilbert (1998:49).

*Nocomis micropogon.* As noted in Gilbert (1998:114), since the species name *micropogon* is based on a hybrid, it is unavailable according to Article 23.8 of the Code. However, the petition of C. R. Gilbert, J. S. Nelson, E. J. Crossman, H. Espinosa-Pérez, L. T. Findley, R. N. Lea, and J. D. Williams, 2000, Bull. Zool. Nomencl. 57(4):214–217, to conserve the specific name *micropogon*, was accepted in Opinion 2002, Bull. Zool. Nomencl. 59(2):147–148. J. R. Stauffer, Jr., C. H. Hocutt, and R. L. Mayden, 1997, Ichthyological Exploration of Freshwaters 7(4):329, recognized a cyprinid population in the Cheat River of West Virginia in its own genus as *Pararhinichthys bowersi* (Goldsborough & Clark, 1908), the Cheat minnow, believing it to represent a valid species of hybrid origin, *Nocomis micropogon* × *Rhinichthys cataractae.* Some earlier authors had recognized it as *R. bowersi* (e.g., Page and Burr 1991). However, we accept the merits of recognizing it, for now, as a hybrid (*N. micropogon* × *R. cataractae*), as suggested by W. J. Poly and M. H. Sabaj, 1998, Copeia 1998(4):1081–1085, while recognizing that further study may favor recognizing self-reproducing populations of hybrid origin as a valid species.

*Notropis albizonatus.* This new species was described from the Tennessee and Cumberland river drainages (Kentucky, Tennessee, and Alabama) by M. L. Warren, Jr. and B. M. Burr, *in* M. L. Warren, Jr., B. M. Burr, and J. M. Grady, 1994, Copeia 1994(4):869.

*Notropis ariommus.* Date of publication correction.

## Page 74

*Notropis bifrenatus.* Date of publication correction.

*Notropis buccatus.* Recognized in the monotypic genus *Ericymba* as *E. buccata* in the 1980 edition and Mayden et al. (1992). See the 1991 edition for reasons for placement in *Notropis*. In addition, M. E. Raley and R. M. Wood, 2001, Copeia 2001(3):638–645, presented molecular data placing this species within the *N. dorsalis* species group.

*Notropis buchanani.* There is a possibility that this species is introduced into Canada (Ontario) and not native.

*Notropis chalybaeus.* Date of publication correction.

*Notropis chlorocephalus.* See *N. lutipinnis.*

*Notropis cumingii.* Formerly called *N. imeldae* Cortés, 1968 (R. R. Miller, personal communication *in* Gilbert 1998:69).

## Page 75

*Notropis jemezanus.* Date of publication accepted as in the 1991 edition from Gilbert (1998:98).

*Notropis lutipinnis.* R. M. Wood and R. L. Mayden, 1992, Copeia 1992(1):68–81, provided evidence that this species is paraphyletic with two undescribed entities, one being more closely related to *N. chlorocephalus.*

*Notropis micropteryx.* Formerly called *Notropis rubellus.* Recognized as a valid species, known from the Green, Cumberland, and Tennessee rivers in the Kentucky to Alabama area, on the basis of genetic evidence presented by R. M. Wood, R. L. Mayden, R. H. Matson, B. R. Kuhajda, and S. R. Layman, 2002, Bulletin of the Alabama Museum of Natural History 22:37–80. This action was anticipated by Gilbert (1998:114).

*Notropis percobromus*. Formerly called *Notropis rubellus*. Recognized as a valid species, known from rivers in the upper Mississippi River basin (including southern Manitoba), Wabash River system, rivers of the Ozark highlands, and the upper Ouachita River system, on the basis of genetic evidence presented by R. M. Wood, R. L. Mayden, R. H. Matson, B. R. Kuhajda, and S. R. Layman, 2002, Bulletin of the Alabama Museum of Natural History 22:37–80.

*Notropis rafinesquei*. This new species was described from the Yazoo River system in Mississippi by R. D. Suttkus, 1991, Bulletin of the Alabama Museum of Natural History 10:1.

*Notropis rubellus*. Formerly recognized as including *N. micropteryx*, *N. percobromus*, and *N. suttkusi*. In addition, R. M. Wood, R. L. Mayden, R. H. Matson, B. R. Kuhajda, and S. R. Layman, 2002, Bulletin of the Alabama Museum of Natural History 22:37–80, noted an undescribed species from the upper Kanawha River system (Ohio River drainage) as part of the *N. rubellus* species group. The range of *N. rubellus* is now restricted primarily to drainages of the Great Lakes and Ottawa River, upper Ohio River, northern Atlantic Slope, and upper Cumberland River.

*Notropis saladonis*. This species is thought to be extinct (S. Contreras-Balderas, personal communication, July 2001).

### Page 76

*Notropis simus*. Date of publication accepted as in the 1991 edition from Gilbert (1998:147–148). Extirpated from Mexico. *Notropis s. simus* now extinct, but subspecies *N. simus pecosensis* Gilbert & Chernoff, 1982, exists in upper Pecos River system of New Mexico (B. Chernoff, R. R. Miller, and C. R. Gilbert, 1982, Occas. Pap. Mus. Zool. Univ. Mich. 698:1–49).

*Notropis stilbius*. Parentheses are removed from the author's name.

*Notropis stramineus*. As noted in the 1991 edition, R. L. Mayden and C. R. Gilbert, 1989, Copeia 1989(4):1084, showed that *N. ludibundus* (Girard, 1856) is a senior synonym of *N. stramineus*. However, the specific name *N. stramineus* is conserved (Opinion 1991, Bull. Zool. Nomencl. 59(1), March 2002), and *N. ludibundus* is suppressed.

*Notropis suttkusi*. This new species was described from the Ouachita Uplands of Oklahoma and Arkansas by J. M. Humphries and R. C. Cashner, 1994, Copeia 1994(1):84.

*Notropis topeka*. As noted in the 1991 edition, R. L. Mayden and C. R. Gilbert, 1989, Copeia 1989(4):1084, showed that *N. tristis* (Girard, 1856) is a senior synonym of *N. topeka*. The specific name *N. topeka* is conserved (Opinion 1821, Bull. Zool. Nomencl. 52, 28 September 1995); therefore, *N. tristis* (Girard, 1856) is suppressed.

*Oregonichthys kalawatseti*. This new species was described from the Umpqua River of Oregon by D. F. Markle, T. N. Pearsons, and D. T. Bills, 1991, Copeia 1991(2):279. Although the species is dace-like in appearance, we retain the name chub as with the other species of the genus.

*Phoxinus eos*. Viable populations of all-female hybrids of *P. eos* × *P. neogaeus* are known (e.g., see R. M. Dawley and K. A. Goddard, 1988, Evolution 42:649–659).

*Phoxinus neogaeus*. Date of publication correction. Also see *P. eos*.

*Phoxinus saylori*. This new species was described from the Tennessee River drainage, Tennessee, by C. E. Skelton, 2001, Copeia 2001(1): 118–128.

### Page 77

*Plagopterus argentissimus*. Almost certainly once occurred in Mexico (lower Colorado River; S. M. Norris, personal communication, April 2003), but confirmed records are lacking. There are collections from the Colorado River at Yuma, Arizona, just upstream from the Mexican border, during the latter part of the 19th century (USNM 48134; CAS 103842, 103845, 105338, 105444).

*Pteronotropis euryzonus*. Formerly classified as a subgenus of *Notropis*, *Pteronotropis* was raised to generic rank by R. L. Mayden, 1989, Univ. Kans. Mus. Nat. Hist. Misc. Publ. 80:30. We adopt this change here. A. M. Simons, K. E. Knott, and R. L. Mayden, 2000, Copeia 2000(4):1068–1075, recognized five species in the genus (*P. euryzonus*, *P. hubbsi*, *P. hypselopterus*, *P. signipinnis*, and *P. welaka*) but stressed that further work is needed to resolve the group's phylogenetic relationships. R. D. Suttkus and M. F. Mettee, 2001, Geological Survey of Alabama Bulletin 170, recognized *P. euryzonus, P. grandipinnis, P. hypselopterus,* and *P. merlini* in the subgenus *Pteronotropis* of *Notropis,* but they expressed uncertainty regarding the affinities of *P. signipinnis* and excluded *P. welaka* and *P. hubbsi* from the group. Suttkus and Mettee (2001) also tentatively recognized *P. metallicus* (Jordan & Meek, 1884) and *P. stonei* (Fowler, 1921), which have previously been considered synonyms of *P. hypselopterus.* We defer recognition of *P. metallicus,* metallic shiner, and *P. stonei,* lowland shiner, pending publication of a separate paper discussing this change (i.e., R. D. Suttkus, B. A. Porter, and B. J. Freeman, in press, Proc. Am. Philos. Soc. 147(4)).

*Pteronotropis grandipinnis.* R. D. Suttkus and M. F. Mettee, 2001, Geological Survey of Alabama Bulletin 170:31, regarded this species, a member of the *P. hypselopterus* complex, as valid and occurring in the Apalachicola River drainage of Florida and southeastern Alabama, but placed it in the genus *Notropis.* See *P. euryzonus.*

*Pteronotropis hubbsi.* See *P. euryzonus.* We include *P. hubbsi* in this genus, rather than *Notropis,* in the belief that it and *P. welaka* are closely related, with *P. welaka* probably being more closely related to this group than to *Notropis.*

*Pteronotropis hypselopterus.* See *P. euryzonus, P. grandipinnis,* and *P. merlini.*

*Pteronotropis merlini.* R. D. Suttkus and M. F. Mettee, 2001, Geological Survey of Alabama Bulletin 170:23, described this species, a member of the *P. hypselopterus* complex, from the upper part of the Choctawhatchee River drainage in Alabama, but placed it in the genus *Notropis.* See *P. euryzonus.*

*Pteronotropis signipinnis.* See *P. euryzonus.*

*Pteronotropis welaka.* See *P. euryzonus* and *P. hubbsi.*

*Ptychocheilus grandis.* Reasons for changing the common names of the four species of *Ptychocheilus* from squawfishes to pikeminnows are given in J. S. Nelson, E. J. Crossman, H. Espinosa-Pérez, C. R. Gilbert, R. N. Lea, and J. D. Williams, 1998, Fisheries 23(9):37. We acknowledge problems with the name pikeminnow in the article and note the desirability of finding a suitable indigenous name. No such name has come to our attention. Other names suggested to the Committee, such as bigmouth minnow, bigmouth chub, or pikefish, are not recommended. The name pikeminnow was proposed by W. Starnes at an AFS/ASIH Fish Names Committee meeting in 1997 in Seattle and also used by him in the draft USGS Vertebrates Checklist.

*Ptychocheilus lucius.* See *P. grandis.* Extirpated from Mexico.

*Ptychocheilus oregonensis.* See *P. grandis.*

*Ptychocheilus umpquae.* See *P. grandis.*

*Rhinichthys atratulus.* Change in common name. See *R. obtusus.*

*Rhinichthys cataractae.* See *Nocomis micropogon* for note on *N. micropogon* × *R. cataractae.* The Nooksack dace is a distinctive form of *R. cataractae* occurring in southwestern British Columbia and western Washington State (J. D. McPhail, 1997, Can. Field-Nat. 111(2):258–262), and *R. cataractae dulcis* (Girard, 1856) is a distinctive form in Wyoming (Gilbert, 1998:73–74).

*Rhinichthys cobitis.* This species was recognized in the 1980 edition as *Tiaroga cobitis.* Reasons for placement in *Rhinichthys* in the 1991 edition are given in Robins et al. (1991:78) and amplified by D. A. Woodman, 1992, Systematic relationships within the cyprinid genus *Rhinichthys,* Pages 374–391 *in* R. L. Mayden, editor, Systematics, historical ecology, and North American freshwater fishes, Stanford University Press, Stanford, California. A. M. Simons and R. L. Mayden, 1999, Copeia 1999(1):13–21, recommended continued placement in *Tiaroga* until relationships are clarified. We provisionally follow the 1991 edition until such additional data are forthcoming. Extirpated from Mexico where it once occurred in the upper Río San Pedro (Gila River drainage) in Mexico (S. M. Norris, personal communication, May 2003, and UMMZ 162682).

*Rhinichthys obtusus.* Recognized as a valid species based on advice of R. E. Jenkins (personal communication, February 2000). This taxon has generally been treated as a subspecies of *R. atratulus,* although information presented in papers such as W. J. Matthews, R. E. Jenkins, and J. T. Styron, 1982, Copeia 1982(4):902–920, and Jenkins and Burkhead (1994), suggested that they may be separate species. This species also includes the nominal species *R. meleagris* Agassiz, 1854, treated by C. L. Smith, 1986 (dated 1985), The inland fishes of New York State, The New York State Department of Environmental Conservation, as a valid species, the western blacknose dace. However, as noted in Jenkins and Burkhead (1994), *R. obtusus* and *R. meleagris* are sister taxa, and we hereby recognize the two as conspecific (both species were described simultaneously by Agassiz in 1854 and D. S. Jordan and C. H. Gilbert, 1883, Synopsis of the fishes of North America, Bulletin of the United States National Museum 16:208, selected *R. obtusus* over *R. meleagris*). *Rhinichthys atratulus*, as now recognized, occurs primarily in Atlantic Slope drainages, from Nova Scotia to South Carolina and Georgia, while *R. obtusus* is found primarily in upper Mississippi and Ohio drainages. Given the recognition of *R. obtusus*, it would be this species of "blacknose dace" that is in Manitoba, Canada (K. W. Stewart, personal communication, November 2002). The common name we recommend for *R. atratulus* in the restricted sense was also used by C. L. Smith. The common name for *R. obtusus* was used by C. L. Smith for the western species and was also recommended by R. M. Bailey (personal communication, November 2002).

*Rhinichthys osculus*. See *R. umatilla*.

*Rhinichthys umatilla*. Usually regarded as a subspecies of *R. osculus*, this taxon, found in southern British Columbia (where it occurs in some areas in sympatry with *R. osculus* but maintains its separate identity), Washington, and Oregon, is recognized here as a valid species based on A. E. Peden and G. W. Hughes, 1988, Can. J. Zool. 66(8):1846–1856, and A. E. Peden and G. W. Hughes, 1989, Can. Field-Nat. 103(2):193–200.

*Scardinius erythrophthalmus*. Occurrence in Canada based on E. J. Crossman et. al., 1992, Can. Field-Nat. 106(2):206–209, and many captures since then in different areas.

### Page 78

*Snyderichthys copei*. A. M. Simons and R. L. Mayden, 1997, Cladistics 13:187–205, presented reasons in their phylogenetic study for raising *Snyderichthys* from a subgenus of *Gila* to a valid genus.

*Yuriria alta*. See *Y. chapalae*.

*Yuriria chapalae*. Formerly regarded as a synonym

of *Y. alta* (Gilbert 1998:58), *Y. chapalae* is recognized in Miller et al. (in press), on the basis of information from C. D. Barbour.

*Catostomus bernardini*. Not seen in the United States (Arizona) since 1967 and considered extirpated, but known in San Bernardino drainage in Mexico from where it could reinvade. It is possible that this sucker will be reintroduced (D. A. Hendrickson and W. R. Radke, personal communication, August 2002).

*Catostomus catostomus*. A distinctive form of the longnose sucker, termed Salish sucker, occurs in southwestern British Columbia and western Washington State (J. D. McPhail, 1987, Can. Field-Nat. 101(2):231–236; J. D. McPhail and E. B. Taylor, 1999, Copeia 1999(4):884–893).

*Catostomus clarkii*. Original spelling ends with -ii. Several species of mountain suckers, namely *C. clarkii*, *C. discobolus*, *C. platyrhynchus*, *C. plebeius*, and *C. santaanae,* form a monophyletic clade and are recognized by some authors in *Pantosteus*; however, as noted by G. R. Smith, 1992, Phylogeny and biogeography of the Catostomidae, freshwater fishes of North America and Asia, Pages 778–826 *in* R. L. Mayden, editor, Systematics, historical ecology, and North American freshwater fishes, Stanford University Press, Stanford, California, this clade cannot be recognized without making the genus *Catostomus* paraphyletic.

*Catostomus commersonii*. Original spelling ends with -ii. Although the original spelling of the specific name is *commersonnii*, a spelling frequently used by early authors, we retain the spelling with one "n," which is in prevailing usage and deemed to be a justified emendation following Article 33.2.3.1 of the Code.

*Catostomus discobolus*. Date of publication correction. Also see *C. clarkii*.

*Catostomus platyrhynchus*. See *C. clarkii*.

*Catostomus plebeius*. See *C. clarkii*.

*Catostomus santaanae*. See *C. clarkii*.

### Page 79

*Chasmistes cujus*. The common name cui-ui is pronounced "kweé-wee".

*Cycleptus elongatus*. See *C. meridionalis*. Populations in the Rio Grande drainage may represent an undescribed species (D. G. Buth and R. L. Mayden, 2001, Copeia 2001(4):899–906).

*Cycleptus meridionalis.* Populations of *C. elongatus* recognized from the Mobile basin of Alabama and Mississippi and the Pascagoula and Pearl river drainages of Mississippi and Louisiana were described as a new species by B. M. Burr and R. L. Mayden, 1999, Bulletin of the Alabama Museum of Natural History 20:44.

*Erimyzon oblongus.* The subspecies *E. oblongus claviformis* (Girard, 1856), western creek chubsucker, from the Gulf Slope, Mississippi Valley, and Great Lakes, is recognized as a valid species in R. M. Bailey, W. C. Latta, and G. R. Smith, in press, An atlas of Michigan fishes with keys and illustrations for their identification, Univ. Mich. Mus. Zool. Spec. Publ. 2. We feel that independent confirmation is required before accepting this proposal.

*Ictiobus niger.* There is a possibility that this species is introduced into Canada and not native.

*Minytrema melanops.* Rarely seen in Canada (Ontario) but is established.

*Moxostoma albidum.* See M. *congestum.*

*Moxostoma anisurum.* See *M. collapsum.*

*Moxostoma ariommum. Scartomyzon,* a subgenus of *Moxostoma,* was raised to generic rank by G. R. Smith, 1992, Phylogeny and biogeography of the Catostomidae, freshwater fishes of North America and Asia, Pages 778–826 *in* R. L. Mayden, editor, Systematics, historical ecology, and North American freshwater fishes, Stanford University Press, Stanford, California, for six species in the 1991 list: *M. ariommum, M. austrinum, M. cervinum, M. congestum, M. lachneri,* and *M. rupiscartes.* However, P. M. Harris and R. L. Mayden, 2002, Mol. Phylogenet. Evol. 20(2):225–237, and P. M. Harris, R. L. Mayden, H. S. Espinosa Pérez, and F. García de León, 2002, J. Fish Biol. 61:1433–1452, suggested that *Scartomyzon* is not a distinct lineage and that its species are within the *Moxostoma* lineage. We do not change the generic placement of the included species from the 1991 list.

*Moxostoma austrinum.* See *M. ariommum.* Parentheses are removed from the author's name (the species was originally described in *Myxostoma,* and parentheses are no longer required according to Article 51.3.1 of the Code). Previously recognized as the west Mexican redhorse, we here drop the inappropriate modifier "west." *Moxostoma mascotae* is considered a separate species based on G.

R. Smith, 1992, Phylogeny and biogeography of the Catostomidae, freshwater fishes of North America and Asia, Pages 778–826 *in* R. L. Mayden, editor, Systematics, historical ecology, and North American freshwater fishes, Stanford University Press, Stanford, California, and P. M. Harris, R. L. Mayden, H. S. Espinosa Pérez, and F. García de León, 2002, J. Fish Biol. 61:1433–1452.

*Moxostoma breviceps.* This species of the Ohio River basin, last listed in the 1960 edition, is elevated from the synonymy of *M. macrolepidotum* on the advice of R. E. Jenkins (personal communication, August 2000), who suggested the common name, and following P. M. Harris, R. L. Mayden, H. S. Espinosa Pérez, and F. García de León, 2002, J. Fish Biol. 61:1433–1452.

*Moxostoma cervinum.* See *M. ariommum.* Common name changed from the misleading "black jumprock" on advice of R. E. Jenkins (personal communication, 2000).

*Moxostoma collapsum.* This species of the Atlantic Slope from Georgia to Virginia, previously listed in the 1960 edition, is elevated from the synonymy of *M. anisurum* on the advice of R. E. Jenkins (personal communication, August 2000), who suggested the common name based on the distinct indentation at each lateral corner of the lower lip, and P. M. Harris and R. L. Mayden, 2002, Mol. Phylogenet. Evol. 20(2):225–237, and following P. M. Harris, R. L. Mayden, H. S. Espinosa Pérez, and F. García de León, 2002, J. Fish Biol. 61:1433–1452.

*Moxostoma congestum.* See *M. ariommum. Moxostoma albidum,* known only from Mexico, was long held to be a subspecies of *M. congestum,* but is recognized as a distinct species based on evidence in P. M. Harris and R. L. Mayden, 2002, Mol. Phylogenet. Evol. 20(2):225–237, and P. M. Harris, R. L. Mayden, H. S. Espinosa Pérez, and F. García de León, 2002, J. Fish Biol. 61:1433–1452; the presence of *M. congestum* in Mexico (the "matalote gris") is now uncertain.

Page 80

*Moxostoma duquesnei.* Although the original spelling of the specific name is *duquesnii,* a spelling used by some authors, we retain the spelling *duquesnei,* which is in prevailing usage and required by the Code whether deemed to be a justified emendation (Article 33.2.3.1) or an incorrect subsequent spelling (Article 33.3.1). As a historical item, R. E. Jenkins (personal communication, October 2000) notes that the species was named after a fort (Fort Duquesne, now Pittsburgh, Pennsylvania, which, in turn, was named after a person, Monsieur Duquesne). See also *M. poecilurum*.

*Moxostoma lacerum.* Recognized in previous editions as *Lagochila lacera*. We accept the latest published evidence of G. R. Smith, 1992, Phylogeny and biogeography of the Catostomidae, freshwater fishes of North America and Asia, Pages 778–826 *in* R. L. Mayden, editor, Systematics, historical ecology, and North American freshwater fishes, Stanford University Press, Stanford, California, that this species should be placed in *Moxostoma*.

*Moxostoma lachneri.* See *M. ariommum*.

*Moxostoma macrolepidotum.* See *M. breviceps* and *M. pisolabrum*.

*Moxostoma pisolabrum.* Elevated from the synonymy of *M. macrolepidotum* based on P. M. Harris, R. L. Mayden, H. S. Espinosa Pérez, and F. García de León, 2002, J. Fish Biol. 61:1433–1452.

*Moxostoma poecilurum.* Parentheses are removed from the author's name. R. E. Jenkins (personal communication, January 2003) has proposed some descriptively appropriate common names for several species of *Moxostoma*, as for example *M. duquesnei* (olive redhorse), *M. poecilurum* (stripetail redhorse), and *M. cervinum* (blacktip jumprock). He also proposed that all species of the subgenus *Scartomyzon* be referred to as jumprocks. Because they required no change from the 1991 list, we have followed his suggestions of common names for *M. albidum* and *M. mascotae*, including the name "jumprock" to indicate their relationship to the Atlantic Slope species of jumprocks. We also have changed the name for *M. cervinum*, but otherwise have adhered to the principle of stability in common names and have not adopted these alternate names.

*Moxostoma robustum.* The species previously recognized as *M. robustum* (Cope, 1870), smallfin redhorse, and as *Scartomyzon robustus* in Mayden et al. (1992) represents an undescribed species of jumprock sucker, *Moxostoma*, referred to as the brassy jump-

rock by R. E. Jenkins (personal communication, 2001), who will describe the species. The name *M. robustum* is transferred to the rediscovered true robust-bodied sucker following Jenkins and Burkhead (1994:491, footnote) and Gilbert (1998:198).

*Moxostoma rupiscartes.* See *M. ariommum*.

*Thoburnia atripinnis.* Formerly classified as a subgenus of *Moxostoma*, *Thoburnia* was raised to generic rank by G. R. Smith, 1992, Phylogeny and biogeography of the Catostomidae, freshwater fishes of North America and Asia, Pages 778–826 *in* R. L. Mayden, editor, Systematics, historical ecology, and North American freshwater fishes, Stanford University Press, Stanford, California, and adopted here. However, acceptance of a monophyletic *Thoburnia*, sister to a monophyletic *Hypentelium*, is not well founded (P. M. Harris, R. L. Mayden, H. S. Espinosa Pérez, and F. García de León, 2002, J. Fish Biol. 61:1433–1452).

*Thoburnia hamiltoni.* See *T. atripinnis*.

*Thoburnia rhothoeca.* See *T. atripinnis*.

*Xyrauchen texanus.* Correction in date of publication follows Gilbert (1998). Extirpated from Mexico (lower Colorado River).

*Astyanax mexicanus.* Correction of spelling of author's name. Synonymized with the more southerly *A. fasciatus* (Cuvier, 1819) in some publications.

### Page 81

*Roeboides bouchellei.* Previously recognized in Mexico as *R. guatemalensis* (Günther, 1864) by several workers. Our listing of *R. bouchellei* as the only species of *Roeboides* present in Mexico is provisional and is based largely on the conclusions of W. A. Bussing, 1998, Freshwater fishes of Costa Rica, Rev. Biol. Trop. 46(Supplement 2):116–122, and R. R. Miller and A. Carr, 1974, Copeia 1974(1):120–125. *Roeboides guatemalensis* is now known only from Panama (W. A. Bussing, personal communication, May 2003). Based on our current knowledge, *R. bouchellei* occurs from southcentral Mexico, from the Usamacinta drainage of the Atlantic Slope, to both slopes of northern Costa Rica.

Ictaluridae. Previous editions have used the common name freshwater catfishes (1948, 1960, and 1970) or bullhead catfishes (1980 and 1991). We now use North American catfishes

(English name) as being more descriptive and similar to that used by many authors. Although there are other catfish families with species in North America, ictalurids are by far the most common. For a discussion of the name "catfishes," see J. S. Nelson, E. J. Crossman, H. Espinosa-Pérez, L. T. Findley, C. R. Gilbert, R. N. Lea, and J. D. Williams, 2002, Fisheries 27(2):38–40.

*Ameiurus brunneus*. Parentheses are removed from the author's name.

*Ictalurus australis*. Recognized following J. G. Lundberg, 1992, The phylogeny of ictalurid catfishes: a synthesis of recent work, Pages 392–420 *in* R. L. Mayden, editor, Systematics, historical ecology, and North American freshwater fishes, Stanford University Press, Stanford, California (p. 393), but we note that Lundberg also indicated (p. 399) that it may be conspecific with *I. punctatus*.

*Ictalurus furcatus*. According to Eschmeyer (1998: Online version, March 2003), the author of this species should be Valenciennes, 1840, and not Lesueur, 1840, with the species originally described as *Pimelodus furcatus* Valenciennes (ex Lesueur) in Cuvier & Valenciennes, 1840. We retain Lesueur, as in the 1960–1991 editions, as being responsible for the description in the interests of nomenclatural stability.

*Ictalurus ochoterenai*. Recognized following J. G. Lundberg, 1992, The phylogeny of ictalurid catfishes: a synthesis of recent work, Pages 392–420 *in* R. L. Mayden, editor, Systematics, historical ecology, and North American freshwater fishes, Stanford University Press, Stanford, California (p. 399), but we note that some consider it a junior synonym of *I. dugesii*.

*Ictalurus pricei*. This species exists in several ponds, in or near the San Bernardino National Wildlife Refuge, Yaqui basin, Arizona, as a result of reintroduction from a stock from the Yaqui basin, Chihuahua, Mexico, obtained about 1987 by Dean Hendrickson and Buddy Jensen. Either progeny reproduced some years later at Uvalde National Fish Hatchery in Texas and/or some of the original stock were then reintroduced in the early 1990s. No reproduction at any of the reintroduction sites has been established (D. A. Hendrickson and W. R. Radke, personal communication, April 2003).

Page 82

*Noturus insignis*. The disjunct nature of this species in Canadian waters suggests that its presence is the result of introduction (N. E. Mandrak, personal communication, April 2003).

*Pylodictis olivaris*. The decision not to list this species from Canada has been controversial. Only two individuals of this catfish are definitely known; it was first reported in Canada (Lake Erie) in 1979, but the only other record we know of is from Lake St. Clair in 2001. However, there are Ohio records of this species from Lake Erie, the oldest of which dates back to 1890. It is possible that its presence in the Lake Erie drainage is natural, but it may also have resulted from introductions.

*Ariopsis felis*. Change in generic placement from *Arius* in the 1991 edition follows general practice (e.g., W. R Taylor, 1987, Bull. Zool. Nomencl. 44(1):31–34). The taxonomy of Castro-Aguirre et al. (1999) is followed in recognizing other species in *Ariopsis* rather than in the Southern Hemisphere genus *Arius*.

Page 83

*Cathorops aguadulce*. *Cathorops* is regarded as a subgenus of *Arius* by some workers. In addition, *C. multiradiatus* (Günther, 1864) and *C. steindachneri* (Gilbert & Starks, 1904) may enter southwestern Chiapas, Mexico.

*Cathorops fuerthii*. See *C. aguadulce*.

*Cathorops melanopus*. See *C. aguadulce*.

*Cathorops spixii*. See *C. aguadulce*.

Doradidae. Added to the list for the species noted.

*Platydoras armatulus*. A doradid thought to be *Platydoras costatus* (Linnaeus, 1758), Guianan striped Raphael, was reported as introduced in Florida (Fuller et al. 1999) and San Felipe Creek, Texas (R. G. Howells, 2001, Texas Parks and Wildlife Department, Management Data Series 188, Austin). It has recently been determined that the San Felipe Creek population is established (G. P. Garrett, personal communication, May 2003). The identity as given is not certain and is based on a Texas specimen sent by R. G. Howells and examined by M. H. Sabaj (personal communication, June 2003). Among nominal forms, the specimen (ANSP 179206) most closely resembles *P. armatulus*. However, uncertainty remains because the genus *Platydoras* is in need of revision.

Pimelodidae. Added to the list for the six species noted.

*Rhamdia guatemalensis.* Although A. M. C. Silfvergrip, 1996, Swedish Museum of Natural History, in a systematic revision of *Rhamdia*, synonymized various species recognized by Mayden et al. (1992) [i.e., *R. guatemalensis* (Günther, 1864) was synonymized with *R. quelen*, and *R. parryi* Eigenmann & Eigenmann, 1888, and *R. reddelli* Miller, 1984, were synonymized with *R. laticauda*], we follow the study of A. Weber and H. Wilkens, 1998, Copeia 1998(4):998–1004, in recognizing five of the species of *Rhamdia* in Mexico, and in addition, we recognize the Pacific Slope species *R. parryi* following Miller et al. (in press).

*Rhamdia laticauda.* See *R. guatemalensis.*

*Rhamdia macuspanensis.* See *R. guatemalensis.*

*Rhamdia parryi.* See *R. guatemalensis.*

*Rhamdia reddelli.* See *R. guatemalensis.*

*Rhamdia zongolicensis.* See *R. guatemalensis.*

Callichthyidae. Added to the list for the species noted.

*Hoplosternum littorale.* Added from information in Fuller et al. (1999), but spelling of specific name corrected following R. E. Reis, 1997, Ichthyological Exploration of Freshwaters 7(4):299–326.

Loricariidae. Change in common name.

*Hypostomus plecostomus.* Correction in date of publication. The identification is highly provisional as L. M. Page, 1994, Fla. Sci. 57(4):171–172, noted that the form in Florida cannot be positively identified to species. In addition, unidentified species of *Hypostomus* are known to be reproducing in Nevada and Texas (L. G. Nico and R. T. Martin, 2001, Southwest. Nat. 46(1):98–104). There are no recent records of *Hypostomus* in Florida, indicating possible extirpation there (Fuller et al. 1999).

*Pterygoplichthys anisitsi.* This species is apparently established and reproducing in the Buffalo Bayou drainage, Houston area, Texas (L. G. Nico and R. T. Martin, 2001, Southwest. Nat. 46(1):98–104). This species and *P. disjunctivus* are very closely related and may be conspecific (L. G. Nico, personal communication, April 2001).

Page 84

*Pterygoplichthys disjunctivus.* L. M. Page, 1994, Fla. Sci. 57(4):171–172, noted that this species is established in Hillsborough County, Florida. Generic placement in *Pterygoplich-*

*thys* instead of *Liposarcus* follows thesis work of J. W. Armbruster noted in Fuller et al. (1999). See *P. anisitsi.*

*Pterygoplichthys multiradiatus.* Addition of Orinoco to the common name (also known in the aquarium trade as the butterfly pleco) after Fuller et al. (1999). See *P. disjunctivus* for generic placement.

*Pterygoplichthys pardalis.* This species is apparently established and reproducing in Lake Julian, a thermally polluted impoundment, Buncombe County, North Carolina (J. W. Armbruster and W. C. Starnes, personal communication, February 2003). The common name is from Fuller et al. (1999).

Gymnotidae. Added to the list for the species noted.

Esociformes. Reasons for recognizing the two included families, listed under Salmoniformes in the 1991 edition, are given in Nelson (1994).

Esocidae. J. A. López, P. Bentzen, and T. W. Pietsch, 2000, Copeia 2000(2):420–431, provided molecular evidence that the families Esocidae and Umbridae, as currently recognized, are paraphyletic. In recognizing the cladistic relationships, they recommended recognizing two subfamilies of Esocidae, with *Esox* and *Novumbra* in Esocinae, and *Dallia* in Dallinae. *Umbra* would be the only genus recognized in Umbridae. Support for *Umbra* being placed in its own family is given in E. J. Crossman and P. Ráb, 2001, Copeia 2001(3):860–865. Other interpretations are possible, and we prefer to await confirmation from other studies before recommending changes in the classification.

*Esox americanus.* Date of publication correction. In this edition, we do not recognize subspecies (even though they are valid—see Principle 7 in the Introduction). Thus, *E. americanus americanus* Gmelin, 1789, redfin pickerel (Fr-brochet d'Amérique), and *E. americanus vermiculatus* Lesueur, 1846, grass pickerel (Fr-brochet vermiculé), are recognized under the species name. The common name redfin pickerel, as used for the nominate subspecies, is also recommended as the common name for the species.

Umbridae. See Esocidae.

*Umbra limi.* Although a publication date of 1841 is given in Eschmeyer (1998:907) and Eschmeyer (1998: Online version, February 2002), the publication date for Volume 3 (1 and 2) of the Boston Journal of Natural History appears to be 1840, as determined by C. R. Gilbert and as in the 1991 edition.

Argentiniformes. We accept the phylogenetic implications of G. D. Johnson and C. Patterson, 1996, Relationships of lower euteleostean fishes, Pages 251–332 *in* M. L. J. Stiassny, L. R. Parenti, and G. D. Johnson, editors, Interrelationships of fishes, Academic Press, San Digeo, California, and recognize this new ordinal name for the three families recognized here (they were given in the 1991 edition under Salmoniformes, and Nelson (1994) placed them and the Osmeridae in the Osmeriformes). The above authors also regarded the Bathylagidae as a subfamily of Microstomatidae. It is because these two families are sister taxa that we view this action, while acceptable, as subjective and provisionally retain family recognition for the bathylagids as in the previous edition.

*Argentina silus.* Parentheses are added to the author's name.

*Argentina striata.* Date of publication correction.

Page 85

Bathylagidae. See Argentiniformes.

*Leuroglossus schmidti.* *Leuroglossus* is considered to be a junior synonym of *Bathylagus* by some authors.

*Leuroglossus stilbius.* See *L. schmidti.*

Salmoniformes. See Esociformes and Argentiniformes.

Osmeridae. See Argentiniformes.

*Hypomesus olidus.* Occasionally enters brackish water (Mecklenburg et al. 2002).

*Hypomesus pretiosus.* Date of publication correction. Occurs in brackish water in United States and Canada, and very rarely in lowermost reaches of rivers in some areas.

*Osmerus mordax.* E. B. Taylor and P. Bentzen, 1993, Evolution 47:813–832 and Molecular Ecology 2:345–357, and E. B. Taylor, 2001, Can. Field-Nat. 115(1):131–137, noted that a freshwater dwarf rainbow smelt and an anadromous normal-sized rainbow smelt occur sympatrically and are reproductively isolated in Lake Utopia, New Brunswick. The two forms appear to coexist elsewhere in similar circumstances. The dwarf form has been recognized as *O. spectrum* Cope, 1870, the pygmy smelt ("éperlan nain" in French), but taxonomic recognition is not recommended

because of apparent multiple independent origins of the dwarf form. Also, E. B. Taylor and J. J. Dodson, 1994, Mol. Ecol. 3:235–248, recognized *O. dentex*, the Arctic smelt (North Pacific and Arctic waters) as a separate species from *O. mordax* (eastern North America). The two are regarded as sister species and together are the sister taxon to the European *O. eperlanus*. We defer recognizing *O. dentex* pending seeing arguments as to why it should be recognized at the species level versus subspecies level.

Salmonidae. Some workers (e.g., C. P. J. Sanford, 1990, Bull. Br. Mus. (Nat. Hist.) Zool. 56(2):145–153; C. P. J. Sanford, 2000, Theses Zoologicae Volume 33, Koeltz Scientific Books, Koenigstein, Germany; and G. D. Johnson and C. Patterson, 1996, Relationships of lower euteleostean fishes, Pages 251–332 *in* M. L. J. Stiassny, L. R. Parenti, and G. D. Johnson, editors, Interrelationships of fishes, Academic Press, San Digeo, California) recognize the families Coregonidae and Salmonidae (to include graylings, which are recognized in Thymallidae by some workers such as Y. S. Reshetnikov, N. G. Bogutskaya, E. D. Vasil'eva, E. A. Dorofeeva, A. M. Naseka, O. A. Popova, K. A. Savvaitova, V. G. Sideleva, and L. I. Sokolov, 1997, An annotated checklist of the freshwater fishes of Russia, J. Ichthyol. 37(9):687–736). However, we regard this as a subjective splitting, not as a cladistic requirement, and see more merit in recognizing the one family (finer relationships can be expressed with the use of lower categories such as subfamily and tribe).

*Coregonus artedi.* In the 1991 edition, this was the one species given two common names; we now use only the name cisco, the one first listed and more commonly used, and drop the name lake herring, although giving "cisco de lac" in French (caution must be used to avoid confusion as to whether reference is being made to this species or to any other species of ciscoes). Anadromous populations are known in large river systems entering James and Hudson bays (L. Bernatchez and J. J. Dodson, 1990, Can. J. Fish. Aquat. Sci. 47:533–543); other species of northern ciscoes, such as the Arctic cisco, may also move into brackish water along the Arctic Coast. J. Turgeon and L. Bernatchez, 2003, Conservation Genetics 4:67–81, proposed that all ciscoes in central Canada and northern United States (e.g., *C. zenithicus* and the Great Lakes endemics) be recognized as *C. artedi*. We accept that postglacial reticulate evolution combined with independent evolution of similar phenotypes has occurred and that not all populations of what has been called *C. zenithicus,* sometimes occurring sympatrically with *C. artedi*, are conspecific. Although they failed to find adequate differences in mitochondrial and microsatellite markers in recognizing species (of extant taxa, *C. kiyi* and *C. reighardi* were not studied) even in the Great Lakes, we prefer to wait for other detailed taxonomic studies before regarding six listed species as conspecific with *C. artedi*. *Coregonus nipigon* (Koelz, 1925), Nipigon cisco, listed in the 1960 and 1970 editions but regarded as a synonym of *C. artedi* in the 1980 edition, was recognized as valid by D. A. Etnier and C. E. Skelton, 2003, Copeia 2003(4):739–749; this publication was received after the list was in press.

*Coregonus clupeaformis*. Several nominal species are probably conspecific with this species, but they could prove to be valid (e.g., *C. nelsonii* Bean, 1884, the Alaska whitefish, which is recognized as a valid species by Page and Burr [1991] and Mecklenburg et al. [2002]).

*Coregonus hoyi*. Change of author from (Gill, 1872). As noted in Eschmeyer (1998:746), the situation is complicated. See *C. artedi*.

Page 86

*Coregonus nigripinnis.* There is a question of authorship of this species, given in the 1991 edition as (Gill, 1872); Eschmeyer (1998:1180) noted it may be Hoy (ex Gill) or Milner, 1874. The 1870–1872 paper by Hoy did not describe any species but gave Gill as the author of *C. nigripinnis*; however, Gill's manuscript was not published, and based on information from W. N. Eschmeyer (personal communication, November 2000), we consider Milner's 1874 paper as the first valid description. Considered extinct in the 1991 edition, this species is extirpated from the Great Lakes, but populations that may be of this species are extant in Lake Nipigon and possibly in other localities in central Canada (J. Turgeon, A. Estoup, and L. Bernatchez, 1999, Evolution 53(6):1857–1871; T. N. Todd, personal communication, 1999). See *C. artedi*.

*Coregonus pidschian*. Date of publication correction.

*Coregonus reighardi*. This Great Lakes species is now considered extinct (S. A. Webb and T. N. Todd, 1995, Arch. Hydrobiol., Spec. Issues Advanc. Limnol. 46:71–77).

*Coregonus zenithicus*. See *C. artedi*.

*Oncorhynchus chrysogaster*. The Pacific trouts were placed in the genus *Parasalmo* by Y. S. Reshetnikov et al., 1997, An annotated checklist of the freshwater fishes of Russia, J. Ichthyol. 37(9):687–736; a taxonomic move we do not follow.

*Oncorhynchus clarkii*. Original spelling ends with -ii. See *O. chrysogaster*.

*Oncorhynchus gilae*. R. J. Behnke, 1992, Native trout of western North America, American Fisheries Society, Monograph 6, Bethesda, Maryland, and R. F. Stearley and G. R. Smith, 1993, Trans. Am. Fish. Soc. 122:1–33, recognized *O. apache* (Miller, 1972), Apache trout (which was included in the 1991 edition of the present list), as a subspecies of *O. gilae*, *O. gilae apache*. We accept this change, consistent with the implications in the overview of F. M. Utter and F. W. Allendorf, 1994, Conserv. Biol. 8(3):864–867, and J. L. Nielsen, M. C. Fountain, J. Campoy-Favela, K. Cobble, and B. Jensen, 1998, Environ. Biol. Fishes 51:7–23, while recognizing the need for further taxonomic work and the need for separate management of the two subspecies. See *O. chrysogaster* and *O. mykiss*.

*Oncorhynchus gorbuscha*. Change in distribution; we lack evidence that this species is established on the Atlantic Coast, but it is established in the Great Lakes (Fuller et al. 1999).

*Oncorhynchus kisutch*. Change in distribution; we lack evidence that this species is established on the Atlantic Coast, but there is reproduction in some Atlantic coastal waters and in the Great Lakes (Fuller et al. 1999). Eschmeyer (1998:837) noted that the original spelling of the specific name was *hisutch/hisatch/kisatch*. As required by the current Code, we continue using the younger name *O. kisutch* (Walbaum, 1792). We know of no use of the senior names after 1899 (Article 23.9.1), and the junior name has been used extensively, exceeding the requirements of Article 23.9.2.

*Oncorhynchus mykiss*. The term steelhead is applied to sea-run rainbow trout and some populations from large lakes in eastern North America where they were introduced. We do not endorse the term "steelhead salmon." R. J. Behnke, 1992, Native trout of western North America, American Fisheries Society, Monograph 6, Bethesda, Maryland, recognized three major groups of rainbow trout: (i) a redband trout of the upper Columbia and upper Fraser River basins, with lake populations commonly called Kamloops trout; (ii) redband trout of the Sacramento River basin, including what was recognized in the 1991 edition of the present list as *O. aguabonita* (Jordan, 1892; date of publication corrected from 1893), golden trout, but now recognized by us as a subspecies, *O. mykiss aguabonita* (also recognized as such by R. F. Stearley and G. R. Smith, 1993, Trans. Am. Fish. Soc. 122:1–33); and (iii) coastal rainbow trout. As with some other trouts, this species has been widely introduced outside its native range (including successful introductions of *O. mykiss aguabonita* outside its native range of the Kern River system in California, in areas such as in Wyoming and Alberta). In accepting the above work of Behnke, we stress that arguments exist for and against the "lumping" of the variable Pacific trout taxa, and future work may require changes to be made. As with *O. gilae* (see above), we recognize the need for separate management of rainbow trout populations. See *O. chrysogaster*.

*Oncorhynchus nerka*. Lacustrine stocks of sockeye salmon are known as kokanee (Fr-kokani, the only one known in Quebec).

*Oncorhynchus tshawytscha*. Reasons for treating the common name as a proper noun and spelling it with a capital letter are given in J. S. Nelson, E. J. Crossman, H. Espinosa-Pérez, L. T. Findley, C. R. Gilbert, R. N. Lea, and J. D. Williams, 2003, Fisheries 28(7):38–39. For help and information on this matter, we acknowledge M. S. Bagdovitz and Chief Cliff Snider (personal communication, July 2001).

*Prosopium coulterii*. Original spelling ends with *-ii*.

*Prosopium cylindraceum*. Change of author from Pallas.

*Salmo salar*. Atlantic salmon are established on the Pacific Coast (J. P. Volpe, B. R. Anholt, and B. W. Glickman, 2001, Can. J. Fish. Aquat. Sci. 58:1–11). Lake populations of Atlantic

salmon are variously known as ouananiche (Fr-ouananiche), lake Atlantic salmon, landlocked salmon, and Sebago salmon.

*Salvelinus alpinus*. The alternate spellings char and charr are used by various authors as the common name for the genus *Salvelinus*, with an appropriate modifier for various species. We are aware that both valid and invalid reasons, in our opinion, are put forth in defense of one or the other orthography, often invoking historical origins of the word that seem debatable. We recommend the simpler spelling char, but acknowledge that some authors/editors will prefer the spelling "charr." Several nominal species may prove to be valid, but are probably conspecific (as advised by C. C. Wilson, personal communication, 1999) with either *S. alpinus* (e.g., *S. aureolus* Bean, 1887, the Sunapee trout [= blueback trout and Quebec red trout], recognized as a valid species by Fuller et al. 1999), or with *S. malma* (e.g., *S. anaktuvukensis* Morrow, 1973, the Angayukaksurak char, recognized as a valid species by Page and Burr 1991).

*Salvelinus confluentus*. Date of publication correction.

*Salvelinus fontinalis*. The extinct *S. agassizii* (Garman, 1885), silver trout, of New Hampshire, considered here to be a subspecies of brook trout, may be a valid species (C. C. Wilson, personal communication, 1999).

*Stenodus leucichthys*. Correction of spelling of author's name. There is good evidence to support inclusion of the inconnu in the genus *Coregonus* (M. Hamada, M. Himberg, R. A. Bodaly, J. D. Reist, and N. Okada, 1998, Arch. Hydrobiol. Spec. Issues Advanc. Limnol. 50:383–389). However, until evidence is published showing its sister-group relationship within *Coregonus*, we prefer to retain it in *Stenodus*.

## Page 87

Sternoptychidae. Added to the list for the species noted.

*Maurolicus weitzmani*. This new species was described from off the southeastern United States by N. V. Parin and S. G. Kobyliansky, 1993, Transactions Institute Oceanology (Russia) 128:95. The common name was suggested in discussion with A. S. Harold (personal communication, 2001).

*Polyipnus clarus.* This new species was described from off the southeastern United States by A. S. Harold, 1994, Bull. Mar. Sci. 54(2):488. The common name was suggested by K. E. Hartel (personal communication, July 2001).

Phosichthyidae. Eschmeyer (1998:2074) noted that the correct spelling of the type genus is the less descriptive *Phosichthys* (Phosichthyidae) and not *Photichthys*. While continued use of the spelling Photichthyidae, by Nelson (1994) and researchers such as A. S. Harold and S. H. Weitzman (personal communication, 1999), might be justified in the interest of stability of past common usage, we use the spelling Phosichthyidae as appearing in several recent publications. Recognized in the family Gonostomatidae (lightfishes, this common name now applied to the Phosichthyidae) in the 1991 edition (the Gonostomatidae as currently recognized has no species in our area of coverage, which includes occurrence at 200 m or less). Strays and early life history stages of additional species of this family may occasionally occur over the continental shelf.

Stomiidae. A number of oceanic species in this and other families normally occur much deeper than 200 m during the day, but migrate above 200 m at night and may occur as strays over our continental shelf. This list thus is somewhat arbitrary, as are those for other mesopelagic fishes. See Myctophidae.

*Aulopus filamentosus.* B. A. Thompson, S. W. Ross, and K. Sulak, in a 2002 manuscript (personal communication, July 2002), provided evidence that *A. nanae* Mead, 1958, is a junior synonym of *A. filamentosus*; this was also adopted by Smith-Vaniz et al. (1999). The common name remains unchanged.

Page 88

*Synodus intermedius.* Correction of author.

*Synodus saurus.* This addition was reported from the Florida Middle Grounds, off the west coast of Florida by G. B. Smith, H. M. Austin, S. A. Bortone, R. W. Hastings, and L. H. Ogren, 1975, Fla. Mar. Res. Publ. 9:1–14, but was overlooked in the 1980 and 1991 editions.

Paralepididae. Spelling of family name corrected.

*Arctozenus risso.* Recognized in *Notolepis* in the 1991 edition, but placed in *Arctozenus* by A. Post *in* O. Gon and P. C. Heemstra, editors, 1990, Fishes of the southern ocean, J. L. B.

Smith Institute of Ichthyology, Grahamstown, South Africa. Original spelling of specific name followed here as required by the Code. Date of publication correction.

*Magnisudis atlantica.* Recognized in *Paralepis* in the 1991 edition, A. Post, 1987, Arch. Fischwiss. 38(1/2):75–131, and A. Post *in* O. Gon and P. C. Heemstra, editors, 1990, Fishes of the southern ocean, J. L. B. Smith Institute of Ichthyology, Grahamstown, South Africa, placed this species in *Magnisudis.* Date of publication correction.

*Anotopterus nikparini.* Recognition of this species in the North Pacific as separate from *A. pharao* is based on E. I. Kukuev, 1998, J. Ichthyol. 38(9):716–729, and followed by Mecklenburg et al. (2002).

Myctophidae. This list is somewhat arbitrary, as are those for mesopelagic or oceanic fishes of other families, because of the uncertainty of which species regularly occur within the 200-m continental shelf contour. Other species could be added, including the Atlantic *Ceratoscopelus maderensis* (Lowe, 1839), *Diaphus dumerilii* (Bleeker, 1856), *D. garmani* Gilbert, 1906, and *D. taaningi* Norman, 1930 (K. E. Hartel, personal communication, July 2001); the Pacific *Nannobrachium ritteri* (Gilbert, 1915) and more than 21 other species; and at least 9 additional species from Pacific Mexico (L. T. Findley, personal communication, June 2001). Although it is known which ones regularly occur above 200-m bottom depth and over the continental shelf, it is difficult to know which ones may be strays. See Anomalopidae below for comment on term flashlightfish used for some myctophids.

*Benthosema glaciale.* This common Atlantic species may also occur in our area in the Pacific portion of the Arctic Ocean (Mecklenburg et al. 2002).

*Diogenichthys laternatus.* Generic name misspelled as *Diogenys* in 1991 edition.

Page 89

*Nannobrachium regale.* Formerly recognized as *Lampanyctus regalis*; change in genus follows B. J. Zahuranec, 2000, Smithson. Contrib. Zool. 607.

*Notoscopelus resplendens.* Added to the Atlantic fauna based on information from K. E. Hartel (personal communication, July 2001).

Lampridiformes. This taxon was placed between the Atheriniformes and Beryciformes in the 1991 edition; reasons for considering it the sister group to all remaining acanthomorphs are given in Nelson (1994). For change in spelling, see Lamprididae.

Lamprididae. Spelling of family and ordinal names corrected following C. Patterson, 1993, Bull. Mar. Sci. 52(1):168–169, and current usage.

*Lophotus capellei.* M. T. Craig, P. A. Hastings and D. J. Pontella II, 2003, Pages 124–125 *in* American Society of Ichthyologists and Herpetologists (ASIH), Program book and abstracts, Manaus, Brazil, (and Bull. South. Calif. Acad. Sci., in press), presented evidence that the North Pacific population of *Lophotus* is specifically distinct from those in both the South Pacific and Atlantic oceans. They further determined that *L. capellei* Temminck & Schlegel, 1845, is the oldest available name for the North Pacific species.

*Lophotus lacepede.* Distribution change. See *L. capellei.*

*Desmodema polystictum.* Date of publication correction.

*Zu cristatus.* Date of publication correction.

### Page 90

*Regalecus glesne.* Parentheses are removed from the author's name. Two other nominal species reported from Pacific Mexico, *R. kinoi* Castro-Aguirre, Arvizu-Martinez, & Alarcón-González, 1991, and *R. russellii* Cuvier, 1816, are provisionally treated as synonyms of *R. glesne.*

Polymixiiformes. See Beryciformes below.

Percopsiformes. The Amblyopsidae, placed in the Percopsiformes in the 1991 edition, was thought to have its relationships within the Anacanthini, possibly near the Ophidiiformes, by A. M. Murray and M. V. H. Wilson, 1999, Pages 397–411 *in* G. Arratia and H.-P. Schultze, editors, Mesozoic fishes 2—systematics and the fossil record, Verlag Dr. Friedrich Pfeil, München. We defer removing it from the Percopsiformes and placing it in its own order, pending confirmation of its relationships.

*Amblyopsis rosae.* Date of publication correction.

*Forbesichthys agassizii.* Previously recognized as *Chologaster agassizi.* We recognize the spring cavefish as *F. agassizii* following Page and Burr (1991; but who used the preoccu-

pied name *Forbesella*), R. L. Mayden et al. (1992), and, with reasons given, D. A. Etnier and W. C. Starnes, 1994 (dated 1993), The fishes of Tennessee, The University of Tennessee, Knoxville.

Ophidiiformes. The recognition of this order separate from the Gadiformes follows general usage (e.g., J. G. Nielsen, D. M. Cohen, D. F. Markle, and C. R. Robins, 1999, FAO species catalogue, Volume 18, Ophidiiform fishes of the world (Order Ophidiiformes), FAO Fish. Synop. 125(18)).

### Page 91

*Brotula barbata.* Correction of author and addition of modifier to common name.

*Neobythites gilli.* Added to the list based on J. G. Nielsen, 1999, Bull. Mar. Sci. 64(2):335–372, who listed numerous records from shallower than 200 m from the Gulf of Mexico.

*Neobythites marginatus.* Added on the basis of one record (73 m) off North Carolina (UF 212327) and as reported by J. G. Nielsen, 1999, Bull. Mar. Sci. 64(2):335–372. This species normally occurs deeper than 200 m and usually deeper than *N. gilli.*

*Ophidion antipholus.* The holotype of the previously listed species *O. beani* Jordan & Gilbert, 1883, is identified as *O. holbrookii.* The species known as the longnose cusk-eel was described by R. N. Lea and C. R. Robins, 2003, Sci. Pap. Nat. Hist. Mus. Univ. Kans. 31:1–9. *Ophidion antipholus* is the new replacement name referred to since the 1970 edition as *O. beani.*

*Ophidion dromio.* This new species, known in our area from the western Atlantic and Gulf of Mexico, was described by R. N. Lea and C. R. Robins, 2003, Sci. Pap. Nat. Hist. Mus. Univ. Kans. 31:1–9.

*Ophidion grayi.* Literature records of *O. grayi* from off the Yucatan Peninsula are based on a transcription error of latitude in the museum catalog and specimen label (TU 82180). The corrected locality is off Louisiana (J. H. Caruso and H. L. Bart, Jr., personal communication, August 2002).

*Ophidion holbrookii.* Parentheses are removed from the author's name (*Ophidium* an unjustified emendation) and original spelling ends with *-ii.*

*Ophidion josephi. Ophidion welshi* (Nichols & Breder, 1922), recognized in previous lists, is probably a synonym of this species (J. G. Nielsen, D. M. Cohen, D. F. Markle, and C. R. Robins, 1999, FAO species catalogue, Volume 18, Ophidiiform fishes of the world (Order Ophidiiformes), FAO Fish. Synop. 125(18).

### Page 92

*Ophidion robinsi.* This new species was described by M. P. Fahay, 1992, Copeia 1992(3):801. The common name was suggested by C. R. Robins.

*Otophidium omostigma.* Specific name modified from *O. omostigmum,* based on J. G. Nielsen, D. M. Cohen, D. F. Markle, and C. R. Robins, 1999, FAO species catalogue, Volume 18, Ophidiiform fishes of the world (Order Ophidiiformes), FAO Fish. Synop. 125(18).

*Calamopteryx robinsorum.* Known depth of occurrence above 200 m not definite.

*Grammonus claudei.* Correction of spelling of author's name. As noted in Eschmeyer and Bailey (1990) and Eschmeyer (1998), *Oligopus*, previously used for *O. claudei* and *O. diagrammus*, is apparently a synonym of *Pteraclis* (Bramidae). *Grammonus* (versus *Oligopodus*, of which *Oligopus* may be a junior objective synonym) is probably the appropriate name.

*Grammonus diagrammus.* See *G. claudei* for note on generic placement.

*Ogilbia cayorum.* Date of publication correction.

*Ogilbia pearsei.* Placed in the genus *Typhliasina* by some authors.

Gadiformes. See Ophidiiformes above.

*Caelorinchus scaphopsis.* Inadvertently omitted from previous lists. A specimen from off Santa Catalina Island, California, from 183 m, reported by T. Iwamoto, 1978, Proc. Calif. Acad. Sci. 41(2):307–337.

*Macrourus berglax.* Date of publication correction.

### Page 93

*Malacocephalus occidentalis.* Added to the list on the basis of two confirmed U.S. records off Florida (UF 46776 at 200 m and UF 228270 at 185.5–192.5 m).

*Nezumia bairdii.* Original spelling ends with -*ii.*

Steindachneriidae. See Gadidae below.

Moridae. *Gadella imberbis* (Vaillant, 1888), placed in the genus *Brosmiculus* by some workers, may occur in our area off the Atlantic Coast, based on UF 46782 and MCZ 75980 and 99522 records, but we await better depth information.

*Laemonema barbatulum.* Added to the list on the basis of at least nine confirmed U.S. records off Florida, taken at an overall depth range of 73–198 m (specimens in UF collection).

Bregmacerotidae. One undescribed species of this family, formerly confused with *Bregmaceros mcclellandii* Thompson, 1840, of the Indian Ocean, may belong in our area off the Atlantic Coast (A. S. Harold, personal communication, March 2002).

*Bregmaceros cantori.* Added to the list on the basis of records from shallower than 200 m off the Atlantic Coast (A. S. Harold and K. E. Hartel, personal communication, March 2002) and in the northern Gulf of Mexico (W. F. Smith-Vaniz and G. D. Dennis, personal communication, January 2002). The common name is based on the description of preserved specimens in D. M. Milliken and E. D. Houde, 1984, Bull. Mar. Sci. 35(1):11–19 and McEachran and Fechhelm (1998:752).

Phycidae. See Gadidae below.

*Ciliata septentrionalis.* See Gadidae below.

*Enchelyopus cimbrius.* See Gadidae below.

*Urophycis chesteri.* Placed in the genus *Phycis* by many recent authors.

*Urophycis cirrata.* The term "Gulf" in the common name is treated as a proper noun, and we infer that the name was originally proposed for the species' occurrence in the Gulf of Mexico.

*Urophycis earllii.* Original spelling ends with -*ii.*

### Page 94

Merlucciidae. See Gadidae below.

*Merluccius hernandezi.* According to D. M. Cohen, T. Inada, T. Iwamoto, and N. Scialabba, 1990, FAO species catalogue, Volume 10, Gadiform fishes of the world (Order Gadiformes), FAO Fish. Synop. 125(10), the taxonomic status of this species is uncertain.

Gadidae. Some species in this family in the 1991 edition are now included in Steindachneriidae, Phycidae, and Merlucciidae, based largely on the works of D. F. Markle (e.g., 1989) and G. J. Howes, and as summarized in Nelson (1994). Some authors (e.g., Eschmeyer 1998), based on a 1991 study of G. J. Howes, recognize the family Lotidae to include a number of genera here placed in either the Gadidae (*Brosme, Lota,* and *Molva*) or Phycidae (*Ciliata* and *Enchelyopus*). We prefer to wait for confirming studies before making these changes.

*Arctogadus borisovi*. Correction of author's name.

*Arctogadus glacialis*. Date of publication correction.

*Brosme brosme*. See Gadidae.

*Gadus ogac*. S. M. Carr, D. S. Kivlichan, P. Pepin, and D. C. Crutcher, 1999, Can. J. Zool. 77:19–26, provided evidence from mtDNA analysis that this species should be considered a junior synonym of *Gadus macrocephalus*, but we await independent confirmation before making this change.

*Lota lota*. See Gadidae.

*Micromesistius poutassou*. Date of publication correction.

*Molva molva*. See Gadidae.

### Page 95

*Opsanus beta*. Date of publication correction. The term "Gulf" in the common name is treated as a proper noun, and we infer that the name was originally proposed for the species' occurrence in the Gulf of Mexico.

*Opsanus pardus*. Date of publication correction.

*Lophiodes spilurus*. Previously known from Mexican waters, this species has been reported by R. N. Lea, T. Keating, G. Van Dykhuizen, and P. B. Lehtonen, 1983, Calif. Fish Game 70(4):250–251, from off California but in depths beyond 200 m. A specimen collected by the Los Angeles County Sanitation District on the Palos Verdes Shelf, 135–142 m, was taken in February 1999. We apply the common name threadfin goosefish from previous usage.

*Lophius americanus*. Called "monkfish" as a food fish.

*Lophius gastrophysus*. Correction of author's name.

### Page 96

*Antennarius striatus*. Correction of author from Shaw & Nodder.

*Dibranchus atlanticus*. Date of publication correction.

*Ogcocephalus cubifrons*. M. G. Bradbury, 1980, Proc. Calif. Acad. Sci. 42:229–285, gave reasons, which we accept, why *O. radiatus* (Mitchill, 1818) should be considered a *nomen dubium* and proposed using the next available name, *O. cubifrons*.

*Ogcocephalus nasutus*. Correction of author and date of publication.

*Himantolophus sagamius*. An exceptionally large specimen (380 mm SL) of this deep-sea species was found in the surf-zone at Del Mar, San Diego County, California in December 2001 (C. Klepadlo, P. A. Hastings, and R. H. Rosenblatt, 2003, Bull. South. Calif. Acad. Sci. 102(3):99–106).

*Cryptopsaras couesii*. Original spelling ends with -*ii*.

Mugiliformes. The one family, Mugilidae, was placed in Perciformes in the 1991 edition. Studies by such workers as M. L. J. Stiassny and G. D. Johnson suggest that it is related to the Atherinomorpha (see Nelson 1994, for references).

*Agonostomus monticola*. Date of publication correction.

### Page 97

*Mugil gyrans*. In the 1991 edition, it was felt that *M. trichodon*, originally described from Cuba, was extralimital. However, McEachran and Fechhelm (1998) noted both species off Florida and in the Gulf of Mexico. We recognize both species until a published paper demonstrates otherwise. However, we use the name whirligig mullet for *M. gyrans* (versus fantail mullet as in the 1991 edition) and fantail mullet for *M. trichodon*, as used in numerous publications over many decades; it seems probable that *M. gyrans* is the young of another species (including possibly *M. trichodon*; I. J. Harrison and W. F. Smith-Vaniz, personal communication, August 2000). We concur with Drs. Harrison and Smith-Vaniz that the common names should be used as noted above, especially considering the nomenclatural and taxonomic problems in this group.

*Mugil* species. Called *M. gaimardianus* Desmarest, 1831, in the 1991 edition; as noted by Eschmeyer 1998:626, this name has been placed on the Official Index of Rejected and Invalid Specific Names in Zoology Opinion 1787, Bulletin of Zoological Nomenclature 51(3) for 1994. L. Alvarez-Lachochere, E. Trewavas, and G. J. Howes, 1992, Bulletin of Zoological Nomenclature 49:271–275, proposed *M. gaimardianus* as a *nomen dubium* because it cannot be applied with certainty to any taxon. Those authors state that *M. gaimardianus* is based only on an inadequate illustration of a specimen from Cuba. The illustration is similar to *M. curema* and *M. trichodon*. A new name, if warranted, has not been proposed; many references to *M. gaimardianus* are misidentifications of *M. curema* (I. J. Harrison, personal communication, September 2000). Rather than deleting the redeye mullet from our list, we make an exception here of listing an unnamed species because of the possibility that this presumed taxon given in the 1991 edition does exist as an undescribed species and could be what Desmarest had before him.

*Mugil trichodon.* See *M. gyrans*.

Atheriniformes. Formal recognition of the Beloniformes and Cyprinodontiformes as separate orders follows the practice of most workers (see Nelson 1994, for references).

Atherinopsidae. See Atherinidae below. Miller et al. (in press) synonymyze *Chirostoma* and *Poblana* with *Menidia*.

### Page 98

*Membras gilberti.* Castro-Aguirre et al. (1999) noted occurrence in Mexico in two estuarine areas bordering the Gulf of California. One of these areas was the Río Mulegé (= Río Santa Rosalia) Estuary, Baja California Sur, with four specimens, USNM 121845, and recorded by L. P. Schultz, 1948, Proc. U.S. Nat. Mus. 98(3220):1–48. These specimens have not been examined to verify their identification (B. Chernoff, personal communication, June 2003), and this listing is provisional.

*Membras martinica.* Distribution change based on voucher specimens in Florida Museum of Natural History collected by C. R. Gilbert well up the St. Johns River in Florida.

*Menidia audens.* We provisionally accept the conclusions of B. A. Thompson and R. D. Suttkus, (1999, American Society of Ichthyologists and Herpetologists [ASIH], Program book and abstracts, Pennsylvania State University, State College [p. 219]) and R. D. Suttkus and B. A. Thompson, 2002, Southeastern Fishes Council Procedings, No. 44:6–10, that this is a valid taxon, separate from *M. beryllina*. It was recognized in the 1960 and 1970 editions.

*Menidia beryllina.* Date of publication correction.

### Page 99

*Menidia conchorum.* Although C. F. Duggins, A. A. Karlin, K. Relyea, and R. W. Yerger, 1986, Tulane Stud. Zool. Bot. 25(2):133–150, recommended that this species be considered a junior synonym of *M. peninsulae*, based on

the absence of electrophoretic differences, we recognize it pending more detailed studies.

Atherinidae. New World silversides are recognized in their own family, Atherinopsidae, separate from the Atherinidae, following B. S. Dyer and B. Chernoff, 1996, Zool. J. Linn. Soc. 117:1–69, and B. S. Dyer, 1998, Pages 519–536 *in* L. R. Malabarba, R. E. Reis, R. P. Vari, Z. M. S. Lucena, and C. A. S. Lucena, editors, Phylogeny and classification of neotropical fishes, Edipucrs, Porto Alegre, Brazil. Change in common name from silversides is a result of change in composition of the family.

*Atherinomorus stipes.* Date of publication correction.

Beloniformes. See Atheriniformes above.

*Tylosurus acus.* Opinion 900, Bulletin of Zoological Nomenclature 26(5/6), April 1970, resulted in suppression of the name *T. acus*, with *T. imperialis* (Rafinesque, 1810) now considered to be the senior name. However, in an analysis of name usage, B. B. Collette (personal communication, April 2003) found that almost all authors continue to use the specific name "*acus*," as earlier advocated by B. B. Collette and F. H. Berry, 1965, Copeia 1965(3):391. In the interest of stability and with the advice of W. N. Eschmeyer (personal communication, April 2003), we continue to use the specific name as used in this list since 1960 (the type locality for *T. acus* is the West Indies, while that for *T. imperialis* is the Mediterranean). It is our understanding that the ICZN will be petitioned to repeal Opinion 900. We add the modifier "Atlantic" to the common name. See *T. pacificus*.

*Tylosurus crocodilus.* Correction of spelling of author's name.

*Tylosurus pacificus.* Formerly recognized as a subspecies of *T. acus* and known from the Gulf of California southward, B. B. Collette and H. M. Banford, 2001, Rev. Biol. Trop. 49 (Supplement 1):51–57, give reasons for recognizing it as a full species.

*Cololabis saira.* Date of publication correction.

### Page 100

Exocoetidae. The recognition of halfbeaks in their own family, Hemiramphidae, follows the practice of most workers, including Nelson (1994).

*Cheilopogon cyanopterus.* N. V. Parin, 1961, Tr. Inst. Okeanol. Akad. Nauk. SSSR 43:92–183, divided *Cypselurus* into two genera, *Cyp-*

*selurus* and *Cheilopogon*, with all species recognized as *Cypselurus* in the 1991 edition now in *Cheilopogon*, except for *C. comatus*. This classification continues to be used by N. V. Parin, 2003 (dated 2002), Exocoetidae (flyingfishes), Pages 1116–1134 *in* K. E. Carpenter, editor, The living marine resources of the western central Atlantic, FAO species identification guide for fishery purposes, Volume 2, FAO, Rome, and by other specialists of the group such as B. B. Collette (personal communication, July 2002).

*Cheilopogon exsiliens*. See *C. cyanopterus*.

*Cheilopogon furcatus*. See *C. cyanopterus*.

*Cheilopogon heterurus*. See *C. cyanopterus*. *Cheilopogon hubbsi* Parin, 1961, included in the previous list, is considered a subspecies of *C. heterurus* in some works (e.g., N. V. Parin *in* Fischer et al. 1995, Volume II:1098), a move that we follow upon the advice of N. V. Parin (personal communication, July 2002).

*Cheilopogon melanurus*. See *C. cyanopterus*.

*Cheilopogon pinnatibarbatus*. See *C. cyanopterus*. *Cheilopogon californicus* (Cooper, 1863), California flyingfish, included in previous list, is considered a subspecies of *C. pinnatibarbatus* in some works (e.g., N. V. Parin *in* Fischer et al. 1995, Volume II:1098), a move that we follow upon the advice of N. V. Parin (personal communication, July 2002). The common name in English follows Smith-Vaniz et al. (1999), although the common name California flyingfish has a long history of use in California and Baja California.

*Fodiator acutus*. The occurrence of this widespread species was inadvertently listed in the 1991 edition as Atlantic.

*Hirundichthys rondeletii*. Original spelling ends with *-ii*. Occurrence of this species on Pacific Coast of United States (off California) needs confirmation.

*Oxyporhamphus micropterus*. *Oxyporhamphus*, usually placed in the Hemiramphidae, is regarded as the sister group of all other exocoetids by J. C. Dasilao, Jr. and K. Sasaki, 1998, Ichthyol. Res. 45(4):347–353.

*Parexocoetus brachypterus*. The subspecies occurring in the Atlantic, *P. brachypterus hillianus* (Gosse, 1851), is recogized at the species level in N. V. Parin, 2003 (dated 2002), Exocoetidae (flyingfishes), Pages 1116–1134 *in* K. E. Carpenter, editor, The living marine resources of the western central Atlantic, FAO

species identification guide for fishery purposes, Volume 2, FAO, Rome.

*Prognichthys occidentalis*. This new species, described by N. V. Parin, 1999, J. Ichthyol. 39(4):281–293, was formerly identified as *P. gibbifrons* (Valenciennes, 1847), a species restricted to waters of the eastern and central Atlantic.

Hemiramphidae. See Exocoetidae above.

## Page 101

*Euleptorhamphus viridis*. Date of publication correction.

*Hemiramphus balao*. Parentheses are removed from the author's name.

*Hyporhamphus meeki*. This new species was described from the Atlantic and Gulf coasts by H. M. Banford and B. B. Collette, 1993, Proc. Bio. Soc. Wash. 106(2):371. We do not employ the patronymic common name Meek's halfbeak as used by B. B. Collette (B. B. Collette and G. Klein-MacPhee, 2002, *in* H. B. Bigelow and W. C. Schroeder, editors, Bigelow and Schroeder's fishes of the Gulf of Maine, Smithsonian Institution Press, Washington, D.C.) for this species because of our Principle 6. Our recommended name in English refers to its past confusion with *H. unifasciatus*.

*Hyporhamphus naos*. This new species, separated from its cognate *H. unifasciatus*, was described from the tropical eastern Pacific (north to Baja California, with strays to San Diego, California) by H. M. Banford and B. B. Collette, 2001, Rev. Biol. Trop. 49(Supplement 1):39–49. We add the modifiers Pacific and Atlantic to the common name of the two species.

*Hyporhamphus unifasciatus*. This species was previously recognized as also occurring in the Pacific. See *H. naos*.

Cyprinodontiformes. See Atheriniformes above.

Aplocheilidae. Change in spelling of common name.

*Rivulus hartii*. Original spelling ends with *-ii*.

Profundulidae. Added to the list for the species noted.

Fundulidae. See Cyprinodontidae below. The name topminnow is also used for a species of Poeciliidae. Species commonly called killifishes are placed in this family and in Cyprinodontidae.

## Page 102

*Fundulus blairae*. We recognize this species described from Texas by E. O. Wiley and D. D. Hall, 1975, Am. Mus. Novit. 2577:3.

*Fundulus cingulatus.* C. R. Gilbert, R. C. Cashner, and E. O. Wiley, 1992, Copeia 1992(3):747–759, determined the holotype of the formerly recognized *F. cingulatus* to be a specimen of *F. lineolatus* (if the type of *F. cingulatus* were accepted as the correct type and not a transposed specimen, then *F. cingulatus* would be a senior synonym of *F. lineolatus).* The above authors recognized the two previously recognized junior synonyms of *F. cingulatus* as representing valid species, the western *F. auroguttatus* found throughout much of the Florida panhandle and northern peninsular Florida and the eastern *F. rubrifrons* found throughout much of peninsular Florida and parts of southeastern Georgia. Arguing that the present holotype of *F. cingulatus* in the MNHN (Paris) does not agree with the original description and probably represents a substituted specimen, K. J. Lazara, 2002, Copeia 2002(1):227–228, designated the lectotype of *F. auroguttatus* (Hay, 1885) as the neotype of *F. cingulatus,* resulting in *F. auroguttatus* becoming a junior synonym of *F. cingulatus.*

*Fundulus dispar.* Page and Burr (1991) and Mayden et al. (1992) recognized *F. dispar* as the northern starhead topminnow, *F. escambiae* as the eastern starhead topminnow, and *F. nottii* as the southern starhead topminnow. The starhead topminnows, five species in all, also include *F. blairae* and *F. lineolatus.*

*Fundulus escambiae.* Date of publication correction. See *F. dispar.*

*Fundulus grandis.* The term "Gulf" in the common name is treated as a proper noun, and we infer that the name was originally proposed for the species' occurrence in the Gulf of Mexico.

*Fundulus kansae.* See *F. zebrinus.*

*Fundulus majalis.* See *F. similis.*

*Fundulus nottii.* See *F. dispar.* Original spelling ends with *-ii.*

*Fundulus rubrifrons.* See *F. cingulatus.*

## Page 103

*Fundulus similis.* Past uncertainty over the validity of the species was expressed in the 1991 edition (p. 83). Although C. F. Duggins, A. A. Karlin, T. A. Mousseau, and K. G. Relyea, 1995, Heredity 74:117–128, gave

evidence supporting treatment of the species as conspecific with *F. majalis,* based on a presumed hybrid zone between these two taxa in northeastern Florida, we continue to recognize *F. similis* based on findings of J. K Blackburn, B. A. Thompson, and R. D. Suttkus, 2002, American Society of Ichthyologists and Herpetologists (ASIH), Program book and abstracts, Kansas City, Missouri (p. 97).

*Fundulus zebrinus.* K. J. Lazara, 2000, The killifish master index, 4th edition, American Killifish Association, Cincinnati, and some other authors placed this species in the genus *Plancterus* (monotypic except for the now recognized *F. kansae*). B. R. Kreiser, 2001, Am. Midl. Nat. 146:199–209, and B. R. Kreiser, J. B. Mitton, and J. D. Woodling, 2001, Evolution 55(2):339–350, presented molecular data supporting the recognition of *F. kansae* as a valid species separate from *F. zebrinus,* with *F. kansae* being found in drainages to the north of the Red River of Texas and the Texas/Oklahoma border and *F. zebrinus* found in the Red River and drainages farther south. These two species were recognized as valid in the 1970 edition but considered conspecific in the 1980 edition.

Anablepidae. Added to the list for the species noted.

*Anableps dowi.* Although originally described by Gill in 1861 as *A. dowei,* and consistently spelled as *A. dowei,* Gill explicitly stated that the species was named for Captain J. M. Dow. To some, the Code can be interpreted in support of retaining the original spelling *dowei, dovii* (M. J. Ghedotti, 1998, *in* L. R. Malabarba, R. E. Reis, R. P. Vari, Z. M. S. Lucena, and C. A. S. Lucena, editors, Phylogeny and classification of neotropical fishes, Edipucrs, Porto Alegre, Brazil [pp. 519–536]), or the commonly used *dowi.* As no explanation for the discrepancy in spelling appeared in the original description, *dowei* is considered by us as an inadvertent error and is emended to *dowi* in agreement with Article 32.5 of the Code. Also, since *dowi* is the spelling overwhelmingly used in the literature, including Miller et al. (in press), this spelling is preserved based on the principle of prevailing usage (Article 33.2.3.1).

## Page 104

*Gambusia panuco.* Considered by R. R. Miller et

al. (in press) to be a probable synonym of *G. regani*.

*Gambusia regani*. See *G. panuco*.

*Gambusia speciosa*. Record for the United States based on reported presence in Devil's River, Texas (M. Rauchenberger, 1989, Am. Mus. Novit. 2951).

*Heterandria formosa*. Although Eschmeyer (1998:600) gave reasons why the original description of this species should date from Girard, 1859, we feel that the reference to small size alone in Agassiz's 1855 description is sufficient to establish the identity of the fish he was describing.

*Poecilia latipinna*. G. D. Williams, J. S. Desmond, and J. B. Zedler, 1998, Calif. Fish Game 84(1):1–17, reported this species introduced in San Diego Bay marsh habitats (intertidal saltmarsh habitats, primarily in hypersaline puddles, where it was also taken with *Acanthogobius flavimanus*, which also occurs in large bays in California).

*Poecilia orri*. In our area, this brackish-water species is thought to occur in the Atlantic Ocean off the Yucatan Peninsula (R. R. Miller, 1983, Copeia 1983(3):817–822; Miller et al., in press).

*Poecilia sphenops*. Added on the basis of information in Fuller et al. (1999), who noted that it is locally established in Montana and Nevada.

### Page 105

*Poeciliopsis gracilis*. Continued occurrence in the United States based on information in P. B. Moyle, 2002, Inland fishes of California, University of California Press, Berkeley (pp. 324–325). See *P. lutzi*.

*Poeciliopsis lutzi*. Considered by Miller et al. (in press) to be a probable junior synonym of *P. gracilis*. See *P. gracilis*.

*Poeciliopsis occidentalis*. P. W. Hedrick, K. M. Parker, and R. N. Lee, 2001, Mol. Ecol. 10(6):1399–1412, provided molecular evidence that *P. occidentalis occidentalis* (Baird & Girard, 1853), Gila topminnow, and *P. occidentalis sonoriensis* (Girard, 1859), "Yaqui topminnow," be recognized as valid species. We do not dispute that *P. sonoriensis* may be a valid taxon but defer species recognition pending further studies. In some works, the two subspecies are collectively referred to as the "Sonoran topminnow" (e.g., Fuller et al. 1999), which form in Spanish is adopted herein.

*Poeciliopsis scarlli*. Considered by Miller et. al. (2003) to be a synonym of *P. turrubarensis*.

*Poeciliopsis turrubarensis*. See *P. scarlli*.

*Xiphophorus couchianus*. Extinct in the wild but maintained in captivity, and reintroduction into the wild is possible.

### Page 106

*Xiphophorus hellerii*. Original spelling ends with *-ii*.

*Xiphophorus meyeri*. *Xiphophorus marmoratus* Obregón-Barboza & Contreras-Balderas, 1988, is considered a junior synonym of *X. meyeri*.

Goodeidae. See Cyprinodontidae below. The common name "splitfins" was used for the goodeids in the 1991 edition (Robins et al. 1991:104).

### Page 107

*Chapalichthys pardalis*. See *C. peraticus*.

*Chapalichthys peraticus*. Considered by Miller et al. (in press) to be a synonym of *C. pardalis*.

*Crenichthys baileyi*. See Cyprinodontidae below.

*Crenichthys nevadae*. See Cyprinodontidae below.

*Empetrichthys latos*. See Cyprinodontidae below.

*Empetrichthys merriami*. See Cyprinodontidae below.

*Goodea atripinnis*. Miller et al. (in press) consider both *Goodea gracilis* and *G. luitpoldii* to be junior synonyms of *G. atripinnis*.

*Goodea gracilis*. See *G. atripinnis*.

*Goodea luitpoldii*. See *G. atripinnis*.

*Ilyodon furcidens*. Miller et al. (in press) consider *I. xantusi* to be a junior synonym of *I. furcidens*.

*Ilyodon lennoni*. Miller et al. (in press) consider *I. lennoni* to be a junior synonym of *I. whitei*.

*Ilyodon whitei*. See *I. lennoni*.

*Ilyodon xantusi*. See *I. furcidens*.

*Skiffia francesae*. Extinct in the wild but maintained in captivity, and reintroduction into the wild is possible.

*Xenotoca eiseni*. S. A. Webb will be erecting a new genus for reception of *X. eiseni* and *X. melanosoma* (Miller et al., in press).

*Xenotoca melanosoma*. See *X. eiseni*.

### Page 108

Cyprinodontidae. Some species in this family in the 1991 edition are now in Fundulidae (see above) and Goodeidae (e.g., species of the genera *Crenichthys* and *Empetrichthys* are in their own subfamily, Empetrichthyinae, of

Goodeidae) following L. R. Parenti, 1981, Bull. Am. Mus. Nat. Hist. 168(4):335–557, and her other works and adopted in Nelson (1994). Change in common name from killifishes is a result of change in composition. Seven Mexican species are extinct in the wild, of which four (*Cyprinodon alvarezi, C. longidorsalis, C. veronicae,* and *Megupsilon aporus*) are maintained in captivity, and reintroduction into the wild is possible (Salvador Contreras-Balderas, personal communication, August 2001). In addition, the continued existence of *C. simus* is doubtful.

*Cyprinodon alvarezi.* See Cyprinodontidae.

*Cyprinodon arcuatus.* This new species was described from the Santa Cruz River basin, mainly Monkey Spring, by W. L Minkley and R. R. Miller *in* W. L Minkley, R. R. Miller, and S. M. Norris, 2002, Copeia 2002(3):699. In the past, it may have occurred in Sonora, Mexico in the uppermost Río Santa Cruz, but records are lacking.

*Cyprinodon eremus.* Formerly recognized as a subspecies of *C. macularius,* A. A. Echelle, R. A. Van Den Bussche, T. P. Malloy, Jr., M. L. Haynie, and C. O. Minckley, 2000, Copeia 2000(2):353–364, recognized this as a distinct species. It is known from the Quitobaquito ciénega (Río Sonoyta drainage), adjacent to the international border, in southwest Arizona, and in the nearby watered stretches of the Río Sonoyta in northwest Sonora.

*Cyprinodon longidorsalis.* See Cyprinodontidae.

*Cyprinodon macularius.* See *C. eremus.*

Page 109

*Cyprinodon pisteri.* This species may also occur in New Mexico, USA, as noted by W. L Minkley, R. R. Miller, and S. M. Norris, 2002, Copeia 2002(3):687–705.

*Cyprinodon simus.* See Cyprinodontidae.

*Cyprinodon variegatus. Cyprinodon hubbsi* Carr, 1936, Lake Eustis minnow, endemic to central Florida, recognized in the 1991 edition, but not recognized as a valid species in Page and Burr (1991) and Mayden et al. (1992), is considered a synonym (and subspecies) of *C. variegatus* based on the unpublished 1974 M.Sc. thesis of W. E. Johnson (Florida Technological University, Orlando) and C. F. Duggins, Jr., A. A. Karlin, and K. G. Relyea, 1983, Northeast Gulf Sci. 6(2):99–107; W. E. Johnson and F. F. Snelson, Jr., 1978, Pages

15–17 *in* C. R. Gilbert, editor, Rare and endangered biota of Florida, Volume II, Fishes, University Press of Florida, Gainesville; C. R. Gilbert, W. E. Johnson, and F. F. Snelson, Jr., 1992, Pages 194–199 *in* C. R. Gilbert, editor, Rare and endangered biota of Florida, Volume II, Fishes, University Press of Florida, Gainesville.

*Cyprinodon veronicae.* See Cyprinodontidae.

*Jordanella pulchra.* Recognized by some workers in the genus *Garmanella,* in which it was originally described.

*Megupsilon aporus.* See Cyprinodontidae.

Beryciformes. The Polymixiidae, placed in the Beryciformes in the 1991 edition, is of uncertain relationship and placed in its own order; it is possibly the sister group to all taxa following its placement (i.e., Percopsiformes and after; see Nelson 1994 for references).

Anomalopidae. Added to the list for the species noted. Although the common name of this family is flashlightfishes, some species of myctophids are also called flashlightfish (e.g., *Protomyctophum crockeri,* California flashlightfish).

*Gephyroberyx darwinii.* Original spelling ends with *-ii.*

*Corniger spinosus.* Date of publication correction.

Page 110

*Myripristis berndti.* Occurrence of this Indo-Pacific species in Mexico is based on sight records by D. Ross Robertson at the Cabo San Lucas region of Baja California Sur and at the Islas Revillagigedo and forms the basis of the report in Allen and Robertson (1994; D. R. Robertson, personal communication to L. T. Findley, January 2003).

*Neoniphon marianus.* Five species recognized in the genus *Holocentrus* in the 1991 edition should be recognized in the genera *Neoniphon* (= *Flammeo*) [masculine] and *Sargocentron* (= *Adioryx*) [neuter], as noted in J. E. Randall and P. C. Heemstra, 1985, Ichthyol. Bull. 49 and J. E. Randall, 1998, Indo-Pacific fishes, No. 27.

*Sargocentron bullisi.* See *Neoniphon marianus.*

*Sargocentron coruscum.* See *Neoniphon marianus.*

*Sargocentron poco.* See *Neoniphon marianus.*

*Sargocentron vexillarium.* See *Neoniphon marianus.*

*Cyttopsis rosea.* Change of author from (Goode & Bean, 1896).

*Xenolepidichthys dalgleishi.* There has been uncertainty whether the specimen forming the basis for listing this species in the 1980 edition (ANSP 68264) was indeed this species or *Grammicolepis brachiusculus.* M. H. Sabaj (personal communication, April 2002) has examined the specimen and has concluded that it represents *X. dalgleishi.*

Caproidae. There is strong evidence that caproids are not zeiforms (e.g., Nelson 1994), but we defer placing them elsewhere pending publication of further studies on their relationships.

Page 111

Aulorhynchidae. See Gasterosteidae below.

*Aulorhynchus flavidus.* Change in common name orthography from tube-snout.

Gasterosteidae. Tubesnouts are recognized in their own family, Aulorhynchidae, separate from the Gasterosteidae.

*Culaea inconstans.* Although a publication date of 1841 was given in the 1991 edition and in Eschmeyer (1998:768), the publication date for Volume 3 (1 and 2) of the Boston Journal of Natural History appears to be 1840, as determined by C. R. Gilbert.

*Gasterosteus aculeatus.* Considerable diversity exists within this species complex and reproductive isolation occurs between sympatric morphs in some lakes in British Columbia (J. D. McPhail, 1993, Can. J. Zool. 71:515–523; E. B. Taylor, 1999, Rev. Fish Biol. Fish. 9(4):299–324; T. Hatfield, 2001, Can. Field-Nat. 115(4):579–583; and T. Hatfield and J. Ptolemy, 2001, Can. Field-Nat. 115(4):591–596).

*Pungitius pungitius.* T. R. Haglund, D. G. Buth, and R. Lawson, 1992, Allozyme variation and phylogenetic systematics of Asian, North American, and European populations of the ninespine stickleback, *Pungitius pungitius,* Pages 438–452 *in* R. L. Mayden, editor, Systematics, historical ecology, and North American freshwater fishes, Stanford University Press, Stanford, California, in a study of allozymal variation, proposed that the North American form of ninespine stickleback be recognized as *P. occidentalis* (Cuvier, 1829). A broader molecular study should be done before accepting the latter name. Y. Keivany

and J. S. Nelson, 2000, Cybium 24(2):107–122, based on morphological evidence, recommended recognizing our form at the subspecies level, *P. p. occidentalis.*

*Halicampus crinitus.* Although two species of the genus *Micrognathus* were recognized in the 1991 list, C. E. Dawson, 1982, Fishes of the western North Atlantic, Memoir, Sears Foundation for Marine Research, Part 8(1):31, felt that differences, primarily in color pattern, between *M. crinitus* (Jenyns, 1842), banded pipefish, and *M. ensenadae* (Silvester, 1916), harlequin pipefish, did not warrant their recognition as separate species. In addition, C. E. Dawson, 1982, Proc. Biol. Soc. Wash. 95 (4):657–687 and C. E. Dawson, 1985, Indo-Pacific pipefishes (Red Sea to the Americas), The Gulf Coast Research Laboratory, Ocean Springs, Mississippi (p. 203), referred *M. crinitus* to the genus *Halicampus.* R. Z. P. Guimarães, 1999, Revue Française d'Aquariologie 26(1–2):7–10, in a study of chromatic and morphological variation in *H. crinitus,* agreed with the change in generic placement and confirmed that *H. crinitus* and *H. ensenadae* are conspecific.

*Hippocampus reidi.* Occurrence in Mexican waters based on four specimens obtained from shrimp trawlers and caught near Tampico (RM 2542) and Lerma (RM 2553) (J. K. Baum and S. A. Lourie, personal communications, June 2003).

Page 112

*Syngnathus scovelli.* The term "Gulf" in the common name is treated as a proper noun, and we infer that the name was originally proposed for the species' occurrence in the Gulf of Mexico.

*Aulostomus maculatus.* Date of publication correction. With the addition of another trumpetfish to the list, we add the geographic modifier Atlantic to the common name of this species.

*Fistularia corneta.* Previously known from Mexico and recently reported from California by R. N. Lea and R. H. Rosenblatt, 2000, CalCOFI Rep. 41:117–129 (some authors use the common name "Pacific cornetfish," a name we prefer not to use in this first-time listing as it is not the only Pacific species on our list).

Macroramphosidae. The snipefishes are recognized in this family and not the Centriscidae (see Nelson 1994).

## Page 113

Synbranchidae. Added to the list for the species noted.

*Monopterus albus.* Added on the basis of information in Fuller et al. (1999).

Scorpaenidae. The classification of this family and of the order Scorpaeniformes is complex and controversial. The Scorpaenidae was split into several families by M. Ishida, 1994, Bull. Nansei Natl. Fish. Res. Inst. 27:1–111, and his classification was used by Eschmeyer (1998) (e.g., Sebastidae with *Helicolenus, Sebastes, Sebastolobus,* and *Trachyscorpia* from our area). Generally, most of the families were recognized earlier as subfamilies (e.g., Nelson 1994), and we recommend retaining the genera in subfamilies until other broad-based studies are done using all genera. According to V. A. Snytko and V. V. Fedorov, 1974, J. Ichthyol. 14:811–818, and V. A. Snytko, 1986, J. Ichthyol. 26(3):124–130, several species on our list may also occur in Mexican waters on the Pacific side of the Baja California peninsula; we do not give their occurrence there pending verification of identity and occurrence of adults versus larval individuals as well as documentation at appropriate depths (records given in the above papers are from depths greater than 200 m).

*Pontinus castor.* Occurrence of this species in Atlantic of United States needs confirmation.

*Pterois volitans.* There have been several reports of adult red lionfish along the east coast of Florida, Georgia, and North Carolina and juveniles off Long Island, New York, resulting from a human-induced introduction (P. E. Whitfield, T. Gardner, S. P. Vives, M. R. Gilligan, W. R. Courtenay, Jr., G. C. Ray, and J. A. Hare, 2002, Mar. Ecol. Prog. Ser. 235:289–297). Based on numbers of individuals seen, along with some young, it seems probable that this Indo-West Pacific species is established in what seems to be the first known successful introduction of a marine fish from the western Pacific to Atlantic coastal waters of the United States.

*Scorpaena agassizii.* Original spelling ends with *-ii.*

*Scorpaena bergii.* Original spelling ends with *-ii.*

## Page 114

*Sebastes aurora.* The record of this species for Mexico noted in W. N. Eschmeyer and E. S. Herald, 1983, A field guide to Pacific Coast fishes of North America, Houghton Mifflin Co., Boston, may be based on an error in field identification; its presence requires verification (W. N. Eschmeyer, personal communication, January 2000).

*Sebastes caurinus.* Date of publication correction.

*Sebastes ciliatus.* Date of publication correction.

*Sebastes dallii.* Original spelling ends with *-ii.*

## Page 115

*Sebastes fasciatus.* Girard, in 1854, first proposed the name *S. fasciatus* for the Pacific Ocean species currently called the China rockfish (type locality: San Francisco [Eschmeyer 1998:569]; signature date August 1854, with date of description 6 October 1854). Girard's name thus is a senior homonym of the Atlantic Ocean *S. fasciatus* Storer, 1854 (the Acadian redfish) (type locality: Provincetown, Massachusetts; signature date October 1854, with date of description 19 December 1854). (*Sebastes fasciatus* Storer was not described in 1856, as had been indicated in Eschmeyer [1998:569].) Under the previous (pre-2000) Code, a petition to the International Commission would have been required to conserve Storer's younger name. However, since Girard's name has not appeared in the recent literature, it appears not to be available under Article 23.9.1.1 of the new Code. Pending confirmation that the conditions of Article 23.9.1.2 of the new Code have also been met, we continue use of the younger name *S. fasciatus* Storer, 1854, for the Acadian redfish. *Sebastes fasciatus* Girard, 1854, in turn, is a junior synonym of *S. nebulosus* Ayres, 1854, as discussed in the appendix account for the latter taxon.

*Sebastes flavidus.* Date of publication correction, although Eschmeyer (1998:589) noted that the year of publication may still be 1863.

*Sebastes gilli.* Two spellings of the specific name were used in the original description (*gillii* and *gilli*). We find both spellings used in recent literature and have not found evidence of a first reviser. Therefore, we herein select *gilli* as the correct original spelling (Article 32.2.1 of the Code). The species is often attributed to Eigenmann & Eigenmann, but the correct author is R. S. Eigenmann.

*Sebastes glaucus.* Added because of occurrence within our area off the western Aleutian Islands (J. W. Orr and D. C. Baker, 1996, Alaska Fishery Research Bulletin 3(2):94–102, and Mecklenburg et al. 2002).

*Sebastes mentella.* Parentheses are added to the author's name.

*Sebastes moseri.* This new species was described from a single specimen taken off San Diego in B. Eitner, C. Kimbrell, and R. Vetter, 1999, Copeia 1999(1):86. Subsequently, a specimen has been obtained off northern Baja California, Mexico (M. S. Love, M. Yoklavich, and L. Thorsteinson, 2002, The rockfishes of the northeast Pacific, University of California Press, Berkeley).

*Sebastes nebulosus.* Fortunately for stability, the name *S. nebulosus* Ayres for the Pacific species (with possible types also from San Francisco, Eschmeyer 1998:1159) appears to be senior to *S. fasciatus* Girard (the description was read 11 September 1854 and published in The Pacific 3(45) 15 September 1854). D. S. Jordan, B. W. Evermann, and H. W. Clark, 1930:369, *in* A checklist of the fishes and fishlike vertebrates of North and Middle America north of Venezuela and Colombia, Report of the United States Commissioner for Fisheries for 1928, Appendix X:1–670, gave *S. fasciatus* Girard "not of Storer" as a junior synonym of *S. nebulosus* Ayres. See also *S. fasciatus.*

*Sebastes ovalis.* Date of publication correction.

### Page 116

*Sebastolobus macrochir.* Date of publication correction. The term broadbanded in the common name used in the 1991 edition was in error for broadhanded (drawn to our attention by C. W. Mecklenburg, personal communication, December 2000). We now adopt the name broadfin thornyhead in allusion to the species name, which refers to its broad pectoral fin.

Triglidae. The family Peristediidae, recognized as a subfamily of Triglidae by some workers, is recognized for *Peristedion* following general practice by authors such as B. B. Washington, W. N. Eschmeyer, and K. M. Howe, 1984, Pages 438–447 *in* H. G. Moser, W. J. Richards, D. M. Cohen, M. P. Fahay, A. W.

Kendall, Jr., and S. L. Richardson, editors, Ontogeny and systematics of fishes, American Society of Ichthyologists and Herpetologists, Special Publication No. 1, Lawrence, Kansas. The two groups are thought to be monophyletic.

### Page 117

*Prionotus ophryas.* Date of publication correction.

*Prionotus roseus.* Date of publication correction.

*Prionotus stearnsi.* Date of publication correction.

Peristediidae. See Triglidae above. The common name "armored gurnards" is used for this group by some authors. *Peristedion brevirostre* Günther, 1860, flathead searobin, has been on the list since 1970 on the basis of a very small specimen collected off the Florida Keys (UF 209974). Since the specimen is now lost and of uncertain identity, this species is removed from the list on the advice of F. F. Snelson (personal communication, June 2002); no material of this species has been obtained within our area of coverage.

*Peristedion greyae.* This deepwater species is added to the list on the basis of specimens collected in our area off Florida, Atlantic side (UF 204496, 79 and 148 mm SL), identified by G. C. Miller, and with the advice of G. C. Miller (personal communication, June 2002).

### Page 118

*Oxylebius pictus.* Recognized in the family Zaniolepididae by G. Shinohara, 1994, Mem. Fac. Fish. Hokkaido Univ. 41(1):1–97.

*Zaniolepis frenata.* See *Oxylebius pictus.*

*Zaniolepis latipinnis.* Date of publication correction. Also, see *Oxylebius pictus.*

Rhamphocottidae. See Cottidae below.

*Rhamphocottus richardsonii.* Original spelling ends with -*ii*.

Cottidae. Some species included in this family in the 1991 edition are now placed in Rhamphocottidae, Hemitripteridae, and Psychrolutidae, based largely on the works of M. Yabe and as followed in Nelson (1994).

*Archistes biseriatus.* Change from the genus *Archaulus* follows Mecklenburg et al. (2002), which in turn is based on the 1941 work of A. Y. Taranetz.

*Artediellus gomojunovi.* Added to the list on basis of occurrence from off Alaska, noted in Mecklenburg et al. (2002) and by J. W. Orr and G. R. Hoff (personal communication, November 2000).

*Artediellus ochotensis*. Added to the list on basis of occurrence from off Alaska, noted in Mecklenburg et al. (2002).

*Artediellus pacificus*. Date of publication correction.

*Asemichthys taylori*. Although Mecklenburg et al. (2002) placed this species in the genus *Radulinus*, we retain it in *Asemichthys*, as done by M. Yabe and S. Maruyama, 2001, Ichthyol. Res. 48:51–63. The two genera are regarded as sister taxa.

*Clinocottus analis*. Date of publication correction.

*Clinocottus globiceps*. Date of publication correction.

### Page 119

*Cottus aleuticus*. There is a limnetic population of uncertain taxonomic status, the Cultus pygmy sculpin, in Cultus Lake, British Columbia; a similar fish also occurs in Lake Washington, Washington (P. A. Coffie, 1998, Can. Field-Nat. 112(1):126–129).

*Cottus bairdii*. Original spelling ends with *-ii*. See *C. bendirei* and *C. hubbsi*.

*Cottus beldingii*. Original spelling ends with *-ii*.

*Cottus bendirei*. This species from the Columbia River basin, formerly recognized as a valid species or as a subspecies in the *C. bairdii* species complex, was recognized as valid by D. F. Markle and D. L. Hill, Jr., 2000, Northwest Sci. 74(3):202–211. Its recognition is supported by the ongoing study of D. A. Neely (personal communication, September 2003). We follow the common name used in the 1960 edition.

*Cottus caeruleomentum*. This new species, previously confused with *C. bairdii*, was described from Atlantic Slope drainages in the United States by A. P. Kinziger, R. L. Raesly, and D. A. Neely, 2000, Copeia 2000(4):1009.

*Cottus hubbsi*. This species from the Columbia River basin, formerly recognized as a valid species or as a subspecies in the *C. bairdii* species complex, was recognized as valid by D. F. Markle and D. L. Hill, Jr., 2000, Northwest Sci. 74(3):202–211. Its recognition is supported by the ongoing study of D. A. Neely (personal communication, September 2003). We follow the common name used in the 1960 edition.

*Cottus paulus*. J. D. Williams, 2000, Copeia

2000(1):302, provided this replacement name for *C. pygmaeus*, Williams, 1968, which is preoccupied.

*Enophrys diceraus*. Date of publication correction.

### Page 120

*Gymnocanthus detrisus*. Added to the list on basis of occurrence from off Alaska noted in Mecklenburg et al. (2002) and by J. W. Orr and G. R. Hoff (personal communication, November 2000).

*Gymnocanthus tricuspis*. Date of publication correction.

*Microcottus sellaris*. Date of publication correction.

*Myoxocephalus niger*. As noted by Eschmeyer (1998:1171), this species was described as a homonym of *Cottus niger* Lacepède, 1801. As required by Article 23.9.1 of the Code, we continue to employ the younger name *M. niger* (Bean, 1881), which has been used since its description. We know of no published use of *Cottus niger* Lacepède, 1801, since its description.

### Page 121

*Myoxocephalus quadricornis*. Recognized in the genus *Triglopsis* by some authors. See *M. thompsonii*.

*Myoxocephalus scorpioides*. As noted by Eschmeyer (1998:1527), the original spelling of the specific name should be rechecked and may be *scorpoides*.

*Myoxocephalus stelleri*. Added to the list on basis of occurrence from off Alaska (occasionally in river mouths), noted in Mecklenburg et al. (2002).

*Myoxocephalus thompsonii*. Original spelling ends with *-ii*. Recognized as a subspecies of *M. quadricornis* by some authors.

*Myoxocephalus verrucosus*. Considered a synonym of *M. scorpius* by some authors (Mecklenburg et al. 2002).

*Porocottus mednius*. Added to the list on the basis of occurrence from Alaska as noted in Mecklenburg et al. (2002). This species was previously known from Alaska as *P. bradfordi* Rutter, 1898, but was inadvertently omitted from earlier versions of this list. It was treated as conspecific with *P. mednius* in Mecklenburg et al. (2002). Although *P. quadrifilis* Gill, 1859, the type of the genus, has been reported from Alaska in some literature, we do not include it because of uncertainty that this species actually occurs in this area (C. W. Mecklenburg, personal communication, April 2001).

*Rastrinus scutiger*. Date of publication correction.

*Stelgistrum beringianum*. Added to the list on basis of occurrence from off Alaska, as noted in Mecklenburg et al. (2002).

*Stelgistrum concinnum*. Added to the list on basis of occurrence from off Alaska, as noted in Mecklenburg et al. (2002).

*Trichocottus brashnikovi*. Added to the list on basis of occurrence from off Alaska, as noted in Mecklenburg et al. (2002) and by J. W. Orr and G. R. Hoff (personal communication, November 2000).

*Triglops macellus*. Date of publication correction.

## Page 122

*Triglops metopias*. Added to the list on basis of occurrence from off Alaska, as noted in original description of C. H. Gilbert and C. V. Burke, 1912, Bulletin Bureau Fisheries 30:31–96. Various other authors have also noted its presence, including T. W. Pietsch, 1994, J. Linn. Soc. Lond. Zool. 109:335–393, and Mecklenburg et al. (2002).

*Triglops pingelii*. Date of publication correction and original spelling ends with *–ii*.

*Triglops xenostethus*. Added to the list on basis of occurrence from off Alaska, as noted in T. W. Pietsch, 1994, J. Linn. Soc. Lond. Zool. 109:335–393, and Mecklenburg et al. (2002).

Hemitripteridae. See Cottidae above. The common name in English is from D. S. Jordan, B. W. Evermann, and H. W. Clark, 1930, Check list of the fishes and fishlike vertebrates of North and Middle America north of the northern boundary of Venezuela and Colombia, Appendix X to Reports of the U.S. Commission of Fisheries for 1928.

*Blepsias cirrhosus*. As noted in Eschmeyer (1998:2886), according to Opinion 212 of the ICZN, the relevant volume (Volume 3) containing the description of this species dates to 1814.

*Nautichthys oculofasciatus*. Date of publication correction.

*Aspidophoroides monopterygius*. T. Kanayama, 1991, Mem. Fac. Fish. Hokkaido Univ. 38(1,2):1–199, treated *A. bartoni* Gilbert, 1896, the Aleutian alligatorfish, of the Pacific, as a junior synonym of *A. monop-*

*terygius*. The expanded distribution reflects this change in species status.

*Bothragonus swanii*. Original spelling ends with *-ii*.

*Chesnonia verrucosa*. Following T. Kanayama, 1991, Mem. Fac. Fish. Hokkaido Univ. 38(1,2):1–199, this species is moved from *Occella* and placed in a monotypic genus.

*Hypsagonus mozinoi*. T. Kanayama, 1991, Mem. Fac. Fish. Hokkaido Univ. 38(1,2):1–199, treated *Agonomalus*, where this species was placed in the 1991 edition, as a junior synonym of *Hypsagonus*.

*Leptagonus frenatus*. T. Kanayama, 1991, Mem. Fac. Fish. Hokkaido Univ. 38(1,2):1–199, found no reason for separating *Sarritor*, where this species was placed in the 1991 edition, from *Leptagonus*, and synonymized the two genera.

*Leptagonus leptorhynchus*. See *L. frenatus*.

## Page 123

*Percis japonica*. Date of publication correction.

*Podothecus accipenserinus*. As noted by Eschmeyer (1998:31), the original spelling of the specific name was *accipenserinus*.

*Podothecus veternus*. M. S. Busby, 1998, National Oceanic and Atmospheric Administration, Technical Report, National Marine Fisheries Service 137:1–88, noted the distribution of this western North Pacific species to extend as far east as St. Matthew Island and Norton Sound, Alaska, and it is therefore added to our list. Busby used the name veteran poacher, which we follow.

*Stellerina xyosterna*. We agree with the conclusions of A. E. Peden, *in* A. C. Matarese, A. W. Kendall, Jr., D. M. Blood, and B. M. Vinter, 1989, National Oceanic and Atmospheric Administration, Technical Report, National Marine Fisheries Service 80:1–652; T. Kanayama, 1991, Mem. Fac. Fish. Hokkaido Univ. 38(1,2):1–199; M. S. Busby, 1998, National Oceanic and Atmospheric Administration, Technical Report, National Marine Fisheries Service 137:1–88, that the previously listed *Occella impi* Gruchy, 1970, the pixie poacher, is a junior synonym of this species.

*Ulcina olrikii*. Following T. Kanayama, 1991, Mem. Fac. Fish. Hokkaido Univ. 38(1,2):1–199, this species is moved from *Aspidophoroides* to the genus *Ulcina* and is corrected to an *ii* ending.

Psychrolutidae. See Cottidae above.

*Cottunculus microps.* Appears to occur only rarely shallower than 200 m in the Gulf of St. Lawrence (Scott and Scott 1988, and J. F. Bergeron and J. Dubé, personal communication, March 2000, based on a 147-m record of 1988 from off Mingan, Quebec, reported by Roberta Miller). Although Scott and Scott (1988) reported *C. thomsonii* (Günther, 1882), pallid sculpin, from 182 to 1,462 m off the North American coast, we lack confirmation of records from depths less than 200 m.

Cyclopteridae. The recognition of snailfishes in their own family (Liparidae) follows the practice of most workers, including Nelson (1994), with appropriate change in family name.

*Aptocyclus ventricosus.* Date of publication correction.

*Cyclopteropsis mcalpini.* Correction of spelling of specific name.

*Eumicrotremus andriashevi.* Removed in error from the 1991 edition (p. 87), this species is restored to the list on the basis of occurrence off Alaska (Mecklenburg et al. 2002, and C. W. Mecklenburg and B. A. Sheiko, 2003, Family Cyclopteridae Bonaparte 1831 – lumpsuckers, California Academy of Sciences Annotated Checklists of Fishes 6 [also available at http://www.calacademy.org/research/ichthyology/]). See *E. terraenovae*.

*Eumicrotremus asperrimus. Eumicrotremus birulai* Popov, 1928, included in the 1991 edition, was considered to be a junior synonym of *E. asperrimus* by C. W. Mecklenburg and B. A. Sheiko, 2003, Family Cyclopteridae Bonaparte 1831 – lumpsuckers, California Academy of Sciences Annotated Checklists of Fishes 6 [also available at http://www.calacademy.org/research/ichthyology/].

*Eumicrotremus eggvinii.* Added to the list on the basis of a specimen collected from shallow water in Saglek Bay, Labrador (Mecklenburg et al. 2002, and C. W. Mecklenburg and B. A. Sheiko, 2003, Family Cyclopteridae Bonaparte 1831 – lumpsuckers, California Academy of Sciences Annotated Checklists of Fishes No. 6 [also available at http://www.calacademy.org/research/ichthyology/]). The common name was suggested by C. W. Mecklenburg (personal communication, October 2003), based on the type locality of the species.

Page 124

*Eumicrotremus phrynoides.* Previously placed in the genus *Cyclopteropsis*; placed in the genus *Eumicrotremus* in Mecklenburg et al. (2002) and C. W. Mecklenburg and B. A. Sheiko, 2003, Family Cyclopteridae Bonaparte 1831 – lumpsuckers, California Academy of Sciences Annotated Checklists of Fishes No. 6 [also available at http://www.calacademy.org/research/ichthyology/].

*Eumicrotremus spinosus.* Correction of the author (previously Müller) and date of publication (C. W. Mecklenburg and B. A. Sheiko, 2003, Family Cyclopteridae Bonaparte 1831 – lumpsuckers, California Academy of Sciences Annotated Checklists of Fishes No. 6 [also available at http://www.calacademy.org/research/ichthyology/]).

*Eumicrotremus terraenovae.* Originally included in the 1960 edition, *E. terraenovae* was regarded as a junior synonym of *E. andriashevi* and thus removed from subsequent editions (see discussion on p. 85 of 1970 edition). C. W. Mecklenburg and B. A. Sheiko, 2003, Family Cyclopteridae Bonaparte 1831 – lumpsuckers, California Academy of Sciences Annotated Checklists of Fishes No. 6 [also available at http://www.calacademy.org/research/ichthyology/], showed it to be a valid species distinct from *E. andriashevi*, and it is accordingly restored here.

*Lethotremus muticus.* Date of publication correction.

Liparidae. See Cyclopteridae above.

*Careproctus ostentum.* Added to the list based on Mecklenburg et al. (2002).

*Careproctus reinhardti.* Added to the list on the basis of records in Scott and Scott (1988).

*Careproctus scottae.* Date of publication correction.

*Careproctus spectrum.* Date of publication correction.

*Liparis bristolensis.* Parentheses are added to the author's name.

*Liparis coheni.* The term "Gulf" in the common name is treated as a proper noun. We infer that the name was originally proposed for the species' occurrence in the Gulf of Maine.

*Liparis fucensis.* Date of publication correction.

Page 125

*Liparis marmoratus.* Added to the list based on M. S. Busby and N. V. Chernova, 2001,

Ichthyol. Res. 48:187–191, who noted the occurrence of this species from Saint Lawrence Island, Alaska. The exact depth of capture is unknown; however, depth in the area of capture appears to be less than 200 m, according to navigational charts. Outside our area, depths of capture when known are 100–165 m. The common name is from B. A. Sheiko and V. V. Fedorov, 2000, Catalog of vertebrates of Kamchatka and adjacent waters, Russian Academy of Sciences, Kamchatskiy Petchatniy Dvor, and the above-mentioned Busby and Chernova paper.

Dactylopteridae. H. Imamura, 2000, Ichthyol. Res. 47(3):203–222, found no support for a close relationship of this family with the Scorpaeniformes and provided cladistic evidence based on morphology that Dactylopteridae and Malacanthidae should be treated as a single percoid family (under the Dactylopteridae). While regarding this study as a valuable contribution, we prefer to recognize the flying gurnards in their own order, Dactylopteriformes, between Scorpaeniformes and Perciformes pending other studies.

Perciformes. Recognized in the 1991 edition as containing one additional family, Mugilidae (see Mugiliformes above), and as excluding one other (see Gobiesocidae below). The sequence of many families is changed from that in the 1991 edition.

Centropomidae. The eight additional species found in Mexican waters and their common names in English, except for that of *Centropomus robalito,* follow L. R. Rivas, 1986, Copeia 1986(3):579–611, and the R. M. Bailey, 1999 manuscript, "A key to the snooks, genus *Centropomus* (Centropomidae)." The latter manuscript, possibly with some modifications of common names, will appear in Miller et al. (in press). The common names in English also follow that of Robins et al. 1991, World fishes important to North Americans, exclusive of species from the continental waters of the United States and Canada, except as noted below for *C. mexicanus.*

*Centropomus mexicanus. See C. parallelus* below.

*Centropomus nigrescens.* Risso (1810) described *Centropomus nigrescens* (presumed to be in the family Moronidae) from Nice, France (Eschmeyer 1998:1175, and Online version, March 2003). Risso's name thus is a senior homonym of *Centropomus nigrescens* Gün-

ther, 1864. Since Risso's name has not appeared in the recent literature, it can be considered not available under Article 23.9.1.1 of the Code. Pending confirmation that the conditions of Article 23.9.1.2 of the Code have also been met, we continue use of *C. nigrescens* Günther, 1864 for the black snook.

*Centropomus parallelus.* Change in common name from "fat snook" to smallscale fat snook, to avoid confusion with the common name in English for *C. mexicanus,* largescale fat snook. The common name of the latter species differs from that in Robins et al. 1991, World fishes important to North Americans, exclusive of species from the continental waters of the United States and Canada, to follow common usage and avoid confusion with the common name in Spanish for *C. pectinatus.*

## Page 126

Moronidae. Species placed in Percichthyidae in the 1991 edition are now recognized in Moronidae, Acropomatidae, and Polyprionidae. In breaking up the Percichthyidae and recognizing these families, we follow G. D. Johnson, 1984, Pages 464–498 *in* H. G. Moser, W. J. Richards, D. M. Cohen, M. E. Fahay, A. W. Kendall, Jr., and S. L. Richardson, editors, Ontogeny and systematics of fishes, Percoidei: development and relationships, American Society of Ichthyologists and Herpetologists, Special Publication 1, Lawrence, Kansas, for Moronidae and Acropomatidae, and C. D. Roberts, 1993, Bull. Mar. Sci. 52(1):60–113, and his 1986 Ph.D. dissertation, for Polyprionidae. The family common name "temperate basses" was used for the species in the former Percichthyidae, but this name is now used for the Moronidae (although some species are striped, we do not use the name "striped basses" for the family, as have some workers). The family Percichthyidae (now termed temperate perches) is now thought to be monophyletic, but species do not occur in our area of coverage.

Acropomatidae. See Moronidae above. The family common name in English follows Eschmeyer (1998) and Smith-Vaniz et al. (1999).

*Synagrops trispinosus.* Added to the list on the basis of 10 specimens taken by trawl from the eastern Gulf of Mexico, off Florida, of which 3 were older museum records previously thought to be *Scombrops oculatus* (R. Ruiz-

Carus, R. E. Matheson, Jr., and F. E. Vose, 2004, Gulf Mex. Sci. MS). The common name was suggested by R. Ruiz-Carus (personal communication, March 2003).

Symphysanodontidae. See Lutjanidae below. W. D. Anderson, Jr. (personal communication, June 2000) suggested the family common name in English.

Polyprionidae. See Moronidae above. The two included genera are thought to be each other's closest relatives, but there is little evidence to relate them to members of other families. However, P. C. Heemstra *in* Fischer et al. 1995, Volume III:1289–1292, included *Stereolepis* in Moronidae.

*Polyprion americanus.* Correction of author.

*Alphestes afer.* Recognition of this species in the genus given, rather than in *Epinephelus*, follows P. C. Heemstra and J. E. Randall, 1993, FAO species catalogue, Volume 16, Groupers of the world (family Serranidae, subfamily Epinephelinae), FAO Fish. Synop. 125(16).

*Alphestes immaculatus.* See *A. afer* and P. C. Heemstra *in* Fischer et al. (1995, Volume III:1578).

*Alphestes multiguttatus.* See *A. immaculatus.*

*Anthias woodsi.* Added to the list on the basis of one specimen (UF 101424) collected off Charleston, South Carolina, in 174 m in 1995 (W. D. Anderson, Jr., personal communication, December 2000). The common name was suggested by P. Heemstra to W. F. Smith-Vaniz (W. F. Smith-Vaniz, personal communication, 1998).

*Centropristis fuscula.* Parentheses are removed from the author's name.

Page 127

*Cephalopholis cruentata.* See *Alphestes afer.*
*Cephalopholis fulva.* See *Alphestes afer.*
*Dermatolepis dermatolepis.* See *Alphestes afer.*
*Dermatolepis inermis.* See *Alphestes afer.*
*Diplectrum maximum.* An adult of this southern species was taken off Newport Beach, California in 1998 (R. N. Lea and R. H. Rosenblatt, 2000, CalCOFI Rep. 41:117–129). We adopt the common name recommended in that publication, rather than "torpedo sand perch" appearing in P. C. Heemstra *in* Fischer et al. (1995, Volume III:1586).

*Epinephelus acanthistius.* The term "Gulf" in the common name is treated as a proper noun. The name was originally proposed for the species' occurrence in the Gulf of California.

*Epinephelus analogus.* Date of publication correction.

*Epinephelus drummondhayi.* Date of publication correction.

*Epinephelus itajara.* Reasons for changing the common name of the species from jewfish to goliath grouper, in reference to its large size, are given in J. S. Nelson, E. J. Crossman, H. Espinosa-Pérez, L. T. Findley, C. R. Gilbert, R. N. Lea, and J. D. Williams, 2001, Fisheries 26(5):31.

*Epinephelus niphobles.* Considered a valid species, distinct from the allopatric *E. niveatus,* by P. C. Heemstra and J. E. Randall, 1993, FAO species catalogue, Volume 16, Groupers of the world (family Serranidae, subfamily Epinephelinae), FAO Fish. Synop. 125(16).

Page 128

*Hemanthias peruanus.* The name splittail bass was used for this species up to the 1980 edition. After it was discovered that the record for this species was a misidentified *H. signifer,* the common name was applied to the latter species in the 1991 edition. We retain the name for *H. peruanus* following general use.

*Hemanthias signifer.* See *H. peruanus.* Change in common name follows W. N. Eschmeyer and E. S. Herald, 1983, A field guide to Pacific Coast fishes of North America, Houghton Mifflin Co., Boston.

*Hemanthias vivanus.* Date of publication correction.

*Hypoplectrus aberrans.* Listed in the 1970 edition but removed from the 1980 edition in the belief that it was a synonym of *H. unicolor,* this species is restored based on M. L. Domeier, 1994, Bull. Mar. Sci. 54(1):103–141. *Hypoplectrus aberrans* and *H. chlorurus* were not specifically mentioned by Domeier as occurring in United States waters but were included in the 1970 edition. The rare *H. aberrans* is known from Alligator Reef, Florida Keys (UF 207085), but the presence of *H. chlorurus* (Cuvier, 1828), the yellowtail hamlet, off Texas (the basis for inclusion in previous editions) is erroneous according to H. D. Hoese and R. H. Moore, 1998, Fishes of the Gulf of Mexico, 2nd edition, Texas A & M University Press, College Station. In addition to the six new hamlets, Domeier's paper noted the occurrence of the undescribed tan hamlet in Florida as *H.* sp #1 (this form is still present, D. B. Snyder, personal communication, June 2001). The difficulty of determining which species of *Hypoplectrus* occur in Mexican waters relates to the recent practice of including all under the name *H. unicolor*. One or more of the four species given in our list as not known from Mexico, in addition to *H. chlorurus* (Cuvier, 1828), may indeed occur there.

*Hypoplectrus gemma.* See *H. aberrans.*

*Hypoplectrus guttavarius.* See *H. aberrans.*

*Hypoplectrus indigo.* See *H. aberrans.*

*Hypoplectrus nigricans.* See *H. aberrans.*

*Hypoplectrus puella.* See *H. aberrans.*

*Hypoplectrus unicolor.* See *H. aberrans.*

*Liopropoma eukrines.* Change in common name from wrasse bass to wrasse basslet for purposes of consistency.

*Liopropoma mowbrayi.* Change in common name from cave bass to cave basslet for purposes of consistency.

*Liopropoma rubre.* Change in common name from peppermint bass to peppermint basslet for purposes of consistency.

*Mycteroperca acutirostris.* Considered a valid species distinct from the eastern Atlantic *M. rubra* (Bloch, 1793) by P. C. Heemstra, 1991, Bol. Mus. Munic. Funchal 43(226):5–71; and P. C. Heemstra and J. E. Randall, 1993, FAO species catalogue, Volume 16, Groupers of the world (family Serranidae, subfamily Epinephelinae), FAO Fish. Synop. 125(16).

*Mycteroperca jordani.* The term "Gulf" in the common name is treated as a proper noun. The name was originally proposed for the species' occurrence in the Gulf of California.

### Page 129

*Paranthias colonus.* Considered a valid species distinct from the allopatric *P. furcifer* by P. C. Heemstra and J. E. Randall, 1993, FAO species catalogue, Volume 16, Groupers of the world (family Serranidae, subfamily Epinephelinae), FAO Fish. Synop. 125(16), and Thomson et al. (2000) (as well as in their 1979 edition).

*Paranthias furcifer.* Change in spelling of common name creolefish (from creole-fish) and addition of modifier Atlantic. See *P. colonus.*

*Pronotogrammus martinicensis.* Placed in *Holanthias* in the 1991 edition. C. C. Baldwin, 1990, Copeia 1990(4):913–955, on

p. 950, placed this species in the older genus *Pronotogrammus.*

*Rypticus saponaceus.* Correction of author.

*Rypticus subbifrenatus.* Parentheses are removed from the author's name.

*Serranus aequidens.* Two specimens of this southern species are known from off California (D. J. Pondella II, 1999, Calif. Fish Game 85(3):130–134).

*Serranus baldwini.* Date of publication correction.

*Serranus phoebe.* Date of publication correction.

### Page 130

*Gramma loreto.* We change the common name of this fish, first listed in the 1991 edition, following advice of P. H. Humann (personal communication, November 1999) that the name fairy basslet, not "royal gramma," is the one in wide use in popular fish identification books and by laypersons. Although this species was included in the 1991 list, its presence in Florida, based on one collection, was due to an introduction; it is native in Mexico off the Yucatan coast.

*Lipogramma evides.* Known depth of occurrence within 200 m not definite (type specimens collected off Arrowsmith Bank, Mexico, in an otter trawl haul covering a depth range of 146–265 m).

Opistognathidae. Previously placed with the trachinoid families, this family is now placed with the percoids following G. D. Johnson, 1984, Pages 464–498 *in* H. G. Moser, W. J. Richards, D. M. Cohen, M. E. Fahay, A. W. Kendall, Jr., and S. L. Richardson, editors, Ontogeny and systematics of fishes, Percoidei: development and relationships, American Society of Ichthyologists and Herpetologists, Special Publication 1, Lawrence, Kansas, and A. C. Gill and R. D. Mooi, 1993, Bull. Mar. Sci. 52(1):327–350.

*Opistognathus lonchurus.* Parentheses are removed from the authors' names.

*Opistognathus macrognathus.* Parentheses are removed from the author's name.

*Opistognathus maxillosus.* Parentheses are removed from the author's name.

*Opistognathus megalepis.* Known depth of occurrence within 200 m not definite (type specimens collected off Arrowsmith Bank, Mexico in an otter trawl haul covering a depth range of 146–265 m).

*Opistognathus melachasme.* The change in occurrence and in common name from yellow-mouth jawfish follows W. F. Smith-Vaniz, 1997, Bull. Mar. Sci. 60(3):1089–1091. Known depth of occurrence within 200 m probable but not definite (type specimens collected off Arrowsmith Bank, Mexico in an otter trawl haul covering a depth range of 146–265 m).

*Opistognathus mexicanus.* W. A. Bussing and R. J. Lavenberg, in press, Rev. Biol. Trop. 51(2), place this species in the synonymy of *O. punctatus* (W. A. Bussing, personal communication, May 2003). They also describe three new species of *Opistognathus, O. brochus, O. fossoris,* and *O. walkeri,* all from the Gulf of California, Mexico.

*Opistognathus nothus.* This new species was described by W. F. Smith-Vaniz, 1997, Bull. Mar. Sci. 60(3):1091. Application of the common name yellowmouth jawfish to this species and not to *O. melachasme,* as in the 1991 edition, follows the above paper.

*Opistognathus punctatus.* See *O. mexicanus.*

*Opistognathus robinsi.* This new species was described by W. F. Smith-Vaniz, 1997, Bull. Mar. Sci. 60(3):1109. Listed in the 1991 edition as *Opistognathus* sp.

*Opistognathus whitehursti.* Authorship given in the 1991 edition as "(Longley, 1931)." W. F. Smith-Vaniz, 1997, Bull. Mar. Sci. 60(3):1118 and Eschmeyer (1998:1791) gave the species as *Opistognathus whitehurstii* Longley, in Longley & Hildebrand, 1940 (originally described in *Opisthognathus*). W. F. Smith-Vaniz (personal communication, May 1999) now advises us that the earliest description actually dates from W. H. Longley, 1927, Carnegie Inst. Wash. Year Book 26:222 (in the genus *Gnathypops*). The authorship, date, and spelling used here are those found in that paper.

## Page 131

Centarchidae. Members of the genus *Elassoma* have been placed in their own family, Elassomatidae (see Elassomatidae below).

*Archoplites interruptus.* As noted by Gilbert (1998:239), *Centrarchus maculosus* Ayres, 1854, appears to have priority; however, as required by Article 23.9.1 of the Code, we continue using the younger name *A. interruptus* (Girard, 1854), which has been used since its description. We know of no usage of *C. maculosus* Ayres, 1854, since its description.

*Lepomis auritus.* There is a possibility that this species is introduced into Canada and not native.

*Lepomis gulosus.* This species was placed in the monotypic genus *Chaenobryttus* by P. C. Wainwright and G. V. Lauder, 1992, The evolution of feeding biology in sunfishes (Centrarchidae), Pages 472–491 *in* R. L. Mayden, editor, Systematics, historical ecology, and North American freshwater fishes, Stanford University Press, Stanford, California, and by P. M. Mabee, 1995, Copeia 1995(3):586–607, who generated a phylogenetic tree that showed *L. gulosus* to be sister to the other *Lepomis,* plus *Enneacanthus.* These conclusions conflict with the results obtained by K. J. Roe, P. M. Harris, and R. L. Mayden, 2002, Copeia 2002(4):897–905, which support placement in *Lepomis.* We accept Roe et al.'s conclusions, and our classification remains the same as in the 1991 edition. This is also as in the list of M. L. Warren, Jr. et al., 2000, Fisheries 25(10):7–31.

*Lepomis megalotis.* The subspecies *L. megalotis peltastes* Cope, 1870, northern longear sunfish, is recognized as a valid species in R. M. Bailey, W. C. Latta, and G. R. Smith, in press, An atlas of Michigan Fishes with keys and illustrations for their identification, Univ. Mich. Mus. Zool. Spec. Publ. 2. We feel that independent confirmation is required before accepting this change.

*Lepomis miniatus.* Previously regarded as a subspecies of *L. punctatus,* M. L. Warren, Jr., 1992, Bulletin of the Alabama Museum of Natural History 12:1–47, provided evidence that this, the western form, should be recognized as a valid species. We accept this conclusion, but note that the area of sympatry comprises what Warren considered to be a broad zone of hybridization; others maintain this as an area of secondary intergradation and that the two forms should more properly be considered subspecies. Although this species was originally described in *Lepiopomus,* that name is considered to be an unjustified emendation of *Lepomis;* consequently, parentheses are not placed around the author's name, following Article 51.3.1 of the Code and on the advice of W. N. Eschmeyer (personal communication, December 2002).

*Lepomis punctatus.* See *L. miniatus.*

*Micropterus cataractae.* This new species was

described from Alabama, Florida, and Georgia by J. D. Williams and G. H. Burgess, 1999, Bull. Fla. Mus. Nat. Hist. 42:83.

*Micropterus salmoides*. T. W. Kassler et al., Pages 291–322 *in* D. P. Philipp and M. S. Ridgway, 2002, Black bass: ecology, conservation, and management, American Fisheries Society, Symposium 31, Bethesda, Maryland, and T. J. Near, T. W. Kassler, J. B. Koppelman, C. B. Dillman, and D. P. Philipp, 2003, Evolution 57(7):1610–1621, elevated *M. salmoides floridanus* (Lesueur, 1822), Florida largemouth bass, to species rank. We defer formal recognition of this subspecies as a valid species pending further work.

*Micropterus treculii*. Original spelling ends with *-ii*. The written description was not published until 1883, and that date was accepted by Eschmeyer (1998:1691) and Gilbert (1998:251) for the species description. However, we accept 1874 in accordance with Article 12.2.7 of the Code, the date a presumed figure was published, and as given in the 1991 edition and in C. R. Gilbert's unpublished revised account of Gilbert (1998).

### Page 132

*Ammocrypta beanii*. Original spelling of *A. beanii* ends with *-ii*. A. M. Simons, 1991, Copeia 1991(4):927–936, and A. M. Simons, 1992, Phylogenetic relationships of the *Boleosoma* species group (Percidae: *Etheostoma*), Pages 268–292 *in* R. L. Mayden, editor, Systematics, historical ecology, and North American freshwater fishes, Stanford University Press, Stanford, California, suggested that the genus *Etheostoma* is monophyletic only with the inclusion of *Ammocrypta* (i.e., as *E. beanii, E. bifascia, E. clarum, E. meridianum, E. pellucidum*, and *E. vivax*), a conclusion we feel requires verification. In addition, although *Ammocrypta* was placed in *Etheostoma* by R. W. Wood and M. E. Raley, 2000, Copeia 2000(1):20–26, their tree does not support this treatment, and T. J. Near, J. C. Porterfield, and L. M. Page, 2000, Copeia 2000(3):701–711, discouraged recognition of *Ammocrypta* in *Etheostoma*.

*Ammocrypta bifascia*. See *A. beanii*.

*Ammocrypta clara*. See *A. beanii*.

*Ammocrypta meridiana*. See *A. beanii*.

*Ammocrypta pellucida*. See *A. beanii*, and correction of author.

*Ammocrypta vivax*. See *A. beanii*.

*Crystallaria asprella*. A. M. Simons, 1991, Copeia 1991(4):927–936, provided evidence that this species, recognized in *Ammocrypta* in the 1991 edition, should be placed in its own genus.

*Etheostoma artesiae*. Known from a broad area in Gulf Coast drainages and previously regarded as a subspecies of *E. whipplei*. However, K. R. Piller, H. L. Bart, Jr., and C. A. Walser, 2001, Copeia 2001(3):802–807, provided evidence that it should be recognized as a valid species.

*Etheostoma basilare*. This new species (subgenus *Catonotus*), formerly considered to be a population of *E. virgatum*, was described from the Caney Fork system of the Cumberland River drainage, Tennessee by L. M. Page, M. Hardman, and T. J. Near, 2003, Copeia 2003(3):522.

*Etheostoma bellator*. This new species (subgenus *Ulocentra*) was described from the Black Warrior River drainage of north-central Alabama by R. D. Suttkus and R. M. Bailey, 1993, Tulane Stud. Zool. Bot. 29(1):18. The species may be a composite of three species (J. P. Clabaugh, K. E. Knott, R. M. Wood, and R. L. Mayden, 1996, Biochem. Syst. Ecol. 24(2):119–134).

*Etheostoma bison*. This new species (subgenus *Oligocephalus*), one of eight species now recognized in the *E. spectabile* species complex, was described from tributaries of the lower Duck and lower Tennessee rivers, Kentucky and Tennessee, by P. A. Ceas and L. M. Page, 1997, Copeia 1997(3):518. The common name is based on occurrence in the Buffalo River.

*Etheostoma blennioides*. See *E. gutselli*.

*Etheostoma brevirostrum*. This new species (subgenus *Ulocentra*) was described from the Coosa River drainage, Alabama River System, of Alabama, Georgia, and Tennessee, by R. D. Suttkus and D. A. Etnier, 1991, Tulane Stud. Zool. Bot. 28(1):15.

*Etheostoma burri*. This new species (subgenus *Oligocephalus*), one of eight species now recognized in the *E. spectabile* species complex, was described from tributaries of the upper Black River system, Missouri, by P. A. Ceas and L. M. Page, 1997, Copeia 1997(3):514.

*Etheostoma cervus*. This new species (subgenus *Ulocentra*), formerly considered to be a population of *E. pyrrhogaster*, was described from the Forked Deer River system of western Tennessee by S. L. Powers and R. L. Mayden, 2003, Copeia 2003(3):577.

*Etheostoma chermocki*. This new species was described from Turkey Creek (Black Warrior River drainage), Alabama by H. T. Boschung, R. L. Mayden, and J. R. Tomelleri, 1992, Bulletin of the Alabama Museum of Natural History 13:12.

*Etheostoma chienense*. This new species (subgenus *Catonotus*) was described from the Bayou du Chien drainage of Kentucky by L. M. Page and P. A. Ceas, *in* L.M. Page, P. A. Ceas, D. L. Swofford, and D. G. Buth, 1992, Copeia 1992(3):627. See also M. L. Warren, Jr., B. M. Burr, and C. A. Taylor, 1994, Trans. Ky. Acad. Sci. 55(1–2):20–27.

## Page 133

*Etheostoma chlorosoma*. The original spelling and grammatically correct *chlorosoma*, treated as an appositional noun, is adopted rather than *chlorosomum* in the 1991 edition and of common usage following advice from C. R. Robins (personal communication, May 2002).

*Etheostoma chuckwachatte*. This new species (subgenus *Nothonotus*), formerly included in *E. jordani*, was described from the Tallapoosa River in Alabama and Georgia by R. M. Wood and R. L. Mayden, 1993, Bulletin of the Alabama Museum of Natural History 16:39.

*Etheostoma collis*. As in the 1991 edition, we follow Jenkins and Burkhead (1994:886) in recognizing *E. saludae* (Hubbs & Cannon, 1935), Saluda darter, as a synonym of *E. collis*.

*Etheostoma colorosum*. This new species (subgenus *Ulocentra*) was described from coastal drainages of southern Alabama and the western Florida panhandle by R. D. Suttkus and R. M. Bailey, 1993, Tulane Stud. Zool. Bot. 29(1):2.

*Etheostoma corona*. This new species (subgenus *Catonotus*) was described from the Cypress Creek system, a tributary of the Tennessee River in southern Tennessee and northern Alabama, by L. M. Page and P. A. Ceas, *in* L. M. Page, P. A. Ceas, D. L. Swofford, and D. G. Buth, 1992, Copeia 1992(3):631.

*Etheostoma denoncourti*. This new species (subgenus *Nothonotus*), formerly included in *E. tippecanoe*, was described from the upper Tennessee drainage by J. R. Stauffer, Jr. and E. S. van Snik, Copeia 1997(1):118. A redescription was provided by C. E. Skelton and D. A. Etnier, 2000, Copeia 2000(4):1097–1103, and a further analysis of lower Tennessee River drainage populations was given by A. P. Kinziger, R. M Wood, and S. A. Welsh, 2001, Copeia 2001(1):235–239.

*Etheostoma derivativum*. This new species (subgenus *Catonotus*), formerly considered to be a population of *E. virgatum*, was described from the middle Cumberland River drainage, south-central Kentucky and north-central Tennessee, by L. M. Page, M. Hardman, and T. J. Near, 2003, Copeia 2003(3):526.

*Etheostoma douglasi*. This new species (subgenus *Nothonotus*), formerly included in *E. jordani*, was described from the upper Black Warrior River system in Alabama by R. M. Wood and R. L. Mayden, 1993, Bulletin of the Alabama Museum of Natural History 16:37.

*Etheostoma duryi*. Robins et al. (1991) changed the common name from blackside snubnose darter to black darter. We recommend changing back to the former name, as the sides of the species have black blotches (as do some other darters) but the species is not generally black. Users must be careful to avoid confusion in names with *E. simoterum*, snubnose darter, and *Percina maculata*, blackside darter.

*Etheostoma etowahae*. This new species (subgenus *Nothonotus*), formerly included in *E. jordani*, was described from the Etowah River system in Alabama by R. M. Wood and R. L. Mayden, 1993, Bulletin of the Alabama Museum of Natural History 16:38.

*Etheostoma forbesi*. This new species (subgenus *Catonotus*) was described from tributaries of Barren Fork of the Collins River, Tennessee by L. M. Page and P. A. Ceas, *in* L. M. Page, P. A. Ceas, D. L. Swofford, and D. G. Buth, 1992, Copeia 1992(3):633.

*Etheostoma fragi*. Known from Missouri and Arkansas and regarded as a subspecies of *E. spectabile* by D. A. Distler, 1968, Univ. Kansas Sci. Bull. 48:143–208. However, P. A. Ceas and L. M. Page, 1997, Copeia 1997(3):512, provided evidence that it should be recognized as a valid species. The common name is based on occurrence in the Strawberry River.

*Etheostoma gutselli.* Formerly considered a subspecies of *Etheostoma blennioides*, this taxon was elevated to species rank following discovery of sympatric occurrence of the two forms, without evidence of massive hybridization, in a restored section of the Pigeon River in eastern Tennessee, in the update for 2001 printing of D. A. Etnier and W. C. Starnes, 1994 (dated 1993), The fishes of Tennessee, The University of Tennessee Press, Knoxville, (pp. 609–610).

### Page 134

*Etheostoma jordani.* See *E. chuckwachatte, E. douglasi,* and *E. etowahae.*

*Etheostoma kantuckeense.* This new species (subgenus *Oligocephalus*), one of eight species now recognized in the *E. spectabile* species complex, was described from tributaries of the upper Barren River system, Kentucky and Tennessee, by P. A. Ceas and L. M. Page, 1997, Copeia 1997(3):517.

*Etheostoma lachneri.* This new species (subgenus *Ulocentra*) was described from the Tombigbee River system in Mobile County, Alabama, by R. D. Suttkus and R. M. Bailey, *in* R. D. Suttkus, R. M. Bailey, and H. L. Bart, Jr., 1994, Tulane Stud. Zool. Bot. 29(2):109.

*Etheostoma lawrencei.* This new species (subgenus *Oligocephalus*), one of eight species now recognized in the *E. spectabile* species complex, was described from Kentucky and Tennessee, by P. A. Ceas and B. M. Burr, 2002, Ichthyological Exploration of Freshwaters 13(3):205.

*Etheostoma maculatum.* Although a publication date of 1841 was given in the 1991 edition and in Eschmeyer (1998:987), the publication date for Volume 3 (1 and 2) of the Boston Journal of Natural History appears to be 1840 as determined by C. R. Gilbert.

*Etheostoma neopterum.* The common name given for this species in the description by W. M. Howell and G. Dingerkus was lollypop darter, as suggested by H. T. Boschung. We now recommend this spelling, which has been used in some regional books, as opposed to that of "lollipop darter" used in the 1980 and 1991 editions.

*Etheostoma nigrum.* See *E. susanae.*

*Etheostoma oophylax.* This new species (subgenus *Catonotus*) was described from most of the tributaries of the lower Tennessee River by P. A. Ceas and L. M. Page, *in* L. M. Page, P. A. Ceas, D. L. Swofford, and D. G. Buth, 1992, Copeia 1992(3):629.

### Page 135

*Etheostoma percnurum.* This new species (subgenus *Catonotus*) was described from Virginia and Tennessee by R. E. Jenkins *in* Jenkins and Burkhead 1994:877

*Etheostoma phytophilum* This new species (subgenus *Fuscatelum*) was described from the upper Black Warrior River system, Alabama, by H. L. Bart, Jr. and M. S. Taylor, 1999, Tulane Stud. Zool. Bot. 31(1):27.

*Etheostoma pseudovulatum.* This new species (subgenus *Catonotus*) was described from four tributaries of the Duck River in Tennessee by L. M. Page and P. A. Ceas, *in* L. M. Page, P. A. Ceas, D. L. Swofford, and D. G. Buth, 1992, Copeia 1992(3):628.

*Etheostoma pyrrhogaster.* See *E. cervus.*

*Etheostoma ramseyi.* This new species (subgenus *Ulocentra*) was described from the Alabama River System, Alabama, by R. D. Suttkus and R. M. Bailey, *in* R. D. Suttkus, R. M. Bailey, and H. L. Bart, Jr., 1994, Tulane Stud. Zool. Bot. 29(2):115.

*Etheostoma raneyi.* This new species (subgenus *Ulocentra*) was described from the Tallahatchie and Yocona river systems, tributaries of the Yazoo River system, of north-central Mississippi, by R. D. Suttkus and H. L. Bart, Jr., *in* R. D. Suttkus, R. M. Bailey, and H. L. Bart, Jr., 1994, Tulane Stud. Zool. Bot. 29(2):98.

*Etheostoma scotti.* This new species (subgenus *Ulocentra*) was described from the Etowah River system, Georgia, by B. H. Bauer, D. A. Etnier, and N. M. Burkhead, 1995, Bulletin of the Alabama Museum of Natural History 17:2.

*Etheostoma sellare.* The Maryland darter is probably extinct, although there is a very remote possibility that it occurs in the mainstem of the Susquehanna River, where sampling is difficult (R. Raesly, personal communication, December 2000).

*Etheostoma spectabile.* See *E. bison, E. burri, E. fragi, E. kantuckeense, E. lawrencei, E. tecumsehi,* and *E. uniporum.* Additional species of the *E. spectabile* species complex await description (P. A. Ceas, personal communication, February 2003).

*Etheostoma susanae.* R. M. Strange, 1998, Am. Midl. Nat. 140(1):96–102, provided molecular evidence supporting recognition of the subspecies *E. nigrum susanae* (Jordan & Swain, 1883) as a valid species. In reaching the decision to recognize this species we have been guided by W. C. Starnes (who suggested the common name, personal communication, May 2000) and additional information from R. M. Strange (personal communication, March 2002).

*Etheostoma swaini.* The term "Gulf" in the common name is treated as a proper noun, and we infer that the name was originally proposed for the species' occurrence in drainages of the Gulf of Mexico.

## Page 136

*Etheostoma tallapoosae.* This new species (subgenus *Ulocentra*) was described from the Tallapoosa River system, Alabama River drainage, of Alabama and Georgia, by R. D. Suttkus and D. A. Etnier, 1991, Tulane Stud. Zool. Bot. 28(1):3.

*Etheostoma tecumsehi.* This new species (subgenus *Oligocephalus*), one of eight species now recognized in the *E. spectabile* species complex, was described from upland tributaries of the upper Pond River, Green River System, Kentucky, by P. A. Ceas and L. M. Page, 1997, Copeia 1997(3):516.

*Etheostoma tetrazonum.* J. F. Switzer and R. M. Wood, 2002, Copeia 2002(2):450–455, note that *E. tetrazonum* is a complex of two species; the one from the Meramec River drainage, Missouri, will be described as a new species.

*Etheostoma tippecanoe.* See *E. denoncourti.*

*Etheostoma uniporum.* Known from Missouri and Arkansas and regarded as a subspecies of *E. spectabile* by D. A. Distler, 1968, Univ. Kans. Sci. Bull. 48:143–208. However, P. A. Ceas and L. M. Page, 1997, Copeia 1997(3):510, provided evidence that it should be recognized as a valid species.

*Etheostoma variatum.* Although a publication date of 1841 is given in Eschmeyer (1998:1741), the publication date for Volume 3 (1 and 2) of the Boston Journal of Natural History appears to be 1840, as determined by C. R. Gilbert.

*Etheostoma virgatum.* See *E. basilare* and *E. derivativum.*

*Etheostoma whipplei.* Although the original spelling ends with –*ii*, we retain the spelling –*ei*, which is in prevailing usage and deemed to be a justified emendation, following Article 33.2.3.1 of the Code, and as noted by Eschmeyer (1998: Online version, February 2002). See *E. artesiae.*

*Percina aurora.* This new species (subgenus *Cottogaster*), formerly included in *P. copelandi*, was described from the Pearl and Pascagoula river drainages in Mississippi by R. D. Suttkus and B. A. Thompson *in* R. D. Suttkus, B. A. Thompson, and H. L. Bart, Jr., 1994, Occasional Papers Tulane University Museum of Natural History (4):15.

*Percina austroperca.* This new species (subgenus *Percina*), formerly included in *P. caprodes*, was described from the Choctawhatchee and Escambia rivers in Alabama and Florida by B. A. Thompson, 1995, Occasional Papers of the Museum of Natural Science Louisiana State University (69):3.

*Percina brevicauda.* This new species (subgenus *Cottogaster*), formerly included in *P. copelandi*, was described from the Mobile Bay drainage, Alabama by R. D. Suttkus and H. L. Bart, Jr., *in* R. D. Suttkus, B. A. Thompson, and H. L. Bart, Jr., 1994, Occasional Papers Tulane University Museum of Natural History (4):20.

*Percina burtoni.* Correction from the 1991 edition; the correct common name is the blotchside logperch, as used in earlier editions.

*Percina caprodes.* See *P. austroperca, P. fulvitaenia, P. kathae,* and *P. suttkusi.*

*Percina copelandi.* See *P. aurora* and *P. brevicauda.*

*Percina crassa.* Parentheses are added to the authors' names.

*Percina cymatotaenia.* See *P. stictogaster.*

## Page 137

*Percina fulvitaenia.* Reasons for elevating *P. caprodes fulvitaenia* to species status were given by B. A. Thompson, 1997, Occasional Papers of the Museum of Natural Science Louisiana State University (73):27. There is some disagreement about whether this taxon, formerly included in *P. caprodes,* is valid at the species level.

*Percina kathae.* This new species, formerly included in *P. caprodes,* was described from the Mobile basin in Mississippi, Alabama, Georgia, and Tennessee by B. A. Thompson, 1997,

Occasional Papers of the Museum of Natural Science Louisiana State University (73):4.

*Percina macrocephala.* Date of publication correction.

*Percina nevisense.* Reasons for recognizing this species from Virginia and North Carolina as distinct from *P. peltata* of the James River, Virginia and northward were given by J. T. Goodin, E. G. Maurakis, E. S. Perry, and W. S. Woolcott, 1998, Va. J. Sci., 49(3):183–194. On the advice of R. E. Jenkins, we recommend the common name chainback darter rather than the geographically inappropriate name Neuse River darter or even the more neutral name Neuse darter.

*Percina peltata.* See *P. nevisense.*

*Percina stictogaster.* This new species, formerly included in *P. cymatotaenia,* was described from the Green and Kentucky river systems of Kentucky and Tennessee by B. M. Burr and L. M. Page, 1993, Bulletin of the Alabama Museum of Natural History 16:19.

*Percina suttkusi.* This new species, formerly included in *P. caprodes,* was described from Louisiana, Mississippi, and Alabama by B. A. Thompson, 1997, Occasional Papers of the Museum of Natural Science Louisiana State University (72):3.

*Percina vigil.* Some authors (e.g., Page and Burr [1991] and Mayden et al. [1992]) prefer to recognize this species as *P. ouachitae* (Jordan & Gilbert, 1887).

*Sander canadensis.* Reasons for changing the generic name from *Stizostedion* to *Sander* are given in J. S. Nelson, E. J. Crossman, H. Espinosa-Pérez, L. T. Findley, C. R. Gilbert, R. N. Lea, and J. D. Williams, 2003, Fisheries 28(7):38–39. Change of author from (Smith, 1834). The specific name is changed from *canadense* to *canadensis* to agree with the masculine *Sander.*

*Sander lucioperca.* At least one specimen of the zander, not part of the original introduction into Spiritwood Lake, north of Jamestown, North Dakota, in 1989, has been found, suggesting that this species is established in North Dakota (R. Bajno, J. D. Reist, and D. G. Wright, personal communication, April 2001). There is the potential that this species could have spread into the Missouri drainage due to flooding in the Spiritwood watershed in 1997 and following years. See *S. canadensis* for generic placement.

*Sander vitreus.* See *S. canadensis* for generic placement. The specific name is changed from *vitreum* to *vitreus* to agree with the masculine *Sander.* Two subspecies have been recognized (last given in the 1980 edition), *S. vitreus vitreus* (Mitchill) and the extinct *S. vitreus glaucus* (Hubbs), commonly called the blue pike.

## Page 138

*Heteropriacanthus cruentatus.* Placed in *Priacanthus* in the 1991 edition, W. C. Starnes, 1988, Bull. Mar. Sci. 43:117–203, concluded that this species belongs in a monotypic genus.

*Apogon pacificus.* This Panamic species is added based on its collection off La Jolla, California in 1998 (R. N. Lea and R. H. Rosenblatt, 2000, CalCOFI Rep. 41:117–129).

*Astrapogon puncticulatus.* Date of publication correction.

*Astrapogon stellatus.* Date of publication correction.

*Phaeoptyx conklini.* Date of publication correction.

## Page 139

Malacanthidae. See Dactylopteridae above, between Liparidae and Centropomidae.

*Caulolatilus affinis.* H. J. Walker, Jr., P. A. Hastings, and R. H. Steele, 2002, Calif. Fish Game 88(3):139–141 report on the capture of this species off Point Loma, California in December 2000.

*Caulolatilus hubbsi.* This species was regarded as a synonym of *C. princeps* in the 1980 edition (p. 83) and by J. S. Grove and R. J. Lavenberg, 1997, The fishes of the Galápagos Islands, Stanford University Press, Stanford, California. Although we acknowledge doubts concerning its validity, we prefer to recognize it, as did W. Schneider and F. Krupp *in* Fischer et al. (1995, Volume III:1268), for reasons stated in R. P. Marino and J. K. Dooley, 1982, J. Zool. (Lond.) 196:151–163, until a thorough study is published demonstrating otherwise.

*Caulolatilus princeps.* Date of publication correction.

*Malacanthus plumieri.* Date of publication correction.

*Echeneis neucratoides.* Spelling of author's name and date of publication correction.

*Remora albescens.* Date of publication correction, and B. O'Toole, 2002, Can. J. Zool. 80(596–

623) showed that the genus *Remora* is paraphyletic without including the genus *Remorina*, where this species was placed in the 1991 edition.

## Page 140

Coryphaenidae. The common name dolphinfish is preferred to the previously used term dolphin to avoid confusion with the cetaceans known as dolphins. The common names mahimahi (with variations in spelling) and dorado are also used in trade.

*Coryphaena equiselis*. Correction of specific name from *equisetis*. See Corphaenidae for change in common name.

*Coryphaena hippurus*. See Corphaenidae for change in common name.

*Caranx bartholomaei*. In some works, certain species of *Caranx* have been placed in other genera (e.g., in *Carangoides, Gnathanodon*, and *Pseudocaranx*). We follow the view expressed in Smith-Vaniz et al. 1999 (p. 237), and await a detailed revision of the group before recommending change. *Caranx bartholomaei* is placed in *Carangoides* by some workers (e.g., W. A. Laroche, W. F. Smith-Vaniz, and S. L. Richardson, 1984, Pages 510–530 *in* H. G. Moser, W. J. Richards, D. M. Cohen, M. P. Fahay, A. W. Kendall, Jr., and S. L. Richardson, editors, Ontogeny and systematics of fishes, American Society of Ichthyologists and Herpetologists, Special Publication No. 1, Lawrence, Kansas).

*Caranx caninus*. Date of publication correction.

*Caranx crysos*. See *C. bartholomaei*.

*Caranx dentex*. This species is sometimes recognized in the genus *Pseudocaranx* (see *C. bartholomaei*).

*Caranx hippos*. Occurs in extremely low salinity and possibly fresh water in parts of western Florida.

*Caranx otrynter*. See *C. bartholomaei*.

*Caranx ruber*. See *C. bartholomaei*.

*Caranx sexfasciatus*. R. N. Lea and H. J. Walker, Jr., 1995, Calif. Fish Game. 81(3):89–95, reported on bigeye trevally from southern California.

*Caranx vinctus*. This species of jack was collected in San Diego Bay, California in 1997 (R. N. Lea and R. H. Rosenblatt, 2000, CalCOFI Rep. 41:117–129). See *C. bartholomaei*.

*Decapterus muroadsi*. *Decapterus scombrinus* (Valenciennes, 1846), Mexican scad, listed in the 1991 edition, was considered a junior synonym of this species by W. F. Smith-Vaniz *in* Fischer et al. (1995, Volume II:965). *Decapterus muroadsi* is a widespread, primarily Indo-Pacific, species to which the name amberstripe scad has been widely applied (e.g., Robins et al. [1991:102, World list]; W. F. Smith-Vaniz *in* Fischer et al. [1995, Volume II:965]; and W. F. Smith-Vaniz *in* Carpenter and Niem [1999, Volume 4:2721]). We here adopt that name in preference to the name "Mexican scad."

*Elagatis bipinnulata*. Date of publication correction.

## Page 141

*Oligoplites saurus*. Correction of author.

*Selene brevoortii*. R. N. Lea and H. J. Walker, Jr., 1995, Calif. Fish Game 81(3):89–95, reported on Mexican lookdown from southern California.

*Selene brownii*. Eschmeyer (1998:287) noted uncertainty in attributing authorship of this species to Cuvier, 1816, or to Spix & Agassiz (ex Cuvier) 1831. We accept the former, based on W. N. Eschmeyer's interpretation (personal communication, November 2000) that Article 12.2 of the Code would serve to validate Cuvier's 1816 description, which was based on P. Browne's 1789 description (from Jamaica), even though the latter work is not available for nomenclatural purposes. The species appears to be valid (W. F. Smith-Vaniz, personal communication, November 2000). *Selene spixii* (Swainson, 1839), the full moonfish, is considered a synonym of this species.

*Selene orstedii*. Specific name often spelled *oerstedii* (see Eschmeyer 1998:1254 and Article 32.5.2.1 of the Code).

*Selene peruviana*. Date of publication correction.

*Seriola fasciata*. Date of publication correction.

*Seriola lalandi*. Although the common name "yellowtail," used in previous lists, has extensive and longtime use on the Pacific Coast in our area, we recommend the added modifier "jack" in order to avoid confusion with other species of "yellowtails," such as the yellowtail rockfish and yellowtail snapper. Allen and Robertson (1994) and W. F. Smith-Vaniz *in* Fischer et al. (1995, Volume II:977) gave the common name as "yellowtail amberjack."

*Trachinotus rhodopus*. Parentheses are removed from the author's name.

*Uraspis helvola.* The taxonomy of *Uraspis* is confusing. In our area, we believe there is one species in the Atlantic and two species with unresolved taxonomic status that may be conspecific in the Pacific (W. F. Smith-Vaniz, personal communication, January 2001). We recognize *U. helvola* as one of the species occurring in the Pacific in our area, based on the opinion of W. F. Smith-Vaniz *in* Fischer et al. (1995, Volume II:986), who gave *U. secunda* as a possible junior synonym. We continue to recognize *U. secunda* following Smith-Vaniz et al. (1999).

*Uraspis secunda.* See *U. helvola.*

*Brama brama.* Date of publication correction.

### Page 142

*Taractes rubescens.* Added to the list on basis of occurrence in Gulf of Mexico, noted by B. A. Thompson and S. J. Russell, 1996, Publ. Espec. Inst. Esp. Oceanogr. 21:185–198. They also discussed a potential taxonomic problem. We accept their recommendation of the common name keeltail pomfret rather than the FAO name "black pomfret."

*Taractichthys longipinnis.* Generic name spelling correction.

*Taractichthys steindachneri.* Generic name spelling and date of publication correction.

*Emmelichthys ruber.* Added to the list on basis of one 8.4-cm-SL specimen regurgitated by a *Lutjanus campechanus* caught at 174 m off Florida in the Gulf of Mexico (R. Ruiz-Carus, R. E. Matheson, Jr., and L. H. Bullock, 2002, Bull. Mar. Sci. 70 (1):241–244).

Lutjanidae. *Symphysanodon berryi,* placed in Lutjanidae in the 1991 edition, is recognized here in its own family, Symphysanodontidae, on the advice of W. D. Anderson, Jr. (personal communication, June 2000).

*Apsilus dentatus.* Although listed in the 1960–1991 editions, based on occurrence on Alligator Reef, Florida Keys, reported by W. A. Starck II, and published in W. A. Starck II, 1968, Undersea Biology 1(1): 5–40 (the only issue published), there were no further reports of this species from United States waters until Trimm and Searcy's (1989, Northeast Gulf Sci. 10(2):157–158) report of a specimen taken off Texas at 40 m.

*Lutjanus apodus.* Date of publication correction.

*Lutjanus jocu.* Correction of authors. Also see *L. novemfasciatus.*

### Page 143

*Lutjanus novemfasciatus.* Long known from Mexican waters, this species was taken off Morro Bay, California in January 2001 (M. T. Tognazzini, 2003, Calif. Fish Game 89(4):201–202). Care must be taken that the common name in English not be confused with the dog snapper of the Atlantic Ocean.

*Lutjanus purpureus.* Date of publication correction based on Eschmeyer (1998: Online version, February 2002); parentheses are also added to the author's name. Presence in United States waters referred to in the 1991 edition now published by F. C. Rohde, S. W. Ross, S. P. Epperly, and G. H. Burgess, 1996, Brimleyana 23:53–64.

*Ocyurus chrysurus.* Several authors, including M. E. Clarke, M. L. Domeier, and W. A. Laroche, 1997, Bull. Mar. Sci. 61:511–539, have synonymized *Ocyurus* with *Lutjanus.* However, we agree with the advice of workers such as W. D. Anderson, Jr. and G. D. Johnson that synonymization of a long-established generic name such as *Ocyurus* is premature until a phylogenetic study is done on the group.

*Pristipomoides freemani.* Change in common name from yelloweye wenchman to the more diagnostic name used here, relative to other western Atlantic species of the genus, as recommended by W. D. Anderson, Jr., 1966, Bull. Mar. Sci. 16(4):816.

*Lobotes pacificus.* J. M. Rounds and R. F. Feeney, 1993, Calif. Fish Game 79(4):167–168, reported on this species, as *L. surinamensis,* from San Pedro, California. During the 1997–1998 El Niño, a number of tripletail were taken off southern California (R. N. Lea and R. H. Rosenblatt, 2000, CalCOFI Rep. 41:117–129). We choose to recognize Atlantic and eastern Pacific populations as distinct at the species level, and therefore, we add the geographic modifiers Pacific and Atlantic to the common name of the two species.

*Lobotes surinamensis.* See *L. pacificus.*

*Diapterus auratus.* Date of publication correction and distribution change. Occurs at extremely low salinities and possibly in fresh water in parts of Florida. R. G. Gilmore (personal communication, June 2000) stated that the common name Irish pompano is seldom if ever used by the public; however, we retain it because of its long history of use in the literature and in the absence of any other name in use in our area brought to our attention.

*Eucinostomus argenteus.* Distribution change. See *E. dowii*, its eastern Pacific cognate, and *E. gracilis*. This species may rarely stray into fresh water in Mexico, but we lack verified museum records, and most literature records of such occurrence are probably referable to *E. harengulus* (R. E. Matheson, Jr., personal communication, June 2001).

*Eucinostomus currani.* This species was reported in the 1970 edition from California as *E. gracilis*. The vernacular name Pacific flagfin mojarra appropriately applies to *E. currani*. D. J. Miller and R. N. Lea, 1972, Calif. Dep. Fish Game Fish Bull. 157:152 used this common name for the species, which at that time was reported on as *Eucinostomus* sp., and noted in the appendix of the 1970 edition "that the specimen of *E. gracilis* listed for California is to receive a new name, because the name *E. gracilis* is identified with *E. californiensis elongatus*." Doubt has existed concerning the authorship of *E. currani* (Eschmeyer 1998); however, since the published original description (*in* A. Yáñez-Arancibia, 1980, Taxonomía, ecología y estructura de las comunidades de peces en lagunas costeras con bocas efímeras del Pacífico de México, Centro de Ciencias del Mar y Limnología [de la] Universidad Nacional Autónoma de México, Publicación Especial 2 [para (for) 1978]:1–306) was translated from Zahuranec, 1967 (B. J. Zahuranec, 1967, The gerreid fishes of the genus *Eucinostomus* in the eastern Pacific, MS thesis, University of California, San Diego), we conclude that the full authorship should be Zahuranec, 1980, *in* Yáñez-Arancibia (see Article 50.1 of the Code).

*Eucinostomus dowii.* Recognized as a valid species by B. J. Zahuranec (1967 thesis, see above) and followed by A. Yáñez Arancibia (1980, see above), M. Tapia-García and G. Ayala-Pérez, 1996–1997, Clave para la determinación de las especies de mojarras de México (Pisces: Gerreidae), Rev. Biol. Trop. 44(3)/45(1):519–525, Castro-Aguirre et al. (1999), and others. R. E. Matheson, Jr. has examined specimens of all eastern Pacific *Eucinostomus* (R. E. Matheson, Jr., 1983, Taxonomic studies of the *Eucinostomus argenteus* complex, Ph.D. dissertation,

Texas A & M University, College Station) and concluded that none are conspecific with western Atlantic forms (R. E. Matheson, Jr., personal communication, November 2000). Therefore, what was recognized on the Pacific Coast in the 1991 edition as *E. argenteus* is treated here as a separate species, *E. dowii*.

*Eucinostomus entomelas.* See *E. currani* regarding authorship.

*Eucinostomus gracilis.* The name Pacific flagfin mojarra, which has been incorrectly applied to this species since the 1970 edition, appropriately applies to *E. currani*. Graceful mojarra is applied here to *E. gracilis*, following W. A. Bussing *in* Fischer et al. (1995, Volume II:1123).

*Eucinostomus harengulus.* Distribution change. Occurs in fresh water in parts of Florida (specimens in the Florida Museum of Natural History) and Mexico.

*Eucinostomus jonesii.* Original spelling ends with -*ii*.

## Page 144

*Eucinostomus lefroyi.* Some authors recognize this species in *Ulaema* (e.g., Castro-Aguirre et al. 1999), but we prefer to retain it in *Eucinostomus* pending a phylogenetic study justifying the former action (as advised by R. E. Matheson, Jr., personal communication, April 2001).

*Eucinostomus melanopterus.* In addition to being known in fresh water in Mexico, there are reports of its occurrence in the lower reaches of rivers in Georgia, Florida, and Texas (R. E. Matheson, Jr., personal communication, September 2002).

*Eugerres plumieri.* Placed in *Eugerres* rather than *Diapterus*, following G. D. Deckert and D. W. Greenfield, 1987, Copeia 1987(1):182–194, and R. Ramon-Carus and M. Uribe-Alcocer, 2003, Caribb. J. Sci. 39(1):109–115. Change in author also made.

*Gerres cinereus.* A. Antuna-Mendiola, J. L. Castro-Aguirre, J. De la Cruz-Agüero, and J. L. Ortiz-Galindo, 2003, American Society of Ichthyologists and Herpetologists (ASIH), Program book and abstracts, Manaus, Brazil (p. 23), presented evidence to indicate that the eastern Pacific *Gerres simillimus* Regan, 1907 is specifically distinct from the western Atlantic *G. cinereus*; we await publication of the evidence before making this change.

*Anisotremus davidsonii*. Date of publication correction and original spelling ends with *-ii*.

*Anisotremus surinamensis*. Date of publication correction.

*Conodon serrifer*. This species was collected at San Onofre Nuclear Generating Station, Orange County, California, in January 1992, as documented by R. H. Moore and K. T. Herbinson, 2002, Calif. Fish Game 88(4):178–180.

*Haemulon flaviguttatum*. R. N. Lea and R. H. Rosenblatt, 1992, Calif. Fish Game 78(4):163–165, reported on this species from southern California.

### Page 145

*Haemulon plumierii*. Original spelling ends with *-ii*.

*Haemulopsis axillaris*. The validity of *Haemulopsis* as a genus is not firmly established, and it is recognized as a subgenus of *Pomadasys* by some authors.

*Haemulopsis elongatus*. See *H. axillaris*.

*Haemulopsis leuciscus*. See *H. axillaris*.

*Haemulopsis nitidus*. See *H. axillaris*.

*Orthopristis cantharinus*. The presence of this species, often mistaken for *O. chalceus*, off Mexico, as noted in R. J. McKay and M. Schneider *in* Fischer et al. (1995, Volume II:1164) and others, requires confirmation. J. S. Grove and R. J. Lavenberg, 1997, The fishes of the Galápagos Islands, Stanford University Press, Stanford, California, regarded it as endemic to the Galápagos.

*Xenistius californiensis*. Date of publication correction.

*Inermia vittata*. Date of publication correction.

### Page 146

*Calamus bajonado*. Correction of author.

*Diplodus holbrookii*. Original spelling ends with *-ii*.

*Stenotomus caprinus*. Change of author from Bean. Castro-Aguirre et al. (1999) regarded this species as a junior synonym of *S. chrysops* (Linnaeus, 1766).

*Bairdiella batabana*. N. L. Chao, 2003 (dated 2002), Sciaenidae, croakers (drums), Pages 1583–1653 *in* K. E. Carpenter, editor, The living marine resources of the western central Atlantic, FAO species identification guide for fishery purposes, Volume 3, FAO, Rome, placed this species in *Corvula*.

*Bairdiella icistia*. In United States, confined to Salton Sea, California, a highly saline environment.

### Page 147

*Bairdiella sanctaeluciae*. N. L. Chao, 2003 (dated 2002), Sciaenidae, croakers (drums), Pages 1583–1653 *in* K. E. Carpenter, editor, The living marine resources of the western central Atlantic, FAO species identification guide for fishery purposes, Volume 3, FAO, Rome, placed this species in *Corvula*.

*Cynoscion arenarius*. Date of publication correction.

*Cynoscion nothus*. Date of publication correction based on W. D. Anderson, Jr. and L. D. Stephens, 2002, John Edwards Holbrook (1794–1871) and his *Southern Ichthyology* (1847–1848), Arch. Nat. Hist. 29(3):317–332.

*Cynoscion parvipinnis*. Date of publication correction.

*Cynoscion xanthulus*. In United States confined to Salton Sea, California, a highly saline environment.

*Equetus punctatus*. Correction of author.

*Isopisthus remifer*. Possibly synonymous with *Ancylodon altipinnis* Steindachner, 1866, described from Peru. N. L. Chao *in* Fischer et al. (1995, Volume III:1466) noted *I. altipinnis* (Steindachner, 1866) as "another scientific name still in use" for *I. remifer* Jordan & Gilbert, 1881 [sic, 1882] described from Panama. However, N. L. Chao later felt (personal communication to LTF, June 2000) that both species are likely valid. We note that the name *I. altipinnis* has been used by some workers in Pacific Central America (e.g., W. A. Bussing and M. I. López S., 1994, Peces demersales y pelágicos costeros del Pacífico de Centro América meridional – guía ilustrada, Rev. Biol. Trop.- Publ. Esp., San José, Costa Rica).

*Menticirrhus littoralis*. See *Cynoscion nothus* above. The term "Gulf" in the common name is treated as a proper noun, and although originally described from outside the Gulf of Mexico (South Carolina), the name applies to an area of primary occurrence.

### Page 148

*Micropogonias ectenes*. Type locality is in the southern Gulf of California at Mazatlán, Mexico. Although considered a valid species by N. L. Chao *in* Fischer et al. (1995, Volume III: 1479), J. D. McPhail, 1960,

Copeia 1960(3):262–263, placed it in the synonymy of *M. altipinnis* (Günther, 1864), based on a comparative study of specimens from Panama (type locality of *M. altipinnis*) and Mexico.

*Pareques acuminatus.* Placed in *Equetus* in the 1991 edition. We follow G. C. Miller and L. P. Woods, 1988, Bull. Mar. Sci. 43(1):88–92, and K. Sasaki, 1998, Mem. Fac. Fish. Hokkaido Univ. 36(1/2):1–137 in according generic recognition of *Pareques* for this and several other species appearing in the 1991 edition. This was also accepted by Smith-Vaniz et al. (1999), who consider *Pareques* to be a sister taxon of *Equetus*. Correction of author.

*Pareques iwamotoi.* See *P. acuminatus* for generic placement.

*Pareques umbrosus.* See *P. acuminatus* for generic placement.

*Pareques viola.* As noted by N. L. Chao *in* Fischer et al. (1995, Volume III:1441) and Thomson et al. (2000), the population heretofore considered to be this species in Mexican waters is probably a new species. This is one of many problems of New World sciaenids under study by N. L. Chao. We follow existing literature in formulating our decisions until these problems are better resolved.

*Roncador stearnsii.* Date of publication correction and original spelling ends with -*ii*.

Page 149

*Mulloidichthys dentatus.* This species, included in previous editions as occurring in the United States, is removed as "P" in distribution, based on R. N. Lea and R. H. Rosenblatt, 2000, CalCOFI Rep. 41:117–129, who noted that specimens forming the historic California record are in fact *Pseudupeneus grandisquamis*. *Mulloidichthys dentatus* is common in the Mexican Pacific.

*Upeneus parvus.* Date of publication correction.

*Pempheris schomburgkii.* Original spelling ends with -*ii*.

*Chaetodon humeralis.* Change in spelling of common name from threeband butterflyfish.

*Prognathodes aculeatus.* Placed in *Chaetodon* in the 1991 edition. We follow W. E. Burgess, 2001, Tropical Fish Hobbyist 49(6):56–63, and the cladistic study of W. L. Smith, J. F. Webb, and S. D. Blum, 2003, Cladistics 19:287–306, in our present generic alloca-

tion (*Prognathodes* was previously recognized as a subgenus of *Chaetodon*).

*Prognathodes aya.* See *P. aculeatus.*

*Prognathodes falcifer.* Placed in *Chaetodon* in the 1991 edition, we follow J. S. Grove and R. J. Lavenberg, 1997, The fishes of the Galápagos Islands, Stanford University Press, Stanford, California, and the two cited papers upon which they based their decision, and the cladistic study of W. L. Smith, J. F. Webb, and S. D. Blum, 2003, Cladistics 19:287–306, in placing it in *Prognathodes.*

*Prognathodes guyanensis.* This species has been photographed and collected off the Florida Keys, 64–94 m, at sites also occupied by *P. aya*, by Forrest A. Young and Ben Daughtry of Dynasty Marine Associates, Inc. (F. A. Young, personal communication, December 2002). We use the common name employed by W. E. Burgess, 1978, Butterflyfishes of the world, TFH Publications, Neptune City, New Jersey.

Page 150

*Holacanthus bermudensis.* Since the subspecies name *bermudensis* is based, at least in part, on hybrid specimens, it is unavailable according to Article 23.8 of the Code. The petition of C. R. Gilbert, J. S. Nelson, E. J. Crossman, H. Espinosa-Pérez, L. T. Findley, R. N. Lea, and J. D. Williams, 2000, Bull. Zool. Nomencl. 57(4):218–222, to conserve the subspecific name *bermudensis* in *H. ciliaris bermudensis* was accepted in Opinion 2003, Bull. Zool. Nomencl. 59(2):149–150.

*Pseudopentaceros wheeleri.* Previously known as *Pentaceros pectoralis* (Hardy, 1983), longfin armorhead. R. L. Humphreys, Jr., G. A. Winans, and D. T. Tagami, 1989, Copeia 1989(1):142–153, concluded that North Pacific armorheads consist of a single, metamorphic species and selected *Pseudopentaceros wheeleri* as the *nomen*. They used the common name North Pacific pelagic armorhead. In the 1991 edition of this list, the committtee regarded *Pseudopentaceros* as a synonym of *Pentaceros*, but most works recognize this species in the genus as given.

*Hermosilla azurea.* Change in spelling of common name from zebra perch.

*Medialuna californiensis.* Date of publication correction.

Kuhliidae. Added to the list for the species noted.

## Page 151

Elassomatidae. See Nelson (1994) for strong evidence, based largely on the work of G. D. Johnson, that this family is not related to the Centrarchidae (in which species of *Elassoma* were placed in the 1991 edition). Whether this taxon is most closely related to other perciforms or to members of other groups, such as the gasterosteiforms/gasterosteids as suggested by G. D. Johnson and V. G. Springer, 1997, American Society of Ichthyologists and Herpetologists (ASIH), Program book and abstracts, Seattle, Washington, p. 176) and G. D. Johnson and V. G. Springer (personal communication, November 2002) is uncertain.

*Elassoma alabamae.* This new species was described from the Tennessee River drainage in Alabama by R. L. Mayden, 1993, Bulletin of the Alabama Museum of Natural History 16:2.

Cichlidae. There is not complete agreement on the genera that should be recognized in this family. In the 1991 edition, most New World species were placed in *Cichlasoma.* Pending a phylogenetic study of all species involved and the addition of species from Mexico, we follow the taxonomy of the 1991 edition in the use of a broad genus *Cichlasoma.* Some of the 49 species may be placed with certainty in the monophyletic genera *Herichthys, Parachromis,* and *Thorichthys.* However, many other species cannot be assigned with reasonable certainty to genera. *Amphilophus, Archocentrus, Paraneetroplus, Theraps,* and *Vieja* are used for some species, but the limits are uncertain. We acknowledge that *Cichlasoma,* as recognized here, is artificial and does not reflect available phylogenetic information found, for example, in S. O. Kullander, 1996, Ichthyological Exploration of Freshwaters 7(2):149–172 and S. O. Kullander and K. E. Hartel, 1997, Ichthyological Exploration of Freshwaters 7(3):193–202 and more recent studies using molecular and morphological analyses. S. O. Kullander, 2003, *in* R. E. Reis, S. O. Kullander and C. J. Ferraris, Jr., editors, Check list of the freshwater fishes of South and Central America, Family Cichlidae (cichlids), Edipurs, Porto Alegre, places species in our list that are in *Cichlasoma* in the following genera: *Amphilophus* (*C. citrinellum, C. macracanthum, C. nourissati, C.*

*robertsoni*), *Archocentrus* (*C. nigrofasciatum, C. spilurum*), *Herichthys* (*C. bartoni, C. carpintis, C. cyanoguttatum, C. deppii, C. labridens, C. minckleyi, C. pantostictum, C. steindachneri, C. tamasopoensis*), *Parachromis* (*C. friedrichsthalii, C. managuense, C. motaguense*), *Paraneetroplus* (*C. bulleri, C. gibbiceps, C. nebuliferum*), *Theraps* (*C. irregulare, C. lentiginosum, C. rheophilus,* and Kullander regards the latter species as a synonym of *C. lentiginosum*), *Thorichthys* (*C. affine, C. callolepis, C. ellioti, C. helleri, C. meeki, C. pasionis, C. socolofi*), and *Vieja* (*C. argenteum, C. bifasciatum, C. breidohri, C. fenestratum, C. guttulatum, C. hartwegi, C. heterospilum, C. intermedium, C. regani, C. synspilum, C. ufermanni , C. zonatum*). Species name endings are changed accordingly to agree in gender for those species originally placed in other genera; we have benefited from the advice of C. R. Robins (personal communication, October 2003) on some of these names. As noted for two species below, the identification of some introduced species is still uncertain.

*Cichla ocellaris.* The specific identity of this species in Florida is uncertain. Listed as peacock cichlid in the 1991 edition, but referred to as butterfly peacock bass in area of introduction (Florida), and in Florida regulations (peacock bass is used for any species of *Cichla*) (J. E. Hill, personal communication, November 2002).

## Page 152

*Cichlasoma managuense.* This species was placed in *Parachromis* by S. O. Kullander and K. E. Hartel, 1997, Ichthyological Exploration of Freshwaters 7(3):193–202 and, as done here, under the more familiar name *managuense* rather than under the senior name *gulosus.* See also Cichlidae.

*Cichlasoma salvini.* Added from information in Fuller et al. (1999).

## Page 153

*Hemichromis letourneuxi.* What was previously thought to be introduced *H. bimaculatus* Gill, 1862, may represent several species, of which *H. letourneuxi* is the most common (P. V. Loiselle, 1979, Annales du Musée Royale de l'Afrique Centrale Série 8 Sciences Zoologiques 228:1–124; W. F. Smith-Vaniz, personal communication, 1999).

*Heros severus*. Added from information in Fuller et al. (1999).

*Oreochromis aureus*. We agree with E. Trewavas, 1981, Buntbarsche Bull. 81:12, E. Trewavas, 1983, Tilapine fishes of the genera *Sarotherodon*, *Oreochromis* and *Danakilia*, British Museum of Natural History, London, and P. Sodsuk and B. J. McAndrew, 1991, J. Fish Biol. 39(Supplement A):301–308, that certain species recognized in the genus *Tilapia* in the 1991 edition should be placed in *Oreochromis* and *Sarotherodon*. Species name endings are changed accordingly to agree in gender.

*Oreochromis mossambicus*. See *O. aureus*.

*Oreochromis niloticus*. Added from information in Fuller et al. (1999).

*Oreochromis urolepis*. Date of publication correction. See *O. aureus*.

*Sarotherodon melanotheron*. See *O. aureus*.

*Tilapia mariae*. Parentheses are removed from the author's name. V. Klett and A. Meyer, 2002, Mol. Biol. Evol. 19:865–883 suggested that only *T. sparrmanii* Smith, 1840, should be placed in *Tilapia*.

*Tilapia zillii*. Original spelling ends with *-ii*. See *T. mariae*.

*Hysterocarpus traskii*. Original spelling ends with *-ii*.

## Page 154

*Abudefduf troschelii*. Reported in California by D. J. Pondella II, 1997, Calif. Fish Game 83(2):84–86.

*Azurina hirundo*. R. N. Lea and F. McAlery, 1994, Bull. South. Calif. Acad. Sci. 91(1):42–44, reported on the occurrence of this species in California.

*Chromis alta*. Long known from Pacific Mexico, this species is added to the United States fauna based on photographic documentation at Santa Catalina Island, California, in November 1998 (D. V. Richards and J. M. Engle, 2001, Bull. South. Calif. Acad. Sci. 100(3):175–185).

*Chromis atrilobata*. The common name in English follows that given in Allen and Robertson (1994); however, the name "scissortail damselfish" is used in many other publications.

*Chromis enchrysura*. Correction of specific name from *enchrysurus*.

*Stegastes adustus*. D. W. Greenfield and L. P. Woods, 1974, Fieldiana, Zoology 65:9–20, showed that *Pomacentrus fuscus* (= *Eupoma-*

*centrus fuscus*), used for the dusky damselfish in the 1970, 1980, and 1991 editions, is confined to Brazil. Acceptance as *S. adustus* rather than as *S. dorsopunicaus* (= *dorsopunicans*) (Poey, 1868) follows Eschmeyer (1998:42, 495). See *S. diencaeus*. See also Smith-Vaniz et al. (1999).

*Stegastes diencaeus*. We recognize the species placed in the 1991 edition in *Pomacentrus* in the genus *Stegastes* (senior synonym of *Eupomacentrus*, as noted by A. R. Emery and G. R. Allen, 1980, Rec. West. Aust. Mus. 8(2):199–206). See also G. R. Allen, 1991, Damselfishes of the world, Mergus Publishers, Melle, Germany. *Pomacentrus* is a valid genus, but we lack species in our area.

*Stegastes leucostictus*. See *S. diencaeus*.

*Stegastes partitus*. See *S. diencaeus*.

*Stegastes planifrons*. See *S. diencaeus*.

## Page 155

*Stegastes variabilis*. See *S. diencaeus*.

*Decodon melasma*. This deepwater species was taken off southern California in 1998 at 60 m and in 1999 at 100 m (R. N. Lea and R. H. Rosenblatt, 2000, CalCOFI Rep. 41:117–129).

## Page 156

*Oxyjulis californica*. Spelling here of common name señorita, as in the 1980 edition; spelled senorita in 1991 edition.

*Xyrichtys martinicensis*. The senior generic synonym *Hemipteronotus* is suppressed according to ICZN Opinion 1799 (Bull. Zool. Nomencl., 1999, 52(1):109–110) and the genus *Xyrichtys* is conserved for the three species formerly recognized in *Hemipteronotus* (Eschmeyer 1998:1031, 1201, 1595, 1963, 2170, 2891). Date of publication correction.

*Xyrichtys novacula*. See *X. martinicensis*.

*Xyrichtys splendens*. See *X. martinicensis*.

*Nicholsina denticulata*. Common in the Mexican Pacific, this species was observed and photographed by Erik Erikson at Santa Catalina Island, California in 1999 (R. N. Lea and R. H. Rosenblatt, 2000, CalCOFI Rep. 41:117–129).

*Nicholsina usta*. Date of publication correction.

*Scarus coelestinus*. Date of publication correction.

*Scarus coeruleus*. This species dates to Edwards, 1771 and not to Bloch, 1786 if the types involved are conspecific, as noted by Eschmeyer (1998: Online version, February 2002) and W. N. Eschmeyer (personal communication, October 2002). We regard *S. coeruleus* Edwards, 1771 as a forgotten name, and we continue to date to Bloch, 1786 following current usage.

*Scarus iseri.* This species name (as *iserti*) was shown by J.E. Randall and G. Nelson, 1979, Copeia 1979(2):210, to be a senior synonym of *S. croicensis*. The 1980 edition noted that the name *S. iserti* had not been used since 1789, and the name *S. croicensis* was retained in the belief that the ICZN was to be petitioned. *Scarus croicensis* was retained without comment in the 1991 edition. As far as we know, no petition was ever submitted, and *S. iseri (iserti*, e.g., Smith-Vaniz et al. 1999*)* has been resurrected in some recent literature. From comments in Eschmeyer (1998: Online version, February 2002), the correct spelling of the specific name should be *iseri*, the name used by P. Parenti and J. E. Randall, 2000, Ichthyol. Bull. J. L. B. Smith Inst. Ichthyol. 68.

*Scarus vetula.* Correction of author.

## Page 157

*Sparisoma aurofrenatum.* Date of publication correction.

*Sparisoma radians.* Date of publication correction.

*Sparisoma rubripinne.* Date of publication correction. We change the common name of this fish from that used in the 1991 edition, following advice of P. H. Humann (personal communication, November 1999) that the name yellowtail parrotfish, not "redfin parrotfish," is the one widely used in popular fish identification books and is more descriptive.

*Rathbunella alleni.* Although recognized in the 1960–1980 editions (as the rough ronquil), together with *R. hypoplecta* (as the smooth ronquil), this species was treated in the 1991 edition as a junior synonym of *R. hypoplecta* (as the stripedfin ronquil). A. C. Matarese, 1990, Systematics and zoogeography of the ronquils, family Bathymasteridae (Teleostei: Perciformes), Ph.D. dissertation, University of Washington, Seattle, recognized both species as valid, and the only two in the genus, and suggested the more descriptive and appropriate common names as given here (we accept stripefin ronquil for *R. alleni* because, as noted in the above dissertation, there is only one stripe in the anal fin).

*Rathbunella hypoplecta.* See *R. alleni*.

*Zoarcidae. Lycodes sagittarius* McAllister, 1976, archer eelpout, of the Arctic Ocean (Pacific side), is deleted from the list because all verified collection records are from depths greater than 200 m (e.g., Mecklenburg et al. 2002).

*Gymnelus popovi.* Correction of spelling of first author's name.

*Lycenchelys verrillii.* Original spelling ends with *-ii*.

## Page 158

*Lycodes esmarkii.* Original spelling ends with *-ii*.

*Lycodes fasciatus.* Added to the list based on Mecklenburg et al. (2002).

*Lycodes pacificus.* Change in genus from *Lycodopsis* (synonym of *Lycodes*) following W. N. Eschmeyer and E. S. Herald, 1983, A field guide to Pacific Coast fishes of North America, Houghton Mifflin Co., Boston (on the advice of M. E. Anderson), and M. E. Anderson, 1994, Ichthyol. Bull. J. L. B. Smith Inst. Ichthyol. 60:1–120.

*Lycodes pallidus.* Date of publication correction.

*Lycodes raridens.* Correction of spelling of first author's name.

*Lycodes rossi.* Date of publication correction.

*Lycodes vahlii.* Original spelling ends with *-ii*.

*Zoarces americanus.* Correction of author. Change in genus from *Macrozoarces* (synonym of *Zoarces*), following M. E. Anderson, 1994, Ichthyol. Bull. J. L. B. Smith Inst. Ichthyol. 60:1–120.

*Acantholumpenus mackayi.* Change in common name from "pighead prickleback," for reasons given in Mecklenburg et al. (2002).

*Anisarchus medius.* Change in genus from *Lumpenus*, based on literature citations in Eschmeyer (1998: Online version, March 2003) and Mecklenburg et al. (2002). Although the above two sources give 1836 as the correct date, work by C. W. Mecklenburg (personal communication, October 2003) suggests that the 1837 date as given in the 1991 edition is correct.

## Page 159

*Chirolophis snyderi.* Added to the list based on Mecklenburg et al. (2002).

*Esselenichthys carli.* Since the generic name *Esselenia* Follett & Anderson, 1990, as originally applied to this fish, is a junior homonym of *Esselenia* Hebard, 1920 in Orthoptera, a replacement name, *Esselenichthys*, has been proposed by M. E. Anderson, 2003, Copeia 2003(2):414.

*Esselenichthys laurae.* See *E. carli.*

*Kasatkia seigeli.* This new species was described from California by M. Posner and R. J. Lavenberg, 1999, Copeia 1999(4):1035.

*Leptoclinus maculatus.* Change in genus from *Lumpenus* follows various works cited in Eschmeyer (1998: Online version, February 2002) and Mecklenburg et al. (2002).

*Lumpenus fabricii.* Change in author and date from "(Valenciennes, 1836)," following Eschmeyer (1998: Online version, March 2003).

*Lumpenus lampretaeformis.* Correction of spelling of specific name (Eschmeyer 1998: Online version, February 2002).

*Plagiogrammus hopkinsii.* Original spelling ends with -*ii*.

## Page 160

*Pholis fasciata.* A. Yatsu, 1981, Bull. Natl. Sci. Mus. (Tokyo) Ser. A (Zool.) 7(4):165–190, considered *P. gilli* Evermann & Goldsborough, 1907, Bering gunnel (listed in the 1991 edition), to be a junior synonym of *P. fasciata*. This has been confirmed by Mecklenburg et al. (2002) and is accepted here. *Pholis gilli* was considered to be restricted to the Pacific of Alaska, and *P. fasciata* as ranging from the Pacific of Alaska through the Arctic to the North Atlantic.

## Page 161

*Ammodytes dubius.* The year of publication may be 1838 (Eschmeyer 1998:2765).

*Ammodytoides gilli.* B. B. Collette and D. R. Robertson, 2001, Rev. Biol. Trop. 49(Supplement 1):111–115, gave reasons for placing this species in *Ammodytoides* rather than in *Bleekeria*, and regarded it as the senior synonym of *A. lucasanus* (Beebe & Tee-Van, 1938), reported from Baja California Sur.

*Astroscopus guttatus.* Date of publication correction.

*Astroscopus zephyreus.* M. de Jesus-Roldán, L. Ellis, and F. Galván-Magáña, 1993, Calif. Fish Game 79(4):171–172, provided a record of this species from off Huntington Beach, southern California.

## Page 162

*Dactyloscopus foraminosus.* C. E. Dawson, 1982, Bull. Mar. Sci. 32:14–85, noted this species (provisionally) from off southeastern Florida.

The common name, related to the color pattern, was suggested by J. T. Williams (personal communictaion, June 2001).

Labrisomidae. See Clinidae below. The family common names in English and Spanish for the Labrisomidae follows Thomson et al. (2000).

*Haptoclinus apectolophus.* Known depth of occurrence within 200 m not definite (of the two type specimens collected off Arrowsmith Bank, Mexico, the paratype, ANSP 121252, was collected in an otter trawl haul covering a depth range of 173–206 m).

*Labrisomus bucciferus.* Parentheses are removed from the author's name.

## Page 163

*Labrisomus socorroensis.* We regard "*soccorrensis*" as an incorrect original spelling (the species was named after Isla Socorro, the type locality, of the Islas Revillagigedo) and follow prevailing usage (the corrected spelling *socorroensis* was first used by V. G. Springer, 1959, Inst. Mar. Sci. Univ. Tex. 5, on p. 425), as defined in Article 29.5 of the Code. The common name in English was suggested by P. A. Hastings (personal communication, September 2002).

## Page 164

Clinidae. The previously recognized Clinidae is now considered to comprise three families: Labrisomidae, Clinidae, and Chaenopsidae. The composition of the Chaenopsidae is modified from Nelson (1994), following P. A. Hastings and V. G. Springer, 1994, Smithson. Contrib. Zool. 558. The new family common name applied to the Clinidae, as now defined, was suggested by V. G. Springer (personal communication, October 2000).

*Gibbonsia elegans.* Eschmeyer (1998:518, 552) regarded the specific name *elegans* of *G. elegans* (Cooper 1864), recognized in the 1991 and earlier editions, as secondarily preoccupied by *Clinus elegans* Valenciennes, 1836, and gave the replacement name as *Gibbonsia evides* (Jordan & Gilbert, 1883). However, we do not regard the nominal species *Clinus elegans* Valenciennes, as congeneric with *G. elegans* (Cooper), nor do we know of any literature reference in which this has been done. In addition, the name *G. evides* (Jordan & Gilbert, 1883) seems not to have been used prior to Eschmeyer (1998). In following Articles 23.2 and 59.3 of the Code, and considering the literature (e.g., C. Hubbs, 1952, Stanford Ichthyol. Bull. 4(2):41–165) and views of other workers, we continue to use the well-known name *G. elegans* (Cooper) for the spotted kelpfish. The advice of W. N. Eschmeyer (personal communication, October 2003) has been helpful in the present decision.

## Page 165

Chaenopsidae. See Clinidae above. The family common name in English for the Chaenopsidae follows the 1979 and subsequent editions of Thomson et al. (2000) and Smith-Vaniz et al. (1999).

*Chaenopsis ocellata.* Although it has been suggested that the author of this species was Gill, W. F. Smith-Vaniz, 2000, Proc. Biol. Soc. Wash. 113(4):918–925, gave reasons for attributing authorship to Poey, 1865, as given in the 1991 edition.

*Chaenopsis roseola.* Not included in the 1991 edition because of doubts about its validity. We include this species of the Gulf of Mexico pending further study.

*Emblemaria pandionis.* Date of publication correction.

*Emblemariopsis bahamensis.* Placed in the genus *Coralliozetus* in the 1991 edition and *Emblemaria* in the 1980 edition. In recognizing *Emblemariopsis,* we accept the conclusions of P. A. Hastings and V. G. Springer, 1994, Smithson. Contrib. Zool. 558, as had J. C. Tyler and D. M. Tyler, 1999, Smithson. Contrib. Zool. 601.

## Page 166

*Emblemariopsis diaphana.* See *E. bahamensis.*

*Hemiemblemaria simula.* Emendation of specific name from *simulus* to *simula* following Eschmeyer (1998:1565).

*Chasmodes bosquianus.* See *C. longimaxilla.*

*Chasmodes longimaxilla.* Included in the 1991 edition under *C. bosquianus* (Lacepède, 1800), the subspecies *C. bosquianus longimaxilla* Williams, 1983, is here recognized as a valid species, following J. T. Williams, 2003 (dated 2002), Blenniidae (combtooth blennies), Pages 1768–1772 *in* K. E. Carpenter, editor, The living marine resources of the western central Atlantic, FAO species identification guide for fishery purposes, Volume 3, FAO, Rome.

*Hypleurochilus caudovittatus.* This new species, from the Gulf of Mexico off Florida, was shown to be distinct from *H. geminatus* by H. Bath, 1994, Senckenb. Biol. 74(1/2):59–85. R. Ruiz-Carus and P. H. Humann (personal communication, November 1999) have given advice on the common names of the new species of *Hypleurochilus.*

*Hypleurochilus geminatus.* See *H. caudovittatus* and *H. multifilis.*

*Hypleurochilus multifilis.* The validity of this species, distinct from *H. geminatus,* was confirmed by H. Bath, 1994, Senckenb. Biol. 74(1/2):59–85. For common name, see *H. caudovittatus.*

*Hypleurochilus pseudoaequipinnis.* This new species, which ranges from Florida southward in the western Atlantic, was shown to be distinct from *H. aequipinnis* (Günther, 1861), now considered to be restricted to West Africa, by H. Bath, 1994, Senckenb. Biol. 74(1/2):59–85. For common name, see *H. caudovittatus.*

## Page 167

*Lupinoblennius vinctus.* The previously recognized *L. dispar* Herre, 1942, was recognized as a junior synonym of *L. vinctus* by H. Bath, 1996, Senckenb. Biol. 76(1/2):88, 91.

*Ophioblennius macclurei.* Recognized as *O. atlanticus* in the 1991 edition and considered a valid subspecies of *O. atlanticus* by V. G. Springer, 1962, Copeia 1962:426–433 and Smith-Vaniz et al. (1999). We now recognize *O. macclurei* as a valid species based on the molecular evidence of A. Muss, D. R. Robertson, C. A. Stepien, P. Wirtz, and B. W. Bowen, 2001, Evolution 55(3):561–572, advice and morphological data of V. G. Springer (personal communication, January 2002), listing by J. T. Williams, 2003 (dated 2002), Blenniidae (combtooth blennies), Pages 1768–1772 *in* K. E. Carpenter, editor, The living marine resources of the western central Atlantic, FAO species identification guide for fishery purposes, Volume 3, FAO, Rome, and advice of W. F. Smith-Vaniz (personal communication, January 2002). *Ophioblennius atlanticus* is now regarded as being restricted to the eastern Atlantic.

*Plagiotremus azaleus.* This species has been observed and collected by D. J. Pondella II, in King Harbor, Redondo Beach, California (R. N. Lea and R. H. Rosenblatt, 2000, CalCOFI

Rep. 41:117–129). The common name in English was suggested by E. S. Hobson, 1968, U.S. Fish Wildl. Serv. Res. Rep. 73.

Gobiesocidae. Recognized in the 1991 edition as a pre-atherininform taxon in its own order, Gobiesociformes. The evidence supporting this as a perciform rather than as a pre-atherinomorph group is weak, but we nevertheless accept the conclusions of L. R. Parenti and J. Song, 1996, Pages 427–444 *in* M. L. J. Stiassny, L. R. Parenti, and G. D. Johnson, editors, Interrelationships of fishes, Academic Press, San Diego, California (also see Nelson 1994).

*Acyrtops beryllinus*. Date of publication correction.

*Acyrtus artius*. J. E. Böhlke and C. C. G. Chaplin, 1993, Fishes of the Bahamas and adjacent tropical waters, University of Texas Press, Austin, and in their 1968 edition regarded *Acyrtus* as a synonym of *Arcos*. We do not make this change and maintain recognition of both genera, as advised by J. C. Briggs (personal communication, September 2002), and as has been done by J. D. McEachran, 2003 (dated 2002), Gobiesocidae (cling-fishes), Pages 1773–1774 *in* K. E. Carpenter, editor, The living marine resources of the western central Atlantic, FAO species identification guide for fishery purposes, Volume 3, FAO, Rome.

*Acyrtus rubiginosus*. See *A. artius*.

## Page 168

*Gobiesox punctulatus*. Date of publication correction.

*Rimicola cabrilloi*. This new species was described from islands off southern California, where it is apparently endemic, by J. C. Briggs, 2002, Copeia 2002(2):441. We base the common name on the geographic name by which these islands are collectively known.

*Foetorepus agassizii*. Original spelling ends with -*ii*.

*Foetorepus goodenbeani*. This new species was described from off the eastern United States and in the northern Gulf of Mexico by T. Nakabo and K. E. Hartel, 1999, Copeia 1999(1):115. The common name was suggested by W. F. Smith-Vaniz and K. E. Hartel (personal communication, 1999).

*Paradiplogrammus bairdi*. Date of publication correction.

*Synchiropus atrilabiatus*. Known before from Mexican waters, this species was taken off Santa Catalina Island in 1998 and off San Diego, California, in 1999 (R. N. Lea and R. H. Rosenblatt, 2000, CalCOFI Rep. 41:117–129).

## Page 169

*Dormitator maculatus*. Date of publication correction.

*Eleotris amblyopsis*. What was given as *E. pisonis* (Gmelin, 1788) in the 1991 edition is now considered to be this species. F. Pezold and B. Cage, 2002, Tulane Stud. Zool. Bot. 31(2):19–63, restricted *E. pisonis* to continental South America from Brazil to eastern Venezuela. The common name in English is from D. W. Greenfield and J. E. Thomerson, 1997, Fishes of the continental waters of Belize, University Press of Florida, Gainesville. *Eleotris abacurus* Jordan & Gilbert, 1896, for which the type locality is the harbor at Charleston, South Carolina, has usually been regarded as a synonym of *E. pisonis*, but has been listed as *abacurus* from fresh water in Mexico (Espinosa-Pérez et al. 1993). It was considered to be a synonym of *E. amblyopsis* by Pezold and Cage in the above 2002 study.

*Eleotris perniger*. Rare in the United States but common in Mexico (F. L. Pezold, personal communication, October 2000).

*Eleotris picta*. Change of author from Kner & Steindachner.

*Guavina guavina*. One specimen has been reported from a freshwater ditch entering Port Canaveral, Florida by D. S. Taylor, 1996, Gulf Mex. Sci. 14(2):120–122. We assume that this record (UF 101745) represents a small established population (with inferred past presence, at least in Florida marine waters), but there is a possibility that *G. guavina* could have been introduced into Florida.

Gobiidae. See Ptereleotridae below.

*Awaous banana*. R. E. Watson, 1996, Ichthyological Exploration of Freshwaters 7(1):1–18, concluded that this species is distinct from *A. tajasica* (Lichtenstein, 1822), recognized in the 1991 edition as occurrence "A-F," with the latter now known only from Brazil in fresh and brackish water. Watson also considered *A. transandeanus* (Günther, 1861), on Pacific slopes, to be a junior synonym of *A. banana* (a conclusion not followed by R. R. Miller et al., in press, who are maintaining recognition of *A. transandeanus*). Therefore, *A. banana*, based on occurrence of adults, is now known from fresh water from northern Florida to Trinidad and Venezuela and from fresh water from northwest Mexico, including Baja California Sur, to northern Peru. Larvae, however, unlike adults which are intolerant of salt water, occur in marine and brackish waters (R. E. Watson, personal communication, August 2002), as is true for many other freshwater gobiids such as the two species of *Sicydium* in Mexico.

## Page 170

*Chriolepis vespa*. This species was described from the notheastern Gulf of Mexico (35–183 m) by P. A. Hastings and S. A. Bortone, 1981, Proc. Biol. Soc. Wash. 94(2):428. It was inadvertently omitted from the 1991 edition.

*Coryphopterus personatus*. Date of publication correction.

*Coryphopterus tortugae*. There is doubt about the validity of this species, and Smith-Vaniz et al. (1999) placed it in the synonymy of *C. glaucofraenum*.

*Ctenogobius boleosoma*. F. L. Pezold III, 1984, A revision of the gobioid fish genus *Gobionellus*, Ph.D. dissertation, University of Texas, Austin, split the New World genus *Gobionellus* into two genera, *Gobionellus* (including *G. microdon* and *G. oceanicus* in our area) and *Ctenogobius* (which includes all other species of *Gobionellus* recognized in the 1991 edition: *C. boleosoma*, *C. pseudofasciatus*, *C. saepepallens*, *C. sagittula*, *C. shufeldti*, *C. smaragdus*, *C. stigmaticus*, and *C. stigmaturus*).

*Ctenogobius claytonii*. Eschmeyer (1998:387) indicated *C. claytonii* (Meek, 1902) to be an objective synonym of *C. fasciatus* Gill, 1858, citing as his source Robins and Lachner (1966:867). However, F. L. Pezold, in an unpublished portion of his Ph.D. dissertation (see *C. boleosoma* for reference) showed these two taxa to be valid species. He also synonymized *Gobionellus atripinnis* Gilbert & Randall, 1979, the blackfin goby, of the 1991 edition, with *C. claytonii* (Meek, 1902). *Ctenogobius claytonii*, which frequents estuaries and lagoons, once had been placed in the synonymy of *C. shufeldti*, but was recognized as distinct by C. R. Gilbert and D. P Kelso, 1971, Bull. Fla. State Mus. Biol. Sci.

16(1):1–54; C. R. Gilbert and J. E. Randall, 1979, Northeast Gulf Sci. 3(1):27–47; and Castro-Aguirre et al. (1999). The English common name of *C. claytonii* is from the above mentioned dissertation of F. L Pezold.

*Ctenogobius fasciatus*. Collected in the Sebastian River, Indian River County, Florida, on several occasions over the past 10–15 years in 0–5 ppt salinity, but not collected at the mouth of the river (R. G. Gilmore, personal communication, November 2000). This species also occurs in marine waters outside our area. See *C. boleosoma* and *C. claytonii*.

*Ctenogobius pseudofasciatus*. Date of publication correction. See *C. boleosoma*.

*Ctenogobius saepepallens*. See *C. boleosoma*.

*Ctenogobius sagittula*. See *C. boleosoma*.

*Ctenogobius shufeldti*. Date of publication correction. See *C. boleosoma* and *C. claytonii*.

*Ctenogobius smaragdus*. See *C. boleosoma*.

*Ctenogobius stigmaticus*. See *C. boleosoma*.

*Ctenogobius stigmaturus*. See *C. boleosoma*.

## Page 171

*Elacatinus horsti*. This and three other species recognized in *Gobiosoma* in the 1991 list are now placed in *Elacatinus*, following D. F. Hoese and S. Reader, 2001, Rev. Biol. Trop. 49(Suplement 1):157–167. We also appreciate the advice of M. S. Taylor in making this change (personal communication, February 2002).

*Elacatinus macrodon*. See *E. horsti*.

*Elacatinus oceanops*. See *E. horsti*.

*Elacatinus xanthiprora*. See *E. horsti*.

*Gnatholepis thompsoni*. Date of publication correction.

*Gobioides broussonetii*. Original spelling ends with *–ii*. Although the original spelling of the specific name is *broussonnetii*, a spelling used by some authors, we retain the spelling with one "n," which is in prevailing usage and deemed to be a justified emendation following Article 33.2.3.1 of the Code.

## Page 172

*Gobiosoma robustum*. Distribution change. Specimens from the St. Johns River, Florida, previously thought to be this species, have been reidentified as *G. bosc* by C. R. Gilbert; elsewhere, we suspect *G. robustum* occurs in no more than brackish water.

*Lophogobius cyprinoides*. Some freshwater occurrences noted in Florida, but none far from salt water (e.g., one specimen noted from a freshwater canal near Boca Raton by W. C. Starnes, personal communication, September 2002).

## Page 173

*Neogobius melanostomus*. This species, which is now widespread in the Great Lakes basin, was probably introduced with ballast water from ships originating in Europe. See D. J. Jude, R. H. Reider, and G. R. Smith, 1992, Can. J. Fish. Aquat. Sci. 92(2):416–421, and E. J. Crossman, E. Holm, R. Chohnondeley, and K. Turininga, 1992, Can. Field-Nat. 106(2):206–209.

*Oxyurichthys stigmalophius*. Placed in *Gobionellus* in the 1991 edition, this species belongs in *Oxyurichthys* (R. S. Birdsong, E. O. Murdy, and F. L. Pezold, 1988, Bull. Mar. Sci. 42(2):174–214; F. Pezold, 1998, Copeia 1998(3):687–695).

*Proterorhinus marmoratus*. This species, which occurs in the St. Clair River to extreme western Lake Erie, was probably introduced with ballast water from ships originating in Europe. See D. J. Jude, R. H. Reider, and G. R. Smith, 1992, Can. J. Fish. Aquat. Sci. 92(2):416–421. In contrast to *Neogobius melanostomus,* this species has moved very little from its original site of introduction. The study of T. A. Bowens and C. A. Stepien, 2003, Abstract, International Aquatic Nuisance Species Conference, Windsor, Ontario, suggests that *Proterorhinus* should be synonymized with *Neogobius* and that the form in the Great Lakes may represent a separate species from *P. marmoratus,* namely *P. rubromaculatus* (which would also be placed in *Neogobius*).

*Psilotris celsus*. Reported off Georgia by M. R. Gilligan, 1989, National Oceanic and Atmospheric Administration, Technical Memorandum, National Ocean Service, Marine Estuarine Management Division 25:57 (W. F. Smith-Vaniz, personal communication, 1999).

*Rhinogobiops nicholsii*. Original spelling ends with -*ii*. Generic change from *Coryphopterus* based on J. E. Randall, 1995, Bull. Mar. Sci. 56(3):795–798; and C. E. Thacker and K. S. Cole, 2002, Bull. Mar. Sci. 70(3):837–850.

*Tridentiger barbatus*. Addition based on Fuller et al. (1999), who noted it to be possibly established in California. The Shokihaze goby is now known to be well established in San Francisco Bay and the Sacramento–San Joaquin Delta system (T. A. Greiner, 2002, Calif. Fish Game 88(2):68–74). The common name was suggested by T. A. Greiner, California Department of Fish and Game, who was involved in the study leading to recognition of this species as distinct from *T. bifasciatus*. For consistency, we add goby to the name, even though "*haze*" means goby in Japanese.

*Tridentiger bifasciatus*. S. A. Matern and K. J. Fleming, 1995, Calif. Fish Game 81(2):71–76, documented the establishment of this exotic goby in the Sacramento–San Joaquin Estuary of California.

## Page 174

Ptereleotridae. The dartfishes (also known as hovering gobies), *Ptereleotris,* were placed (under the name *Ioglossus*) in the Gobiidae in the 1991 edition and were recognized as a subfamily of Microdesmidae in Nelson (1994), based on the original 1984 study of D. F. Hoese. Although no clear evidence is yet available to show that this taxon is more closely related to some other family, we here follow the classification of C. Thacker, 2000, Copeia 2000(4):940–957, who placed them in their own family, Ptereleotridae. *Ioglossus*, with two western Atlantic species, is a junior synonym of *Ptereleotris* (J. E. Randall and D. F. Hoese, 1985, Indo-Pacific Fishes, No. 7).

*Ptereleotris calliura*. See Ptereleotridae. Change of author, as *Ioglossus calliurus* Bean, 1882 in the 1991 edition, based on Eschmeyer (1998: Online version, February 2002).

*Ptereleotris helenae*. See Ptereleotridae.

Zanclidae. Added to the list for the species noted.

*Zanclus cornutus*. *Zanclus cornutus* and *Z. canescens* were both described by Linnaeus (1758), are conspecific, and both names have subsequently appeared in the published literature. We accept the decision of J. E. Randall (personal communication, 2000), who has determined that G. Cuvier (1831), as first reviser, selected *cornutus*.

*Acanthurus achilles*. The basis for listing this species is a sighting by A. N. Kerstich in the Cabo San Lucas region, Baja California Sur, Mexico (noted in the 1979 and subsequent editions of Thomson et al. 2000).

*Acanthurus bahianus*. W. F. Smith-Vaniz, H. L.

Jelks, and J. E. Randall, 2002, Gulf Mex. Sci. 20(2):98–105, established that *A. randalli* Briggs & Caldwell, 1957, the gulf surgeonfish, which was recognized in the 1991 and earlier editions, is conspecific with *A. bahianus*.

*Acanthurus coeruleus*. Correction of author.

### Page 175

*Sphyraena barracuda*. Change of author and year from Walbaum, 1792. We follow Eschmeyer (1998: Online version, March 2003) and note that B. C. Russell, 2003 (dated 2002), Suborder Scombroidei, Sphyraenidae (barracudas), Pages 1807–1811 *in* K. E. Carpenter, editor, The living marine resources of the western central Atlantic, FAO species identification guide for fishery purposes, Volume 3, FAO, Rome, adopted the change.

*Sphyraena ensis*. Several examples of this species were taken off southern California in 1997 (R. N. Lea and R. H. Rosenblatt, 2000, CalCOFI Rep. 41:117–129).

*Sphyraena picudilla*. This species is considered by Smith-Vaniz et al. (1999) and B. C. Russell, 2003 (dated 2002), Suborder Scombroidei, Sphyraenidae (barracudas), Pages 1807–1811 *in* K. E. Carpenter, editor, The living marine resources of the western central Atlantic, FAO species identification guide for fishery purposes, Volume 3, FAO, Rome, to be a synonym of *S. borealis*. We continue to recognize it pending detailed studies.

Gempylidae. See Trichiuridae below. Additional deepwater species may occasionally occur at less than 200 m within our area.

*Diplospinus multistriatus*. Added to the list on the basis of five specimens (UF 217715) taken in the Florida Straits at a depth of 104–155 m and a specimen (MCZ 67281) taken within our area off South Carolina from 128 m.

*Neoepinnula americana*. G. W. Mead, 1951, Copeia 1951(4):301, reported *Epinnula orientalis* Gilchrist & von Bonde, 1924 from the northern Gulf of Mexico, and it was added to the 1980 edition under the name sackfish. M. Grey, 1953, Copeia 1953(3):135–141, described the subspecies *E. orientalis americanus*. The two taxa (*orientalis* and *americanus*) were considered distinct species by I. Nakamura and N. V. Parin, 1993, FAO species catalogue, Volume 15, Snake mackerels and cutlassfishes of the world (families Gempy-

lidae and Trichiuridae), FAO Fish. Synop. 125(15), with *N.* (formerly *Epinnula*) *americana* confined to the western Atlantic and *N.* (formerly *Epinnula*) *orientalis* to the Indo-Pacific region. The common name is changed to reflect the distribution of the species, as determined by Nakamura and Parin, 1993 (above).

*Ruvettus pretiosus*. Date of publication correction.

Trichiuridae. Recognition of the Gempylidae as separate from the Trichiuridae follows the practice of most workers, including Nelson (1994). The change in family common name reflects this change in classification.

*Benthodesmus pacificus*. Considered by I. Nakamura and N. V. Parin, 1993, FAO species catalogue, Volume 15, Snake mackerels and cutlassfishes of the world (families Gempylidae and Trichiuridae), FAO Fish. Synop. 125(15), to be a valid species distinct from *B. elongatus* (Clarke, 1879), which is confined to the Southern Hemisphere. The change in common name reflects the geographic distribution. The 1991 edition added "A" to occurrence because of records reported by Scott and Scott (1988); however, Nakamura and Parin, 1993, made no reference to such records but did note that *B. tenuis* (Günther, 1877) and *Evoxymetopon taeniatus* Gill, 1863, come within or close to our depth of coverage (see below for latter species).

*Benthodesmus simonyi*. Added to list on basis of records in Scott and Scott, 1988 (as *B. elongatus simonyi*) and presence in Mexico. I. Nakamura and N. V. Parin, 1993, FAO species catalogue, Volume 15, Snake mackerels and cutlassfishes of the world (families Gempylidae and Trichiuridae), FAO Fish. Synop. 125(15), recognized *B. simonyi* as separate from *B. elongatus* of the Southern Hemisphere.

*Evoxymetopon taeniatus*. Added to the list based on specimens brought to our attention by K. E. Hartel (personal communication, March 2002), one from 144 m in Toms Canyon, east of Cape May, New Jersey (MCZ 160934) and identified by B. B. Collette (personal communication, June 2002), one from off North Carolina (NCSM 28581) is from our area (W. C. Starnes, personal communication, May 2002), and two from off Georgia from 110 m (UF 41304). *Evoxymetopon taeniatus* was recorded off Florida, but not necessarily within our area of coverage, by I. Nakamura and N. V. Parin, 1993, FAO species catalogue, Volume 15, Snake mackerels and cutlassfishes of the world (families Gempylidae and Trichiuridae), FAO Fish. Synop. No. 125(15). We accept Poey as the author, rather than Gill, based on our interpretation of T. Gill, 1863, Proc. Acad. Nat. Sci. Phila. 15:224–229 (following Article 50.1.1 of the Code).

*Lepidopus altifrons*. This new species was described by N. V. Parin and B. B. Collette, 1993, Arch. Fischwiss. 41(3):189. Although normally found below 200 m, it was noted above that depth within our area. The common name crested scabbardfish (versus Atlantic scabbardfish preferred by some workers) is from I. Nakamura and N. V. Parin, 1993, FAO species catalogue, Volume 15, Snake mackerels and cutlassfishes of the world (families Gempylidae and Trichiuridae), FAO Fish. Synop. 125(15).

## Page 176

*Trichiurus lepturus*. I. Nakamura and N. V. Parin, 1993, FAO species catalogue, Volume 15, Snake mackerels and cutlassfishes of the world (families Gempylidae and Trichiuridae), FAO Fish. Synop. 125(15), considered *T. nitens* to be a junior synonym of *T. lepturus*, with the common name largehead hairtail. They noted that the eastern Pacific "form differs from all other populations of *T. lepturus*" and that it is considered as a valid species by many authors. Until the systematics of *Trichiurus* are better understood, we recognize the Atlantic and Pacific populations as specifically distinct, as done in the 1991 edition and as supported by I. Nakamura (personal communication, June 2001).

*Trichiurus nitens*. See *T. lepturus*.

*Scomber australasicus*. The English common name was suggested by B. B. Collette (personal communication, January 2002).

*Scomber colias*. B. B. Collette, 1999, Pages 149–164 *in* B. Séret and J. -Y. Sire, editors, Société Française d' Ichtyologie, Proceedings of the 5th Indo-Pacific Fish Conference, Nouméa, 1997, Paris, and B. B. Collette, C. Reeb, and B. A. Block, 2001, Pages 1–33 *in* B. A. Block and E. D. Stevens, editors, Fish physiology, Volume 19, Academic Press, San Diego, California, recognized Atlantic and Pacific populations of chub mackerels as separate species.

In the 1960 edition, the Atlantic *S. colias* and the Indo-Pacific *S. japonicus* were recognized as distinct, with the former called the chub mackerel and the latter the Pacific mackerel. In the 1970 edition, they were synonymized as *S. japonicus,* following T. Matsui, 1967, Copeia 1967(1):71, and chub mackerel was selected as the common name. We herein recognize both species and adopt descriptively appropriate common names in English most similar to those in use on both coasts.

*Scomber japonicus*. See *S. colias*.

*Scomberomorus concolor*. The term "Gulf" in the common name is treated as a proper noun. Although originally described from off California, the name applies to the species' primary occurrence in the Gulf of California.

*Thunnus atlanticus*. Date of publication correction.

*Thunnus orientalis*. B.B. Collette, 1999, Pages 149–164 *in* B. Séret and J. -Y. Sire, editors, Société Française d' Ichtyologie, Proceedings of the 5th Indo-Pacific Fish Conference, Nouméa, 1997, recognized Atlantic and Pacific subspecies of the bluefin tuna as full species.

*Thunnus thynnus*. See *T. orientalis*.

## Page 177

*Istiophorus platypterus*. Correction of author from Shaw & Nodder. Some authors, for example, I. Nakamura, 2003 (dated 2002), Istiophoridae (billfishes), Pages 1860–1866 *in* K. E. Carpenter, editor, The living marine resources of the western central Atlantic, FAO species identification guide for fishery purposes, Volume 3, FAO, Rome, recognized the Atlantic form as a separate species, *I. albicans* (Latreille, 1804). We await further studies before making this change.

*Makaira mazara*. There is good evidence that this species should be recognized as distinct from *Makaira nigricans*, and we follow I. Nakamura *in* Fischer et al. (1995, Volume II:1191) and I. Nakamura, 2003 (dated 2002), Istiophoridae (billfishes), Pages 1860–1866 *in* K. E. Carpenter, editor, The living marine resources of the western central Atlantic, FAO species identification guide for fishery purposes, Volume 3, FAO, Rome, in making this change.

*Makaira nigricans*. See *M. mazara*.

Centrolophidae. See Stromateidae below.

*Centrolophus medusophagus*. Date of publication correction.

*Centrolophus niger*. Date of publication correction.

Nomeidae. See Stromateidae below.

*Cubiceps capensis*. Added to the list on the basis of T. B. Agafonova, 1994, J. Ichthyol. 34(5):116–143, who noted that the large specimen washed up on the New Jersey shore identified by R. G. Arndt, 1981, Fla. Sci. 44 (1):35–39, as *C. baxteri* is really this species. The common name is capitalized, based on the assumption that it refers to the type locality being north of Cape Town.

*Nomeus gronovii*. Date of publication correction.

### Page 178

Ariommatidae. See Stromateidae below.

Tetragonuridae. See Stromateidae below.

Stromateidae. Some species in this family in the 1991 edition are now included in the Centrolophidae, Nomeidae, Ariommatidae, and Tetragonuridae (Nelson 1994), based largely on the works of R. L. Haedrich (e.g., 1967, Bull. Mus. Comp. Zool. 135:31–139).

*Peprilus burti*. The term "Gulf" in the common name is treated as a proper noun, and we infer that the name was originally proposed for the species' occurrence in the Gulf of Mexico.

*Peprilus paru*. *Peprilus alepidotus* (Linnaeus, 1766), included in the 1991 and in previous editions, was earlier synonymized by M. H. Horn, 1970, Bull. Mus. Comp. Zool. 140:165–262, with *P. paru* (Linnaeus, 1758). We adopt this change here.

Belontiidae. The recognition of this family for species previously placed in the Anabantidae is based on the works of K. F. Liem and is followed in Nelson (1994).

Channidae. Added to the list for the species noted.

*Channa marulius*. Reproducing and established in a canal system in the Tamarac area, Broward County, Florida. Possibly brought in through the Asian food market, along with *C. argus* (Cantor, 1842), which has also been reported from Florida but with no evidence of establishment (P. Shafland, personal communication, April 2001). Common name suggested by P. Shafland, W. R. Courtenay, Jr., and P. Musikasinthorn (personal communication, October 2001). Various other species of snakeheads are also turning up in the wild elsewhere in the United States, where establishment is possible, as noted by W. R. Courtenay, Jr. and J. D. Williams, 2004, Snakeheads (Pisces, Channidae)—a biological synopsis and risk assessment, U.S. Geological Survey Circular 1251, Denver, Colorado.

Bothidae. Some species in this family in the 1991 edition are now included in the Scophthalmidae and Paralichthyidae (Nelson 1994), which is based largely on the works of F. Chapleau and D. A. Hensley. *Chascanopsetta lugubris* Alcock, 1894, the pelican flounder of the Atlantic, is deleted from the list as all verified collection records are from depths greater than 200 m.

### Page 179

*Engyophrys sanctilaurentii*. Formerly known from Mexico, this flatfish was taken off southern California in 1998 (R. N. Lea and R. H. Rosenblatt, 2000, CalCOFI Rep. 41:117–129).

Scophthalmidae. See Bothidae above. Common name in English suggested by F. Chapleau (personal communication, 1999).

Paralichthyidae. See Bothidae above. Common name in English from Smith-Vaniz et al. (1999).

*Ancylopsetta quadrocellata*. Date of publication correction.

*Citharichthys dinoceros*. Added to the list based on many collections in the Florida Museum of Natural History (e.g., UF 108880 and UF 109054) above 200 m from off Florida and Mexico. Common name based on the spines on the head.

*Citharichthys fragilis*. The term "Gulf" in the common name is treated as a proper noun. The name was originally proposed for the species' occurrence in the Gulf of California.

### Page 180

*Etropus crossotus*. Considered to be the same species in Atlantic and Pacific oceans. Occurs in U.S. waters in the Atlantic but in the Pacific only in Mexican waters in our area of coverage.

*Paralichthys albigutta*. The term "Gulf" in the common name is treated as a proper noun; we infer that the name was originally proposed for the species' occurrence in the Gulf of Mexico.

*Syacium micrurum*. Date of publication correction.

### Page 181

*Atheresthes evermanni*. Although J. A. Cooper and

F. Chapleau, 1998, Fish. Bull. 96(4):686–726, placed species of *Atheresthes* within *Reinhardtius*, we recognize both genera, as did J. W. Orr and A. C. Matarese, 2000, Fish. Bull. 98:539–582, because of their many differences. In addition, N. Suzuki, M. Nishida, and K. Amaoka, 2001, Bull. Fish. Sci. Hokkaido Univ. 52(1):39–46, using molecular data, found that *A. evermanni* is not closely related to *Reinhardtius* and supported the retention of *Atheresthes* as a valid genus.

*Atheresthes stomias.* See *A. evermanni.*

*Embassichthys bathybius.* J. A. Cooper and F. Chapleau, 1998, Fish. Bull. 96(4):686–726, placed this species within *Microstomus.* We feel, as did J. W. Orr and A. C. Matarese, 2000, Fish. Bull. 98:539–582, that the differences those authors presented (p. 712) do not warrant the change. The phylogenetic conclusions of Cooper and Chapleau, such as the monophyly of this clade, are not in question.

*Glyptocephalus zachirus.* As a result of the cladistic study of J. A. Cooper and F. Chapleau, 1998, Fish. Bull. 96(4):686–726, many changes in generic placement are required from the 1991 edition. *Glyptocephalus zachirus* was formerly recognized in *Errex*, and parentheses are now removed from the author's name.

*Isopsetta isolepis.* See *Glyptocephalus zachirus.* Formerly placed in *Pleuronectes.*

*Lepidopsetta bilineata.* See *Glyptocephalus zachirus.* Formerly recognized as *Pleuronectes bilineatus.*

*Lepidopsetta polyxystra.* This new species of flatfish was described from the North Pacific, from Puget Sound to the Sea of Okhotsk, by J. W. Orr and A. C. Matarese, 2000, Fish. Bull. 98:539–582.

*Limanda aspera.* See *Glyptocephalus zachirus.* Formerly recognized as *Pleuronectes asper*; parentheses are now added to the author's name.

*Limanda ferruginea.* See *Glyptocephalus zachirus.* Formerly recognized as *Pleuronectes ferrugineus.*

*Limanda proboscidea.* See *Glyptocephalus zachirus.* Formerly recognized as *Pleuronectes proboscideus.*

*Limanda sakhalinensis.* D. E. Kramer, W. H. Barss, B. C. Paust, and B. E. Bracken, 1995, Guide to Northeast Pacific flatfishes, Alaska Sea Grant College Program, Mar. Advis. Bull. 47,

included this species, under the name *Pleuronectes sakhalinensis*, since it ranges as far east as the Pribilof Islands.

*Lyopsetta exilis.* See *Glyptocephalus zachirus.* Formerly placed in *Eopsetta.*

*Parophrys vetulus.* See *Glyptocephalus zachirus.* Formerly placed in *Pleuronectes.* The original spelling *vetulus* (versus *vetula,* as used in some works) is retained as required in Article 34.2.1 of the Code (the name is a noun in apposition and is also the original spelling). This change was also discussed by J. W. Orr and A. C. Matarese, 2000, Fish. Bull. 98:footnote p. 559.

*Platichthys stellatus.* Date of publication correction.

*Pleuronichthys guttulatus.* Formerly recognized as *Hypsopsetta guttulata.* Although this species could be retained in *Hypsopsetta,* since it is the sister species of all other species of *Pleuronichthys* (J. A. Cooper and F. Chapleau, 1998, Fish. Bull. 96(4):686–726), we follow Cooper and Chapleau, who placed it in *Pleuronichthys.* Parentheses are now removed from the author's name.

### Page 182

*Pseudopleuronectes americanus.* See *Glyptocephalus zachirus.* Formerly placed in *Pleuronectes.*

*Reinhardtius hippoglossoides.* For a discussion of the reasons for retention of the common name, see the Annual Report of the Committee on Names of Fishes, 1969, Trans. Am. Fish. Soc. 98(1):179, and Scott and Scott (1988:559). The current official market name both in the United States and Canada is Greenland turbot.

Poecilopsettidae. This family is recognized following J. A. Cooper and F. Chapleau, 1998, Copeia 1998(2):477–481. The family common name in English was suggested by F. Chapleau (personal communication, 1999).

*Poecilopsetta beanii.* Now known to occur off North Carolina in waters shallower than 200 m, as reported by F. C. Rohde, S. W. Ross, S. P. Epperly, and G. H. Burgess, 1995, Brimleyana 23:53–64.

Achiridae. This family is recognized for the species of *Achirus, Gymnachirus,* and *Trinectes,* formerly placed in Soleidae (in the 1991 edition), following F. Chapleau and A. Keast, 1988, Can. J. Zool. 66:2797–2810.

*Achirus klunzingeri.* Listed on report of a specimen from the coast of Guerrero, Pacific Mexico by A. Yáñez-Arancibia, 1980, Centro de Ciencias del Mar y Limnología [de la] Universidad Nacional Autónoma de México, Publicación Especial 2 [para (for) 1978]:1–306 (p. 117 and Lam. 31); the same record noted in Castro-Aguirre et al. (1999:493).

*Achirus zebrinus.* Listed on authority of Castro-Aguirre et al. (1999:496). The status of this species remains in doubt.

*Gymnachirus melas.* Parentheses are removed from the author's name.

Soleidae. Species in this family in the 1991 edition are transferred to Achiridae and Cynoglossidae. We now have only one species of Soleidae, in the strict sense, in our area (Pacific Mexico). See Achiridae and Cynoglossidae.

Cynoglossidae. This family is recognized for species of *Symphurus* formerly placed in Soleidae (in the 1991 edition), following F. Chapleau and A. Keast, 1988, Can. J. Zool. 66:2797–2810, and followed by Nelson (1994). *Symphurus nebulosus* (Goode & Bean, 1883), the freckled tonguefish of the Atlantic, is deleted from the list as all verified collection records are from depths greater than 200 m (T. A. Munroe, 1998, Fish. Bull. 96(1):1–182).

*Symphurus atricaudus.* Specific name spelling correction from *atricauda*.

*Symphurus billykrietei.* This new species was described from the continental shelf of the western North Atlantic by T. A. Munroe, 1998, Fish. Bull. 96(1):38. The English and Spanish common names were chosen with the help of T. A. Munroe (personal communication, October 2002).

## Page 183

*Symphurus civitatium.* Specific name spelling correction. T. A. Munroe, 1991, Fish. Bull. 89:247–287, gave reasons for rejecting the previously used spellings *civitatus* and *civitatum* and preferred the emended spelling *civitatium* upon advice of G. C. Steyskal (Ginsburg spelled this *civitatum*). This was followed by T. A. Munroe, 1998, Fish. Bull. 96(1):1–182, Smith-Vaniz et al. (1999), and Eschmeyer (1998: Online version, February 2002).

*Symphurus diomedeanus.* Date of publication correction and specific name spelling correction.

*Symphurus pterospilotus* Ginsburg, 1951, daubed tonguefish, noted in our area by Scott and Scott (1988), is a synonym of this species (T. A. Munroe, 1998, Fish. Bull. 96(1):97).

*Symphurus marginatus.* This species, known from the Atlantic from off New Jersey to Brazil, is added based on T. A. Munroe, 1998, Fish. Bull. 96(1):1–182; its presence in Mexico above 200-m depth is uncertain.

*Symphurus piger.* Date of publication correction.

*Symphurus stigmosus.* This new species was described from the tropical Atlantic in the Gulf Stream and Straits of Florida by T. A. Munroe, 1998, Fish. Bull. 96(1):45. Most records are from deeper than 200 m, but one lot, UF 213917, is from 192 m off Florida.

*Symphurus urospilus.* Parentheses are removed from the author's name.

Balistidae. Change in common name of family from leatherjackets (the recommended common name for the superfamily comprising triggerfishes and filefishes). See Monacanthidae.

## Page 184

Monacanthidae. Although forming a monophyletic group with triggerfishes, the recognition of filefishes in their own family follows the practice of most workers and Nelson (1994). See Balistidae.

*Aluterus heudelotii.* Original spelling ends with *-ii*.

*Aluterus schoepfii.* Original spelling ends with *-ii*.

*Cantherhines macrocerus.* Date of publication correction.

*Stephanolepis hispidus.* Formerly placed in the genus *Monacanthus*.

*Stephanolepis setifer.* Formerly placed in the genus *Monacanthus*. Date of publication correction.

*Acanthostracion polygonia.* Included in *Lactophrys* in previous editions. J. C. Tyler, 1965, Proc. Acad. Nat. Sci. Phila. 117(8):261–287, J. C. Tyler, 1980, National Oceanic and Atmospheric Administration, Technical Report, National Marine Fisheries Service Circular 434, and G. J. Klassen, 1995, Bull. Mar. Sci. 57:393–441 recognized *Acanthostracion* as a genus distinct from *Lactophrys*.

*Acanthostracion quadricornis.* See *A. polygonia.*

*Lactoria diaphana.* Change in generic placement from *Ostracion* follows general usage, as given in Eschmeyer (1998: Online version, March 2003).

## Page 185

Tetraodontidae. The recognition of porcupine-fishes, separate from puffers, in their own family follows the practice of most workers and Nelson (1994).

*Canthigaster jamestyleri.* This new species was described from off South Carolina at depths of 38–42 m by R. L. Moura and R. M. C. Castro, 2002, Proc. Biol. Soc. Wash. 115(1):32–50. The species is also known from the Florida Keys and several Gulf of Mexico localities as far west as Texas, and may range to the Yucatan Peninsula (W. F. Smith-Vaniz, personal communication, April 2002); the common name is that used in P. Humann and N. Deloach, 2002, Reef fish identification, New World Publications, Inc., Jacksonville, Florida, 3rd edition, and is supported by W. F. Smith-Vaniz (personal communication, April 2002).

*Canthigaster rostrata.* Date of publication correction.

*Lagocephalus laevigatus.* F. J. Schwartz, 2001, J. Elisha Mitchell Sci. Soc. 117(4):280–285, noted this species in estuarine waters in North Carolina.

*Sphoeroides spengleri.* Date of publication correction.

Diodontidae. See Tetraodontidae.

*Chilomycterus antennatus.* Date of publication correction. See *C. reticulatus.*

*Chilomycterus antillarum.* See *C. reticulatus.*

*Chilomycterus atringa.* This spelling of the specific name (versus *atinga*) is the one used in the original species description by Linnaeus. Consideration was given to continued use of *atinga*, based on prevailing usage (Article 33.3.1), since this was the spelling appearing in previous editions and in certain recent publications; however, this has been rejected because the original spelling (*atringa*) has appeared with frequent usage in recent publications (Eschmeyer 1998: Online version, March 2003). See *C. reticulatus.*

*Chilomycterus reticulatus.* J. M. Leis, 1986, *in* M. M. Smith and P. C. Heemstra, editors, Smith's sea fishes, Diodontidae, Macmillan South Africa, Johannesburg, synonymized *C. affinis* Günther, 1870, Pacific burrfish, with *C. reticulatus.* The common name in English is changed accordingly. In addition, Leis distinguished *Cyclichthys* from *Chilomycterus*, with *Chilomycterus* being monotypic (for the worldwide *C. reticulatus*). Our remaining species previously in *Chilomycterus* thus are now in *Cyclichthys*; however, we choose to maintain these sister taxa in *Chilomycterus*, following Smith-Vaniz et al. (1999).

*Chilomycterus schoepfii.* See *C. reticulatus.*

## Page 186

*Mola lanceolata.* Correction of spelling of author's name. In the first report of occurrence from the eastern Pacific, one specimen was reported stranded on a beach near La Paz, Mexico, by E. F. Balart, J. L. Castro-Aguirre, and E. Amador-Silva, 2000, Calif. Fish Game 86(2):156–158.

# Appendix 2
# Names Applied to Hybrid Fishes

Many fish species hybridize in nature and others have been crossed in the laboratory or in fish hatcheries. Scientists routinely refer to hybrids by the names of both parental species, as for example, *Luxilus cornutus* × *Notropis rubellus*, a fairly commonly occurring natural cyprinid hybrid. This hybrid combination when first collected was not recognized as such and was described as a new species, *Notropis macdonaldi* Jordan & Jenkins, 1888. Following Article 23(h) of the International Code of Zoological Nomenclature, 3rd edition, 1985 (and Article 23.8 of the 4th edition, 1999), scientific names based on hybrids have no nomenclatural validity, and *Notropis macdonaldi* is, therefore, an unavailable name.

Hybrid fishes generally are not given common names. In a few instances, hybrids have been recognized and named by anglers, and several are listed in such sources as Fuller et al. (1999) and the *2001 World Record Game Fishes* published by the International Game Fish Association. Others have become important in fish management or are marketed from aquaculture fisheries and have been accorded common names. The U.S. Food and Drug Administration has required specific labeling of such cultured fishes being sold in consumer markets.

The common names of crosses between species of *Morone* have been approved by the Striped Bass Committee of the Southern Division of the American Fisheries Society (and confirmed most recently by Scott Van Horn, personal communication, June 2001). Although various authors give the male or the female first, when parental sexes are known, we follow the systematists' practice of listing parental species alphabetically. Hybrid moronids of unknown parentage are called "wipers."

In the table below, we list the parental species (arranged by family) and common name applied to the hybrid fish for those that are established in fishery literature. We stress that this is not a list of all hybrid fishes known from our area.

PARENTAL SPECIES                                                        COMMON NAME

### Salmonidae—trouts and salmons

*Oncorhynchus clarkii* × *O. mykiss* ............................................................................ cutbow trout
*Salmo trutta* × *Salvelinus fontinalis* ............................................................................ tiger trout
*Salvelinus fontinalis* × *S. namaycush* ............................................................................ splake
(The cross of *S. namaycush* × splake has the name "backcross," which we acknowledge can cause confusion.)

### Esocidae—pikes

*Esox lucius* × *E. masquinongy* .............................................................................. tiger muskellunge

### Moronidae—temperate basses

male *Morone americana* × female *M. saxatilis* ............................................................... Virginia bass
female *Morone americana* × male *M. saxatilis* ............................................................. Maryland bass
female *Morone chrysops* × male *M. saxatilis* ................................................................. sunshine bass
male *Morone chrysops* × female *M. saxatilis* ................................................................. palmetto bass
male *Morone mississippiensis* × female *M. saxatilis* ..................................................... paradise bass

### Centrarchidae—sunfishes

*Lepomis macrochirus* × *Micropterus salmoides* ..................................................................... blue bass

## Percidae—perches

*Sander canadensis* × S. *vitreus* ................................................................................................................ saugeye

## Cichlidae—cichlids

*Oreochromis mossambica* × *O. urolepis* ...................................................................................... red tilapia

## Pleuronectidae—righteye flounders

*Parophrys vetulus* × *Platichthys stellatus* ........................................................................... forkline sole

# PART III

## References

Most references to literature sources are in abbreviated form, omitting the title but giving enough information for the publication to be found, but some are given here as regular text citations by author and year. Asterisks (*) denote principal references consulted for potential adoption of common names in Spanish and/or English for Mexican species new to the list.

*Allen, G. R., and D. R. Robertson. 1994. Fishes of the tropical eastern Pacific. University of Hawaii Press, Honolulu. [*Spanish translation by M. I. López, 1998, Peces del Pacífico oriental tropical, CONABIO, Agrupación Sierra Madre y CEMEX, México, D.F.]

*Amezcua-Linares, F. 1996. Peces demersales de la plataforma continental del Pacífico central de México. Instituto de Ciencias del Mar y Limnología, Universidad Nacional Autónoma de México, México, D.F.

*Applegate, S. P., L. Espinosa-Arrubarrena, L. B. Menchaca-López, and F. Sotelo-Macias. 1979. Tiburones mexicanos. Secretaría de Educación e Investigación Tecnológica, Dirección General de Ciencia y Tecnología del Mar, México, D.F.

*Bussing, W. A., and M. I. López S. 1994. Peces demersales y pelágicos costeros del Pacífico de Centro América meridional, guía ilustrada. Rev. Biol. Trop., Publ. Especial, San José, Costa Rica.

*Carta Nacional Pesquera. 2000. Diario Oficial de la Federación (Organo del Gobierno Constitucional de los Estados Unidos Mexicanos), Tomo DLXIII, No. 20, Segunda Sección, 28 de agosto de 2000, Carta Nacional Pesquera, México, D.F.

*Castro-Aguirre, J.L., and H. Espinosa Pérez. 1996. Apéndice 2, Pages 74–75 in Listados faunísticos de México VII. Catálogo sistemático de las rayas y especies afines de México (Chondrichthyes: Elasmobranchii: Rajiformes: Batoideiomorpha). Instituto de Biología, Universidad Nacional Autónoma de México, México, D.F.

Castro-Aguirre, J. L., H. Espinosa Pérez, and J. J. Schmitter-Soto. 1999. Ictiofauna estuarino-lagunar y vicaria de México. Editorial Limusa, México, D.F.

*Chirichigno, N., W. Fischer, and C. E. Nauen (compilers). 1982. INFOPESCA. Catálogo de especies marinas de interés económico actual o potencial para América Latina. Parte 2 – Pacífico centro y suroriental. FAO/PNUD, SIC/82/2, Roma.

*Claro, R., and L. Parenti. 2001. The marine ichthyofauna of Cuba, Appendix 2.1, Pages 33–57 in R. Claro, K. C. Lindeman, and L. R. Parenti, editors. Ecology of the marine fishes of Cuba. Smithsonian Institution Press, Washington, D.C.

Compagno, L. J. V. 1999. Checklist of living elasmobranchs. Pages 471–498 in W. C. Hamlett, editor. Sharks, skates, and rays—the biology of elasmobranch fishes. The John Hopkins University Press, Baltimore, Maryland.

*Cudney Bueno, R., and P. J. Turk Boyer. 1998. Pescando entre mareas del alto Golfo de California. Una guía sobre la pesca artesanal, su gente y sus propuestas de manejo. Serie Técnica No. 1, Centro Intercultural de Estudios de Desiertos y Océanos, Puerto Peñasco, Sonora, México.

*De la Cruz-Agüero, J., M. Arellano-Martínez, V. M. Cota-Gómez, and G. De la Cruz-Agüero. 1997. Catálogo de los peces marinos de Baja California Sur. Instituto Politécnico Nacional-Centro Interdisciplinario de Ciencias Marinas, La Paz, B.C.S.

Desrosiers, A., F. Caron, and R. Ouellet. 1995. Liste de la faune vertébrée du Québec. Nouvelle édition. Gouvernement du Québec. Ministère de l'Environment et de la Faune. Les Publication du Québec, Sainte Foy, Québec.

Eschmeyer, W. N., editor. 1998. Catalog of fishes. Special Publication 1, California Academy of Sciences, San Francisco. Volume 1:1–958, Volume 2:959–1820, Volume 3:1821–2905. [Online access (most recent): http://www.calacademy.org/research/ichthyology/]

Eschmeyer, W. N., and R. M. Bailey. 1990. Part 1, Genera of recent fishes. Pages 7–433 *in* W. N. Eschmeyer. Catalog of the genera of recent fishes. California Academy of Sciences, San Francisco.

*Escobar-Fernández, R., and M. Siri. 1998. Nombres vernáculos y científicos de los peces del Pacífico mexicano. Universidad Autónoma de Nuevo León, Monterrey, N.L., México [para (for) 1997: Universidad Autónoma de Baja California, Mexicali, B.C., y Sociedad Ictiológica Mexicana, A.C., San Nicolás de los Garza, N.L.].

*Espinosa-Pérez, H., M. T. Gaspar-Dillanes, and P. Fuentes-Mata. 1993. Listados faunísticos de México III. Los peces dulceacuícolas mexicanos. Instituto de Biología, Universidad Nacional Autónoma de México, México, D.F.

*Findley, L. T., M. E. Hendrickx, R. C. Brusca, A. M. van der Heiden, P. A. Hastings, and J. Torre. In press. Macrofauna del Golfo de California [Macrofauna of the Gulf of California]. CD-ROM version 1.0. Macrofauna Golfo Project. Center for Applied Biodiversity Science, Conservation International, Washington, D.C.

*Fischer, W., F. Krupp, W. Schneider, C. Sommer, K. E. Carpenter, and V. H. Niem, editors. 1995. Guía FAO para la identificación de especies para los fines de la pesca. Pacífico centro-oriental. Vertebrados. Volume II:647–1200, Volume III:1201–1813. FAO, Roma.

Fuller, P. T., L. G. Nico, and J. D. Williams. 1999. Nonindigenous fishes introduced into inland waters of the United States. American Fisheries Society, Special Publication 27, Bethesda, Maryland.

*Garibaldi, L., and S. Busilacchi (compilers). 2002. Aquatic Sciences and Fisheries Information System (ASFIS) list of species for fishery statistics purposes. ASFIS Reference Series. No. 15. FAO, Rome. [Online access (most recent): http://www.fao.org/fi/statist/fisoft/asfis/asfis.asp]

*Garrison, G. 2000. Peces de la Isla del Coco [Isla del Coco fishes]. INBio, Santo Domingo de Heredia, Costa Rica.

Gilbert, C. R. 1998. Type catalogue of recent and fossil North American freshwater fishes: families Cyprinidae, Catostomidae, Ictaluridae, Centrarchidae and Elassomatidae. Florida Museum of Natural History, Special Publication 1, University of Florida, Gainesville.

*Grove, J. S., and R. J. Lavenberg. 1997. The fishes of the Galápagos Islands. Stanford University Press, Stanford, California.

*Hastings, P. A., and L. T. Findley. In press. Marine fishes of the biosphere reserve, northern Gulf of California. In R. S. Felger and B. Broyles, editors. Dry borders: great natural areas of the Gran Desierto and the upper Gulf of California. University of Utah Press, Salt Lake City.

*Humann, P. 1993. Reef fish identification: Galápagos. New World Publications, Jacksonville, Florida, and Libri Mundi, Quito, Ecuador.

*Humann, P. 1994. Reef fish identification: Florida, Caribbean, Bahamas (2nd edition). New World Publications, Jacksonville, Florida.

Jenkins, R. E., and N. M. Burkhead. 1994. Freshwater fishes of Virginia. American Fisheries Society, Bethesda, Maryland.

Mayden, R. L. 1991. Cyprinids of the New World. Pages 240–263 *in* I. J. Winfield and J. S. Nelson, editors. Cyprinid fishes: systematics, biology and exploitation. Chapman and Hall Ltd., London.

Mayden, R. L., B. M. Burr, L. M. Page, and R. R. Miller. 1992. The native freshwater fishes of North America. Pages 827–863 *in* R. L. Mayden, editor. Systematics, historical ecology, and North American freshwater fishes. Stanford University Press, Stanford, California.

McEachran, J. D., and J. D. Fechhelm. 1998. Fishes of the Gulf of Mexico. Volume 1. University of Texas Press, Austin.

Mecklenburg, C. W., T. A. Mecklenburg, and L. K. Thorsteinson. 2002. Fishes of Alaska. American Fisheries Society, Bethesda, Maryland.

*Miller, R. R., W. L. Minckley, and S. M. Norris. In press. Freshwater fishes of Mexico, University of Chicago Press, Chicago.

Nelson, J. S. 1994. Fishes of the world. 3rd edition. John Wiley & Sons, New York.

Page, L. M., and B. M. Burr. 1991. A field guide to freshwater fishes of North America north of Mexico. The Peterson Field Guide Series. Houghton Mifflin Co., Boston.

*Pérez-Mellado, J., and L. T. Findley. 1985. Evaluación de la ictiofauna acompañante del camarón capturado en las costas de Sonora y norte de Sinaloa, México. Pages 201–254 *in* A. Yáñez-Arancibia, editor. Recursos pesqueros potenciales de México: la pesca acompañante del camarón. Programa Universitario de Alimentos, Instituto de Ciencias del Mar y Limnología/Instituto Nacional de la Pesca, Universidad Nacional Autónoma de México, México, D.F.

* Schaldach Jr., W. J., L. Huidobro C., and H. Espinosa P. 1996. Lista de peces marinos. Pages 463–471 *in* E. González, R. Dirzo, and R. C. Vogt, editors. Historia natural de Los Tuxtlas. CONABIO, IBUNAM, Centro de Ecología, Universidad Nacional Autónoma de México, México, D.F.

Scott, W. B., and M. G. Scott. 1988. Atlantic fishes of Canada. Canadian Bulletin of Fisheries and Aquatic Sciences 219.

Smith-Vaniz, W. F., B. B. Collette, and B. E. Luckhurst. 1999. Fishes of Bermuda: history, zoogeography, annotated checklist, and identification keys. American Society of Ichthyologists and Herpetologists, Special Publication No. 4, Lawrence, Kansas.

* Thomson, D. A., L. T. Findley, and A. N. Kerstitch. 2000. Reef fishes of the Sea of Cortez, the rocky-shore fishes of the Gulf of California. Revised edition. University of Texas Press, Austin.

* Walford, L. A. 1937. Marine game fishes of the Pacific coast from Alaska to the equator. University of California Press, Berkeley.

## Editions of the Names List
### (given in chronological order)

Chute, W. H. (chairman), R. M. Bailey, W. A. Clemens, J. R. Dymond, S. F. Hildebrand, G. S. Myers, and L. P. Schultz. 1948. A list of common and scientific names of the better known fishes of the United States and Canada. American Fisheries Society, Special Publication 1, Ann Arbor, Michigan (and Transactions of the American Fisheries Society 75:355–398).

Bailey, R. M. (chairman), E. A. Lachner, C. C. Lindsey, C. R. Robins, P. M. Roedel, W. B. Scott, and L. P. Woods. 1960. A list of common and scientific names of fishes from the United States and Canada. 2nd edition. American Fisheries Society, Special Publication 2, Ann Arbor, Michigan.

Bailey, R. M. (chairman), J. E. Fitch, E. S. Herald, E. A. Lachner, C. C. Lindsey, C. R. Robins, and W. B. Scott. 1970. A list of common and scientific names of fishes from the United States and Canada. 3rd edition. American Fisheries Society, Special Publication 6, Washington, D.C.

Robins, C. R. (chairman), R. M. Bailey, C. E. Bond, J. R. Brooker, E. A. Lachner, R. N. Lea, and W. B. Scott. 1980. A list of common and scientific names of fishes from the United States and Canada. 4th edition. American Fisheries Society, Special Publication 12, Bethesda, Maryland.

Robins, C. R. (chairman), R. M. Bailey, C. E. Bond, J. R. Brooker, E. A. Lachner, R. N. Lea, and W. B. Scott. 1991. Common and scientific names of fishes from the United States and Canada. 5th edition. American Fisheries Society, Special Publication 20, Bethesda, Maryland.

## Edition of the World List

Robins, C. R. (chairman), R. M. Bailey, C. E. Bond, J. R. Brooker, E. A. Lachner, R. N. Lea, and W. B. Scott. 1991. World fishes important to North Americans, exclusive of species from the continental waters of the United States and Canada. American Fisheries Society, Special Publication 21, Bethesda, Maryland.

# Personal Communications

W. D. Anderson, Jr., Grice Marine Biological Laboratory, Charleston, South Carolina (retired)

M. Bagdovitz, U. S. Fish and Wildlife Service, Portland, Oregon

R. M. Bailey, Museum of Zoology, University of Michigan, Ann Arbor (retired)

R. Bajno, Fisheries and Oceans Canada, Winnipeg, Manitoba

H. L. Bart, Jr., Tulane Museum of Natural History, Belle Chasse, Louisiana

J. K. Baum, Department of Biology, Dalhousie University, Halifax, Nova Scotia

J. F. Bergeron, Lac-Supérieur, Québec (retired)

H. T. Boschung, Biology Department, University of Alabama, Tuscaloosa

J. C. Briggs, Georgia Museum of Natural History, University of Georgia, Athens (retired)

G. H. Burgess, Florida Museum of Natural History, University of Florida, Gainesville

W. A. Bussing, CIMAR, Universidad de Costa Rica, San José, Costa Rica

D. G. Buth, Department of Organismic Biology, Ecology and Evolution, University of California-Los Angeles

J. H. Caruso, Department of Biology, University of New Orleans, Lakefront, Louisiana

P. A. Ceas, St. Olaf College, Northfield, Minnesota

N. L. Chao, Universidade do Amazonas, Manaus, Brazil

F. Chapleau, Department of Biology, University of Ottawa, Ottawa, Ontario

B. Chernoff, Wesleyan University, Middletown, Connecticut

B. B. Collette, National Marine Fisheries Service, National Museum of Natural History, Washington, D.C.

S. Contreras-Balderas, Universidad Autónoma de Nuevo León, Monterrey, México

W. R. Courtenay, Jr., U. S. Geological Survey, Gainesville, Florida

M. R. de Carvalho, Department of Ichthyology and Herpetology, American Museum of Natural History, New York

G. D. Dennis, U. S. Fish and Wildlife Service, Vero Beach, Florida

T. E. Dowling, Department of Biology, Arizona State University, Tempe

J. Dubé, Société de la Faune et des Parcs du Québec, Gouvernement du Québec, Longueuil, Québec

D. J. Eisenhour, Department of Biological and Environmental Sciences, Morehead State University, Morehead, Kentucky

W. N. Eschmeyer, Department of Ichthyology, California Academy of Sciences, San Francisco

L. T. Findley, Centro de Investigación en Alimentación y Desarrollo-Unidad Guaymas, Sonora, México

J. P. Gallo, Centro de Investigación en Alimentación y Desarrollo-Unidad Guaymas, Sonora, México

G. P. Garrett, Texas Parks and Wildlife Department, Ingram

R. G. Gilmore, Dynamac Corporation, Kennedy Space Center, Florida

A. S. Harold, Grice Marine Biological Laboratory, Charleston, South Carolina

P. M. Harris, Department of Biological Sciences, University of Alabama, Tuscaloosa

I. J. Harrison, Department of Ichthyology, American Museum of Natural History, New York

K. E. Hartel, Museum of Comparative Zoology, Harvard University, Cambridge, Massachusetts

P. A. Hastings, Scripps Institution of Oceanography, University of California-San Diego, La Jolla

D. A. Hendrickson, Texas Memorial Museum and Section of Integrative Biology, University of Texas, Austin

J. E. Hill, Fisheries and Aquatic Sciences, University of Florida, Gainesville

G. R. Hoff, NMFS/NOAA, Alaska Fisheries Science Center, Seattle, Washington

R. G. Howells, Texas Parks and Wildlife Department, Ingram

P. H. Humann, Davie, Florida

R. E. Jenkins, Department of Biology, Roanoke College, Salem, Virginia

G. D. Johnson, Division of Fishes, National Museum of Natural History, Washington, D.C.

W. J. Jones, Monterey Bay Aquarium Research Institute, Moss Landing, California

S. A. Lourie, Department of Biology, McGill University, Montreal, Québec

N. E. Mandrak, Great Lakes Laboratory for Fisheries & Aquatic Sciences, Burlington, Ontario

D. F. Markle, Department of Wildlife & Fisheries, Oregon State University, Corvallis

R. E. Matheson, Jr., Florida Marine Research Institute, St. Petersburg

J. D. McEachran, Department of Wildlife and Fisheries Sciences, Texas A&M University, College Station

C. W. Mecklenburg, Point Stephens Research, Auke Bay, Alaska

G. C. Miller, St. Simons Island, Georgia (retired)

R. R. Miller, Museum of Zoology, University of Michigan, Ann Arbor (deceased)

T. A. Munroe, National Marine Fisheries Service, National Museum of Natural History, Washington, D.C.

P. Musikasinthorn, Faculty of Fisheries, Kasetsart University, Bangkok, Thailand

I. Nakamura, Fisheries Research Station, Kyoto University, Japan

D. A. Neely, Department of Biology, Saint Louis University, St. Louis, Missouri

L. G. Nico, U. S. Geological Survey, Gainesville, Florida

S. M. Norris, Biology Department, California State University-Channel Islands, Camarillo

J. W. Orr, NMFS/NOAA, Alaska Fisheries Science Center, Seattle

N. V. Parin, P. P. Shirsov Institute of Oceanology, Russian Academy of Sciences, Moscow

F. L. Pezold III, Museum of Zoology, University of Louisiana, Munroe

H. Plascencia, Centro de Investigación en Alimentación y Desarrollo-Unidad Mazatlán, Sinaloa, México

S. P. Platania, Department of Biology, University of New Mexico, Albuquerque

S. G. Poss, Gulf Coast Research Laboratory, Ocean Springs, Mississippi

W. R. Radke, U. S. Fish and Wildlife Service, Douglas, Arizona

R. Raesly, Department of Biology, Frostburg State University, Frostburg, Maryland

J. E. Randall, B. P. Bishop Museum, Honolulu, Hawaii

J. D. Reist, Fisheries and Oceans Canada, Winnipeg, Manitoba

C. B. Renaud, Canadian Museum of Nature, Ottawa, Ontario

C. R. Robins, Museum of Natural History and Biodiversity Research Center, University of Kansas, Lawrence (retired)

R. H. Rosenblatt, Scripps Institution of Oceanography, University of California-San Diego, La Jolla (retired)

R. Ruiz-Carus, Florida Fish and Wildlife Conservation Commission, Florida Marine Research Institute, St. Petersburg

M. H. Sabaj, Academy of Natural Sciences, Philadelphia, Pennsylvania

P. Shafland, Non-Native Fish Research Lab, Florida Fish and Wildlife Conservation Commission, Boca Raton

D. G. Smith, Division of Fishes, National Museum of Natural History, Washington, D.C.

W. D. Smith, Moss Landing Marine Laboratories and Pacific Shark Research Center, Moss Landing, California

W. F. Smith-Vaniz, U. S. Geological Survey, Gainesville, Florida

F. F. Snelson, Florida Museum of Natural History, University of Florida, Gainesville

Chief C. Snider, Portland, Oregon

V. G. Springer, Division of Fishes, National Museum of Natural History, Washington, D.C.

W. C. Starnes, North Carolina State Museum of Natural Sciences Research Lab, Raleigh

K. W. Stewart, Department of Zoology, University of Manitoba, Winnipeg

R. M. Strange, Department of Biology, Southeast Missouri State University, Cape Girardeau

M. S. Taylor, Department of Biological Sciences, Louisiana State University, Baton Rouge

T. N. Todd, U. S. Geological Survey, Ann Arbor, Michigan

A. M. van der Heiden, Centro de Investigación en Alimentación y Desarrollo-Unidad Mazatlán, Sinaloa, México

R. E. Watson, Gainesville, Florida

S. H. Weitzman, Division of Fishes, National Museum of Natural History, Washington, D.C.

J. T. Williams, Division of Fishes, National Museum of Natural History, Washington, D.C.
C. C. Wilson, Ontario Ministry of Natural Resources, Aquatic Ecosystems Science Section, Peterborough, Ontario
D. G. Wright, Fisheries and Oceans Canada, Winnipeg, Manitoba
F. A. Young, Dynasty Marine Associates, Inc., Marathon, Florida

# Index

**D**

# J

## W

## X

WALFORD LIBRARY
NOAA, NMFS, NORTHEAST FISHERIES CENTER
J.J. HOWARD MARINE SCIENCES LABORATORY
74 MAGRUDER ROAD
HIGHLANDS, NJ 07732

NOAA-NMFS/SANDY HOOK LABORATORY
LIONEL A. WALFORD LIBRARY

3 9288 1001 3602 3